COMPUTER FUNDAMENTALS AND PROGRAMMING IN C

COMPUTER FUNDAMENTALS AND PROGRAMMING IN C

(As per revised syllabus 2009 for Ist year students of Andhra Pradesh Polytechnic Institutions)

Contains Lab Assignments for:
Computer Fundamentals and Programming in C Labs &
Information Technology Labs.

Second Edition

RAJIV KHANNA
Technical Director
Bell Infotech Systems (P) Ltd.

PUBLISHING FOR ONE WORLD

NEW AGE INTERNATIONAL (P) LIMITED, PUBLISHERS
New Delhi • Bangalore • Chennai • Cochin • Guwahati • Hyderabad
Jalandhar • Kolkata • Lucknow • Mumbai • Ranchi
Visit us at www.newagepublishers.com

Published by New Age International (P) Ltd., Publishers
First Edition: 2006
Second Edition: 2010

Branches:

- 36, Malikarjuna Temple Street, Opp. ICWA, Basavanagudi, **Bangalore.** ✆ (080) 26677815
- 26, Damodaran Street, T. Nagar, **Chennai**. ✆ (044) 24353401
- CE-39/1016, Carrier Station Road, Near Paulson Park Hotel, Ernakulam South, **Cochin**. ✆ (0484) 4051303
- Hemsen Complex, Mohd. Shah Road, Paltan Bazar, Near Starline Hotel, **Guwahati**. ✆ (0361) 2543669
- No. 105, 1st Floor, Madhiray Kaveri Tower, 3-2-19, Azam Jahi Road, Nimboliadda, **Hyderabad**. ✆ (040) 24652456
- RDB Chambers (Formerly Lotus Cinema) 106A, Ist Floor, S.N. Banerjee Road, **Kolkata**. ✆ (033) 22275247
- 16-A, Jopling Road, **Lucknow**. ✆ (0522) 2209578
- 142C, Victor House, Ground Floor, N.M. Joshi Marg, Lower Parel, **Mumbai**. ✆ (022) 24927869
- 22, Golden House, Daryaganj, **New Delhi**. ✆ (011) 23262368, 23262370

ISBN : 978-81-224-2755-4

Rs. 275.00

C-09-06-3751

Printed in India at Ajit Printers, Delhi.
Typeset by author

PUBLISHING FOR ONE WORLD
NEW AGE INTERNATIONAL (P) LIMITED, PUBLISHERS
4835/24, Ansari Road, Daryaganj, New Delhi - 110002
Visit us at **www.newagepublishers.com**

PREFACE

Modern advancements and developments in the field of computer have brought the world into new era. Computer has emerged as a powerful tool that is continuously transforming the shape of our working methodologies and day-to-day services. There is hardly any sphere of life left now, in which computers are not being used. Be it any area of operations, computer knowledge is must. This is the reason, why most of the education institutions have introduced computer as a subject in their course curriculum.

This book is specially written for the **first year** students of **Andhra Pradesh Polytechnic** institutions. It is as per **revised syllabus** mentioned in **"Scheme of Instructions and Examination Curriculum 2009"**, released by concerned authorities. However, at some places, sequences of the topics have been changed with the objective of explaining the topics in gradual manner and making the learning easy.

This book titled **"Computer Fundamentals and Programming in C"** comprises of 3 parts. First part (**CM-105**, as mentioned in the syllabus) deals with the theory of Computer Fundamentals and C Programming Language. Second part (**CM-107**, as mentioned in the syllabus) deals with Computer Fundamentals and C programming lab sessions. Third part (**CM-110**, as mentioned in the syllabus) deals with Information Technology lab sessions.

First part (CM-105) of the book comprises of 18 chapters and contains in-depth contents on all the topics mentioned in the syllabus. No topic of the syllabus has been left unexplained. To make the learning easy, examples are liberally used throughout the book. In C language chapters, large numbers of programs for wide variety of problems are included to explain fine issues related to logic development and programming. **All the programs of the book are working programs.** They have been tried and tested in our lab. Students can directly enter them on their computer, compile and execute them to get the output.

At the end of each chapter, a question bank, titled "Exercises" is there. **Solving these questions correctly**, on self-knowledge basis, will generate confidence and **will ensure good marks in the examination**.

Second part (CM-107) of the book provides practical solutions for all the assignments that are suggested in the syllabus. These solutions are given in terms of instructions. Following these instructions, students will be able to complete the assignment, without any confusion and in best possible way.

Third part (CM-110) of the book comprises of self study material and solution for Information Technology lab assignments. It is suggested in the syllabus that theory of IT topics will not be taught in regular classes. Students will have to complete the assignments without them. This is the reason, why we have included self study material of easy-to-understand nature before the lab assignments. Topics like **MS-Word, MS-Excel, MS-Access, MS-PowerPoint** etc. are part of this section. This material is so well written that students will be able to understand it in single round of study and will be in a position to complete related assignments without any external assistance. Solutions for lab assignments of this module also are of instructional nature.

We want that readers of this book should get an edge over others. With this objective in mind, we have included many working C programs at the end of the book. To gain confidence in programming, these programs can be executed and analyzed in practical sessions.

We are sure that this book will turn out to be a perfect teaching guide for the teachers and good reference book for the students. It is expected that both of them will take full advantage of our knowledge and experience.
Although enough care has been taken to make the book error free but some mistakes may have gone unnoticed. Feedbacks and suggestions in this regard, on our address, will be highly appreciated.

Rajiv Khanna
Technical Director
Bell Infotech Systems (P) Ltd.

SYLLABUS

COMPUTER FUNDAMENTALS AND PROGRAMMING IN C

Subject : **Computer Fundamentals and Programming in C**
Subject Code : **CM - 105**
Periods per Week : **5**
Periods per Year : **150**

TIME SCHEDULE

S.No	Major Topics	Periods	Weightage of marks	Short Questions	Essay Questions
1	Fundamentals of Computer	25	16	2	1
2	Features of DOS& Windows	25	13	1	1
3	Features of Internet	20	13	1	1
4	Concept of Programming Methodology	05	3	1	
5	Programming Constructs	20	23	1	2
6	Arrays and Strings	20	18	1	1½
7	Modular Programming	15	10		1
8	Pointers	10	8	1	½
9	Structures, Unions	5	3	1	
10	Bitwise Operators and Files	5	3	1	
	Total	**150**	**110**	**10**	**08**

1.0. Understand the fundamentals of Computer

1.1 Draw the block diagram of a Computer. (1)
1.2 Explain the interaction between the CPU, Memory, Input / Output devices. (2)
1.3 Describe the function of CPU and major functional parts of CPU. (11)
1.4 Describe the function of memory. (10)
1.5 Describe the function of input/output devices. (2-7)
1.6 State the relevance of speed and word length for CPU Performance. (12)
1.7 Recognize the current family of CPUs used in Computers. (13)
1.8 State the use of storage devices used in a Computer. (7)
1.9 List types of memory used in a Computer. (10)
1.10 State the importance of cache memory. (11)
1.11 Generations of computers. (19)
1.12 Classification of computers - based on size, processor. (23)
1.13 Know importance of binary number system for use in Digital Computers. (30)
1.14 List the various number systems used in digital Computer. (34-40)
1.15 Convert decimal number into binary number. (31)
1.16 Convert binary number into decimal number. (33)
1.17 Convert binary number into hexadecimal number. (39)
1.18 Convert hexadecimal number into binary number. (38)
1.19 Understand the ASCII coding scheme. (42)
1.20 Understand the EBCDIC coding scheme. (42)

2.0 DOS & Windows Operating Systems

2.1 Describe the need for an operating system. (45)
2.2 List the various operating systems used presently. (46)
2.3 DOS Prompt, Types of commands, Internal & External Commands. (47)
2.4 Directories and files, wild cards, autoexec.bat, config.sys, (48-50)
2.5 List the features of Windows desktop. (65)
2.6 List the components of a Window. (72)
2.7 State the function of each component of a Window. (73)
2.8 Explain the Method of starting a program using start button. (71)
2.9 Understand maximize, minimize, restore down and close buttons. (73)
2.10 State the meaning of a file. (79)
2.11 State the meaning of a folder. (79)
2.12 Explain the Method of viewing the contents of hard disk drive using Explore option. (80)
2.13 Explain the Method of finding a file using search option. (84)
2.14 Explain formatting a floppy disk using explore option. (87)
2.15 Describe installing new software using control panel. (88)
2.16 Describe uninstalling software using control panel. (90)
2.17 Explain installing a new hardware using control panel. (90)
2.18 Explain uninstalling a hardware using control panel. (91)
2.19 Narrate finding out drive space using system tool option of accessories group. (96)
2.20 Explain the procedure of disk defragmentation using System tools. (96)
2.21 Narrate installing a printer using control panel.(92)
2.22 Explain the procedure for changing resolution, colour, appearance, and screensaver options of the display. (97-99)
2.23 Narrate the process of changing the system date and time. (99)

3.0 Fundamentals of Internet

3.1 Explain meaning of a computer network. (104)
3.2 Describe the concept of a local area network. (105)
3.3 Explain the concept of the wide area network. (106)
3.4 Compare Internet & Intranet. (107-108)
3.5 Describe the relevance of an internet service provider. (114)
3.6 Explain the role of a modem in accessing the Internet. (106)
3.7 Explain the installation procedure of a MODEM using control panel. (94)
3.8 Explain the purpose of web browser software. (117)
3.9 Explain the structure of a Universal Resource Locator (URL). (113)
3.10 Describe the purpose of World Wide Web, FTP, telnet and E-mail. (113)
3.11 Explain the process of sending and receiving E-mail. (122-127)
3.12 Understand different Connection methods. (115-117)
3.13 Describe address format and IP address. (110)
3.14 Describe DNS. (111)
3.15 Understand the role of search engines with examples. (120)

4.0 Understand Programming Methodology.

4.1 State the different steps involved in problem solving. (131)
4.2 State the steps involved in algorithm development. (136)

4.3 Differentiate algorithm and flowchart. (138-139)
4.4 Develop algorithms for simple problems. (136-138)
4.5 Draw the symbols used in flowcharts. (139)
4.6 Draw flowcharts for simple problems. (142-145)

5.0 Programming Constructs in C

5.1 Understand Sequential structure.

5.1.1 Know about C. ((159)
5.1.2 Know the character set. (165)
5.1.3 Keywords, Identifiers, Constants and Variables. (165-168)
5.1.4 Classify data types and explain them with examples. (168)
5.1.5 Know different arithmetic operators. (170)
5.1.6 Define an expression and show how to evaluate it. (171)
5.1.7 Mention about assignment statement. (173)
5.1.8 Explain an increment and decrement operators. (174)
5.1.9 Know shortcut assignment operators. (173)
5.1.10 Know about nested assignments. (173)
5.1.11 Explain I/P and O/P functions printf and scanf. (180-187)
5.1.12 Know various type conversion techniques and discuss them. (171)
5.1.13 Know about Preprocessor Directives and Macros. (389-396)

5.2 Understand selective structure.

5.2.1 Know various relational operators with their precedence. (175)
5.2.2 List various logical operators and their Precedence. (175)
5.2.3 Know how to evaluate a logical expression. (176)
5.2.5 Explain various conditional statements. (189-198)
5.2.5 Stress on conditional operator. (176)
5.2.6 Stress on multi way conditional statements. (192)
5.2.7 Know the switch statement. (198)

5.3 Understand repetitive structure.

5.3.1 Explain Various Loop Statements. (207)
5.3.2 Define nesting and implement it. (214)
5.3.3 Differentiate break and continue statements. (215-216)
5.3.4 Mention about null statement and comma operator. (217)

6.0 Understand Arrays and Strings

6.1 Know about arrays

6.1.1 Define Array. (220)
6.1.2 Declaration and Initialization of One Dimensional Array. (221)
6.1.3 Accessing the elements in the Array. (221)
6.1.4 Reordering an array in ascending order.(226)
6.1.5 Declaration and Initialization of Two Dimensional Arrays. (234)
6.1.6 Programs on Matrices. (238-245)

6.2 Know about Strings

6.1.1 Define String. (248)

6.1.2 Declaration and Initialization of a String. (249)

6.1.3 Explain about various String functions. (253-254)

6.1.4 Programs on Strings.(250-255)

7.0 Understand modular programming

7.1 Define a function. (267)

7.2 Stress on return statement. (267)

7.3 Types of functions. (262)

7.4 Write programs using function call techniques. (270)

7.5 Stress on function Proto types in programming. (269)

7.6 Differentiate Local and External Variables. (276)

7.7 Know how to pass array elements as arguments. (271)

7.8 Know about Call by value and Call by reference. (270 & 275)

7.9 Know about Storage Classes. (283)

7.10 Define Recursion and Explain with examples. (288)

8.0 Understand basics of Pointers.

8.1 Differentiate address and de-referencing operators. (293-294)

8.2 Declaration and Initialization of Pointers. (293)

8.3 Stress on Pointer Arithmetic. (301)

8.4 Know precedence of address and de-referencing operators. (177)

8.5 Discuss on pointer comparison and pointer conversion. (296-297)

8.6 Know Relationship between Arrays and Pointers. (301)

8.7 Accessing array elements using pointers. (301)

8.8 Pointers as Function Arguments. (316)

8.9 Discuss pointer Arrays with examples. (316)

8.10 Know various dynamic memory management functions and illustrate with examples to use these functions..(305-308)

9.0 Understand basics of Structures and Unions.

9.1 Define a structure. (324)

9.2 Know about structure variable. (325)

9.3 Know structure initialization. (326)

9.4 Know how to access structure members. (326).

9.5 Illustrate concept of structure assignment. (328)

9.6 Explain how to find size of a structure. (328)

9.7 Discuss nested structure concept. (331)

9.8 Summarize concept of pointer to structure. (333)

9.9 Structure as function arguments and structures as function values. (336)

9.10 Arrays of structures, structures containing arrays, arrays of structures containing arrays. (328)

9.11 Illustrate concept of structures containing pointers. (325)

9.12 Explain Self referential structures with examples. (343)

9.13 Define the Union and illustrate use of a union. (346)

10.0 Understand Bitwise operators, File processing techniques

10.1 List bitwise logical operators and explain them in detail. (352-354)

10.2 Know about bitwise shift operators. (354-355)

10.3 Know various file processing facilities in C and explain them in detail. (362-380)

10.4 Write program to create a data file and random access to data. (365-385)

COURSE CONTENTS

1. Organization of a Digital Computer

Block diagram of a digital computer (1), functional parameters of CPU(11), Clock speed and word length(12), Functional blocks of a CPU: ALU and Control unit(12), types of memory RAM, ROM(10), purpose of cache memory(11), Binary Number system(29), Decimal(29), Binary(30), hexadecimal and octal codes(34-36), Conversion from one number system to another number system(31-40), ASCII(42), BCD and EBCDIC code for characters(42), concept of a byte and word(12 & 41).

2. Advanced Windows Features

Formatting disks (87), install/uninstall new software/hardware(88-95), using system tools-drive and disk defragmentation(96); control panel features-installing printer(92), changing display(98-99), keyboard, mouse, date/time settings(99).

3. Fundamentals of Internet

Basics of a computer network (103), local area network and wide area network (105-106), Basics of E-mail(122). Exposure to Web browsers (177). Structure of Universal Resource Locator (113). Type of web sites .com, .gov etc.(110), functions of an Internet service provider(114), role of a modem in accessing the Internet(104), Connection Methods(115), IP address(110), DNS and search engines(111 & 120).

4. Concept of Programming methodology

Steps involved in solving a problem (131). Concept of Structured program (150) , Flow chart(139) , Algorithm(136).

5. Programming constructs

Sequential structure: Various types of data(168)– Arithmetic operators(170) – Expressions(171)- Assignment statement(173) - Assignment operators(173) – printf(183), scanf(182) – Type conversion techniques(171) – Macro define(391) – Selective Structure: Relational operators(175) - Logical operators(175) - Logical expressions(176) - Conditional operator(176) - Conditional statements(189-192) - Multi way condition statement(192) - Switch statement(198) Repetitive structures: Iterative loops(207-214) – Nesting(214) – break(215), continue statements(216) –null statement(217) – comma operator(176).

6. Arrays and Strings

Array (220) - Array declaration(221) - Access to array elements(221) - Initialization of Array elements(225) and - String(248) – Declaration of Strings(249) – various String Functions(253-254).

7. Modular programming:

Function: return statement(267) – function prototypes(269) - local and external variables(276) – Automatic and static variables(283 & 286), Recursion(288).

8. Pointers:

Pointer (292) - Address and de-referencing operators(293-294) - Declaration, Assignment & Initialization of a pointer(293) - Pointer Arithmetic(301) - Pointer comparison(296), conversion parameter passing by reference(298) – Relation between arrays and pointer(301) –Pointer arrays(316) - Pointer to function(318)- Dynamic memory management functions(305-308).

9. Structures, Unions

Structures initialization (326), access concept (326) - Size of a structure(328) - Pointers to structure(333) – Relationship between structure and function(336)- Structures function arguments and function values (336-343)- Relation between structure and arrays(328) –Structure containing pointers(333) –self Referential structure(343) – Unions(346)

10. Bitwise operators, File processing

Operation on bitwise operators (352-358) – File processing facility(361-385)

Subject wise modification table for restructuring of the syllabus.

Branch…Computer Engineering I Year…

Sub-Code as per C-05	CM-106	Sub-Code as per C-09	CM-107
Name of the subject as per C-05	Office Automation Lab	Name of the subject as per C-09	Computer Fundamentals & Programming in C Lab
No. of periods allotted as per C-05	180	No. of periods allotted as per C-09	180

S. No	Name of the Chapter	No. of periods As per C_05	Topics proposed for Addition / deletion	No. of periods added / deleted	No. of periods As per C_09	Justification for Addition / Deletion
1	Windows	20	--	--	20	---
2	Install and Uninstall a Software and Hard ware	20	--	--	20	---
3	Usage of System Tools	15	--	--	15	---
4	Text Manipulation	24	All Topics are deleted	-22	--	The Topics are placed in Information Technology Lab in C-09
5	Exercises on Worksheet	24		-22	--	
6	Create and run PPT Presentation	21		-21	--	
7	Exercise on Ms-Access	24		-24	--	
8	Run browser Software to access websites.	21		-21	--	
9	DOS	15	--I	--	15	---
10	C Programming	--	Added	+110	110	All Topics are brought from CM-308, C & UNIX Lab in C-05
	Total	**180**		**00**	**180**	

Computer Fundamentals and Programming in C Lab

Subject Title	**: Computer Fundamentals and Programming in C Lab**
Subject Code	**: CM - 107**
Periods per Week	**: 6**
Periods per Year	**: 180**

1.0 Windows

1.1 Start the windows Operating system. (399)
1.2 Start a program using the program option of the start menu. (499)
1.3 Minimize, maximize, and close a window. (400)
1.4 Resize and move a window. (400)
1.5 Open multiple windows and switch between windows. (400)
1.6 Locate a file using the Search option of the Start menu. (401)
1.7 Operate the calculator in the accessories. (401)
1.8 Open notepad, paint and WordPad programs. (402)
1.9 Practice locating Files stored on the hard disk drive. (401)
1.10 Know the various options in "My Computer "icon. (405)

2.0 Install and Uninstall the software and hardware.

2.1 Install new software using control panel. (406)
2.2 Uninstall software using control panel. (406) (407)
2.3 Install a new hardware using control panel. (407)
2.4 Uninstall a hardware using control panel. (407)
2.5 Install a modem using control panel. (407)
2.6 Install a printer using control panel. (407)

3.0 Usage of system tools.

3.1 Find out drive space. (407)
3.2 Carryout Disk Defragmentation. (407)
3.3 3.3 Change resolution, color, appearance, screen server options of Display. (408)
3.4 3.4 Change the system date and time. (408)

4.0 DOS

9.1 Practice on Internal & External commands. (408)
9.2 Create and use Batch Files. (408)
9.3 Know the usage of Edlin Editor. (408)

5.0 C Programming

5.1 Acquaintance with editing, compiling and executing programs. (410)
5.2 Exercise on printf and scanf functions. (410)
5.3 Exercises on Selective Structures. (410)
5.4 Exercises on Repetitive Structures. (411)
5.5 Exercises on arrays and Strings. (411)
5.6 Exercises on functions. (412)
5.7 Exercises on recursion . (412)
5.8 Exercises on global variables. (412)
5.9 Exercises on C preprocessor Directives. (412)
5.10 Exercises on Pointers. (413)
5.11 Exercise on structures unions and files. (413)

Information Technology Lab

Subject Title :Information Technology Lab
Subject Code :CM-110
Periods/Week :06
Periods per Semester :90

SPECIFIC OBJECTIVES

On completion of this subject the student would be able to

- Identify the various components of a Computer system
- Differentiate between hardware and software
- State the functions of each component of a computer a system
- State the configuration of a computer system
- Identify the various peripherals
- Know how to open an application program
- Know how to create a folder in a specified location
- Open MS-word and Identify the components on the screen
- Create a document using MS-word and save it
- Create a table using MS-Word and save it
- Create mailing letters using mail merge tool of MS-word
- Open MS-Excel and identify the components on the screen
- Create a Worksheet in MS-Excel and save it
- Generate a Chart using the data in Excel-worksheet
- Automate calculations in a worksheet using formula
- Sort and filter data in a worksheet
- Create a simple Power point presentation for a small topic
- Backup required files and folders to a CD-ROM
- Introduction to the internet technology and imparting training to use searching of required sites and using e-Mails etc

COURSE CONTENT:

1. Study of a computer system
2. Familiarise with basic MS-WINDOWS facilities like opening programs, searching, creating folders, copying and shifting data ,etc.
3. Create a formatted word document using MS-Word
4. Familiarise with spell checker facility of MS-Word
5. Print the Word document using page setup and Print facilities
6. Create a soft copy of a given table using MS-Word
7. Create mailing letters for a given information using MS-Word
8. Create a soft copy of the given statistical data using MS-Excel
9. Generate Appropriate Chart for the statistical data using MS-Excel
10. Generate the soft copy of a worksheet using formula facility of MS-Excel
11. Create a soft copy of a simple database using Excel. Run sort and filter facilities for the database
12. Create a power point presentation for a simple technical topic using MS-PowerPoint
13. Create a backup CD for a data using NERO or similar CD writing software
14. Create an user account on the Internet and e-mail and sending a document to from a given e-mail address. To another e-Mail ID as attachment.
15. Using different search engines finding required sites to collect information on engineering related topics including down loading the contents.

Table Of Contents

Table Of Contents

CHAPTER 1

Organization Of A Digital Computer

INTRODUCTION

Computer is electronic equipment. It is mainly used for automating manual tasks. Using computer you can perform tasks quickly, effectively and in error free manner. Be it any organization, office, factory or institution, you can find people making use of computer there. In offices, computers are used for preparing letters, documents and reports. In hotels, computers are used for advance booking of rooms, preparing bills and providing enquiry services. In railways, computers are used for rail reservation, printing of tickets and preparation of reservation charts. Doctors use computers for diagnosing illness and treatment of deceases. Architects use them for map designing and city planning. In meteorology department, computers are used for weather forecasting. In short you can say that there is hardly any sphere of life left now, in which computers are not being used. What computer is, what are its main units, how does it function are the issues, which are described in this chapter.

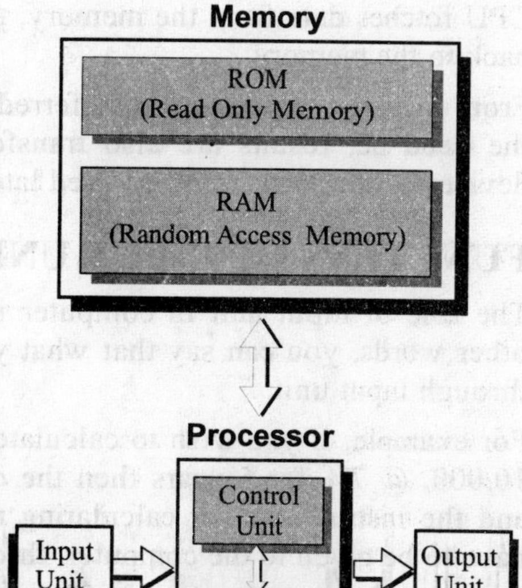

Figure 1.1

BLOCK DIAGRAM OF A DIGITAL COMPUTER

As you know, computer is an electronic device, it comprises of many units. These units work in coordination with each other to perform the given task. Block diagram of computer is shown in figure 1.1.

Refer this figure and note that computer comprises of following units:

1. Input Unit
2. Output Unit
3. Input/Output Unit
4. Central Processing Unit
   (a) Memory Unit
   (b) ALU
   (c) Control Unit

Physically these units exist in the form of electronic devices in computer.

When a task is given to the computer, each unit performs its function in co-ordination with other unit. Thus collectively all the units work together to complete the task and it is said that computer has finished the given work.

INTERACTION BETWEEN THE PARTS OF COMPUTER

To perform a task through computer, data and instructions are provided to the computer, using its Input Units.

Data provided to the computer, travels internally within computer on dedicated path, called Bus and gets stored in memory.

CPU fetches data from the memory, processes it as per given instructions and sends results back to the memory.

From memory, results are transferred to any of the Output Unit, where user can view it. If the need be, results are also transferred from memory to any of the computer storage devices so that they could be used later.

FUNCTION OF INPUT UNITS

The role of input unit in computer is to provide data or instructions to the computer. In other words, you can say that what you supply to the computer for processing is supplied through input unit.

For example, if you wish to calculate simple interest on Rs. 10,000, @ 7% for 5 years then the data 10,000, 7, 5% etc. and the instructions for calculating the simple interest will have to be given to the computer, through input unit.

All those devices, using which input is provided to the computer are termed as input units. Following are few commonly used input units that can be found attached with almost every computer.

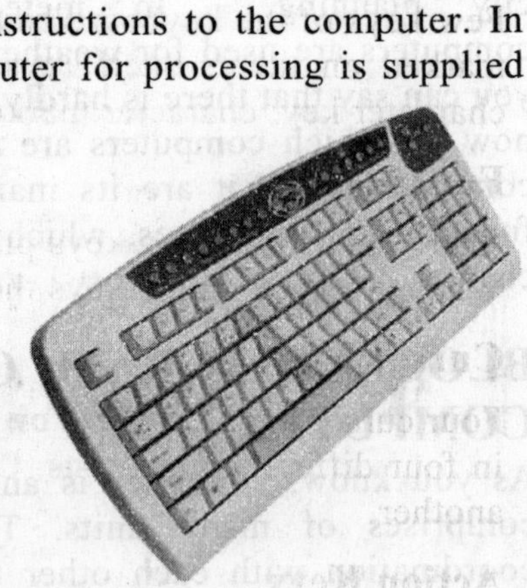

Figure 1.2

Keyboard

Keyboard consists of many keys. Keys have alphabets, numbers, characters or words written on them. Keyboard is illustrated in figure 1.2.

When keyboard is connected to the computer, a blinking sign (| or –) appears on the monitor. This sign is called cursor. When you press an alphabet or number key, the character written on the key gets typed at current cursor position and the cursor moves forward.

Keys

Keys of the keyboard are broadly classified into following categories:

- ❑ Alphabet keys
- ❑ Number keys
- ❑ Special character keys
- ❑ Function keys
- ❑ Cursor keys
- ❑ Action keys

Alphabet Keys

Alphabet keys have alphabets, from A to Z, written on them. By pressing these keys, you can type alphabets, words, sentences etc. in lower case. For example, when you press 'A' key, 'a' gets typed. To type the alphabet in upper case, you need to press Shift key along with the alphabet key. For example, if you press 'A' key along with Shift key, letter 'A' gets typed.

Number Keys

Number keys have digits, from 0 to 9, written on them. These keys are used for typing the numbers. Note that each number key also has a special character written just above the number. To type this character, you will have to press the number key along with the Shift key. For example, number 5 key has % sign marked on it. When you press number 5 key, 5 will get typed. If you pres the same key, along with Shift key % sign will get typed.

Special Character Keys

Few keys of the keyboard have special characters like semicolon (;), comma (,), dot (.) etc. marked on them. Such keys are called special character keys. When you press special character key, character marked on it gets typed at current cursor position.

Function Keys

There are 12 function keys present on the keyboard. They are named as F1, F2, F3 .....F12. When you press these keys they perform special functions.

Cursor Keys

Four cursor keys are there on the keyboard. They are marked with arrows on them, pointing in four different directions. Using cursor keys, you can move the cursor from one place to another.

Action Keys

Keyboard has many action keys. When you press an action key, a special event takes place. Most commonly used action keys of the keyboard are described below.

Caps Lock Key

When you press this key, capital lock becomes on. When you press an alphabet key, while capital lock is on, the letter written on it gets typed in upper case.

Shift Key

Shift key is always pressed along with other keys. When you press this key along with number key then the symbol written on upper part of the key gets typed. When you press Shift key along with alphabet key then the alphabet gets typed in upper case.

Enter Key

Enter key is used to start a new line. When you press this key; cursor comes to the next line. Whatever you type now, gets typed in the next line.

Space Bar

This key is used to put blank spaces between the two characters.

DEL Key

This key is used to rub a character from current cursor position.

Backspace Key

This key removes one character from the left side of the cursor.

Insert Key

This key is used to insert characters in between the two characters, which have already been typed.

Page Keys

There are two page keys on the keyboard, named as PgDn (i.e. Page Down) and PgUp (i.e. Page Up). When you press PgUp key, previous page gets displayed on the screen. When you press PgDn key, next page gets displayed on the screen.

Tab Key

This key is used for making the cursor jump in forward direction, by many places.

ESC Key

This key is called Escape key. Currently on-going activity gets cancelled when this key is pressed.

Mouse

Mouse is an input device. It is shown in figure 1.3. It looks like a real mouse with few buttons placed on its back. When mouse is connected to the computer, an arrow sign appears on the monitor screen. This sign is called Mouse Pointer.

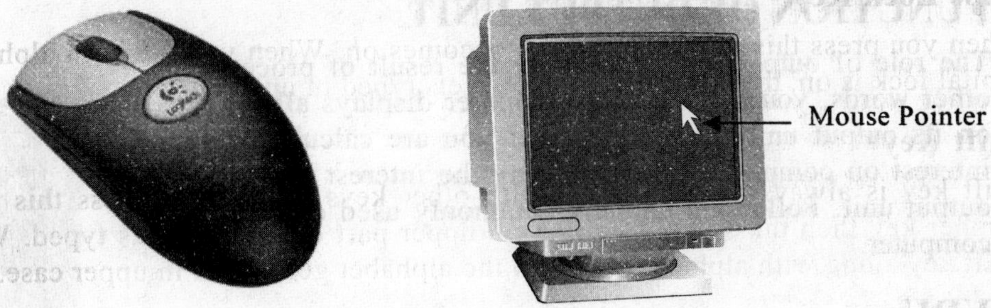

Figure 1.3

When you move the mouse on plane surface, mouse pointer also moves in the same direction. Thus by moving the mouse, you can make the mouse pointer point to anything present on the screen. After pointing the mouse on any desired object, following actions can be performed:

Clicking The Mouse

Pressing the left button of the mouse and releasing it is called clicking the mouse.

Double Clicking The Mouse

Pressing the left button of the mouse twice, in quick succession, is called double clicking the mouse.

Dragging The Mouse

Moving the mouse, with its left button pressed is called dragging the mouse.

Dropping

Moving the finger away from the mouse after dragging it is called dropping.

CD-ROM Drive

CD is acronym for Compact Disk. It works as a medium for storing data or instructions. It looks like circular plastic disk. Huge amount of data can be stored on CD. For example, single CD can hold personal data of all the students studying in a college.

CD-ROM drive is an input unit that reads data from CD. As the name indicates, CD-ROM (Compact Disk Read Only Memory) can only read the data from CD, it cannot write on it. CD and CD-ROM drive are shown in figure 1.4.

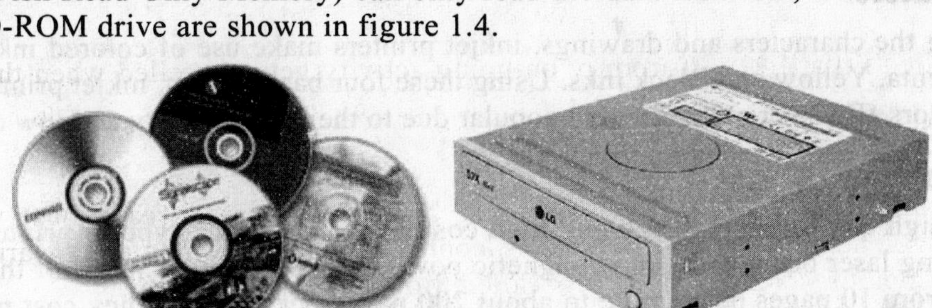

Figure 1.4.

FUNCTION OF OUTPUT UNIT

The role of output unit is to show the result of processing. In other words, you can say that computer displays all the results on its output unit. For example, if you are calculating simple interest on computer, it will display the interest amount on its output unit. Following are few commonly used output units of computer.

VDU

VDU is acronym for Visual Display Unit. It looks like portable TV. VDU is illustrated in figure 1.5. It is primarily used for following two purposes:

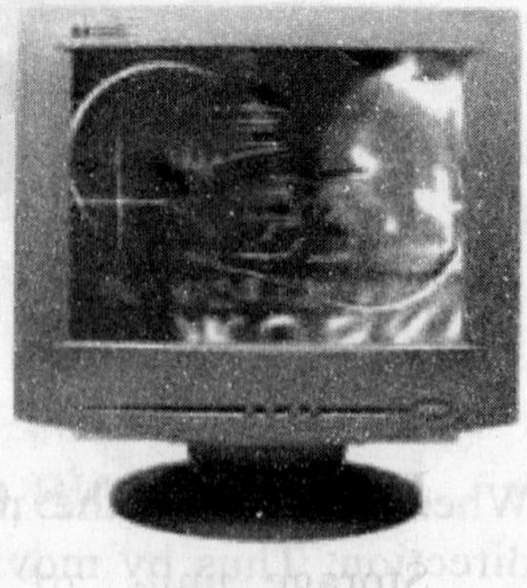

Figure 1.5

- ❑ To display the contents that are being typed through keyboard.
- ❑ To display the result of processing (output).

Printer

Printer is an output device. It prints the output on paper. Different types of printers print differently. Their quality and speed of printing differ from each other. Following are different types of printers, which are being commonly used these days:

1. Dot Matrix Printer
2. Inkjet Printer
3. Laser Printer

Dot Matrix Printers

These printers are very versatile printers and drive their name "Dot Matrix" from the fact that they print the characters making dots. Pins of the printer print these dots so close to each other that the gap between them is hardly visible. Viewer gets an impression of full continuity. These printers are versatile printers and are capable of printing not only text, but up to some extent graphics also. They are relatively fast printers and their speed varies from 300 Character Per Second (CPS) to 600 CPS.

Inkjet Printers

For printing the characters and drawings, inkjet printers make use of colored inks. They use Cyan, Magenta, Yellow and Black inks. Using these four basic colors, inkjet printers generate all other colors. These printers are very popular due to their high quality and low cost.

Laser Printers

These are high quality, high speed and high cost printers. In such type of printers, printing is done, using laser beam and black magnetic powder, called Toner. Speed of these printers can range from 10 pages per minute to about 200 pages per minute. They cost much higher than dot matrix and inkjet printers. All the three types of printer are shown in figure 1.6.

Dot Matrix Printer Inkjet Printer Laser Printer

Figure 1.6

FUNCTIONS OF STORAGE UNITS

Storage units are those devices, which hold the data, instructions, information etc. permanently within computer. Whatever is written on them remains there till the time someone removes it deliberately from there. This is the reason, why they are also called permanent storage units.

Whatever is required for longer durations is stored in storage units. Later whenever stored item is required, it is read from there. Unlike input and output units, they allow users to perform both, input and output operations. This is the reason they are also called Input/Output units.

Floppy drives and hard disks are the two, very common storage units, which are found in most of the computers. Using floppy drive read/write operations are performed on a media called floppy.

Floppy Drive

Floppy drive is an Input/Output unit. It is basically an assembly, in which you put the floppy, close its door and then perform read / write operations on the floppy. For analogy, you can think of tape recorder's cassette housing assembly, in which you put the cassette, close the door and then perform read / write operations on the cassette. Similarly you either write the data on the floppy or read the data from the floppy. Whatever you write on floppy, it gets permanently stored there, until you delete it yourself or mishandle the floppy. Floppy and floppy drive are shown in figure 1.7.

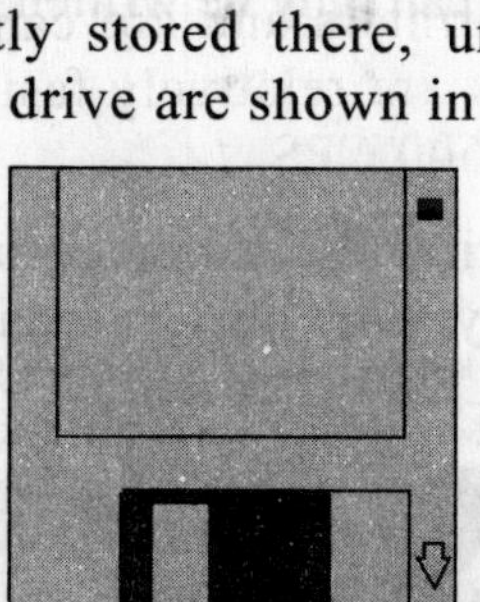

Floppy
(a)

Floppy Drive
(b)

Figure 1.7

Floppy is basically a data storage medium, on which you record the data or programs to read them later. Floppy consists of flexible plastic coated with magnetic material iron oxide. This plastic is enclosed in a thick black gasket cover, which protects it from heat, dust, sun etc. Most commonly used floppies are of 3 ½" size.

Hard Disk

Hard disk is another unit, which stores the data permanently in computer. Externally it looks like a box and remains fixed within computer chassis. Its internal composition is shown in figure 1.8.

Refer this figure and note that hard disk consists of multiple dish like units, on which the data is stored. These dishes are called platters. Each platter has a corresponding read-write head.

Read-write heads write the data or instructions on the platters. Thus they get permanently stored there.

Note that floppy and hard disk both are used for storing data but the capacity of the hard disk is generally many times more than that of a floppy. Floppy is a removable storage medium while hard disk is a fixed medium.

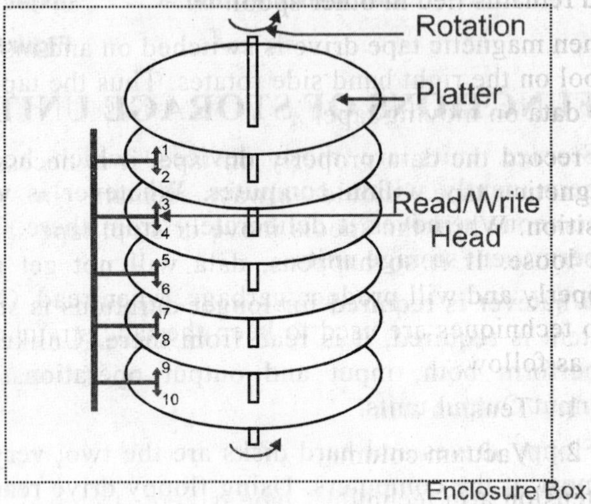

Figure 1.8

CD-Writer

CD writer is another Input/Output device, which stores data, instructions, results etc. permanently on medium called CD-R and CD-R/W.

CD-R

CD-R is acronym for Compact- Disk Readable. It resembles CD, on which data can be written. Data is written on CD-R through a device called CD Writer. CD-R looks like CD but its internal composition remains different. But note that data can only be written once on CD-R but not again and again.

CD-R/W

CD-R/W is acronym for Compact Disk Re-Writeable. It looks similar to CD-R but data can be written multiple times on it. If you wish, you could write data on it, read data from it and erase the data as many times as required. CD-Writer and CD-R are shown in figure 1.9.

Figure 1.9

Magnetic Tape Drive

Magnetic tape drive is another input/output unit, which is used for storing the data permanently. It accesses the data sequentially. Using this unit, data is recorded on magnetic tapes. Magnetic tape drive in its appearance looks like older spool based tape records. Its block diagram is illustrated in figure 1.10.

In magnetic tape drive, magnetic tape from feeder spool passes below the Read/Write head and remains tied in other spool.

When magnetic tape drive is switched on and instructions for writing the data are given, the spool on the right hand side rotates. Thus the tape moves forward. Read/Write head records the data on moving tape.

To record the data properly on tape, it is necessary that magnetic tape should always remain in stretched position. While the spools move or stop, tape should not get loose. If it so happens, data will not get recorded properly and will produce garbage, when read. Generally two techniques are used to keep the tape stretched. They are as follows:

1. Tension arm
2. Vacuum column.

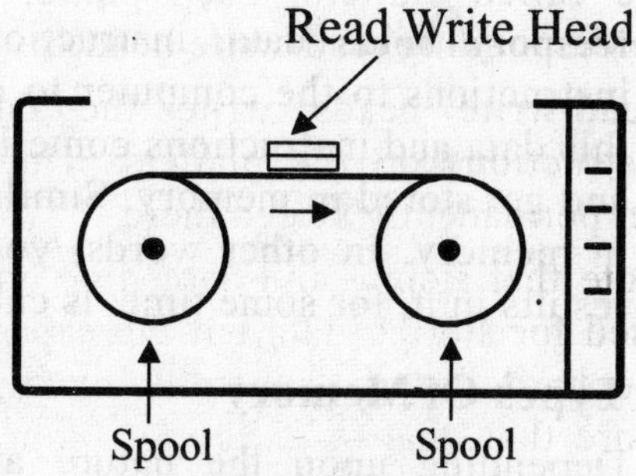

Figure 1.10

In tension arm technique, tape is kept stretched, with the help of mechanical arms while in vacuum column technique tape is kept stretched by creating vacuum. Those tape drives, which use tension arm technique, are called tension arm tape drives. Those tape drives, which use vacuum technique, are called vacuum column tape drives.

Magnetic Tape

Magnetic tape is a medium to record the data. Generally it is 12.5 mm. to 25 mm wide and 500 meters to 1200 meters in length. It is made of magnetic material coated plastic. When the tape passes below read/write head, it creates magnetic waves and writes data on the tape. Note that data does not get continuously written on the tape. It gets recorded in blocks. There remains a gap (blank space) between the two blocks. This block is called Inter Block Gap or IBG in short. The way data gets stored on the tape, is illustrated in figure 1.11.

Figure 1.11

Magnetic Cartridge Tape Drive

Figure 1.12

Like magnetic tape drive, magnetic cartridge tape drive is also an Input/Output unit, which records the data on tape. Cartridge tape drives are much smaller in size than magnetic tape drives. They do not store the data on spool tapes. They store it on cartridge tapes. Cartridge tape resembles small video tape that is used in handy cams. The shape of cartridge tape is shown in figure 1.12.

Memory

Memory holds data, instruction or results temporarily. For example, when you give instructions to the computer to compute simple interest on Rs. 10,000, @ 7% for 3 years, this data and instructions come into computer from any of the input or Input/output devices and get stored in memory. Similarly result (simple interest in this example) also gets stored in memory. In other words, you can say that the unit, which holds data, instructions or results in it, for some time, is called Memory.

Types Of Memory

Depending upon the nature and behavior of memory, computer memories could be categorized into following categories:

1. Primary Memory
2. Cache Memory

Characteristic behavior of each type of memory is described below.

Primary Memory

That memory, which is utilized by the computer for its internal functioning, is called primary memory. Since it plays an important role in internal functioning of computer hence it is often referred to as internal memory. Primary memory is further categorized into two categories:

1. Read Only Memory (ROM)
2. Random Access Memory (RAM)

Read Only Memory (ROM)

This memory by its nature is quite special. Computer cannot write data in it. Using special devices, such as ROM programmer, instructions are written in it. Once instructions are written in it, it is put inside the computer. As and when required, computer reads instructions from it. Since data can only be read from it hence it is called Read Only Memory or ROM in short. ROM physically exists in the form of blank electronic chip, in which programs or data are written, using special devices. Those ROMs, in which data once written, cannot be erased by any means are called Programmable Read Only Memory or PROM in short. Other type of ROM, in which data is written or erased, using ultraviolet rays is called Erasable Programmable Read Only Memory or EPROM in short.

Random Access Memory

In short, Random Access Memory is called RAM. It differs from ROM in nature. It provides both, reading and writing facilities. As and when required, computer writes data or instructions in it and reads them whenever necessary. This is the reason why they are also called Read/Write memory.

Note that whatever data or instructions are given to the computer for processing, computer writes them in RAM. As and when required, it reads them from there and processes them to generate the result. Computer first writes all the results in RAM and then whenever necessary, it transfers them to output unit.

The data written in Random Access Memory remains there till the time computer power is on. As soon as the power goes off, data written in RAM gets erased. This is the reason why they are also called Temporary memory.

Cache Memory

In cache memory reading and writing operations take place at very fast speed but it costs very high. When it is introduced into computer, it increases its speed and cost also. For best cost-performance ratio, sufficient amount of cache memory (less then the size of RAM) is introduced in the computer, in between the processor and Random Access Memory, as shown in figure 1.13.

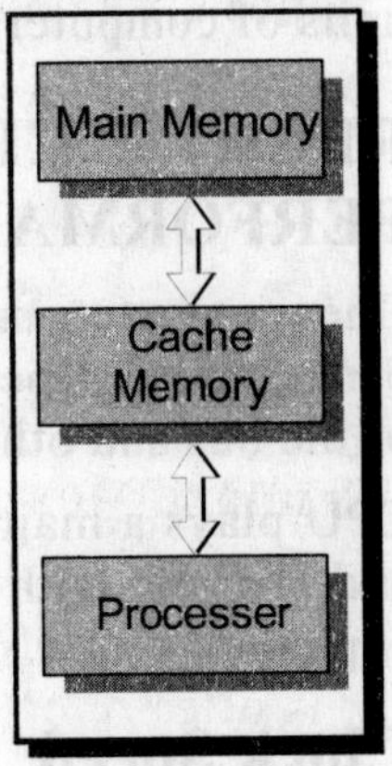

Figure 1.13

First time, when computer requires data/instructions/results from RAM, it reads them from there. But at the same time, many more of them are read and put in cache memory. Next time, whenever computer requires something from RAM, it reads it from cache memory. Since the speed of cache memory is faster than RAM hence reading is done in much shorter time. When computer doesn't get the required item in cache memory, it goes back to RAM and reads it from there along with many more items. The whole mechanism of reading and writing, in computers, is implemented in such a way that most of the time required items are found in cache memory. On the other hand, if computer has to write the data in RAM, it writes it in cache memory, from where it is transferred to RAM.

Thus cache memory improves the speed of computer. In short, it can be said that the memory, which is introduced in the computer with objective of increasing its speed, is called cache memory.

CPU AND ITS MAJOR FUNCTIONAL PARTS

CPU is acronym for Central Processing Unit. It is called heart of computer because it not only performs major functions in computer, like heart does in human body but it also controls other devices.

Physically, CPU exists in the form of an electronic chip, called Microprocessor. Microprocessor comprises of two major parts i.e. ALU and Control Unit. An introduction to both the units is given below.

ALU

ALU is acronym for Arithmetic and Logic Unit. It performs arithmetic and logical calculations in computer.

Recall that calculations like, addition, subtraction, multiplication division etc. fall into the category of arithmetic calculations and operations like a>b, c>=d etc. are logical operations.

In computer terminology, the activity of performing arithmetic and logical calculations is called processing. Thus it can be said that ALU performs data processing functions in computer.

Control Unit

While computer functions, data moves from one unit to another unit. For example, when input is given to the computer, data and instructions move from input unit to memory. When data is processed, it moves from memory to ALU. Similarly when processing is over, results move from ALU to memory and memory to output unit.

Now the question is, which part of computer organizes data movement within the computer? Well, Control Unit is the unit, which performs traffic police like task. It ensures movement of right data from right source, to right destination at right time so that all the units of computer perform their functions in coordination with each other.

RELEVANCE OF CLOCK SPEED AND WORD LENGTH ON CPU PERFORMANCE

One computer may process the data fast and the other may take times. Computer's performance depends upon several factors like the CPU being used, size of memory, width of the bus and other architectural details of computer.

CPU plays a major role in deciding the internal architecture of the computer. Clock speed and Word Length are the major attributes that govern CPU performance. These factors are explained below.

Clock Speed

Each computer has a clock inside. Clock ticks at a very fast rate, such as 800 Mega Hertz (MHz), 900 Metz, 1 Giga Hertz (GHz), 1.8 GHz etc. Recall that 1 Hz means 100 ticks per second. That means if the clock speed is 1 Hz then the clock will tick after every 10^{-2} seconds. Similarly a clock of 100 MHz speed will tick after every 10^{-8} seconds. That means, as the frequency of clock increase, time between the two ticks reduces.

The time between two ticks of the clock is called CPU cycle. In each cycle, CPU performs a task. Now it is quite obvious that a microprocessor, which has higher clock speed, will perform more tasks in the same time than the microprocessor, which has lower speed. In other words it can be said that microprocessor clock speed affects the processing speed.

Word Length

Within computer, all the digits (0-9), alphabets (a-z) and symbols (like *, @, $ etc.) are represented using group of 0s and 1s. Each such unit (0 and 1) is called bit. That means 1 is one bit and 0 is another bit.

In most of the computers, it takes 8 bits to represent a character. For example, A will require 8 bits for representation, within in computer. Similarly the digit 7 or 5 will also require 8 bits. The word BELL will thus require 32 bits.

In computers, Bit is the most basic unit but most commonly used unit is Byte. 8 bits put together are called 1 Byte. That means it takes 1 Byte to represent alphabets like A, B, C, D etc. within computer. Similarly other characters like 1, 2, *, $ etc also take up 1 byte for their representation within computer.

Now the question is what is word length? Well! Word Length is the number of bits that can be moved in a single operation from storage to a processor for processing.

In a computer with 8 bit word length, 8 bits (i.e. one character) are moved in a single operation while in 64 bit word length 64 bits (i.e. 8 characters) are be moved from memory to processor for processing.

It is quite clear that larger the word length, faster is the processing or speed of the computer.

Which computer will have what word length, depends upon many factors like, the type of microprocessor being used, bus width and the architecture of the computer.

Bus Width

As mentioned earlier, data from one place to another, within the computer, travels on Bus. Bus is basically a set of parallel conducting track. The speed of data travel depends upon the number of tracks that run parallel to each other. A bus with 8 parallel tracks is called 8 bit bus. Similarly 16 bit bus will have 16 bit parallel tracks for data communication.

On 8 bit bus, 8 bits can be transmitted simultaneously. Thus, if two characters A and B have to be transferred from memory to CPU on 8 bit bus, the process will take two CPU cycles. In first cycle, 8 bits of A will transferred and in the second cycle another 8 bits of B will get transmitted. On the other hand, on a 16 bit bus both the characters (8 bits of A and 8 bits of B) will get transferred. This clearly states that higher the bus width faster is the data transfer. Faster data transfer obviously results into faster data processing.

Now a days computer have 32 bit to 64 bit bus width. That means 4 to 8 characters can be simultaneously transferred from one place to another.

CURRENT FAMILIES OF CPUs USED IN COMPUTER

A microprocessor or CPU is always identified by its manufacturer, name and a number. For example, Intel Pentium IV is a popular microprocessor that was used in microcomputers. Intel is the manufacture's name, Pentium is name of the model and IV is the number.

A processor is typically characterized by its number of transistors packed into the chip, clock speed, data bus width and number of registers (memory) in it.

There are many companies, which manufacture microprocessor for microcomputers. Intel IBM, Free Scale, Advanced Micro Devices (AMD), Motorola etc. are famous manufactures of microprocessors.

They manufacture wide verity of microprocessor, with many variations in them. A detailed description of the processors, manufactured by some of the companies is given below.

Pentium Series

In 1993 Intel introduced its latest microprocessor. It was supposed to be named as 80586, in continuation to Intel 80x86 family but the company opted for the name Pentium. Originally Pentium was introduced with 60 and 66 MHz but later, in a very short span of time the speed was enhanced to 166 MHz. In 1996 Intel further improved its design and introduced Multimedia Extension Technology called MMx to make the Pentium microprocessor suite best for multimedia operations. Thus sound and graphics operations were made possible at very reasonable speed. In fact Pentium processor brought a revolution in multimedia field. Those applications, which previously required higher end computers, were now able to run on desktop computers. Pentium processor had following things incorporated in it:

Super Scalar Technology

Pentium had the capability to execute two instructions at the same time. Whereas all preceding chips performed only one instruction at a time. Pentium had 64 bit data, but 32 bit of internal registers. So the instructions, 64 bit data channel got broken down into two 32 instructions and processed in the same way as in 80486. Some people thought that Intel was misleading them by calling the Pentium a 64-bit processor, but 64-bit transfer did take place. But internally, however, the Pentium had 32 bit registers that were fully compatible with 80486.

Bus Width

Pentium had 32 bit address bus width i.e. it could access up to 4 GB of memory. Pentium had the 64 bit wide data bus i.e. it could move 64 bit of data in one clock cycle whereas in the same clock cycle, 486 processor could move only 32 bits of data.

Cache

Pentium had two separate internal caches of 8 KB instead of a single 16 KB cache in 486. This cache was of Level 1, i.e. its speed was faster than RAM. It also had cache of Level 2.

System Management Mode

Pentium processor incorporated the System Management Mode (SMM) to provide full control over power management features, which helps to reduce power consumption. The second generation of Pentium processor (75 MHz and faster) had even the feature to stop the clock, putting the processor in a state of suspension, which requires very little power. Note that second generation Pentium processor runs on 3.3 V power (instead of 5 Volt).

Maths Coprocessor

Pentium had an internal math coprocessor or floating-point unit. The Pentium CPU was 10 times faster than the CPU in the 80486.

Pentium Series Enhancements

Pentium-I, Pentium-II, Pentium-III and Pentium IV are the member processors of Pentium series, which are gradually enhanced versions of original Pentium processors. In what way the enhancements have taken place in Pentium series, has been summarized in the following table.

Name	Date	Transistors	Microns	Clock speed	Data width	MIPS
Pentium	1993	3,100,000	0.8	60 MHz	32 bits 64-bit bus	100
Pentium II	1997	7,500,000	0.35	233 MHz	32 bits 64-bit bus	~300
Pentium III	1999	9,500,000	0.25	450 MHz	32 bits 64-bit bus	~510
Pentium IV	2000	42,000,000	0.18	1.5 GHz	32 bits 64-bit bus	~1,700

Note that in above table the **date** is the year in which the processor was introduced. **Transistors** are the number of transistors on the chip. You can see that the number of transistors on a single chip has risen steadily over the years. **Micron** is the width, in microns, of the smallest wire on the chip. For comparison, a human hair is 100 microns thick. **Clock speed** is the maximum rate that the chip can be clocked at. **Data width** is the width of the ALU. **MIPS** stand for "Millions of Instructions Per Second" and is a rough measure of the performance of a CPU.

Intel Dual-Core Processor

It is Intel's relatively new creation with latest technology packed into it to improve microprocessor's performance, increase its speed and cut upon power requirements.

The dual core processor consists of two complete execution cores packed into one physical processor. Each execution core has its own cache. While one processes the other one fetches data. They are not held up while working with same resources. They work in parallel coordination to deliver improvised throughputs.

To conceptualize its design, consider a four lane highway. Note that 4 lane highway can accommodate 2 times more traffic than 2 lane highway, without making each car drive twice as fast. Dual core processor works like 4 lane highway and delivers better results than single core processor.

With Intel dual-core processor, users can do more at once than ever before, without slowing down the performance. It's performance can be quite appreciated in highly multithreaded and compute-intensive applications.

Intel Dual Core processor makes use of Intel® Core™ microarchitecture that greatly reduces the costs and uses less power and is energy-efficient.

It provides flexibility and performance to handle robust content creation or intense gaming with multimedia-enabling technologies built in.

Intel Core 2 Duo Processor

Intel Core 2 Duo processor is next gen processors from Intel. It is Intel's latest creation in the series for delivering high performance at much reduced cost, with high energy saving.

It is Up-High version of Intel Dual-Core processor. It consists of two complete execution cores packed into one physical processor with single cache shared by both the cores. Single cache improves efficiency of the processor and delivers better throughputs than dual core processors.

Celeron Series Of Microprocessors

Intel Corporation not only manufactures Pentium series of processors but also manufactures Celeron processors. Celeron processor came into existence when Pentium II processor was released. Pentium II was high in price and performance, so Intel came out with a scaled down version of Pentium II, which was much lower in price but slightly lower in speed (due to removal of L1 cache). Such a processor was named Celeron. Scaled down version came on account of reducing processor's internal cache memory. Celeron processor was very well accepted in the market. Ever since then Intel has been releasing Celeron processors in parallel with their Pentium processors.

Xeon Series Of Microprocessors

Intel Corporation also manufactures Xeon series of processors. They came into existence after the release of Pentium II processor. Pentium II had a shortcoming that not more than 2 processors could be used in multiprocessor applications. To overcome this shortcoming, Xeon processor was designed and released by Intel. The design of Xeon processor was such that 8 processors could be combined to work together. The design was improved by introducing bigger and faster cache memory (up to 2MB).

Intel Mobile Series Of Microprocessors

Intel mobile processors are the processors, which are basically energy efficient processors and have been designed by Intel for the use in smaller computers. In its mobile series, Intel has already released versions like Pentium II-M, Pentium III-M and Pentium IV-M.

Special small size components are manufactured by companies, to make smaller computers like laptops and palmtops. Manufacturing of smaller sized microprocessors was possible by reducing the size of transistors. Such special type of manufacturing is quite costly which increases the price of processors and other components to many folds.

Motorola CPUs

Motorola is another company that manufactures microprocessors. Its microprocessors are named after the company and are referred as Motorola series. Motorola's initial microprocessor introduction was the 6800 in 1975. It was strictly an 8-bit processor capable of addressing 64 kilobytes of memory. Probably the most striking difference between the Motorola and Intel architectures is that early members of the 6800 family tended to minimize register usage in favor of general purpose RAM.

Motorola introduced numerous variations of the 6800. The 6802 incorporated 128 bytes of RAM on the CPU itself. The 6803/6808 ran faster (3.58 MHz), incorporated 128 bytes of RAM, and included both a UART (universal asynchronous receiver/transmitter) for serial communications, and a counter/timer. The last variation of the 8-bit Motorola family was the 6809. It was similar to the 6802, but offered an enhanced instruction set, including what was probably the first multiply instruction on an 8-bit CPU.

In 1978, Motorola introduced its first 16-bit CPU: the 68000. Unlike Intel's 8086/8088, which could address only one megabyte of physical RAM, the 68000 had 24 address lines that could access 16 megabytes of RAM directly. It was an almost inconceivable amount of memory at that time. In addition, the 68000 ran faster than mainstream Intel processors of the day: 16 MHZ. Also, Motorola abandoned the idea of RAM-based registers and incorporated 16 general-purpose registers in the 68000. It would be four years until Intel could approach the technology of the 68000.

Motorola entered the 32-bit CPU arena with the 68020. Like the 68000, the 68020 had 16 general-purpose registers, and could address four gigabytes of RAM directly. A first for the 68020 was the inclusion of an internal 256-byte instruction cache - negligible by today's standards, but a true architectural advance at the time.

The 68030 is Motorola's second generation 32-bit CPU. It is very similar to the '020, but is available in faster speeds, and with one 256-byte cache each for data and instructions.

The 68040 is the third generation. It increases the data and instruction caches to 4 kilobytes each, and, for the first time, includes an on-board math coprocessor and memory-management unit.

One of the latest members of the 680x0 family is the 68060. The 68060 is a super scalar design that has multiple instruction pipelines, and on-board memory and power management.

PowerPC

After more than a decade of development, the 680x0 architecture simply ran out of stream, so Motorola teamed up with IBM and Apple to produce a new microprocessor with improved performance. The MPC601, or PowerPC, is a 64-bit super-scalar CPU that can effectively execute up to three instructions per clock cycle. The PowerPC is the first implementation of reduced instruction set computing (RISC) for personal computers. (The 680x0 and 80x86 families use complex instruction set computing (CISC) technology.) With RISC, most instructions execute in only one clock cycle. Instructions can even be completed out of order, but the CPU will make them appear sequential. The MPC601 has a 32-bit address bus, 32 kilobytes of cache memory, and an internal maths coprocessor. After MPC601 came the processors, MPC603, MPC604 and MPC620 which were gradual improvements of the original processors in terms of speed, number of transistors, bus width and memory accessibility.

AMD Series Of Microprocessors

AMD is the short name of the company called Advanced Micro Devices. It was founded in 1969 and manufactures microprocessors in a big way. AMD processors are quite famous and are named as AMD&&. AMD processors are used by many computer manufacturers, including IBM. AMD processors are RISC based processors.

In the year 1975 AMD released reversed engineering version of Intel 8080 chip. Later AMD released all equivalents of Intel x86 processors. AMD K5 is a fifth generation processor offered by AMD. It is a 64-bit processor equivalent to Intel's Pentium processor. It uses 4-instruction pipeline architecture, which is two times more than Pentium.

The latest AMD processor is AMD Opteron. It is eighth generation processor that makes use of integrated memory controller, which reduces memory bottlenecks, and Hyper Transport (TM) technology. This technology increases overall performance by removing or reducing I/O bottlenecks, increasing bandwidth and reducing latency.

Cyrix Series Of Microprocessors

Cyrix is another company that manufactures microprocessors. It introduced its microprocessors, which were named as 486DLC and 484SLC. These processors were designed to be compatible with Intel's 486 microprocessor.

Later Cyrix produced many microprocessors that were in competition with Intel processors. Cyrix 6x86 was sixth generation processor and was designed to provide better results than Intel's Pentium and that too at lower cost. It used 7-stage pipeline architecture to avoid lags in execution process and increase the flow of information. The latest Cyrix processor is M-II 733 MHz, which is available in the market.

RISC And CISC Processors

RISC stands for Reduced Instruction Set Computer and CISC stands for Complex Instruction Set Computer. The processors, which are designed, based on reduced instruction set are called RISC processors and the processors which are designed, based on complex instruction set are called CISC Processors.

To understand the concept of reduced and complex instruction set, consider a fact that a processor's architecture is governed by its instruction set. If instruction set is complex the design of the processor will also be complex and the complexity will result into high performance and high price. On contrary, if the instruction set is simple the design of the processor will also be simple and the price of the processor will obviously be low. As far as the performance of such processors is concerned they will be able to do all the simple functions with same efficiency, but for doing complex operations they will take more number of cycles.

The fact about the normal processors is that they make use of only 20% instructions of their instruction sets, rest 80% of the instructions are seldom used in rare circumstances. But the fact is that normally the provision is made, in the processor, for all the 100% instructions. Thus price goes high. Now think of a situation, if somehow an instruction set could be reduced to only those instructions, which are mostly used and a processor could be designed for this instruction set then this processor would have lower price and high performance. RISC based processors are the processors that are designed and developed on this philosophy. They have reduced instruction set to work with. All the tasks are resolved through reduced instruction set only. Whenever such a task is to be performed which cannot be directly resolved through the instructions present in the instruction set then the task is broken down into multiple steps of execution, which takes longer duration. It is quite obvious that such type of tasks are rarely needed thus in the normal circumstances these processors provide best price performance ratio.

Examples of RISC processors are the Berkeley RISC, HP-PA, Clipper, i960, AMD 29000, MIPS R2000 and DEC Alpha. IBM's first RISC computer was the RT/PC (IBM 801), they now produce the RISC-based RISC System/6000 and SP/2 lines.

The processors that are designed to work with complex instruction sets are called CISC processors. Examples of CISC processors are the Motorola 680x0 family and the Intel 80186 through Intel 486 and Pentium.

GENERATIONS OF COMPUTER

Computer being an electronic device, its size, capabilities and power at any time are greatly influenced by the existing state of electronics of that time.

If electronic components and devices of any time were big, slow and unreliable then computers of that time were also big, slow and unreliable. On the other hand fast, reliable and smaller electronic components made the computers small, reliable and fast in operations.

You know that technological developments of electronics passed through few major phases. For example, there was a time when vacuum tubes were quite popular. They were freely used in majority of electronic equipments. After some time, they were replaced by transistors. Later Integrated Circuits came and set a new path for electronic developments.

Computers of specific electronic era are often referred to as a generation. Various generations of computer that came into existence, are described below.

First Generation Computers (1942-1955)

First generation computers were voluminous in size. **They were made using vacuum tubes**. Vacuum tube was a fragile glass device that could control and amplify electronic signals.

First generation computers used the idea of execution of stored programs. Following were the main drawbacks of first generation computers:

1. Their size was very large.
2. Speed of instruction-execution was very slow.
3. They generated lot of heat.
4. Switching through vacuum tubes was not reliable.
5. Heavy air conditioning was required.
6. Only scientists and engineers were able to use these computers and that too in limited areas due to their high cost.

Figure 1.14

7. They needed a constant maintenance, which was very expensive.

Some of first generation computers are ENIAC, EDSAC and UNIVAC I etc.

Second Generation Computers (1955-1964)

Transistor was invented as a smaller and more reliable successor of the vacuum tube. Although transistor was invented in 1948, its application in computers started in the year 1958. The transistor was more reliable, less expensive, and smaller than the smallest vacuum tube. It consumed very little power and produced much less heat.

A transistor is also called a solid-state device. It is made of a material whose principal part is silicon element. It is also called semiconductor device. It performs all the functions of a vacuum tube i.e. switches circuit on and off at a very high speed. **Second generation computer made use of transistors.**

Figure 1.15

Apart from the above listed advantages, the second generation computers used better devices such as card readers, printers etc. This generation is also important from the point of view of language development and use. First generation computers used machine level language or low-level language i.e. program was written directly in binary digits, which was very cumbersome and tedious. Later the development of Assembly Language helped the programmers to some extent. The high level language FORTRAN was also developed for this generation of computers. This development brought the computers very close to man and made it a very popular machine. Some of the names of second generation computers are IBM series, UNIVAC III, CDC 1400 series, Honeywell etc.

Third Generation Computers (1964-75)

The development of integrated circuit was another milestone in the history of computer science. It was micro electronic technology, in which it was possible to integrate large number of circuit elements into very small surface area (less than 5 mm square) of silicon known as Chip. This generation was based on Integrated Circuits (IC) technology and the **computers that were designed with the use of integrated circuits were called third generation computers.**

Figure 1.16

These computers had better storage devices and improved input / output devices, such as Visual Display Unit (VDU), Magnetic Ink Character Reader (MICR) and high-speed line printers. These computers were 10,000 times faster than the first generation computers and arithmetic and logical operations could be performed in nano seconds (1 nano second=10^{-9} seconds). It was this time, around which major advancement in the field of hardware as well as software took place. Many useful high-level languages were developed. These computers used operating system. The use of faster input and output devices enhanced the capabilities of these computers and made multi-programming possible, in which a number of programs could be executed simultaneously by a single processor. Some of the popular computers of this generation are IBM 360 series, 370 series, UNIVAC, HOG 9000 series etc. Some of them are still in use.

Fourth Generation Computers (1975 Onwards)

The development of microprocessor chip that contains entire central processing unit (CPU) on a single silicon chip led to the invention of fourth generation computers. The technology that was used in third generation computers in the form of Integrated Circuit (IC) was known as Small-Scale Integration (SSI). This IC contained about ten to twenty transistors on it. Later, the Medium Scale Integration (MSI) was developed, in which it was possible to assemble up to hundred transistors on a single chip. After this, came the era of Large-Scale Integration (LSI) in which, it was possible to integrate 30,000 transistors on a single chip. Efforts were made and now the era of VLSI (Very Large Scale Integration) has come, in which millions of transistors can be assembled on single chip. **Current generation computers are fourth generation computers and are making use of VLSI chip.** This has made the size of current computer very small. Fourth generation of computers can be called microcomputer generation. The input/output devices used with fourth generation computers are quite advanced. These devices are optical readers, which can transfer the contents of CD within few microseconds to the computers. This generation's computers are compact, faster, and more reliable.

Figure 1.17

Fifth Generation Computers

Till fourth generation computers, the main stress was on hardware technology. Though these computers are faster, more accurate, reliable, smaller in size and very cheap, still they lack thinking power. **The fifth generation computers will have thinking power and capability to make decisions like human beings,** and may prove better than man in certain aspects. They will be more useful in the field of knowledge processing rather than in data processing.

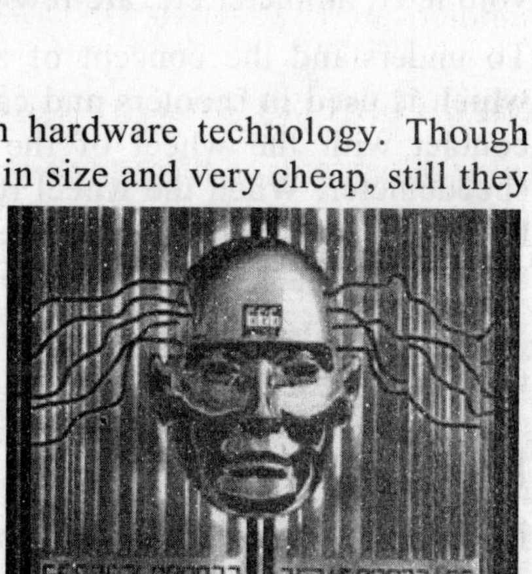

Figure 1.18

In fact fifth generation computers are dreams of Japanese scientists. They have started work in this direction few years ago. The concept of Artificial Intelligence (AI) is being used in these computers. These computers will have Knowledge Information Processing System (KIPS) rather than the present Data/Logic Information Processing System. Japan has chosen the PROLOG (Programming in logic) language as its operating software and plans to have the final machine, which will talk with human beings, see and deliver pictures and hear man's natural language.

CLASSIFICATION OF COMPUTERS ON THE BASIS OF INPUT THAT THEY ASCCEPT

A device, which computes is called computer. For computation, computer takes some input, performs computation on it and gives result.

The type of input that computer accepts, decides its nature and capabilities and the type of computation that it will be able to perform. For example, some of the computers accept input in the form of signals. On the other hand, majority of computers take input in the form of digits. Some computers accept input in both the forms i.e. in the form of digits and signals. On the basis of input type, computers have been classified into following three categories:

1. Analog computers
2. Digital Computers
3. Hybrid computers

A brief description of all these types of computers is given below:

Analog Computers

Let's first understand what is signal. Signals can be defined as continuous flow of physical identity. Temperature, pressure, water level, speed, voltage, current etc. are few examples of signals.

Those computers, which operate upon signals (by accepting temperature, pressure, speed etc. as input) **are called analog computers.** Speedometer, thermometer, barometer, voltmeter, ammeter etc. are few examples of analog computers.

To understand the concept of analog computers, let's take the example of speedometer, which is used in scooters and cars. It makes use of cable. One end of the cable remains in contact with the wheel of the vehicle. The other end of the cable is inserted in the speedometer. When the wheel rotates, cable also rotates. Cable's rotation is thus passed to the internal assembly of the speedometer, which in turn rotates the needle on a calibrated scale. Thus when the vehicle moves, its speed gets displayed on the speedometer's scale.

The slide rule is hand-operated analog computer for doing arithmetic operations like multiplication, division etc.

Digital Computers

In computer terminology, alphabets, numbers, special characters etc. are called digits. Those computers, which accept digits (like name, age, e-mail address etc.) as input, are called digital computers. Computers that we see in offices, shops, hotels etc. are digital computers.

Hybrid Computers

Those computers, which accept both types of inputs i.e. signals and digits are called hybrid computers. For example, computers placed in ICU (Intensive Care Unit) are examples of hybrid computers. They accept heartbeats of the patient (signals) as input. They also accept instructions that need to be carried out (digits). Similarly computers placed in atomic reactors (taking radioactivity level and instructions as input) and mines (which take carbon monoxide level and instructions as input) are other examples of hybrid computers.

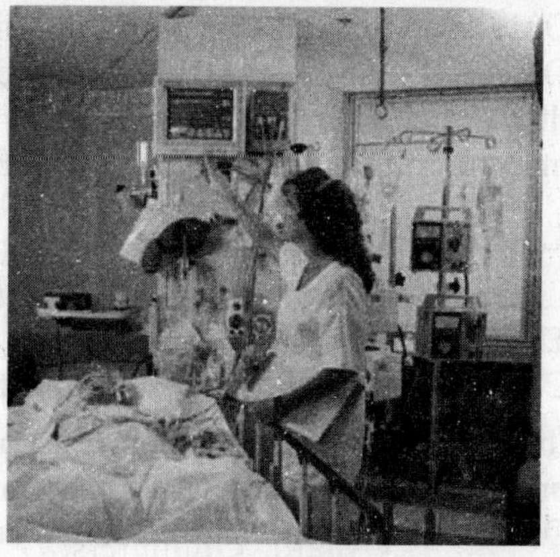

Figure 1.19

Note that in this book, we will mainly deal with digital computers. All the aspects, explained now onwards would mainly apply to digital computers unless stated otherwise.

CLASSIFICATION OF DIGITAL COMPUTERS ON THE BASIS OF SIZE, PROCESSOR ETC.

Digital computers can be classified into various categories, on the basis of their sizes. When we say, size of the computer, it refers to multiple factors like, size of the memory, number of terminals that can be connected to the computer, storage capacity of the hard disk, type of processor used in the computer etc. Digital computers are generally classified into following categories:

1. Microcomputers
2. Mini computers
3. Mainframe computers
4. Supercomputers

Micro Computers

Microcomputer is the smallest category of computers, in which single microchip is used for two basic units i.e. ALU and Control Unit. This microchip is often referred to as microprocessor. Microcomputers are further classified into following categories:

1. Personal computers
2. Laptop computers
3. Tablet PC
4. Personal Digital Assistant (PDA)

Personal Computers (PC)

Computers that you commonly see these days are examples of Personal Computers. In short, they are called PC. Their outward appearance is shown in figure 1.20. They mainly comprise of four units i.e. CPU box called chaises, keyboard, VDU and mouse.

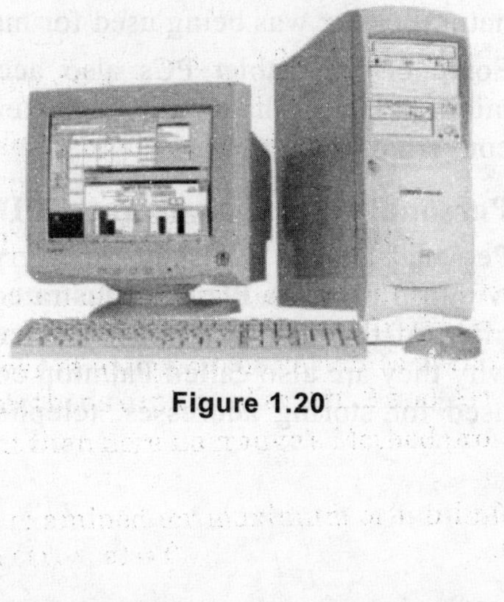

Figure 1.20

Only one person can work on them at a time, so they are called single user computer. Originally they were designed and manufactured by IBM. Later, as they became popular, other manufacturers also started manufacturing similar type of computers called IBM clones.

Figure 1.21

Laptop Computers

Laptop computers also fall into the category of microcomputers. They possess same capabilities and resources that of Personal Computers. A laptop is shown in figure 1.21.

In their outward appearance, Laptop computers look like a briefcase. Upper panel of the briefcase comprises of LCD screen. Lower panel contains keyboard and mouse arrangement. Other components and circuitry remain packed inside the briefcase. They are deliberately designed to be light in weight. They run on chargeable battery, which resides inside. Due to their size, weight and independence from power (for two to three hours) people carry them while traveling in car, train or airplane and work on them.

Figure 1.22

Tablet PCs

Tablet PC is the latest development in the field of computers. Its physical appearance is illustrated in figure 1.22. Note that it looks like laptop computer with many more enhancements and additional facilities packed, within same space.

Display system of Tablet PC, vertically rotates, by 180^0. When rotated, it starts accepting input through a special light pen, called light pen. Whatever is written on Tablet PC's screen, with the pen, in natural handwriting, is taken as input. Thus writers need not write their articles on paper and then give it to typists to get its formatted copy. They can directly write the text on Tablet PC's screen, using light pen. Tablet PC will recognize their handwriting and save the document in predefined format, in desired font, as if typist typed it on computer. Similarly artists can now draw figures, directly on Tablet PC's screen and color them too. Light pens also have provision for removing written text or drawing lines, as if natural eraser was being used for making corrections.

Some of the Tablet PCs also accept voice input, through microphone. Whatever is spoken in front of them is converted into text file.

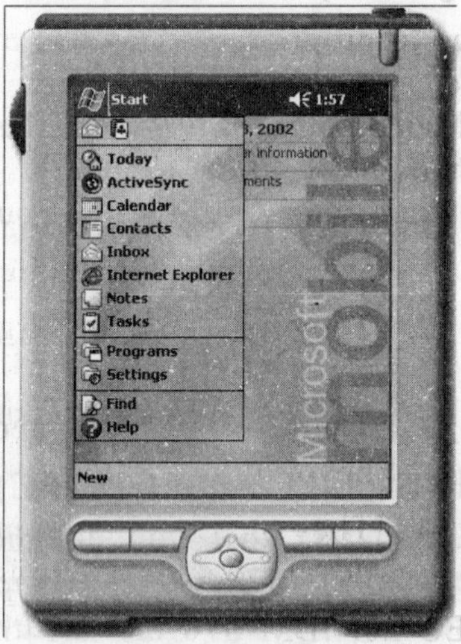

Figure 1.23

Personal Digital Assistants (PDA)

Personal Digital Assistants are very small computers that fit within a palm. A PDA is illustrated in figure 1.23. They are often of the size of scientific calculator. This is the reason, why they are also called Palmtop computers. They are mostly used for storing addresses, telephone numbers, maintaining personal appointments etc. They can also be connected to higher range computers either through cable or wireless link, for the exchange of data and information.

Minicomputers

Minicomputers are relatively larger and faster computers. Apart from single user environment, they also support multi user environment. They are generally used for automating those applications, which are large in size, require fast processing capabilities and demand for resource sharing among multiple users. Main characteristics of minicomputers are described below.

1. They are built, using high performance and high capability processors.
2. Memory size in such type of computers is generally very large.
3. They support multiple terminals, which may range from 2 to 16.
4. Large capacity disks are used in multiple numbers so that the data and programs of all the users could be put on-line.
5. They provide facility to connect multiple printers.
6. They possess the capability of performing computer network related major operations.

Mainframes

Mainframes fall into next higher category of computers. Their internal architecture and circuitry remains different from minicomputers. They use specially designed proprietary circuits instead of just single microprocessor as their CPU. Their circuitry promotes higher connectivity, faster throughputs and large data processing capabilities.

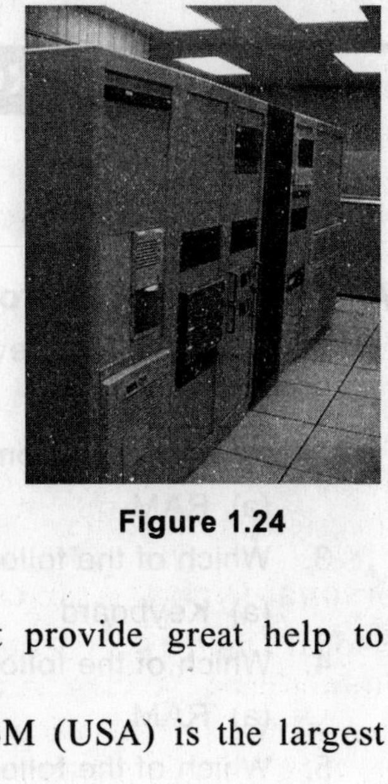

Figure 1.24

Due to proprietary circuitry, mainframes become quite big in size and provide facility for connecting minicomputers and microcomputers with them. Few characteristics of mainframes are listed below.

1. They possess the capability of addressing larger memory sizes than that of minicomputers.
2. They also support larger capacity disks like optical disks etc.
3. Their terminal connectivity can go as high as 256 or beyond.
4. They possess large number of application libraries that provide great help to developers in developing useful applications.

DEC 20, IBM 370 etc. are the examples of few mainframes. IBM (USA) is the largest manufacturer of Mainframe computers.

Supercomputers

Supercomputer is the largest category of computers. They use multiple CPUs for processing the data and executing the instructions. While performing a task through Supercomputer, the complete task gets divided into multiple independent tasks. Each CPU takes up individual task and completes it in parallel. This methodology of processing is called parallel processing.

Figure 1.25

Due to parallel processing, Supercomputers become capable of processing large volumes of data at very fast speed. They process multi million to few trillion commands per second. Applications like weather forecasting, nuclear weapon design, projection system modeling, aero modeling etc., which require tremendous processing capabilities, can be very well executed on Supercomputers. CRAY, XMP 24 and NEC 500 are few examples of Supercomputers.

EXERCISES CHAPTER 1

Short Type Questions

A. Select most appropriate answer for following questions:

1. Which type of device, a computer is?
   (a) Mechanical (b) Electrical (c) Magnetic (d) Electronic
2. Which part of computer stores data temporarily?
   (a) RAM (b) ALU (c) CU (d) CPU
3. Which of the following device will be used for displaying the result?
   (a) Keyboard (b) ALU (c) VDU (d) Mouse
4. Which of the following can be used for storing the data permanently?
   (a) RAM (b) Hard disk (c) Mouse (d) VDU
5. Which of the following processes data in computers?
   (a) ALU (b) Memory (c) Control Unit (d) BUS

B. Fill in the blanks:

6. RAM is acronym for ....
7. ROM is acronym for ....
8. PROM is acronym for ....
9. EPROM is acronym for ....
10. ALU is acronym for ....

C. State, true or false for following statements:

11. Keyboard is the main input unit for computers.
12. Floppy drive is an output device.
13. Data, instructions or results can be permanently stored on hard disk.
14. In computer, Control Unit performs all arithmetic and logical operations.
15. Random Access Memory is always faster than Cache Memory.

D. Differentiate between the following:

16. Input and output units of computer.
17. RAM and ROM.
18. Secondary Memory and Cache Memory.
19. Microcomputers and Minicomputers.
20. Analog computers and Digital computers.

Detailed Answer Type Questions

E. Answer the following questions in detail:

21. What is computer? For what purpose it is used?
22. Write characteristics of first and fourth generation computers.
23. Draw a block diagram of computer and label its component.
24. Describe the role of keyboard and mouse in computer. What are the fundamental similarity and differences between them?
25. Name any two output devices.
26. What is the role of memory in computer? Name any two medium, which serve the purpose of permanent memory.
27. What do you understand by logical operations? Which part of computer performs arithmetic and logical operations?

28. Describe the interaction of different peripherals of computer. Explain how data moves input unit to output unit.
29. Describe the role of control unit in computer.
30. What is bus in computers and what role does it play?
31. Describe Mainframe and Supercomputers.
32. What is microprocessor? What is its function in computer?
33. Name any three latest processors that are being used in computers these days.
34. Describe the role of cache memory in computer.
35. Describe clock speed and how does it affect the speed of computer?
36. Describe the role of hard disk in computer.
37. Differentiate between floppy and hard disk.
38. Write a short note on interaction between parts on computer.
39. Describe any two removable storage media that are used in computers.
40. What is hybrid computer? Name any two applications of hybrid computers.

****

CHAPTER 2

Number System

INTRODUCTION

The number system that we use in day-to-day life is called Decimal Number System. As you know, it makes use of 10 fundamental digits i.e. 0, 1, 2, 3, 4, 5, 6, 7, 8 and 9. All the numbers in this number system are formed by the permutation and combination of these digits. All the calculations that we do in this number system are done on the basis of these 10 digits only.

Although we follow decimal number system and we use computer to do calculations for us but computer doesn't make use of decimal number system. Internally it makes use of another number system, called binary number system. What is binary number system, which digits are used, as fundamental digits in this number system are the topics, which have been described in detail in this chapter.

INTRODUCTION TO BINARY NUMBER SYSTEM

Binary number system is the fundamental base of computers. It makes use of two digits only i.e. 0 and 1. All other numbers in binary number system are formed using these digits. For example, 101 is a binary number. Now the question is how to be sure that this is a binary number, not one hundred one of decimal number system? Well, to avoid the confusion, generally binary numbers are written within the bracket and 2 is written at the base of the closing bracket. For example, $(101)_2$ is definitely a binary number. There is no confusion of any type now. For more familiarity with binary numbers, a table illustrating few initial numbers of binary number system and their equivalent decimal numbers is given below.

Binary Number	Decimal Number
0	0
1	1
10	2
11	3
100	4

Binary Number	Decimal Number
101	5
110	6
111	7
1000	8
1001	9

Refer above illustrated table and note that it illustrates equivalent binary numbers for fundamental digits of decimal number system. Now the question is how other numbers of decimal number system are represented in binary number system? Well, the process is quite simple and is described later in this chapter.

IMPORTANCE OF BINARY NUMBER SYSTEM FOR USE IN DIGITAL COMPUTER

For performing any activity, computer accepts data from its input devices, processes it, using its processor and displays the result on its output devices.

Usually the data that is given to the computer consists of alphabets, numbers, special characters etc. But computer being electronic device doesn't really recognize the characters (a, b, c 1,9,*% etc). What it recognizes is absence or presence of current, called plus. That means if the current is flowing through computer circuitry, it will be able to acknowledge the situation. Similarly if the current is not following through the circuit, it will recognize it as another situation, which is quite different from the previous situation.

It is quite obvious that if data (or instructions or as a matter of fact, any other object such as graphics, sound video etc.) is to be handled using computer then all the arrangements will have to be made to represent it in the from of absence of pulse and presence of pulse. For example, we may decide that 2, 3, 5 and + sign will be represented as follows:

2: Presence of a pulse and absence of a pulse.

3: Presence of a pulse and presence of a pulse.

5: Presence of a pulse, absence of a pulse and presence of a pulse.

+: Presence of a pulse, absence of a pulse and presence of a pulse, absence of a pulse, presence of a pulse and presence of a pulse.

Under this decision, the two digits 2 and 3 can be represented in electronic form, within the computer and it can be said that computer has been provided with the data and it is holding it.

In addition to this, instruction to add these two numbers (i.e. + sign) can also be represented in computer, in terms of absence of current and presence of current, as mentioned above.

The result of addition can also be represented as mentioned above.

It is quite clear that if computer is to be used for processing the data, all the alphabets, numbers and characters, using which data and instructions are given to the computer will have to be represented in terms of absence of current and presence of current. Well, this is what is done in computers.

Note that absence of current and presence of current are two different states. Binary number system makes use of only two digits i.e. 0 and 1. All the numbers in binary number system are formed using these two digits only.

In the event of associating 0 with absence of current and 1 with presence of current, Binary Number System starts serving as base number system for computers and a very well

working ground is made for representing all the digits, alphabets and special characters within the computer using two electronic states i.e. absence of current and presence of current. This is the reason why binary number system is important for computers.

Conversion Of Decimal Number Into Binary Number

A given decimal number can be converted into equivalent binary number by following method:

1. **Since binary number system makes use of only two digits hence divide the decimal number by 2. Write the quotient below the number and remainder on the right hand side.**
2. **Now divide the quotient by 2 and repeat above-mentioned process till the time quotient becomes 0.**
3. **Now arrange the remainders (x1, x2, x3 …. etc.) in reverse order (…. x3, x2, x1)**

The number thus obtained will be binary equivalent of given decimal number. To understand the procedure of conversion, consider following examples:

Example -1

Convert decimal number $(231)_{10}$ into equivalent binary number.

2	231	
2	115	1
2	57	1
2	28	1
2	14	0
2	7	0
2	3	1
2	1	1
	0	1

Number = $(11100111)_2$

Thus above mentioned process yields: $(231)_{10} = (11100111)_2$

Example - 2

Convert decimal number $(109)_{10}$ to equivalent binary number.

2	109	
2	54	1
2	27	0
2	13	1
2	6	1
2	3	0
2	1	1
	0	1

Number = $(1101101)_2$

Thus above mentioned process yields: $(109)_{10} = (1101101)_2$

You are now familiar with the process of converting integer decimal numbers (those numbers which do not include decimal point) into equivalent binary numbers. Now the question is how do you convert fractional numbers (that have decimal point in them) into equivalent binary numbers? Well, such conversions take place in three steps. In first step, integer part (i.e. number towards left of the decimal point) is converted into equivalent binary number (using procedure mentioned above). In second step, fractional part (i.e. number towards right hand side of the decimal point) of the number is converted to equivalent decimal number. In third step both the parts are put together. Procedure for converting fractional part into equivalent binary number is given below.

1. Since binary number system consists of only two digits hence multiply fractional decimal part by 2. When you do so, integer part obtained on the left hand side of the decimal number will either be 1 or 0. Whatever you get, write it separately (say you write x1. Here x can either be 1 or 0).
2. Now take the resultant fractional part and multiply it by 2 again. Repeat the process, as many times as number of digits are required on the right hand side of the binary point (thus obtaining x2, x3, x4 etc.). For example, if 4 digits are required on the right hand side of the binary point, repeat above-mentioned process 4 times.
3. Arrange the digits that were written separately in the sequence, in which they were obtained (e.g. x1, x2, x3, and x4). The number thus obtained (x1x2x3x4) will be binary equivalent of given fractional decimal number.

To understand the process of conversion of fractional decimal numbers into equivalent binary numbers, let's consider following example:

Example -3

Convert decimal number $(0.862)_{10}$ to equivalent binary number.

$0.862 \times 2 = 1.724$	1	
$.724 \times 2 = 1.448$	1	
$.448 \times 2 = 0.896$	0	
$.896 \times 2 = 1.792$	1	
$.792 \times 2 = 1.584$	1	Number = $(.110\,111)_2$
$.584 \times 2 = 1.168$	1	

Thus above mentioned process yields: $(0.862)_{10} = (0.110111)_2$

Example –4

Convert decimal number $(0.235)_{10}$ to equivalent binary number.

$0.235 \times 2 = 0.47$	0	
$0.47 \times 2 = 0.94$	0	
$0.94 \times 2 = 1.88$	1	Number = $(.0011)_2$
$0.88 \times 2 = 1.76$	1	

Thus above mentioned process yields: $(0.235)_{10} = (0.0011)_2$

Example –5

Convert decimal number $(122.486)_{10}$ to equivalent binary number.

First Step

In first step, integer part of the number is taken:

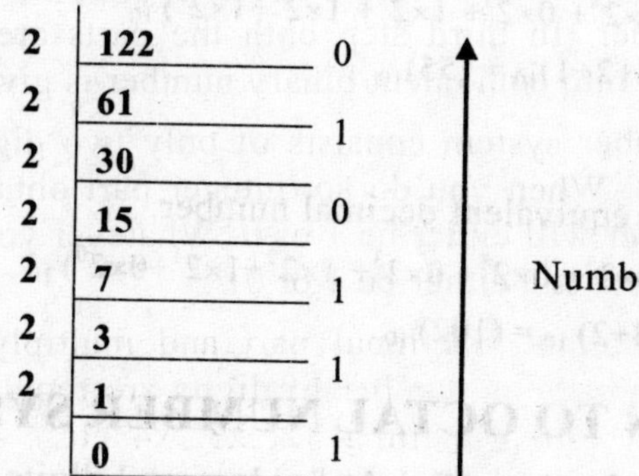

Thus $(122)_{10} = (1111010)_2$

Second Step

In second step, fractional part of the number is taken:

$.486 \times 2 = 0.972$ 0

$.972 \times 2 = 1.944$ 1

$.944 \times 2 = 1.888$ 1

$.888 \times 2 = 1.776$ 1

Number = $(0.0111)_2$

Third Step

Joining both the parts together will result in following number:

$(122.486)_{10} = (1111010.0111)_2$

Converting Binary Numbers into Equivalent Decimal Numbers

Positional values for different positions in binary number are illustrated below:

......	2^5	2^4	2^3	2^2	2^1	2^0	.	2^{-1}	2^{-2}	2^{-3}	2^{-4}	2^{-5}	.....

↑ Binary Point

Perform following steps to convert a binary number into equivalent decimal number:

1. **Multiply each digit of the number, by its positional value.**
2. **Now add all the products to get the sum.**

The sum, thus obtained will be the equivalent decimal number of given binary number.

To understand the procedure of conversion of binary numbers into equivalent decimal numbers, consider following examples:

Example -6

Convert binary number $(110111)_2$ into equivalent decimal number.

$(110111)_2 = (1\times2^5 + 1\times2^4 + 0\times2^3 + 1\times2^2 + 1\times2^1 + 1\times2^0)_{10}$

$= (32+16+4+2+1)_{10} = (55)_{10}$

Example -7

Convert $(1100110)_2$ into equivalent decimal number.

$(1100110)_2 = (1\times2^6 + 1\times2^5 + 0\times2^4 + 0\times2^3 + 1\times2^2 + 1\times2^1 + 0\times2^0)_{10}$

$= (64+32+4+2)_{10} = (102)_{10}$

INTRODUCTION TO OCTAL NUMBER SYSTEM

Octal number system makes use of eight fundamental digits i.e. 0, 1, 2, 3, 4, 5, 6 and 7. All other numbers in octal number system are formed using these digits. For example, 154 is an octal number. Now the question is how to be sure that this is an octal number, not one hundred fifty four of decimal number system? Well, to avoid the confusion, generally octal numbers are written within the bracket and 8 is written at the base of right bracket. For example, $(154)_8$ is definitely an octal number. There is no confusion of any type now. For more familiarity with octal numbers, a table illustrating few initial numbers of octal number system and their equivalent decimal numbers is given below.

Octal Number	Decimal Number
0	0
1	1
2	2
3	3
4	4

Octal Number	Decimal Number
5	5
6	6
7	7
10	8
11	9

Now the question is, how other numbers of decimal number system are represented in octal number system? Well, the process is quite similar to that of binary numbers and is described below.

Conversion Of Decimal Number Into Octal Number

A given decimal number can be converted into equivalent octal number by following method:

1. Since octal number system makes use of 8 digits hence divide the decimal number by 8. Write the quotient below the number and remainder on the right hand side.

2. **Now divide the quotient by 8 and repeat above-mentioned process till the time quotient becomes 0.**
3. **Now arrange the remainders (y1, y2, y3 …. etc.) in reverse order (…. y3, y2, y1)**

The number thus obtained will be octal equivalent of given decimal number. To understand the procedure of conversion, consider the following examples:

Example -8

Convert decimal number 231 into equivalent octal number.

Divisor	Dividend	Remainder
8	231	
8	28	7
8	3	4
	0	3

Number = $(347)_8$ (remainders read from bottom to top, ↑)

Thus above mentioned process yields: $(231)_{10} = (347)_8$

Example -9

Convert decimal number $(109)_{10}$ to equivalent octal number.

Divisor	Dividend	Remainder
8	109	
8	13	5
8	1	5
	0	1

Number = $(155)_8$ (remainders read from bottom to top, ↑)

Thus above mentioned process yields : $(109)_{10} = (155)_8$

Converting Octal Numbers Into Equivalent Decimal Numbers

Positional values for different positions in octal number are shown below.

…….	8^5	8^4	8^3	8^2	8^1	8^0	.	8^{-1}	8^{-2}	8^{-3}	8^{-4}	8^{-5}	…..

↑ Octal Point

Perform following steps to convert an octal number into equivalent decimal number:

1. **Multiply each digit of the number, by its positional value.**
2. **Now add all the products to get the sum.**

The sum, thus obtained will be the equivalent decimal number for given octal number.

To understand the procedure of conversion of octal number into equivalent decimal number, consider the following example:

Example -10

Convert octal number into equivalent decimal number.

$$(125)_8 = (1 \times 8^2 + 2 \times 8^1 + 5 \times 8^0)_{10} = (64 + 16 + 5)_{10} = (85)_{10}$$

INTRODUCTION TO HEXADECIMAL NUMBER SYSTEM

Hexadecimal Number System makes use of 16 fundamental digits i.e. 0, 1, 2, 3, 4, 5, 6, 7, 8, 9, A, B, C, D, E and F. All other numbers in hexadecimal number system are formed using these digits. For example, 275 is a hexadecimal number. Now the question is how to be sure that this is a hexadecimal number, not two hundred seventy five of decimal number system? Well, to avoid the confusion, generally Hexadecimal numbers are written within the bracket and 16 is written at the base of right bracket. For example, $(275)_{16}$ is definitely an octal number. Similarly $(14F)_{16}$ is also a hexadecimal number. There is no confusion of any type now. For more familiarity with hexadecimal numbers, a table illustrating few initial numbers of hexadecimal number system and their equivalent decimal numbers is given below.

Hexadecimal Number	Decimal Number
0	0
1	1
2	2
3	3
4	4
5	5
6	6
7	7

Hexadecimal Number	Decimal Number
8	8
9	9
A	10
B	11
C	12
D	13
E	14
F	15

Refer above illustrated table and note that it illustrates equivalent hexadecimal numbers for decimal digits and numbers. Conversion of decimal numbers into hexadecimal numbers and vice versa can be done by following the procedures mentioned in octal number system, but making use of 16 as base number, instead of 8.

CONVERSION OF NUMBERS OF ONE NUMBER SYSTEM INTO ANOTHER NUMBER SYSTEM

You are now familiar with the process of converting decimal numbers into equivalent binary, octal and hexadecimal numbers. You are also familiar with their reverse processes. Now the question is how to convert the numbers of binary, octal or hexadecimal number systems into equivalent numbers of each other number systems. Well, the methods are described below.

Conversion Of Octal Numbers Into Binary Numbers

Binary equivalents of octal digits, i.e. 0, 1, 2, 3, 4, 5, 6 and 7 are given in the following table. This table is used for converting octal numbers into equivalent binary numbers and vice versa.

Binary	**Octal**
000	0
001	1
010	2
011	3
100	4
101	5
110	6
111	7

To convert any octal number into binary number, take the least significant digit from the given octal number and write its binary equivalent, using above-mentioned table. Take the next octal digit and write its equivalent binary number on the right hand side of the previous binary number. Repeat the process till most significant digit of the octal number is reached. The number obtained in this way will be the equivalent binary number of the given octal number.

For example, $(56)_8$ is an octal number. To convert this number into binary number, get the binary equivalent of 6 and 5 from above mentioned table and write them in same sequence. By doing so, you will get the number $(101110)_2$. The process is illustrated below.

$(6)_8=(110)_2$ and $(5)_8 = (101)_2$

Thus $(56)_8 = (110101)_2$

Similarly equivalent of Octal $(423)_8$ can be derived as follows:

$(4)_8 = (100)_2$, $(2)_8 = (010)_2$ and $(3)_8 = (011)_2$

Thus $(423)_8 = (100010011)_2$

Conversion Of Binary Numbers Into Octal Numbers

Perform following steps to convert the binary number into octal number:

1. Take the given binary number and count total number of digits in the number. If they are in multiples of 3, leave the number as such else add required number of zeros on the left hand side to make the total number of digits in multiples of 3. For example, if there are 4 digits in the given binary number, put two zeros on the left, so that total number of digits, now, become 6.
2. Take three binary digits from right most place of the binary number.
3. Write their octal equivalent digit, using above mentioned table.

4. Take next three binary digits and write their octal equivalent in the same way, but on the left hand side of previously written number.
5. Repeat the process till the left most digit of the given number is reached.
6. The number thus formed will be octal equivalent of given binary number.

Let's convert $(101100)_2$ to equivalent octal number to get familiar with the method. The process of taking three binary digits and writing their octal equivalent, can be performed as follow:

(100)2=(4)8

(101)2=(5)8

Thus (101100)2=(54)8

Let's take another example. Say you have to convert $(1010111)_2$ to equivalent octal number. The process of converting this number into equivalent octal number can take place as mentioned below:

(1010111)2 = 01010111)2

(111)2 = (7)8

(010)2 = (2)8

(001)2 = (1)8

Thus (1 010 111)2 = (127)8

Conversion Of Hexadecimal Numbers Into Binary Numbers

Binary equivalents of 16 fundamental hexadecimal digits are given in the following table. This table is used for converting binary numbers into equivalent hexadecimal numbers and vice versa.

Hexadecimal	Binary	Hexadecimal	Binary
0	0000	8	1000
1	0001	9	1001
2	0010	A	1010
3	0011	B	1011
4	0100	C	1100
5	0101	D	1101
6	0110	E	1110
7	0111	F	1111

To convert any hexadecimal number into binary number, take the least significant digit from the given hexadecimal number and write its binary equivalent, using above mentioned table. Take the next hexadecimal digit and write its equivalent binary number on the left hand side of the previous binary number. Repeat the process till you reach most significant digit of the hexadecimal number. The number obtained in this way will be binary equivalent number of the given hexadecimal number.

For example, if $(A6)_{16}$ is a hexadecimal number. To convert this number into binary number, get the Binary equivalent of 6 and A from above mentioned table and write them in same sequence. In this way, you will get the number $(10100110)_2$. Similarly $(BCD)_{16}$ will be equivalent to $(101111001101)_2$

Conversion Of Binary Numbers Into Hexadecimal Numbers

Perform following steps to convert a binary number into hexadecimal number:

1. **Take the given binary number and count total number of digits in the number. If they are in multiples of 4, leave the number as such else add required number of zeros on the left hand side so as to make the total number of digits in multiples of 4. For example if there are 7 digits in the given binary number, put one zero on the left, so that total number of digits, now, become 8.**
2. **Take four binary digits from right most place of the binary number.**
3. **Write their Hexadecimal equivalent digit, using above mentioned table.**
4. **Take next four binary digits and write their hexadecimal equivalent in the same way, but on the left hand side of previously written number.**
5. **Repeat the process till the left most digit of the given number is reached.**

The number thus formed will be hexadecimal equivalent of given binary number. To understand the procedure, let's convert $(101101011)_2$ into equivalent hexadecimal number.

$(101101011)_2 = (000101101011)_2$

$(1011)_2 = (B)_{16}$

$(0110)_2 = (6)_{16}$

$(0001)_2 = (1)_{16}$

$(000101101011)_2 = 16B)_{16}$

Conversion Of Octal Number Into Hexadecimal Numbers

You are already familiar with the process of converting octal numbers into binary numbers and binary numbers into equivalent hexadecimal numbers. Note that binary is common in both the conversions. To convert an octal number into hexadecimal number you can first convert the octal number into binary number and then binary number into equivalent hexadecimal number.

Let's convert $(175)_8$ into equivalent hexadecimal number to get familiar with the process.

$(175)_8$ can be converted to equivalent Binary number as follows:

$(5)_8 = (101)_2$

$(7)_8 = (111)_2$

$(1)_8 = (001)_2$

Thus $(175)_8 = (001\ 111\ 101)_2$

Now $(001\ 111\ 101)_2$ can be converted to equivalent Hexadecimal number as follows:

$(0\ 0111\ 1101)_2 = (0111\ 1101)_2$

$(1101)_2 = (D)_{16}$

$(0111)_2 = (7)_{16}$

Thus $(175)_8$ will be equivalent to $(7D)_{16}$.

Conversion Of Hexadecimal Numbers Into Octal Numbers

You are already familiar with the process of converting Hexadecimal numbers into Binary numbers and Binary numbers into Octal numbers. Note that Binary is common in both the conversions. To convert a Hexadecimal number into Octal number you will have to first convert Hexadecimal number into Binary number and then Binary number into equivalent Octal number.

To get familiar with the process, let's convert $(2B)_{16}$ to equivalent octal number.

$(2B)_{16} = (00101011)_2$

$(00101011)_2 = (101011)_2$

$(011)_2 = (3)_8$

$(101)_2 = (5)_8$

Thus $(2B)_{16}$ will be equivalent to $(53)_8$

ONE'S COMPLEMENT

In computers, one's complement is used for representing negative numbers.

When 0's in a binary number are replaced by 1s and 1s are replaced by 0s then the resultant number is said to be 1's complement of the number. For example, 1's complement of 100110 will be 011001. Similarly 01011100's one's complement will be 10100011.

TWO'S COMPLEMENT

Two's Complement is another method of representing negative numbers in computer. Two's complement is achieved by adding 1 in one's complement. Few examples of Two's Complement are given below.

Example -11

Number=1011

One's Complement = 0100

Two's Complement = 0100 +1= 0101 = 101

Example -12

Number = 1100100

One's Complement = 0011011 = 11011

Two's Complement = 11011+1 = 1110

BIT

Computer stores all its data in the form of 0s and 1s. Digit 0 and 1 and called Bits. That means 0 is one bit and 1 is another bit. The data 1100 comprises of 4 bits. You can say that bit is the smallest storage unit of computer.

BYTE

8 bit put together form 1 byte. For example, 10101011 will occupy one byte space.

HOW COMPUTER REPRESENTS DATA

You are now familiar with binary number system and know that it makes use of only two digits i.e. 0 and 1 to represent any number. You also know that computer recognizes only two states i.e. absence of pulse and presence of pulse. For all practical purposes, absence of pulse is considered as 0 and presence of pulse is taken as 1.

Thus decimal number $(2)_{10}$ will be represented as binary number $(10)_2$ and in computer, it will be recognized as presence of pulse and absence of pulse. Similarly all other decimal numbers will be represented by difference permutation and combinations of absence of pulses and presence of pulse and for that binary number system will provide the base.

Text Codes

Representing digits and numbers, using binary number system is OK. But the question is, how do you represent alphabets and special characters, using binary number system, because whichever combination of 0_s and 1_s you make, it will be a binary number and it will have a decimal equivalent number. Thus if you make use of pure binary number system, it will represent numbers, numbers and numbers only. There will be no place for alphabets and special characters. Thus the system, which is used in computers, for representing numbers, is a combination of binary number system and decimal number system. The rules of representation are as follows:

1. Each digit of decimal number is expressed using 4 binary digits. For example, 2 is not represented as $(10)_2$ but it is represented as $(0010)_2$. Similarly 5 is not represented as $(101)_2$ but it is represented as $(0101)_2$.

2. For expressing representing a decimal number in binary number system, all digits are represented individually into binary number system, and their positional values are maintained. For example, in pure binary expression $(15)_{10}$ is represented as $(1111)_2$. But in modified method to express $(15)_{10}$, 1 and 5 will be expressed individually to have the number expressed as (00010101). Similarly $(102)_{10}$ will represented as (000100000010).

Now the question is, how this arrangement makes provision for representing alphabets and special characters? Well, note that 4 digit combination can represent 2^4 i.e. 16 numbers. But you required only 10 combinations to represent 10 decimal digits. Balance 16-10 i.e. 6 digits can be utilized to represent 6 alphabets as illustrated in the table.

Sr. No.	Binary Combination	Character Represented
1.	0000	0
2.	0001	1
3.	0010	2
4.	0011	3
5.	0100	4
6.	0101	5
7.	0110	6
8.	0111	7
9.	1000	8
10.	1001	9
11.	1010	A
12.	1011	B
13.	1100	C
14.	1101	D
15.	1110	E
16.	1111	F

BCD Scheme

This scheme, which makes use of 4 digits is called Binary Coded Decimal (BCD) scheme. But note that this scheme represents only 10 numeric digits and 6 alphabets only. Other alphabets and special characters cannot be represented by this scheme.

EBCDIC Scheme

Another scheme, called Extended Binary Coded Decimal Interchange Code, was introduced to represent numbers, alphabets and special characters. This scheme, instead of 4 digits makes use of 8 digits. Thus it can represent 2^8 i.e. 256 characters. This scheme is still popular in IBM mainframes. Characters represented by EBCDIC are illustrated in a table given in Appendix-1.

ASCII Scheme

Another coding scheme, called American Standard Code for Information Interchange (called ASCII in short) makes use of 8 digits combinations. Thus 28 i.e. 256 characters are represented through this scheme. Out of these 256, American National Standards Institute (ANSI) has standardized first 128 combinations. These standardized combinations and the characters represented by ASCII scheme are illustrated in Appendix-2.

UNICODE

Unicode standard is the Universal Character-Encoding standard, used for representation of text for computer processing. Unicode standard provides the capacity to encode all of the characters used in the languages of the world. The Unicode standards provide information about the character and their use. Unicode standard is very useful for computer users, who deal with multilingual text, business people, linguists, researchers, scientists, mathematicians and technicians. Unicode uses a 16 bit encoding that provides code for more than 65000 characters (65536). Unicode standard assigns each character a unique numeric value and name. The Unicode standard and ISO10646 standards provide an extension mechanism called UTF-16 that allows for encoding as many as a million characters. Presently Unicode standard provides codes for 49194 characters.

Unicode is being widely accepted as a standard for information interchange worldwide, as most of the major IT companies have declared their support for it. Unicode for Indian languages uses ISCII-88 and not ISCII-91, which is the latest official standard. It was felt necessary that Indian Government should represent UNICODE consortium for necessary modification in the code pertaining to Indian languages script and hence department of Information Technology became full member of Unicode consortium with voting right.

EXERCISES CHAPTER 2

Short Type Questions

A. Select most appropriate answer for following questions:

1. Which number system is used for representing numbers within the computer?
   (a) Decimal (b) Octal (c) Binary (d) Hexadecimal
2. Which of the following is a valid octal number?
   (a) $(893)_8$ (b) $(125)_8$ (c) $(786)_8$ (d) $(679)_8$
3. Which number system makes use of alphabets to represent numbers?
   (a) Decimal (b) Octal (c) Binary (d) Hexadecimal
4. How many fundamental digits are used in binary number system?
   (a) 0 (b) 1 (c) 2 (d) 10
5. Which of the following is not a binary number?
   (a) $(10)_2$ (b) $(20)_2$ (c) $(11)_2$ (d) $(100)_2$

B. Fill in the blanks:

6. The base of binary number system is ....
7. The base of octal number system is ....
8. The base of hexadecimal number system is ....
9. Binary equivalent of decimal (100)10 will be ....
10. 1's complement of (110011)2 will be ....

C. State, true or false for following statements:

11. In our day-to-day functioning, we make use of binary number system.
12. Computer makes use of binary number system for doing all calculations.
13. Two's complement represents negative numbers in computer.
14. Binary equivalent of (22)10 is (10110)2
15. 1's complement of (1110)2 will be 1.

D. Answer the following questions in short:

16. How many digits are used in binary number system?
17. How many digits are used in hexadecimal number system?
18. Write all basic digits of octal number system.
19. Convert $(55)_{10}$ into equivalent binary number.
20. Convert $(11)_{10}$ into equivalent decimal number.

Detailed Answer Type Questions

E. Answer the following questions in detail:

21. Convert following binary numbers into equivalent decimal numbers.
    (a) $(1011)_2$ (b) $(11100)_2$ (c) $(11001111)_2$
22. Convert following decimal numbers into equivalent binary numbers.
    (a) $(175)_{10}$ (b) $(575)_{10}$ (c) $(975.55)_{10}$
23. Convert following octal numbers into equivalent decimal numbers.
    (a) $(124)_8$ (b) $(246)_8$ (c) $(357)_8$
24. Convert following binary numbers into equivalent octal numbers.
    (a) $(110011)_2$ (b) $(111000)_2$ (c) $(111)_2$
25. Convert following octal numbers into equivalent binary numbers.
    (a) $(234)_8$ (b) $(126)_8$ (c) $(374)_8$
26. Convert following binary numbers into equivalent hexadecimal numbers.
    (a) $(1100)_2$ (b) $(11001100)_2$ (c) $(1101111)_2$
27. Convert following octal numbers into equivalent hexadecimal numbers.
    (a) $(123)_8$ (b) $(4567)_8$ (c) $(6574)_8$
28. Convert following hexadecimal numbers into equivalent octal numbers.
    (a) $(1F2)_{16}$ (b) $(2A6)_{16}$ (c) $(126)_{16}$
29. What is one's complement? Explain by giving a suitable example.
30. What is Two's complements? Explain by giving a suitable example. What is its purpose in computers?
31. Describe BCD scheme that is used to represent data within computers.
32. Why binary number system is used in computers? What is its relevance?
33. What is EBCDIC Code? How many digits it represents? Where it is used?
34. What is ASCII? How it is different from EBCDIC? How many characters can be represented in this scheme?
35. What is Unicode? Describe few important aspects of it.

****

CHAPTER 3

MS-DOS Operating System

INTRODUCTION

A computer system is basically combination of hardware and software. For its functioning it requires different types of hardware devices, electronic components and various types of software. Operating system is one of the software, which computer uses for its internal functioning. What operating system is, what are its functions and what types of operating systems are commonly available for use are the issues that are described in this chapter.

NEED FOR OPERATING SYSTEM

Operating System is essential software that is required for a computer to become operational. It provides functionality to computer hardware so that electro-mechanical components of it perform read, write and processing functions as human beings do.

Without operating system, computer cannot work. In the absence of operating system, neither input devices will be able to provide data to the computer nor memory will be able to store anything in it nor processor will be able to process the data nor output devices will be able to show the result. Managing computer's resources and making them work in coordination with each other is the responsibility of operating system.

Any instruction given by the user to the computer to perform a function is actually carried out by operating system. It is the operating system, which on receiving instructions from the user invokes all internal units to perform their duties and workout the result. Details of operating system are described below.

SIGNIFICANCE OF OPERATING SYSTEM

Operating system is essential software, purpose of which is to activate the computer and:

1. perform internal management functions
2. provide services.

Internal management functions are the functions that have to be essentially performed to make the computer work. For example, managing the processor, memory, devices, input / output functions, data etc.

Services are bunch of commands and utilities that operating system provides to its users to have better control over computer. Block diagram, showing the basic structure of operating system is shown in figure 3.1. It also depicts its purpose.

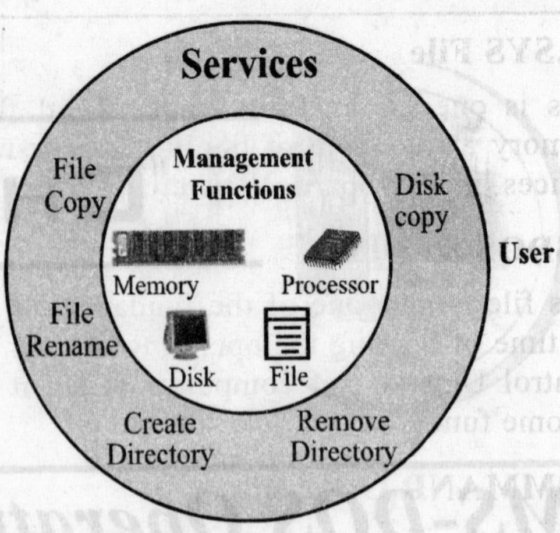

Figure 3.1

EXAMPLES OF OPERATING SYSTEM

To activate the computer and to perform different types of activities on computer, many operating systems are available these days. MS-DOS, Windows, Linux, UNIX etc. are few popular operating systems of modern time. Each operating system has its own advantages and disadvantages. As per its design and features each operating system offers its own style of working and commands. In this book, we will mainly describe MS-DOS and Windows operating systems.

INTRODUCTION TO MS-DOS

MS-DOS is one of the most popular, powerful and useful operating system. It was designed and developed in the initial days of Personal Computers (PC) by Microsoft Corporation of USA. Due to its versatility and ease of operations, it became quite popular, within short span of time.

MS-DOS is Character User Interface (CUI) based operating system. To execute any command in MS-DOS, you need to know the command and its format. Any mistake in its spelling or format leads to error.

MS-DOS not only activates computer resources and controls them but it also provides many commands for performing day-to-day tasks. Internal architecture of MS-DOS and its commands are explained in this chapter.

CONSTITUTION OF MS-DOS

MS-DOS is a modular operating system and comprises of many files. It utilizes these files as and when required. Following files put together constitute MS-DOS operating system:

1. IO.SYS
2. MSDOS.SYS
3. COMMAND.COM
4. Many external command files

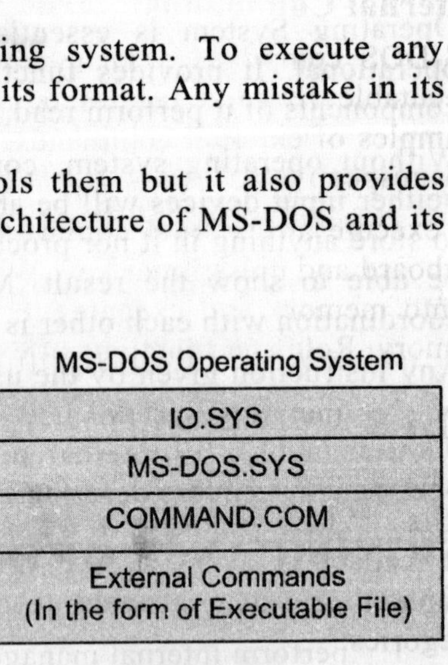

Figure 3.2

Basic architecture of MS-DOS operating system is shown in figure 3.2 and role of each file is explained below.

IO.SYS File

This is one of the most fundamental files of MS-DOS. It gets loaded into computer's memory at the time of booting the system. It primarily activates basic input and output devices like keyboard, VDU etc. and makes them functional.

MSDOS.SYS File

This file is also one of the fundamental files of MS-DOS. It automatically gets loaded at the time of booting the operating system. It controls internal resources like memory, ALU, Control Unit etc. of computer. When it gets executed, memory, ALU, Control Unit etc. become functional.

COMMAND.COM File

This is the third fundamental file of MS-DOS operating system. It comprises of few frequently used MS-DOS commands. When you boot the system, it gets automatically loaded into computer's memory. After booting the system, commands contained in it, remain present in main memory. This is the reason, why they are called internal commands. For example, DIR, COPY, TYPE, REN etc. are internal commands of MS-DOS and reside in COMMAND.COM file.

To execute an internal command, you need to type the command from the keyboard in its recommended format. When you do so, it is directly read from the memory and executed. Role and function of each internal command are described later in this chapter.

External Commands

MS-DOS comprises of many external commands. Each command exists in the form of executable file and resides on the disk. For example, FORMAT, XCOPY etc. are the examples of external commands. They exist in the form of FORMAT.COM, XCOPY.EXE files respectively.

To execute an external command, you need to type the name of the command from the keyboard and press Enter key. When you do so, computer reads the file from the disk, loads it into memory and executes it. When its execution is complete, it is removed from the memory. Role and functions of external commands are described later in this chapter.

FILES AND FILE TYPES

Whatever computer has to store on media like floppy hard disk or CD, it stores in the form of files. Whenever it has to make use of the contents, stored in the file, it accesses the file and reads them from it. In other words you can say that all read/write operations, in computer are done through files. Computer files can be broadly classified into two categories:

1. Executable files
2. Data files

Executable files are basically command files, which when executed perform specific task. For example, DISKCOPY.COM is a command file, which copies the contents of a floppy on another floppy.

Data files are the files, which contain data, program or some information in them.

Files are identified by their names. Each operating system follows a fixed file naming convention. All files of that operating system need to follow the convention. MS-DOS file naming convention is described below.

FILE NAMING CONVENTION

As per rules of MS-DOS operating system, file name comprises of two parts. First part is called primary name and second part is called extension. Both the parts remain separated from each other by a dot (.). Thus following pattern is used for naming the files:

<Primary Name>.<Extension>

For example, DELL.DAT is a valid file name. Here DELL is the primary name and DAT is extension. Following are the restrictions that are imposed by MS-DOS, on file names:

1. Primary name can be at most 8 characters long. The name can either be written in upper case or lower case letters but operating system stores all the file names in upper case only. For example, file names like AMOUNT.DAT, Amount.Dat, amount.dat etc. will be treated as, same and will be stored as AMOUNT.DAT.
2. Extension can be at most 3 characters long and can be given in lower case or upper case letters. It will also get stored in upper case.
3. Mathematical signs like +,-,*,/ etc. can not be used in constituting the name.

Following is the general format of MS-DOS file name:

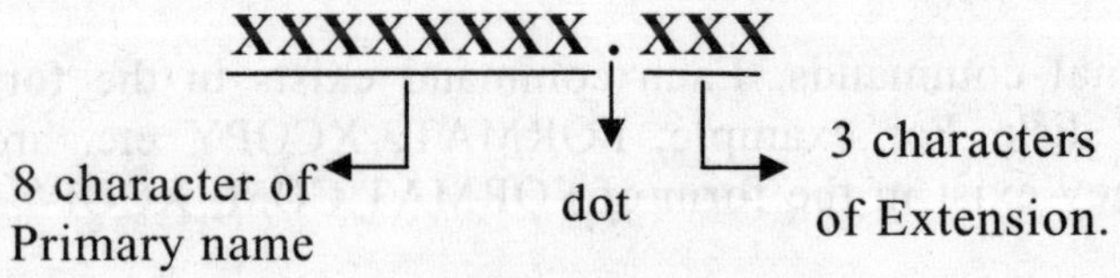

Following are few valid file names:

DELL.COM, PLOT.DAT, MONTH12.BAK, YR.AS, RIGHT.DOC

Wild Cards Are Their Usage

As you know, each file is assigned a unique name. Thus when you refer a file by its name, single file is referenced. Wild card is a mechanism, using which you can refer a group of files.

Wild cards are basically special characters that can be used while specifying a file name. These characters carry special meaning for computer. Following are the wild card characters and their meaning:

1. The character "*" denotes any character after this place.
2. The character "?" denotes any character at this place.

To understand the concept of wild card character, assume that following files are present on the disk:

1. DAT
2. ADC.BAK
3. A1.TXT
4. S.BAK
5. WORK.DAT
6. WORK.BAK
7. MONEY.TXT
8. MY.FIL
9. AXP.EXE
10. ART.WRK

1. If you wish to refer all the files with extension .BAK, you can refer them by the name *.BAK
2. If you wish to refer all those files, in which names start with A and have any extension, you can refer them by the name A*.*.
3. All file names starting with A, three characters long, ending with C and any extension, can be referred by the name A?C.*.

CONCEPT OF DIRECTORY

Directory can be conceptualized as special file, which can hold files and directories in it. Concept of directory is illustrated in figure 3.3. Refer this figure and note that D1 is a directory, which holds two files F1 and F2 in it. It also contains a directory D2 in it. D2 holds Files F3 and F4 in it.

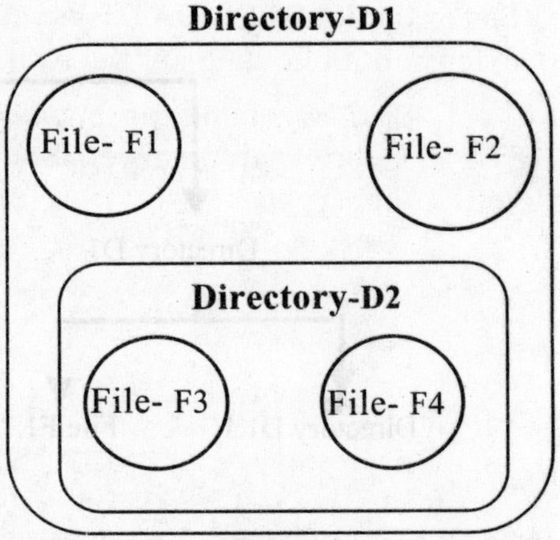

Figure 3.3

From this figure, it is quite clear that directories can be utilized for classified storage of files on the disk. For example, directory named LETTER could be utilized for storing all letters in it. Similarly the directory CPROGRAM could be used for storing all the programs written in C language.

Concept Of Root Directory

Root directory can be conceptualized as the top most directory, which holds other directories and files in it.

Whenever you use any disk for the first time, root directory gets automatically created on it. Other files and directories that are created thereafter are created within root directory. In MS-DOS, root directory is denoted by back slash(\) sign.

Concept Of Parent Directory

Parent directory is the directory, in which you create another directory. For example, if directory D2 is created in directory D1 then D1 directory will be called parent directory of D2. Similarly if directory D3 is created in directory D2 then D2 will be the parent directory for D3. Parent directory is denoted by double dot (..) symbol.

Current Directory

Once you have directories within directory, you can always change your position from one directory to another directory. The directory within which you are currently placed is called current directory. For example, if you are currently placed in directory D1 then D1 will be called current directory. When you have moved from directory D1 to D3 then D3 will be the current directory.

MS-DOS FILE SYSTEM

The mechanism of arranging the files and directories on the disk is called file system. In MS-DOS, file system looks like an inverted tree. Root directory appears at the top of the tree. Other directories branch off from there and files act as leafs.

Such a file arrangement is often referred to as Hierarchical File System. A hierarchical file system consisting of few files and directories is illustrated in figure 3.4.

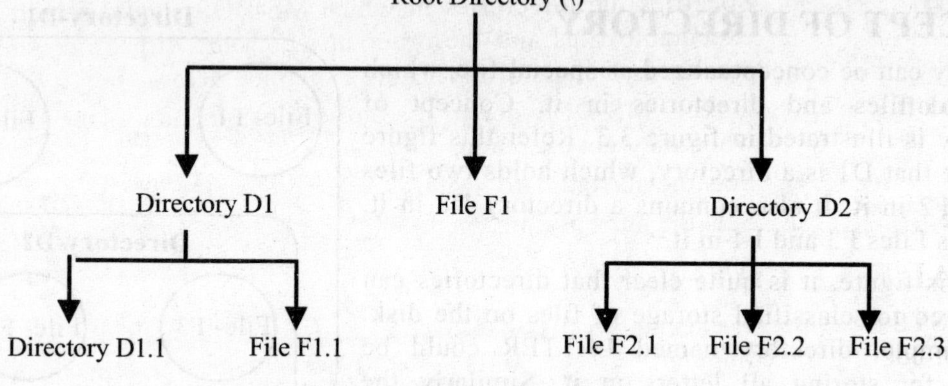

Figure 3.4

Refer hierarchical file system illustrated in figure 3.4 and note that root directory is at the top of the tree. Root directory contains two directories D1, D2 and a file, named "File1" in it. D1 and D2 further contain subdirectories and files in them. Note that directories in MS-DOS follow the same naming convention that files do. Generally the directories are assigned a name, which gives an indication of the type of files contained in them. For example, the name DOCUMENT could be used for storing document files in it. Similarly SALARY directory could be used for storing pay relates files.

CONCEPT OF PATH

Path of a file or directory is the list of directory names in descending sequence, starting from root and each directory name separated by a back slash (\), following which you reach to the desired file or directory. For example, refer figure 3.4. The path for file F1.1 will be \D1\F1.1. Similarly the path name for F2.2 file will be \D2\F2.2. Note that first backslash in the path name denotes root directory, while other backslashes serve the purpose of separators.

You know that MS-DOS provides numerous internal and external commands for performing different tasks. To make use of these commands, it is necessary that computer should be booted with MS-DOS. The procedure of booting the computer is described below.

SPECIAL BATCH FILE AUTOEXEC.BAT OF MS-DOS

AUTOEXEC.BAT is a special batch file that is executed at the time of booting. All the executable statements written in it, get executed line by line automatically and the desired working environment is created for the user.

Now the question is what do you write in this batch file? Well, all those commands that are to be executed at the time of booting are written in it. Following are some commonly used commands that are put in AUTOEXEC.BAT file:

Prompt	Sets the appearance of the system prompt. For details refer PROMPT command.
PATH	Specifies the directories in which MS-DOS should search for the executable files and the order in which the directories should be searched. Details of PATH are explained below.
Echo off	Directs MS-DOS not to display the commands in the batch file, when they get executed.
Date	Sets the current date. Refer DATE command.
Time	Sets the current time. Refer TIME command.

SPECIAL FILE CONFIG.SYS OF MS-DOS

CONFIG.SYS is a special executable file of MS-DOS that gets automatically executed at the time of booting the computer.

When it gets executed, all the system configuration commands written in it are executed one by one in sequence and the system is configured accordingly.

For example, you may wish to handle the dates in mm-dd-yy format instead of dd-mm-yy format. For this, MS-DOS provides a system configuration command which cannot be executed from the command prompt but can be put in a CONFIG.SYS file. When config.sys file gets executed, system will be configured accordingly.

Its main purpose is to configure the system as per requirements. It can be edited by the user and system configuration commands can be written in it. Mostly used system configuration commands are described below.

Break (ON\OFF)

Recall that when you give a command from the system prompt, system gets busy in executing the command. In this duration keyboard gets held up and you cannot give any other command. "BREAK ON" system turns CTRL C check ON and you can abort the execution of the command in the middle by pressing CTRL and C keys together. If Break is OFF then this key gets defended and you can abort the execution by pressing CTRL+ C.

Buffers

A buffer is the memory area which system keeps, reserved for reading and writing purposes. More are the buffers, faster is the system performance but lesser is the area for our use. So we have to optimize the memory area for best system - user performance.

Buffer command in CONFIG.SYS specifics how much memory, MS-DOS has to reserve for buffers. The syntax for setting the buffers is as follows :

Buffer = x

Where x ranges from 2 to 255

Default value of buffer is 2

Files

Files is a command using, which you specify how many files can be opened at a time. The syntax for declaration is as follows :

Files = X

Where x ranges from 5 to 255.

Default value of files is 8

COUNTRY

Using this command you can change the data format. The command for setting the date format is as follows :

COUNTRY = x

Where

x=1 means USA and format is mm-dd-yy

x=2 means France and format is yy-mm-dd

x=3 means Spanish and format is dd-mm-yy

Device

This command is for loading the device driver for a particular device.

Recall that device driver is a software for controlling any device that you attach to your system. For example, if you attach CD ROM to your system then you will have to load the corresponding device driver. This can be done by including following lines in CONFIG.SYS file

DEVICE= <device driver file name>

Rem

This command enables you to add comments in CONFIG.SYS file and AUTOEXEC.BAT file also. Adding the comments increases readability of the file.

e.g. Rem This is configuration file.

Rem This batch file deletes 0 size files.

BOOTING COMPUTER USING MS-DOS

To boot the computer, using MS-DOS, follow the following steps:

1. Switch on the VDU.
2. Switch on the power, using power switch present in computer cabinet.

When you switch on the computer, it performs self-test. If self-test passes through correctly, operating system is read from the disk and loaded in computer's memory. Immediately after that following sign appears on VDU screen:

C:\>

Above mentioned sign is called system prompt. Different characters in system prompt signify different things. C: indicates that the system was booted from C drive. Character \ indicates that root is the current directory. The > sign is a terminator. Any thing written after this sign is treated as command. The dash sign is called cursor. It keeps blinking. It acts like tip of the pen. Whatever you type from the keyboard, gets typed at current cursor location and it shifts towards right.

BOOTING SEQUENCE

You are already familiar with booting process, CONFIG.SYS and AUTOEXEC.BAT files, so let's have a look into Personal computer's booting sequence. The complete booting sequence of MS-DOS is illustrated in figure 3.5.

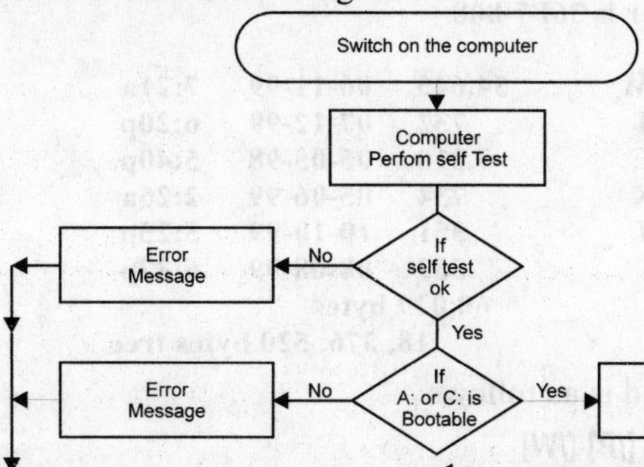

Figure 3.5

INTERNAL COMMANDS

All those commands, which are part of COMMAND.COM file and remain resident in memory from the time of booting to the time of shutdown, are called internal commands. For example, DIR, COPY, EDIT, CLS, PROMPT, REN, DEL etc. are all, internal commands. Formats and functions or internal commands are described below.

DIR Command

DIR command is used for displaying the names of all the files residing on media like floppy hard disk, CD etc. In its simplest form, it can be executed in following format:

C:\> DIR [Enter]

This command will display the names of all the files present on C: disk, in the following format:

```
Volume in drive C is RAMESH
Volume Serial Number is 36F7-808
Directory of C:\
COMMAND     COM     54,645   06-11-99   7:21a
DATA        DAT        732   07-12-99   6:20p
REPORT      DOC      3,210   05-05-98   5:40p
DOIT        BAK        734   05-06-99   2:25a
TOTAL       DAT        351   10-10-99   5:25p
EXAM        LET        357   08-08-99   6:37p
        6 file(s)   60,029 bytes
                    18, 376, 520 bytes free
```

General format of DIR command is as follows:

DIR [drive:] [file name] [/P] [/W]

Explanation of each notation used in above mentioned format is given below:

drive is the name of that drive, for which, the file names are to be displayed. For example, if "A:" drive name is specified then the names of all those files will be displayed, which are present on the floppy that is currently present in A: drive.

file name If file name is specified then its presence is reported. For example, if "DATA.JAN" file name is specified and if this file is not present in the drive then a message saying that this file is not present on the disk will be displayed. On the other hand if the file is present then its name will be displayed along with other details, confirming its presence on the disk.

/P It is an optional switch. If it is specified in the command, output of DIR command is displayed page wise. That means after displaying one screen of output, display halts and at the bottom of the screen, a message "Press any key to continue..." gets displayed. When you press a key, next screen gets displayed.

/W	It is an optional switch. It displays the file names, width wise, instead of one file name in one line.
/O	It is an optional switch. It sorts the output of DIR command.

Following are few examples of DIR commands and their results:

DIR	Displays names of all the files, present in default drive.
DIR A:	Displays names of all the files, present in A: drive.
DIR A: /P	This command displays names of all the files, present in A: drive, page wise.
DIR /W	This command displays names of all the files, present in default drive, width wise i.e. 5 file names per line.
DIR A.DAT	It reports presence or absence of A.DAT file in default drive. If it is found, its name along with other details is displayed else "No such file" message is displayed.
DIR *.BAK	Names of all those files are displayed, which have .BAK extension.
DIR B*.DAT	All those file names, which start with 'B' and have .DAT extension get displayed.
DIR Z???.*/P	All those file names, which are 4 characters long, start with Z and have any extension, get displayed, page wise.
DIR AB??.DAT	All those file names, which are 4 characters long, start with "AB" and have ". DAT" extension, get displayed.

EDIT Command

EDIT command is used to create a text file and type text in it. It is executed in the following format:

EDIT [drive:] [file name] [Enter]

Here, in this format, **"drive:"** is the name of that drive, on which the file is to be created and "file name" is the name, by which the file is to be created. For example, following command will create MYFILE.TXT file on default drive:

EDIT MYFILE.TXT [Enter]

After execution of this command, following window will appear on the screen:

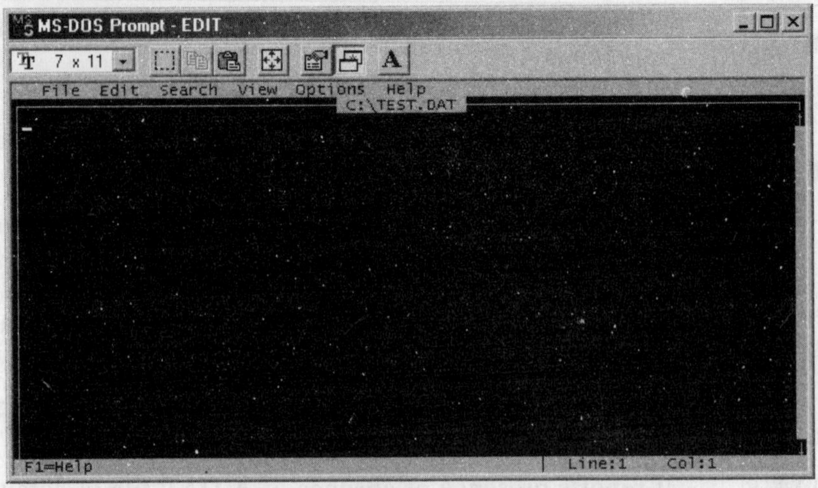

Figure 3.6

After getting the window on the screen, type the text as per instructions given in the following table:

Sr. No.	Task	Action
1.	Type the text	Use character keys of the keyboard to type the text.
2.	Take the cursor to the desired line and column.	Use arrow keys.
3.	Delete a word	Take the cursor to the beginning of the word and press CTRL and T keys together.
4.	Delete a line	Take the cursor to the line, which is to be deleted and then press CTRL and Y keys together.
5.	Insert text	Take the cursor to the place where text is to be inserted and start typing the text.
6.	Inserting a line between two lines	Take the cursor to the line, which is to be shifted below. After this, press Enter key.
7.	Save the file	Press ALT and F keys together and then press S key.
8.	Come out of EDIT	Press ALT and F keys together and then press X key.

TYPE Command

TYPE command is used for displaying the contents of a file on VDU. It is executed in the following format:

TYPE <file name.> [Enter]

Here, in this format, <file name> is the name of that file, contents of which are to be displayed on the screen. For example, if you wish to view the contents of MYFILE.TXT then following command is to be given:

TYPE A:TEST [Enter]

COPY Command

COPY command is used to make a duplicate copy of a given file. It is executed in the following format:

COPY <Source file name> <Destination file name> [Enter]

Here in this format, "Source file name" is the name of the file, which you wish to copy and "Destination file name" is the name of the file, in which the contents have to be copied. For example, if the contents of "MYFILE.TXT" file are to be copied in "MYFILE.BAK" then COPY command will have to be executed, as mentioned below:

COPY MYFILE.DAT MYFILE.BAK

General format of COPY command is as follows:

COPY [/-y] [Source file] [+Source file] [+.........} [destination file] /V.

Explanation of each notation used in above mentioned format is given below:

/-Y It is an optional switch. It makes the COPY command interactive. That means if the destination file already exists, it displays a confirmation message.

In above mentioned format, many source file names with + sign indicate that multiple files can be copied into one file so as to add them together.

/V It is an optional switch. It makes COPY command, verify the contents after copying the file.

To understand the usage of different switches in COPY command, consider below given commands:

COPY /-Y A:JAN.DAT C:JAN.BAK /V

If file C:JAN.BAK file already exists on C: drive then following confirmation message will get displayed:

Overwrite A:JAN.BAK (YES / NO / ALL)

Against this message, if you opt for "YES", computer will overwrite on the existing, JAN.BAK file. If you opt for "NO" then the file will not be copied. "ALL" option will behave as "YES" option, when multiple files are copied. /V switch in the command will verify the contents of JAN.BAK file from the original file, after copying the file. Following command will add three files i.e. ONE.DAT, TWO.DAT and THREE.DAT into one file named ALL.DAT.

COPY ONE.DAT+ TWO.DAT+ THREE.DAT ALL.DAT

REN Command

REN command is used for renaming an existing file. General syntax for REN command is as follows:

REN <Existing file name> <New file name> [Enter]

To understand the usage of REN command, consider the following examples:

REN DATA.DAT INFO.TXT [Enter]

This command will change the name of DATA.DAT file to INFO.TXT.

REN *.NEW *.OLD [Enter]

This command will change all extension names, ".NEW" to ".OLD". For example, JAN.NEW file will be renamed as JAN.OLD. Similarly, TEST.NEW file will be renamed as TEST.OLD.

DEL Command

DEL command is used for removing a file from the disk. In its simplest form, it can be executed as follows:

DEL <File name> [Enter]

Here, in this format, "File name" is the name of the file along with drive reference, which is to be removed from the disk. To understand the usage of DEL command, consider the following examples:

DEL A:DATA.DAT [Enter]

This command will remove DATA.DAT file from A: drive.

DEL *.* [Enter]

This command will remove all the files from the default drive. It is quite obvious that this command can be disastrous. So as a precautionary measure, whenever you make use of DEL *.* command, computer displays following confirmation message and removes or doesn't remove files as per your confirmation:

All files in directory will be deleted !
Are you sure (Y/N)?

It you opt "Y", all the files are deleted else the command is ignored.

General format of DEL command is as follows:

DEL <File name> [/P]

Here, in this format, /P is an optional switch. It makes DEL command interactive. That means before deleting the file, a confirmation message is displayed. As per the choice opted against this message, action is performed. For example, following confirmation message will get displayed when you give DEL ABC.DAT /P:

ABC.DAT, Delete (Y/N) ?

If you opt for "Y", file will get deleted. If you opt for "N" then file will remain intact.

CD Or CHDIR Command

CD is short form of Change Directory. It is used for moving from one directory to another directory. General format for CD command is as follows:

CD <Directory name> [Enter]

Here, in this format, "Directory name" is the name of that directory, to which you wish to move. To understand the usage and functioning of CD command, consider the following examples:

If current directory has a directory named SECOND in it and you wish to move to that directory, CD SECOND command will have to be given.

If you wish to move to root directory, CD \ command will have to be given.

If you wish to move to the parent directory, CD .. command will have to be given.

If you execute CD command, without any file name, the name of current directory gets displayed.

MD Or MKDIR Command

MD is short form of Make Directory. This command is used for creating a new directory. It is used in the following format:

MD <Directory name> [Enter]

Here, in this format, "Directory name" is the name that is to be assigned to the newly created directory. For example, if you wish to make a new directory with the name "LETTERS", following command will have to be given:

MD LETTERS [Enter]

Note that when you make a directory, it is made in the current directory. For example, if you are in root and execute above-mentioned command, LETTERS directory will be created in root. On the other hand, if you are in DOC directory and you execute that command, LETTERS directory will get created in DOC directory.

RD Or RMDIR Command

RD is short form of Remove Directory. This command is used for removing the directory from the disk, provided it is blank. It is used in the following format:

RD <Directory name> [Enter]

Here, in this format, "Directory name" is the name of that directory, which is to be removed. For example, if you wish to remove LETTERS directory, following command will have to be given:

RD LETTERS [Enter]

For example, it you wish to remove NEWS directory from the media then you can give the following command:

RD NEWS [Enter]

PROMPT Command

PROMPT command is used for changing the system prompt. It is used in the following format:

PROMPT String

Here, in this format, "String" can either be few special-meaning characters or a simple message. For example, if "YourChoice" has to be set as system prompt then PROMPT YourChoice command will have to be given.

Special meaning characters that can be used in PROMPT commands are listed in the following table:

Special Character	Their Effect
$Q	Equal Sign gets included
$T	System prompt changes to current time.
$D	System prompt changes to current date
$P	System prompt changes to current $ drive and path
$G	Greater than Sign

For example, following command will change the system prompt to current drive, current directory name and a greater than sign:

PROMPT PG

CLS Command

This command erases all the contents, currently present on the screen and puts the system prompt in left hand upper corner of the screen. It is executed in the following format:

CLS [Enter]

SYS Command

SYS command is used to make a media, like floppy, hard disk etc. bootable. While making it bootable, it copies IO.SYS, MSDOS.SYS and COMMAND.COM files at specific location on the media. Since these files are copied at specific location hence the media becomes bootable. On the other hand, if you copy these files to the media, using COPY command, media will not become bootable. SYS command is used in following format:

SYS <Drive name> [Enter]

Here, in this format, "Drive name" is the name of the drive that contains the media, which is to be made bootable. For example, if floppy in drive A: is to be made bootable, following command will have to be executed:

SYS A: [Enter]

LABEL Command

Label is basically an identification name, which can be assigned to any media like floppy, hard disk etc. In MS-DOS, LABEL command is used for putting labels on the media. It is used in the following format:

LABEL <Drive name> [Enter]

Here, in this format, "Drive name" is the name of that drive, which holds the media, on which the label is to be marked. For example, if you wish to put the label on the floppy, present in A: drive, following command will have to be given:

LABEL A: [Enter]

This command will show the existing label and display the following message:

Volume label (11 characters ENTER for name) ?

Here you need to type the identification name of the floppy, consisting of maximum 11 characters. If you do not type the name and simply press Enter key then the existing volume label, will get deleted.

VOL Command

VOL command is used for displaying the label that has been put on the media. It is used in the following format:

VOL <drive name> [Enter]

Here, in this format, "Drive name" is the name of that drive, which holds the media, whose label is to be displayed. For example, if you wish to display the label of the floppy, which has been put in A: drive, following command will have to be given:

VOL A: [Enter]

Floppy's label will get displayed in the following format:

Volume in drive A: is <Volume name>

EXTERNAL COMMAND

All those commands of MS-DOS, which are not part of COMMAND.COM file and reside on the disk, in the form of executable files, fall into the category of external commands. For example, FORMAT, MOVE, MORE, TREE, DISKCOPY etc. are external commands.

Functions and formats of these commands are described below.

FORMAT Command

Format command makes internal logical arrangement on the media like floppy, hard disk etc. to store the data. This arrangement is made by dividing the surface of the media into concentric circles and concentric circles into small segments, called sectors. Internal logical format of a typical floppy is illustrated in figure 3.7.

The floppy that we generally use is called 135 TPI double sided high density 3.5" floppy. Data is recorded on both the sides of the floppy. Each side consists of 80 tracks and each track contains 18 sectors in it. Each sector stores 512 bytes in it. Thus capacity of the floppy turns out to be 1.44 MB. FORMAT command, in its simplest form can be executed as follows:

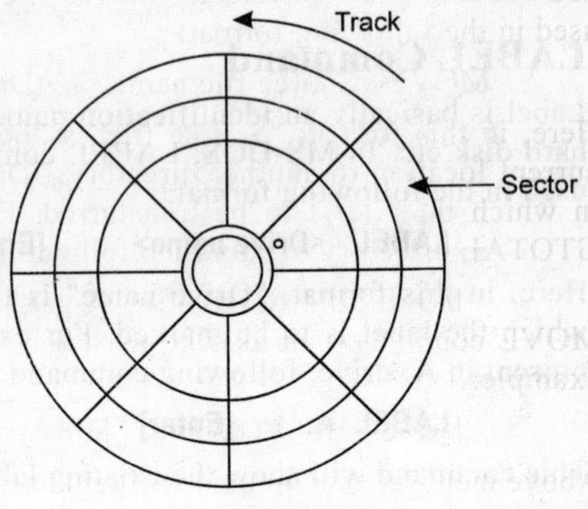

Figure 3.7

FORMAT [Drive name]

Here, in this format, "Drive name" is the name of the drive that holds the media, which is to be formatted. For example, if you execute "FORMAT A:" command, the floppy present in A: drive will get formatted. After giving this command, computer will display the following message on the screen and wait for your intervention:

Insert new diskette for drive A:

and press ENTER when ready...

Now you will have to put the floppy, which is to be formatted, in A: drive and press Enter key. When you do so, following message will be displayed on the screen:

Checking existing disk format

Saving UNFORMAT information

After formatting the floppy, FORMAT command will display following message on the screen:

Volume label (11 characters, ENTER for none) ?

You can type any string of characters (not more than 11 characters) as label, against this message. At last, following message will get displayed:

Format Complete

Format another disk (Y/N)

If you wish to format another disk, type "Y" else type any other character. Note that this was the simplest form of FORMAT command. The general format of FORMAT command is as follows:

FORMAT <drive name> [Switch]

Following switches can be used in FORMAT command:

/S : This switch makes the floppy bootable.

/U : Formats the floppy unconditionally.

MOVE Command

MOVE command, physically moves files and directories from one place to another. It is used in the following format:

MOVE <Source file name> <Destination directory>

Here, in this format, "Source file" is the name of the file, which is to be moved from its current location to another directory. "Destination directory" is the name of that directory, in which the file is to be transferred. For example, if you wish to move SUM file into GTOTAL directory of root then following command will have to be given:

MOVE SUM \GTOTAL [Enter]

MOVE command can also be used for renaming the directories, as done in the following example:

MOVE JAN MONTH [Enter]

Above mentioned command will rename JAN directory to MONTH.

TREE Command

TREE command displays the file system, present on the disk, in graphical form. In its simplest form, it is executed in the following format:

TREE [Enter]

A sample output of this command is illustrated in figure 3.7.

Refer figure 3.8 and note the following points:

1. Directory names that are at equal distance denote that these directories are at same hierarchical level, in the file system. For example, EXPENSE, BOOK and MONTH directories are subdirectories of ROOT and are at same level. Similarly subdirectories like, SALARY, TOUR and WEEK are at equal level.
2. File names do not get displayed in the output.

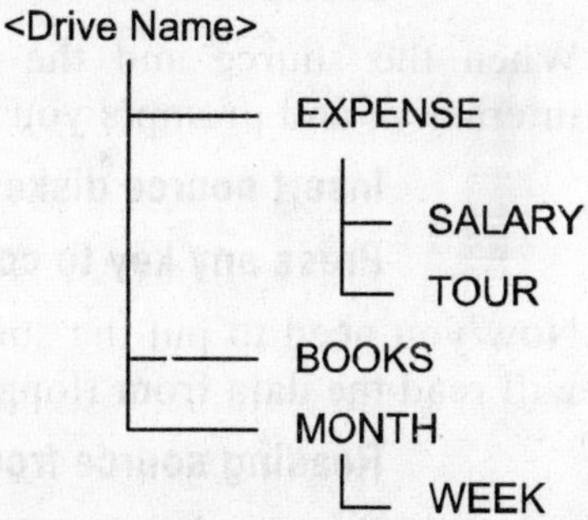

Figure 3.8

General format of TREE command is as follows:

TREE [drive:] [path] [/ F]

Here, in this format, "Drive:" is name of that drive, for which you wish to see the directory structure. Path is the full path name for the directory, for which the directory structure is to be seen. If you specify /F switch file names are also displayed along with the directory tree structure.

DELTREE Command

DELTREE command is used for deleting the directory tree. When you delete the directory tree, all files and directories, in it get deleted. It is used in the following format:

DELTREE <name of the directory to be removed> [Enter]

This command will remove the complete branch of the directory structure that starts from the specified directory. This means that this directory and all the files and directories in it will get deleted.

DISKCOPY Command

DISKCOPY command is used for duplicating the contents of a given floppy. When you make use of this command, all files and directories of one floppy get copied to another floppy. In its simplest form, it can be executed as follows:

DISKCOPY <Source drive> <Destination drive>

Here, in this format, "Source drive" is the name of that drive, which contains the floppy, whose contents are to be duplicated. "Destination drive" is the name of that drive, which holds the floppy, on which the contents have to be copied. For Example, if you wish to copy the contents from drive A: to B: drive then following command will have to be given:

DISKCOPY A: B: [Enter]

Note that DISKCOPY makes a mirror image of the source on the destination, so it is essential that both the drives should be of the same size and both should contain the floppy of the same capacity. Any difference will result into an error and DISKCOPY will not copy the files.

If there is only one floppy drive in the computer and you wish to execute this command then it will have to be executed as follows:

DISKCOPY A: A: [Enter]

When the source and the destination drive are same, DISKCOPY command becomes interactive and prompts you as follows:

Insert source diskette in drive A:

Press any key to continue.

Now you need to put the source floppy in A: drive and press any key. After this, computer will read the data from floppy and display the following message on the screen:

Reading source from the diskette.....

After reading the data, computer will again displays the following message on the screen:

Insert TARGET diskette in drive A:

Press any key to continue.

Now you have to take out the source floppy from A: drive and put the destination floppy (on which you wish to copy the files) in the same drive. After this, copying process will start when you press any key. Note that copying may not get completed in one cycle. In that case above-mentioned messages will keep on appearing as many times as required. You will have to keep on inserting source and destination floppies as and when asked for.

General format of the DISKCOPY command is as follows:

DISKCOPY <source drive> <destination drive> [/V]

/V switch, when included in DISKCOPY command, verifies the contents after copying. Obviously inclusion of this switch will slow down the procedure.

EXERCISES CHAPTER 3

Short Type Questions

A. Select most appropriate answer for following questions:

1. Which of the following file gets automatically loaded at the time of booting the computer?
   (a) TYPE.COM (b) FORMAT.COM (c) IO.SYS (d) DIR
2. Which of the following file is not part of MS-DOS operating system?
   (a) COMMAND.COM (b) IO.SYS (c) FORMAT.COM (d) DIR.DAT
3. Which of the following character doesn't represent a directory?
   (a) \ (b) / (c) . (d) ..
4. Which of the following character represents a wild card in MS-DOS?
   (a) * (b) $ (c) % (d) !
5. Which of the following command does not operate upon file?
   (a) EDIT (b) COPY (c) CLS (d) DEL

B. Fill in the blanks:

6. Loading the operating system into computer's memory is called ....
7. Those commands of MS-DOS, which remain resident in computer's memory are called ....
8. External commands of MS-DOS reside on ....
9. Primary name of MS-DOS file can be up to .... characters long while extension could be........................ characters long.
10. .... command of MS-DOS can be used for renaming a file.

11. The character .... represents root directory in MS-DOS
12. In MS-DOS, ... command is used for displaying the names of all the files present on disk.
13. .... command of MS-DOS is used for displaying the contents of a file.
14. .... command of MS-DOS could be used for typing your personal details on computer.
15. .... command could be used for making mirror image of a floppy.

C. State, true or false for following statements:

16. IO.SYS file of MS-DOS contains all internal commands of MS-DOS.
17. COMMAND.COM file of MS-DOS contains all external commands of MS-DOS.
18. DEL is an external command of MS-DOS.
19. FORMAT command of MS-DOS erases all the files present on the disk.
20. REM command of MS-DOS renames a given file.

D. Differentiate between the following:

21. IO.SYS and MSDOS.SYS files of MS-DOS.
22. FORMAT /S and SYS commands of MS-DOS.
23. COPY and XCOPY commands of MS-DOS.
24. VOL and LABEL commands of MS-DOS.
25. DELTREE and RD commands of MS-DOS.

E. Describe the functioning and format of following MS-DOS commands:

26. (a) DIR (b) REN (c) PROMPT (d) MOVE (e) MD (f) DISCOPY

Detailed Answer Type Questions

E. Answer the following questions in detail:

27. Draw a block diagram of MS-DOS and describe the role of COMMAND.COM file.
28. What do you understand by wild cards? Name the characters that are used as wild cards in MS-DOS. What do they signify?
29. Name any three internal commands and write their general format.
30. Name any three external commands of MS-DOS and write their general format.
31. How will you make A: drive as default drive in MS-DOS?
32. How will you FORMAT a floppy in MS-DOS and make it bootable?
33. How will you rename the file, A.DAT to A.BAK in MS-DOS?
34. How will you check the presence of DATA.DAT file on a floppy, which is present in A: drive?

35. How will you make a mirror image of a floppy, if you have only one floppy drive in your computer?
36. How will you see the contents of A.DAT file on VDU?
37. What is operating system? Name any three popular operating systems.
38. Describe the role of operating system in computer? Why it is required?
39. What is booting and what is bootable disk? Name the files that are related to MS-DOS booting.
40. Describe the role of AUTOEXEC.BAT and CONFIG.SYS files in MS-DOS.
41. Draw booting sequence diagram of MS-DOS, clearly mentioning the names and sequence of the files that participate in MS-DOS booting.
42. Name any three functions of operating system.
43. Name any three files that get executed automatically at the time of booting the computer with MS-DOS.
44. What is the function of EDLIN command of MS-DOS.
45. Out of internal commands and external commands of MS-DOS, which of the two will execute fast and why?

****

CHAPTER 4

Windows Operating System

INTRODUCTION

Windows is the most popular operating system of modern times. It has been designed and developed by Microsoft Corporation of USA. Windows not only activates computer and makes its devices functional, it also provides applications for performing wide variety of tasks on computer. For example, its Notepad program enables you to write letters and notes. Using its Paint program you can draw pictures on computer and color them too. Likewise there are many more programs in Windows. An introduction to its features, functions and applications is given in its chapter.

FEATURES OF WINDOWS OPERATING SYSTEM

Following are the features of Windows operating system:

GUI Based Operating System

GUI is acronym for Graphical User Interface. Windows is Graphical User Interface based operating system. It provides very simple, yet powerful and interesting mechanism for interacting with computer.

In GUI interaction, you don't interact with computer by typing commands, as you do in MS-DOS. Instead of this you make use of graphical items like icons, menus, buttons, dialog boxes etc. As and when required, these items appear on computer screen and you click, double click or right click the mouse on them to carryout required tasks. Thus in GUI mode of interaction, you need not remember the commands and their formats to perform the task, rather you should know the method of clicking, right clicking, dragging and dropping the items.

Multitasking Operating System

Windows is multitasking operating system. Thus in Windows, you can perform multiple tasks simultaneously. For example, while typing the letter through keyboard, you can view a movie on VDU and print the report on printer too.

Drag And Drop

Drag and Drop is a powerful feature of Windows operating system. Using this feature, you can drag objects like files, folders etc. from their original location and drop them at some other place, so that they could either be copied or moved there. For example, dragging the file A from folder F1 and dropping it on folder F2 will move the file A from F1 to F2.

CUT COPY And PASTE

Cut, Copy and Paste are powerful features of Windows operating system. Using these feature, selected item like text, graphics, icons etc. can either be copied from their original place to a temporary memory location called Clipboard or from Clipboard to the desired location. Thus you can either move these items from one place to other or make duplicate copies of them. For example, when you select an item and perform CUT operation on it, it physically moves from its original place to the Clipboard. When you move to some other location and perform PASTE operation there, the item from Clipboard gets copied to the current location. Thus at the end of CUT-PASTE operation, selected item changes its place. Similarly when you perform COPY operation on a selected item, it get copied into Clipboard (doesn't get removed from its original place, as it happens in the case of CUT operation). After this, when you change your current location and perform PASTE operation there, contents of Clipboard get copied to the new location. Thus a duplicate copy of the selected item gets made.

Object Embedding

This is one of the most powerful features of Windows operating system. It enables two or more programs to exchange objects like text, graphics etc. among them. For example, a drawing made in Paint program could be brought into the document, created through WordPad program so that figure could be embedded in the text. For example, you may type the description of Kutubminar in WordPad program and draw its figure in Paint program. Using object embedding feature of Windows, you can place the figure of Kutuminar in Kutuminar text, so that it becomes complete text in itself.

Object Linking

Object Linking is yet another powerful feature of Windows operating system. Using this feature, one object can be linked to the other object. Thus whenever linked object is modified or changed, modifications/changes get visible in other object also. For example, you may type the description of Personal Computer in WordPad program and draw its figure in Paint program. Using Object Linking feature you may link the computer figure to computer description so that it appears in the document (as it did in case of Object Embedding). Now whenever you will make modifications/changes in computer figure they will automatically get reflected in the description. You may note that overall effect of Object Embedding and Object Linking is same but automatic reflection of changes/modifications does not take place in case of Object Embedding.

Plug And Play

It is an important feature of Windows operating system. It makes the operating system, slightly intelligent. Whenever a new device is attached to the computer, operating system automatically senses its attachment and loads its device driver. Thus due to plug and play feature, new devices become automatically operational in Windows operating system.

Command Prompt

Using this feature, Windows provides MS-DOS working environment, within Windows environment. Thus all MS-DOS commands could be executed from Windows.

WINDOWS-A SERIES OF OPERATING SYSTEMS

Windows is now, quite popular operating system. Long back, it came into existence. It was continuously updated to enhance its power and to incorporate more and more features into it. With the result of this, it has become world's most favorite operating system.

Development of Windows operating system has taken place in two streams. First stream deals with stand alone environment while second stream deals with network environment.

Different versions of Windows, which gradually came into existence, in stand alone environment are Windows-95, Windows-98, Windows-me, Windows-XP etc. Each version that came later was improved and enhanced version of the previous one. These operating systems were designed and developed for single user environment.

For network environment, Windows-NT, Windows-2000, Windows-3000 etc. came into existence. They all are network operating systems. They not only provide base networking facilities but also provide network administration utilities.

In this book, we will mainly deal with Windows-XP, which is the latest operating system for stand alone working environment. All throughout the book, we will refer it with the name Window.

BOOTING COMPUTER WITH WINDOWS

To boot the computer with Windows operating system, first switch the monitor on and then switch on the CPU, using ON/OFF switch present in its chassis.

When you do so, computer will check all its peripherals, if they are functioning properly or not. If any unit is found faulty, an error message appears on the screen and booting process stops. On the other hand, if all the units are found OK, booting process continues. Computer reads the operating system from the disk, loads it into memory and displays a dialog box, as shown in figure 4.1.

Figure 4.1

This dialog box is part of Windows security system. It asks for login name and password to ensure that only authorized persons use the system. To boot the system, enter your login name and password correctly and click the mouse on OK button. After a while, display on the monitor will turn as shown in figure 4.2.

Figure 4.2

INTRODUCTION TO WINDOWS DESKTOP COMPONENTS

After booting the system with Windows, the first screen that appears on the monitor is called Desktop. Desktop is illustrated in figure 4.2. A brief introduction of each component of Windows desktop is given below.

Desktop Icons

Icons are graphical pictures. They represent objects like programs, files, folders etc. Initially few icons appear on desktop. Later, if the need be, more icons are placed on the desktop. To activate any icon, you need to double click the mouse on it.

Start Button

Start button is the starting point of Windows menu system. When you click the mouse on "Start" button, Start menu, as shown in figure 4.3 appears on the screen.

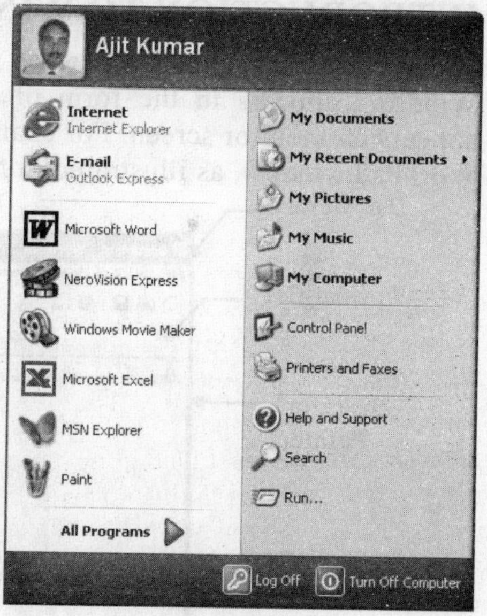

Figure 4.3

Refer Start menu, shown in figure 4.3 and note the following points:

1. Some of the options in Start menu have an arrow marked in front of them. This

arrow indicates that when you click the mouse on the option, a submenu will appear on the screen.

2. Some of the options have few dots (...) marked in front of them. These dots indicate that when you click the mouse on the option, a dialog box will appear on the screen.
3. Those options that neither have arrow nor dots marked in front of them get directly executed when you click the mouse on them.

Quick Launch Toolbar

As illustrated in figure 4.2, Quick Launch toolbar comprises of many buttons. Each button represents a program. When you click the mouse on any button, corresponding program gets executed.

Task Manager

Initially, Task Manager appears as blank area but when you execute any program, a button for that program gets created in this area. This button identifies the program and provides means for performing different operations on the running program. For example, using the button you could terminate the program.

System Tray

Initially system tray displays few icons and system time in it. Each icon of the system tray represents a program, which is invisibly running in the background. To operate upon a background program, you can double click the mouse on its icon. For example, to set the system date and time, you can double click the mouse on system time icon.

INTRODUCTION TO WINDOW

Windows operating system drives its name from the fact that each running program, in Windows appears in the form of a window. When you execute a program, a window appears on monitor screen. For example, when you execute WordPad program of Windows, WordPad window, as illustrated in figure 4.4 appears on monitor screen.

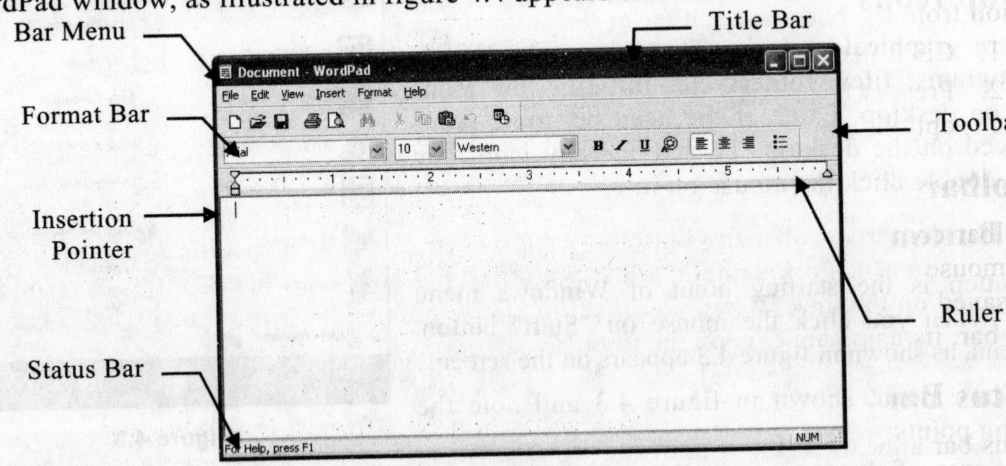

Figure 4.4

Refer figure 4.4 and note that window comprises of many components. Role and function of each component of the window is given below.

Title Bar

Title bar acts as window header. It comprises of following items:

System menu button : When you click the mouse on this button, system menu, as illustrated in figure 4.5 appears on the screen.

Program Name : Name of the program, with which window is related, appears in the title bar. This name identifies the windows. When you have many windows present on the screen, program name in title bar helps you in identifying the window.

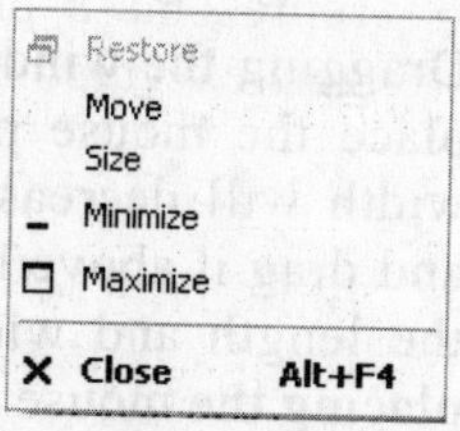

Figure 4.5

Minimize Button : It shrinks the window to a button, placed in task bar, when you click the mouse on it.

Maximize Button : When you click the mouse on this button, window enlarges to the size of the monitor screen and the button gets converted to Restore button. When you click the mouse on Restore button, enlarged Window gets back to its original size.

Close Button : When you click the mouse on this button, program terminates. Its window and task bar button, both get removed from the monitor screen.

Bar Menu

Bar menu appears as broad strip with multiple options in it. Each option has an underlined character in it. For example, File option has F character, underlined in it. When you select any option, a pull down menu (submenu) appears on the monitor screen. To select any option from the bar menu, either of the following operations could be performed:

1. Click the mouse on the option, which you wish to select.
2. Press Alt key and underlined character key together. For example, to select File option, you could press Alt and F keys together.

Toolbar

Toolbar comprises of many buttons. Each button performs a specific task, when you click the mouse on it. For example, when you click the mouse on Save button, current contents get saved on the disk. When you rest the mouse pointer for some time on any button of the tool bar, its name appears on the monitor screen.

Status Bar

Status bar appears at the foot of the window. Relevant information, help messages, current activity status etc. get displayed in it.

OPERATING UPON A WINDOW

Any window that appears on the screen can be operated upon in many ways. Following are the operations that can be performed on a window.

Moving The Window

Window can be moved from one place to another on the screen by dragging it with its title bar and dropping it at the desired location.

Changing The Size Of The Window

Dragging the window by its border, changes its length, width or both. For example, if you place the mouse pointer on window's right borderline and drag it towards left/right, its width will decrease/increase. Similarly if you place the mouse pointer on top borderline and drag it above/below, its length will increase/decrease. If you wish to increase/decrease the length and width of the window simultaneously, in proportion, drag the window by placing the mouse pointer on any of its corners.

Minimizing The Window

To minimize a window, click the mouse on its Minimize button. When you do so, it shrinks to a button in Task Manager Area and gets removed from VDU.

Restoring The Minimized Windows

To restore a minimized window, right click the mouse on its button present in Task Manager Area. When you do so, a short cut menu, as illustrated in figure 4.5 appears on the monitor screen.

Select "Restore" option from this menu. When you do so, minimized window returns back to its original status.

Maximizing The Windows

To maximize a window, click the mouse on its Maximize button. When you do so, its size gets enlarged to the size of monitor screen and Maximize button gets converted into Restore button.

Restoring The Maximized Windows

To restore the maximized window, click the mouse on Restore button. When you do so, it returns back to its original size and Restore button gets converted into Maximize button.

Closing The Windows

To close the window and terminate the program, click the mouse on its Close button.

GUI COMPONENTS OF WINDOWS

Windows is Graphical User Interface (GUI) based operating system. While working with this operating system, you interact with the computer through many GUI components. A brief description of commonly used GUI components of Windows is given below.

Program Icons

All those icons that represent program are called Program icons. Some of the program icons are illustrated in figure 4.6. To run the program, you need to double click the mouse on its program icon. For example, to execute Date/Time program, you will have to double click the mouse on its icon.

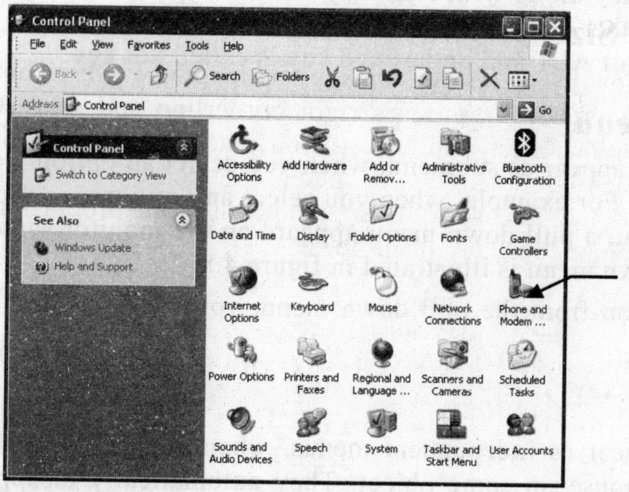

Figure 4.6

Objects Icons

All those icons that represent objects like devices, files, folders etc. are called object icons. Some of the object icons are illustrated below.

Represents Floppy drive.

Represents hard disk.

Represents a folder.

Represents executable file.

Represents non-executable files.

Represents data file.

Bar Menu

Bar menu appears in the form of a horizontal strip, with options written inside. A typical bar menu, is illustrated in figure 4.7.

Figure 4.7

To select an option from the bar menu, you need to either click the mouse on the option or press underlined key along with ALT key. For example, to select Edit option from the bar menu, you can either click the mouse on Edit option or press ALT and E keys together. This combination of ALT and underlined key is called hot key.

Pull Down Menu

Pull down menus appear as submenu, when you select an option from some other menu. For example, when you select any option (say Edit) from the bar menu, a pull down menu appears on the monitor screen. A typical pull down menu is illustrated in figure 4.8.

To select an option from the pull down menu, you need to click the mouse on it.

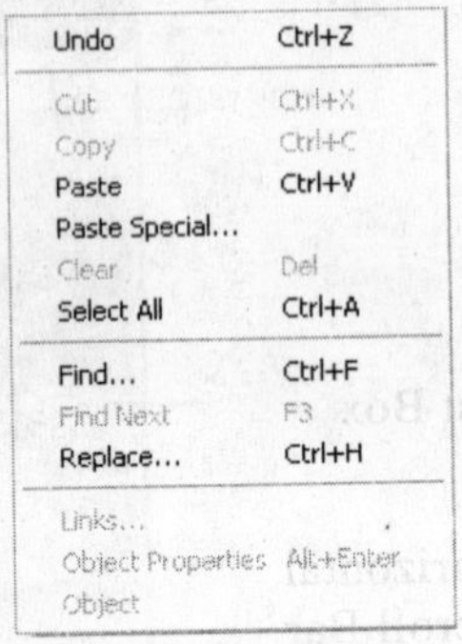

Figure 4.8

Popup Menu

These menus appear as independent menus, when you click the left button of your mouse on some object. They automatically disappear when you click the mouse at some other place. For example, when you click the mouse on "Start" button, Start menu pops up as an independent menu. These menus do not appear everywhere but remain available at some special location. A popup menu is illustrated in figure 4.3.

Shortcut Menu

Shortcut menus appear when you right click the mouse. For example, when right click the mouse on desktop, a shortcut menu appears on the monitor screen. Such a shortcut menu is shown in figure 4.9.

To select an option from the shortcut menu, you need to click the mouse on the option. When you select the option, corresponding activity takes place and popup menu disappears from the screen.

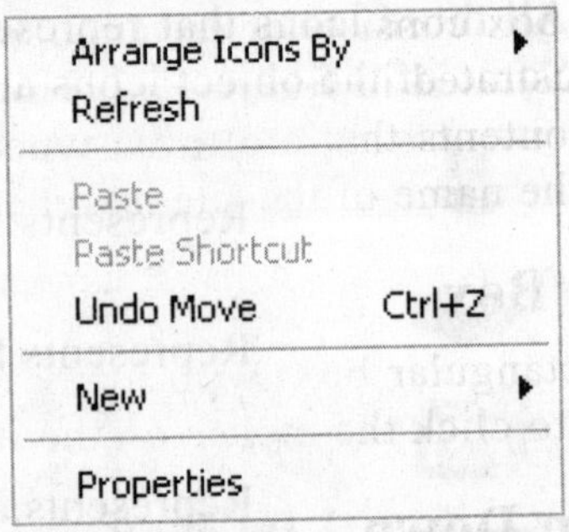

Figure 4.9

Toolbars

A row of small buttons, with icons in them forms a toolbar. Each button performs a specific task when you click the mouse on it. A typical toolbar is illustrated in figure 4.10.

Figure 4.10

To find out, what a button of toolbar does, rest the mouse pointer on the button for a while. Don't click on it, a label called tool tip will appear near the button. Generally labels are such that they give idea of button's function.

Dialog Box

A dialog box is special type of window that allows you to enter specifications for performing a task, as per your choice. For example, when you open a file, a dialog box, as illustrated in figure 4.11 appears on the screen. Using this dialog box, you can specify drive, folder, file name etc. of the file, which you wish to open.

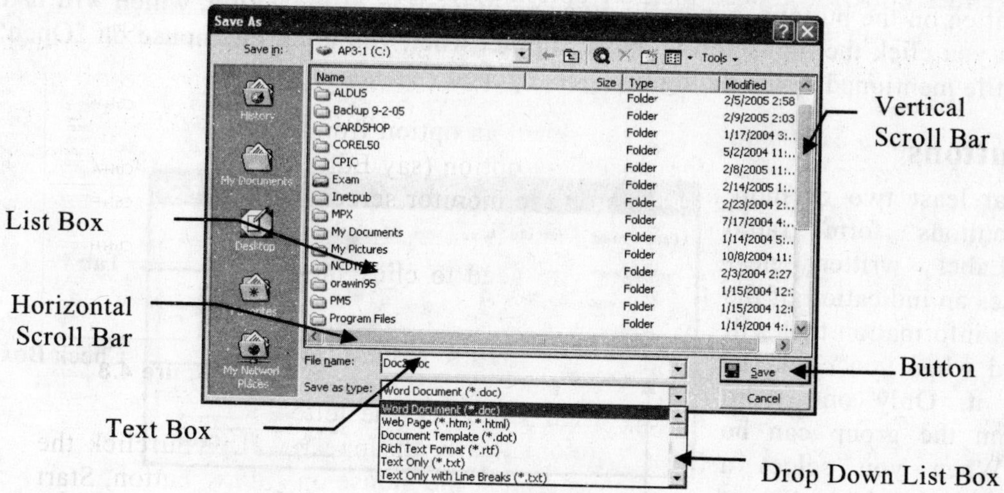

Figure 4.11

Text Box

Text box consists of rectangular blank area, in which contents are typed. A typical text box is illustrated in figure 4.11. Note that the label written beside the text box gives the idea of the contents that are to be typed in text box. For example, the label "File name" indicates that the name of the file is to be typed in this text box.

List Box

A rectangular box, with many items in it, forms a list box. To select an item from it, you need to click the mouse on the item. A list box is illustrated in figure 4.11.

Drop Down List Box

Drop down list box is another type of list box that looks like a text box with a down pointing arrow on its right hand side. A list of options drops down when you click the mouse on the arrow. To select any option from this list, you need to click the mouse on it. A drop down list is shown in figure 4.11.

Scroll Bar

Whenever items to be displayed do not get accommodated in the given space, blank columns with arrow buttons at their end and a slider inside appear on the screen. These columns are called scroll bars. Vertical columns of such type are called vertical scroll bars and horizontal columns are called horizontal scroll bars. Horizontal scroll bar is illustrated in figure 4.11. Either by clicking the mouse on arrow buttons or by dragging the slider, you can display the items of the list, which are not being currently displayed on the screen.

Buttons

Rectangular labels, with some text written on them form buttons. Few buttons are illustrated in figure 4.11. When you click the mouse on the button, an action takes place. The text written on the buttons, generally gives an indication of the action, which will take place, when you click the mouse on it. For example, when you click the mouse on "Open" button, the file mentioned in the dialog box gets opened.

Radio Buttons

Group of at least two or more rounded buttons form radio buttons. Label written near buttons gives an indication of the type of data/information that will get selected when you click the mouse on it. Only one radio button, from the group can be selected. When you select a button, a black dot appears within the selected button. Radio buttons are illustrated in figure 4.12.

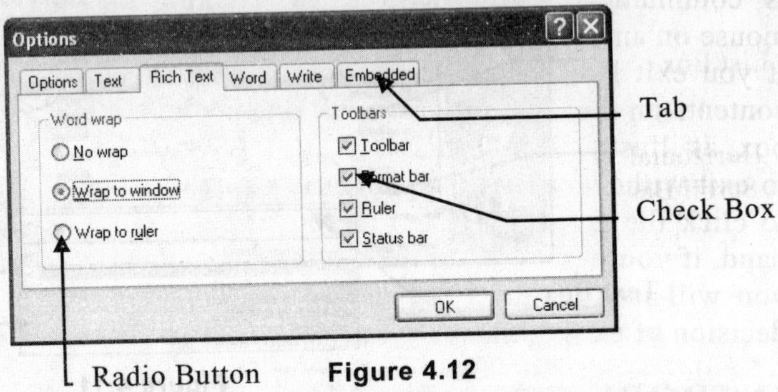

Figure 4.12

Check Boxes

Small square shaped buttons (could be one or more) form check boxes. Label written near the button gives an indication of the type of data/information that will get selected, when you click the mouse on it. When you select a check box, a tick mark gets placed within the check box. If you wish, you could select more than one check box from the group. Check boxes are illustrated in figure 4.12.

Tab

The shape of tab resembles the shape of half opened button. Tabs are basically the medium to display categorized information of different subjects in the same dialog box. Tabs are illustrated in figure 4.12. Each tab has some subject written on it. When you click the mouse on a tab, it gets selected and information or options related to the selected subject get displayed in the dialog box.

Spinner

A spinner consists of two arrow buttons and text box, with some value written into it. One arrow points up and the other points down. The value in the text box increases when you click the mouse on up arrow. When you click it on down arrow the value in the text box decreases. A typical spinner is illustrated in figure 4.13.

Figure 4.13

Alert Boxes

Alert box comprises of rectangular area with an icon, a message and few buttons in it. A typical alert box is illustrated in figure 4.14. Alert boxes generally appear to attract user's attention in the event of some error or failure. Further course of action, which needs to be taken, is communicated to windows by clicking the mouse on any of the desired buttons. For example, if you exit Notepad program, without saving the contents on the disk, program will display an alert box, as illustrated in figure 4.14. Thus if you wish to exit without saving the contents, you will have to click the mouse on "No" button. On the other hand, if you wish to exit after saving the contents, you will have to click the mouse on "Yes" button. If somehow you wish to cancel the decision of exiting the program, you will have to click the mouse on "Cancel" button.

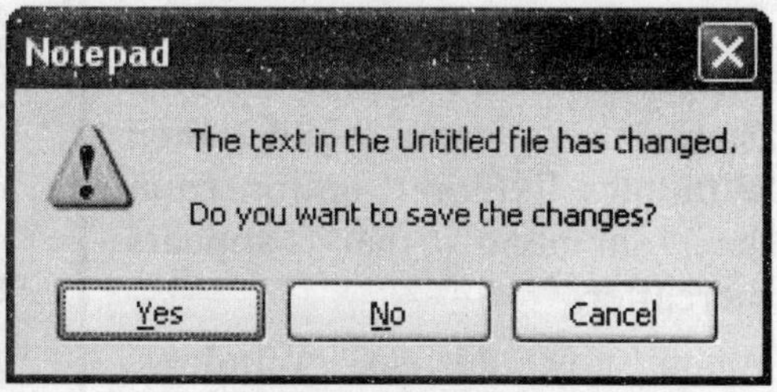

Figure 4.14

INTRODUCTION TO FILE

File is a medium to store data and information on computer. File is always identified by its name and the same name is used while operating upon it. Following points apply for Windows file names:

(i) File name can be up to 255 characters long.

(ii) Blank and dot (.) can also be used in file names. For example, "My File" is a valid file name.

(iii) Characters like + ; [=] etc. can also be used in file names.

(iv) Characters like \ / : * ? " are prohibited in file names.

Figure 4.15

FOLDER

Folder is basically a special file, which is capable of holding other files and folders into it. At any given point of time a folder can either remain closed or open. When it is closed, only its name and icon get displayed on VDU. A closed folder is denoted using a symbol, shown in figure 4.15.

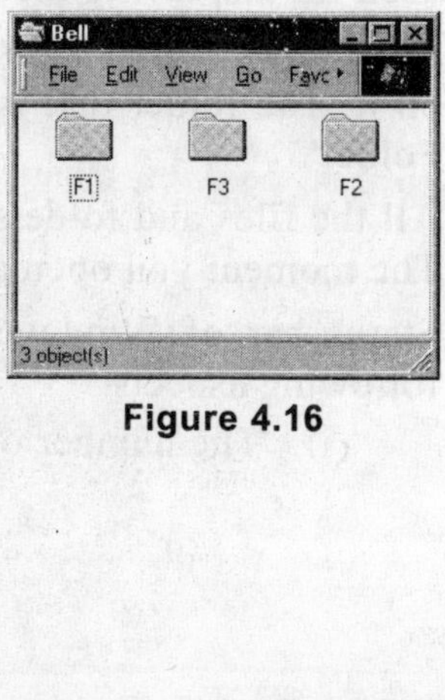

Figure 4.16

When a folder is open then its own window gets displayed on the screen. Window displays all files and folders contained in it in the form of icons. A folder window is shown in figure 4.16.

WINDOWS EXPLORER

Windows Explorer is a file and folder maintenance program of Windows. It is mainly used for viewing the contents of folder tree and arranging the files and folders on the disk. Some of the operations like copying file, moving files, deleting file etc. can be very easily done with the help of Windows Explorer. Details of Windows Explorer are explained below.

To invoke Windows Explorer program, click the mouse on 'Start' button. When you do so, Start menu, as shown in figure 4.3 will appear on the screen. Now select 'Programs' option from this menu and then 'Windows Explorer' option from the submenu that appears thereafter.

When you do so, Windows Explorer will get loaded into the memory and a window, as shown in figure 4.17, will appear on the screen.

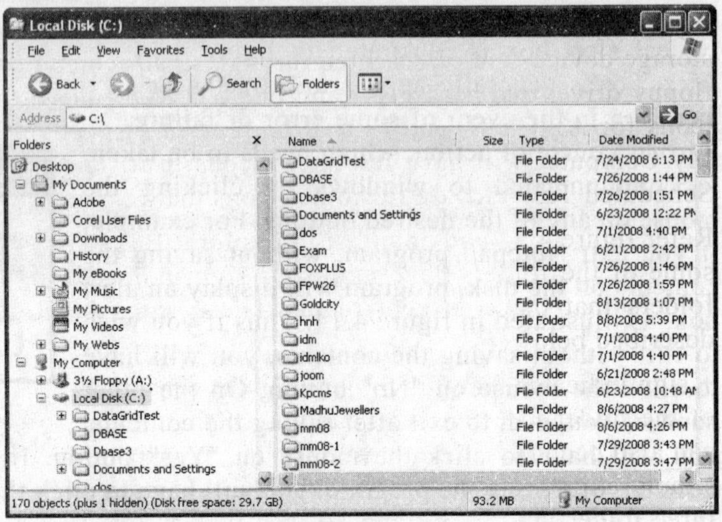

Figure 4.17

Note that, Explorer window gets displayed in this format only if the settings have been made for small icons. If the settings are done for large icons then the same windows will appear in a different manner. To change the icon settings, select 'View' option from the bar menu and then select large icon or small icon option from the submenu.

EXPLORER WINDOW

Refer Explorer window and note that it remains divided into two parts. These parts are generally called Pane. The left pane of Explorer window is referred to as Explorer Bar. It is used for displaying the folder tree and its branches.

Any folder that gets displayed in Explorer bar can be opened by double clicking the mouse on it. The folder that is currently opened is sometimes called, 'Selected Folder' or 'Current Folder'.

All the files and folders contained within the current folder get displayed in the right pane. The moment you open any folder (in the left pane), the display in the right pane changes.

Status bar of Windows Explorer window displays the status of the disk describing the following aspects:

(i) The number of folders are contained within the current folder.

(ii) The disk space occupied by the current file or folder.

(iii) The disk space free for use.

FOLDER TREE STRUCTURE

Refer figure 2.34 and note that the folder tree gets displayed in the Explorer bar. Desktop always resides at the top of the folder tree. Just below the desktop, icons for My Computer, My Document, Internet Explorer, Recycle bin etc. are shown.

My Computer icon

My Computer icon refers to all the storage devices that are present in your computer. These storage devices are represented through small icons. For example, if your computer has one floppy drive, two hard disks and one CD ROM drive then under My Computer, the object icons for A:, C:, D: and E: will be present respectively. Note that, apart from these icons My Computer will have few more icons in it. For example, Printer, Dial Up Networking, Scheduled Task etc. are few other icons that remain present under My Computer icon.

Refer figure 4.34 and note that in Explorer Bar some of the folders have a plus (+) sign and some of the folders have minus (-) sign indicated on their left-hand side. In some of the folders that place is kept blank. These signs practically convey a special meaning, as described below.

Figure 4.18

+ sign indicates that this folder contains other folders in it and this branch of the folder tree can be expanded, so that all the folders contained in it can also become visible on the screen. To expand any branch you have to simply click the mouse on + sign. For example, if there is a folder named Bell and it has three folder viz. F1, F2 and F3 in it then initially Bell folder will look as shown in figure 4.18.

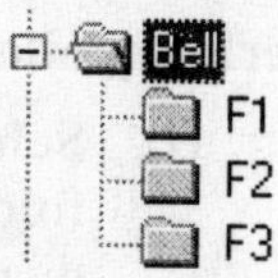

Figure 4.19

When you click the mouse on + sign then it will get expanded, as shown in figure 4.19.

When you expand any folder then its + sign gets automatically converted to '-' sign.

A minus sign, present towards left side of the folder icon indicates that the expanded branch of this folder can be collapsed or reduced to a single folder icon. To collapse the branch you have to simply click the mouse on - sign. For example, if you click the mouse on minus sign shown in figure 4.19 then the complete branch will collapse to an icon as shown in figure 4.18.

Those folders that do not have any sign on their left, can neither be expanded nor collapsed.

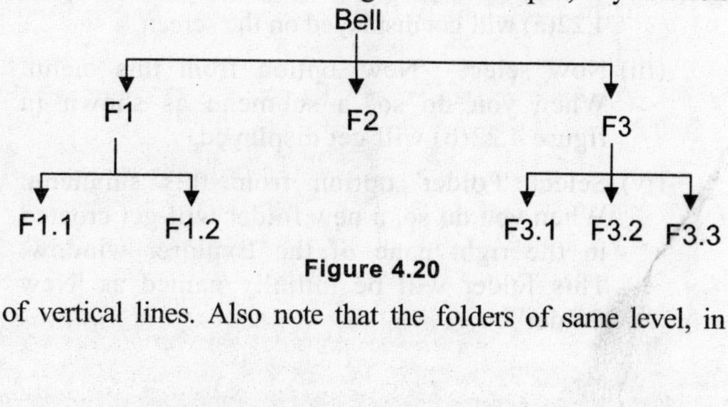

Figure 4.20

Refer figure 4.21 and note that folder tree icons get displayed in the form of vertical lines. Also note that the folders of same level, in hierarchy get arranged in same vertical line. To understand the concept, refer folder structure that is illustrated in figure 4.20.

Note that in above illustrated diagram, folders F1, F2 and F3 are at the same level. Folders F1.1, F1.2, F3.1, F3.2, F3.3 are one level down in hierarchy but at same level. When this branch of the folder tree is displayed in the Explorer Bar then it will look as shown in figure 4.21.

Compare this figure with figure 4.20 and note that folders of same hierarchical level arrange themselves in same vertical line.

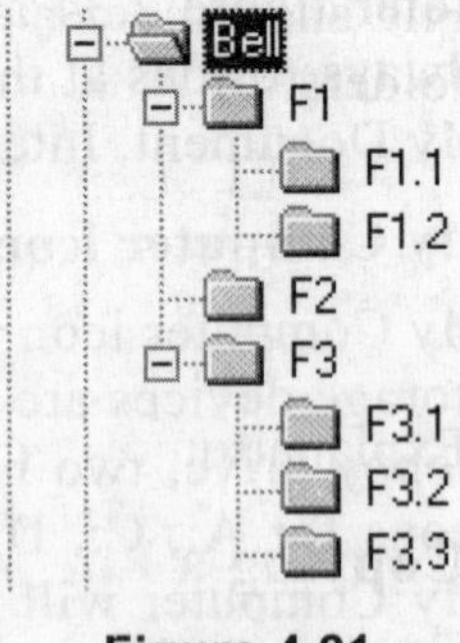

Figure 4.21

SELECTING FILES AND FOLDERS

To select any folder in Explorer Bar, click the mouse on its icon. When you do so, contents present in the folder (files and folder) get displayed in the right pane.

To select a file or folder in the right pane, click the mouse on it. A selected folder gets highlighted. If you wish to select more than one file or folder in sequence then press the shift key and click the mouse on the first icon of the sequence and then on the last icon of the sequence (shift key pressed). This process will select all the icons of the sequence. For example, if you wish to select tenth, eleventh, twelfth, thirteenth and fourteenth icon then you click the mouse on tenth icon and then on fourteenth icon with shift key pressed.

If the files to be selected are not in sequence then press control key and click the mouse on each icon that you wish to select. For example, if you wish to select second, fifth and twentieth icon press control key and click the mouse on these icons, one by one.

CREATING A NEW FOLDER

Perform following steps to create a new folder, within an existing folder:

(i) Select the folder, in which you wish to create a new folder. When you select this folder, all its files and folders will get displayed in right pane of the Explorer window.

(ii) Now select 'File' option from the bar menu. When you do so, a submenu, as shown in figure 4.22(a) will get displayed on the screen.

(iii) Now select 'New' option from this menu. When you do so, a submenu as shown in figure 4.22(b) will get displayed.

(iv) Select 'Folder' option from this submenu. When you do so, a new folder will get created in the right pane of the Explorer window. This folder will be initially named as 'New Folder'.

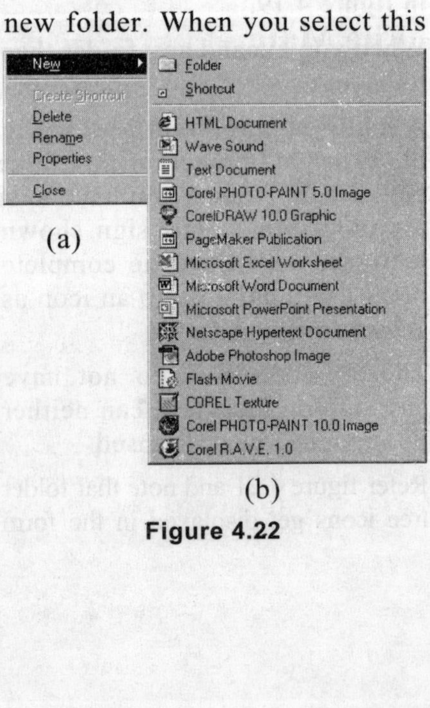

Figure 4.22

(v) Now type the new name of the folder and press Enter key.

This process will create a new blank folder with the name, specified by you.

FILE AND FOLDER MAINTENANCE

File and Folder maintenance means performing copy, move, delete operations on files and folders. In Windows Explorer, these operations can be performed in following three ways:

- ❑ Using Drag and Drop feature.
- ❑ Through Toolbar.
- ❑ Through Bar menu.

Explanation of each type is given below:

Copying a File or Folder

To copy the file or folder from one place to another press 'CTRL' key and drag it from its source location and drop it in the destination folder.

Moving the File

To move the file from one folder to another, simply drag the file from its source location and drop it at the destination folder.

Copying a File or Folder to another Disk

To copy the file or folder from its original location to another disk, drag the file icon from its original location and drop it at the drive icon, that is present in the Explorer bar. For example, if you wish to copy Bell.txt file from its original location to drive. **D:** then drag the file icon from its original place and drop it at the icon that represents D: drive in Explorer bar.

File Maintenance through Toolbar

Various types of file maintenance tasks can be performed through 'Edit' option of Bar menu as follows:

Deleting a File

To delete a file or folder, first select it and then click the mouse on 'Delete' button of Standard Toolbar. When you do so, an alert box, as shown in figure 4.23 will get displayed on the screen.

(i) If you wish to delete the file then select "Yes" button, if you don't want to delete the file, select "No." button.

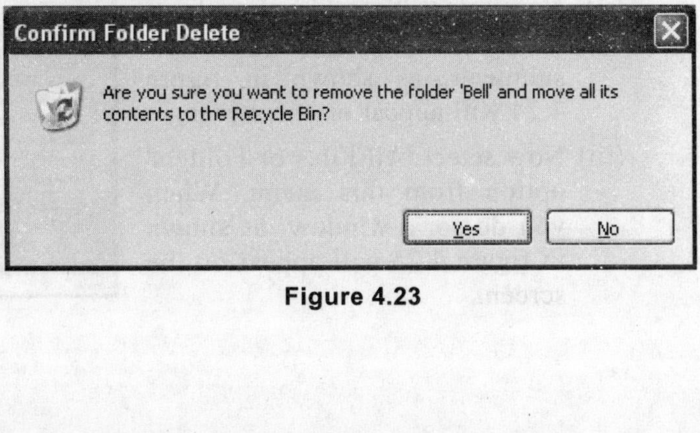

Figure 4.23

On selecting "Yes" button, the selected file will be removed from the folder.

Renaming a File or Folder

To rename a file or folder right click the mouse on the object, which is to be renamed. When you do so, a popup menu will appear on the screen. Select Rename option from that menu. When you do so, the current name of the selected object will get highlighted. Now type the new name and press enter key. This process will rename the selected object.

Undo Using Bar menu

If you so wish, you can cancel the effect of the command, which was recently given and bring back the situation in original state. For example, say you copied a file named 'Bell' from 'org'" folder to 'dest' folder. Now if you cancel the effect of copy command then Bell file will be automatically removed from 'dest' folder and situation will be brought back to original state.

For canceling the effect of recently done operation, select 'Edit' option from Window Explorer bar menu. When you do so, a submenu will appear on the screen. Select 'Undo' option from that submenu.

Note that Undo operation can also be done by clicking the mouse on Undo button that remains present in the Standard Bar.

EXITING FROM WINDOWS EXPLORER

To come out of Windows Explorer, click the mouse on 'Close' option from 'File' submenu or 'Close' option from System menu or click the mouse on window's close button.

SEARCHING A FILE OR FOLDER ON DISK

Windows provides file searching facility. Using this facility, you can search a file with given name. Perform following steps for searching the file on disk:

(i) Click the mouse on 'Start' button. When you do so, Start menu, as shown in figure 4.3 will appear on the screen.

(ii) Now select 'Search' option from this menu. When you do so, a submenu, as shown in figure 4.24 will appear on the screen.

(iii) Now select 'All Files or Folders' option from this menu. When you do so, a window, as shown in figure 4.25 will appear on the screen.

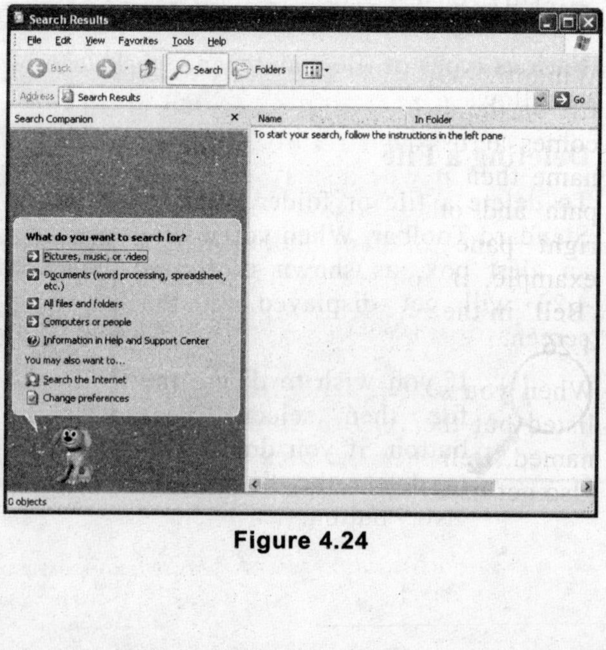

Figure 4.24

Using this dialog box, you can search any file or folder at desired location, like disk, Internet etc. How do you use this dialog box for searching desired files and folders, in different ways is explained below.

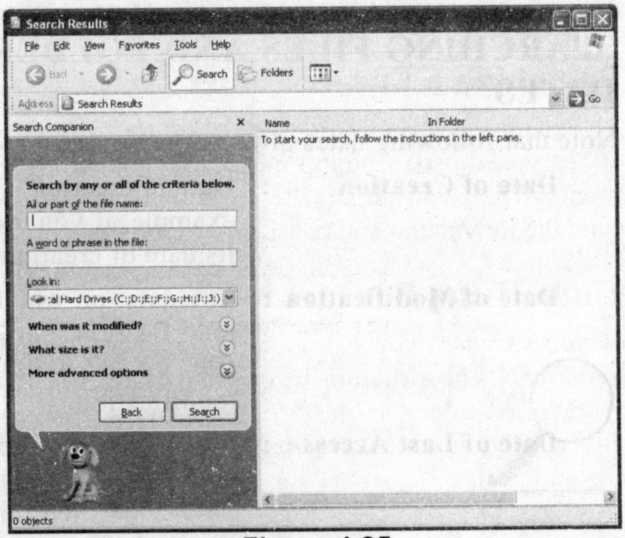

Figure 4.25

SEARCHING FILE BY ITS NAME

Perform following steps to search a file on the basis of its name:

(i) Enter the name of that file, which is to be searched in the text box that has been titled as 'Search for Files or Folders named'

(ii) To specify the search begin point (that location of the folder tree from where the search has to start), either choose the location from 'Look in' drop down list or enter the complete path of that point (folder) yourself, in its edit box. For example, if you wish to begin the search from the root folder of D: disk then enter D:\.

(iii) At last, click the mouse on 'Search' Now' button.

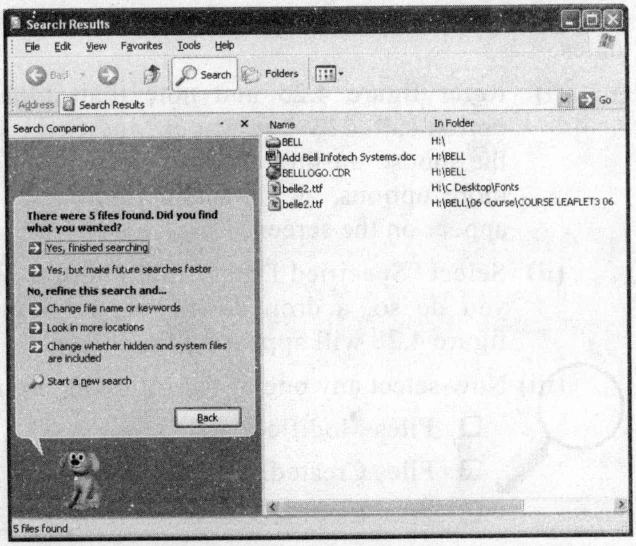

Figure 4.26

Windows will now start searching the file on the disk. During the search, if it comes across any file of the specified name then it will display its complete path and other related details in the right pane of the dialog box. For example, if you search the file named 'Bell' in the root folder of C: disk then search results may get displayed as shown in figure 4.26.

When you search a file, using this facility then not only the files of specified name get listed but the files of similar names also get listed. For example, if you search the file named, Bell then the files having names like Bell1, AbcBell95, Bell.Text, inbell etc. will also get listed.

SEARCHING FILES AND FOLDERS ON THE BASIS OF THEIR DATES

Note that following dates always remain associated with all the files:

Date of Creation : Date of creation is the date, on which you create the file. For example, if you create the file on 22-8-2008 then this will be its date of creation.

Date of Modification : The date, on which you modify the file, becomes its date of modification. For example, if you make some changes in the file on 22-9-2008 then this date will be its date of modification.

Date of Last Access : The date, on which you accessed the file last, becomes its date of last access. For example, if you accessed the file on 24-9-2008 then this date will become its date of last access. Similarly if you again access this file on 26-9-2008 then its last date of access will get modified to 26-9-2008.

Note that using any of these dates, files can be searched on the disk. Perform following steps to search the files on the basis of any of these dates:

(i) Refer figure 4.25 and note that it has an option called "When was it Modified". Click the mouse on this option. When you do so, more options, as shown in figure 4.27 will appear on the screen.

(ii) Select "Specified Dates" radio button. When you do so, a drop down list, as shown in figure 4.28 will appear on the screen.

(iii) Now select any one of the following options:

- ❑ Files Modified.
- ❑ Files Created.
- ❑ Files Last Accessed.

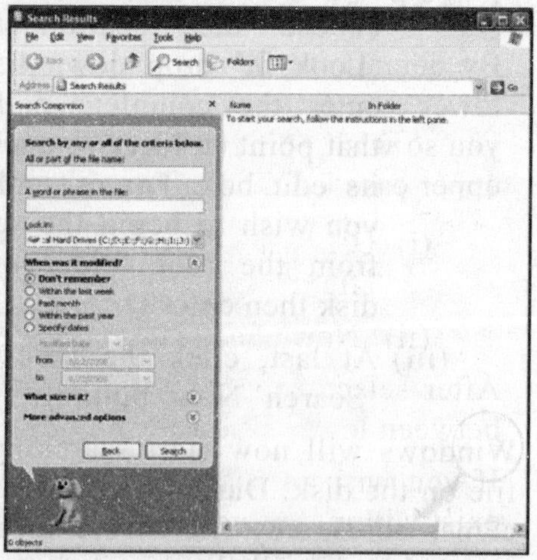

Figure 4.27

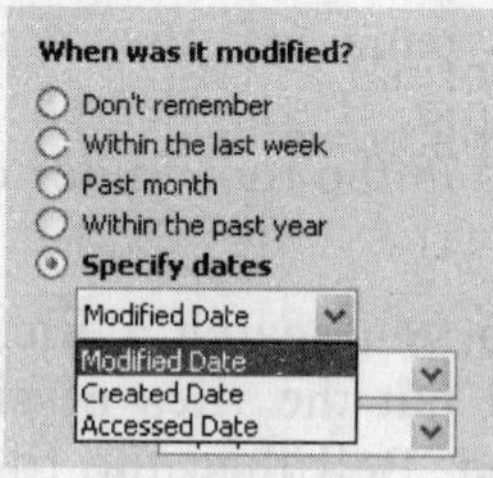

Figure 4.28

(iv) Refer dialog box illustrated in figure 4.28 and note that using various options, you can specify the specific date on the basis of which you would like to search the file. For example, using 'From' and 'To' options you can specify those dates, in between which falls the desired date. Say you wish to search all those files, which were modified between 10/03/96 and 1/1/97 then you will have to select "files Modified" option in step (i) and specify these dates in "between" and "and" edit boxes respectively. Similarly you can choose 'in the last months' option and specify number of months or you can select 'in the last days' option and specify number of days.

(v) At last, click the mouse on 'Search' button.

SEARCHING THE FILES ON THE BASIS OF THEIR CONTENTS

Windows provides you the facility to search the files, on the basis of their contents. For doing this, perform following steps:

(i) Refer figure 4.25 and note that it has a text box, which has been titled as "A word of phrase in the file:". Type those contents (words) on the basis of which you wish to search the files in this text box. For example, if you wish to search those files which have the word "'Beautiful' written in them, then type the word 'Beautiful' in Content text box.

(ii) Now click the mouse on 'Search' button.

When you do so, Windows will search all those files, which have the given word (Beautiful in this example) written in them and display the details as before.

CASE SENSITIVE SEARCH

By default, Windows search facility does not differentiate between upper case letters and lower case letters. For example, it would treat bell, BELL and BeLl, as same words. But if you so wish, you can force the search facility to differentiate between lower case letters and upper case letters. To do this, perform following steps:

(i) Choose 'More Advanced Options' option from the dialog box, which is shown in figure 4.25. When you do so, case sensitive check box will appear on the screen.

(ii) Now check "Case Sensitive" check box.

After selection, case sensitive option gets set and search facility will start differentiating between lower case letters and upper case letters.

If you wish to search the file not only in the specified folder but also in subfolders that exist within the specified folder then you should check "Search Subfolders" check box.

FORMATTING FLOPPY DISK USING EXPLORE OPTION

To format a floppy disk, using Windows Explorer, first invoke Windows Explorer on your computer and then perform following steps:

(i) Insert the floppy in floppy drive.

(ii) Right click on "31/2 Floppy (A:)" option present in left pane of Explorer window. When you do so, a popup menu, as shown in figure 4.29 (a) will appear on monitor screen

(iii) Now select "Format…" option from this menu. When you do so, a dialog box as shown in figure 4.29 (b) will appear on monitor screen.

(iv) Enter volume label in "Volume Label" text box.

(v) If you wish to quick format the floppy, check "Quick Format" check box.

(vi) If you wish to make the floppy, bootable floppy, check "Create MS-DOS startup disk" check box.

(vii) Now click the mouse on "Start" button of the dialog box. When you do so, an alert box as shown in 4.29 (c) will appear on monitor screen. This is basically a warning message box, indicating that formatting will erase all the contents of the disk.

(viii) At last, click the mouse on “OK" button.

When you do so, computer will start formatting the floppy and on completion it will display a message that formatting is complete.

Note that other drives of the system like hard disk; pen drive etc. can also be formatted in the same way, by clicking the mouse on corresponding icons, present in Explorer window.

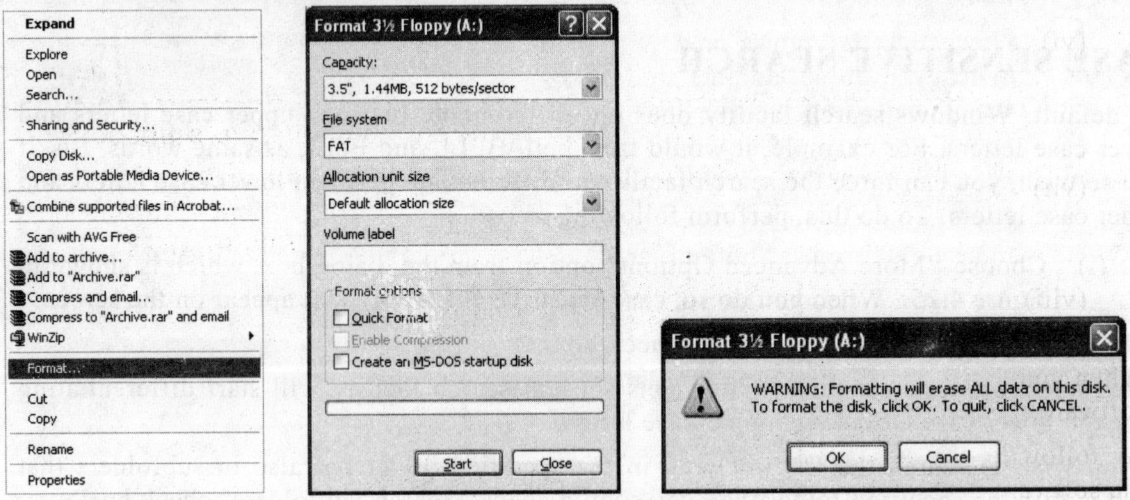

(a) (b) (c)

Figure 4.29

INSTALLING A NEW SOFTWARE FROM CONTROL PANEL

Windows provides various facilities to add new software to the system. Control Panel method is one of the methods.

Perform following steps to install new software through control panel:

(i) Click the mouse "Start" button present on desktop. When you do so, Start menu will appear on monitor screen.

(ii) Select "Control Panel" option from this menu. When you do so, control panel window, as shown in figure 4.30 will appear on monitor screen. If somehow the appearance of the window looks different, select "Switch to classic view" option.

(iii) Select "Add Or Remove Programs" icon from this window by double clicking the mouse on it.

When you do so, another window, as shown in figure 4.31 will appear on monitor screen.

(iv) Select "Add New Programs" option from this window. When you do so, scenario, within the window will change and "CD or Floppy" button will appear within the window.

(v) Now insert the installation CD or floppy in the drive and click the mouse on this button. When you do so, a dialog box, as shown in figure 4.32 will appear on monitor screen.

(vi) Now click the mouse on "Next" button. When you do so, another dialog box of the installation wizard, as shown in figure 4.33 will appear on the screen.

(vii) Select the correct location of the installation software by clicking the mouse on "Browse" button.

(viii) At last, click the mouse on "Finish" button.

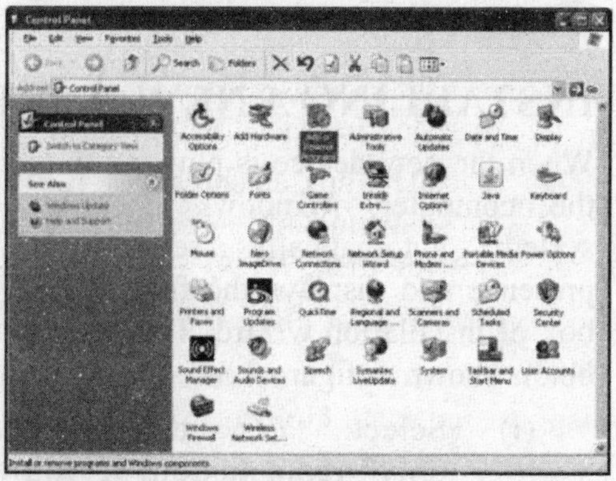

Figure 4.30

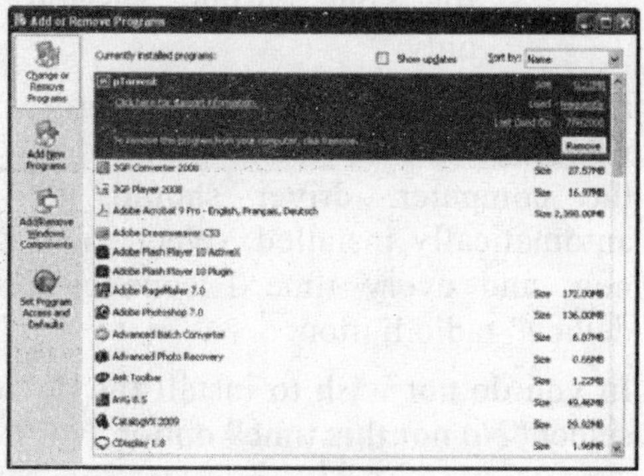

Figure 4.31

When you do so, installation program will start and software specific screens will appear on the monitor screen.

By following the messages of these screens and providing relevant information, correctly, the software installation can be completed.

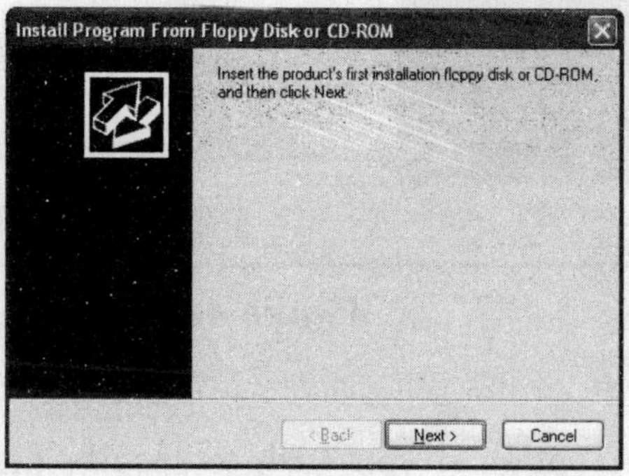

Figure 4.32

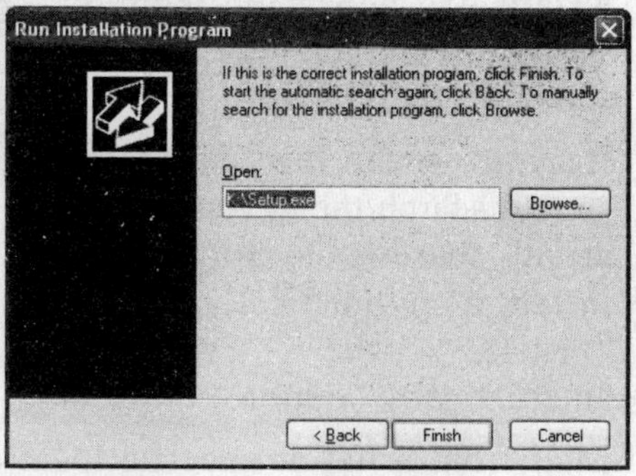

Figure 4.33

UNINSTALLING SOFTWARE FROM CONTROL PANEL

Note that windows and screens mentioned above also have options for removing the software. Thus by selecting the same option from the Start menu but different options, you can remove a program from the computer that was installed previously.

INSTALLING A NEW HARDWARE

When the new device is plugged in to the computer, Windows operating system automatically senses its presence and displays the first dialog box of installation wizard. This dialog box is shown in figure 4.34.

Figure 4.34

(i) Select "Yes, this time only" radio button, if you wish to install the device for your current session only.

If you wish that from now onwards, whenever this device is plugged to the computer, driver should get automatically installed, select "Yes, now and every time I connect a device" radio button.

In you do not wish to install the device, select "No not this time" option.

When you do so, "Next" button of the dialog box will get activated.

(iii) Click the mouse on "Next" button. When you do so, next dialog box of the installation wizard will appear on monitor screen. This dialog box is shown in figure 4.35.

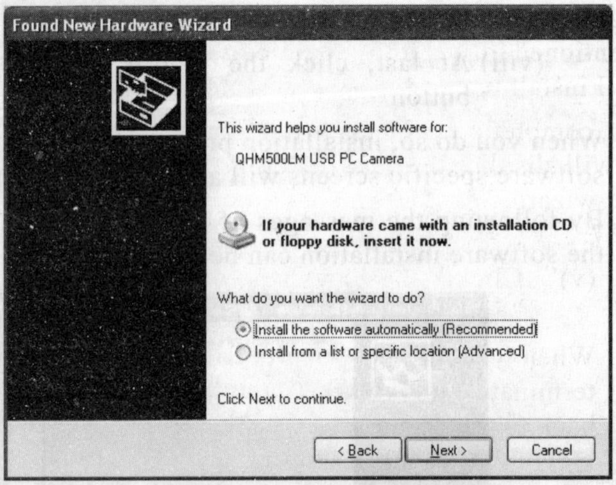

Figure 4.35

(iv) If you wish that windows should search the device driver at all feasible locations and install it automatically, select "Install the software automatically" option.

Select "Install from a list or specific location" option if you wish to specify the location where Windows should specifically look for the device driver,

Say you select “Install from a list or specific location” option. When you do so, "Next" button of the dialog box will get activated”.

(v) Click the mouse on "Next" button”. When you do so, next dialog box of the installation wizard will appear on monitor screen. This dialog box is shown in figure 4.36.

(v) If you have an installation CD / DVD, put it in the drive and check "Search removable media" check box.

If you wish to install the driver from any other location, check "Include this location in the search” check box and specify the exact location either by selecting the location from the drop down list or by clicking the mouse on "Browse" button and selecting the location through the dialog boxes that appear thereafter. When you do so, "Next" button of the dialog box will get activated.

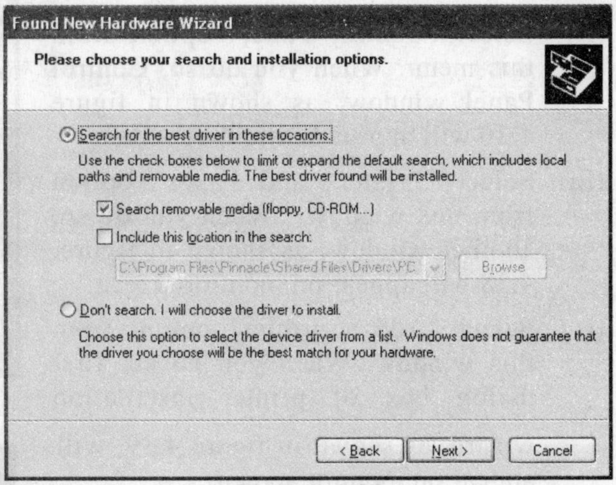

Figure 4.36

(vi) Click the mouse on "Next" button.

When you do so, Windows will search the device driver on mentioned drive and if found, it will install it also.

On completion of the installation, it will display the last dialog box of wizard, as shown in figure, 4.37.

(v) Click the mouse on "Finish" button.

When you do so, wizard will terminate and you will return back to the desktop.

Figure 4.37

Note that some of the installations require that system should be rebooted to invoke the device driver and make the device work. If that is the case, reboot the system else start using the device.

INSTALLING A PRINTER FROM CONTROL PANEL

(i) Click the mouse on "Start" button. When you do so, Start menu will appear on monitor screen.

(ii) Select "Control Panel" option from this menu. When you do so, Control Panel window, as shown in figure 4.30 will appear on monitor screen.

(iii) Select "Printers and Faxes" option from this window. When you do so, another window, as shown in figure, 4.38 will appear on monitor screen.

(iv) Select "Add a printer" option from this window. When you do so, first dialog box of printer installation wizard, as shown in figure 4.39, will appear on monitor screen.

(v) Click the mouse on "Next" button. When you do so, next dialog box of printer installation wizard, as shown in figure 4.40, will appear on monitor screen.

(vi) Select "Local printer attached to this computer" option, if you wish to install a printer, local to your system and click the mouse on "Next" button.

When you do so, Windows will search a plug and play printer attached to the system, if it finds one of that type, it will search for its driver in its database and if it finds a suitable device driver, it will install it automatically.

If it doesn't find the driver of plug and play printer in its database, it will ask for device driver disk. When you insert the disk in the drive, it will install the driver from there and make the printer ready.

If Windows doesn't find a plug and play printer attached to the computer, it will display next dialog box of the installation wizard. This dialog box is shown in figure 4.41.

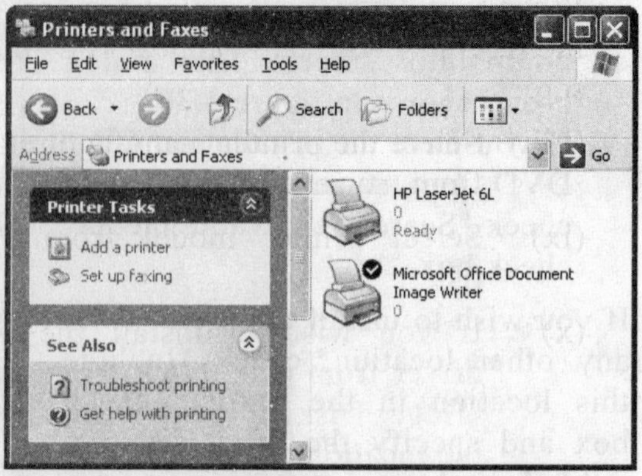

Figure 4.38

Figure 4.39

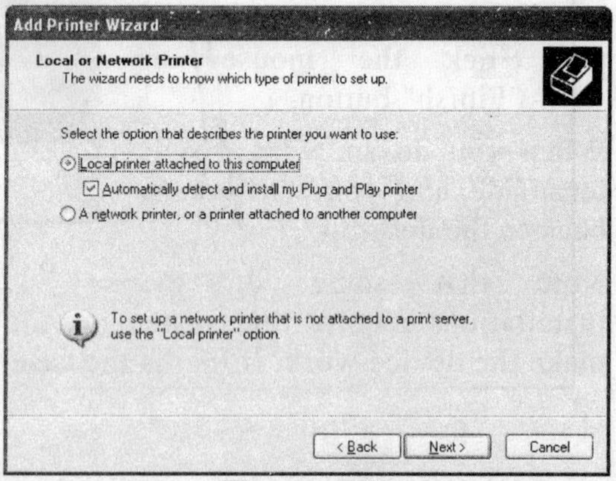

Figure 4.40

(vii) Select the port, on which the printer has been connected and click the mouse on "Next" button.

When you do so, next dialog box, as shown in figure 4.42, will appear on monitor screen.

(viii) Select the printer manufacturer name from manufacturer list.

(ix) Select printer model from Printer list.

(x) If you wish to install the printer driver from disk, click the mouse on "Have Disk..." button and specify the location of the driver on the disk.

(xi) Click the mouse on "Next" button. When you do so, a dialog box, as shown in figure, 4.43 will appear on monitor screen.

(i) If you wish to make this printer the default printer for the system, select "Yes" radio button else select "No" option and click the mouse on "Next" button.

When you do so, next dialog box of the wizard, as shown in figure 4.44 will appear on monitor screen.

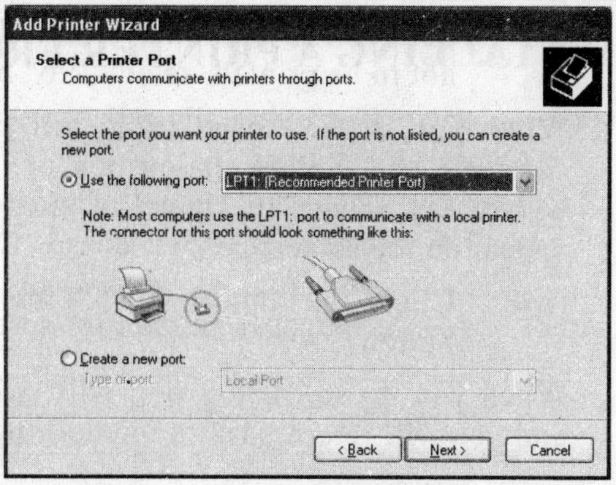

Figure 4.41

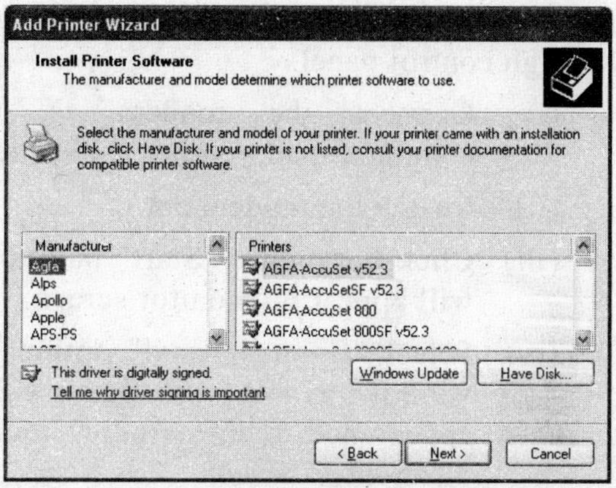

Figure 4.42

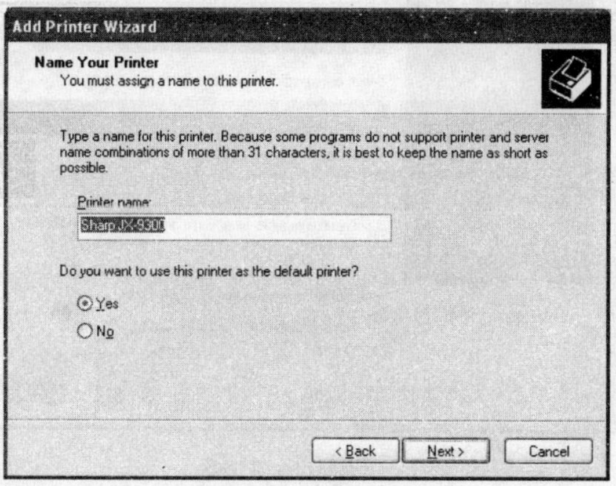

Figure 4.43

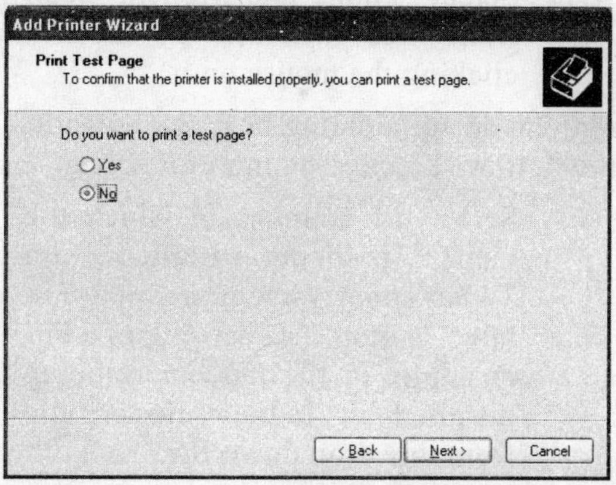

Figure 4.44

(ii) Select "Yes" option if you wish to print the test page after installation. If it is not to be printed, select "No" option and click the mouse on "Next" button.

When you do so, installation will get complete and the last dialog box of the wizard, as shown in figure, 4.45 will appear on the screen.

(iii) Click the mouse on "Finish" button.

When you do so, dialog box will close and you will return back to the desktop.

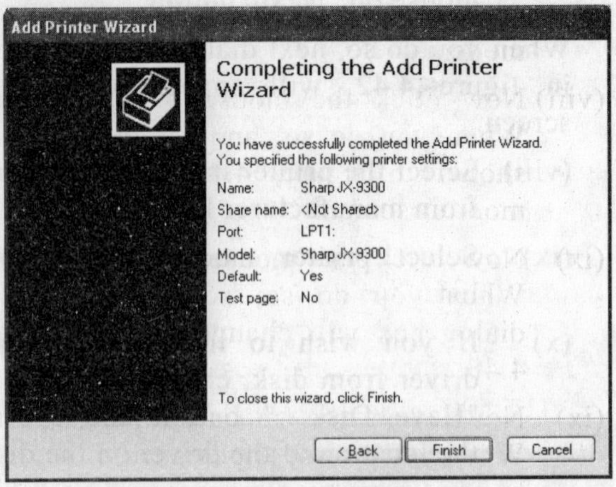

Figure 4.45

INSTALLING A MODEM FROM CONTROL PANEL

Perform following steps to install a modem through control panel:

(i) Connect the modem to the computer using proper cable and then connect the telephone line to the modem.

(ii) Switch the modem on.

(iii) Click the mouse "Start" button present on desktop. When you do so, Start menu will appear on monitor screen.

(iv) Select "Control Panel" option from this menu. When you do so, control panel window, as shown in figure 4.30 will appear on monitor screen. If somehow the appearance of the window looks different, select "Switch to classic view" option.

(iv) Select "Phone and Modem" icon from this window by double clicking the mouse on it.

When you do so, a dialog box, as shown in figure 4.46 will appear on monitor screen.

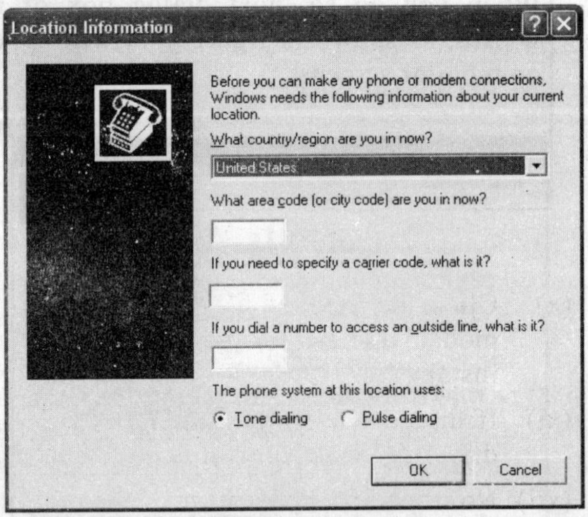

Figure 4.46

(v) Select the country, in which the modem is being installed from "What country / region you are in now" drop down list. For example, in the modem is being installed in India, select India from this drop down list.

(vi) Now enter, area code of the city in "What area code" text box, for example, if the modem is being installed in Delhi, enter 011 or if it is being installed in Hyderabad, enter 040.

(vii) Select "Tone dialing" or "Pulse dialing" option, as per the nature of telephone connection that is being connected to the modem.

(viii) Now click the mouse on "OK" button. When you do so, another dialog box, as shown in figure, 4.47, will appear on monitor screen.

(ix) Now click the mouse on "Modem" tab. When you do so, scenario, within the dialog box will change, as shown figure, 4.48.

(ix) Now click the mouse on Add button. When you do so, appearance of the dialog box will change, as shown in figure 4.49.

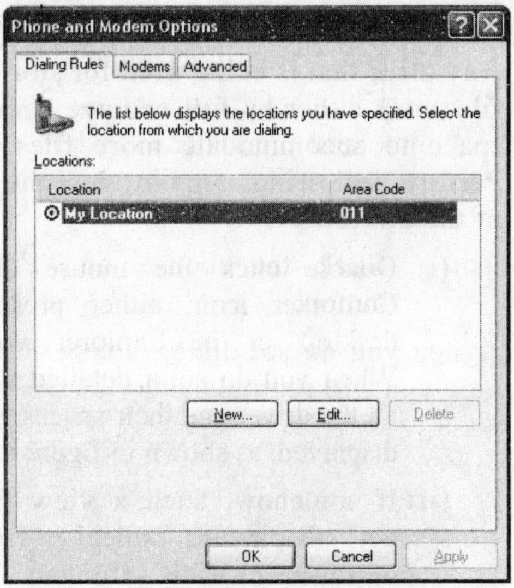

Figure 4.47

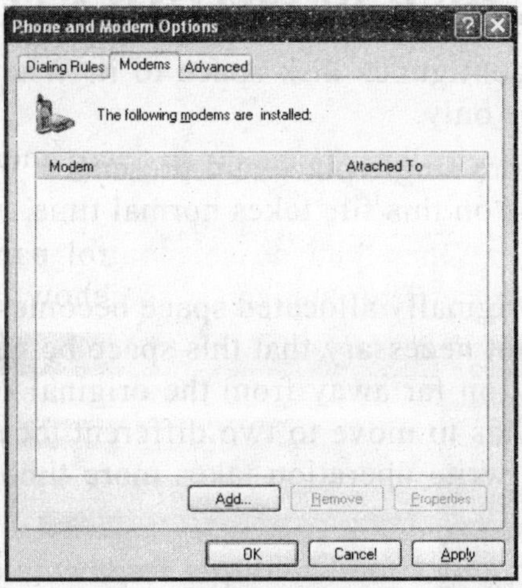

Figure 4.48

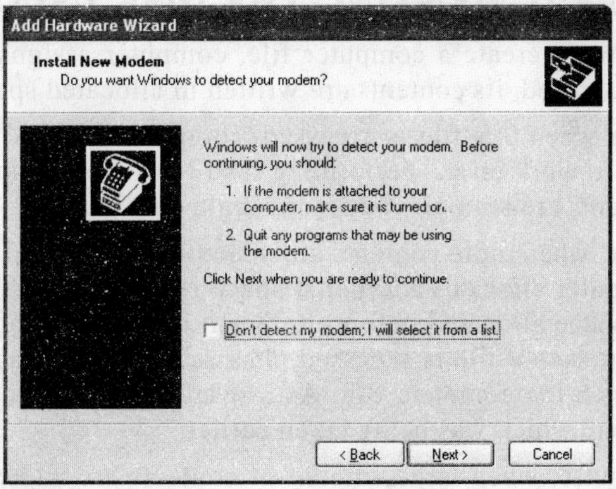

Figure 4.49

(x) Click the mouse on "Next" button. When you do so, Windows will detect the modem and ask for the location of its device driver, as it had asked in case printer installation.

(xi) If the device driver is on CD / DVD / Floppy, insert the disk, containing device driver in the drive. If it is on the hard disk move on to next step.

(xii) Now specify the location of the driver.

When you do so, Windows will read the device driver from the specified location, install the driver and make the modem operational.

VIEWING THE DRIVE SPACE

Any drive that is being used for storing the files may either be full or have some free space to accommodate more files on it. Perform following steps to view the status of the drive:

(i) Double click the mouse on My Computer icon, either present on desktop or in Explorer window. When you do so, a detailed view of all the drives and their spaces will get displayed, as shown in figure 4.50.

(ii) If somehow, such a view doesn't get displayed, select "Details" option from View submenu.

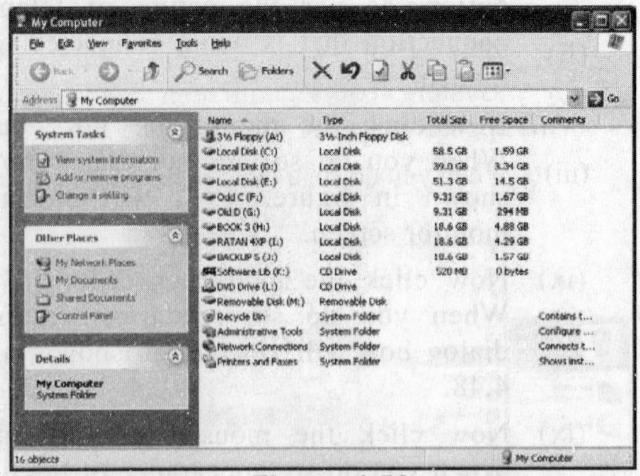

Figure 4.50

DEFRAGMENTING THE DISK USING DISK DEFRAGMENTER

When we create a computer file, computer assigns contiguous disk space to it. When the file is saved, its contents are written in allocated space only.

Later when this file is accessed, computer reads it from single place and presents it before user to work on it. Performing read / write operations on this file takes normal time, as the contents are read or written on single disk location.

Later, when more contents are added in the file and originally allocated space becomes full, computer allocates additional space for it. But, it is not necessary that this space be next to the space allocated before. Rather it can be at a location far away from the original space. When such a file is accessed, disk read / write head has to move to two different locations to fetch the complete file. As a result of this, read / write operation takes more time than the one which was being taken earlier.

Likewise, when large amount of contents are added many times, multiple fragments come into existence. As the number of fragments increase, read / write operations become slower.

When population of such fragmented files becomes large on the disk, system performance decreases drastically.

Defragmentation is a process, in which fragmented files are read from the disk and are reallocated new space on the disk, so as to store the files in the form of contiguous blocks. Contiguous files are read in single stroke without moving disk read / write head here and there. Thus in this process, read / write time is resorted back to normal and system throughputs increase considerably.

Windows provides Disk Defragmenter utility, using which files can be defragmented on any of the disks of computer.

Perform following steps for defragmenting the disk, using disk defragmenter:

(i) Click the mouse on "Start" button. When do so, Start menu, as shown in figure 4.51 (a), will appear on the screen.

(ii) First select "All Programs" option from this menu and then "Accessories", then "System Tools" and then "Disk Defragmenter" option from the submenus that appear one after the other.

(iii) When you do so, a dialog box, as shown in figure 4.51 (b), will appear on the screen.

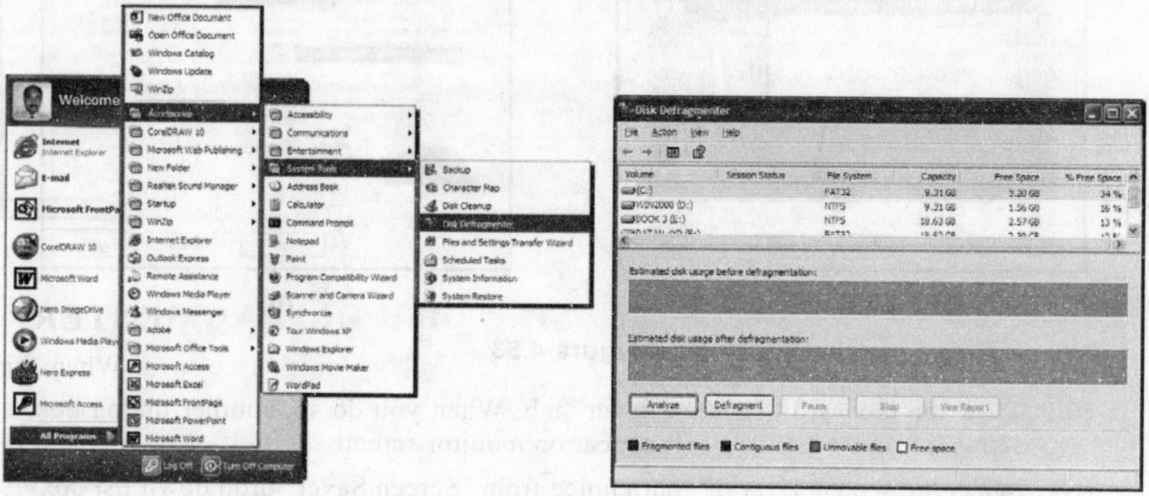

(a) (b)

Figure 4.51

(iv) Click the mouse on "Defragment" button.
When you do so, Windows will start the defragmentation process. Note that defragmentation is a long and time-consuming process. Total time taken to defragment the whole disk will depend upon the size of the disk and file population on it.

INSTALLING A SCREENSAVER

Screensavers are the moving patterns that automatically appear on computer screen when no input / output activity takes place for some time. Screensavers are used to save the monitor screen from visual dents.

Perform following steps to set the screensaver:

(i) Right click the mouse on any empty place of Desktop. When you do so, a menu, as shown in figure 4.52 will appear on monitor screen.

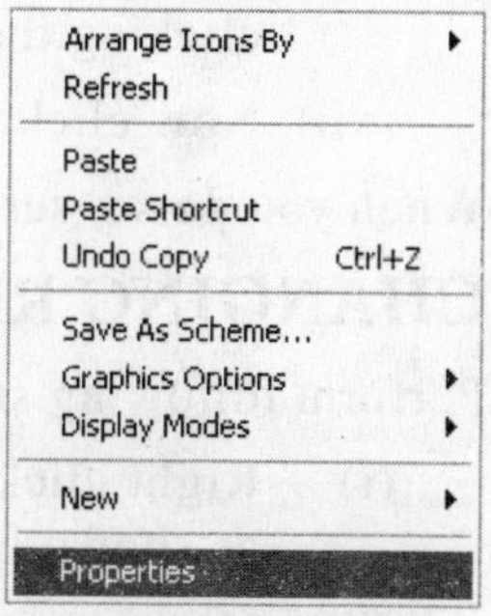

Figure 4.52

(ii) Now select "Properties" option from this menu. When you do so, a dialog box, as shown in figure 4.53 (a) will appear on monitor screen.

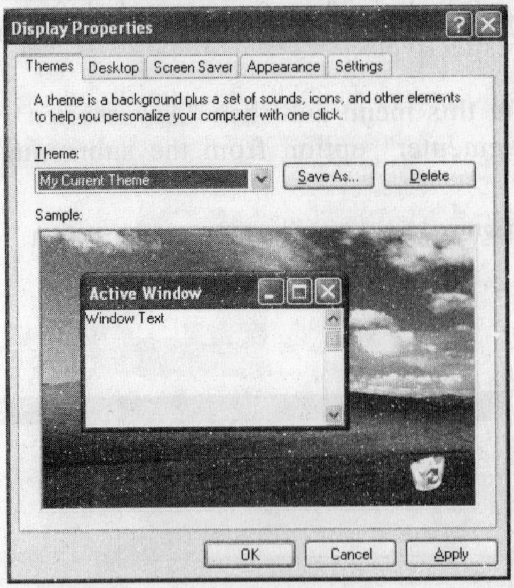

(a)

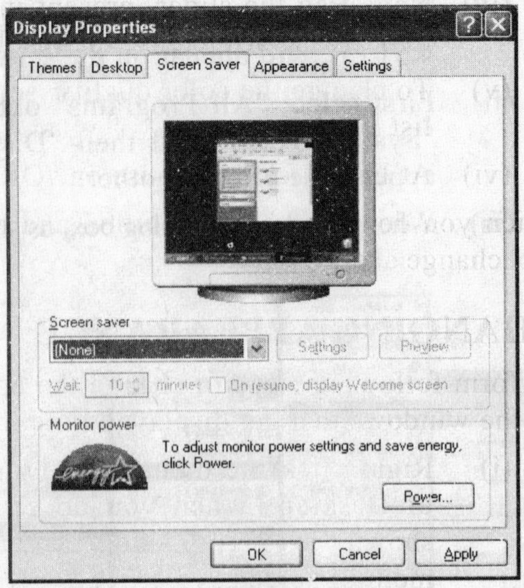

(b)

Figure 4.53

(iii) Click the mouse on "Screen Saver" tab. When you do so, another dialog box, as shown in figure 4.53 (b) will appear on monitor screen.

(iv) Select the screen saver of your choice from "Screen Saver" drop down list box.

(v) Now make use of "Wait" spinner and specify the time after which the screen saver should get activated, if no input/output activity takes place.

(vi) For example, if you specify this limit as 10 minutes and no input/output activity takes place for 10 minutes then screensaver will automatically get activated.

(vi) Using "Settings" button, set other related options. For example, what should be the speed of moving patterns, what should be their shape etc, can be set by clicking the mouse on this button.

(vii) Now click the mouse on "OK" button.

When you do so, screensaver will get set for the system.

CHANGING RESOLUTION AND COLOR

Perform following steps to change the screen resolution:

(i) Right click the mouse on any empty place of Desktop. When you do so, a menu, as shown in figure 4.52 will appear on monitor screen.

(ii) Now select "Properties" option from this menu. When you do so, a dialog box, as shown in figure 4.43 (a) will appear on monitor screen.

(iii) Click the mouse on "Settings" tab. When you do so, another dialog box, as shown in figure 4.54, will appear on monitor screen.

(iv) Now drag the slider, present in "Screen Resolution" section towards left or right to decrease or increase the resolution, respectively.

(v) To change the color quality, select desired option from "Color quality" drop down list box.

(vi) At last, click the mouse on "OK" button.

When you do so, screen resolution and color quality will change accordingly.

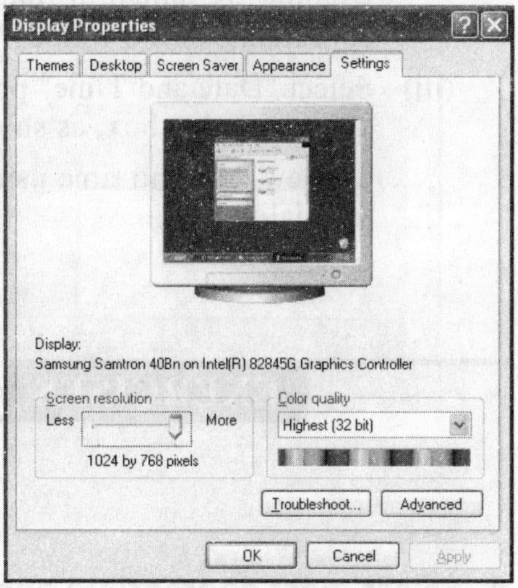

Figure 4.54

CHANGING APPEARANCE

Perform following steps to change the appearance of all the windows that get displayed time to time:

(i) Right click the mouse on any empty place of Desktop. When you do so a menu, as shown in figure 4.52 will appear on monitor screen.

(ii) Now select "Properties" option from this menu. When you do so, a dialog box, as shown in figure 4.53 will appear on monitor screen.

(iii) Click the mouse on "Appearance" tab. When you do so, another dialog box, as shown in figure 4.55 will appear on monitor screen.

(iv) If you wish to change the appearance of outer structure of the window and the buttons, select desired option from "Windows and buttons" drop down list.

(v) If you wish to change the color scheme of the window, select desired option from "Color scheme" drop down list.

(vi) If you wish to change the font size of the text that appears within the window, select desired option from "Font size" drop down list.

(vii) At last, click the mouse on "OK" button.

When you do so, window appearance will change accordingly.

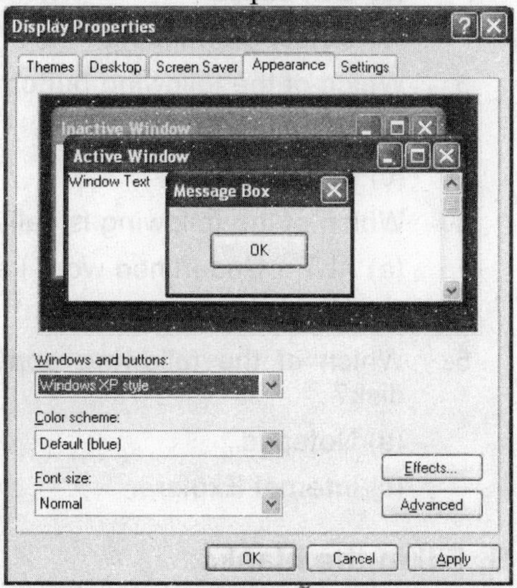

Figure 4.55

SETTING SYSTEM DATE AND TIME

Perform following operations to set new date and time for system clock:

(i) Click the mouse "Start" button present on desktop. When you do so, Start menu will appear on monitor screen.

(ii) Select "Control Panel" option from this menu. When you do so, control panel window, as shown in figure 4.30 will appear on monitor screen. If somehow, the appearance of the window looks different, select "Switch to classic view" option.

(iii) Select "Date and Time" program by double clicking the mouse its icon. When you do so, a dialog box, as shown in figure 4.13 will appear on the screen.

Set new date and time using corresponding drop down list and spinners present in the dialog box.

EXERCISES CHAPTER 4

Short Type Questions

A. Select most appropriate answer for following questions:

1. What is Windows?
   (a) An operating system (b) Computer hardware
   (c) A command (d) A program
2. Which of the following is not applicable for Windows?
   (a) GUI based (b) Multitasking
   (c) Object Embedding (d) Multi user
3. Which of the following button will bring a maximized window to its original size?
   (a) Minimize (b) Restore
   (c) Recover (d) Start
4. Which of the following is called Hot Key combination?
   (a) ALT + Underlined word key (b) CTRL + Underlined word key
   (c) Shift + Underlined key (d) ALT + DEL keys
5. Which of the following application could be used for file/folder maintenance on disk?
   (a) Notepad (b) WordPad
   (c) Internet Explorer (d) Windows Explorer

B. Fill in the blanks:

6. GUI stands for ....
7. .... is a feature of Windows, which enables multiple programs to run simultaneously.

8. To move an object from one application to another, you will have to make use of .... and .... options of Windows.
9. To copy an object from one place to another in document, you will have to make use of .... and .... options of Windows.
10. .... is that place in a window, where the name of the application gets displayed.

C. State, true or false for following statements:

11. Windows is Graphical User Interface based operating system.
12. Windows is multitasking operating system.
13. If a graphics is embedded in a document then change in graphics will get automatically reflected in the picture, present in the document.
14. Using Plug and Play feature of Windows you can copy a file from one folder to another folder.
15. A device driver can be installed by selecting Control Panel option from Start submenu.

D. Answer the following questions in short:

16. What is Windows?
17. Which feature of Windows enables automatic loading of device driver, when a new device is plugged to the computer?
18. Name the place, where system time gets displayed in desktop.
19. Name that button of Windows, which enables you to work with Windows menu system.
20. Name any two components that remain present on Windows desktop.

E. Differentiate between the following:

21. Minimize and Maximize button of Windows.
22. Radio buttons and Check boxes.
23. List box and Drop down list box.
24. Object Embedding and Object Linking.
25. Popup menu and Shortcut menu.
26. In which type of user interface, user has to type the command to interact with computer?

Detailed Answer Type Questions

E. Answer the following questions in detail:

27. What do you understand by the term GUI? Name any two GUI items of Windows.

28. Explain the term multitasking. How it is related to Windows?
29. Write two applications of CUT, COPY, PASTE features of Windows.
30. Explain Drag and Drop feature of Windows, by taking a suitable example.
31. Explain Plug and Play feature of Windows, by taking a suitable example.
32. What Command Prompt feature of Windows does?
33. How will you move a Window from one place to another?
34. How will you change length and width of a window? If the window is to be enlarged in proportion, how will you do it?
35. How will you restore a minimized window?
36. Write any two methods of selecting an options from the Bar menu.
37. What do you understand by Object Embedding? Explain in detail.
38. What do you understand by Object Linking? Explain in detail using an example.
39. What is screensaver, why do you require it and what role does it play in computer?
40. What is defragmentation? How do you do it in Windows?
41. How will you install a new device in computer? Describe the process.
42. How will you search a file or folders on disk? Describe the process.
43. Describe the advantages of defragmentation process. When should it be performed?
44. How will you format a floppy in Windows?
45. How will you change monitor resolution in Windows?

****

CHAPTER 5

Internet

INTRODUCTION

Internet is the most useful development of computer world. It comprises of millions of interconnected computers that are geographically located in every nook and corner of the world. Computers of Internet remain connected with each other through telecommunication medium. Thus sharing of information and resources becomes possible among them.

Computers of Internet hold very large volumes of information and offer wide variety of services. Any person willing to avail information or services can get his / her computer connected to Internet and acquire them.

Many useful applications like e-mail, chatting, Internet Telephony, Electronic Shopping, Internet Banking, Movie, Music and Gaming etc. are quite popular these days. Popularity of Internet is increasing day by day. Number of Internet users is continuously increasing and the size of Internet is growing.

The way Internet is expanding and its services are getting popular, the day is not far when Internet, like water, electricity, telephone etc., will become basic necessity of our life. An introduction to Internet and its services is given in this chapter.

INTRODUCTION TO NETWORK

When two or more objects of same kind join together to work in co-ordination with each other, they form a network. For example, when many marketing persons unite together to sell a product, they form a marketing network. Network marketing team is shown in figure 5.1.

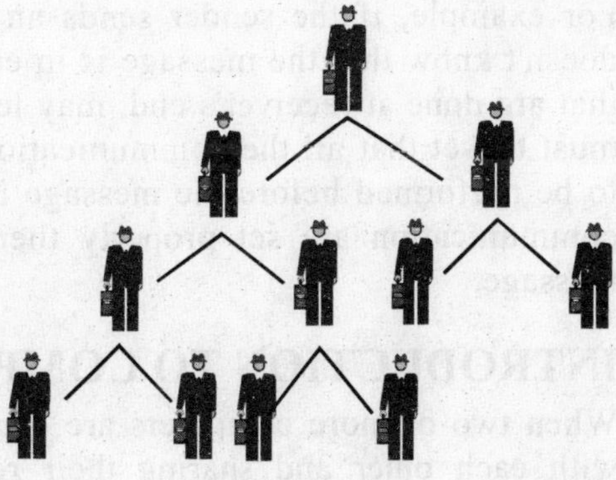

Figure 5.1

NETWORKING BASICS

Basic model of network is illustrated in figure 5.2. It shows that network comprises of following essential components:

1. Sender
2. Receiver
3. Medium
4. Message
5. Protocol

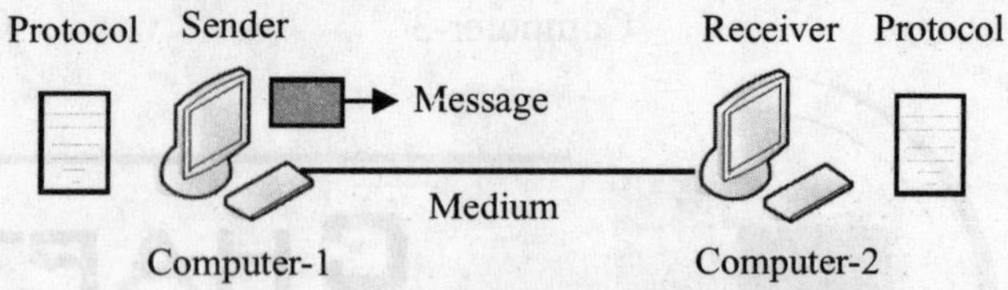

Figure 5.2

A brief description of each component is given below.

Sender

The computer, which sends the message (or starts the communication) is called sender. For example, if computer-1 sends message to computer-2 then computer-1 will be termed as sender.

Receiver

That computer of network, which receives the message is called receiver. For example, if computer-2 receives the message sent by computer-1 then computer-2 will be termed as receiver.

Medium

Medium is basically that substance through which message propagates and reaches the destination (receiver). In some of the networks, it could be wire. In other networks it could be air.

Message

What travels from sender to receiver is called message. As an essential rule of communication, message should reach the destination in its original form. No deformation or manipulation should take place in the middle.

Protocols

A protocol is basically a set of standards that are decided between the sender and receiver for error free communication between them. A message, though received in its original form, is of no use, if receiver cannot understand the message.

For example, if the sender sends an encrypted message to the receiver and the receiver doesn't know that the message is in encrypted form, then in this case all the manipulations that are done at receiver's end, may lead to errors. Thus before communication starts, rules must be set that all the communication will be done in encrypted form and decryption has to be performed before the message is manipulated. It is quite obvious that if the rules of communication are set properly there will not be any problem in interpretation of the message.

INTRODUCTION TO COMPUTER NETWORK

When two or more computers are connected together with the objective of communicating with each other and sharing their resources, they form a computer network. A simple computer network is illustrated in figure 5.3

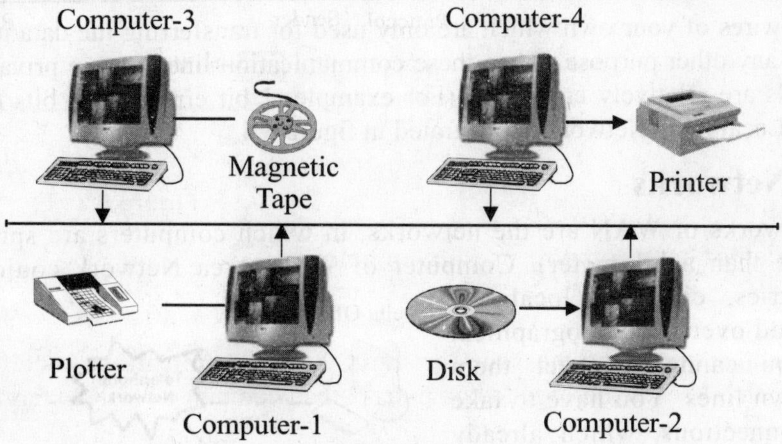

Figure 5.3

Refer figure 5.3 and note that in this network, four computers are connected together to form a computer network.

In this network, any computer can communicate with any other computer. For example, computer-1 can send message to computer-4 and computer-4 can replay back. Similarly, computer -2 and computer-4 can exchange data among them.

In computer network, computers share their resources among them. For example, computer-3 can print its documents on the printer that is attached to computer-4. Similarly computer-1, computer -3 and computer-4 can store their data on computer- 2's disk.

TYPES OF COMPUTER NETWORKS

Computer networks are broadly classified into two categories:

1. Local Area Networks (LAN).
2. Wide Area Networks (WAN).

Other networks are variations of these two networks. A detailed, description of both types of networks is given below.

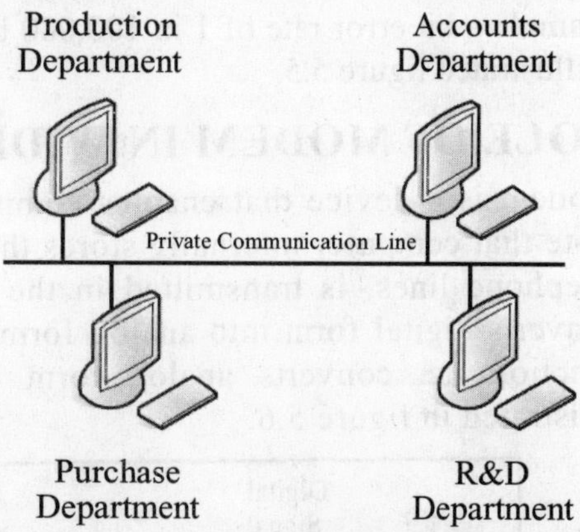

Figure 5.4

Local Area Network

Local area networks are the networks that spread within a short distance of a kilometer or so and are generally confined to a building or a campus. For example, computers of various departments of an organization that confine within the factory building itself, if connected together, will form a Local Area Network.

The data transfer speed of Local Area Network is generally high i.e. large amount of data can be transferred from one computer to the other in a very short span of time. Roughly the data transfer rate in LANs is generally of the order of Mega bits per second (MBPS). In Local Area Networks you connect the computers using dedicated wires of your own which are only used for transferring the data/information and are not used for any other purpose. Since these communication lines run, in private, undisturbed area hence LANs are relatively error free. (For example, 1 bit error in 10^9 bits transmitted). A rough sketch of Local Area Network is illustrated in figure 5.4.

Wide Area Networks

Wide Area Networks or WAN are the networks, in which computers are spread over long distances (more than a kilometer). Computer of Wide Area Network could either be in different countries, cities or localities. Since they spread over wide geographical area hence you cannot connect them through your own lines. You have to take help of the connections, which already exist in one form or the other. For example, telephone connection is one type of link that is already available in ready-made form. It can be used to connect the computers, which are far apart. Similarly microwave link and satellite link are other types of links that can be used to connect the computers that are in remote locations or are situated across the countries.

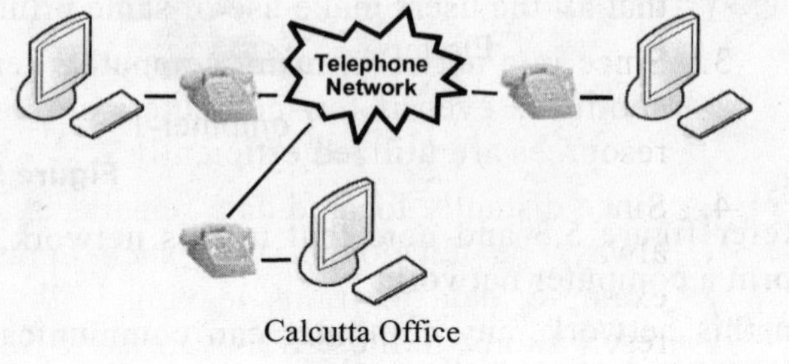

Figure 5.5

Note that these ready-made links were originally designed for some other purpose not for connecting computers, so their transfer speeds are not as high as that of dedicated lines (LAN lines). Roughly their speed is of the order of few Kilo bits per second say 32 Kbps or 64 Kbps.

Since these lines run into noisy environment where humidity, heat and electrical signals cannot be controlled hence Wide Area Networks are more error prone than Local Area Networks (For example a bit error rate of 1 in 100,000 bits transmitted). A rough sketch of Wide Area Network is illustrated figure 5.5.

ROLE OF MODEM IN WIDE AREA NETWORK

Modem is a device that enables computer to transmit data over telephone or cable lines. Note that computer internally stores the data in digital form, whereas data transmitted over telephone lines, is transmitted in the form of analog signals. A modem at sender's end converts digital form into analog form and the modem at receiver's end performs opposite function i.e. converts analog form into digital form. The functioning of modem is illustrated in figure 5.6.

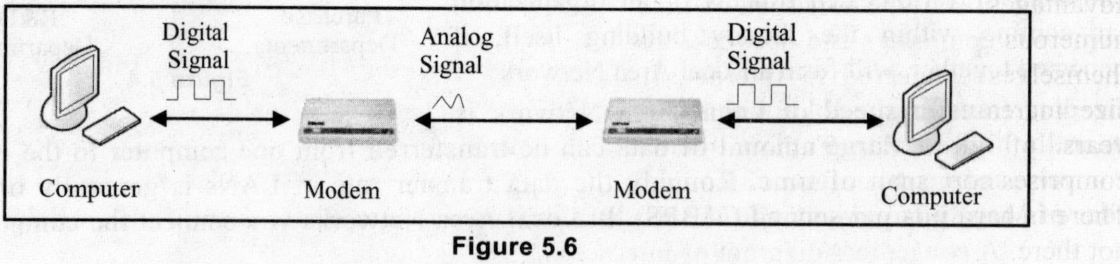

Figure 5.6

ADVANTAGES OF COMPUTER NETWORK

There are many advantages of computer network. Few of them are described below:

1. Distantly located information becomes available in no time. For example, if computer-A at Delhi is connected with computer-B at Mumbai over WAN then information among them can be exchanged within few seconds. This enables efficient working and fast decisions.
2. Costly devices such as magnetic tapes, printers etc. can be shared among different computers of the network. For example, one printer can be connected in LAN, so that all the users make use of same printer. This saves operational cost.
3. Since in a network, many computers remain available for use hence on-going work continues even if few computers are down. Thus in a computer network, time and resources are utilized efficiently.
4. Since distantly located data remains available locally, hence useful applications can always be developed. One such application is railway reservation system. For example, data of trains leaving Delhi remains accessible from Lucknow so train reservations, in those trains are done from Lucknow also.
5. Fast communication takes place among different users of the network. They can exchange words, messages or letters among them. Electronic mail is the best example of fast communication. Electronic mail neither gets delayed nor gets lost in transit, as usual mail does.

WHAT IS INTERNET

When many computer networks of the world were connected together, with the objective of communicating with others and sharing their resources, Internet was formed. In other words, you can say that Internet is network of computer networks, which spreads all across the globe.

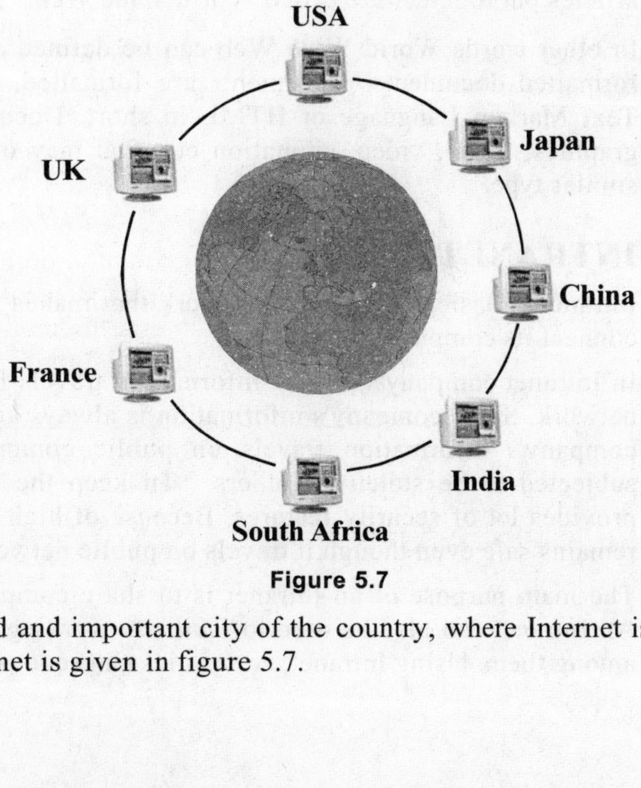

Figure 5.7

Initially the size of Internet was small, it was limited to few geographical locations only. But soon, people become aware of its utility and advantages. Within short span of time, numerous computers and networks got themselves connected to Internet. Its size increased multi fold within few years of its birth. Today Internet comprises of many million computers. There is hardly any country of the world and important city of the country, where Internet is not there. A conceptual diagram of Internet is given in figure 5.7.

Internet is basically a large computer network, which extends all across the globe. In Internet, millions of computers remain connected together through well-laid communication system. Recall that telephone communication system is well-defined, time proven system. Computers of Internet are connected to each other through this system. Thus like a telephone, any computer of any city can establish a connection with any other computer of any other city and exchange data or messages with it.

UNDERSTANDING WORLD WIDE WEB

Internet and World Wide Web are often mistakably used as synonyms, but the fact is that their existence is very closely associated with each other, but they are different. To understand the concept of world wide web, consider two objects, Say a piece of text "Keyboard is the main input unit of computer" and the figure of the keyboard. There exists a mechanism by which both these objects could be linked together, in such a way that whenever required, one can be accessed through other irrespective of their geographical location. For example, text and graphics could either be on same computer or on different computers (one in India and other in USA) connected over Internet/network.

This mechanism of linking does not restrict itself to text and graphics linking. Other objects like sound, animation, video etc. may participate in linking. Linking mechanism also doesn't put any restriction on the length of the chain. First can be linked to second objects. Second object could be linked to third object and so on. The growing chain can involve other computers of Internet/network.

Note that volumes and volumes of such linked objects exist over Internet. All such linked articles put together are called World Wide Web.

In other words World Wide Web can be defined as part of Internet that support specially formatted documents. Documents are formatted, using a special language, called Hyper Text Markup Language or HTML in short. Documents may consist of objects like text, graphics, audio, video, animation etc. that may or may not be linked to other objects of similar type.

INTRANET

Intranet is basically a private network that makes use of public communication network to connect its computers.

In Intranet company's private information travels from one place to another through public network. Since company's information is always kept hidden from outsiders and in Intranet company's information travels on public communication network hence it is always subjected to be stolen by others. To keep the information away from others, Intranet provides lot of security features. Because of high security features company's information remains safe even though it travels on public network.

The main purpose of an Intranet is to share company's information among its employees. An Intranet can also be used to facilitate working in-groups and arranging teleconferences among them. Using Intranet, companies can send private messages to each other.

CLASSIFICATION OF INTERNET COMPUTERS

Computers of Internet can be broadly classified into following two categories:

1. Web Servers
2. Web Clients

Role and requirements of both types of computers are explained below.

Web Servers

Those computers of Internet, which provide information or services to other computers, are called web servers. For example, if a computer in an organization named Hotmail provides electronic mail services to Internet users then that computer will be categorized as web server.

Web servers provide services/data to millions of Internet users, so they generally possess following characteristics:

1. They are fast.
2. They are equipped with large memory and large disk space.
3. They remain connected to Internet all through the day i.e. seven days a week, 31 days a month and 365 days a year.
4. They make use of fast communication lines.

Web Clients

Those computers of Internet, which take information or services from web servers are called web clients. For example, if you make use of Hotmail's web server to send electronic mail to your friends or relatives then your computer will be termed as web client.

Since web clients interact with web servers on one-to-one basis and that too when service/information is required hence they possess following characteristics:

1. They need not be very fast computer.
2. They need not have large memory and disk space as servers have.
3. They get connected to Internet, when they need information/service from it. After taking it, they disconnect from Internet.
4. They generally make use of slow connection like telephone lines, to get connected to Internet.

IDENTIFICATION OF COMPUTERS ON INTERNET

There are two ways of identifying computers of Internet. First is by a number called IP address and another is by their names, called Domain Name.

On Internet computer identification mechanism is same as that of indentifying a student in a class. Just like each student in the class has a unique name and a unique roll number is assigned to him similarly, each computer of Internet is assigned a unique name and a unique IP address.

Details of IP address format and Domain naming convention are described in coming sections.

IP Address

Like houses of any city are identified by a unique address, similarly computers of Internet are identified by a unique address called IP address.

IP address comprises of four numbers separated by dots(.). For example, 150, 075,100.085 is a valid IP address. Each of the four numbers is called a quad. As they are connected by dot, it's called dotted quad notation.

Each number in IP address can range from 0 to 255. So IP address can range from 0.0.0.0 to 255.255.255.255. Thus if IP address of a computer is known, it can be accessed over Internet.

Servers of Internet always have fixed IP address. Their IP addresses never change. For example, IP address of google.com, yahoo.com, excite.com will never change.

IP addresses of internet clients remain fixed for a session. When they get connected to internet, working IP address is assigned to them. When they disconnect from internet, their IP address is made free and is allotted to other client which connects to Internet. Next time when this client connects to Internet, a new IP address is assigned to it and process continues.

Domain Name

As mentioned above, each computer of Internet is identified by a number called IP address. But for all practical purposes they can also be assigned a unique name. This name is called Domain Name. Computers of Internet can also be accessed using their domain names.

Domain name comprises of two or more strings of characters separated by dots (.). First string of characters is called domain name. It identifies the name of the server, For example, in indianrail.gov.in, indianrail identifies the name of the server. Second string of characters identifies the nature of the server. For example in hotmail.com, com indicates that it is commercial server. Standard strings that are used at second place in the domain name are as follows:

String	Type of web site
com	Commercial organizations (profit making)
edu	Educational institutes
gov	Government organization
mil	Military
net	Network service providers
org	Non profit making organizations

Third string in the domain name is always indicative of country. For example, "**in**" is used for India. "au" is used for Australia, "uk" is used for United Kingdom, "fr" is used for "France" etc.

DNS

DNS is acronym for Domain Name System. It is a basically a collection of servers that perform the task of translating domain names into corresponding IP addresses.

Note that it is easy for human beings to remember a name rather than number. For example, I can remember the names like google.com, yahoo.com, bispl.com etc. but it will be very difficult for me, if someone says remember the numbers 178.100.95.101, 220.045.180.111 and 145.212.001.200 assigned to them respectively. To make the computer access easy in Internet environment (where millions of computers remain accessible) computers are assigned a unique name called Domain Name and users are can access them by these names.

On the other hand, computers identify each other, using numbers rather than names. It is really very difficult to implement a mechanism by which computers would identify each other on the basis of their domain names like google.com, yahoo.com etc. rather than numbers (IP addresses) like 178.100.95.101, 220.045.180.111 etc. In Internet environment computers make use of IP addresses to communicate with each other.

To make Internet system work with ease, a translation system has been introduced in the environment. This translation system is called DNS. This system hosts a directory mentioning which domain name corresponds to which IP address. It is just like a telephone directory, in which we search a person's name and find his telephone number for talking to him.

When a user accesses a computer, using its domain name (like google.com) DNS translates this name into corresponding IP address (like 178.100.95.101) and returns it back to the computer to use it for accessing it.

DNS system is implemented into Internet through dedicated servers called DNS Servers. Whenever a new domain name is assigned, corresponding, IP address is added to DNS system directory. Unless this is done, domain name remains inaccessible.

WEB SITE

Web site is basically, well-identified location on web server, which holds the information of an individual or an organization or place etc. Each web site is identified by a unique name, called domain name. For example, hotmail.com, yahoo.com, indianrail.gov.in, sanchar.net etc. are valid web sites.

Physically a website may consist of single or multiple web pages. Details of web page are described below.

WEB PAGE

Information or services on any web site are arranged in the form of web pages. A web page consists of elements like text graphics, sound, animation video and hyper links in it, arranged in attractive manner.

A web site may consist of interlinked multiple web pages. When you access a web site, its first page gets displayed on you computer. Since web pages of a web site remain interlinked through hyperlinks hence you can always access other web pages, after accessing the first web page.

Web pages are generally developed using special markup language called HTML (Hypertext Markup Language). Generally their names are of the type index.html, intro.htm, contact.html etc.

HYPERLINK

When a link between two objects, is maintained in such a way that when you click the mouse on first object, second object gets displayed then such a link is called hyperlink. Concept of hyperlink is illustrated in figure 5.8.

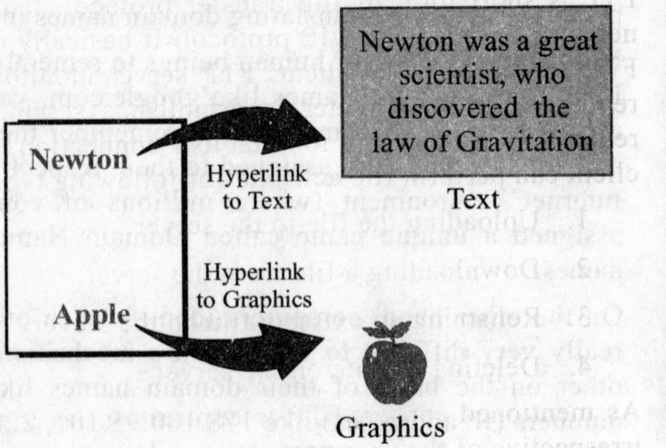

Figure 5.8

HYPERTEXT

The text that remains linked to other objects like text, graphics, audio etc. through hyperlink is called hypertext. For example, the words "Newton" and Apple are hypertext.

HYPERMEDIA

As hypertext allows you to link the text with another text, in the similar manner, hypermedia allows the user to create a link from a particular document to either another program, or to another movie or sound clip or to Internet related facilities (like e-mail, chat etc.). When such types of links are created, they are known as Hypermedia.

HYPER TEXT TRANSFER PROTOCOL (HTTP)

Hyper Text Transfer Protocol is an Internet protocol, using which communication between web client and web server takes place. Dynamics of this protocol proceeds as follows:

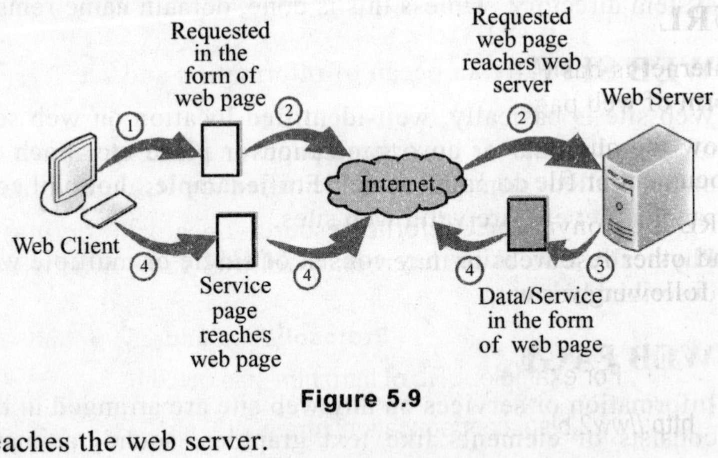

Figure 5.9

1. When web client requires any information/service from web server, it makes a request to the web server in the form of a web page.
2. Request-web-page travels over Internet and reaches the web server.
3. Web server generates a web page containing requested information/service in it and sends it to web client.
4. Service web page travels over Internet and reaches the client.

Concept of HTTP is illustrated in figure 5.9.

FTP

FTP is short form of file transfer protocol. It is mainly used for transfer of files over a network that uses TCP/IP protocol. It basically comprises of two main components, called FTP server and FTP client. FTP server monitors the network to find out if there is any request from a computer to establish a session. Other component, FTP client, sends a request to FTP server to establish connection. Once the connection is established, FTP client can perform file activities of following types:

1. Uploading the file to the server.
2. Downloading a file from the server.
3. Renaming an existing file on the server.
4. Deleting the file on the server.

As mentioned earlier, FTP is application layer protocol hence it allows all file activities, irrespective of the operating systems being used on both the computers.

Telnet

Telnet is a protocol, which is used for accessing remote computers. Using telnet a person can access another computer remotely. Note that FTP allows a user to manipulate files on other computer, but Telnet allows a user to log-on to another computer as a user, by supplying correct login name and password. Thus he can use applications and other resources, present on that computer, as per permissions granted to him.

In this protocol communications is established, using TCP/IP protocol and the communication is based on a set of facilities know as Network Virtual Terminal (NVT).

URL

Internet is basically an ocean of information and services. All these exist on Internet in the form of web pages.

Now the question is, how these pages are addressed and located on Internet? Well, each document or file on Internet is identified by its unique address called URL.

URL is acronym for Uniform Resource Locator. It defines the global address of documents and other resources on Internet. It follows same format all across the world and is written in following format:

Protocol://site address/path/filename

For example, URL of intro.html file could be

http://ww2.bispl.com/education/intro.html. This URL consist of following components:

- Protocol: **http**
- Host computer name: **ww2**
- Domain name: **bispl**

- Domain type: **com**
- Path: **/education**
- File name **intro.html**

Protocols

In addition to the http protocol, mentioned above, there are few other protocols on the Internet. Few commonly used protocols are described below.

File	: Enables a hyperlink to access a file on a local system.
FTP	: Used to download files from remote machines.
Gopher	: Helps in accessing a gopher server.
mailto	: Calls SMTP (the Simple Mail Transport Protocol) and enables a hyperlink to send an addressed email message.
news	: helps in accessing a USENET newsgroup.
telnet	: Provides the means for a hyperlink to open a telnet session on a remote computer.

Site Address

The site address consists of the host computer name, the domain name and the domain type and country identification tag. For example, indianrail.gov.in.

Path Name

Path name specifies the hierarchic location of the said file on the computer. For instance, in http://ww2.bispl.com/education/intro.html the file intro.html is located in education subdirectory under the server root directory.

File Name

File name is the name of the file that contains the document that is to be accessed.

INTERNET SERVICE PROVIDER

An Internet Service Provider (ISP) is a company that provides individuals and other companies, access to the Internet and other related services.

Using their services, web clients can navigate through Internet and access any of the desired web servers present on Internet.

An ISP has the equipment and the telecommunication line access required to have a point-of-presence on the Internet for the geographic area served. The larger ISPs have their own high-speed leased lines so that they are less dependent on the telecommunication providers and can provide better service to their customers.

BSNL, VSNL, Airtel, Reliance etc. are few Indian service providers. AT&T WorldNet, IBM Global Network, MCI, Netcom are the names of few international ISPs.

ISPs provide Internet connection on monthly fees. When user takes Internet connection from them they provide modem and other accessories, necessary to connect the client to the telephone line.

INTERNET CONNECTION METHODS

As mentioned earlier, to acquire any information/service, the server, client has to get connected to Internet. This can be done using:

1. Dialup connection.
2. Broadband connection.
3. ISDN connection.
4. Digital Subscriber Line (DSL) connection.
5. Cable Modem connection.
6. Wireless connection.

A brief introduction of each type of connections is given below.

Dialup Connection

In dial-up connection, client is connected to Internet through ordinary telephone line, using a modem, as illustrated in figure 5.10.

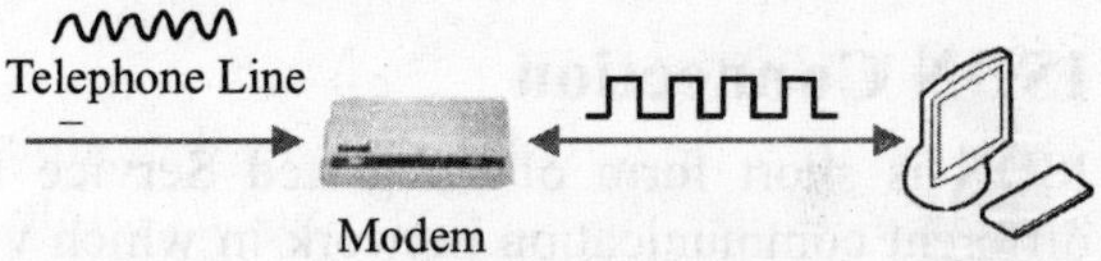

Figure 5.10

To connect the computer to Internet, user should have following with him:

1. An account (called connection) on Internet Service Provider's server (which is generally provided by ISP on paid basis).
2. A valid login name and password to access ISP's server (provide by ISP at the time of subscribing dialup service).
3. ISP's telephone number.
4. A dialup connection made on the client, preferably on desktop, in the form of an icon.

To get connected to Internet, user executes the dialup connection program on client. A dialog box, asking for ISP's phone number, users login name and password appears on the screen. The dialog box, which appears in Windows operating system, is illustrated in figure 5.11.

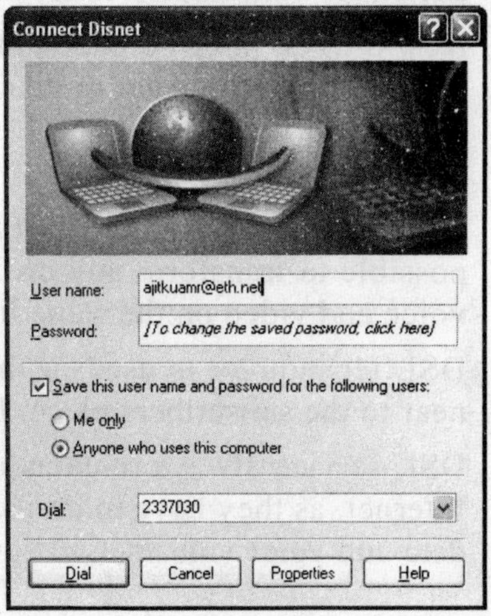

Figure 5.11

This program dials ISP's phone number and if call gets through establishes a link with ISPs server.

As soon as link gets established, client gets connected to Internet.

Note that dialup connection is slow speed connection. ISP's claim to provide 56 kbps transfer speed, which is often very less.

Broadband Connection

Broadband connection basically refers to a connection, which uses a medium, which can carry several channels at once. Concept of broadband is illustrated in figure 5.12. Note that the single broadband cable can carry signals related to various services. It becomes possible, due to broad bandwidth of the cable.

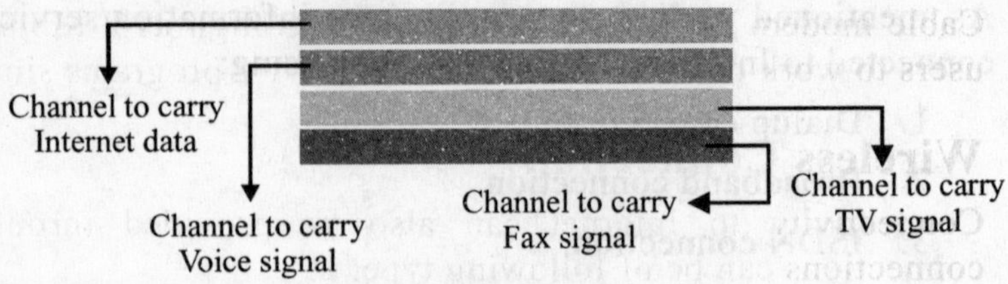

Figure 5.12

Broadband connections are faster connections in comparison to dialup connection. Their speed generally varies from 64 kbps to 256 kbps.

When you connect your computer to broadband service through ADSL modem, it gets automatically connected to Internet when you boot the system. It remains connected to it till the time computer is switched off. While making use of Internet through broadband connection, you can use other services such as telephone service etc. available on broadband line.

ISDN Connection

ISDN is short form of Integrated Service Digital Network. As the name indicates, it is a different communication network in which voice / data signals are transmitted in digital form. You can say that it supports digital transmission, as against normal telecommunication network, which supports analog transmission of voice / data. Thus it provides higher quality and better transmission rates. Its supports up to 128 kbps data transfer speeds.

Now-a-days good broadband services are available at very nominal rates, so ISDN connections, which are quite costly, are getting out.

DSL Connection

DSL is short form of Digital Subscriber Line. It is a telephone service that makes it possible to transform any ordinary phone line into a high-speed line for transmitting data, voice and video on the same line.

DSL technology is used in the areas, where services provider's switching equipments are near to the subscribers place. Both of them cannot be very far away.

DSL service always remains on. Users don't need to dial a connection to get connected to Internet, as they have to do in dialup connection. It also allows user to use the same line for data and voice signals.

Cable Modem Connection

You know that cable TV service is provided to home subscribers through coaxial cable.

This cable's bandwidth is much more than the bandwidth of telephone line. In spite of many frequencies for multiple channels passing through cable, a large amount of bandwidth remains free. Often this bandwidth is utilized to provide connectivity to Internet.

A modem designed to operate over TV line is called cable modem. Internet service provided through cable network, using cable modem, is called cable modem Internet service.

Cable modem connection offers speed as high as 2 Mbps. This type of connection allows users to work on Internet and view cable TV programs simultaneously.

Wireless Connection

Connectivity to Internet can also be provided through wireless connections. These connections can be of following type:

1. Using mobile phones.
2. Wireless LANs (i.e. WLAN)
3. Wireless Wide Area Network (WWAN)
4. Satellite Connection

WEB BROWSER

The software, using which you traverse over Internet and access web sites to avail different types of services being provided by it, is called Web Browser.

Internet Explorer, Netscape, Mozila etc. are few famous web browsers. Most of the Internet operations are done, using web browser.

WORKING WITH INTERNET EXPLORER

Internet Explorer is a web browser. Most of the Internet operations are performed through Internet Explorer. Perform following steps to invoke Internet Explorer on your computer:

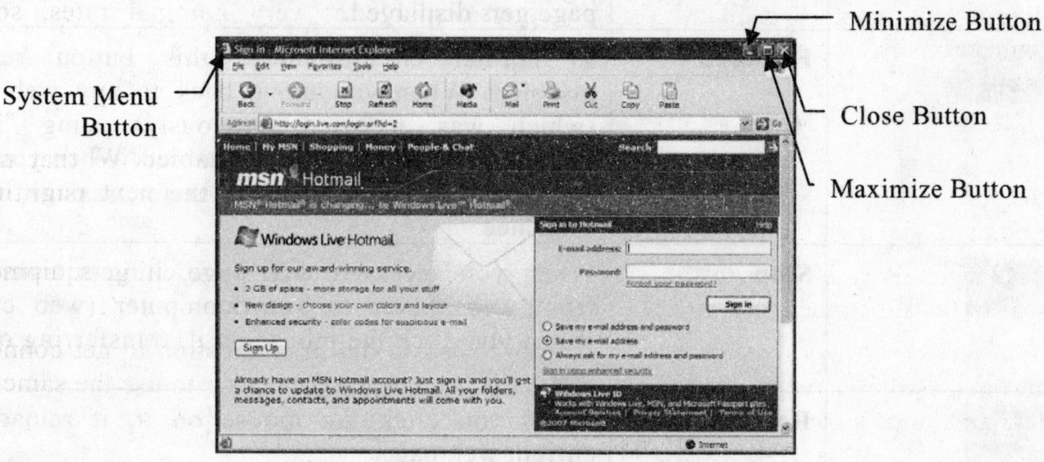

Figure 5.13

1. Click the mouse on "Start" button. When you do so, Start menu will appear on the screen.

2. Select "All Programs" option from that menu. When you do so, a submenu containing "Internet Explorer" option in it, will appear on the screen.
3. Select "Internet Explorer" option.

When you do so, Internet Explorer will get loaded in computer's memory and Internet Explorer window, as shown in figure 5.13, will appear on the screen.

When Internet Explorer window gets displayed for the first time, Home page gets displayed in it. Home page is the web page, which by default get displayed, whenever Internet Explorer is loaded. Any web page, present on the disk can be set as home page for Internet Explorer.

INTRODUCTION TO INTERNET EXPLORER WINDOW

Refer figure 5.13 and note that Internet Explorer window comprises of many components. Some of the components like System Menu button, Minimize button, Maximize button, Close button etc. are usual window components. They need no explanation now. Other components are local to Internet Explorer. Their roles and functions are described below.

Address Bar

Address bar is used for entering the domain name of the web site that you wish to access.

Toolbar

Toolbar comprises of many buttons. Each button performs a specific function, when you click the mouse on it. Roles and functions of commonly used buttons are explained below.

Button	Name	Action
	**Back**	When you click the mouse on Back button, the web page, which was accessed, prior to the current web page gets displayed.
	**Forward**	In normal circumstances, this button remains disabled. When you move back to any web page, (which was accessed previously) using "Back" button, Forward button gets enabled. When you click the mouse on it, it displays the next page, in the sequence.
	**Stop**	When you access a web page, it gets transferred from web server to your computer (web client). When you click the mouse on it, transferring of web page stops.
	**Refresh**	When you click the mouse on it, it reloads the current web page.
	**Home**	When you click the mouse on it, home page that has been set for the web browser, gets displayed.

Button	Name	Action
	**Favorites**	Internet Explorer maintains a folder, with the name Favorites. If you wish you can maintain links to all your favorite web pages/sites in this folder. When you click the mouse on this button, it provides easy access (within the browser) to favorite links, so that associated web pages could be re accessed.
	**History**	Internet Explorer maintains a categorized list of the web sites that you visit. This list remains alive, for the duration set for the browser (a tunable parameter). When you click the mouse on this button, history list appears within the browser window. If you wish, you can again access any of the web pages, using this list.

Link Toolbar

Link toolbar consists of many buttons. Each button remains linked to web site or web page on Internet. When you click the mouse on any of the buttons, it takes you to the linked object.

Status Bar

Status bar is the place where, information related to current object, current web page or down loading appears.

Now you are familiar with Internet and Internet Explorer, so let's make use of Internet Explorer to utilize different services of Internet.

WEB SURFING

Moving from one web site to another web site is called web surfing or web browsing. Perform following steps to access a web site:

1. Get connected to Internet.
2. Invoke Internet Explorer (using the process mentioned above) and get Internet Explorer window (illustrated in figure 5.13) on the screen.
3. Enter domain name in address bar and press "Enter" key.

When you do so, Internet Explorer will search the web site and if it gets it, it will display its first page, called opening page in the browser window. For example, if you access yahoo.com web site, its opening page, as shown in figure 5.14, will appear in Internet Explorer window.

Refer figure 5.14 and note that web page contains few icons, a text box with button and many text items in it. Truly speaking, each icon and each text message is a link. When you click the mouse on any of the links, linked item or service gets displayed. For example, there is a Mail icon in the upper portion of the web page. When you click the mouse on it, a web page offering e-mail service appears in Internet Explorer window. Similarly, you can click the mouse on other links to avail associated services.

While traveling through links, if you wish to go to a specific web site, enter the desired domain name in address bar and press "Enter" key. If you do so, current service will get terminated and you will be taken to the opening web page of the mentioned web site. For example, if, while working with yahoo's e-mail service, you enter **hotmail.com** in the address bar and press "Enter" key, e-mail service will get terminated and opening web page of hotmail.com will get displayed in Internet Explorer window.

Figure 5.14

SEARCHING CONTENTS ON INTERNET USING SEARCH ENGINES

Internet is an ocean of information. Be it any topic, science, culture, entertainment, tourism, medical or aviation, volumes of information can be found on Internet. This information remains available on web sites and can be availed by visiting the web site

Now the questions is, there are millions of web sites on Internet so how do you come to know, which information is available on which site and what is its domain name? Well, Internet itself provides solution for this problem. There are certain web sites, which provide search facility for searching the content on Internet. For example, yahoo.com is a web site, which provides search facility. Refer figure 5.14 and note that search facility remains available in the form of a text box and a button titled "Search" To get the information on any desired topic, perform following steps:

1. Enter the search term in text box. For example, if you wish to get the information on "Examination Taking Techniques" enter this term (called, search term) in the text box and click the mouse on "Search" button.

2. When you do so, a program called Search Engine will search its information database and find the links to the information. Found links will get displayed in the form of a list, as shown in figure 5.15. In technical term, this list is called "Hit List".

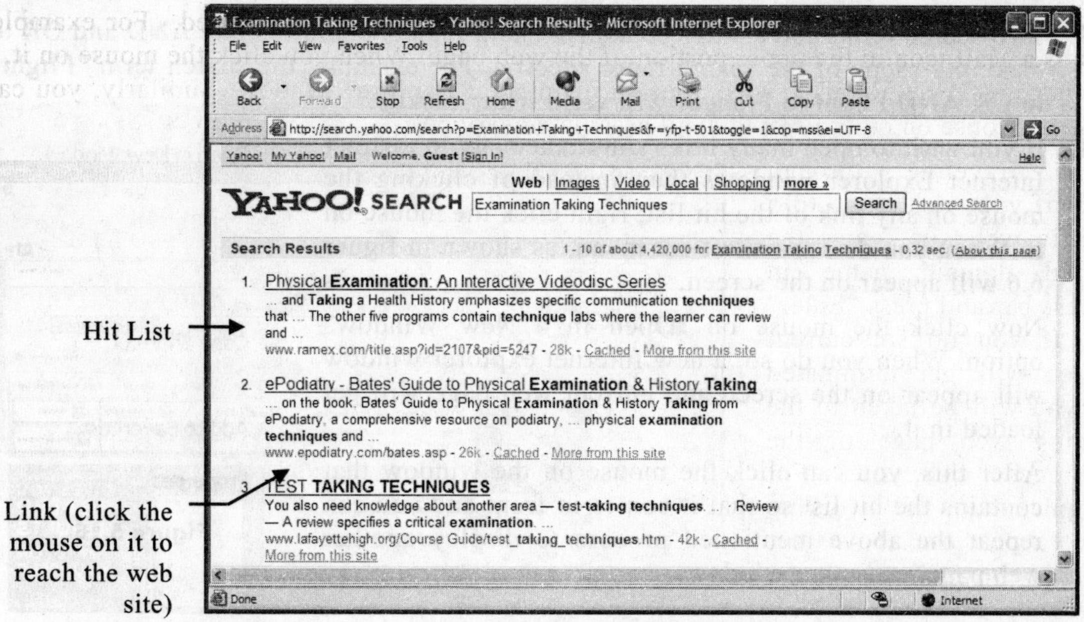

Figure 5.15

3. To reach the web site that contains the information, click the mouse on any desired link of the hit list.
4. After reaching the web site, you can make use of browser's "Back" button, to get back to the hit list.
5. Now click the mouse on another link to get more information on the same topic, but from another web site.

Important Points Related to Internet Search

Following are few important points that should be kept in mind, while searching the information on Internet:

1. Different search engines provide different hit lists. Thus if the results of one search engine are not satisfactory, different search engines can be tried for better results.
2. Search term plays an important role in the process of acquiring the information from the Internet so search term should be framed carefully. For example, you may wish to get information on life style of Gandhi ji. For this, if you use the search term Gandhi, you may get lot of irrelevant information, which may not be of any use to you. For example, links related to Gandhi park, Gandhi restaurant, Gandhi club etc. may appear in the hit list. But if you use the search term, "Gandhi life style", it is likely that you may get the desired information.

   Other search terms, may also relate to same topic so they should also be tried, while searching the information. For example, search term "Gandhian Philosophy" may also, fetch the desired information.

3. Two search terms can always be added, using logical operators like AND and OR to make the scope of the search more specific. For example, the search term "Flights to UK AND Flight to France" will yield wider results.

4. If you wish to open many links simultaneously in distinct Internet Explorer windows then instead of clicking the mouse on any link of the hit list, right click the mouse on it. When you do so, a short cut menu, as shown in figure 6.6 will appear on the screen.

   Now click the mouse on "Open in a New Window" option. When you do so, a new Internet explorer window will appear on the screen and current web page will get loaded in it.

   After this, you can click the mouse on the window that contains the hit list so that it comes in front and you can repeat the above mentioned process to display another web page in another window.

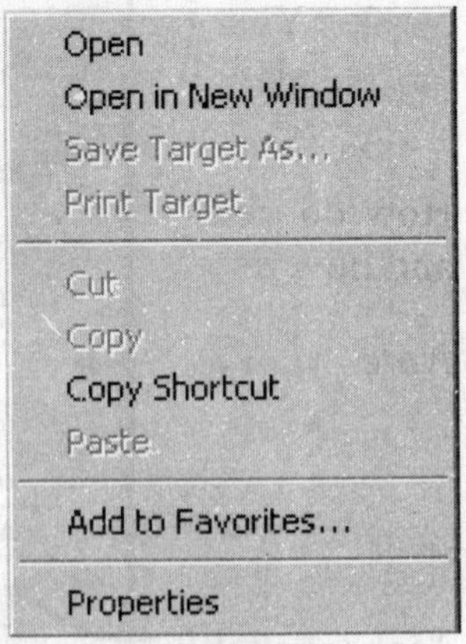

Figure 5.16

INTRODUCTION TO E-MAIL

E-mail is a service, using which you can send letters and documents to your friends and relatives. You can also receive reply from them over Internet within few seconds. For example, if a letter is sent from India to America by normal post, it takes around 15 to 20 days. But if the same letter is sent, using e-mail, it reaches America within 15 to 20 seconds. On top of this, there remains no possibility of letter getting lost in the way.

Figure 5.17

e-mail software remains available in different forms. Most of the commercial web sites provide the use of this software free to their visitors. For example, yahoo.com, hotmail.com, rediffmail.com are the names of few web sites, which provide free e-mail services to their visitors. A web page offering e-mail service is shown in figure 5.17. If the visitors wish to avail e-mail facility of any web site then, once forever, they have to open an e-mail account on that web site. After that they are assigned a unique e-mail address. Using this e-mail address they can then send and receive letters.

USING E-MAIL

Following points should be kept in mind, before you make use of e-mail service:

1. Your computer should be connected to Internet.
2. You must have an e-mail account on a web site that provides e-mail facility. You should know your e-mail login name and password.
3. You should also know e-mail address of the person to whom you wish to send the e-mail.

How do you create an e-mail account, how do you read the letters that you have received and how do you send the letters to others, is explained below.

Note

- *As mentioned above, each web site provides an e-mail program of its own. E-mail program of one web site may differ from the program of other web site. It is not possible to explain the procedural details of each famous e-mail program in this book. The idea is to make you familiar with the general steps of operating e-mail. With this objective in mind, we have taken yahoo e-mail program as base program. All the steps for operating e-mail have been explained in relation to this program only. If you understand the basic idea, you will be able to operate all other programs, as well.*
- *Note that the physical appearance of the web pages keeps on changing from time to time. It is quite possible that when you access the web sites, mentioned in this chapter, you may come across different appearances of the web pages. So it is essential that you should mainly focus your attention on procedures rather than on the appearance of the web pages.*

Opening An E-mail Account

Perform following steps to open an e-mail account on yahoo.com:

1. Connect to Internet and access yahoo.com. When you do so, a web page as shown in figure 5.14 will get displayed in browser window.
2. Now click the mouse on "Mail" link. When you do so, a web page, as shown in figure 5.18, will appear in browser window.

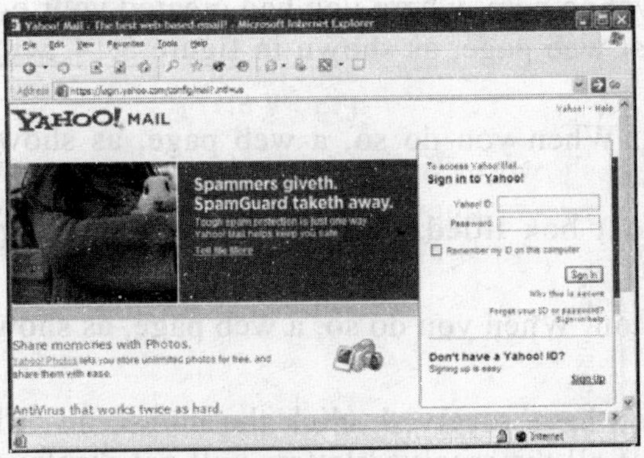

Figure 5.18

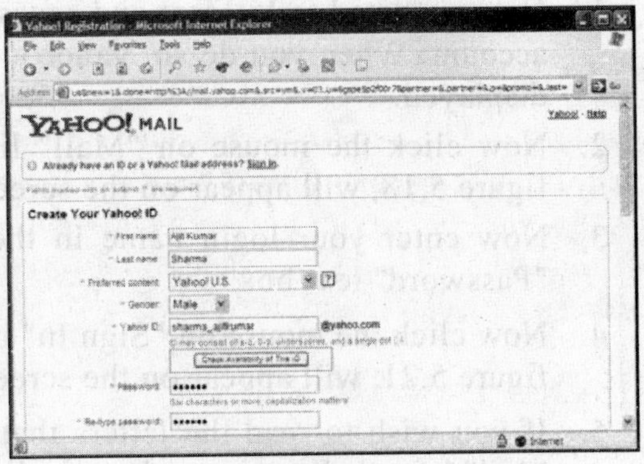

Figure 5.19

3. Now click the mouse on "Sign Up" link. When you do so, a web page, as shown in figure 5.19 will get displayed in the browser window.
4. Refer web page shown in figure 5.19 and note that this is basically a form, which accepts details from the user for creating his account. Enter your details in each field.
5. After filling the form, click the mouse on "Submit This Form" button (not shown in the figure, as it appears at the bottom of the web page. It will appear when you scroll the page.) When you do so, your e-mail account will be created and a web page, as shown in figure 5.20, will be displayed.
6. After creating the account, yahoo sends a test mail into your account to confirm that mail transactions are taking place correctly in that account. To check your test mail (described above), click the mouse on "Continue to Yahoo Mail" button. When you do so, a web page, as shown in figure 5.21 will get displayed in your browser window, showing you that you have one unread message in your account.

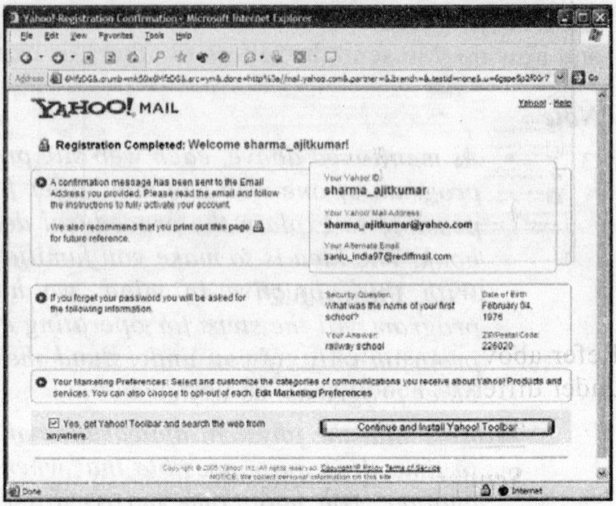

Figure 5.20

7. Now you can either check your test mail by clicking the mouse on Inbox(1) link or exit from e-mail by clicking the mouse on "Sign Out" link.

Reading E-Mail

Perform following steps for reading e-mail:

1. Get connected to Internet and access yahoo.com, where you had created your e-mail account. When you do so, yahoo's first web page, as shown in figure 5.14, will get displayed.
2. Now click the mouse on "Mail" link. When you do so, a web page, as shown in figure 5.18, will appear on the screen.
3. Now enter your login name in the text box titled, "Yahoo ID" and password in "Password" text box.
4. Now click the mouse on "Sign In" button. When you do so, a web page, as shown in figure 5.21, will appear on the screen.
5. If you wish to read the letters that you have received, click the mouse on "Check Mail" button. When you do so, a list of all the received letters will get displayed in the form of a web page, as shown in figure 5.22.

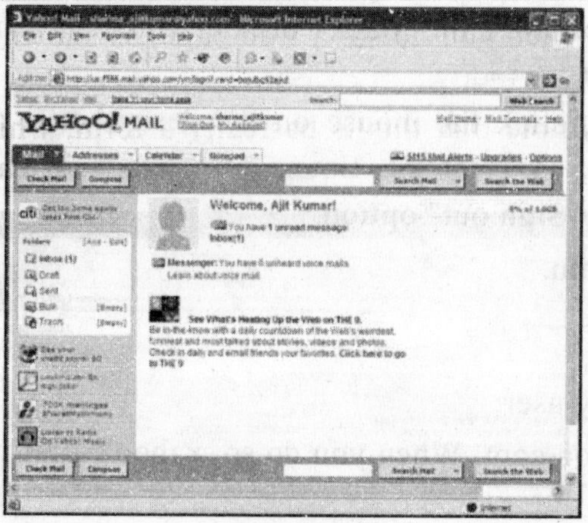

Figure 5.21

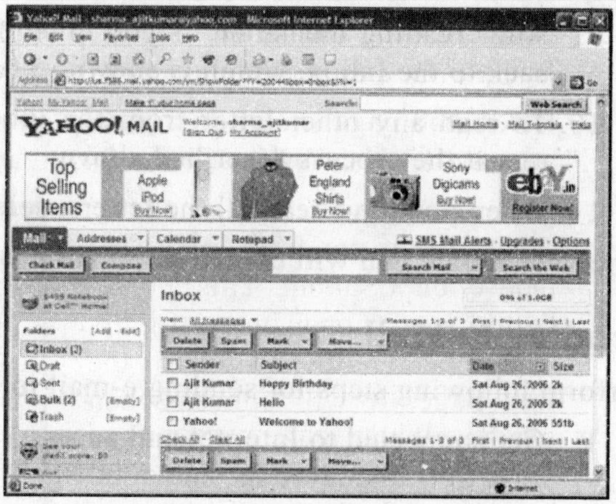

Figure 5.22

Refer above-illustrated figure and note that the details of the received letters are displayed under different headings. Description and meaning of all the headings are as follows:

Title	Meaning
Sender	It signifies the name of the person who has sent the e-mail.
Subject	This is the title of the letter, which gives an idea of the contents of the letter.
Date	It specifies the date, on which the e-mail was received.
Size	It signifies the size of the mail in Kilobytes.

Note that in this list, certain titles are displayed in bold letters, while some of them are displayed in the normal. The title displayed in bold letters, signifies that this letter has not yet been read. On the other hand, the letters, which have been read, are displayed in the normal text.

6. In order to read any letter, click the mouse on its title. As soon as you do so, the letter will get displayed on the screen and you will be able to read it. A sample letter that gets displayed in this way, is shown in figure 5.23.
7. Refer figure 5.23 and note that there is a button titled as "Reply". This button, when clicked, allows you to send the reply of the letter, without coming out of the letter.
8. If, after reading the letter, the letter is to be deleted from the inbox, select appropriate checkbox and click the mouse on "Delete" button.

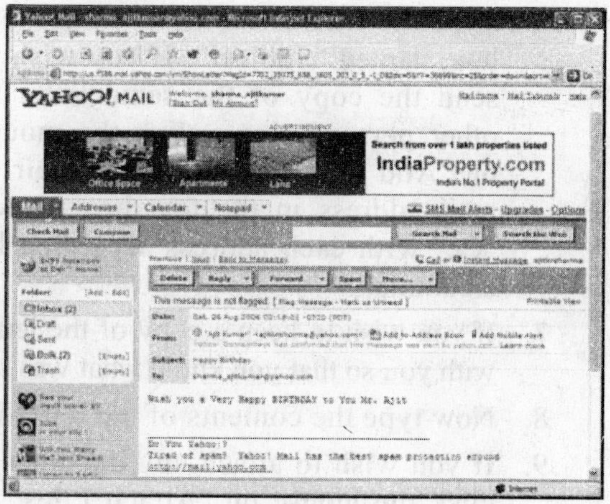

Figure 5.23

9. After reading the letter, if you click the mouse on "Back" button, you will return back to the Inbox, which is shown in figure 5.22.
10. To read any other letter from the inbox, click the mouse on the desired title and repeat the process described above.
11. When you have read all the letters, select "Sign out" option.

When you do so, you will exit from e-mail program.

Sending E-Mail

Perform following steps for sending e-mail to any user:

1. Get connected to Internet and access yahoo.com. When you do so, yahoo's first web page gets displayed as shown in figure 5.14.
2. Now click the mouse on "Mail" link. When you do so, a web page, as shown in figure 5.18 will appear on the screen.
3. Now enter your login name in the text box titled "Yahoo ID" and password in "Password" text box.
4. Click the mouse on "Sign In" button. When you do so, browser will display a web page, which is shown in figure 5.21.
5. Now click the mouse on "Compose" option. When you do so, a web page that facilitates you to write the letter, appears in browser window. This web page is shown in figure 5.24.
6. Now enter e-mail address of the person to whom you want to send the mail in the text box, titled "To". Type the title of the letter in the text box, named "Subject". If you wish to send the copy of the same letter to other persons also, click the mouse on "Add CC" link and enter their e-mail address in the text box named "Cc" with each address separated by a comma.

Figure 5.24

7. If you wish to keep a copy of the letter with you so that you know what was sent to whom, select "Save copy" check box.
8. Now type the contents of the letter in letter writing area.
9. If you wish to attach any document with your letter (that is present on your disk), click the mouse on "Attach Files" button. When you do so, you will be asked to specify the location and name of the document that you wish to attach. Specify the details, as per requirement.

10. After entering the contents of the letter, click the mouse on "Send" button. This will transmit the letter to the desired address and you will get a message on your screen (in the form of a web page) that your letter has been sent.

Exiting From E-Mail

After finishing all e-mail related activities, you should come out of email program. For this, make use of "Sign Out" option.

OTHER SERVICES OF INTERNET

As mentioned earlier, Internet is an ocean of information and services. Wide variety of services remain available on Internet. Whosoever wishes, can avail these services by visiting the website. Few popular services of Internet are described below.

1. Internet telephony is a service that enables its users to communicate with other persons. Using this service an Internet user can ring other person's normal telephone. If other person picks up his phone, communication path between the two gets established and they talk in the same way as two telephone users do. This type of telephony is called Net-To-Phone telephony.
2. News group is very popular service of Internet, in which a person has to become a member of a predefined group. Each group relates to a specific topic like wind surfing, multimedia, physics, video gaming, vintage cars etc. Members of the group exchange information, news, problems, solutions etc. among them.

   Due to the categorization of group, likeminded people become the member of the group. This keeps the discussion inline and helps members in seeking solutions for their questions and problem from other group members.
3. These are various web sites on Internet, which provide electronic greeting cards for all occasions and all reasons. These cards are generally very colorful, attractive and often animated. People access these web sites and send card to their friends and relatives.
4. There are various web sites on Internet, which provide facility for reading newspapers, magazines and articles on Internet.
5. Astrological web sites of Internet provide horoscope, future predictions and suggestions to the visitors, who visit the web site.
6. There are various web sites on Internet, which provide job opportunities to the persons seeking job. They also help employers in searching the right candidate.
7. Music, songs and radio can also be enjoyed over Internet.
8. There are various web sites, which sell different kinds of products. These web sites can be visited and products can be purchased from there. These web sites are often referred to as e-mall. Payment for the purchased items is made on-line through credit cards.
9. Numerous, free and paid computer games are available on Internet. They can be downloaded and played.
10. Advance booking in hotels, trains, aero planes etc. can be done through Internet.

EXERCISES CHAPTER 5

Short Type Questions

A. Select most appropriate answer for following questions:

1. In which type of network, computers are placed very near to each other?
   (a) LAN (b) WAN (c) Internet (d) World Wide Web
2. Which of the following is not the objective of computer network?
   (a) Share data (b) Share devices
   (c) Exchange messages (d) Share secret information.
3. What name is given to those computers of Internet, which provide information and services to other computers?
   (a) Web Client (b) Web Servers (c) Web Browsers (d) Web Sites
4. Which of the following requires 24 hours connectivity to Internet through fast data communication lines?
   (a) Web Client (b) Web Server (c) Both (d) None
5. How many numbers put together, constitute IP address of a web site?
   (a) 2 (b) 3 (c) 4 (d) Any number

B. Fill in the blanks:

6. LAN is acronym for ....
7. WAN is acronym for ....
8. Network of computer networks is known as ....
9. .... is the software, using which Internet related activities are performed.
10. Full form of DNS is ....

C. State, true or false for following statements:

11. A computer network, in which its computers are placed in different cities, is an example of Internet.
12. Internet Explorer is a web browser.
13. The text, which displays another piece of text, when mouse is clicked on it, is called hypertext.
14. Two or more web pages are linked together with the help of super links.
15. DNS server converts IP address into domain name.
16. The domain name xyz.com indicates that xyz is a commercial organization.

17. Web clients get connected to Internet for short durations. They only take information from it and get disconnected.
18. Broadband Internet connection is faster than Dialup connection
19. Users of e-mail service are identified by their login name and password.
20. yahoo.com is a website, which provides search facility.

D. Answer the following questions in short:

21. What name is given to the activity of visiting web sites?
22. Which software is used for web surfing?
23. Write a valid IP address.
24. Which two words will be essentially there in the domain name of Indian government web site?
25. Which protocol is used for transferring files from server to client?
26. What is yahoo.com?
27. Name any two famous services of Internet.
28. What name is given to those computers of Internet, which take information from other computers?
29. What is search engine and what it is used for?
30. Is Internet an example LAN or WAN?

E. Differentiate between following:

31. LAN and WAN.
32. Web Server and Web Client.
33. IP address and domain name.
34. Web Surfing and Web Browsing.
35. Web Site and Web Page.

Detailed Answer Type Questions

F. Answer the following questions in detail:

36. Define the term Internet. Name any three services of Internet.
37. What is IP address? What it is used for? How it is constituted?
38. What is domain name? Write general format of domain name.
39. How do you search information on a given topic on Internet?
40. What is e-mail? Write at least 2 advantages of e-mail.
41. Why users prefer domain name over IP address when they can access the sites by specifying the IP address? Explain by giving a suitable example.

42. What is Internet Telephony? What advantage it has over normal telephony?
43. What is web browsing? How do you perform it through Internet Explorer?
44. Explain the term hypertext, by taking a suitable example.
45. Write two advantages of Internet.
46. Describe the role of ISP in Internet.
47. Describe any three types of Internet connectivity.
48. Describe the role of DNS server in Internet.
49. What is protocol? Describe telnet and ftp.
50. Describe HTTP using a suitable diagram.

****

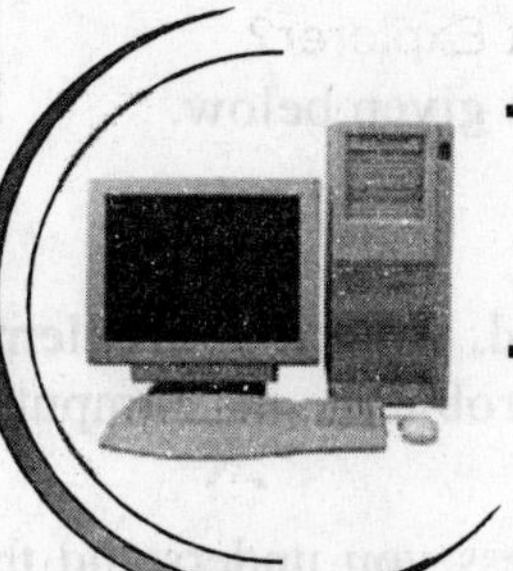

CHAPTER 6

Concepts Of Programming Methodology

INTRODUCTION

Computers are basically dumb devices. They cannot do anything on their own. Be it their internal tasks or user's application, they require step-by-step instructions for performing the task.

The set of instructions that is required to perform a given task is called program or computer program. For example, 20 instructions that would be required for finding the roots of a quadratic equation will be called a program. Similarly there could be another program for printing railway reservation tickets.

Computer programs are written in computer languages. Over the years many computer languages have come into existence. Each computer language is different from other but it has its own advantages and disadvantages and suits well for automating a particular type of task. C, C++, Java, Visual Basic etc. are few examples of popular computer languages.

The process of writing computer programs is called programming. Programming requires knowledge of computer language and aptitude for programming. In practice, many popular tools and techniques are followed for writing correct, efficient and maintainable programs. In this chapter, we will describe all important aspects of programming.

STEPS INVOLVED IN PROBLEM SOLVING

Problem solving is not a single activity but a multi step process. Each step comprises of specific type of activities.

All the steps of problem solving put together are often referred to as program development life cycle. Steps of program development life cycle are listed below.

(a) Understanding the problem

(b) Planning a solution (developing algorithm)

(c) Coding

(d) Editing, compiling and executing

(e) Debugging

(f) Documentation

Detailed description of each step of program development life cycle is given below.

Understanding the Problem

Before we describe the activities of this phase, let us first understand, what is a problem? Any task that is to be performed using computer is called Problem, in computer terminology.

For writing a program, you have to understand the problem first. Unless you understand the problem clearly you will not be able to write the program. For example, by simply, saying "Write a program to calculate the salary of all the employees, working in the organization", does not provide enough details for writing the program. The statement only conveys that a salary statement has to be generated but it does not provide any detail on the following issues:

- ❑ Which are the earning heads?
- ❑ Which are the deduction heads?
- ❑ In which format the output is to be printed.

Without knowing these details, if somebody starts writing the program then program will be totally hypothetical and it may not be of any use for the person for whom it is being written. In order to provide a useful solution, you will have to understand the problem in detail and find out all the aspects, which are closely associated with the problem. For example, if you have to write the program for the above-mentioned problem then you will have to find complete details of the problem i.e. all the earnings and all the deduction heads. A detailed study of these factors may reveal that:

(a) Earning heads include Basic pay, D.A at the rate of 150% of the basic pay, House rent at a fixed rate of Rs. 2000 and Overtime at the rate of Rs. 150 per hour worked etc.

(b) Deduction heads include, P.F at the rate of 11% of the Basic Pay and Income tax as per the rules stated by the government.

It is quite obvious that after knowing these details, gross and net salary can be calculated but on the other hand, these details are insufficient to generate the output in the desired format. You will also have to study the format of the output. Say the output report has the following format.

Employee Name	Basic Salary	DA	House Rent	Over Time	Total Earning	P.F.	Income Tax	Total Deduction	Net Salary

Figure 6.1

Once you have studied the problem in detail and gathered all the information, which is sufficient for writing the program, you can move to the next step of program development life cycle i.e. planning the solution.

Planning the Solution (Developing Algorithms)

Planning the solution means finalizing all those steps that are to be carried out for solving the problem. This step is often referred to as algorithm development or logic development phase.

In algorithm development phase, all the steps following which the problem will be solved are written on paper, in simple English like sentences.

In order to understand the activities of this phase, let's consider the above-mentioned example (preparation of salary statement) and plan a solution for it. To provide the solution to this problem, you will have to identify the following:

(a) What are the minimum number of inputs that are required for the solution and how the data will be accepted within the program? For example, in the above-mentioned example, Name and the Basic salary are the two inputs that will be required for completely solving the problem. To acquire this data in the program, you may decide to accept it either through keyboard (if the data is small) or you may decide to read it from the data file (if the data volume is large).

(b) How will other information get generated or you can say, how the processing will be done.

For example here, DA will be calculated by multiplying Basic salary by 150 /100. Similarly other earning heads will also be calculated. Thus Gross-pay will be calculated by adding Basic pay, DA, House rent and Overtime.

For deduction, PF will be calculated at the rate of 11% of the basic pay. Similarly income tax will be calculated on the basis of basic pay, as per the rules of the government. Thus total deductions will be calculated by adding all the deduction heads.

At last Net pay will be calculated by subtracting total deductions from the gross salary.

(c) How and where printing will be done and what methods will be required for generating the desired output. For example, you may decide to print the above-mentioned report on the printer.

(d) If the data has to be processed for many identities then you will have to decide the strategy for repeating the steps. For repeating the steps, you will have to form a loop by incorporating a suitable condition, using which loop executes as many times as required and after that it breaks for finishing the task.

For example, if the salary has to be calculated and printed for 1000 employees then salary calculation and printing steps will have to be repeated by forming a loop that executed 1000 times.

Coding

Refer all above mentioned steps and note that these steps are simply a plan on paper for attaining a solution, not the exact solution. The exact solution has to exist in the form of commands written in computer language. While planning the solution above-mentioned steps are written in general English. In the coding phase of programming cycle, you have to translate the steps of solution plan into computer language. These translated steps in the form of computer language are called "Program" and this procedure of translation is called Coding.

Editing, Compiling and Executing

In this phase, program is written on computer, using a text editor. After entering the program it is compiled so that the sentences of the program get converted into machine language. When the program has been compiled you have to execute the program. When you execute the program, all the steps of the program come into action and produce the result accordingly.

Debugging

Newly developed program may have few errors in it. These errors can occur due to various reasons. Either you may have forgotten some of the steps or you may have performed wrong operations or you may have used wrong logic in the program. For example, while calculating the gross pay you may subtract gross pay from the total deductions thus getting the negative value. All such types of errors have to be found out in the program and corrected so that the program gives correct results. The process of finding mistakes in the program and correcting them is called debugging.

Documentation

A correct program is of very little use, unless it is supported by full description in writing. Detailed description of the program is called documentation. Program documentation is done with two objectives. First is to enable the user to operate the program correctly and the second is to enable the other person to understand the program, so that if necessary, he could modify or correct the program.

CONCEPT OF ALGORITHM

Algorithm is basically a step-by-step solution for solving a given problem. When solution is sought for solving the problem through computer, all the steps are framed in the light of basic operations that computer can perform. What computer can do is described below.

WHAT COMPUTER CAN DO

Basic operations that computers can perform are very limited. These operations are:

1. Read data
2. Write data
3. Make comparison
4. Create variables and assign values to them
5. Do processing
6. Loop formation

An introduction of all these activities is given below.

Read Data

Computer can read the data from three sources i.e. either from program itself or from the keyboard or from data file. It totally remains on the discretion of the programmers to select the source from where the data will be fetched in the program. All the programming languages provide commands for reading the data from all the three sources.

Write Data

Computer can display data and print it too. Data can either be printed on printer or in a file. All the programming languages provide commands for all these activities.

Make Comparison

Computer can compare only two given values at a time. For example, if A and B are two given values then it can make comparisons like "IS A>B", "IS A<B", "IS A=B" etc.

The result of comparison is either true or false. If the given condition holds good, the result of comparison is true. On the other hand, if the condition doesn't hold good, result is false. For building the conditions, following types of operators are used:

Conditional Operators

Sign	Meaning	Sign	Meaning
=	Equal to	>=	Greater than or equal to
>	Greater than	<=	Less than or equal to
<	Less than	<>	Not equal to

Relational Operators

OR	Joins two conditions and gives true if either of the condition is true or both of them are true. In all other cases it gives false.
AND	Joins two conditions and gives false if either of the condition is false or both of them are false. In all other cases it gives true.
NOT	If the condition is true, it gives false. If it is false, it gives true.

Create Variables And Assign Values

Variables can be defined as memory locations, which are assigned a name for reference. For example, Number1=0 means Number1 is a variable whose value is 0. Similarly Pay=10000 means Pay is a variable, which holds 10000 in it.

Note that in computers, statements like Pay=Pay+1000 are used. Statements of such type are algebraically wrong but in reference to computer, they are correct. This statement simply increases current values of Pay variables by 1000. For example, if its value was 10000 then after execution of this statement, it will become 11000.

Do Processing

Computers can do calculations. Calculations that they do are called processing. For processing, computer languages provide following operators:

Operator	Meaning	Operator	Meaning
+	Addition	/	Division
-	Subtraction	*	Multiplication
^	Raised to the power of (Exponentiation)	()	Brackets

Loop

Computer can process a single or more steps repeatedly. When it does so, it is said that a loop has been formed. Following is an example of loop:

1. A=0
2. B=A+10
3. Display B
4. Repeat Step 2 and 3, 4 more times.

Here step 4 forms a loop and makes a provision that the value of B gets increased and displayed five times.

CHARACTERISTICS OF AN ALGORITHM

Following are the characteristics of algorithm:

1. Algorithms always have a definite starting point and an end point. These points are generally marked with the words like Start, Begin, End, Stop etc.
2. They consist of finite number of steps.
3. They always relate to a specific problem or you can say that they are written for a given problem.
4. They serve as foundation stone for programming.
5. They are written in easy language. Their sentences are always unambiguous and are easy to understand.

WRITING ALGORITHMS TO DEPICT LOGIC

You are now familiar with algorithm and their characteristics, so let's write few algorithms for following problems:

Problem-1

Let's write algorithm for swapping contents of two variables.

Algorithm-1

1. Start
2. Read value of A
3. Read value of B
4. C=A
5. A=B
6. B=C
7. Print A
8. Print B
9. End

This algorithm makes use of intermediate variable C. It holds value of A in it, temporarily and later assigns it to B variable. Thus values of variable A and B get interchanged.

There is another way of interchanging the values i.e. without making use of intermediate variable. Algorithm for it is given below.

1. Start
2. Read value of A and B
3. A=A+B
4. B=A-B
5. A=A-B
6. Print A, B
7. End

Problem-2

Let's write an algorithm to find the largest of given three numbers.

Algorithm-2

1. Start
2. Read three numbers A, B and C
3. Let Big=0
4. IF A>B Then Big=A Else Big=B
5. IF C>Big Then Big=C
6. Print Big
7. End

Problem-3

Let's write an algorithm for calculating and printing factorial of a given number.

Algorithm-3

1. Start
2. Read a number, A
3. Let I=1
4. Let Sum=1
5. Sum=Sum*I
6. I=I+1
7. If I is not > A perform step 5, 6 and 7
8. Print Sum
9. End

Problem-4

Let's write an algorithm for solving a given quadratic equation, $ax^2+bx+c=0$. Note that roots are determined by following formula:

$$x = \frac{-b \pm \sqrt{b^2 - 4ac}}{2a}$$

Algorithm-4

1. Start
2. Read value of a, b and c
3. If a=0 Stop
4. Calculate values of discriminate $D=b^2-4ac$
5. If D=0 then there is one root p=-b/2a
6. If D>0 then there are two real roots

   $p = \frac{b+\sqrt{D}}{2a}$ and $q = \frac{-b-\sqrt{D}}{2a}$
7. If D<0 then there are two complex roots

   $p = \frac{-b+i\sqrt{-D}}{2a}$ and $q = \frac{-b-i\sqrt{-D}}{2a}$
8. Print p and q
9. Stop

PROBLEMS WITH ALGORITHMS

As mentioned earlier, algorithms are written in English like sentences. Sentences are always subject to misinterpretation.

If the sentence is complex, different readers may interpret it differently. This definitely leads to problems at the time of coding.

To overcome this problem, often the solution of the problem is provided in pictorial form. Pictures carry more meaning and don't lead to ambiguity. Such type of step-by-step solution, provided in pictorial form is called flowchart. Details of flowchart are given below.

FLOWCHARTS

When a step-by-step solution of a given problem is illustrated in the form of graphical chart that chart is called flowchart.

FLOWCHARTS SYMBOLS

Flowchart is a universal tool, using which solution providers communicate the solution of a given problem to the programmers so that they can translate the steps (of flowchart) into computer language and transform it into a computer program. To make the process universal and unambiguous, symbols of flowcharts have been standardized. These symbols and their meaning are explained below.

Read

A parallelogram is used to depict reading process in the flowchart. To make the process more illustrative, the word "Read" is written along with variable names, within the parallelogram. For example, the word "Read Pay", written within the parallelogram states that value of Pay has to be read and stored in Pay variable. Similarly "Read Number" states that a number has to be read and the value has to be stored in a variable named, Number. Use of read symbol is illustrated in Figure 6.2.

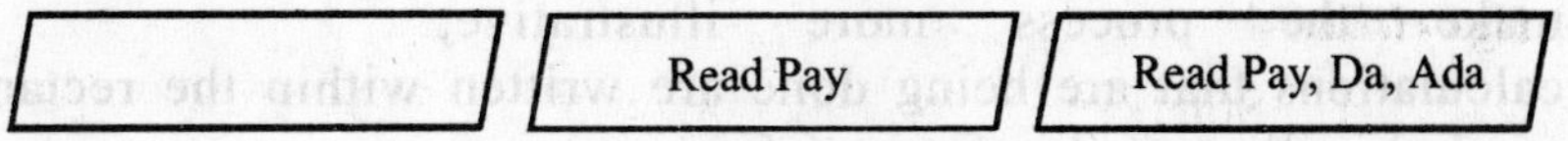

Figure 6.2

Often multiple values have to be read one after the other. In such cases, instead of making use of multiple read symbols and making the flowchart lengthy, one read symbol is used and names of all the variables are written in it. This is illustrated in last symbol of Figure 6.2.

Write

In flowcharts, parallelogram is also used to depict writing / displaying process. To make the writing process more illustrative, the word Write, along with names of the variables (whose values have to be printed / displayed) are written within the parallelogram. Use of write symbol is illustrated in figure 6.3.

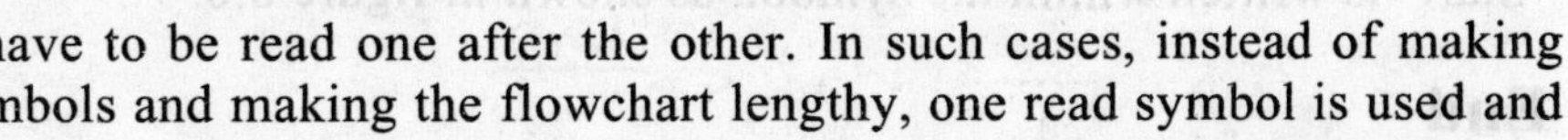

Figure 6.3

Values of multiple variables can also be displayed / printed, using single symbol, as illustrated in figure 63.3.

Condition Checking / Decision

Symbol shown in figure 6.4 is used for depicting comparison of two values or condition checking or decision-making etc. The condition that is to be checked is written within the figure.

It is quite obvious that whenever a condition will be checked there will be two outcomes i.e. either the condition will be true (condition holds good) or it will be false (condition doesn't hold good).

These two outcomes are shown as two branches coming out of the symbol. To clearly illustrate, which branch relates to true and which branch relates to false, the words Yes (or Y or True or T) and No (or N or False or F) are written near the branches. This process is illustrated in figure 6.4.

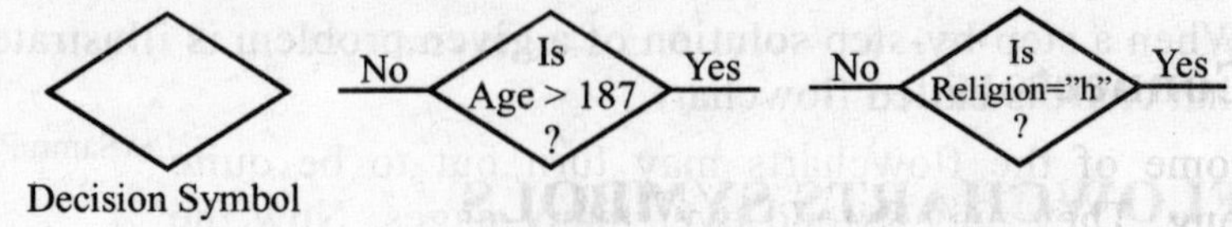

Figure 6.4

Processing

In flowcharts, processing or calculation activities are depicted, using a rectangle. To make the process more illustrative, calculations that are being done are written within the rectangle. The use of processing symbol is illustrated in figure 6.5.

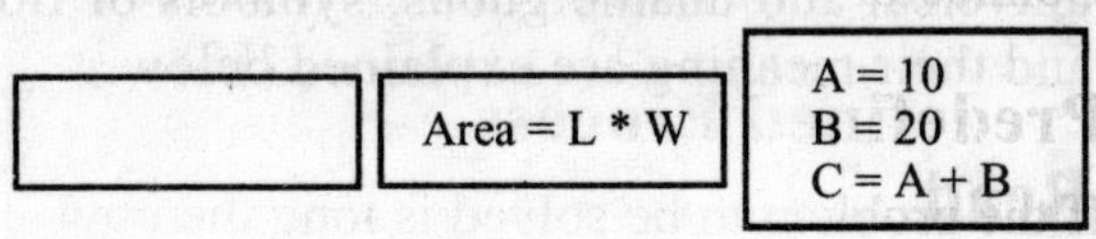

Figure 6.5

Start

Like algorithm, flowchart must have a definite starting point. Starting point of the flowchart is depicted through a flat oval shape symbol, as shown in figure 6.6. To make the symbol more illustrative, the word "Start" is written within the symbol, as shown in figure 6.6.

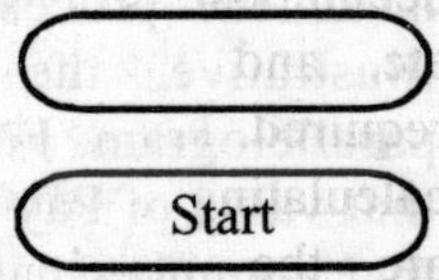

Figure 6.6

End

Like algorithm, flowchart must have a definite end point. End point of the flowchart is depicted through a flat oval shape symbol, as shown in figure 6.7. To make the symbol more illustrative, the word "End" is written within the symbol, as shown in figure 6.7.

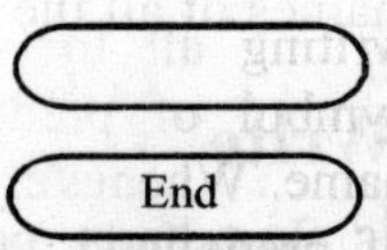

Figure 6.7

Flow Lines

Joining many symbols together makes a flowchart. As you know, each symbol of the chart represents an activity. Which activity will be conducted after which activity, is depicted with help of flow lines. A flow line is a simple line with an arrow at its front end. The head of the arrow depicts the direction of flow. Flow lines are illustrated in figure 6.8.

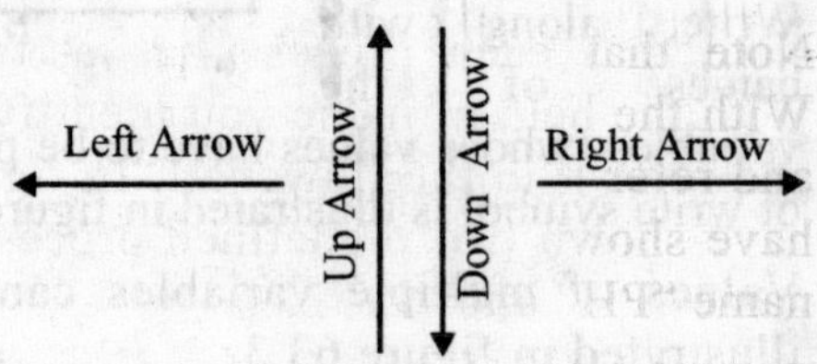

Figure 6.8

For example, if the third step is connected to seventh symbol, using a flow line, it will indicate that after executing third step seventh step is to be executed. Step four, five and six are not to be executed in this case.

An up arrow is used for depicting a loop in the flowcharts. For example, if fifth step is connected to the third step, using an up arrow flow line, it will mean that after executing fifth step, third step is to be executed again. Note that this is nothing but a loop.

Connectors

Figure 6.9

Some of the flowcharts may turn out to be quite long. They may extend over many pages. Now the question is, how do you connect the processes, which are either far apart or are off the pages? For such type of requirements, two types of connectors are used. One is called same page connector and another is called "Off Page Connector". Both the connectors are shown in figure 6.9.

Predefined Process

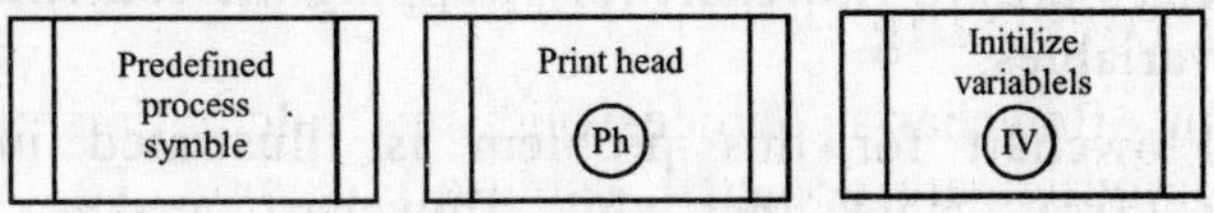

Figure 6.10

If the problem to be solved is long then by showing all the steps in the same flowchart may make the chart complex. To avoid the complexity and keep the flowchart simple, you have to decompose the problem. In decomposition, you identify the group of mundane routines, such as initialization of variables etc. and the routines, which are repeatedly required. For example, printing the header lines, calculating a value based on certain formula etc. are the tasks that have to be performed repeatedly. You draw a flowchart for these processes separately and declare them as predefined processes and assign them name for reference. In the main flowchart, instead of writing all the steps, you simply include the symbol of predefined process along with the name. Whenever one wants to go into the details of predefined process, he refers corresponding chart separately. The symbol and use of predefined process is illustrated in figure 6.10.

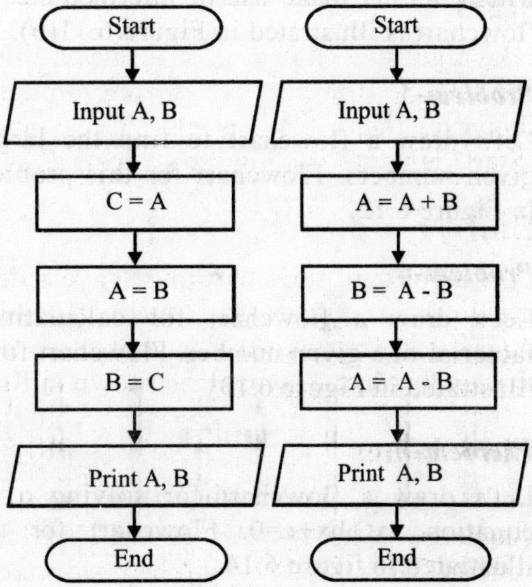

Figure 6.11

Note that each process has a unique name. With the help of name you identify the process and refer it in the flowchart. In figure 6.10, we have shown two predefined processes with the name "PH" and "IV".

From the description of flowchart, given above, it is quite clear that flowchart is nothing but a graphical representation of the solution for a given problem, in which you make use of standard graphical symbols and within the symbol, you write the details of the operation. For communicating the details of the activities of a particular step, you have to include some text within the symbol. For this, you have to often make use of different types of operators. A list of arithmetic, relational and conditional operators is given in algorithm section.

DRAWING THE FLOWCHART

Now you are familiar with flowchart definition and flowchart symbols, so let's draw few flowcharts for given problems.

Problem-4

Let's draw a flowchart for swapping the contents of two variables.

Flowchart for this problem is illustrated in figure 6.11(a). Note that this flowchart makes use of intermediate variable, C to interchange the values of two variables A and B.

This flowchart can be redrawn to depict the method, which doesn't make use of intermediate variable. Such a flowchart is illustrated in Figure 6.11(b).

Problem-5

Let's draw a flowchart to find the larger of the three given numbers. Flowchart for this problem is illustrated in Figure 6.12.

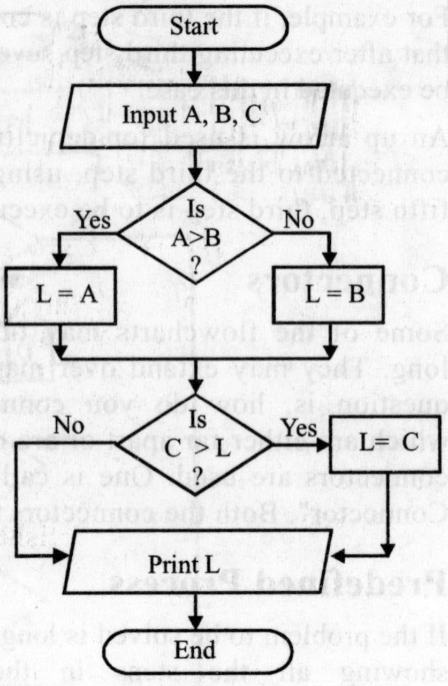

Figure 6.12

Problem-6

Let's draw a flowchart for calculating and printing factorial of a given number. Flowchart for this problem is illustrated in Figure 6.13

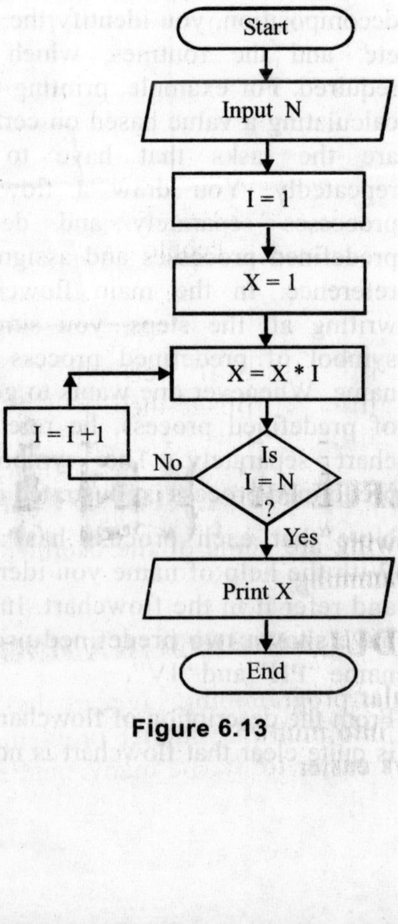

Figure 6.13

Problem-7

Let's draw a flowchart for solving a given quadratic equation $ax^2+bx+c=0$. Flowchart for this problem is illustrated in figure 6.14.

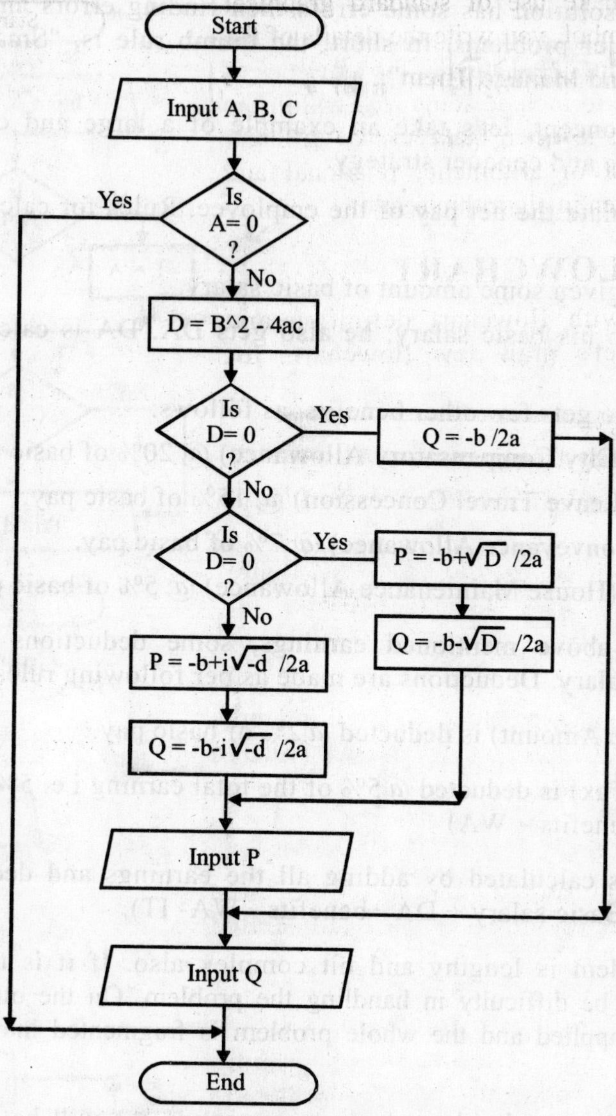

Figure 6.14

USEFUL PRACTICES IN PROGRAMMING

Following are some of the useful practices, which need to be followed religiously while programming:

MODULAR PROGRAMMING

Modular programming suggests that a large or complex problem, should always be broken down into multiple smaller problems and each problem should be dealt individually. It is always easier to handle many smaller problems rather than one large problem. In addition to this, if suggested solution has some errors then finding errors and fixing them is also easy in case of smaller problems. In short, the thumb rule is, "Small Is Manageable, so Make Many Smalls and Manage Them".

To understand the concept, let's take an example of a large and complex problem and handle it, using divide and conquer strategy.

Say we have to calculate the net pay of the employee. Rules for calculating the pay are as follows:

1. Employee is given some amcunt of basic salary.
2. In addition to his basic salary, he also gets DA. DA is calculated @150% of his basic salary.
3. Employee also gets few other benefits, as follows:
   (a) CCA (City Compensatory Allowance) @ 20% of basic pay.
   (b) LTC (Leave Travel Concession) @ 15% of basic pay.
   (c) CA (Conveyance Allowance) @ 7% of basic pay.
   (d) HMA (House Maintenance Allowance) @ 5% of basic pay.
4. Apart from above mentioned earnings, some deductions are also made from employee's salary. Deductions are made as per following rules:
5. WA (Welfare Amount) is deducted @2% of basic pay.
6. IT (Income Tax) is deducted @5% of the total earning i.e. 5% of (basic pay + DA + Sum of all benefits – WA)
7. Net salary is calculated by adding all the earnings and deducting all deductions from it (i.e. Basic salary + DA +benefits - WA- IT).

Note that this problem is lengthy and bit complex also. If it is treated as single large problem, there may be difficulty in handling the problem. On the other hand, if divide and conquer strategy is applied and the whole problem is fragmented into small units, it can be handled easily.

To handle this problem in divide and conquer manner, we will have three modules. First module will be the main module, which will take care of primary activities. Other two modules will handle benefit calculation and income tax calculations. This strategy is applied in the given flowchart, show in figure 6.15.

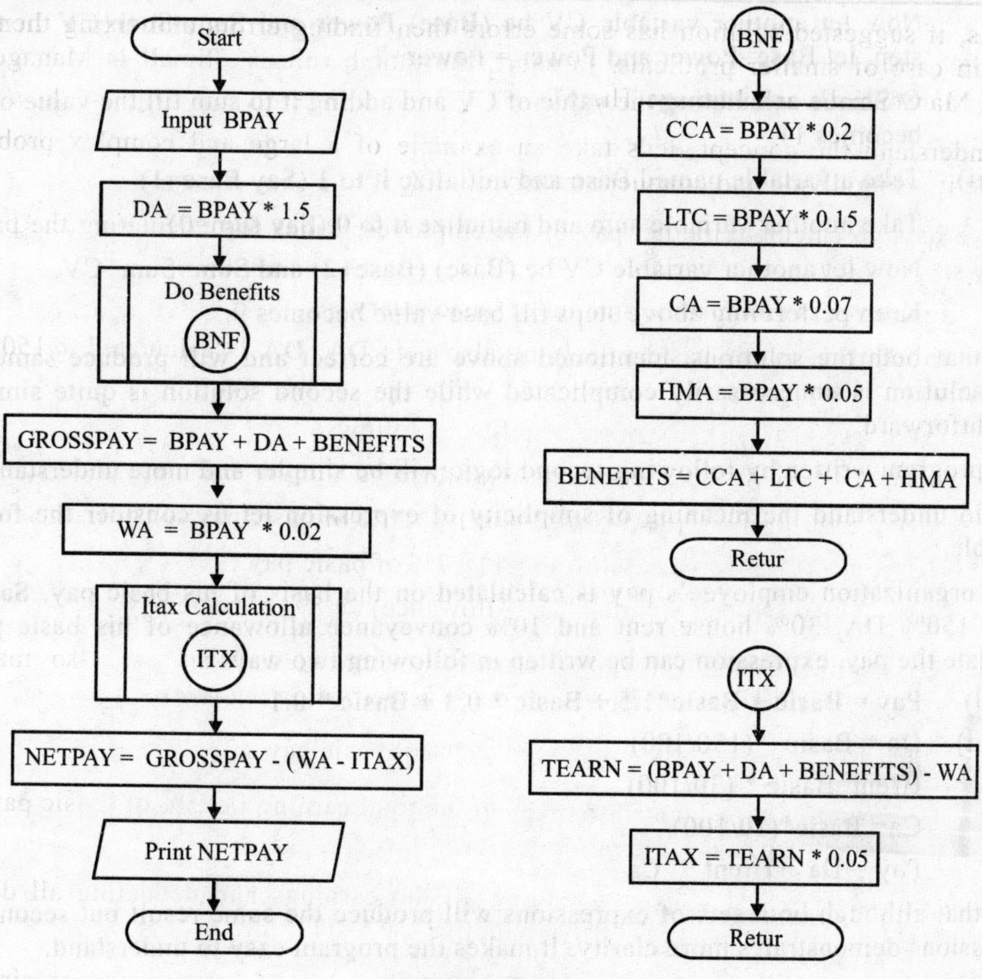

Figure 6.15

Clarity and Simplicity of Expressions

For providing computerized solution of any given problem, logic has to be built into the program and various expressions need to be built. To make the program understandable, logic should always be kept simple and expressions should be built in such a way that they convey the meaning at first glance. To understand the concept of simplicity of logic, consider following problem:

Say you are supposed to find out the sum of the following series:

$1^3 + 3^5 + 5^7 + 7^9 + 9^{11}$

Logic for solving above problem can be built in two ways:

(i) Take a variable for the base number and initialize it to 1 (say base=1).
Take another variable for the power and initialize it to 3 (Say Power=3).
Take a variable sum and initialize it to 0 (Say Sum=0)

Now let another variable CV be (Base) Power and Sum=Sum+CV In the next step, let Base=Power and Power = Power+2

Continue calculating the value of CV and adding it to sum till the value of Power becomes 11.

(ii) Take a variable named Base and initialize it to 1 (Say Base=1)

Take another variable sum and initialize it to 0 (Say sum=0)

Now let another variable CV be (Base) (Base+2) and Sum=Sum+CV.

Keep performing above steps till base value becomes 9.

Note that both the solutions, mentioned above are correct and will produce same result. First solution is unnecessarily complicated while the second solution is quite simple and straightforward.

Thus program written by following second logic will be simpler and more understandable.

Now to understand the meaning of simplicity of expression let us consider the following example.

In an organization employee's pay is calculated on the basis of his basic pay. Say, he is given 150% DA, 30% house rent and 10% conveyance allowance of his basic pay. To calculate the pay, expression can be written in following two ways :

(i) Pay = Basic + Basic*1.5 + Basic * 0.3 + Basic * 0.1

(ii) Da = Basic *(150/100)
Hrent=Basic * (30/100)
Ca= Basic*(10/100)
Pay = Da + Hrent + Ca

Note that although both sets of expressions will produce the same result but second set of expressions demonstrates more clarity. It makes the program easy to understand.

You are now familiar with the concept of clarity and simplicity in reference to programming. Following are few guidelines for bringing clarity in logic and making the expression simple.

(i) Avoid pushing too may operations in single line of the program.
(ii) Avoid using tricky logic, which cannot be followed by other persons.
(iii) Make use of brackets liberally to make the expression more meaningful.
(iv) Make use of standard library functions to improve the readability of the program.
(v) While writing the program, keep the focus on simplicity rather than on making the program short.

Proper Names for Identifiers

Identifiers, identify different components of a program, thus their names play an important role in the understandability of the program. For example, if the variable name is such that it gives an idea of what it is then obviously it will improve the readability of the program.

For example A=r*q does not convey any meaning while Amount = Rate * Quantity gives a complete idea of the activity being performed. Similarly when you write GOTO Err it gives an idea that the program control is being transferred to error handling routine. Following are few guidelines for choosing the names for identifiers.

(i) The names should be meaningful and should identify the nature of subjects to which they are related. For example, variable names, like Name, Address, Telephone No are more meaningful rather than variable names like, N, A,T etc.

(ii) All identifier names should look different from others at first sight, so that no confusion takes place. For example, to store two different types of totals variables like sum and sun could be used. But most likely they may be mistakenly read as same by other persons. So a better way would be to use two variables, which in no way look similar. For example, Sum1, Sum2 etc.

Using Comments

Each programming language provides the facility for writing comments in the program. Comments do not initiate action, but they serve as remarks. It is a good practice to use comments liberally in the program. For example, a comment line, like "Income Tax Calculations" within pay calculation program will make it very clear that following logic is for income tax calculations. It is quite obvious that the use of comment lines within the program will improve the readability and understandability of the program.

Use of Indentation

Most of the programming languages that are being used today are format free languages. Format free languages do not impose restrictions on starting and finishing points of the line. They allow you to start the line from any place and end it at any place. This liberty can be utilized for indenting the lines and enhancing the clarity and readability of the program. To understand the concept of indentation consider following piece of code.

```
if (a<b)
{
    a=a*2
    b=b*2
    if (a<c)
    {
        d=c-a
        e=c+a
    }
    else
    {
        d=c+a
```

```
        e=c-a
    }
    else
    {
        a=a*a
        b=b*b
    }
}
```

Note that not all the lines of the program start from the same place. They have been shifted towards right to clearly indicate the following things:

(i) Which are the steps that are being performed when a < b and which steps are being carried out when a is not less than b.

(ii) Which else is related to which if.

(iii) Which closing bracket is for which opening bracket.

It is quite obvious that such practice of indentation will make the program logic more clear and automatically remove confusions of various kinds.

Using Line Breaks

Putting many commands in one line makes the program complex. Make use of line breaks to improve the readability of the program.

EXECUTING A PROGRAM

Once the translation of an algorithm into computer language is complete, paper program gets ready. Now this program has to undergo following steps:

1. Entering program into computer
2. Compiling
3. Linking
4. Execution
5. Debugging

Entering Program into computer

In this phase the program, written on paper in entered into computer. For this we make use of some text editor program.

Text editor enables us to type the program in computer, make changes in it and save it in the computer in the form of a file so that it could be reused, whenever required. The program file that is saved on computer is known as source program or source file. It serves as input for the next step.

Compilation

Compilation is a process in which source program is converted in machine language so that it could be executed.

The process of compilation is performed by special software called compiler. For example, C language compiler will be required for compiling C language programs.

Each language suggests standard syntax for all those statements that you write in a program. The language remains rigid about the syntax and accepts no variation in that. It is likely that while writing the program, programmer may write the syntax incorrectly. Such mistakes may go unnoticed at the time of writing the program, but they are clearly pointed out at the time of compilation by the compiler. **All those errors, which occur due to wrong syntax, are called syntax errors or compilation errors.**

Unless all compilation errors are removed, the program cannot be executed. To remove syntax errors from any program, you have to again edit the given program and correct the mistakes. Following are some of the examples of syntax errors:

(i) a= =b //double = is not valid for assignment.

(ii) a * b = c //on the left hand side of equality, only variable can appear not the expression

Linking

Most of the computer languages provide wide variety of pre-written programs, for performing common tasks. For example, C language provides pre-written programs to find absolute value of a given number, comparing the equality of two strings etc. Such programs are referred to as functions. Generally these functions remain available to the programmers in the form of standard libraries.

Any programmer can make use of these functions in his program by just writing their names in specified syntax.

Linking is the process in which all the library functions are assembled into complied program and one final executable program is generated.

Executing the Program

Once executable program is ready, it can be executed whenever required. When program is executed, it gets loaded into computer's memory and the execution starts from its first line. After first line second line gets executed and the process continues line by line till the end of the program.

Debugging

It is not necessary that the program may run efficiently and produce correct results in first run. Some logical errors may go unnoticed in the program. Due to the logical errors, program gives wrong results. For example, instead of using + sigh in a statement programmer may, by mistake, use some other sign like – or * etc. Obviously this mistake will not surface out at the time of compilation, but it will give wrong results at the time of execution.

The process of identifying such errors and removing them is called debugging. Certain types of bugs do not surface out in normal working conditions. Such bugs are hard to find. They require rigorous testing.

Once run time error is found, you have to again go back to the source program, modify it and execute all other steps thereafter.

In short, it can be said that writing correct, efficient and maintainable program is an iterative process. It requires step-wise refinement of the program.

STRUCTURED PROGRAMMING

Structured programming is basically a style of programming that provides means by which, programmers can easily follow code written by other programmers. In other words it can be said that structured programming is a procedure oriented method of designing and coding a program.

To understand the concept of structured programming, let's first understand what non structured programming is. In non structured programming, programmer remains free to arrange the logical sentences of the program, in any order and in any way, as far as it performs the given task. Following is a pseudo code that illustrates non structured programming:

```
10 Start
20 Get Basic salary data
30 GoTo Line 1000
40 Get Saving data
50 GoTo Line 1020
60 Calculate Net Salary
70 Print Tax and Net Salary
80 Stop
1000 Do Salary calculation
1010 GoTo line 40
1020 Do Tax calculations
1030 GoTo line 60
1040 End
```

Observe the use of GoTo statement in this pseudo code, which transfers the program control from here to there several times within such a small program. Had the program been long (say 1000 lines extending over multiple pages), it would have been very difficult to trace the logic of the program.

In the earlier days of programming, this approach was practiced by most of the programmers. But later strict rules were suggested and programmers were encouraged to practice those rules. All those rules put together were given the name, structure programming. If you write the program following those rules, it results into structured program.

Structured programming avoids the use of unconditional jumping (GoTo statement) and suggests number of constructs that are used to define the sequence, in which the program statements are to be executed. These constructs are described below.

Consecutive

Concept of consecutive construct is illustrated in figure 6.16. Statements, within a structured program are normally executed in the same sequence as they are written within the program. For example, if a code fragment comprises of three statements then statements-1 will be executed first, statements-2 second and statements-3 last. To change the sequence, programmer can easily make use of GoTo statement. But structured programming restricts use of GoTo statements. It suggests other constructs, which are described below.

Illustration	Algorithm	Example
1	Statements-1	Get value of A
2	Statement-2	B=500+A*2
3	Statement-3	Print B

Figure 6.16

Block

Block comprises of group of statements. A group always has a well defined beginning and end. The symbol or keywords are used to mark the beginning and end of the block. The keywords or marks differ from one language to other. For example, in C language, beginning of the block is marked by opening curly brace ({) and the end is marked by closing curly brace (}). All the statements written within opening and closing brace are identified as one block. Following is a block in C language:

```
{
Statement-1;
```

```
Statement-2;
Statement-3;
}
```

Subroutine

A subroutine is basically a code that is written for performing a specific task. For example, in pay calculation program, income tax is to be calculated. Income tax calculation, logic could be separated from the preceding and following code and placed at appropriate place within the program (say at the end of the program).

Subroutines are identified by their name. Whenever, whenever required, within the program they can be called by writing their name.

Whenever subroutine is called, program control is transferred to the subroutine. When program control reaches subroutine, its first statement gets executed then second and then third and so on. Execution gradually proceeds further line by line till the end of the subroutine. After executing the last statement of the subroutine, program control returns back to the next statement form where it had come to the subroutine.

Concept of subroutine is illustrated in figure 6.17.

Illustration	Algorithm	Result
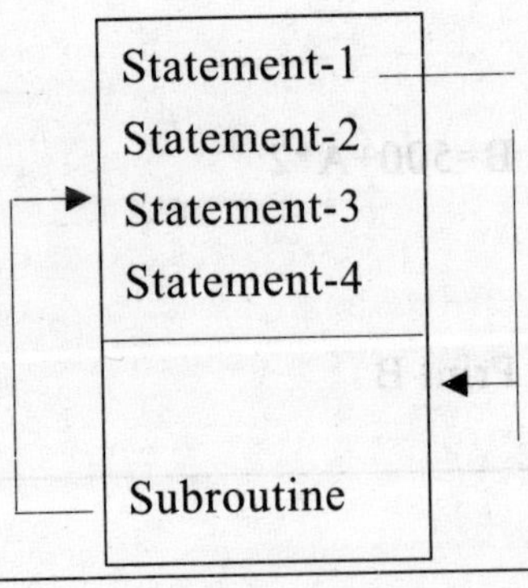	A=100 Call DISP Print (A*2) Print (A*3) End DISP Print A*4 Print A*5 Return	400 500 200 300

Figure 6.17

Once the subroutine has been defined, it can then be called from one or more places within the program. This allows a program to perform the same task number of times without re-writing the same code.

Note that a single call statement replaces all of the statements contained within the subroutine.

Function

A function is similar to subroutine, except that the function always returns a single value to the calling program. Function is generally called implicitly by embedding the function in a statement. Concept of function is illustrated in figure 6.18.

Illustration	Algorithm	Example	Result
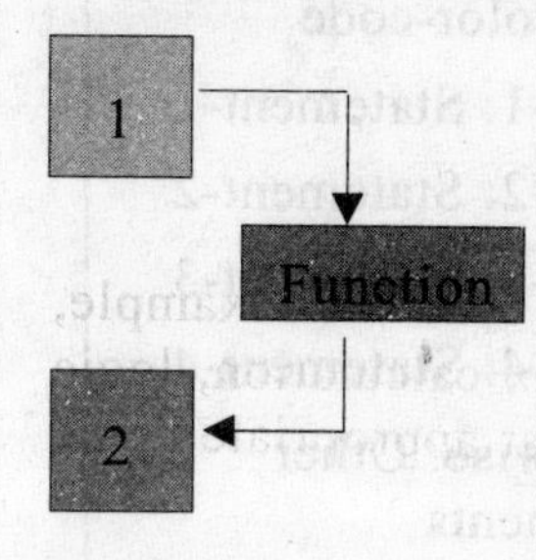	var 1= function-x(var2) ------------ ------------ ------------ Function-x(var2) Statement-1 Statement-2 Return var3	a=square(b) print a square(c) d=c*c Return d	if b=3 then 9 will be printed.

Figure 6.18

Branching

In branching construct, a given condition is evaluated. If the given condition is found true, a set of statements is executed. On the other hand, if it is found false, another set of statements is executed. Concept of branching is illustrated in figure 6.19.

Illustration	Algorithm	Example

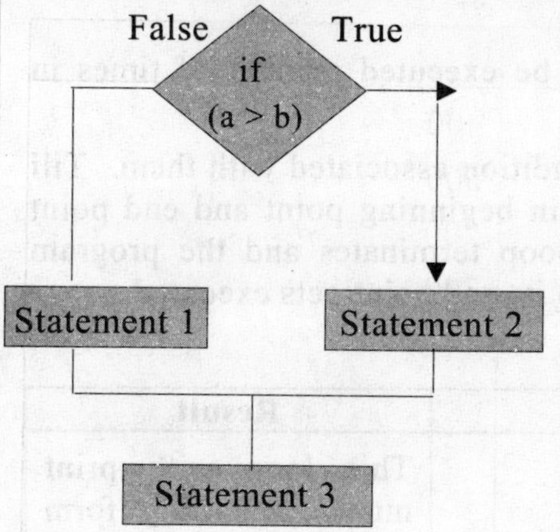	if (condition-1)
	Statement 1
	else
	Statement 2
		if (a>b)
		Print a is bigger than b.
		else
		print b is bigger than a.

Figure 6.19

Case

Case construct is similar to branch construct, except that in branching there are only two outcomes from the evaluation of the given condition, i.e. True or False but in case construct there could be may outcomes. For example, color code may either be r (red) or g (green) or b (blue) or y (yellow). If you wish to execute different segments (branches) of the program, in the event of finding different color codes then case construct comes handy. Case construct evaluates current code value and depending upon its value, transfers the program control to the respective branch of the program. Concept of case construct is illustrated in figure 6.20.

<table>
<tr><td>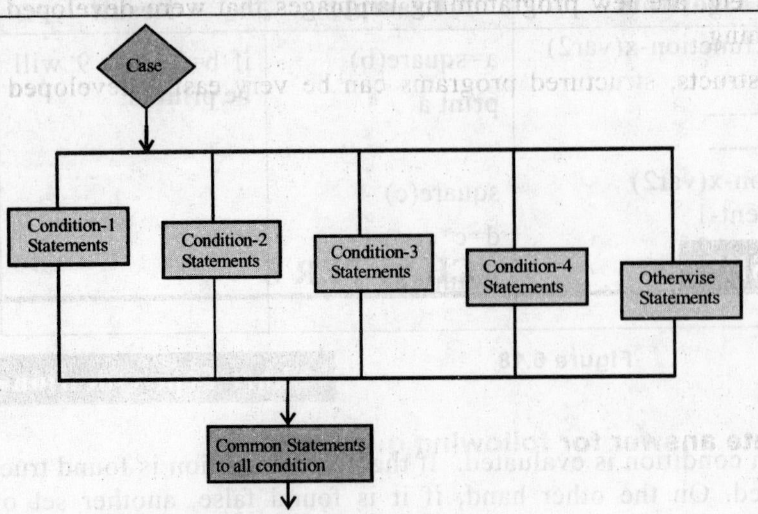
</td><td>Algorithm
Case color-code
Value-1: Statement-1
Value-2: Statement-2
Value-3: Statement-3
Value-4: Statement-4
Otherwise: Other Statements</td></tr>
</table>

Figure 6.20

Loops

Loops allow single statement or multiple statements to be executed number of times in succession.

All the loops have a beginning point, end point and a condition associated with them. Till the time condition remains true, statements written within beginning point and end point are executed. The moment condition becomes false, loop terminates and the program control come out of the loop and statement written next to its end point gets executed.

Concept of loop is illustrated in figure 6.21.

<table>
<tr><th>Illustration</th><th>Example</th><th>Result</th></tr>
<tr><td>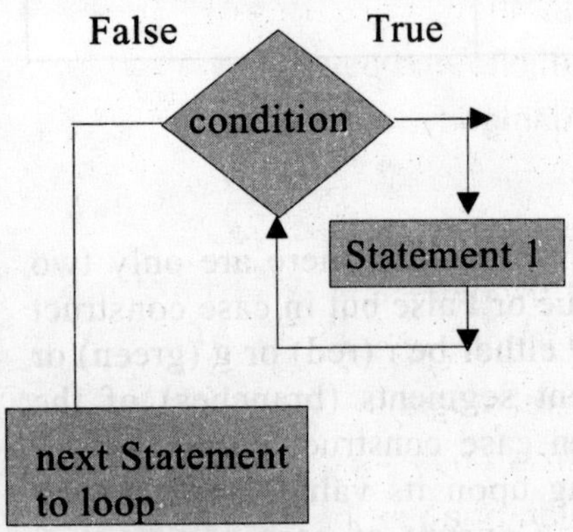
</td><td>a =1
While (a<=10)
{
print a
a=a+1;
}</td><td>This loop with print numbers starting form 1 to 10.</td></tr>
</table>

Figure 6.21

COBOL, PASCAL, ADA, C etc. are few programming languages that were developed to promote structured programming.

Using above mentioned constructs, structured programs can be very easily developed in these languages.

EXERCISES CHAPTER 6

Short Type Questions

A. Select most appropriate answer for following questions:

1. What is an algorithm?
   (a) A Computer program (b) A plan for Computer
   (c) An error in program (d) A Computer language
2. Which of the following is the first step of program development life cycle?
   (a) Planning the solution (b) Coding
   (c) Under sting to problem (d) Debugging
3. In which phase of program development paper plan is translated into computer language?
   (a) Debugging (b) Algorithm development
   (c) Coding (d) Compilation
4. In which of the following, solution of a problem is depicted using graphical symbol?
   (a) Flowchart (b) Algorithm
   (c) Top-Down development (d) Debugging
5. Which of the following should not be there in an algorithm?
   (a) Definite start point (b) Definite end point
   (c) English sentences (d) Ambiguity
6. Which symbol is not used while making flowchart?
   (a) Ellipse (b) Parallelogram
   (c) Polygon (d) Arrow lines
7. Which of the following symbol depicts starting point in a flowchart?
   (a) Ellipse (b) Parallelogram
   (c) Polygon (d) Arrow lines
8. Which of the following is related to repeated execution of a part of a program?
   (a) Loop (b) Conditional Checking
   (c) Sequential Construct (d) Case Construct

9. Which of the following software converts high level language in machine language?
   (a) Operating system (b) Compiler
   (c) Debugger (d) Text editor
10. Using which programming techniques, complex problem is divided into smaller problems?
   (a) Structured programming (b) Normal programming
   (c) Modular programming (d) Top-down programming
11. Which of the following is not a good programming practice?
   (a) Writing comments in program (b) Using Indentation
   (c) Using alphabets for variable names (d) Using line breaks
12. Which of the following activity is performed immediately after entering into Computer?
   (a) Linking (b) Compiling
   (c) Debugging (d) Execution
13. Which of the following is strictly restricted in structured programming?
   (a) GoTo Statement (b) Looping
   (c) Subroutines (d) Functions
14. Which of the following doesn't relate to reusability of Code?
   (a) Subroutine (b) Loop
   (c) Function (d) Decision
15. Which of the following doesn't makes use of condition in its execution?
   (a) Case (b) Loop
   (c) Decision (d) Function

B. Fill in the blanks:

16. .... high level programming language into machine language.
17. ....makes use of symbols to depict solution of a problem.
18. ....converts high level language program into machine language program, step by step and executes it also.
19. ....are always written in English like sentences for depicting the solution of a given problem.
20. Rectangle figures in a flowchart shows................
21. For branching.........................symbol is used in flowchart.
22. In...................... phase of program development life cycle, programming errors are found and corrected.
23. After compilation of the program .... activity is performed and then comes execution of the program.
24. Case, Loop, Function constructs etc. are used in ....

25. ....constructs checks a single condition and can transfer the program control to more than tow sections of the programs.

C. State, true or false for following statements:

26. Before writing the program, problem should be understood properly.
27. Algorithm is written immediately after coding.
28. In coding phase, high level computer language commands are converted to machine language.
29. In documentation phase all program errors are corrected.
30. Compilation errors and runtime errors, both occur because of wrong logic.
31. Library routines are assimilated into source program, during Linking phase.
32. Purpose of flowchart and algorithm is same.
33. Steps of algorithm can always be depicted using flowcharts.
34. Computer cannot compare three values at a time, it can compare only two.
35. Algorithm and flowcharts, both should have finite number of steps.
36. Parallelogram in a flowchart represents condition checking.
37. Ellipse symbol in flowchart represents pre defined process.
38. all program are first converted to the language of 0 and 1 and then they become executable.
39. Structured programming is basically a set of rules that are suggested for writing maintainable programs.

D. Answer the following questions in short:

40. Name the first step of program development life cycle.
41. In which part of program development life cycle Algorithm is translated in computer language?
42. Name at least two software which convert high level language commands into machine language commands.
43. List all those basic activities of computer, which are taken into account, while developing an algorithm.
44. Which symbols are used for depicting start and end of a flowchart?
45. Which symbols are used to show reading and writing activates in a flowchart?
46. Which symbols are used to depict flow of data and loops in a flowchart?
47. Give an example of a construct which relates to repetition.
48. In which type of programming a big problem is divided into multiple small problems.
49. Is modular programming closely related to top-down development?
50. Name any 4 constructs suggested by structured programming.
51. What activity is performed during compilation?
52. Write all steps of program development life cycle.
53. Is modular programming necessary for all programs?

Detailed Answer Type Questions

F. Answer the following questions in detail:

54. What do you understood by program development cycle? Describe its all phases.
55. What is algorithm? What are its advantages?
56. Write an algorithm for checking if a given number is a prime number.
57. Write an algorithm to calculate factorial of a given number.
58. Write an algorithm to convert inches into centimeters.
59. What is a flowchart? What are its advantages over algorithm?
60. Describe symbols that are used for reading, writing, branching, processing and looping in flowchart.
61. Draw a flow chart to check and print if a given year is leap year or not.
62. What is structured programming?
63. Describe subroutine and function constructs that are suggested in structured programming?
64. What is structured programming?
65. What programming practices are suggested for writing correct, efficient and maintainable programs?

****

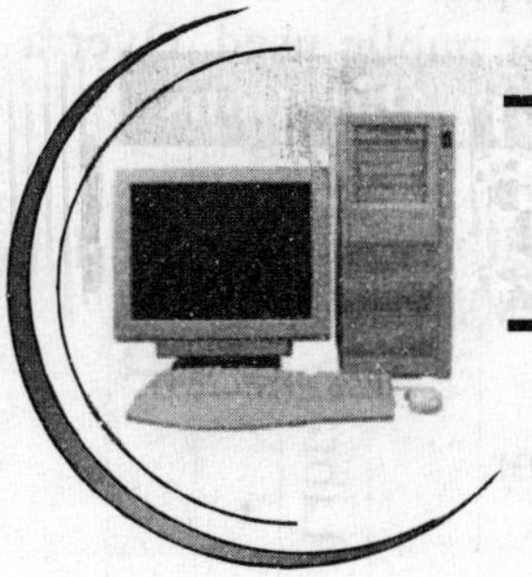

CHAPTER 7

Fundamentals of C Programming

INTRODUCTION

Computers are basically dumb electronic equipments. Be it their internal functioning (like transferring data from keyboard to memory, from memory to processor or from memory to output device) or automation of a manual task (like computerization of examination system, railway reservation system etc.), they require proper instructions. Without instructions they don't do anything.

Obviously they do not accept instructions in natural languages (like English, Hindi, Tamil etc). They follow the instructions, provided to them in computer languages.

Quite some time back, low level languages, like Machine language, Assembly language etc. were used for providing instruction to the computer for performing its internal functions. On the other hand, high level languages were exclusively used for automating human tasks. Truly speaking, that was an era, when no single computer language was available; using which both types of tasks could be performed.

In the year 1970, two computer scientists Dennis Ritchie and Brain Kernighan, at Bell Laboratories of USA, developed C language. It was quite powerful computer language. Its scope of operations was very wide. It not only provided means and commands for writing programs for computer's internal functioning but it also provided instructions for automating manual tasks. In other words you can say that it had the penetrating power of low level language and had the features of high level language too. Within short span of time, C language became quite popular all across the world. Although it came into existence, long time back, but it is still being used. In the remaining part of this book, we will describe the commands, features and programming aspects of C language.

KNOW ABOUT C LANGUAGE

C language is basically a very small instruction set, coupled with few standard rules and predefined formats. To write a C program, one needs to use appropriate instructions and follow the standard rules.

To make the C programming easy, many programs for primitive functions (that need to be performed in most of the cases) have already been written and compiled in the form of libraries (also called header files). These libraries remain available for public used. Over a period of time these libraries have become industry standard. Programs of these libraries are so commonly used that they are almost considered as part of C language. stdio.h, string.h, stdlib.h etc. are the names of few standard C libraries. Likewise there are many other libraries, which are considered as part of C language. Complete shape of C language is illustrated in figure 7.1.

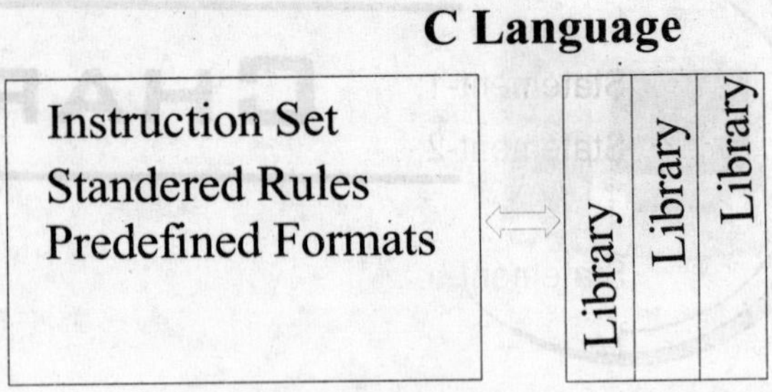

Figure 7.1

To make use of any program (called function), available in library, the name of the library need to be included in the main program. Following is the format, using which function libraries are included in any program:

```
#include <library-name>
```

Here #include is keyword, which is to be written as such and library-name is the name of that library, which is to be included in the program. For example, to include stdio.h library in the program, following statement will be written, at the beginning of the program.

```
#include<stdio.h>
```

STANDARD I/O IN C

Reading the data into computer and providing results are the two activities that each program performs. To perform these activities, most of the computer languages provide commands. By writing those commands in specified syntax, activities like reading the data or displaying the result can be very easily performed through program. But note that C language does not provide any command for such operations; rather it provides functions for them. For example, getchar, scanf etc. are few functions that read the data from the standard input (i.e. Keyboard). Similarly putchar, printf etc. are few functions that display data on standard output (i.e. VDU). In C language, all standard input, output related functions have been compiled and put in a library, named stdio.h. This library is often referred to as standard I/O library.

To make use of standard input output functions in your program, you have to include this library at the beginning of the program. Following is the command, using which this library can be included in the program:

```
#include <stdio.h>
```

A detailed description of standard input/output functions will be described in coming chapter.

STRUCTURE OF C PROGRAM

All C programs are written in the form of function. Structure of C program is illustrated below.

```
#include<library-name>
main()
{
Statement-1;
Statement-2;
:
Statement-n;
}
```

Refer above illustrated structure of C program and note that all the libraries that need to be used within the program are include at the beginning of the program, using #include statement. The function, from where the execution will start is named as main(). The scope of main() function extends from open curly bracket ({) to closing curly(}) bracket.

PROGRAMMING RULES

Following are the rules of C programming. They should be strictly followed. In case of any violation, compilation error occurs and the program doesn't execute.

1. A C program may consist of one or more functions. One of them must be named as main(). Execution of the program always starts from main() function.
2. All the statements of main() function should be written, within the opening and closing brackets, which mark the beginning and end of the function, respectively.
3. Practically there is no limit to the number of statements that could include in the main() function. However to make the program manageable, use of multiple functions should be promoted instead of too many lines in one function.
4. Each statement should be terminated with a semicolon sign (;).
5. C is case sensitive language. A differentiation is always made between upper case and lower case letters. For example, Andhra, ANDHRA andhra will be treated as three different identities in C language.
6. Comments can always be included in the program by placing the matter in between /* and */ delimiters. Following is the general format for placing comments in the program:

```
/* Comments */
E.g. /* This program calculates simple interest */
```

WRITE AND EXECUTE THE FIRST PROGRAM

PROGRAM-1

```
#include<stdio.h>
main() {
```

```
/* This program calculates distance
   for given speed and time. It also demonstrates the
   the general structure of C program */
int speed , time, distance ;
speed = 75 ;
time = 4 ;
distance = speed * time ; /* Calculating distance */
printf("\nDistance is %d ", distance) ; /* Displaying distance */
}
```

Read above mentioned program carefully and note the following points:

1. The speed, time and distance are the variables, which are utilized in the program for holding the values.
2. As a rule of C programming, all the variables that are used in the program, should be declared before they are used. Note that this is done through the statement, "**int speed, time, distance**". This statement states that these three variables will hold integer (int) values.
3. printf is standard output function, which displays the value of said variable on the VDU. It remains available in stdio.h library, which has been included at the beginning of the main() function.

LIFE CYCLE OF C PROGRAM

Now the question is how do you execute the C program on computer? Well, the program that you write on paper has to follow following steps:

1. Entered into computer.
2. Compiled.
3. Run (executed).

For entering the program in computer, any text editor can be used. After entering the program it should be saved for future use.

Once the program has been written and saved on the disk, it should be complied. At the time of compilation, all grammatical errors are checked and if found, they are clearly illustrated by the compiler. In computer terminology these errors are called compilation Time Errors. Note that a program having compilation errors, doesn't execute. Thus program should be re-edited and all the mistakes should be removed.

When all the compilation errors are removed and compiler compiles the program successfully, it can be executed.

When you execute the program, execution starts from the main() function. All the steps written in it get executed one after the other, till end of the function is reached. All printf statements display the result on the VDU.

TURBO C PROGRAMMING ENVIRONMENT

Numerous, compilers and interpreters of C language are available in market. You can select any one of them and work with it. For all practical purposes, we have chosen Turbo C compiler and will describe all the programs in relation to that.

Borland International Inc developed Turbo C compiler. It is menu driven package that provides complete environment for C programming. Program can be entered, compiled, linked to the libraries, executed and debugged without leaving the package.

Invoking Turbo C Compiler

To invoke turbo C compiler, give the command, TC from the system prompt and press Enter key. After giving the command, system reads the software from the default drive, loads it into computer's memory and displays a screen, as illustrated in figure 7.2.

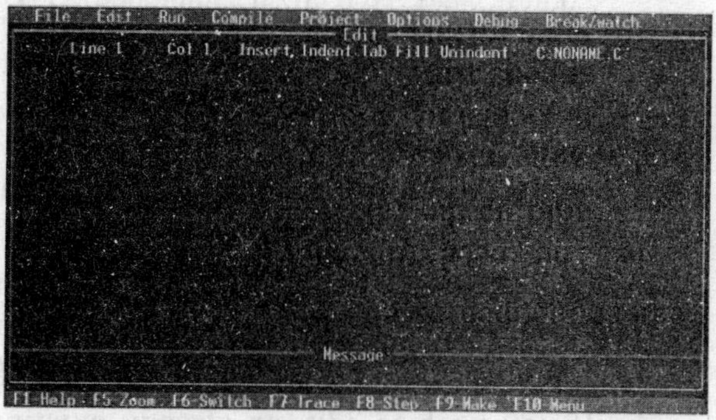

Figure 7.2

Refer above illustrated figure, which clearly states that Turbo C is menu driven software. Some of the important aspects of the screen are described below.

1. The top line of the screen is the main menu. You can invoke any option of the menu by pressing ALT key and the first letter key of that option, together. For example if you wish to invoke Run option then you will have to press ALT and R keys together.
2. When you choose any option of the main menu, it displays a submenu. Any option of the submenu can also be chosen in the same way.
3. The second line from the top displays editing related details. For example, Line and Col headings display the current position of the cursor.

Other items of the line are self-explanatory and need no further clarification. Note that the last item of the second line illustrates the name of the current file. If you do not assign any name to the file then Turbo C automatically assigns a default name, "NONAME.C" to it.

4. Below the second line is the blank area, in which you can write the program.
5. At the bottom of the screen there is a message line, which explains the function of different function keys.

Editing the Program

In editing phase you enter the program into computer and save it in a file. For editing the program you can make use of the following keys:

1. Arrow keys, to move the cursor in the respective directions.
2. CTRL + F to move the cursor to the next word.

3. CTRL + A to move the cursor to the previous word.
4. Backspace and DEL keys to delete a character.
5. CTRL + T to delete the current word.
6. CTRL + Y to delete the current line.

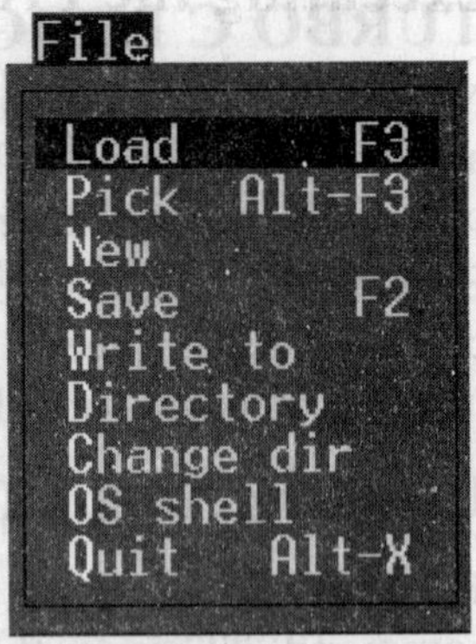

Figure 7.3

To save the current editing in the file, follow the following steps:

1. Select "File" option from the main menu, by pressing ALT and F keys together or by pressing F10 key first and then pressing F key. On pressing these keys, Turbo C will display a submenu, which is illustrated in figure 7.3.
2. Select either "Save" option or "Write to" option. If you are saving the file for the first time, then both the options ask you, the name of the file, in which you wish to save the contents of the current editing session. As soon as you type the file name, the contents will be saved on the media.
3. After editing the current file, if you wish to write another program then you can select "New" option from the File submenu. A fresh screen will be presented to you and you could start entering a new program.
4. If you wish to edit, an already existing program, then you will have to load it into memory by choosing "Load" option of the File submenu (figure 7.3).
5. To exit from the Turbo compiler, you need to choose "Quit" option from the File submenu (figure 7.3).

Compiling the Program

After editing the program, you have to compile the program. To compile the program load the program, if it is not presently loaded. After loading the program, follow the following steps:

1. Select "Compile" option from the main menu.
2. On selecting compile option, Turbo C will display a submenu, which is illustrated in figure 7.4.
3. Now select "Compile to OBJ" option.

Figure 7.4

During compilation, Turbo C checks all the syntax problems, and points out all the mistakes. In case of errors, you will have to again go back to editing mode (press F6 key) and correct all the errors and recompile the program. The cycle will have to be repeated, till all the errors have been removed. When there are no mistakes in the program, Turbo C will compile the program successfully and link it also to the libraries and thus produce an executable file, with the name a.out.

Executing the Program

To execute the program, follow the following steps:

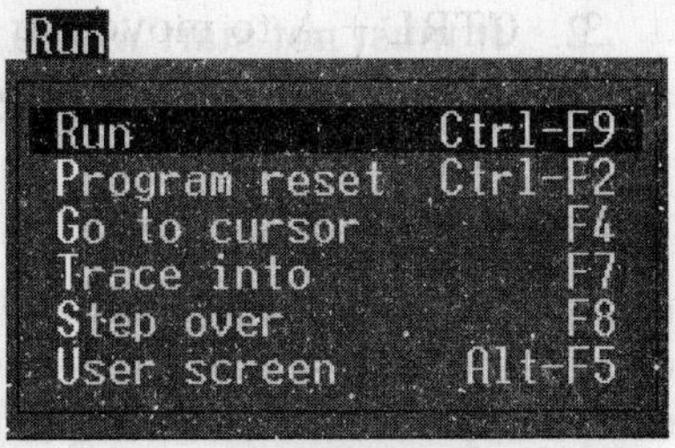

Figure 7.5

1. Select "Run" option from the main menu. When you do so, Turbo C will display a submenu, which is illustrated in figure 7.5.
2. Now choose Run option to execute the program. Note that the program does not get executed in Turbo C window. It gets executed on user screen. When you run the program the control gets transferred to the user screen, it's output gets displayed there and when the program finishes, control is transferred back to the Turbo C window.
3. After running the program, if you wish to go back to the user screen, for some reason or the other then you will have to select, User Screen option, from Run submenu (figure 7.5).

C CHARACTER SET

In computer terminology, a letter, digit, or special symbol is called character. All those characters that can be used within C programs are called C character set. C character set is described below:

Letters:	A-Z, a-z
Digits:	0-9
Special symbols:	+ - * / ^ \ () [] {} =! = < >. , " $; %! ~? & _(under score) # < = > = @ horizontal tab, white spaces, blank space, carriage return (↵), new line, form feed.

C TOKENS

Tokens are group of characters that are used for representing an identity. They can very well be used while writing C programs. In C language, following types of tokens are used:

1. Identifiers
2. Keywords
3. Literals or Constants
4. Operators

An introduction to these tokens is given below.

Identifiers

Identifiers are basically the names that are used for identifying an entity. These entities can be anything like variables, functions etc. For example, if roll number and age of the students have to be referred in the program then two identifiers, such as Rol and Age could be used in the program. The rules that apply on identifiers are as follows:

1. An identifier can consist of alphabets, digits, and /or underscore.
2. It must not start with a digit, however it can start with underscore.
3. C is case sensitive so ROL and Rol will differ from each other.

Keywords

In C language some words are reserved for specific task. They carry special meaning for C complier. Thus these words should not be used as identifiers. These reserved words are called keywords. Following is a partial list of C keyword:

asm	continue	float	new	singed	try-
auto	default	for	operator	sizeof	typedef
break	delete	enum	integer	static	union
case	do	goto	return	struct	unsigned
catch	double	if	this	switch	void
char	else	inline	register	template	while
const	extern	long	short	throw	

LITERALS OR CONSTANTS

Data items that do not change their valves while the program executes, are called literals or constants. C allows following types of literals:

1. Integer constants
2. Character constants
3. Floating point constants
4. String constant

Constants in C program can be defined as follows:

```
const   data type   variable name =  value;
```

Following are few valid constant declarations:

```
const int speed = 75 ;  const distance = 100.55 ; const char = 'A' ;
```

C language supports integer constants, floating-point constants, character constants and string constant. A detailed description of these is given below.

Integer Constants

Integer values that do not change during the course of the program are termed as integer constants. Following are few examples of valid integer constants:

```
0, -10, 276, 5968, 32767, - 230
```

Floating-Points Constants

Those real values, which do not change during the course of the program, are called Floating Point Constants. Following are few examples of valid floating-point numbers:

0.1	345.	0.77	906.07
2E5	0.50e-21	288E+8.	121214e12

Character Constants

A character constant is a single character, enclosed in single quotes. Following are example of character constants:

'A' 'B' '3' '#' '@'

Note that following are invalid character constants:

'AB'(has two characters), '100' (has three characters)

Note that characters are internally represented as numerical values in computers. A complete chart of these values is given in annexure 1.

C language provides the facility to operate upon the alphabets as alphabets and as numbers too. To understand this, first of all note printf("%d", variable-name) is the command for printing integer values and printf("%c", variable-name) is the command for printing character values. Now consider following two examples:

1. char disp ;

   disp = 'Z' ;

   printf ("%c", disp) ;

When this piece of code will get executed, it will display 'Z'

2. int disp ;

   disp = 'Z'

   printf ("%d", disp);

When this piece of code will get executed, it will display 90.

The advantage of operating upon characters, as numbers, is that you can apply number mathematics on characters also.

Non-printable Character Constants

Note that A, B, C, 17, 9 etc. are printable characters, they physically appear on the screen when you either type them or print them through program. But apart from these characters, there exist various characters, which cannot be seen, but when printed, they produce special effects. In C language a backslash on left hand side of the character represents these characters. Few examples of non-printable characters are given below.

Character	Name	Effect
\n	new line	Puts the cursor in next line.
\a	bell	Gives a beep sound.
\b	backspace	Takes the cursor back by one space.
\t	tab	Takes the cursor to next tab position.
\f	form feed	Ejects a paper on printer.
\o	null	Returns null value.

String Constants

In C language, characters enclosed within double quotes form string constants. Following are few examples of string constants:

"Sachin"

"Indian Cricket Team"

To understand the usage of string constants clearly, go through the following piece of code:

```
printf("Sun") ;
printf("Rises in East") ;
```

This program will display "SunRises in East". Note that although there are two printf statements, but the result gets displayed in a single line. This is because there is no new line character in the first statement. If the result of each statement is to be printed in a new line, a new line character (non printable character) will have to be introduced in printf statement, as illustrated in following piece of code:

```
printf("Sun\n") ;
printf("Rises in East") ;
```

This piece of code will produce the following result:

```
Sun
Rises in East
```

VARIABLES

Variables are basically memory locations, which hold some value in them. They are always assigned a unique name for identification. When you refer a variable, in the program, you basically access its contents. For example, if the variable, speed has been assigned the value, 100 and you write the statement speed = speed + 50 in your program then the value of this variable will get incremented by 50 and thus value of speed variable will become 150. Statements of this kind may appear to be algebraically wrong but they are correct as far as computer languages are concerned. They signify that new value of the variable will now be equal to the old value plus the constant value written in the statement (which is 50 in this example).

CLASSIFICATION OF DATA TYPES

Different types of data that could be used in any language are referred to as Data Types. For example, name will always be alphabetic data, age will be numeric, date of birth will be date, time of arrival will always be time. In short, it can be said that these are different data types. Note that not all the languages support all the data types. For example, C language doesn't support Date and Time data types. In order to handle such type of data in the program, you need to make manipulations of some kind. Now the question is, which are the data types that are supported in C language? Well, C supports wide variety of data types. They are broadly classified as follows:

1. Basic (fundamental) data type
2. Derived data types

Derived data types make use of basic data types and will be described later in this book. However basic data types are described below.

BASIC DATA TYPES

The int, char float and double are the four basic data types that are supported in C language. int represents integer data i.e. whole numbers (like 125, 200 etc.). char represents single character (like a, 1, * etc.). float represents real numbers i.e. the numbers containing decimal points (like 125.50, 200.67 etc). double represents numbers with double precision i.e. more accurate numbers.

Few qualifiers, such as short, long, signed and unsigned etc. can augment int data type. For example, integer quantities can be defined as:

```
short int
long int
unsigned int
signed int
```

Short int will require less memory space than long int because long int requires double the amount of memory.

Signed integers represent integers in the range -32,768 to +32767. Unsigned integers represent numbers in the range 0 to 65,535.

If the need be, two qualifiers could be used together so as to make a logically correct statement:

```
unsigned short int
unsigned long int
```

DECLARING VARIABLES

As mentioned earlier, all the variables must be declared, before they are used in the program. Following format is used for declaring variables in C program:

```
data type variable name ;
```

For example, a variable named speed can be declared as integer type, using following statement:

```
int speed;
```

This declaration signifies that speed variable will always hold integer values in it. Any attempt to store values of other data types will always result into error.

More than one variables of the same data type can be declared through single declaration statement, as mentioned below.

```
int rate, quantity, amount ;
float area, radius, perimeter ;
char religion_code1, religion_code2, religion_code3, religion_code4 ;
```

Initializing the Variables While Declaring

Variables can also be initialized at the time of their declaration. This is done in following format:

```
int speed = 100 ;
```

This statement will declare the variable speed as integer type and it will also assign it an initial value 100. To understand the process of initialization more clearly, consider the following declaration statement:

```
int rate, quantity, amount = 100;
```

This statement will only initialize the value of amount variable, to 100. Variables, rate and quantity will not be initialized. Uninitialized variables initially contain garbage value in them. When you make use of uninitialized variables in your program, compiler gives warning at the time of compilation. If you still run the program, you may get wrong results.

Correct method of initializing multiple variables in single declaration statement is illustrated below.

```
int rate=10, quantity=50, amount = 0;
```

ARITHMETIC OPERATORS

To operate upon numerical values, C provides, following operators:

Operator	Symbol	Purpose
Addition operator	+	Adds given values.
Subtraction operator	–	Subtracts one value from other value.
Multiplication operator	*	Multiplies given values.
Division operator	/	Divides one value by other.
Modulus operator	%	Provides remainder value that results from integer division

ARITHMETIC FUNCTIONS

C language does not provide any operator for square root cube root, raised to the power of etc. Now the question is how do you perform these operations in C language? Well, for these operations, C language provides standard functions. These functions remain available in math.h library. Some of these functions are described below.

Function and Usage	Description	Example
sqrt(n)	Gives square root of n.	sqrt(144) will give 12.
abs(n)	Gives absolute value of n.	abs(-95) will give 99.
pow(2,3)	Gives value of 2 raised to the power of 3.	pow(2,3) will give 8.
log(n)	Gives log of n.	log(10) will give natural logarithm of 10.

ARITHMETIC EXPRESSIONS

When two or more arithmetic constants or variables or functions are combined together, using, arithmetic operators, they form arithmetic expression. For example (a+b)*100 is an arithmetic expression.

To understand the concept, assume that there are two integer variables, p=25 and q=7. Using these variables, following expressions can be formed:

1. p+q : This expression will give 32.
2. p-q : This expression will give 18.
3. p*q : This expression will give 175.
4. p/q : This expression will give 3.
5. p%q : This expression will give 4.

Following table illustrates few more arithmetic expressions:

	Mathematical Expression	Equivalent C expression
1.	$c = a \div b$	c = a / b
2.	$m = p^2 + q^2 + r^2$	m = (p * q * r)
3.	$z = (a + b + c) \div (x + y)$	z = (a + b + c) / (x + y)
4.	$d = \sqrt{}(a + b + c)$	d = sqrt((a+b+c))
5.	$x = a^b$	x = pow(a,b)

Rules for forming Arithmetic Expressions

Rules for the use of arithmetic operators are as follows:

1. All the operands of arithmetic expressions should be numeric.
2. Second operand in the Division operator should be non-zero. That means you cannot divide the number by zero.
3. While making use of modulus operator, both the operands should be integer (whole number) and the second operator should be non-zero.

Type Conversion

When operands of different data types participate in an expression they undergo automatic type conversion before final evaluation takes place. The conversion takes place in such a way that the final result is expressed in the highest precision possible, as mentioned below.

If one of the participating operand is long double and another is simply double then the result will be long double.

If one of the operand is floating point and other is floating point or int then the result will be floating point.

Point to be Noted

While making use of arithmetic operators, following points should be kept in mind:

1. When an integer is divided by another integer, the result obtained is always an integer. For example, when you divide 9 by 2(9/2) logically the result should be 4.5, but in C program the result will be 4.
2. While making use of division operator even if one of the operands is real number, the result obtained will be a real number. For example, 9/2.0 will result into 4.5 in C program.
3. Rules of algebra follow, when participating operands happen to be negative. For example, if p=17, q= -5, and r= -35, then:
   (a) p+q=12
   (b) p-q=22
   (c) p*q= -85
   (d) p/q= -3
   (e) p%q=2
   (f) r%p= -3

Evaluation of Arithmetic Expressions

When an operator is applied on one or more operands, an expression is said to be formed.

An expression is never limit to the number of operands and operators. It could involve multiple operators and operands. Now the question is, which operator will execute first and which will operate later?

For example, will the result of 5+3*2 be 16 or 11? Well, in C language, operators execute in predefined sequence. This predefined sequence is called "Order of Precedence". Following is the order in which arithmetic operators get executed:

1. Arithmetic operator *, / and % have the same precedence but definitely have higher precedence than + and - operators. Thus in an expression, having * and + operators, * will get executed first. Thus in the expression, 5+3*2, first multiplication will take place and then the addition. This it will give 11.
2. With the operators of same precedence, execution takes place, from left to right.
3. Order of execution can be altered with the use of brackets. Expressions, written within the bracket get executed first. For example, 5+3*2 will give 11 but the expression (5+3)*2 will give 16.
4. If the need be, brackets within the brackets (called nested brackets) could also be used in the expression. In that case expression within the inner most bracket get evaluated first and then the evaluation moves from inner bracket to other bracket.

SIMPLE ASSIGNMENT OPERATOR AND STATEMENT

In C language the symbol "=" is known as simple assignment operator. It sets the value of the variable written on left hand side to the value written on right hand side of it. Expression thus formed is called simple assignment statement. Following are few simple assignment:

```
A=100 ;
B=200 * 3 ;
C=(A*B) + 50 ;
```

It sets the value of the variable, on left hand side, to the value on right hand side. Value o

NESTED ASSIGNMENT STATEMENTS

In C language same value can be assigned to more than one variables of same type, using multiple assignment statement. Multiple assignment statements are written in following format:

Variable1 = Variable2 = Variable3 = Constant;

Here Variable1, Variable2, Variable3 are variable names and constant is the value that is to be assigned to all the three variables.

For example, if variable a, b and c are of the same type and all the three have to be assigned the value 700 then following type of multiple assignment statement can be written in C:

```
a = b = c = 700;
```

Note that in multiple assignment statement the values are assigned to the variables from right to left i.e. in the above statement, first the variable c will acquire 700 value then b and then a.

ARITHMETIC ASSIGNMENT STATEMENTS

When the variable itself takes part in the assignment statement and stores the result in itself then arithmetic assignment statement is said to be formed. Following are few arithmetic assignment statements:

```
x = x + 100;
y = y - 200 ;
```

To understand the functioning of arithmetic assignment statement, let's assume that initially m=100. When statement m=m-10 will be executed, the new value of m will become 90, because this statement will subtract 10 from original value of m (which was 100) and store the result (90) in variable m. Thus the old value of m (100) will get lost.

SHORTCUT ASSIGNMENT OPERATORS

Assignment operators, operate upon operands and assign the resultant value to a variable. Following are the assignment operators, available in C language. Their usage, with example is summarized in the following table:

Assume thatx=100, y=200

Operator	Expression	Equivalent Expression	Result
+=	x+=50	x=x+50	x=150
-=	y-=10	y=y-10	y=190
*=	x*=3	x=x*3	x=300
/=	y/=2	y=y/2	y=100
%=	a%=3	a=a%3	a=1

Note that if the two operands in the statement are of different data type then the expression on the right hand side will be automatically converted to the type, on left.

UNARY OPERATORS

Those operators, which operate upon single operand, are called Unary operators. Following Unary operators, are available in C language:

Unary Minus (-)

Unary Minus operator is denoted by minus sign (-).

Although arithmetic subtraction operator and Unary Minus appear to be same but truly speaking, they are different. Subtraction operator requires two operands, while Unary Minus requires only one operand. Unary Minus converts positive value to negative value. For example, -150, -(-700) etc are the examples of Unary Minus.

Increment Operator (++)

Increment operator operates upon numerical values or numerical expressions. It increases their values by one. For example, if i=100 then i++ will give 101.

Note that ++ operator can either be used as ++i (pre increment) or i++ (post increment). In both the forms, same result is obtained but the time of execution differs.

In pre increment case (ie ++i) the value of the operand (ie i) gets incremented before the execution of the statement, in which it is used. For example, if i=100 then print ++i will print 101

In post increment case (ie i++) the values of the operand (ie i) gets incremented after the execution of the statement, in which it is used. For example, if i=100 then print i++ will print 100 and then increment the value of i to make it 101.

Decrement Operator (--)

Decrement operator works in the same way as increment operator does, except that it decreases the value of its operand. --i and i-- are the examples of pre decrement and post decrement operators.

RELATIONAL OPERATORS, EXPRESSIONS AND PRECEDENCE

Relational operators operate upon an expression and evaluate it to find whether it is true or false. In the event of expression being true, they return 1 else if it is found false they return 0.

Following relational operators are available in C language. Their usage with examples and results is illustrated in following table.

Assume a=100, b=50, c=150, d=50

Operator	Symbol	Usage	Result	Value Returned
<	Less than	a<b	False	0
<=	Less than or equal to	b<=c	True	1
>	Greater than	a>b	True	1
>=	Greater than or equal to	b>=c	False	0
Note that all these logical operators have the same order of precedence but definitely have lower precedence than arithmetic operators.				
= =	Equal to	a= =b	False	0
		b= =d	True	1
!=	Not equal to	a!=b	True	1
		b!=d	False	0
Note that Equal to and Not Equal to operators have the same precedence but definite have lower precedence than above mentioned, four relational operators.				

The operator = = is quite different from = operator. The = operator assigns a value of an expression in a variable, while = = operator check for equality. You can say that its function is opposite to that of Not Equal To operator (!=).

LOGICAL OPERATORS

Logical operators operate upon two logical expressions to build more complex logical expressions, which are either true or false. Following are the logical operators, which are available in C language.

Logical AND Operator (&&)

Logical AND operator combines two logical expressions in such a way that the resultant expression gives true only if both the expressions (being combined) are true. In any other condition it gives false. Logical AND operator is denoted by && sign.

To understand its usage, assume that S1 and S2 are two logical expressions. The expression S1&&S2 will be a complex logical expression. It will be true if and only if S1 and S2 are true. In the event of S1 or S2 or both being false, this expression will evaluate to false.

Logical OR (||)

Logical OR operator combines two logical expressions in such a way that the resultant expression gives false only if both the expressions (being combined) are false. In any other condition it gives true. Logical OR operator is denoted by || sign.

To understand its usage, assume that S1 and S2 are two logical expressions. The expression S1||S2 will be a complex logical expression. It will be false if and only if S1 and S2 are false. In the event of S1 or S2 or both being true, this expression will evaluate to true.

Logical NOT (!)

This operator negates the value of the expression. For example, if the expression is true, it will return false and if it is false then it will return true. Fir example, !(100>50) will return false.

LOGICAL EXPRESSIONS AND PRECEDENCE OF LOGICAL OPERATORS

When two or more relational expressions are combined together, using logical operators, a logical expression is said to be formed. For example (a.>200) AND (b<500) is a logical expression. Similarly (C>1000) OR (d<2000) is another logical expression.

The logical AND operator (&&) and logical OR operator (||) have lower precedence than relational operators.

The logical negation operator has higher precedence over any relational or arithmetic operator.

The precedence among logical operators is NOT, AND and lastly OR.

THE CONDITIONAL OPERATOR (?:)

Conditional operator, denoted by ? sign, is ternary operator. It requires three expressions and is used in the following format:

```
expression1 ? expression 2 : expression3 ;
```

While evaluating the conditional expression, expression1 is evaluated first. If expression1 is found to be true then expression2 is evaluated and its value becomes the value of the whole expression. If expression1 is found false then expression3 is evaluated and its value becomes the value of the whole expression. To understand the usage of conditional operator, consider the following code:

```
total = (x==y) ? 700 : 900 ;
```

When x will be equal to y then the expression will evaluate to 700. Thus the value of total will become 700 (i.e. total=700). On the other hand, if x is not equal to y then the expression will evaluate to 900. Thus the value to total will become 900.

COMMA OPERATOR

The comma operator is used to join together several expressions. The complex expression, thus formed is evaluated from left to right, in sequence. The result of the right most expression in the complex expression becomes the value of the expression. To understand the concept, consider the following expression, formed with the use of comma operator:

```
x =(a=4*5, a+100)
```

When this statement gets executed, first 4 will be multiplied by 5 and the result, 20, will be assigned to the variable a. After this, the right most expression i.e. a+100 will get executed and the value 120 will be obtained. This value will be assigned to the variable x.

Note that Comma operator falls last in the sequence of order of precedence.

OPERATOR PRECEDENCE AND ASSOCIATIVITY

As mentioned earlier, C expression may have different types of operators present in the expression. In that case operators will get executed in the following sequence.

1. Unary operator.
2. Arithmetic multiply, Division and Modulus.
3. Arithmetic Add and Subtract.
4. Relational operators.
5. Equality operators.
6. Logical AND.
7. Logical OR.
8. Conditional operator.
9. Assignment Operator.
10. Comma operator

STATEMENTS AND COMPOUND STATEMENTS

A statement makes the computer perform an action. As, you know all the statements, in C language have to be terminated with a semicolon (;) sign. C statements can be broadly classified into following two categories:

1. Simple statements.
2. Compound statements.

Simple statement comprises of single statement, followed by a semicolon. For example, "int speed ; " is a simple statement. Similarly, distance=speed*time; and printf("%d",distance) ; are other two statements.

Compound statement comprises of more than one statements enclosed within { and }. For example, following is a compound statement:

```
{
    distance=speed*time ;
    printf("%d",distance) ;
}
```

EXERCISES CHAPTER 7

Short Type Questions

A. Select most appropriate answers for the following questions:

1. Which type of programming can be done, using C language?

   (a) High level (b) Low level (c) Both of the above (d) None of the above.

2. Which of the following clause is used for including i/o function library in C programs?

   (a) #include <io.h> (b) #include<stdio.h>

   (c) include # <io.h> (d) include#<stdio.h>

3. Which character marks the end of each statement in C language?

   (a) ; (b) : (c) { (d) }

4. Which of the following operator is used for checking the equality of two variables?

   (a) ! (b) <> (c) = (d) ==

   Which of the following will be used to write an equivalent C expression for 237?

   (a) * (b) ^ (c) exp() (d) pow()

B. Fill in the blanks.

5. At the time of .... all the grammatical mistake in the program are checked and displayed on the screen.
6. .... is valid data type of C language, which deals with the numbers that contain decimal point.
7. To find out the remainder after dividing one number by other number .... operator is used. It is denoted by .... sign.
8. The expression, m+=100 is equivalent to ....
9. The expression 2+7-3*6 will give ....on evaluation.

C. State true or false.

10. C language was designed and developed at Microsoft Corporation of USA.
11. All mathematical functions of C language remain available in stdio.h library.
12. A C program must have main() function in it.
13. A C program can have more than one function in it.
14. Any statement written in between /# and #/ is treated as comments in C program.

D. Answer the following questions in one or two words:

15. Who invented C language?
16. Which operators are used for multiplication and division in C language?

17. How do you denote Not Equal To operator in C language?
18. Write a statement, showing the use of Conditional operator.
19. Name any four, basic data types available in C Language.

Detailed Answer Type Questions

E. Answer the following questions in detail:

20. Describe the general structure of a C program.
21. Differentiate between i++ and ++i.
22. Differentiate between simple C statements and compound C statements.
23. What do you understand by compilation and compile time errors? How do you remove them from the program?
24. What is role and characteristic of AND operator? Explain, using a suitable example. Which symbol is used for denoting AND operator in C Language?
25. Write an equivalent expression for $\sqrt{a^1+b^2+c^3+d^4+e^4}$
26. Differentiate between = and == operator.
27. Write a program in C language that initializes rate and quantity values of an item in the program and prints the amount.
28. Write a program in C Language, which converts 25^0 Centigrade into Fahrenheit.
29. Write a program in C Language, which initializes three character variables a, b and c to A, B and C respectively and prints their ASCII values.
30. Write the results of the expression (x==y)? 5+3*2:(5+3)*2 when x=100 and y=100 and when x=100, y=200.
31. If x=100 then what will be the value of the expressions x*=2 and x+=2?
32. What will be the result of x=y%3 when y=-103 and x=3.
33. Evaluate the expression sqrt(pow(12,2)).
34. Write a program, which converts 10 centimeters into equivalent inches.
35. Write at least two advantage and disadvantages of using C language.
36. What are C tokens? Describe different types of tokens available in C language.
37. Describe different data types available in C language.
38. Differentiate between integer and double data types and tell the difference between short and long integers.
39. Write a short note on precedence of C operators.
40. Explain the functioning of conditional operator, using suitable examples.

****

CHAPTER 8

Input & Output Functions

INTRODUC TION

Be it any program, it requires data to operate upon, so that it could process it and produce the results as per requirements. One method of providing data to the program is to assign the values to the variable, within the program and access the variables whenever required. You are already familiar with this method. Note that this method suites well for the situations, in which data is of fixed type and happens to be very small in volume. You cannot afford to deal with this method if data, such as roll number, name, address, subjects, marks etc. of fifty students, has to be processed. It is quite obvious that for such situations, program should accept the data from other sources like, keyboard, etc. Well, C language provides wide variety of input output functions for accepting the data from the keyboard n the program and displaying the results on VDU. These functions remain available in function library and can always be accessed from there by using appropriate statements. Details of this library and input output functions are described in this chapter.

ACCESSING FUNCTION LIBRARY

"stdio.h" is the function library, (also called header file) in which all the input output functions of C language remain available for use. As a rule, this header file has to be included in the program by writing # include statement at the beginning of the program. So if you intend to make use of input out statements in your program (which in any case you will) then you have to write the following statement at the beginning of the program:

```
# include <stdio.h>
```

READING A CHARACTER (getchar function)

Using getchar function, you can accept single character from the keyboard into the program. This function doesn't require any argument. It has to be simply followed by a pair of empty parentheses. In general, getchar function would be used as follows:

```
character variable = getchar()
```

```
e.g.    p=getchar()
```

Here p is a character variable. Whenever, above statement will get executed, the program execution will halt and the program will wait for an input from user's side. Whichever character will be entered from the keyboard will be assigned to the variable, p.

To understand the functioning of getchar() function let's write a program for the following problem:

PROBLEM-1

Say we have to write a program, which takes student's category code from the keyboard. If code is 'r' i.e. reserved then fees to be paid is set to Rs. 200. Other candidates pay Rs. 1000. The fees amount is displayed on the VDU.

PROGRAM-1

```
#include <stdio.h>
main()
{   char code ;
    int fees ;
    code = getchar() ;
    fees = (code == 'r') ? 200 : 1000 ;
    printf("\nFees to be paid %d ",fees) ;
}
```

WRITING A CHARACTER (putchar function)

The putchar function displays single character on VDU. The character or the character variable that is to be displayed is passed as an argument to the function. Following is the general format for putchar function:

```
        putchar (character variable)
e.g:    putchar (code) or putchar('A')
```

Here code is a character variable and 'A' is a character constant. On execution, putchar function will display the contents of the code variable or the character 'A' respectively.

Now you are familiar with getchar and putchar functions so let's write a program for the following problem:

PROBLEM-2

Write a program to accept one character color code from the keyboard and display it on the VDU.

PROGRAM-2

```
#include <stdio.h>
main()
{
```

```
    char code ;
    code = getchar() ;
    putchar (code);
}
```

PROBLEM-3

Let's write a program, which accepts one alphabet color code from the keyboard. If color code is 0 then it prints B (black) else it prints W (white).

PROGRAM-3

```
#include <stdio.h>
main()
{
    char code ;
    code = getchar() ;
    (code=='0') ? putchar('B') : putchar('W') ;
}
```

You are now familiar with one character input output functions of C language. Now the question is, how do you accept and display data, which comprises of many characters? Well, for those types of data items, C provides two functions i.e. scanf and printf. Function scanf accepts multiple character data items from the keyboard and printf displays them on the VDU. Usage of scanf and printf functions is described below.

FORMATTED INPUT (scanf function)

Function scanf accepts all types of data in the program. General format for scanf function is as follows:

```
scanf (control string, variable1, variable2, variable3---------)
```

Here control string is a string of characters, which contains information of the format, in which data will be accepted from the keyboard. The variable1, variable2, etc. are the variables, which will hold the values that will be given from the keyboard, when the program runs.

Control string may consist of multiple % signs and conversion characters. One % sign and one conversion character put together is called character group. Note that one character group will hold formatting information for one data item only (i.e. one variable only). For example, if four data items are to be accepted from the keyboard then scanf statement will have four character groups and four variables in it. Each character group will consist of one % sign and one conversion character. Thus control string of such a statement will have the following format:

```
%conversion character %conversion character %conversion character%conversion character
```

First character group (i.e. % conversion character) will be associated with first variable, second character group will be associated with second variable and so on.

Now the question is, what are conversion characters? Conversion characters are the characters that indicate the type of data that the corresponding variable has to hold. In other words you can say that it indicates the type of data that is supposed to be entered from the keyboard, for this variable. For example, first conversion character will indicate the type of data that first variable has to hold. The second conversion character will indicate the type of data associated with second variable and so on. Note that different characters are used for different types of data. Following table illustrates a list of conversion characters that are used for accepting different types of data.

Conversion Character	Meaning
c	Data item is a single character.
d	Data item is a decimal number.
e	Data item is a floating point value in scientific notation.
f	Data item is a floating point value in normal notation.
i	Data item is an integer.
h	Data item is a short integer.
s	Data item is a string followed by white space characters.
u	Data item is an unsigned decimal integer.

So if the first value to be entered is an integer, second is floating point, third value is again a floating point and the fourth value is a character then the control string will have to be written as follows:

```
"%i %f %f %c"
```

Note that control string is always written within double quotes. Another important point to be noted for scanf function is that, while writing the variables within the bracket, in scanf statement, each variable name is preceded by an & sign. For example, variable names for above mentioned control string will be written, as mentioned in the following scanf statement:

```
scanf ("%i %f %f %c", &pay &da &itax, &religion);
```

Here pay, da, itax and religion are the variables of int, float, float and char type respectively, which will hold the respective values.

FORMATED OUTPUT (printf function)

Function printf displays all types of data on the screen. General format for printf function is as follows:

```
printf (control string, variable1, variable2------------)
```

Here control string contains formatting information and variable1, variable2 etc. are the variables, values of which have to be displayed. Control string of printf function is formed in the same way as that of scanf function (explained in the last section). The characters used for forming the control string of printf statement are listed in the following table:

Conversion Character	Meaning
c	Data item is displayed as a single character.
d	Data item is displayed as decimal number.
e	Data item is displayed as floating point value with an exponent.
g	Data item is displayed as a floating point value, using either e-type or f-type conversion, depending upon the value. Trailing zeros and trailing decimal points will not be displayed.
f	Data item is displayed as floating point value without an exponent.
i	Data item is displayed as integer.
s	Data item is displayed as string.
u	Data item is displayed as an unsigned decimal integer.

For example, for printing four variables i.e. pay, da, itax and religion, which are of integer, float, float and character data types espectively, following printf statement will be written:

```
printf ("%i %f %f %c",  pay da itax, religion);
```

Note that here in printf function, variable names are not preceded by & sign as they are in scanf function.

In order to be familiar with these functions, let's write a program for the following problem:

PROBLEM-4

Write a program to accept roll number and physics, chemistry, maths marks of a student. This program should calculate and print total marks and percentage achieved, assuming that maximum marks for each subject are 100.

PROGRAM-4

```
#include <stdio.h>
main()
{   int roll, phy, chem, maths, total ;
    float per ;
    printf ("\n Give Roll number");
    scanf ("%i", &roll);
    printf("\nGive Physics, Chmistry and Maths marks ");
    scanf ("%i %i %i", &phy, &chem, &maths);
    total = (phy + chem + maths) ;
    per = total * 100.00 / 300.00 ;
```

```
    printf ("\nTotal  marks are %i + %i + %i  %i ", phy, chem, maths ,total) ;
    printf ("\n Percentage = %f ", per) ;
    printf ("\n Percentage = %g ", per) ;
}
```

Notice the following points in relation to scanf and printf functions:

1. **Notice blank spaces in between %i and %i and i% in scanf function. Due to these spaces data will have to be entered as 70 80 90.**
2. **If the control string would have been written as "%i%i%i" i.e. without any space in between two character groups then it will be required that the data should be entered as 708090. Note that this data is confusing. It could also be interpreted as 708 09 0 or 70 809 0 etc. Thus if you use character groups without blank in between, compiler may produce confusing results.**
3. **If you want that individual data item should be entered on a separate line then the control string should be written as: "%i \n %i \n%i".**
4. **If you wish that each data item should be separated by a comma (like 70,80,90), at the time of entering the values then control string should be written as : "%I,%I,%i"**
5. **Refer printf ("\nTotal marks are %i + %i + %i %i ", phy, chem, maths ,total) statement and note the blank spaces and + sign in between the character groups. Blank spaces and + sign gets displayed as such.**
6. **If you do not include any gap between the character groups of printf function, the numbers will get displayed as 708090. Note that, if the numbers are printed in this manner then you will not be able to interpret them.**
7. **If the value of each variable is to be displayed in a new line then new line character i.e.\n will have to be included between the two character groups, as shown below.**

   "%i \n \%i"
8. **If you wish that each value, printed through printf function, should be separated by a comma then each character group in printf function should also be separated by comma (,) as shown below.**

   "%i, %i".

EXECUTION AND RESULT

When you execute, above mentioned program, it will ask for the data by displaying following lines:

Give Roll number   (say you enter 10 here)
Give Physics, Chmistry and Maths marks (say you enter 70 80 90 here)

After entering the data, it will display following result on the screen:

Total marks are 240
Percentage = 80.000000
Percentage = 80

Note the first percentage value and the second value. The first value is printed through character f in control string (float) and other value is printed through g (float with trailing zeros suppressed).

PROBLEM-5

Say we want to accept three numbers from the keyboard and then print the largest number, out of these three numbers.

PROGRAM-5

```
#include <stdio.h>
main()
{
    int n1, n2, n3, largest;
    printf ("Give three numbers");
    scanf ("%i, %i, %i", &n1, &n2, &n3);
    largest = (n1>n2)? n1 :n2;
    largest = (n3>largest)? n3 : largest;
    printf ("The largest No is %i", largest);
}
```

While entering the data for this program (against scanf function), you will have to enter the data as : 100, 200, 500. On the other hand if you wish to enter each data item in separate lines then you will have to write the scanf function in the following format:

```
scanf ("\n%i\n%i\n%i, &n1, &n2, &n3);
```

To write the next program, let's get familiar with the following functions and values:

1. A function named toupper(), used as toupper(character), converts the given lower case character to upper case character. For example, if the given character is 'a' then toupper('a'), will convert it to 'A'.
2. The other function named tolower(), used as tolower(character), converts the given upper case character to lower case character. For example, if the given character is 'A' then tolower('A') will convert it to 'a'.
3. A given character is a lower case character or upper case character, can be known from its ASCII value. Recall that ASCII value of an alphabet can be obtained by equating the alphabet to an integer variable. ASCII values of all the upper case characters and lower case characters are given in annexure 1.

PROBLEM-6

Let's write a program that takes an alphabet from the keyboard. If the alphabet is lower case alphabet, it converts it to upper case and if it is upper case alphabet, it converts it to lower case alphabet. It also prints the converted alphabet.

PROGRAM -6

```
#include <stdio.h>
main()
```

```
{ char alphabet, converted_alphabet ;
  printf("\nType an alphabet " ) ;
  scanf ("%c",&alphabet) ;
  converted_alphabet = (alphabet>96) ? toupper(alphabet) : tolower(alphabet) ;
  printf("\n Converted character is %c" , converted_alphabet ) ; }
```

EXERCISES CHAPTER 8

Short Type Questions

A. Select most appropriate answers for the following questions:

1. In which of the following library, does the function, getchar() exist?
   (a) iostream.h (b) stdio.h (c) function.h (d) getchar.h
2. Which of the following function will take single character input from the keyboard?
   (a) getchar (b) getch (c) givechar (d) charget
3. Which of the following function will display the value on VDU, without the use of control string?
   (a) getchar (b) putchar (c) scanf (d) printf
4. Which of the following statement will print the output in two different lines?
   (a) printf("Hello you"); (b) printf("\nHello you);
   (c) printf("Hello you\n"); (d) printf("Hello \n you");
5. Which of the following character will be used to print a real number, with trailing zeros suppressed?
   (a) \ (b) f (c) g (d) 0

B. Fill in the blanks.

6. One character input can be taken using .... function.
7. .... is function, which displays a single character on the screen.
8. To accept data in a and b variables, which are of integer and float type,............................ will be used as control string in printf statement.
9. .... statement will accept an integer value in price variable.
10. .... is a function, which converts an upper case character to lower case character.

C. State true or false.

11. putchar is an output function.
12. a=putchar() is a valid statement.
13. x=getchar (b) is a valid statement.
14. If a and b are float and integer type of variables then their values can be displayed on the screen, using print("\n%i%f",a,b);

15. If a value is to be accepted in variable named var then this variable should be written as &var in scanf function.

D. Answer the following questions in one or two words:

16. Name the function, using which one character input can be taken in the program.
17. Name the function, using which three integer values could be accepted within the program.
18. Name the function, using which three float values could be displayed on the screen.
19. Using which formatting character, value stored in character variable could be displayed on the screen?
20. F is a float variable and F=100.000. Which character, f or g, would be used as control string character to display the value as F=100?

Detailed Answer Type Questions

E. Answer the following questions in detail:

21. Describe the usage of getchar function, taking a suitable example.
22. Describe the usage of putchar function, taking a suitable example.
23. Explain the role of scan function, taking a suitable example.
24. Explain the role of printf function, taking a suitable example.
25. How will you convert an upper case alphabet to lower case alphabet?
26. Write a program, which accepts basic pay, from the keyboard and then calculates and prints da and income tax amount. The da amount is calculated as 150% of the pay and itax is calculated as 3% of the pay. It should also calculate the net pay.
27. Write a program, which accepts purchase amount and calculates discount @7.5%. It should print the net payable amount (purchase amount - discount).
28. Write a program, which takes a date in ddmmyy format from the keyboard and prints it in yymmdd format. For example, the date 25/10/80 will be printed as 80/10/25.
29. Write a program that accepts age from the keyboard. If age is <18, it prints "Minor" and if age is >=18 then it prints "Major".
30. Write a program, which takes previous and current meter readings of an electrical meter. On the basis of these two readings, it calculates units consumed and prints the payable amount, considering that per unit cost is Rs. 4.45.
31. Write a program to print following figure:

```
    #
   ###
  #####
 #######
#########
  ****
```

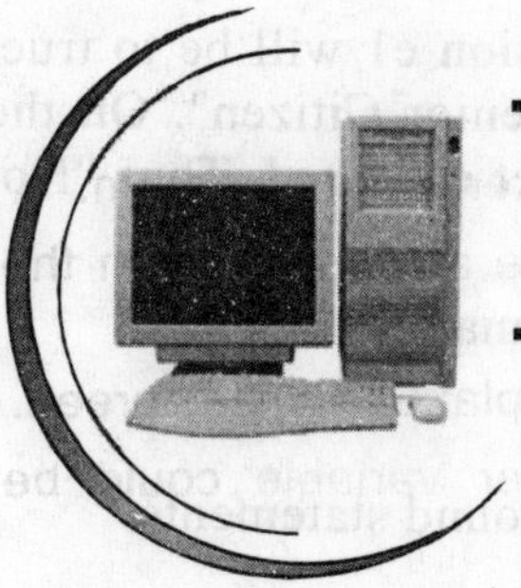

CHAPTER 9

Conditional Statements

INTRODUCTION

As mentioned earlier in C language, program execution starts from the first line of the main() function and continues line after line, till the end of the function is reached. Often while writing programs for real life problems, this normal flow of execution need to be altered. To do this, C language provides many control commands.

Control commands provide means to alter the normal flow of execution and turn it into some other direction. For example, after executing first 10 lines of the program, you may wish to evaluate a logical expression. If it is found true then only you may wish to execute other lines of the program else you may like to terminate the program. Similarly, in some other situation, you may wish to execute first 20 lines of the program repeatedly 7 times. Such types of programming requirements are normal requirements and occur in almost all the programs. Usage of C language control commands is explained in this chapter.

IF ELSE STATEMENT

If else statement is basically decision making command. It involves one condition (say e1) and two courses of actions (say s1 and s2). When this statement gets executed, given condition (e1) is evaluated. If it is found true (1) then first action (s1) gets executed. On the other hand if the given condition evaluates to false (0), second statement (s2) gets executed. Characteristic behavior of if else statement is illustrated in figure 9.1.

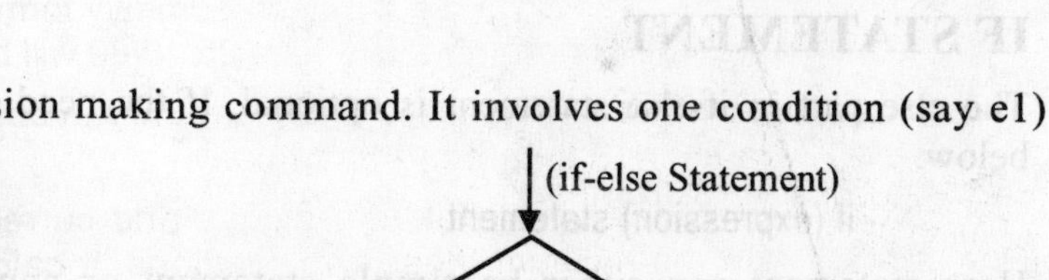

Figure 9.1

To understand the characteristic behavior of if else statement, assume that:

1. Expression e1 is (age>=60)

2. Statement S1 is printf("Senior citizen")
3. Statement S2 is printf ("Not an old person")

At the time of execution of it else statement, if age=75 then expression e1 will be to true. Thus S1 statement will get executed and the program will print "Senior Citizen". On the other hand if age = 45 then e1 will be false and S2 statement will get executed. Thus "Not an old person" will get printed.

In its simplest form, if else statement is executed in the following format:

```
if (expression) Statement 1 else statement2
```

Statement 1 and Statement 2 can either be simple statements or compound statements.

For example:

```
if (age>=60) printf ("Sinor Citizen") else
printf ("Not an old person")
if (status = ='p')
    {   pay=10000;
        bonus=5000;
        leave=30;
    }
    else
    {
        pay=5000;
        bonus=0;
        leave=10;
    }
```

IF STATEMENT

The else part in if-else statement is optional. If the need be, it could be omitted as illustrated below.

```
if (expression) statement
```

Here statement can either be simple statement or compound statement as mentioned in following examples:

```
if (marks>75) printif ("Distinction")
if (Sale>=10000)
{ comm=1000;
incentive=200;
increment=30; }
```

PROBLEM-1

Let's write a program, which accepts roll number, physics, chemistry and math marks of a student. It calculates percentage marks, assuming that maximum marks for each subject are 100. If percentage is found to be less than 50 then it prints "Student has Failed" else it prints "Student has Passed".

PROGRAM-1

```
#include <stdio.h>
main()
{   int roll, phy, chem, maths, total ;
    float per ;
    printf ("\n Give Roll number");
    scanf ("%i", &roll);
    printf("\nGive Physics, Chmistry and Maths marks ");
    scanf ("%i %i %i", &phy, &chem, &maths);
    total = (phy + chem + maths) ;
    per = total * 100.00 / 300.00 ;
    printf ("\nPercentage achieved = %g ", per) ;
    if ( per > 49)
    printf ("\n Student has Passed ") ;
    else
    printf ("\n Student has Failed") ;
}
```

PROBLEM -2

In a company, employee's total pay is governed by his basic pay and the category, to which he belongs. He could either be of reserved category (i.e. category_code='r') or general category (i.e. category_code='g'). If he is of reserved category then he gets 50% of his basic pay as bonus, Rs. 5000 for LTC and 25% of his basic pay as house rent. On the other hand, if he is of general category then he gets 30% of his basic pay as bonus, Rs. 2000 for LTC and 10% of his basic pay as house rent.

Write a program that takes necessary inputs, calculates total pay for the employee and prints it.

PROGRAM-2

```
#include <stdio.h>
main()
{   int empno, ltc ;
```

```
float bpay, bonus, hra, total=0.0 ;
char category ;
printf("\nGive category ");
scanf ("%c", &category);
printf ("\n Give  Employee number");
scanf ("%i", &empno);
printf("\nGive Basic pay ");
scanf ("%f", &bpay);
if (category=='r' )
{
    bonus = bpay * 50.00/100.00 ;
    ltc = 5000 ;
    hra = bpay * 25.0 / 100.0 ;
    total = bpay + bonus + ltc + hra ;
}
else
{
    bonus = bpay * 30.0/100.00 ;
    ltc = 2000 ;
    hra = bpay * 10.0 / 100.0 ;
    total = bpay + bonus + ltc + hra ;
}
printf ("\nBasic Salary  = %g ", bpay) ;
printf ("\nBonus         = %g ", bonus) ;
printf ("\nLTC           = %i ", ltc) ;
printf ("\nHouse rent    = %g ", hra) ;
printf ("\nTotal salary = %g ", total) ;
}
```

Nested if Statements (Multiway Conditional Statements)

You know that in if else statement if branch gets executed when given condition is true and else branch gets executed when condition if false. Now the question is, what happens if few other conditions need to be test in if branch or in else branch or in both the branches? Well, for such type of complex situations, C language provides nested if statements.

In nested if statements, another if statement is places either in if branch or in else branch or in both the branches. Thus there are various versions of nested if statement. Their formats and examples are given below.

FORMAT-1

```
if (expression-1) if (expression-2)
    Statement-1 ;
    else
    statement-2;
e.g. if (marks>=90) if (phy_marks>=95)
        award_amount=10000 ;
        else
        award_amount=5000 ;
```

Note that in this format, there are two if statements and one else statement. Second if statement is being checked in if branch of the first if statement. Now the question is, with which of the two if statements, else statement is associated with? Well, as a general rule, any else statement remains associated with the nearest if statement. Thus in this example award_amount=5000; is associated with phy_marks>=95 not with marks>=90.

To understand the dynamics of this format of nested if statement, consider the following conditions and the results obtained for them:

1. If marks=95 and phy_marks=98 then the award-amount will be 10000.
2. If marks=95 and phy_marks=80 then else branch will get executed and award_amount will be 5000.
3. If marks=80 then none of the statements, mentioned above will get executed.

FORMAT-2 (THE ELSE IF LADDER)

```
if (expression1) statement1
else if (expression2) statement2
```

e.g.

```
if (marks>=90)
award_amount=1000;
else if (category = ='r')
award_amount=500;
```

Note that in this format, second if condition is being evaluated in else branch. Thus this condition gets checked only if first condition is false.

To understand the dynamics of this format, consider the following conditions and results obtained under them.

1. If marks=95 then award amount_amount=1000
2. If marks are less than 90 but category is r then the award_amount will be 500.
3. If marks are less than 90 and the category is not r then no statement in the above mentioned code gets executed.

FORMAT-3

```
if (expression1) if (expression2) statement1
else statement2;
else statement3;
```

e.g.

```
if (marks > 50) if (maths_marks > 75)
    maths_award_amount=1000;
    else
    maths_award-amount=0;
    else
    printf("Student failed the test");
```

Note that in this format there are two if and else statements. First else statement is associated with second if statement and the second else statement is associated with first if statement. Thus if the first expression becomes true then only the second expression gets evaluated otherwise the second else statement gets executed. If second expression becomes true then first statement gets executed. On the other hand, if this expression become false then the statement under first else branch gets executed.

To understand the dynamics of this format, consider the following conditions and the results obtained under them:

1. If marks are 40 then first expression becomes false. Under this situation, its associated else branch (which happens to be second else) gets executed. Thus "Student failed the test" message gets displayed.
2. If marks=60 then first expression becomes true thus second if statement gets evaluated.

Say maths_marks=80 then the second expression becomes true and thus the statement maths_award_amount=1000 gets executed.

On the other hand if maths_marks=60 then the second expression becomes false and thus the statement maths_award_amount=0 in first else branch gets executed.

FORMAT-4

```
if (expression1) statement1
else if(expression2) statement2;
    else statement3;
```

e.g.

```
if (marks>50) printf ("Pass")
else if (marks>45) printf ("Can Get Grace Marks")
else
printf("Failed Badly");
```

Note that in this format there are two if and two else statements. First else statement is associated with first if statement. Similarly second else statement is associated with second if statement.

If the first expression evaluates to true then first statement (under if branch) gets executed otherwise the second expression (under else branch) gets evaluated. In this case if the second expression evaluates to true then second statement (under second if branch) gets executed, otherwise statement-3 under second else branch gets executed.

To understand the dynamics of this format, consider above mentioned example and consider the following cases and the results obtained under them.

1. If marks=60 then the first expression becomes true so statement-1 i.e printf("Pass") gets executed.
2. If marks=46 then the first expression becomes false and thus second expression i.e. "marks>45" gets evaluated. Since marks=46 hence this expression evaluates to true. Thus second statement i.e. printf ("Can Get Grace Marks") gets executed.
3. If marks=40 then the first expression becomes false and thus second expression i.e. "marks>45" gets evaluated. Since marks=40 hence this expression evaluates to false. Thus third statement i.e. printf("Failed Badly) gets executed.

Now you are familiar with if else statement and its various variations, so let's write few programs for the given problems.

PROBLEM-3

A college awards scholarship to its meritorious students. If the student is a female candidate and has secured more than 74% marks then she gets 75 times the amount of the percentage that she has secured. On the other hand, male students get the same amount if they have secured more than 85% marks. Write a program to accept roll number, marks and sex of the student and print the scholarship amount.

PROGRAM-3

```
#include <stdio.h>
main()
{
    int roll, marks;
    float amount=0.0 ;
    char sex;
    printf("\nGive sex i.e. m or f ");
    scanf ("%c", &sex);
    printf ("\n Give  Roll Number");
    scanf ("%i", &roll);
    printf("\nGive Marks");
    scanf ("%i", &marks);
```

```
        if (sex=='f') if (marks>75)
            {  amount = marks * 75.0 ;
               printf("\nScholarship for this girl = %g", amount) ;
            }
        else printf("No Scholarship for this girl") ;
        else if (marks>85)
            {
               amount = marks * 75.0 ;
               printf("\nScholarship for this boy = %g", amount) ;
            }
        else printf("No Scholarship for this boy") ;
    }
```

PROBLEM - 4

A company promotes saving habits among their employees who get higher salaries. If employee's salary is less than Rs.10000 then they do not deduct any tax. But if the salary is greater than or equal to Rs. 10000 and the savings are more than 50% of the salary then they do not deduct any tax otherwise a tax amount, equivalent to 3% of their salary is deducted.

PROGRAM - 4

```
#include <stdio.h>
main()
{   float salary, saving, tax=0.0, chkamt  ;
    printf("\nGive salary ");
    scanf ("%f", &salary);
    printf ("\n Give  Savings ");
    scanf ("%f", &saving);
    chkamt = salary * 50.0 /100.00  ;
    if (salary < 10000 )
    printf("\nNo tax deducted for this person ") ;
    else if (saving < chkamt)
  { tax = salary * 3.00 / 100.00 ;
    printf("\nTax = %g", tax) ;
  }
  else printf("No tax deductude for this person") ;
}
```

PROBLEM-5

An examining body charges a fees of Rs. 5000 from all the candidates, but gives fees discount as follows:

1. Rs. 500 discount to all reserved candidates.
2. Rs. 700 discount to all the female candidates.
3. Rs. 1000 discount to all the handicapped candidates.

These discounts are given on mutually exclusive basis. That means a general category handicapped girl will get a discount of Rs. 1700.

Write a program to accept all relevant details of the candidate and print his / her fees amount.

PROGRAM-5

```
#include<stdio.h>
main()
{
    int roll ;
    char res,sex,handi,junk;
    int discount=0, fees ;
    printf("\nGive Roll Number ");
    scanf("%i",&roll) ;
    printf("\nGive sex i.e. m or f");
    scanf("%c%c",&junk,&sex);
    printf("\nIs he a reserved candidate ? give y or n");
    scanf("%c%c",&junk,&res) ;
    printf("\nIs he a handicapped candidate ? give y or n ");
    scanf("%c%c",&junk,&handi) ;
    if(res=='y')
    discount = discount + 500 ;
    if(sex=='f')
    discount = discount + 700 ;
    if (handi=='y')
    discount = discount + 1000 ;
    fees = 5000 - discount ;
    printf("\nTotal discount %i", discount);
    printf("\nFees to be paid %i",fees );
}
```

ANALYSIS

Note that all those statements, which are accepting character data, have an extra variable named junk (arbitrary name given). This variable is used because of the fact that when Enter key is pressed against last data entered, a new line character is entered. This character remains there in the buffer. So when you include an extra variable, like junk, in scanf statement, new line character is assigned to junk and the next character that you enter goes into proper variable and thus input activity takes place properly.

SWITCH STATEMENT

Switch statement provides means for checking a given expression and selecting one course of action among various actions available. For example, think of a code, (character data type), which can attain any one value out of four given values (say 'h', 'm', 's' or 'c'). If code takes the value 'h', you may wish to print Hindu. Similarly you may wish to print Muslim, Sikh or Christian, if code attains the value 'm', 's' or 'c' respectively. For such a situation, switch statement comes handy. It will check the code, get its value (whether it is 'h', 'm', 's' or 'c') and transfer the program control to the matching section, where meaning of the code (Hindu, Muslim etc.) gets printed.

Switch statement, comprises of two sections, First section is identified by switch keyword and contains the expression that is to be evaluated. Second section comprises of multiple case statements, which clearly associate all possible outcomes (say 'h', 'm', 's', 'c') of the expression and the actions to be formed in each case. General format, for switch statement is as follows:

```
switch (expression)
{
    case(value-1) Statement;
    case(value-2) Statement;
    :
    :
    case (value-n) Statement;
}
```

Here statement can either be single statement or compound statement. To understand the format and functioning of case statement, let's write a program for the following problems:

PROBLEM-6

Say we have to write a simple, program, which accepts roll number and category code of the student and prints his roll number and category as follows:

1. If code is 's' then prints "SC/ST".
2. If code is 'b' then prints "Backward".
3. If code is 'h' then prints "Handicapped".
4. If code is 'a' then prints "Army".

5. If code is 'g' then prints "General".

PROGRAM- 6

```
#include<stdio.h>
main()
{
        int roll ;
        char code, junk ;
        printf("\nGive Roll Number ");
        scanf("%i",&roll);
        printf("\nGive code ");
        scanf("%c%c",&junk,&code);
        switch(code)
        {
                case 's' :
                printf("\nSC/ST ");
                break ;
                case 'b' :
                printf("\nBackward ");
                break ;
                case 'h' :
                printf("\nHandicapped ");
                break ;
                case 'a' :
                printf("\nArmy ");
                break ;
                case 'g' :
                printf("\nGeneral ");
                break ;
        }
}
```

Refer above mentioned program and visualize a situation that wrongly an in valid code is entered (such as y, z, x etc.). Now the question is, what happens in that case? Well, in that situation no case will match and nothing will be printed. But practically speaking, some action may be required, in such cases. For example, in the above program, you may wish to display a message, "Wrong Code". Well, for such type of situations, when no case matches, switch statement offers default: case. So if no match takes place, instructions written in default case: get executed.

The usage of default case, in switch statement is illustrated below.

PROBLEM-7

Modify previous program, so that, if a code other than's', 'b', 'h', 'a' or 'g' is entered, program displays a message "Wrong code".

PROGRAM-7

```
#include<stdio.h>
main()
{
    int roll ;
    char code, junk ;
    printf("\nGive Roll Number ");
    scanf("%i",&roll);
    printf("\nGive code  ");
    scanf("%c%c",&junk,&code);
    switch(code)
    {
        case 's' :
        printf("\nSC/ST ");
        break ;
        case 'b' :
        printf("\nBackward ");
        break ;
        case 'h' :
        printf("\nHandicapped ");
        break ;
        case 'a' :
        printf("\nArmy ");
        break ;
        case 'g' :
        printf("\nGeneral ");
        break ;
        default:
        printf("Wrong code ");
    }
}
```

PROBLEM-8

Let's write a program, which accepts month in number and prints it name in words. For example prints January for 1 or June for 6.

PROGRAM-8

```
#include<stdio.h>
main()
{
    int mth ;
    char code, junk ;
    printf("\nGive Month in number");
    scanf("%i",&mth);
    switch(mth)
    {
        case 1 :
            printf("\nJanuary");
            break ;
        case 2 :
            printf("\nFebruary");
            break ;
        case 3 :
            printf("\nMarch");
            break ;
        case 4 :
            printf("\nApril ");
            break ;
        case 5 :
            printf("\nMay");
            break ;
        case 6:
            printf("\nJune");
            break ;
        case 7 :
            printf("\nJuly ");
            break ;
        case 8 :
```

```
                printf("\nAugust ");
                break ;
            case 9 :
                printf("\nSeptember ");
                break ;
            case 10 :
                printf("\nOctober ");
                break ;
            case 11 :
                printf("\nNovember ");
                break ;
            case 12 :
                printf("\nDecember ");
                break ;
                default:
                printf("Wrong month ");
        }
    }
```

GOTO STATEMENT

The goto command makes the program control jump from its current location to some other, named location.

General format of goto statement is as follows:

```
goto label ;
```

Here label is the named line, to which the program control has to jump. For example, to transfer the program control to a line named merit, goto command will have to be used as follow:

```
goto merit ;
```

The labels can be marked in the program in following manner:

```
label name:
```

e.g. merit:

To get familiar with the usage of goto statement, let's consider the following program:

PROBLEM-9

Let's write a program that accepts religion code (**h** or **m** or **s or c**) from the keyboard and prints Hindu if the given code is h. Muslim, Sikh or Christian is printed if the religion codes are m, s or c respectively. The program should not accept any other code than these four codes. Any attempt to enter other codes should flash an error message, "Wrong Code".

PROGRAM-9

```
#include<stdio.h>
main()
{
    char code, junk ;
    start:
    printf("\nGive code ") ;
    scanf("%c%c",&code,&junk) ;
    if (code!='h'&& code!='m' && code!='s' && code!='c')
    goto err ;
    if(code=='h')
    {
        printf("\nHindu") ;
        goto last ;
    }
    if(code=='m')
    {
        printf("\nMuslim") ;
        goto last ;
    }
    if(code=='s')
    {
        printf("\nSikh") ;
        goto last ;
    }
    if(code=='c')
    {
        printf("\nChristian") ;
        goto last ;
    }
    err:
    printf("\nWrong Code") ;
    goto start ;
    last:
    printf("\nEnd of program") ;
}
```

ANALYSIS

To understand the dynamics of the program, go through the following points:

1. Notice the first if condition. In this condition, through the use of && operator user is forced to enter either h or m or s or c codes only.
2. If any other character than those, which are allowed, is entered then goto err: statement is executed.
3. The err: is a label. When program control comes here, the message, "Wrong Code" gets displayed and after that goto start: statement gets executed. Thus program control is transferred to err: label.

If the entered code is among one of those codes, which are allowed then corresponding religion in words gets displayed and the statement, "goto last ;" gets executed. Notice that last is a label. When program control comes here, a message, "End of program gets displayed.

EXERCISES CHAPTER 9

Short Type Questions

A. Select most appropriate answers for the following questions:

1. When will if branch of if else statement get executed?
   (a) When condition is true (b) When condition is false
   (c) When error occurs (d) None of the above
2. If a=100 and b=200 then which branch of if (a>100).......statement will get executed?
   (a) if branch (b) else branch (c) both (d) next statement
3. Which of the following is correct statement for checking a condition in if statement?
   (a) if (a=b) (b) if (a==b) (c) if (a , b) (d) if (a b)
4. A variable can acquire many values and depending upon the value a course of action has to be chosen. Which of the following will suit best for this situation?
   (a) If statement (b) Goto statement
   (c) Case statement (d) else statement
5. Which of the following command will place the program control at the end of the loop, when it gets executed?
   (a) goto (b) break (c) continue (d) end

B. Fill in the blanks.

6. Switch statement is always associated with ....l.
7. If a=10 and b=20 then c will be .... when the statement if (a==b) c=(500+a) ; else c=(1000+b) ; gets executed.
8. If branch of an if else statement gets executed, when the associated condition is ....
9. A loop placed in another loop is called .... loop.
10. .... statement transfers the program control to another part of the program.

C. State true or false.

11. An if statement can be placed in else branch of other if statement.
12. An if statement can be placed in if branch of other if statement.
13. Switch statement is like if else statement.
14. err; is a valid level.
15. Each switch statement should have at least one matching case statement.

D. Answer the following questions in short:

16. Can one if statement have multiple else statements?
17. Can a switch statement be replaced by multiple if ... else statements?
18. Which case is written to take care of the values that do not match the given case values in switch statement?
19. Which statement is used in switch statements to prevent the program control to enter into other case choices?
20. Which statement of C language transfers program control to jump unconditionally to some other statement of the program?
21. If a=100 and c= 5 then what will be the value of c, when if (a>50) c= 100 ; else if (a <100) c=150 ; statement gets executed?
22. If a=1000 and c= 500 then what will be the value of c, when if (a>50) c= 100 ; else if (a <1000) c=150 ; else (c= c+ a) gets executed?
23. Which statement will you use if one course of action is to be decided among 20 courses of actions available, depending upon the result obtained after evaluation of a condition?

Detailed Answer Type Questions

E. Answer the following questions in details:

24. What is the function of if statement? Explain with example.
25. Describe the two different forms of if-else statement. How they are different from each other? Explain giving suitable examples.
26. Give an example of nested if statements.

27. What is the format of case command? Write its general format.
28. Write a program, which accepts sales figures of 10 executives and prints their commission @13%. It also prints total of commission.
29. Write a program to accept 3 numbers and print the smallest number among them.
30. Write a program, which accepts salary of a person. If salary is greater than Rs. 10,000 but less than 20,000 then it should print "Executive". If the salary is greater than or equal to 20,000 then it should print "Manager". In rest of the conditions, it should print "Worker".
31. Write a program to print odd numbers starting from 1 to 10 and printing their sum also.
32. Write a program to accept religion code that can either be h, m, s or c. Check the code in the program and print Hindu, Muslim, Sikh and Christian respectively for the code.

****

Chapter 10

Repetitive Structure Using Loops

INTRODUCTION

In reference to programming, loop means, executing a group of lines (or a line) repeatedly. For example, if line 10,11,12 and 13 are being executed continuously 5 times then it will be said that program has a loop. Now the question is, how do you form a loop in C program?

Well, C language provides many commands for forming different types of loops within the program. These loops and associated commands are described below.

WHILE LOOP

While loop aways has an expression and one or more than commands associated with it. Till the time, expression evaluates to true, commands associated with it get executed repeatedly. The moment expression becomes false, while loop terminates. General format of while loop is given below.

```
while(expression)                while (expression)
or {
command;                         command-1;
                                 command-2;
                                 command-3;
                                 }
```

Note that in while loop, expression remains placed at the beginning of the loop. At the time of execution of while statement, expression is evaluated. If it is found true all the commands associated with it get executed one after the other. After executing the last statement of the loop, program control returns back to the beginning of the loop. Now again expression is evaluated, if it is found true the body of the loop is executed again else the loop terminates. When the loop terminates, the statement placed next to the while loop gets executed.

Following points, need to be taken care for proper execution of while loop:

1. The expression should be so framed that its value should change in each iteration of loop.
2. If the expression is ill framed and its value doesn't change within the loop, loop will never terminate. The loops, which do not terminate are called infinite loops.

   As a general rule of programming, infinite loops have to be avoided at any cost.
3. Initially if the expression is found false, loop will not execute even once.

To understand the functioning of while loop, let's write few programs for the given problems.

PROBLEM -1

Using while loop, write a program to print even numbers starting from 1 to 20 and their squares.

PROGRAM-1

```
#include<stdio.h>
main()
{    int start=2, limit = 20, sq=0 ;
     while (start <= limit)
     {
          printf("\nNunber = %i",start) ;
          sq = start * start ;
          printf("  Its square  = %i",sq) ;
          start = start + 2 ;
     }
}
```

ANALYSIS

To understand the dynamics of the program, note the following points:

1. Initially the condition associated with while loop is true, so the loop starts.
2. Since initial value of start variable is 2 so incrementing it by two in each iteration yields even numbers, starting from 2.
3. When value of start becomes more than 20 then the condition, start <= limit becomes false (because value of limit was initially initialized to 20) and the loop breaks.
4. Since printf statements are placed within the loop hence they get executed in each iteration and thus even numbers and their squares get printed.

PROBLEM-2

Let's write a program that accepts roll number, physics chemistry and math marks from the keyboard and prints total and percentage, assuming that all the marks are awarded out of 100 marks. This program should work in loop so that it works for as many students as required.

PROGRAM-2

```
#include <stdio.h>
main()
{   int roll, phy, chem, maths, total ;
    float per ;
    char q='y', junk ;
    while(q!='n')
    {
        printf ("\n Give Roll number");
        scanf ("%i", &roll);
        printf("\nGive Physics, Chmistry and Maths marks ");
        scanf ("%i %i %i", &phy, &chem, &maths);
        total = (phy + chem + maths) ;
        per = total * 100.00 / 300.00 ;
        printf ("\nTotal  marks are %i + %i + %i  %i ", phy, chem, maths ,total) ;
        printf ("\nPercentage = %f ", per) ;
        printf("\nDo you wish to continue ? ") ;
        scanf("%c%c",&junk,&q);
    }
}
```

DO WHILE LOOP

The do while loop is variant of while loop. In this loop, expression is placed at the end of the loop rather than at the beginning General format of do while loop is given below.

```
do
{
    Statement1;
    Statement2;
    etc.
}
while (expression) ;
```

Note that the keyword, do marks the beginning of the loop and while (expression) marks its end. All the statements written between do and while, form the body of the loop. Since the expression is evaluated at the end of the loop hence this loop gets executed at least once even if the expression is false.

Like while loop, this loop also gets executed, till the time given expression remains true.

The moment expression becomes false, loop terminates and the statement next to it gets executed.

To understand the functioning of do while loop, let's write few programs, for the given problems.

PROBLEM -3

Let's write a program, which accepts a target number and prints the sum of the series of the following type:

$1 + 2^2 + 3^3 + 4^4 + 5^5 + \ldots\ldots. + (\text{Target\_No})^{\text{Target\_No}}$

PROGRAM -3

```
#include<stdio.h>
#include<math.h>
main()
{   int start=0, target, value;
    int tot=0 ;
    printf("\nGive target value ");
    scanf("%i",&target);
    do
    {   value = pow(start,start);
        tot = tot + value;
        printf("\n%i",value);
        ++start ;
    }
    while(start <= target) ;
    printf("\nTotal=%i",tot) ;
}
```

ANALYSIS

To understand the functioning of this program, go through the following points:

1. Initially the loop starts with start=0 and the target value is entered through keyboard.
2. The function pow(x,y) gives the value of the expression x^y. This function remains present in math.h library, which need to be included at the beginning of the program.
3. The loop starts with start=0 and keeps on iterating till the time condition "start <= target" remains true. Loop breaks when condition is checked and found false.
4. Since the condition is being checked at the bottom of the loop hence this loop will get executed at least once, even if the condition is false.

FOR LOOP

The for command of C language is another means of forming a loop within the program. General format of for command is as follows:

```
for(expression1; expression2; expression3)
Statement or Group of statements
```

Here in this loop, all the there expressions involve a control variable of integer type, say x.

Expression1, initializes the value of the control variable and is generally of the type x=value e.g. x=100.

Expression3 increments or decrements the value of control variable, say x in each iteration and is generally of the type x=x+value or x=x-value. If the value of the control variable is to be incremented by 1 in each iteration then it is of the type, x++. On the other hand, if the value is to be decremented each time then it could be of the type x--.

Second expression is used for framing the target value for the control variable. That means the loop will continue till the time expression is true. The moment this expression becomes false the loop terminates. To understand the functioning of for loop, consider the following example:

```
for (x=1; x<25; x++)
{
    sq=x*x ;
    printf("%i",sq) ;
}
```

In this example, for loop will start with x=1. In the body of the loop, squre of x(i.e. 1 at present) will be calculated and assigned to the variable, sq. The printf statement will display the square (of 1).

After printing, the value, x will be incremented by 1 and the second expression (x=25) will be evaluated to check if value of x has reached 25 or not. Since current value of x will be 2 hence this expression will be true. Thus the loop statements will be executed again. Again the value of x will be incremented and process will continues, till the time x becomes 25.

The moment x becomes 25, loop will break and the statement next to for statement will get executed.

To understand the functioning of for loop more clearly, let's write program for the given problems.

PROBLEM -4

Let's write a program, which prints the sum of the following series:

(1+2) + (2+3) +(3+4)+..........................+(10+11)

PROGRAM-4

```
#include<stdio.h>
#include<math.h>
main()
{    int i, value, total=0;
     printf("\nSeries Total\n");
     for(i=1 ; i<=10 ; i++)
     {
          value = (i+(i+1)) ;
          (printf("(%i+%i)+",i,(i+1));
          total = total + value ;
     }
     printf(" =%i",total) ;
}
```

OUTPUT

This program will give the following output:

(1+2) + (2+3) +(3+4)+ (4+5) + (5+6) +(6+7)+ (7+8) + (8+9) +(9+10)+(10+11)+ = 120

PROBLEM-5

Notice the last term (10+11) in the above given output, it has an extra + sign, which should not be there. Modify the program to get rid of this sign.

Also make modifications in the program, so that it works for the target number given by the user. At present it is working for target number 10.

PROGRAM-5

```
#include<stdio.h>
#include<math.h>
main()
{
     int i, value, total=0, target;
     printf("\nGive the target number");
     scanf("%i",&target);
     printf("\nSeries Total\n");
     for(i=1 ; i<=target ; i++)
     {
          value = (i+(i+1)) ;
          if (i!=target)
          printf("(%i+%i)+",i,(i+1));
```

```
            else
            printf("(%i+%i)",i,(i+1));
            total = total + value ;
        }
        printf(" =%i",total) ;
    }
```

PROBLEM-6

Let's write a program to take roll number and marks of 5 students and print the details of that student, who secured highest marks.

PROGRAM-6

```
    #include<stdio.h>
    main()
    {
        int i, roll, roll_save, marks ;
        int big=0 ;
        for (i=0 ; i<5 ; i++)
        {
            printf("\nGive roll number ") ;
            scanf("%i",&roll) ;
            printf("\nGive marks ") ;
            scanf("%i",&marks) ;
            if (marks > big)
            big=marks ;
            roll_save = roll ;
        }
        printf("\nHighest marks %i secured by roll no. %i" , big, roll_save) ;
    }
```

PROBLEM-7

Let's write a program that takes a number from the user and prints its table.

PROGRAM-7

```
    #include<stdio.h>
    main()
    {   int j, no ;
        printf("\nGive the number whose table is to be printed") ;
        scanf("%i",&no) ;
```

```
        for (j=1 ; j<11 ; j++)
        printf("\n%i * %i = %i ", no,j,(j*no)) ;
    }
```

Nested for Loops

When one for loop is fully placed within other for loop then they are said to be nested. A simple example of nested for loop is given below.

1. for (x=1; x<2; x++)
   for (y=1; y<4; y++)
   printf ("%i,%y); }
   The execution of nested loop takes place as follows:
   Outer loop starts with initial value x=1.
2. In the next step inner loop starts, with initial value of y i.e. y=1 and continues till y<5. Thus for x=1 the inner loop gets executed three times (i.e. y=1, y=2 and y=3).
3. When inner loop gets completed then control is transferred to the outer loop and then for next value of x (i.e. x=2) the inner loop is again executed three times. (i.e. y=1, 2 and 3).
4. The process continues till the outer loop terminates. Thus for each value x the inner loops gets fully executed.

Thus following this sequence of operations, above mentioned loop will generate following output.

```
1,1
1,2
1,3
2,1
2,2
2,3
```

To understand the dynamics of nested for loops, let's write a program for the following problem:

PROBLEM-8

Five companies, manufacture the same product. Write a program to accept their profit figures for the first three months of the year. This program should print total profit of each company and at last print which company made maximum profit and the amount of profit made by it.

PROGRAM-8

```
#include<stdio.h>
main()
{
```

```
        int i,j, profit,comp_save, total_profit=0 ;
        int big=0;
        for( i=1 ; i<6 ; i++)
        {
            printf("\nGive profit figures for company %i ", i) ;
            for (j=1 ; j<4 ; j++)
            {
                printf("\nGive profit for %i month ", j ) ;
                scanf("%i",&profit) ;
                total_profit = total_profit + profit ;
            }
            if(total_profit>big)
            {
                big=total_profit ;
                comp_save = i ;
            }
            printf("\ntotal profit = %i ", total_profit) ;
            total_profit = 0 ;
        }
        printf("\nMaximum profit %i earned by %i " , big, comp_save );
    }
```

JUMP IN LOOPS

In the normal circumstances a loop continues till the time target condition is not achieved. For example, while loop continues, till the time given expression evaluates to true and for loop continues till the time, second expression doesn't hold good. The moment target condition is achieved, the loop breaks. Now the question is, can a loop be terminated in a given condition? Well, C language provides many jump commands for that. These commands are explained below.

Break Statement

The break command abruptly terminates the loop. As soon as it gets executed, program control comes out of the loop and the first statement after the loop gets executed. To understand the functioning of break statement, let's write a program for the given problem.

PROBLEM-9

Let's write a program that takes total amount present in a bank account and the amount that is to be withdrawn per month from that account. The program should calculate and print the number of months the amount will last (Assume that the months will never exceed 100 months). It should also print, how much amount will be left in the account, after withdrawing the last installment.

PROGRAM-9

```
#include<stdio.h>
main()
{
    float amount, pm_amount;
    int i ;
    printf("\nGive total saving amount ") ;
    scanf("%f",&amount) ;
    printf("\nGive per month widthdrawal amount ") ;
    scanf("%f",&pm_amount) ;
    for(i=1 ; i<100 ; i++)
    {
        amount = amount - pm_amount ;
        if (amount < pm_amount)
        break;
    }
    printf("\nThe amount will last for %i months", i) ;
    printf("\nAt last you will be left with %g amount", amount) ;
}
```

Continue Statement

The continue command, when executed breaks the current cycle of the loop and places the program control at the end of the loop. Thus all the statements written after continue command, within the loop, get bypassed in the current iteration. To understand the role of continue command, consider the following program and its result:

PROBLEM-10

Let's write a program to generate a series of the following type and print the sum of it:

$1^2+2^3+3^4+4^5+5^6+6^7$

PROGRAM-10

```
#include<stdio.h>
#include<math.h>
main()
{   int i,j ;
    float total=0.0 ;
    for( i=1 ; i<7 ; i++)
    {
```

```
            for (j=1 ; j<7 ; j++)
            {
                if (i!=j)
                continue;
                else
                {
                    total = total + pow(i,(j+1)) ;
                }
            }
        }
        printf("\nSum = %g ", total) ;
    }
```

NULL Statement

The null statement does nothing. To include a null statement in the program, simply a semicolon is written. For example, following piece of code illustrates the use of null statement:

```
for(i=0 ; i<100 ; i++);
/* Null statement */
printf( "\The prosess got delayed") ;
```

Note that null statement in the third line, above does nothing. Due to this, for loop simply iterates 100 times and doesn't do any thing.

EXERCISES CHAPTER 10

Short Type Questions

A. Select most appropriate answers for the following questions:

1. Which of the following will not form a loop?
   (a) for statement (b) while statement
   (c) 2 goto statements (d) 2 if statements
2. In which of the following loop the number of iterations remain known prior to the execution of the loop?
   (a) for (b) while (c) do while (d) in none of the above.

3. When will a while loop get terminated?
   (a) When given condition is true (b) When given condition is false
   (c) After 10 iterations (d) Depends upon other factors
4. Where in do while loop, condition is placed?
   (a) At top (b) At bottom (c) In middle (d) No where
5. Which of the following command will place the program control at the end of the loop, when it gets executed?
   (a) goto (b) break (c) continue (d) end

B. Fill in the blanks.

6. A loop, which never ends is called ....loop.
7. The statement for (i=1; i<9 ; i++) will iterate the loop .... times.
8. Minimum .... times while loop can get executed.
9. Minimum .... times do while loop can get executed.
10. A loop placed in another loop is called .... loop

C. State true or false.

11. A for loop can be placed within a while loop.
12. While loop gets executed till the time given condition is not attained.
13. The first statement in for loop is always of i++ type.
14. Assume that a=10 and b=20. A condition (a>b) is associated with do while loop. A statement, c=a+b, written in it will get executed, in this situation.
15. A for loop that is made to iterate 10 times, has another for loop in it, which iterates 5 times. A statement written within inner loop will get executed 15 times.

D. Answer the following questions in short:

16. Outer for loop is designed to get executed 5 times and the inner nested for loop is designed to execute 4 times. If printf statement is written just above inner for loop, how many times will it get executed?
17. Outer for loop is designed to execute 5 times and the inner nested for loop is designed to execute 3 times. If a scanf statement is written within inner for loop, how many times will it execute?
18. How many times for(i=2 ; i<10 ; i++) loop will iterate?
19. Which command breaks the loop and brings the program control to the statement, written just after the loop?
20. Minimum how many times a while loop can get executed?
21. Minimum how many times a do while loop can get executed?
22. Minimum how many times a for loop can get executed?
23. Where in do while loop, condition is placed?

Detailed Answer Type Questions

E. Answer the following questions in details:

24. What is the function of for statement? Explain with example.
25. Give an example of nested for statements.
26. Differentiate between do while and while loops. Write their general formats.
27. What is the format of while command? Write its general format.
28. Write the general format of for loop. Explain its functioning with example.
29. Differentiate between break and continue commands.
30. Write a program, which accepts sales figures of 10 executives and prints their commission @13%. It also prints total of commission.
31. Write a program to accept 50 numbers and print the smallest number among them.
32. Write a program to generate the following series:

    $1^9+2^8+3^7+$......................$+10^0$.
33. Write a program to print the all the even numbers, starting for 1 to 100 in reverse order i.e. 100, 98, 96 and so on.
34. Write a program to accept value of N and print the sum of N term Fibonacci series.

****

CHAPTER 11

Arrays

INTRODUCTION

Array, in general, can be defined as similar type of items placed side by side. For example, an array of students, an array of elements or an array of cars. In reference to programming, array comprises of group of variables that are of same data type (int, float, char etc.) Such an array is illustrated in figure 11.1(a).

An array is identified by its name and the number of variables it consists of. For example, the array shown in figure 11.1(a) comprises of 5 variables and its name is x. Thus this array will be identified as x[5].

Individual element in the array is identified by the array name and its position in the array. Position in the array starts from 0 i.e. the first element will be on oth position, second element will be on 1st position and so on. The name of the element is written in the following format:

Array name[element's position in the array]

Following this format, all the element of the array x, will be named as illustrated in figure 11.1(b).

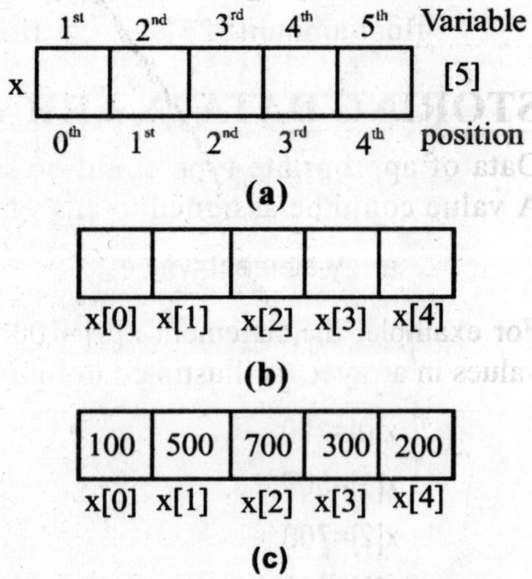

Figure 11.1

Note that the first element will be at oth position and will be named as x[0]. Similarly the last element will be at fourth position and will be named as x[4].

After all, all the elements of the array are variables and variables are utilized for storing some value. Thus an array of integer variable will be able to store integer values. Similarly a character array will be utilized for storing character values. Any mismatch in the array type and the data being stored in it, leads to error. Now the question is, how do you decide the array type? Well, that is done at the time of defining the array. As a general rule, all the arrays must be defined before they are used in the program. The procedure for defining the array is described below.

DECLARING ONE DIMENSION ARRAY

In C programs, arrays are defined in the following format:

```
storage class data-type array-name [No-Of-Elements]
```

Here storage class could either be auto, extern or static. These keywords have their usual meaning and the array defined with these storage classes, behaves in the manner, as described in previous chapter.

The data-type could be int, float, char etc. Data type of an array, obviously defines the data type of its elements. For example, if an array is of int data type then all its elements will also be of int data type. Thus this array will store only integer values in it.

The array-name is the name of the array and No_Of_Elements signifies maximum number of elements that the array will comprise of. Following are few valid array declarations:

```
int mat[20];            /* integer array, mat of 20 elements */
char name[50];          /* character array, name of 50 elements */
static int sum [10];    /* static integer array sum of 10 elements */
float amount [25];      /* float array amount of 25 elements */
```

STORING DATA IN ARRAY

Data of appropriate type could be stored in array, by assigning values to the each element. A value could be assigned to any element of the array in the following format:

```
array element=value
```

For example, the statement x[0]=100 will store 100 in the first element of the array, x. To store values in array x, as illustrated in figure 14.1(c), following statements will have to be written:

```
x[0]=100;
x[1]=500;
x[2]=700;
x[3]=300;
x[4]=200;
```

ACCESSING ARRAY ELEMENTS

Array elements are accessed, simply by their names. For example x[2] refers third element of the array. When you refer this element, you are basically referring to its value. For example, following statement will print 700, because the value stored in x[2] is 700.

```
printf("%i", x[2])
```

Accessing Array Elements Using For Loop

Now think of a situation, in which all the elements of array x have to be printed. For this, you will have to write 5 different printf statements. This situation will become worse if the array comprises of 100 or more.

So to make the task simple, array elements are often accessed, using for loop. Controlling variable (such as i) of for loop varies from 0 to the maximum number of elements in the array and is utilized as index of the array, as illustrated in the following example:

```
for(i=0 ; i<5 ; i++)
    printf ("%i" x[i]) ;
```

Obviously this loop will print all the five elements of the array. Use of such loop is illustrated in the following program.

PROGRAM-1

```
#include<stdio.h>
main()
{
    int x[5] ;
    int i ;
    x[0]=100 ;
    x[1]=500 ;
    x[2]=700 ;
    x[3]=300 ;
    x[4]=200 ;
    for(i=0 ; i<5 ; i++)
    printf("\n%i",x[i]) ;
}
```

RESULT

When executed, this program will produce following output:

```
100
500
700
300
200
```

DECLARING ARRAY USING SYMBOLIC CONSTANTS

Array handling becomes very easy when symbolic contents are used for defining the array, in a program. The use of symbolic contents for defining the array is illustrated in the following example:

```
# define lngth 10
int mat [lngth] ;
```

The first statement above defines the variable named length as 10. When this variable is utilized in second statement, an integer array of 10 gets created.

The use of symbolic constant can be appreciated by visualizing a program, which has been written for operating upon an array of 10 elements. Obviously this program will have multiple spots, where provision for reading, writing and processing 10 elements will be there.

Now, if this program is to be modified to work for 100 elements then a single change, in the statement, #define length 10 ; will have to be made (changing 10 to 100), if symbolic constant has been used in the program. If it has not been used then such changes (10 to 100) will have to be done in all those lines, which are governed by the size of the array.

To understand the usage of array, let's write few programs for the given problems:

PROBLEM-2

Say we have to write a program that takes 5 numbers from the keyboard and prints the average and those numbers, which are above average. This program should make use of symbolic constant and define the array, using it.

PROGRAM-2

```
#include<stdio.h>
# define size 5
main()
{
    int x[size] ;
    int i, total=0 ;
    float avrg=0.0 ;
    for (i=0 ; i<size ; i++)
    {
        printf("\nGive number %i ", (i+1)) ;
        scanf ("%i",&x[i]) ;
        total = total + x[i] ;
    }
    printf("\nTotal %i ", total) ;
```

```
        avrg = total / size ;
        printf ("\nAverage is %g",avrg) ;
        printf("\nNumbers that are above average are :") ;
        for (i=0 ; i<size ; i++)
        {
            if (x[i] >= avrg)
            printf("\n%i ", x[i]) ;
        }
    }
```

PROBLEM-3

Let's write a program, which accepts elements of two arrays (each of 5 elements) and adds them to form a new array. It also prints the new array.

PROGRAM-3

```
    #include<stdio.h>
    # define size 5
    main()
    {
        int a[size], b[size], c[size] ;
        int i ;
        printf("\nGive Elements of first array" );
        for (i=0 ; i<size ; i++)
        {
            printf("\nGive element %i ", (i+1)) ;
            scanf ("%i",&a[i]) ;
        }
        printf("\nGive Elements of second array" );
        for (i=0 ; i<size ; i++)
        {
            printf("\nGive element %i ", (i+1)) ;
            scanf ("%i",&b[i]) ;
        }
        for (i=0 ; i<size ; i++)
        {
            c[i] = a[i] + b[i] ;
```

```
        }
        printf("\nTotals of the sum array are :\n" ) ;
        for(i=0 ; i<size ; i++)
        printf("%i  ",c[i]) ;
    }
```

INITIALIZATION OF ARRAY

Elements of the array can also be initialized at the time of defining the array. This is done by including the values of the elements within the curly brackets, in the array definition statement, in the following format:

```
int x[5]={100, 500, 700, 300, 200};
```

Following points hold good while initializing an array at the time of defining it:

1. Values with which array elements have to be initialized are separated by comma and are written within curly brackets.
2. The first value is assigned to the first element of the array, second values is assigned to the second element and so on.
3. If the number of values given in the curly bracket happen to lesser in number than the number of elements in the array then those elements are set to zero, which do not have corresponding value, within the bracket (if the array is of int type). For example, in a statement int x[5]={100, 500, 700}; elements x[3] and x[4] will be set to zero.

   An array could also be defined and initialized in the following manner.

   ```
   int array-name[]={list of values, separated by comma};
   ```

e.g.

```
int x[]={100, 500, 700, 300, 200};
```

Note that in this format, maximum number of elements in the array is not mentioned. It is automatically set to the number of values listed within the bracket. For example, in above statement, it will be set to 5. Following are few valid array definitions with initializations:

```
float amt[] = {115.55, 227.68, 350.50};
char color[]={'c', 'y', 'm', 'x'};
int mat[10]={-5, -3, 2};
```

To understand the usage of these definitions and the methods of initialization, consider the following program, which prints cube of five numbers.

PROGRAM-4

```
#include<stdio.h>
main()
{
    int a[5]={3,5,7,9,11}  ;
```

```
int i, cube ;
for (i=0 ; i<5 ; i++)
{
    cube = a[i] * a[i] * a[i] ;
    printf("\nCube of %i is %i ", a[i], cube) ;
}
}
```

REORDERING ELEMENTS OF ARRAY (SORTING)

Sorting means arranging elements in a particular way, If you sort the elements in increasing order then such type of sorting is called ascending order sorting and if you arrange elements in decreasing order then such type or sorting is called descending sorting. Unsorted Array, sorted Array in ascending order and descending order are shown in figure 11.2.

4	9	7	2	12

Unsorted Array

2	4	7	9	12

Ascending Order Sorted Array

12	9	7	4	2

Descending Order Sorted Array

Figure 11.2

There are many sorting algorithms present today but we will deal with three main sorting algorithms, which are as follows:

(i) Selection sort

(ii) Bubble sort

(ii) Insertion sort

Selection Sort

The insertion sort starts from the first element and searches the entire Array until it finds the minimum value. The sort places the minimum value at the first place and writes the first place value at the place from where it had picked up the minimum value. After this it selects the second element and searches for the second smallest element. This process is repeated until the complete Array is sorted. The algorithm for selection sort of an Array RAY [N], which has N elements in it, is given below.

Algorithm-1

Steps

1. FOR x=1 to N-1 repeat steps 2 to 7
2. Smallest=RAY [x]; Location=x
3. FOR y=x+1 to N repeat step 4
4. If (RAY [y]>smallest) then

   [Smallest = RAY [y];

   Location=y];

5. Temp=RAY [x];
6. RAY [x]=RAY [Location];
7. ARRAY [location]=Temp;
8. END

This algorithm uses two loops. To compare N elements N-1 comparisons are made in the outer x loop, which terminates at N-1 value. There is one more loop, which is y loop which starts from (x +1th location, which is the 2nd element of unsorted part of the Array. In case of selection sort two things are important to be noted. First is selection and second is exchange. The selection of the smallest element and its position in the unsorted part of Array can be done in the body of a loop. It should be noted that the interchange takes place outside the body of j-loop i.e. from step 5 to 7.

PROGRAM -5

Implementation of this algorithm is shown below in a C program:

```
#include<conio.h>
#include<stdio.h>
void bubble_sort(int[],int);
void main()
{
    int a[30],n,i;
    printf("\nEnter no of elements :");
    scanf("%d",&n);
    printf("\nEnter array elements :");
    for(i=0;i<n;i++)
        scanf("%d",&a[i]);
    bubble_sort(a,n);
        printf("\nSorted array is :");
    for(i=0;i<n;i++)
        printf("%d\t",a[i]);
    getch();
}
void bubble_sort(int a[],int n)
{
    int i,j,temp;
    for(i=1;i<n;i++)
        for(j=0;j<n-i;j++)
            if(a[i]>a[j])
```

```
            {
              temp=a[i];
              a[i]=a[j];
              a[j]=temp;
            }
    }
```

Bubble Sort

As a bubble, in water when rises up, it keeps on growing and it becomes of maximum size, when it reaches at the top level of water. Based on this behavior, the name Bubble sort is assigned to the technique, which works fine for small arrays. Although this sorting technique does not work efficiently when Array size is big. Suppose you have to sort the elements in the Array and move the biggest element to the top of the Array. Say the Array to be sorted is as given below:

Pass 1

I[st] Iteration

40	30	50	20	10

Figure 11.3

Now element 40 is selected and sorting starts. This element 40 is compared with next element and checked if it is smaller. Since 40 is greater than 30 so swapping takes place and 40 is shifted to 2nd place and 30 to first place. After this Array becomes as shown below.

IInd Iteration

30	40	50	20	10

Figure 11.4

Now 40 is again compared to 3rd element and since it is smaller than 50 so no swapping takes place. Thus the Array gets arranged as shown below.

IIIrd Iteration

30	40	50	20	10

Figure 11.5

Now 50 is compared with 20 and swapping takes place again. The Array gets arranged as follows:

IVth Iteration

30	40	20	10	50

Figure 11.6

Now 50 is compared with 10 and again swapping takes place, so as to have the Array arrange as follows:

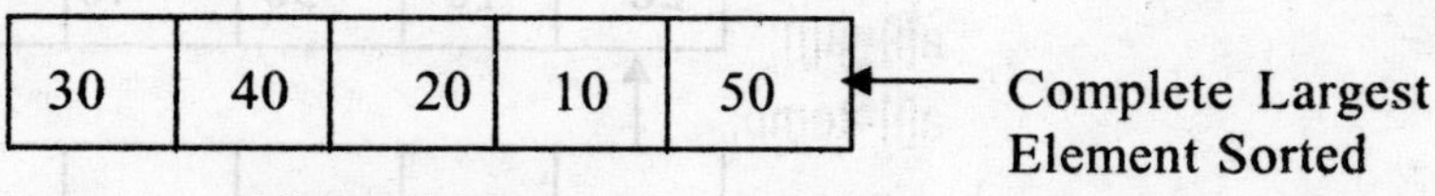

Figure 11.7

All these steps make largest element, come to top. These steps put together are called one pass. So here one pass has made 4 comparisons. Similarly in second pass same steps are repeated but up to (5-1) th position. After this comparison are made till (4-1) th position and the cycle continues till the comparison is made between second and the first element. The arrangement of Array after each pass is shown in the following figure:

Pass 2

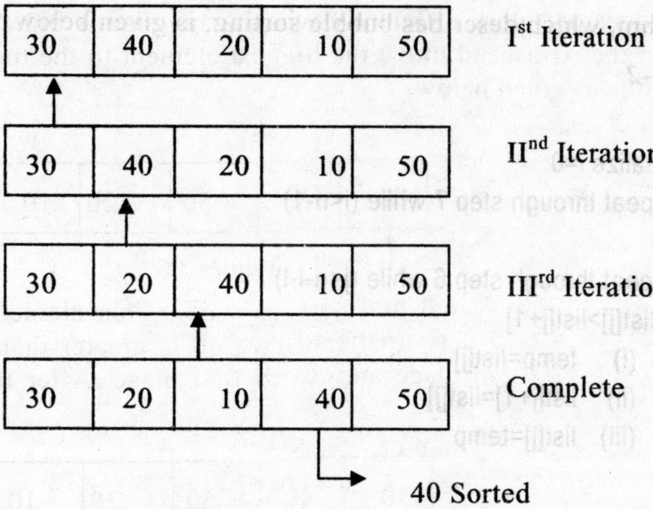

Figure 11.8

Pass 3

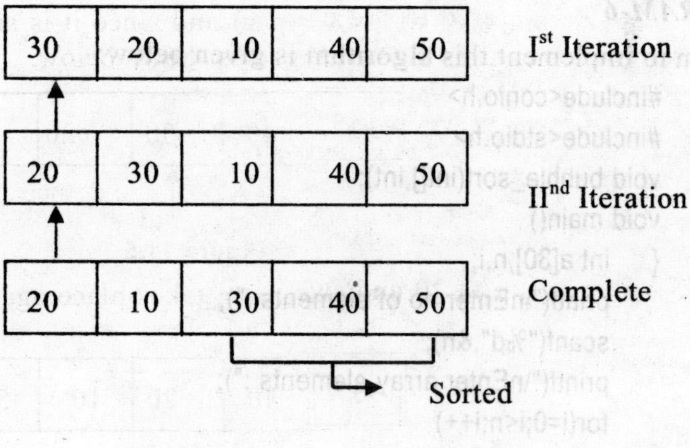

Figure 11.9

Pass 4

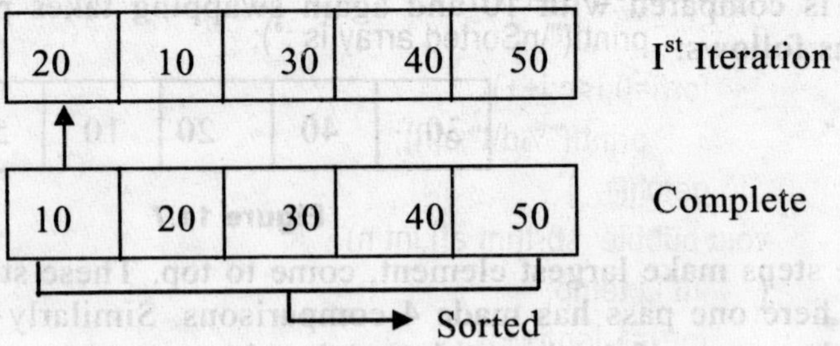

Figure 11.10

This slows that if you have n elements in Array then number of passes will be (n-1).

An algorithm, which describes bubble sorting, is given below:

Algorithm-2

Steps:

1. Initialize i=0
2. Repeat through step 7 while (i<n-1)
3. j=0
4. Repeat through step 6 while (j<n-I-I)
5. if (list[j]>list[j+1]
   (i) temp=list[j]
   (ii) list[j+1]=list[j]
   (iii) list[j]=temp
6. j++
7. i++
8. END

PROGRAM-6

Program to implement this algorithm is given below:

```
#include<conio.h>
#include<stdio.h>
void bubble_sort(int[],int);
void main()
{   int a[30],n,i;
    printf("\nEnter no of elements :");
    scanf("%d",&n);
    printf("\nEnter array elements :");
    for(i=0;i<n;i++)
        scanf("%d",&a[i]);
```

```
        bubble_sort(a,n);
            printf("\nSorted array is :");
        for(i=0;i<n;i++)
            printf("%d\t",a[i]);
        getch(); }
    void bubble_sort(int a[],int n)
    {   int i,j,temp;
        for(i=1;i<n;i++)
            for(j=0;j<n-i;j++)
                if(a[j]>a[j+1])
                {  temp=a[j];
                   a[j]=a[j+1];
                   a[j+1]=temp; } }
```

Insertion Sort

In this method, we do not take up all the numbers (which are to be sorted) at once, for sorting. Rather we start from the first element and assume it to be the only element, which is to be sorted at present. Since at present there is no other element hence it is assumed to be sorted. Now we take up the next element, for consideration and try to sort these two numbers.

When they get sorted we take-up third number along with the first two numbers for sorting and try to sort them. In this way, we continue to sort the Array by taking the next element, along with the previous elements and keep on sorting the numbers till the time there is no next element to be taken up i.e. the end of the Array.

Note that this method of sorting is quite analogous to the arrangement of cards that you make in your hand, when a player distributes cards to you while playing a card game. Recall that when he gives you the first card, you simply pickup the card and hold it in your hand. You assume this card to be sorted, because at this moment there is no other card present. When the card distributor gives you next card, you pick it up and place it either on left hand side or on right hand side, depending upon the type of arrangement (i.e. ascending or descending) you would like to make. Now when you get the next card you place this card either on the left, right or in the middle of the card, so that all the cards that you have in your hand remain in sorted state. Note that, in all, if 13 cards have to come in hand then, not all the 13 cards are being sorted, together but the sorting is taking place gradually between 1, 2,3,4,.............. cards that you have in your hand. The process continues till the last card comes in your hand. Insertion sorting method is similar to card sorting method as mentioned above. This methodology of sorting is implemented as follow:

Say you have an Array of five elements as follows:

50	30	20	10	60

Figure 11.11

Along with this Array you have to have a variable, which will denote the position, till which the Array elements are to be considered for sorting. For example, if the variable has the value 4 then first four element will be taken up for sorting. Note that initially we will take its value to be 1, so that sorting starts from the first element.

Gradual increment and arrangement of Array elements will take place as shown below:

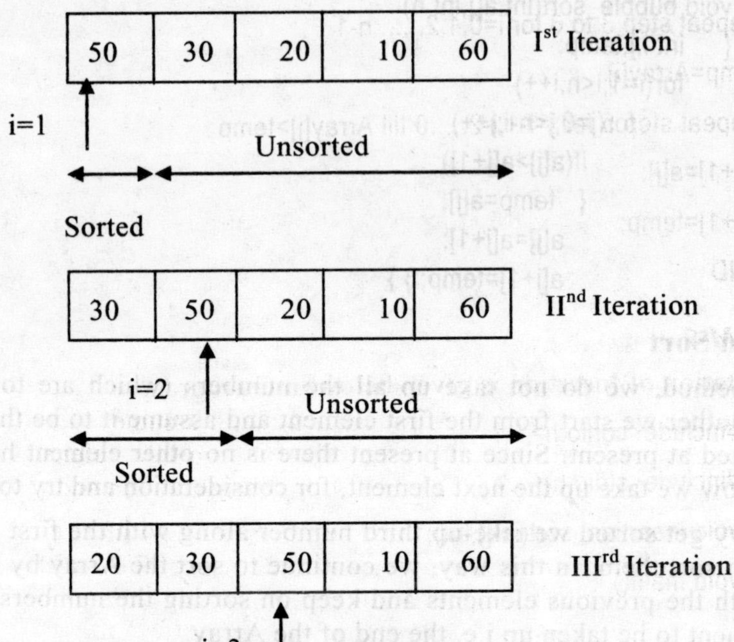

Figure 11.12

An algorithm for Insertion sort is given below:

Algorithm-3

Steps:

1. Initialize i=0
2. Repeat step 3 to 6 for i=0,1,2..... n-1
3. temp=Array[i]
4. Repeat step 5 for j=i-1,i-2.....0 till Array[j]>temp
5. a[j+1]=a[j];
6. a[j+1]=temp;
7. END

PROGRAM-7

Implementation of Insertion is given below in C program.

```
#include<conio.h>
#include<stdio.h>
void insertion_sort(int[],int);
void main()
{
    int a[50],n,i;
    printf("\nEnter no of elements :");
    scanf("%d",&n);
    printf("\nEnter array elements :");
    for(i=0;i<n;i++)
        scanf("%d",&a[i]);
        insertion_sort(a,n);
            printf("\nSorted array is :");
    for(i=0;i<n;i++)
        printf("%d\t",a[i]);
    getch();
}
void insertion_sort(int a[],int n)
```

```
{   int i,j,temp;
    for(i=1;i<n;i++)
    {   temp=a[i];
        for(j=i-1;j>=0 && a[j]>temp;j--)
            a[j+1]=a[j];
        a[j+1]=temp;
    }
}

/*
        *** OUTPUT ***
Enter no of elements :5

Enter array elements :57 89 64 56 77 333

Sorted array is :56    57    64    77    89
*/
```

TWO DIMENSIONAL ARRAYS

Recall that the elements of the array, which we had been dealing up till now, were spread in one direction only, so those arrays are often referred to as single dimension arrays. Now the question is, what happens, if you have multiple such arrays placed one below the other, as shown in figure 11.12(a). Such an arrangement is called two dimensional array. Horizontal arrangement of elements, in such an array is called row and vertical arrangement is called column. Refer figure 11.12(a) and note that this array consists of 3 rows and four columns.

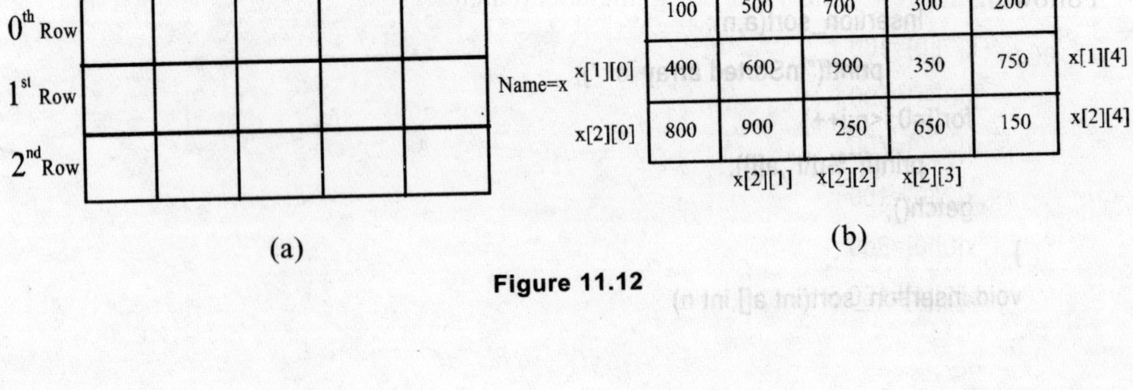

(a) (b)

Figure 11.12

Two dimensional arrays are identified by their names and the number of rows and columns in them. For example, x[3][5] is a valid two dimensional array. Note that first number within the bracket denotes number of rows in the array while the second number denotes number of columns in the array. Thus x[3] [5] denotes an array, x which comprises of 3 rows and 5 columns. Similarly y[10][7] will denote an array y that consists of 10 rows and 7 columns.

As illustrated in figure 10.2(a), the first row is denoted by 0, second row is denoted by 1 and so on. Similarly the first column is denoted by 0, second column is denoted by 1 and so on. Individual elements in the array are identified by the array name and their position in row and column.

For example, the first element of the array x will be x[0][0], second element in the first row will be x[0][1]. Similarly first elements in the second and third row will be denoted as x[1][0], x[2][0] respectively. Few other elements of x[2][4] array are listed in figure 12.2(b), for your reference.

Declaring Two Dimensional Arrays

Two dimensional arrays can be defined in the following format:

```
storage class data-type array-name[No. of rows] [No. of columns]
```

Following are few valid definitions of two dimensional arrays:

```
int summary[12][30] ;

float monthly_amount[12]6] ;

Static int x[3][4] ;

char status [10] [10] ;
```

Assigning Values to the Elements of Two Dimensional Array

Any value can be assigned to elements of two dimensional array, in following format, provided the value matches with the array data type:

```
element-name=value ;
```

Following are few valid value assignment statements:

```
x[0][0]=100 ;

x[0][1]=500 ;

x[0][2]=700 ;

x[2][0]=100 ;

x[0][0]=800 ;

x[2][4]=150 ;
```

Accessing Elements of Two Dimensional Array

Individual elements of two dimensional array can be accessed by referring their names. For example, jut by writing x[1][2] you would refer the value 900. But when it comes to accessing all the elements of the array, one by one, two nested for loops are utilized. Controlling variable of one loop (say i) is utilized for accessing rows of the array and controlling variable of other loop (say j) is utilized for accessing columns of the array. Thus both the variables put together x[i][j], access the complete array. To get familiar with the process of accessing the elements of two dimensional arrays, let's write a program, which accepts elements of two dimensional array (3 row, 4 columns) and prints them.

PROGRAM-8

```
#include<stdio.h>
main()
{   int arry[3][4] ;
    int i, j ;
    for (i=0 ; i<3 ; i++)
    {   printf("\nGive elements of row %i \n", (i+1)) ;
        for (j=0 ; j<4 ; j++)
        {   printf("\Give element %i ", (j+1)) ;
            scanf ("%i",&arry[i][j]) ;
        }
    }
    for (i=0 ; i<3 ; i++)
    {   for (j=0 ; j<4 ; j++)
        printf("%i ",arry[i][j]) ;
        printf("\n") ;
    } }
```

Initializing Two Dimensional Arrays

Two dimensional arrays can also be initialized at the time of their definition, in the following format:

data type array-name [rows] [columns]={list of values separated by comma}

For example, the array illustrated in figure 14.2(a) can be initialized at the time of its definitions, so as to have the element values, as shown in figure 14.2(b), by including following statement in the program.

```
int x[2][4]={100,500,700,300,200,400,600,900,350,750,800,900,250,650,150}
```

Note the following points, in relation to the initialization of two dimensional array at the time of its definition:

1. Values with which array is to be initialized have to be separated by comma and need to be written within the curly brackets.

2. Value assignment is done row wise. That means first value will be assigned to the first element of the first row, second value will be assigned to the second element of the first row and so on till the last element of the first row is assigned the value.

   After last element of the first row, first element of the second row gets initialized and then the second element of the second row. The process continues till the last element of the last row gets initialized.

3. If the number of values fall short, remaining elements are initialized with 0 (if array is of int type and with null if array is of char type). Alternatively the two dimensional array can also be initialized by providing one set of values within the curly brackets, for each row of the array. This method is illustrated below.

```
int x[3][5]={
{100,500,700,300,200},
{400,600,900,350,750},
(800,900,250,650,150}
};
```

Now you are familiar with the definition and initialization methods of two dimensional arrays, so let's write few programs for the given problems.

PROBLEM-9

Write a program, which initializes an array of 3 rows and 4 columns within the program. It takes the values of other array's elements (3 rows and 4 columns) from the keyboard. After accepting the values it adds the two arrays and prints them.

PROGRAM-9

```
#include<stdio.h>
main()
{
    int mat [3][4]={ {10,20,30,40},
    {50,60,70,80},
    {90,100,110,120} } ;
    int arry[3][4] ;
```

```
int sum[3][4] ;
int i, j ;
for (i=0 ; i<3 ; i++)
{
    printf("\nGive elements of row %i \n", (i+1)) ;
    for (j=0 ; j<4 ; j++)
    {
        printf("\Give element %i ", (j+1)) ;
        scanf ("%i",&arry[i][j]) ;
    }
}
for (i=0 ; i<3 ; i++)
{
    for (j=0 ; j<4 ; j++)
    {
        sum[i][j]=mat[i][j] + arry[i][j] ;
        printf("%i ",sum[i][j]) ;
        printf("\n") ;
    }
}
}
```

PROBLEM-10

Write a program to accept sales figures of three products (say, AC, Fridge and Cooler) being manufactured by a company, for first three months of the year (i.e. Jan., Feb. and Mar.). This program, should present the data in tabular form and print row totals and column totals as follows:

Product	Jan	Feb	Mar	Total
AC	10000	15000	25000	50000
Fridge	5000	6000	5500	16500
Cooler	11000	7000	8000	26000
Total	26000	28000	38500	92500

PROGRAM STRATEGY

Note that an array of 3 rows and three columns will be sufficient to hold the figures. But

since we have to generate row totals and column totals also hence we will add one row and one column in the array, so as to have an array of 4 rows and four columns.

PROGRAM-10

```
#include <stdio.h>
# define row 4
# define col 4
initmat(float mat[ ][ ]) ;
main()
{
    float mat[row][col] ;
    int i , j ;
    initmat(mat) ;
    for (i = 0 ; i < row-1; ++i )
    {
        printf("\nGive sales figurs for product %i ",(i+1));
        for (j = 0 ;  j < col-1 ; ++ j )
        {
            printf("\nGive figure for month %i ",(j+1) ) ;
            scanf("%f",&mat[i][j]);
            mat[i][col-1] += mat[i][j] ;
            mat[row-1][j] += mat[i][j] ;
            mat[row-1][col-1] += mat[i][j] ;
        }
        printf("\nGive Value for the next Item");
    }
    for (i = 0 ; i < row; ++i )
    {
        printf("\n");
        for (j = 0 ;  j < col ; ++ j )
        printf("%g ",mat[i][j] ) ;
    }
}
initmat(float mat[row][col])
```

```
{    int i , j ;
     for (i = 0 ; i < row ; ++i )
     for (j = 0 ; j < col ; ++j)
     mat[i][j] = 0.0;
}
```

PROGRAM-11

Let's write a program that reads elements of an integer array and then counts and prints even and odd numbers in it.

```
#include<stdio.h>
#include<conio.h>
void main()
{
    int i,a[50],sum,n, even, odd;
    printf("\n Enter no of elements :");
    scanf("%d",&n);
    /* Reading values into Array */
    printf("\n Enter the values :");
    for(i=0;i<n;i++)
    scanf("%d",&a[i]);
    /* computation of total */
    sum=0; even = odd = 0;
    for(i=0;i<n;i++)
    {    sum = sum+a[i];
         if(a[i]%2==0)
              even++;
         else
              odd++;
    }
    /* printing of all elements of array */
    for(i=0;i<n;i++)
    printf("\n a[%d]=%d",i,a[i]);
    /* printing of total */
    printf("\n sum=%d\n even=%d\n odd=%d", sum, even, odd);
}
```

PROGRAM-12

Let's write a program to read an array of integers and insert an element at specified location.

```
#include<stdio.h>
#include<conio.h>
void main()
{
    int a[30],x,n,i,loc;
    /*
        x   - element to be inserted
        n   - no.of elements in the array
        i   - for scanning of the array
        loc - place where the new element is to be inserted      */
    printf("\n Enter no of elements :");
    scanf("%d",&n);
    /* read n elements in an array  */
    for(i=0;i<n;i++)
    {
        printf("\nGive Element %i ",(i+1));
        scanf("%d",&a[i]);
    }
    printf("\n Enter the element to be inserted :");
    scanf("%d",&x);
    printf("\n Enter the location");
    scanf("%d",&loc);
    /* create space at the specified location */
    for(i=n-1;i>=loc-1;i--)
        a[i+1]=a[i];
    n++;
    a[loc-1]=x;     /* Element inserted  */
    /* Printing of result */
    for(i=0;i<n;i++)
        printf("\n %d",a[i]);
}
```

PROGRAM-13

Let's write a program to copy all elements of an array into another array.

```
#include<stdio.h>
#include<conio.h>
void main()
{
    int a[30],b[30],i,n;
    /* Element of an array 'a' will be copied into array 'b'
    i -> for scanning of an array
    x -> no. of elements in the array */
    printf("\n Enter no of elements :");
    scanf("%d",&n);
    /* Reading values into Array */
    printf("\n Enter the values :");
    for(i=0;i<n;i++)
    scanf("%d",&a[i]);
    /* Copying data from array 'a' to array 'b */
    for(i=0;i<n;i++)
    b[i]=a[i];
    /* printing of all elements of array */
    printf("the copied array is :");
        for(i=0;i<n;i++)
    printf("b[%d]=%d\t",i,b[i]);
    getch();
}
```

PROGRAM-14

Let's write a program to search a given elements in the array.

```
#include<stdio.h>
#include<conio.h>
void main()
{
    int a[30],x,n,i;
    printf("\n Enter no of elements :");
```

```
        scanf("%d",&n);
        /* Reading values into Array */
        printf("\n Enter the values :");
        for(i=0;i<n;i++)
            scanf("%d",&a[i]);
        /* read the element to be searched */
        printf("\n Enter the elements to be searched");
        scanf("%d",&x);
        /* search the element */
        i=0;      /* search starts from the location zero */
        while(i<n && x!=a[i])
        i++;
        /* search until the element is not found i.e. x!=a[i] */
        /* search until the element could still be found i.e. i<n */
        if(i<n)     /* Element is found */
        printf("found at the location =%d",i+1);
        else
        printf("\n not found");
        getch();
    }
```

PROGRAM-15

Let's write a program for merging the elements of two array.

```
    #include<stdio.h>
    #include<conio.h>
    void main()
    {
        int a[30],b[30],c[30],i,j,k,n1,n2;
        /*
        n1 - no of elements in the array 'a'
        n2 - no of elements in the array 'b'
        */
        printf("\n Enter no of elements in 1'st array :");
        scanf("%d",&n1);
```

```
for(i=0;i<n1;i++)
scanf("%d",&a[i]);
printf("\n Enter no of elements in 2'nd array :");
scanf("%d",&n2);
for(i=0;i<n2;i++)
    scanf("%d",&b[i]);
i=0;j=0;k=0;  /* merging starts */
while(i<n1 && j<n2)
{
    if(a[i]<=b[j])
    {
        c[k]=a[i];
        i++;k++;
    }
    else
    {
        c[k]=b[j];
        k++;j++;
    }
}
/* Some statements in array 'a'are still remaining
   where as the array 'b' is exhausted
*/
while(i<n1)
{
    c[k]=a[i];
    i++;k++;
}
/* some elements in array b are still remaining
   whereas the array 'a'is exhausted
*/
while(j<n2)
{
    c[k]=b[j];
```

```
        k++;j++;
    }
    /* Displaying elements of array 'c' */
        printf("\nMerged array is :");
    for(i=0;i<n1+n2;i++)
    printf("\n %d",c[i]);
}
```

EXERCISES CHAPTER 11

Short Type Questions

A. Select most appropriate answers for the following questions:

1. How many elements will be there in X[7] array?
   (a) 7 (b) 8 (c) Initally 0 (d) 6
2. Which of the following will be the last element of X[9] array?
   (a) x[9] (b) x[0] (c) x[8] (d) None of the above
3. How many elements will be there in x[10][5] array?
   (a) 15 (b) 5 (c) 50 (d) 20
4. Which of the following will correctly define an array, if it is to be initialized by {'a', 'b', 'c'} values?
   (a) int x['a'] (b) char x['a'] (c) char x[2] (d) char x[3]
5. Mat[10] is an array. Which statement will pass this array to the function, named prt_array?
   (a) prt-array(mat(10)) (b) prt-array[mat10] (c) prt-array(mat)
   (d) prt-array(mat[]);

B. Fill in the blanks.

6. .... is an example of single dimension array.
7. .... is an example of two dimensional array.
8. To initialize an integer array x[2] with 10, 20 and 30, at the time of defining it, statement .... will be written.
9. Array A[20] will have ....elements in it.
10. All elements of x[20] [30] can be accessed using .... loops.

C. State true or false.

11. Arrays are passed to the function, by reference.
12. To initialize A[5][4] array, you need to provide 20 values.
13. A() is an array of 10 elements.
14. Scanf function can be used to read array elements in the program.
15. getchar can be used to print array elements in the program.
16. Arrary int B[5] can be used to store five character the a, b, c, d and e into it.
17. To store 10 numbers in the program, so that they could be sorted, you require an array, say char x[9].
18. An array int B[5][5].will have 25 elements in it.
19. If X[10]=Y [10] is a valid statement.

D. Answer the following questions in short:

20. Write a statement to define a character array of 5 elements.
21. How many elements will be there in A[100] array?
22. Can while loop be used for accessing elements of an array?
23. Which function will you use to print elements of character array?
24. Which function will you use to accept elements of an integer array?
25. Write declaration statement of an array that would hold 7 double precision numbers.
26. Write a statement to declare 3 by 7 array that will hold characters in it.
27. How many elements will be there in A[10][20] array?
28. In a notation, A[10][4], what [4] represents ?
29. Are arrays always passed to the function by value?

Detailed Answer Type Questions

E. Answer the following questions in details:

30. What is an array? How will you define an array of 20 integer elements?
31. Write the general syntax for initializing a two dimensional array at the time of defining it.
32. What is meant by the statement, "Arrays are passed to the function by reference"? Explain with example.
33. Write a program to accept 10 characters from the keyboard and print total number of vowels in it.
34. Write a program to accept 10 characters from the keyboard and print total number of consonants in it.
35. Write a program to accept 10 numbers and print them in reverse order.
36. Write a program to accept values for all the elements of 10x10 array, from the keyboard. Program should print its diagonal elements.

37. Write a program to subtract two arrays of 3 rows and 3 columns.
38. Write a program to accept marks and names of 10 students. The program should print the marks and name of the student, who secured highest marks.
39. Write a program to read 10 numbers and print, how many of them are prime numbers.
40. Write a program to accept 10 principal amounts and print the interest amount for 5 years if the rate of interest is 12% per year. The interest amounts should be stored in another array, before printing.
41. Write a program to print row and column totals of 10 x 10 array.
42. Write a program to sort an array of 10 elements, using Bubble Sort method.
43. Write a program to accept roll number and marks of 100 students and prepare a merit list of 10 students who got maximum marks.
44. Differentiate between Bubble, Insertion and Selection sort methods.
45. Write a program to add the corresponding elements of two arrays, which are of the same size and store the sum in the third array.

CHAPTER 12

Strings

INTRODUCTION

Data items like, Manmohan, Hydrabad, Computer, Rol-105 etc. are examples of strings. Now the question is how do you handle strings in your program? Because C language doesn't directly support string data type as it does for integer numbers (int data type), real numbers (float data type), characters (char data type) etc. Well, in C language, strings are indirectly handled through character arrays. Complete methodology of handling strings in C language and related functions are described in this chapter.

DIFFERENCE BETWEEN CHARACTERS AND STRINGS

In reference to C language, difference between characters and string need to be understood at two levels. First at external level i.e. how they are written or identified within the program. Second at internal level, i.e. how they are represented internally, within the computer.

Note that a character, written within single quotes is treated as character in C language. For example, 'a' is a character. On the other hand a single or multiple characters written within double quotes are treated as strings. For example "a" is a string. Similarly "Manmohan" is another string.

Another point to be noted is that, in C language all the strings are terminated by a special invisible charcater\0. Thus when you write 'a', single character a gets written in computer's memory. But when you write "a" two characters i.e. a and \0 get stored in memory. Similarly when you write "Manmohan", Manmohan\0 gets stored in memory.

CHARACTER ARRAYS AND STRINGS

You know that an array of char data type is called character array. Such arrays are utilized for storing characters in them. For example, following is a character array definition:

```
char name[10] ;
```

If you store 8 characters M, a, n, m, o, h, a, n in them. They will get stored, as illustrated in figure 12.1(a). Thus name[0] will have 'M' stored in it name[1] will have 'a' stored in it and name[7] will have 'n' stored in it. Elements after this will have nothing in them.

M	A	n	m	o	h	a	n		

(a)

M	a	n	m	O	h	a	n	\0	

(b)

Figure 12.1

As mentioned earlier, in C language, strings are handled through character arrays. For example, the character array, name can be utilized to store the string "Manmohan" in it. When stored, it will get stored as illustrated in figure 12.1(b). Thus name[0] will have 'M' stored in it, name[1] will have 'a' stored in it and name[8] (which had nothing in it, in case of character array) will have '\0' stored in it. The element name[9] will have nothing in it.

In other words, you can say that when the character '\0' is stored in name[8], element of the array, shown in figure 12.1(a), becomes a string.

DEFINING STRINGS AND INITIALIZING

A string can be stored in character array, at the time of defining it. For this following format is used:

```
        char array-name[size]="string";
e.g.    char name[10]="Manmohan";
```

This statement will initialize the name array by the string Manmohan, as illustrated in figure 12.1(b).

Now the question is, what happens, when following statement gets executed.

```
char name[5]="Manmohan";
```

Well, elements of the array will get initialized as follows:

```
name[0]='M', name[1]='a', name[2]='n', name[3]='m',name[4]='o'
```

Since the elements of this character array are not terminated by '\0' character hence this array will not represent a string. It will store characters. Thus proper care has to be taken while defining the length of the array and the length of the string that has to be stored in the array. A safe method of defining and initializing character array is as follow:

```
char array name[]="string"
```

Note that this format does not mention any thing about the length of the string. When it gets executed, the length is automatically set to the length of string, taking care of the termination character, '\0' also. For example, following is valid statement, which defines name array and initializes it with the string "Manmohan".

```
char name[]="Manmohan";
```

This statement will define the length of the array as 9 and initialized it as illustrated in figure 12.1(b).

DISPLAYING STRING, USING FORMAT

You know printf() is the function, using which int, flot and char values are printed on VDU. Now the question is, how do you print a string? Well, the same printf() function is used for printing strings also. To print a string, you need to make use of %s format. For example, if name is a character array, holding the string, "Manmohan" in it then printf("%s", name); will display the string on VDU. To get familiar with string printing operations, consider the following program:

PROGRAM-1

```
#include <stdio.h>
main()
{
    char x[ ] = "I live in India" ;
    printf("\n%s",x) ;
}
```

ACCEPTING STRING FROM THE KEYBOARD

You know that scanf() function is used for accepting integer, float, character values etc. from the keyboard. Now the question is how do you accept, string, in the program, from the keyboard? Well, the same scanf() function is used for accepting strings from the keyboard. Note that to accept strings, using scanf() function, you need to make use of %s format in the function. In addition to this you need not prefix string variable, with & sign, as you do in case of integers, float, characters etc. For example, if name is a character array then using scanf("%s", name); statement a string can be accepted in the array, from the keyboard. To get familiar with string input operations, consider the following program:

PROGRAM-2

```
#include <stdio.h>
main()
{
    char x[25] ;
    printf("\nGive a string ") ;
    scanf("%s",x) ;
    printf("\n%s",x) ;
}
```

RESULT

To understand the functioning of scanf() function properly, consider the following inputs and the result produced for them (by above written program).

1. In you input the string "Manmohan" through keyboard it will be printed as such on the VDU.
2. If you input Manmohan Singh, it will again print Manmohan on VDU.

This happens because scanf function has been designed to accept strings that have no blanks in them. As soon as, blank appears in the string, following part is rejected by scanf() function. On contrary to this, if you input "ManmohanSingh". This string will get displayed on VDU because it doesn't have blanks in it. Now the question is, how do you accept strings with blanks, from the keyboard? Well for that you will have to make use of getchar() function.

Recall that getchar() function accepts one character from the keyboard. Well, to accept all the characters of the string, you will have put getchar() function in loop. Now the question is, how long the loop should continue? Because nobody knows, in advance that how many characters will be there in the coming string. Well, but one thing is sure that after inputting the string Enter will be pressed. Note that when you press Enter '\n' character gets passed. Thus the loop, can continue till '\n' character is pressed. This logic has been transformed into C statements in the following program:

PROGRAM-3

```
#include <stdio.h>
main()
{
    char x[30];
    int i=0;
do {
        x[i]=getchar();
    }
    while(x[i++]!='\n');
    x[i]='\0';   /* Adds \0 character at the end*/
    printf ("\n%s",x );
}
```

RESULT

If you provide "Manmohan Singh" as input string to this program, it will display the string, as such (with blank in between) on the VDU.

MULTIPLE STRING HANDLING

Now you know that a single string can be very well handled, using one dimensional array, in C program. Now the question is, how do you handle multiple strings? Well, the method is quite simple, they are handled through two dimensional arrays.

Recall that two dimensional arrays are conceptualized as many single dimension arrays, placed one below the other. Thus each single dimension array (which is nothing but the row of elements) can be utilized to store a different string. A two dimensional array with multiple strings stored in it is illustrated in figure 12.2.

D	e	l	h	I	\0			
M	u	m	b	A	i	\0		
C	h	e	n	N	a	i	\0	
H	y	d	r	A	b	a	d	\0
K	o	l	k	O	t	t	a	\0

Figure 12.2

Now to get familiar with multiple string handling operations, let's write a program for the given problem.

PROBLEM-4

Say we have to write a program, which accepts names of 10 students and their marks from the keyboard and prints them.

PROGRAM-4

```
#include <stdio.h>
#include <string.h>
#define row 10
#define col 101
main()
{
    int i;
    char x[row] [col];
    int marks[row] ;
    printf ("\n Enter Student's  \n");
    for (i=0; i<row; ++i)
    {
        printf ("Name %d", i+1);
        scanf("%s",x[i]);
        printf ("Marks ");
        scanf("%i",&marks[i]);
    }
    for(i=0 ; i<row; ++i)
    {
        printf("\n %s", x[i]);
        printf("  %d", marks[i]) ;
    }
}
```

STRING HANDLING FUNCTIONS

While operating upon strings, operations of following type need to performed, quite often:

1. Equating the two strings i.e. assigning the value of one string to other string.
2. Comparing two strings to know, which of them is lexically high, in order. For example, "Amit" will be lower in order than "Boy".
3. Find the length of a string.
4. Concatenate two given string, so as to have a single string.

To perform such operations, C language provides few string functions. These functions remain available in "string.h" library. So to make use of these functions, you need to include this library, in the beginning of your program, as follows:

```
#include<string.h>
```

A detailed description and usage of string related function is given below.

The strcpy Function

This function copies one string into other string. It is used in the following format:

```
strcpy (string-1, string-2) ;
```

Here string-2 is that string, which is to be copied and string-1 is the string, in which copying is to be done. Thus at the end of the execution, string1 will hold string-2 in it.

To understand the concept assume that x[5] [30] is a two dimensional array and x[1]="" and x[2]="Sachin". Following statement will copy the string "Sachin" into x[1].

```
strcpy (x[1],x[2]);
```

The strcmp Function

This function compares two given strings and finds, which of them comes first in lexicographical order. It is used in the following format:

```
strcmp (string-1, string-2);
```

This function gives following results:

1. Negative value if string-1 falls lower in lexicographical order.
2. 0 if both the strings are same.
3. Positive value if string-2 falls lower in lexicographical order.

For example, the statement strcmp(x[1], x[2]) will produce results as stated in following table:

x[1]	x[2]	Result
Amit	Boy	Negative value (say -5)
Amit	Amit	0
Boy	Amit	Positive value (say 10)
Arti	Zenat	Negative
Pramod	Prashant	Negative

The strlen Function

This function returns the length of the given string i.e. how many characters constitute the string (excluding '\0' character). It is used in the following format:

```
strlen (string-1);
```

Here string-1 is that string, whose length is to be determined.

For example, if x[1]="Delhi" then strlen(x[1]); statement will give 5. Similarly if x[1]="Hydrabad" then it will return 8.

The strcat Function

This function concatenates two strings and forms a single string out of them. It is used in the following format:

```
strcat (string-1, string-2)
```

For example, if x[1]="Manmohan" and x[2]="Singh" then strcat(x[1],x[2]) will give "ManmohanSingh".

To understand the usage of these functions, let's write a program, which makes use of these functions.

PROBLEM-5

Write a program that takes 20 names from you and prints them in sorted ascending order. The program should have the provision to take less than 20 names also, thus terminating the input process if name is given as "Last".

PROGRAM-5

```
#include <stdio.h>
#include <string.h>
print(int n , char a[][15]) ;
sort(int n , char a[][15]) ;
main()
{
int i, n = 0 ;
char array[20][15] ;
printf("\nEnter a name name\n") ;
do {
    printf("Name %d ",n+1) ;
    scanf ("%s",array[n]) ;
    }
while (strcmp(array[n++], "Last"));
```

```
        n= n-1 ;
        printf("\n\nUnsorted array") ;
        print(n,array) ;
        sort(n,array) ;
        printf("\n\nSorted Array") ;
        print(n,array) ;
      }
      sort(int no, char a[][15])
      {
      int i , j ;
      char tmp[15] ;
      for ( i = 0 ; i < no-1 ; i++ )
      for ( j = 0 ; j < no-1 ;  j++ )
        {
           if (strcmp (a[j],a[j+1]) > 0 )
           {
              strcpy (tmp,a[j+1]) ;
              strcpy (a[j+1],a[j]) ;
              strcpy (a[j],tmp) ;
           }
        }
      return ;
      }
      print(int no, char a[][15])
      {
      int i = 0 ;

      for ( i = 0 ; i < no ; i++ )
           printf("\n%s",a[i]);
      return ;
      }
```

EXERCISES CHAPTER 12

Very Short Answer Type Questions

A. Select the most appropriate choice for the following questions:

1. Which character terminates strings in C?

   (a) /0 (b) \0

   (c) "\0" (d) !0

2. What will be the maximum length of the string that would get stored in char array, A[10]?

   (a) 9 (b) 10

   (c) 11 (d) 0

3. Say s1="Bell" and s2="bell" then what value will be returned by the function. strcmp(s1,s2)?

   (a) Positive (b) Negative

   (c) 0 (d) Null

4. Which of the following functions will not read string from keyboard?

   (a) get() (b) scanf

   (c) gets() (d) getchar()

5. Which of the following functions will not write a string?

   (a) write (b) printf

   (c) puts (d) putchar()

6. How many elements will be there in X[7] array?

   (a) 7 (b) 8 (c) Initally 0 (d) 6

7. Which of the following will be the last element of X[9]?

   (a) x[9] (b) x[0] (c) x[8] (d) None of the above

8. How many elements will be there in x[10][5] array?

   (a) 15 (b) 5 (c) 50 (d) 20

9. Which of the following will correctly define an array, if it is to be initialized by {'a', 'b', 'c'} values?

   (a) int x['a'] (b) char x['a'] (c) char x[2] (d) char x[3]

10. Mat[10] is an array. Which statement will pass this array to the function, named prt_array?

    (a) prt-array(mat(10)) (b) prt-array[mat10]

    (c) prt-array(mat) (d) prt-array(mat[]);

B. State True or False

11. In C language, strings are declared, as character arrays.
12. In C language, each string has to be terminated by \n.
13. To manipulate a string of 20 characters you require an array of at least 22 elements.
14. If a[] represent a string and b[] represents another string then string b[] can be copied to a[] by writing a[]=b[].
15. If you have to accept the name of 25 students then you will have to make use of two-dimensional arrays in your program.
16. Arrays are passed to the function, by reference.
17. To initialize A[5][5] array, you need to provide 25 values.
18. "s" is a string.
19. Strings can be accepted in the program, using printf function.
20. getchar can be used to accept strings with blanks in them.
21. To store the string TATA, you need to have a character array, with, at least, 5 elements in it.
22. To store 10 city names (of maximum 10 characters) in the program, so that they could be sorted, you require an array, say char x[10].
23. The strcat function copies one string into other string.
24. If x[]="Hello" and y[]="Dear" then the statement x[]=y[] will put Dear in x[].

C. Fill in the Blanks:

25. In C, language each string is terminated by .... character.
26. .... is the function that copies one string to another.
27. To copy strg1[] string to strg2 [] you will have to write .... in your program.
28. To compare two strings strg1 [] and strg [] to see if they are equal, you will have to write .... in your program.
29. To handle 25 characters long name in your program you will have to make declaration of array as ....
30. .... is an example of single dimension array.
31. .... is an example of two dimensional array.
32. To initialize an integer array x[2] with 10, 20 and 30, at the time of defining it, statement .... will be written.
33. In C language, strings are terminated with .... character.
34. All elements of x[20] [30] can be accessed using .... for loops.

Short Answer Type Questions

D. Answer the Following Questions in Short :

35. What is the basic relationship between array and string in C?
36. What is the basic difference between storing characters and strings in an array?
37. Which character terminates a string in C?
38. What should be the minimum length of the array, which will store names that are15 characters long?
39. Is there any problem in following declaration of the array?

    char[10]="India Is The Best";
40. Is there any problem in following declaration of the array?

    char[]="India Is The Best";
41. Is there any problem in following declaration of the array?

    int[5]="12345";
42. Write the statement to print the string, which has been stored in one dimensional array named NM.
43. Write a statement to accept a string from the keyboard and to store it in an array named ARI.
44. The word BellInfotech is stored in an array named ARY. Which function will you use to print four left most characters of this string?
45. You need to store 10 names of 50 characters long in your program. How will you declare a suitable array for this?
46. In a two dimensional array of strings, what will columns of the array store? What will rows of the array store?
47. A and B are two arrays which have been initialized with different strings. What is the problem with following code segment?

    A=B ;
48. Which header file will have to be included in the program for making use of string related function?
49. Which function will you use in your C program, if you wish to hold the current value of a string in a temporary string variable?
50. The statement strcmp(x, y) returns a negative value. What inference will you draw from this?
51. The statement strcmp(x, y) returns a positive value. What inference will you draw from this?
52. While making use of strcmp() function, how do you come to know that the two given strings are identical?
53. Which function and header file will you use if you are asked to add two given strings in your C program?

54. An array of 10 elements has been initialized with the word BEST. What will be the value of 7th element?
55. Write a statement to define a character array of 5 elements.
56. Can while loop be used for accessing elements of an array?
57. Which function will you use to print a string?
58. Which function will you use to accept a string in your program?
59. Which type of array will be required to operate upon single string?
60. Which type of array will be required to operate upon multiple strings in your program?
61. Which function returns the length of the given string?
62. Which function copies one string into other?
63. Are arrays passed to the function by value?

Long Answer Type Questions

E. Answer the Following Questions in Detail :

64. What do you understand by a string?
65. What is the basic difference between string and char?
66. Which data type is provided in C for storing strings?
67. Which special character is inserted at the end of string and why this provision is made?
68. What is the difference between storing a character and a string? Explain with example.
69. In which way does initialization of character array take place?
70. Which method is used to print a string on screen?
71. What method do you adopt for inputting string in program? Explain with example.
72. How do you handle multiple strings in a program?
73. What are string-manipulating functions? Write examples of any three such functions.
74. Which string function will you use to copy one string to another?
75. Which string function will you use to compare two strings? Give an example.
76. Which string function will you use to calculate the length of a given string?
77. Which function is used for concatenating two strings?
78. Write the general syntax for initializing a two dimensional array at the time of defining it.
79. What is meant by the statement, "Arrays are passed to the function by reference"? Explain with example.
80. Differentiate between character and string. How a character array x, containing c, i, r, c, l, e in it, could be converted to a string.

81. Write a program to accept a string and display its length.
82. Write a program to accept a string and print its each character in a new line.
83. Write a program to subtract two arrays of 3 rows and 3 columns.
84. Write a program to accepts marks and names of 10 students. The program should print the marks and name of the student, who secured highest marks.
85. Write a program, which accepts a string and finds, if it is palindrome or not. For example, abeba is such a string.

F. Write C Programs For Following Problems:

86. Write a program for accepting two strings from the keyboard and printing them on the terminal.
87. Write a program, which displays the use of get function for accepting your home address, which can be of maximum 100 characters long.
88. Write a simple program, which accepts 3 names of the students, from the keyboard (length not exceeding 20 characters) and then simply prints them on the terminal.
89. Write a program for initializing second string from an already existing string.
90. Write a program that accepts a string and converts it to uppercase and calculates its length.
91. Write a program that accepts name and marks of five students and then prints the name of the student who got the highest marks.
92. Write a program that takes names of 10 cities and their population. It sorts the names of the cities in such a way that the city having lowest population comes first and the city having highest population comes last. Display the sorted list on VDU.
93. Write a program that accepts 10 names and then finds out, which of the 10 names are same. Display the same names on VDU. At last, also count the number of names that were found to be the same.
94. Write a program to take five characters from the keyboard and convert them to a string and check that, this string is "India" or not.
95. Write a program to accept 10 city names and the names of the state to which they belong. The program should accept a city name and search for its state name and display it.
96. Write a program to accept a sentence from the keyboard and count the number of occurrences of each vowel.
97. Write a program to take a string from the keyboard and print it in the reverse order.
98. Write a program to accept names of 10 countries and print them in descending sorted order.
99. Write a program to accept a string with blanks. Program should remove the blanks and print the string. For example the string "Bell Infotech" should be printed as "BellInfotech".

100. **Take a string of 5 characters from the keyboard and print it in diminishing manner as shown, for the string India, below.**

India
Indi
Ind
In
I

101. **Write a program to accept a string and print it in incrementing fashion. For example, Infotech should be printed as :**

I
In
Inf
Info
Infot
Infote
Infotec
Infotech

*****

CHAPTER 13

Modular Programming

INTRODUCTION

Functions are basically special type of programs, which perform a specific task, but don't work independently, as main function does. They get executed only when some other program calls them. If required, they receive data from the program that had called them. After processing the data they may or may not return back some value to the program, which had called them. The concept of function is illustrated in figure 13.1.

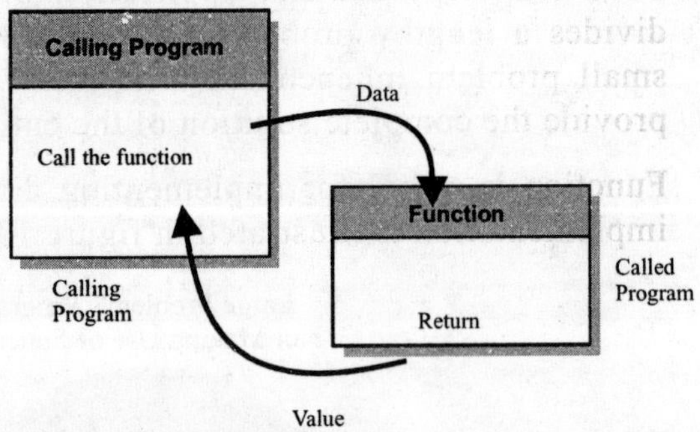

Figure 13.1

Functions are identified by their names and a list of variables, (separated by comma) through which they transact data with the calling program. For example, following is a function, which adds given five numbers:

sumlist(a,b,c,d,e)

As a matter of fact, functions, once written can be called anywhere, any number of times, by as many calling programs as required. For example, a function, say convert_num_2_words, which converts, numbers into word (e.g. 11 to Eleven etc.) can be written and called within the main function, as many times as required. Similarly another function, say pay(), which prints pay slips for the employees of the organization, may use the function for converting their pay amount into words.

TYPES OF FUNCTIONS

C functions can be broadly classified into two categories:

1. Standard C library functions.
2. User defined functions.

Standard C library functions, like printf, scanf, getchar, putchar etc. remain available in standard libraries like <stdio.h> etc. You are already familiar with such type of libraries and functions. Note that many more functions like pow(a,b), sqrt(n) etc. remain available in other libraries of C.

User defined functions are written by the user for performing a task of his requirement. A detailed description of user-defined functions is given below.

NEED FOR USER DEFINED FUNCTION

Not all the times, problems to be programmed are simple. They are often complex and involve many issues. A single program (as we had been writing, up till now) written for such problems becomes very large.

Lengthy programs are always difficult to write, test and maintain. Long monolithic code is likely to have errors in it. Finding errors and fixing them in long code is a difficult and sometimes challenging task.

In lengthy program, effect of an error ripples down the remainder portion of the program, creating a snowball effect. Thus even a small error may produce entirely wrong results, giving an impression that the whole program is incorrect.

Often in lengthy program, similar type of activities have to be performed at multiple places. Writing same code at each place makes the program lengthier and the problems of lengthy program get increased.

Such situations demand application of divide and conquer strategy. A strategy, which divides a lengthy problem into multiple small problems and promotes handling of each small problem independently in such a way that their individual solutions put together provide the complete solution of the entire problem.

Function is a tool for implementing divide and conquer strategy, within the program. Its implementation is illustrated in figure 13.2.

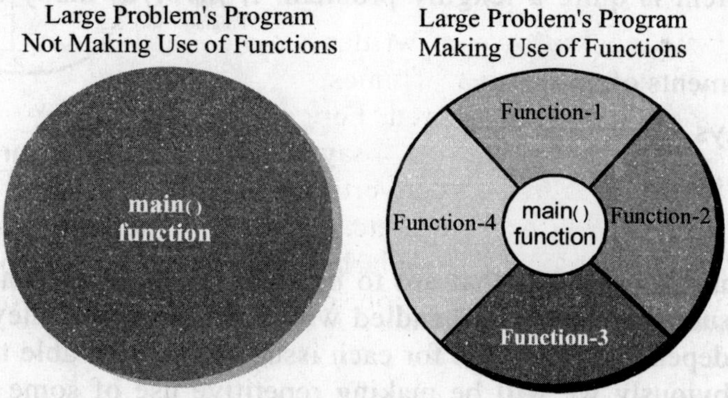

Figure 13.2

ADVANTAGES OF USING FUNCTIONS

Advantages of using functions are many. Some of them are listed below.

1. With the use of functions, modularity gets automatically incorporated in the program. Thus a single long program gets divided into small modules, obviously maintaining small modules is much easier than maintaining a single large program.
2. If function is being used then to perform the same function again within the program, the code need not be written again. Only one line for calling the function can be written, which would perform the task. This not only saves efforts and time but also reduces the length of the program.
3. Since function written for one program, can be used in other programs also hence programming becomes easy. Time and efforts reduce to a considerable extent.

A MULTI-FUNCTION PROGRAM

When you implement divide and conquer strategy, using function, the complete program becomes multi-function program. In such a program each function will be an independent unit dealing with specific segment of the problem. Say, we have to write a program, which performs following functions:

1. Accepts elements of first array.
2. Accepts elements of second array.
3. Prints first array.
4. Prints second array.
5. Calculates sum of the two arrays.
6. Prints sum of the arrays.
7. Calculates difference of the two arrays.
8. Prints difference of the two arrays.

Note that this problem is quite a lengthy problem. It involves many issues of following types:

1. Reading elements of array.
2. Adding arrays.
3. Subtracting arrays.
4. Printing the array.

Now compare the number of tasks that are to be done (as mentioned above, they are 8 in number) and the issues that are to be handled within the program (they are 4 in number). Thus if we write independent functions for each issue, we will be able to handle 8 tasks by just 4 functions. Obviously we will be making repetitive use of some of the functions to perform the complete task. Skeleton of such a program is illustrated in figure 13.3.

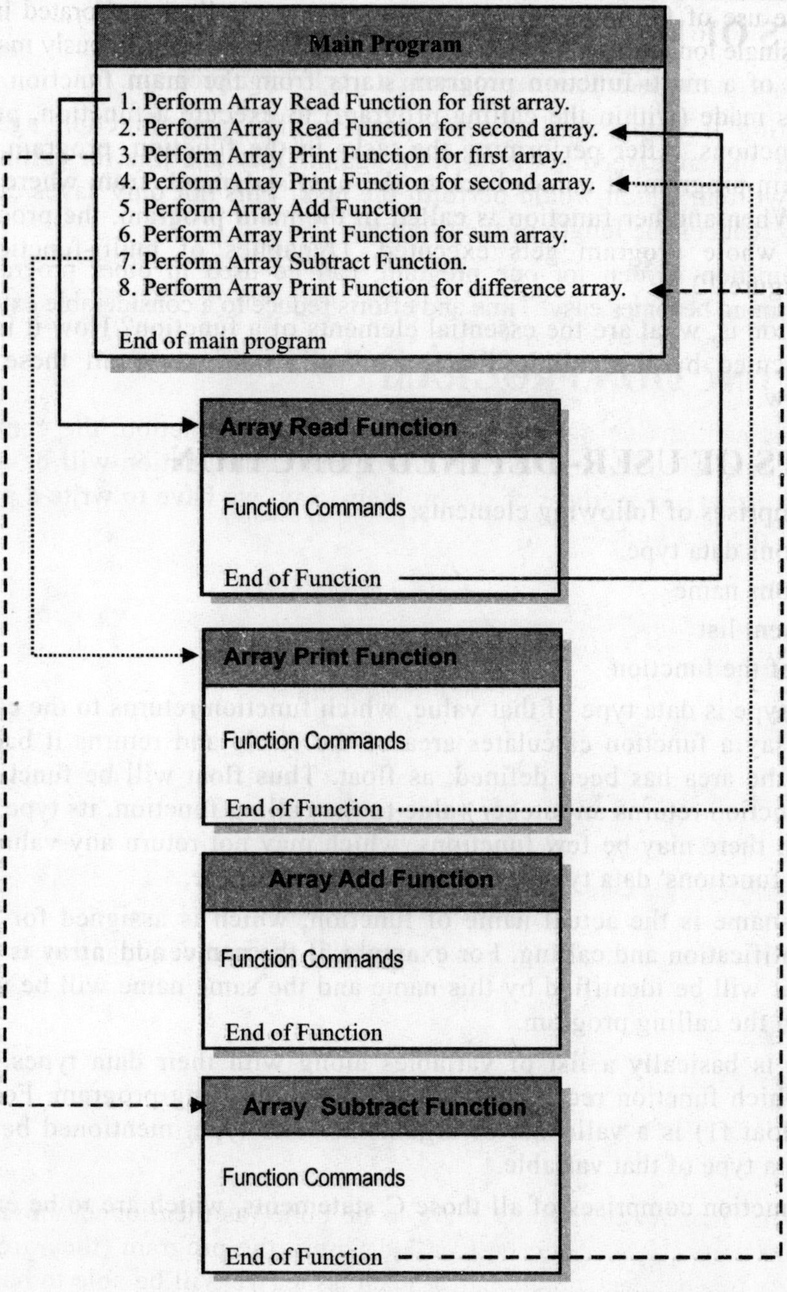

Figure 13.3

This is a skeleton of multi-function program, which clearly states role, functioning and advantages of use of function.

DYNAMICS OF MULTI-FUNCTION PROGRAM

The execution of a multi-function program starts from the main function. As and when function call is made (within the calling program) to execute a function, program control goes to the functions. After performing the tasks in the function, program control comes back to the main program. It comes back to the next statement, from where it had gone to the function. When another function is called in the main program, the process repeats. In this way the whole program gets executed. Dynamics of multi-function program is illustrated in figure 13.3.

Now the question is, what are the essential elements of a function? How it is defined? And how it is executed by the calling function? Well, answers of all these questions are explained below.

ELEMENTS OF USER–DEFINED FUNCTION

A function comprises of following elements:

1. Functions data type.
2. Functions name
3. Argument list
4. Body of the function.

Function data type is data type of that value, which function returns to the calling program. For example, say a function calculates area of the circle and returns it back to the main program. Say the area has been defined, as float. Thus float will be function's data type. Similarly if function returns an integer value to the calling function, its type will be int. On the other hand, there may be few functions, which may not return any value to the calling function, such functions' data type is said to be void data type.

Here function-name is the actual name of function, which is assigned for the purpose of function's identification and calling. For example, if the name, add_array is assigned to the function then it will be identified by this name and the same name will be used for calling this function in the calling program.

Argument list is basically a list of variables along with their data types. These are the variables in which function receives the data from the calling program. For example, (int a1, char c1, float f1) is a valid list of arguments. The type, mentioned before a variable name is the data type of that variable.

Body of the function comprises of all those C statements, which are to be executed, within the function.

USING FUNCTIONS

Using functions in C program is two-step process.

1. First you need to define the function.
2. Second, you need to call the function in some other program.

A detailed description of defining and calling the user-defined functions is given below.

DEFINITION OF FUNCTION

In C language, function is defined in the following format:

```
data-type function-name (type1 arg1, type2 arg2............. type-m argm)
```

Here data-type, name and variables written within the bracket (argument list) have the same meanings, which were explained above.

The variables, in which function receives data, are called formal arguments or formal parameters. These arguments are said to be local to the function. That means they come into existence when function starts and loose their existence when function ends. This is the reason, why values of formal parameters remain inaccessible outside the function

FUNCTION CALL

As mentioned earlier, function doesn't execute on its own. It gets executed, when the calling function calls it. Now the question is, how do you call a function, which has already been defined? Well, a function can be called by writing a statement of the following type, in the calling program:

```
function name (argument list) ;
```

For example, to call the function, big, in a program, following statement will have to be introduced at that point in the program, where the function has to be called.

```
big (a1, b2);
```

Here a1 and b2 are the variables, whose values have to be passed to the function, for processing. Variables of calling statement are called actual parameters or actual arguments. Now refer, calling statement mentioned above and the definition of the function, big and note the following points:

1. Number of formula parameters in the function and actual parameter in calling program should match. For example, if there are two formal parameters then there will have to be two actual parameters. Any mismatch in number will lead to error.
2. Data types of formal parameters should match with data type of actual parameters. For example, if the first formal parameter is of int type and second is of float type then first actual parameter should also be of int type and the second actual parameter should be of float type. In short, you can say that there should be one to one correspondence between them. Any mismatch between them leads to an error.

When a function is called the value of first actual argument is copied in first formal argument, value of second actual argument is copied in second formal argument and so on.

RETURN STATEMENT

They body of the function can terminate with a return statement. If function doesn't return any value to the calling function, either return statement is omitted or a simple statement, "return" is written. On the other hand, if the function returns a values to the calling function, statement "return(value)" is written. Here value could be a variable or expression, which evaluates to the value that need to be sent back to the calling program. For example, if x=100 and the value of x is to be returned to the calling program then the statement return(x); will have to be written.

To understand the usage of function, let's write a function, named big, which receives two integer values from the main function and returns back the larger value to it.

```
int big (int n1, int n2)
{
    if n1>n2
    eturn(n1) ;
    else return (n2) ;
}
```

Note that it is not necessary that function should always return a value to the calling program. It may or may not return the value, depending upon the requirement.

Limitation with return statement is that it can return only a single value to the calling program. Multiple values can't be returned through it. For example "return(a,b)" is a wrong statement.

FUNCTION DECLARATION

Now you know that to make use of function, you have to have a function and a calling program (function). Now the question is, in which sequence these two items should be placed? Should the definition be placed before the calling function or after calling function? Well, C language supports both the methods. Both these methods are explained below.

Placing the Function Definition Before Calling Program

Say there is a function named big, which receives two numbers from the calling program. It compares them and returns back the larger number.

Assume that main() is the calling function, it accepts two numbers from the keyboard and passes them to a function named big. The big function returns the larger number to the main function, where it gets printed on the screen.

When function definition is placed before calling program (which is main() function, in this case) the whole arrangement will appear as shown in the following program:

PROGRAM-1

```
#include<stdio.h>

int big(int n1, int n2)
{
if (n1>n2)
  return(n1) ;
```

```
else
    return(n2) ;
}
main()
{
    int no1, no2, no3 ;
    printf("\nGive First number" ) ;
    scanf("%i",&no1) ;
    printf("\nGive Second number" ) ;
    scanf("%i",&no2) ;
    no3 = big(no1,no2) ;
    printf("\nLarger of the two numbers is %i ",no3);
}
```

Note that in this type of arrangement, since function definition exists before calling program hence at the time of calling the function, compiler already knows that a function of this name exists and its return type and argument list is of such type. So it matches actual parameters with formal parameters and if any discrepancy is found, it reports error. Thus no extra arrangement is made to educate the compiler regarding function details.

Placing the Function Definition After Calling Program (Use of Function Prototype)

As mentioned earlier, function definition can also be placed after the calling program. For example, definition of big function can also be placed after the main() function.

In such arrangement, when a call is made in the calling program, compiler would never know, that a function with such name exists and its return type and argument lists are of such type. Since compiler will be ignorant of function's existence hence it will immediately given an error. To overcome this problem, C language suggests that in such cases (in which the function definition is placed after calling program) a function prototype should be used at the beginning of the calling program. A function prototype is written in the following format.

```
data type function-name (type arg1, type-2arg2, .....type-n argn);
```

Note that function prototype is functions definition, terminated by a colon(;). Thus if the function is placed after main() function then the whole arrangement, including use of function prototype will be as follows:

PROGRAM-2

```
#include<stdio.h>
int big(int n1, int n2) ; /* Function Prototype */
main()
{
    int no1, no2, no3 ;
    printf("\nGive First number" ) ;
    scanf("%i",&no1) ;
    printf("\nGive Second number" ) ;
    scanf("%i",&no2) ;
    no3 = big(no1,no2) ;
    printf("\nLarger of the two numbers is %i ",no3);
}
int big(int n1, int n2)  /* Function definition */
{
    if (n1>n2)
    return(n1) ;
    else
    return(n2) ;
}
```

CALLING FUNCTION BY VALUE (FUNCTION CALL TECHNIQUE)

As mentioned earlier, when you make use of a function in calling program, values of actual parameters get copied in formal parameters. Thus at that point of time, two values exist. Function operates upon the second copy (value received in formal parameters). After returning the required value to the calling program, formal parameters die. Thus the modifications done on the second copy remain unavailable to the calling function. What remains available is the original copy of values i.e. actual parameters.

This method of calling the function is called "Call By Value" or "Calling The Function By Value".

The concept of calling the function by value is illustrated in the following program and becomes clearer by following its logic and tracing its results.

PROGRAM-3

```
#include <stdio.h>
int fun (int speed_in)
{
```

```
        printf ("\nValue received in function is %i",speed_in');
        speed_in = 2* speed_in ;
        printf ("\nValue after modification is %i",speed_in );
        return (speed_in) ;
    }
    main()
    {
        int speed=250;
        printf ("\nValue of speed variable in main function is %i",speed );
        fun (speed);
        printf ("\nValue of speed variable after coming back from function is %i",speed );
    }
```

RESULT

Value of speed variable in main function is 250
Value received in function is 250
Value after modification is 500
Value of speed variable after coming back from function is 250

PASSING ARRAY ELEMENTS AS ARGUMENTS

Array elements can be passed as arguments to the other functions. The procedure for this is the same as that, which is followed for normal variables. Here instead of mentioning the variable names, you mention array elements. For example, say int a[5] is an array and sqr is a function, which calculates square of the given number. Array elements can be passed to this function in the following format:

Calling program

```
for (i=0 ; i<5 ; i++)
sqr(a[i] ) ;
```

Function

```
sqr( int x1 )
{
    x2 =  x1 * x1 ;
    return (x2) ;
}
```

PASSING ARRAYS AS ARGUMENT

As you pass variables to the function, whole array can also be passed to the function but in a slightly different way. You know that making use of functions involves following:

1. Function definition.
2. Calling the function.
3. Some times function prototype.

Function Definition

If array is being passed as argument then function definition is written in the following format:

```
data-type-f function-name (data-type-a array-name[])
```

Here data-type-f is function's data type. The function-name is the name of the function, by which it will be called in the calling program.

The data-type-a is the data type of array, which will be passed by the calling function. For example, if the calling program is passing integer type or character type array then data-type-a will be int or char respectively.

The array-name could be any name (same or different than that being passed by the calling function). Note that, array name is to be followed by [] but with nothing written in it. Following are few valid function definitions, which accept array as arguments.

```
int max(int array[])
{
    Statements
}
void select_color (char color[])
{
    Statements
}
```

Calling the Function

To call a function, which accepts array as arguments, following format is used:

```
function-name(array-name) ;
```

Here function name is the name of that function, which is to be called and array-name is the name of that array, which is to be passed as argument to the function. Note that no bracket or number is written along with the array name. Following are the two statements, which would be used for calling the functions mentioned in definition section:

```
max(x) ;
select_color(array) ;
```

Prototype Function

As mentioned earlier, if the function definition appears, after the calling function then you would be required to make use of function prototypes. Function prototypes are used in the following format:

data-type-f, function name(data-type-a array-name[]);

For example, function proto types for the functions mentioned in definition section, will be written as follows:

int max(int array[]) ;

void select-color(char C[]) ;

Now you are familiar with the methods and procedures of passing array as argument to the functions. So let's apply these concepts to write few programs for the given problems.

PROBLEM-4

Write a program which accepts 10 numbers from the keyboard and prints them in reverse order, through a function named reverse.

PROGRAM-4

```
#include<stdio.h>
# define size 10
void reverse_print(int b[]);
main()
{    int a[size] ;
     int i ;
     printf("\nGive Elements of thearray" );
     for (i=0 ; i<size ; i++)
     {
          printf("\nGive element %i ", (i+1)) ;
          scanf ("%i",&a[i]) ;
     }
     reverse_print(a);
}
void reverse_print(int b[])
{    int i ;
     for (i=(size-1) ; i>-1 ; i--)
     printf("\n %i",b[i]) ;
}
```

PROBLEM-5

Write a program that accepts 10 numbers from the keyboard and then sorts them in descending order. It should also print sorted numbers.

PROGRAM-5

```
#include <stdio.h>
# define size 10
int sort_array(int n[]);
main()
{
    int i , nmbr[size] ;
    for (i = 0 ; i < size ; ++i)
    {
        printf("\nGive a Number ") ;
        scanf("%i", &nmbr[i]) ;
    }
    sort_array(nmbr) ;
    for (i = 0 ; i < size ; ++i )
    printf("%i ",nmbr[i] ) ;
}
sort_array(int n[])
{
    int i,j, temp;
    for (i=0 ; i < (size -1) ; ++i )
    {
        for (j=0 ; j < (size-1); ++j )
        if (n[j] < n[j+1])
        {
            temp = n[j] ;
            n[j] = n[j+1] ;
            n[j+1] = temp ;
        }
    }
}
```

WHAT IS PASSING ARGUMENTS BY REFERENCE?

When you pass an array as argument to any function then actual arguments are not copied on formal arguments (that means no duplicate copy is made, as it is done in normal cases). Instead of copying, address of the array (reference) is passed to the function.

So for all practical purposes, function operates upon original values. Thus any change made in array element, remains available to calling function also. This method of passing arguments to the function is called Passing Arguments By Reference.

To understand the concept of passing arguments by reference, consider the following program:

PROBLEM-6

Let's write a program, which accepts 10 number from the keyboard and later doubles them through the use of a function, called double calling function prints the doubled values.

PROGRAM-6

```
#include<stdio.h>
# define size 10
void double_value(int b[]);
main()
{
    int arry[size] ;
    int i ;
    printf("\nGive Elements of thearray" );
    for (i=0 ; i<size ; i++)
    {
        printf("\nGive element %i ", (i+1)) ;
        scanf ("%i",&arry[i]) ;
    }
    double_value(arry);
    for (i=0 ; i<size ; i++)
    printf("\n %i",arry[i]) ;
}
void double_value(int b[])
{
    int i ;
    for (i=0 ; i<size ; i++)
    b[i]= b[i] * 2 ;
    return;
}
```

LOCAL AND EXTERNAL VARIABLES

Variables that are used in functions can be broadly classified into two categories. First category of variables is called Local Variables. Other category is called External Variables.

Local variables remain accessible within the function, in which they are declared. Their values remain inaccessible out side the function i.e. to the other functions of the program.

Unlike local variables, values of external variables remain accessible outside the function also. How do you create such type of variables, is explained in later part of this chapter.

CATEGORY OF FUNCTIONS

It is not mandatory on function's part to always receive and return values from / to calling program. Some of the functions may receive the value from the calling function and may not return any result to it. On the other hand, some other function may not receive any value but still return some result to the calling program.

Truly speaking lot of permutations and combinations could be there. Thus on the basis of arguments received or not received and the value returned or not returned, functions are categorized in many categories. These categories are as follows:

1. Functions with no arguments and no return value.
2. Functions with arguments and no return value.
3. Functions with arguments and one return value.
4. Functions with no arguments and one return value.
5. Functions that return multiple values.

Functions of each category are described below.

Function With No Arguments And No Return Values

As the name indicates, these functions neither take any input from the main function, nor they return any value to it. They simply perform the task for which the commands have been written in their body.

Since these functions do not return any value to the main function hence their data type is declared as void.

Since they do not receive any value from the main function hence their argument list remains blank and their definition is written in the following format:

```
        void function-name()
e.g.    void print_command()
```

To understand the usage of such type of functions, let's write a program for following problem.

PROBLEM-7

Write a program, which accepts roll number, name and age of 10 students. If the age of any student is found to be less than 21 years, a function named remarks prints "Not Eligible".

PROGRAM-7

```
#include <stdio.h>
void remarks() ;
main()
{
    int i ;
    int roll, age ;
    char name[20] ;
    for(i=0 ; i<5 ; i++)
    {
        printf("\nGive Roll Number " );
        scanf("%i", &roll) ;
        printf("\nGive Name " );
        scanf("%s", name) ;
        printf("\nGive age " );
        scanf("%i", &age) ;
        if (age < 21)
            remarks() ;
    }
}

void remarks()
{
    printf("\nNot Eligble") ;
}
```

Function With Arguments And No Return Value

These functions receive values from the calling function. They work upon the received-values within their body and generate some results. They utilize the result them selves. They do not send back any value to the calling program.

Since they do not send back any result so their data type is declared as void.

Since they receive the value from the calling function hence they are defined as follows:

```
void function-name (argument_list)
```

e.g. void print_square_n_cube (int x)

To understand the usage of such type of functions, let's write a program for the following problem.

PROBLEM-8

Let's write a program, which accepts numbers from the user and print its square and cube through a function.

PROGRAM-8

```
#include <stdio.h>
void print_square_n_cube(int x) ;
main ()
{
    int i ;
    int number;
    for(i=0 ; i<5 ; i++)
    {
        printf("\nGive a number " );
        scanf("%i", &number) ;
        print_square_n_cube(number) ;
    }
}
void print_square_n_cube(int x)
{
    int sq , cu ;
    sq = x * x ;
    cu = x * x * x ;
    printf("\nSquare of %i is %i " , x, sq) ;
    printf("\nCube of %i is %i " , x, cu) ;
}
```

Function With Argument And One Return Value

Such functions receive values from the calling program through arguments. They operate upon the values and workout some result. They return the result to the calling program.

Since they return back some value to the calling program hence their data type is decided by the data of the value that they return to the calling program. For example, if they return integer value, their data type will be int. If they return a character value their data type will be declared as char.

Since they receive values from the calling program through argument list hence they are declared in the following format:

data-type function-name (argument_list);

e.g. int area (int length, int width);

To understand the usage of such type of function, let's write a program for the given problem.

PROBLEM-9

Write a program, which accepts length and width of a rectangle and prints the area. The values of length and width are accepted from the keyboard, within the main program. The function calculates the area and returns it to the main program, where it gets printed.

PROGRAM-9

```
#include <stdio.h>
int calculate_area(int x, int y) ;
main ()
{
    int  length , width,  area ;
    printf("\nGive Length " );
    scanf("%i", &length) ;
    printf("\nGive Width " );
    scanf("%i", &width) ;
    area=calculate_area(length, width) ;
    printf("\nArea is %i", area) ;
}
int calculate_area(int x, int y)
{   int ar ;
    ar = x * y ;
    return (ar) ;
}
```

Function With No Argument And One Return Value

Such functions do not get any input from the calling program but still provide some output to it. Since they return some value to the calling program hence their data type is governed by the value they return to the calling program.

Since they do not receive any value from the calling program hence their argument list remains empty. Thus they are declared in the following format:

data type function-name( )

e.g. int getsum( )

To understand the usage of such type of functions, lets' write a program for the given problem.

PROBLEM-10

Let's write a program, which, accepts basic pay, da and income tax of 10 employees.

It calculates net pay as follows:

Net pay = basic pay + da – Income tax

The process of accepting the values is performed in a function. This functions also calculations the net pay and returns it to the calling functions, where it gets, displayed.

PROGRAM-10

```
#include <stdio.h>
int net_pay() ;
main ()
{   int i ;
    int npay;
    for(i=0 ; i<5 ; i++)
    {   npay = net_pay() ;
        printf("\nNet pay of Eemployee No. %i is %i", (i+1) , npay );
    }
}

int net_pay()
{
    int bpay, da, itax, tot ;
    printf("\nGive basic pay " );
    scanf("%i", &bpay) ;
    printf("\nGive Da" );
    scanf("%i", &da) ;
    printf("\nGive income tax" );
    scanf("%i", &itax) ;
    tot = bpay + da - itax ;
    return (tot) ;
}
```

Functions That Return Multiple Values

Up till now we had been dealing with the functions that returned single value to the calling program. For this, they made use of return statement. Recall their limitation that they cannot return multiple values. They can return only one value to the calling function. Now the question is, how it is possible to return multiple values to the calling program? Well, this is made possible by making some additions in the argument list and sending them back through argument list itself. Such a modified list is illustrated below.

Function-name(Argument-list2, Argument_list2)

Here Argument-list1 represents all those arguments that are passed to the function by the calling program to operate upon them. Argument-list2 represents all those arguments that are to be sent back to the calling program by the function. In other words you can say that Argument-list1 is input list and Argument-list2 is output list for the function. For example, if you wish to pass the radius of the circle to the function and want the values of circumference and area back, then there will be three arguments in the function definition. One argument will be for sending radius to the function and other two will be for receiving back the values of circumference and area respectively.

Note that the arguments of Argument-list1 are written in normal way, as we had been writing up till now, but arguments of Argument-list2 are written in slightly different way. They are written using two special operators, called address operator and indirection operators. They both are related to pointers. While dealing with pointers in function, following things need to be remembered:

1. A pointer variable is declared as follows:

   ```
   data-type *variable-name
   e.g.  int * pa ;
         char * pb ;
   ```

2. Address operator is denoted by & sign. When it is operated upon a variable, it gives its address. For example if a is a variable then &a will gives address of variable a (i.e. the memory location where a has been stored). Thus following statements will hold good:

   ```
   Int a= 100 ;
   Int *pa ;
   pa=&a;
   ```

3. Indirection operator is denoted by * sign. When it is operated upon pointer variable. It returns the value of that variable, which pointer points to. For example, following statement will hold good:

   ```
   int a= 100;
   int * pa;
   ```

pa = &a

*pa will give 100

Now the question is how return of multiple values is made possible using pointer concept. Well, this is done in the following manner:

1. **Calling program sends the address of those variables in which it wants to get multiple values from the function.**
2. **Upon receiving the values, function operates upon the values and calculates all those values, which it has to send back to the calling function. These values are calculated, making use of * operator instead of normal variables so that the relationship between addresses sent and the values being calculated remains maintained.**
3. **When control returns back to the calling function, calling function extracts values from the addresses and thus receives multiple values from the function, which was not possible through return statement.**

To understand the usage, let's write a program for the following problem.

PROBLEM-11

Say we have to write a program, in which main function accepts value of circle's radius and sends it to a function. The function calculates circumference and area of the circle and returns back to the main function, where they get printed.

PROGRAM-11

```
#include <stdio.h>
void calculate(int r, float *cir, float *area ) ;
main ()
{
    int i ;
    int radius;
    float circum , area  ;
    for(i=0 ; i<5 ; i++)
    {
        printf("\nGive Radius of the circle " );
        scanf("%i", &radius) ;
        calculate(radius , &circum , &area) ;
        printf("\nCircumfrence is %f" , circum );
        printf("\nArea is %f" , area );
    }
}
```

```
void calculate(int r, float *cir, float *ar)
{    *cir = 2 * (22.0 / 7.0) * r ;
     *ar = (22.0 / 7.0) * r * r ;
}
```

SCOPE OF VISIBILITY

That span of the program, over which a variable remains accessible, is called its scope of visibility. To understand the concept of scope of visibility (of variables), consider a program, which consists of a main() function and at least one more function. In such cases you must have observed the following points:

1. The variables that you declare, within the calling function (say main()) cannot be accessed by function.
2. The variables that you declare, within the function remain inaccessible in calling function.
3. The variables that you declare in function loose their identity and value as soon as the function ends. Their values cannot be retained for utilization.

From here it is clear that the scope of visibility of the variables, generally spans over the function, in which they are declared. Now the question is, can any arrangement be made, to enhance their scope of visibility so that they remain accessible beyond the boundaries of the function, in which they were declared? Well, C language provides the facility to declare the storage class of a variable, along with its declaration. Depending upon its storage class, variable's scope of visibility gets decided, Different types of storage classes that could be defined in a C program, are described below.

TYPES OF STORAGE CLASSES

Following types of storage classes can be declared in C application programs:

1. Automatic
2. External
3. Static

What these storage classes are, how they are declared within the program etc. are the subjects that are explained below.

Automatic Variables

Automatic variables are the variables, which come into existence, when the function starts and loose their existence when the function ends. This is the reason why they remain inaccessible in other functions. In other words, you can say that their scope of visibility remains only within the function, in which they are declared.

A variable can be declared as Automatic by qualifying its definition by the keyword, auto in the following format:

```
auto data-type variable-name ;
```

Following are few valid examples of automatic storage class declaration:

```
auto int i ;
auto int i, j, x ;
auto int i = 0, j = 100, k = -5 ;
auto char flag;
```

Following are the points that apply for automatic variables:

1. Since their scope of visibility extends over the function, in which they are declared hence same variable name can be used in more than one function. For example, say there are three functions, f1, f2 and f3. A variable say pay can be declared as automatic variable in all the three functions. Its value in one function will never clash with its value in other function.
2. If you do not qualify the declaration of a variable, with any storage class, by default, it will get declared as automatic.
   For example, recall that up till now, we did not use any storage class for any of the variable in any of the programs of this book. Thus they all where taken as automatic. This is the reason that their scope of visibility was limited to the function, in which they were declared.

External Variables

External variables come into existence when they are declared and remain alive till the end of the program (complete program, not the function). Thus not only the function in which they are declared but the functions defined after their definition are also able to access them.

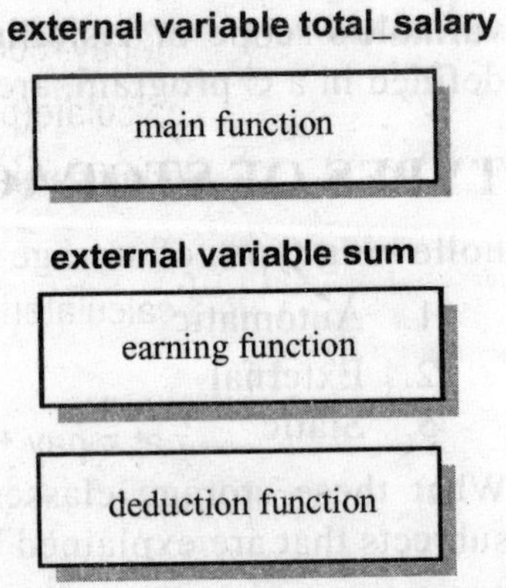

Figure 13.4

To understand the nature of external variables, refer figure 13.4 and note that.

Complete program comprises of three functions i.e. main function, earnings function and deduction function.

Two variables, i.e. total_salary and sum have been declared as external variables. The total_salary has been declared before main function. Thus it will be accessible by main function and the other two functions (i.e. earnings and deduction functions), which are defined after the main function. On the other hand, other variable, sum has been declared after main function. Thus main function will not be able to access it. But other two functions, i.e. earnings and deductions will be able to access it.

A variable can be declared external by qualifying its declaration with the extern keyword, in the following format:

```
extern data-type variable_name ;
```

Following are few examples of valid external variable declarations:

```
extern int total_salary ;
extern float net_earning, net deduction ;
extern char check='0' ;
extern int x=0, y=500, z=1000 ;
```

Following are the points that apply for external variables:

1. All those variables that are defined before the function are taken as external variables.
2. Just the position of the declaration of variable makes it external variable. The keyword extern is optional.

To understand the usage of external variables, go through the following program and its result.

PROGRAM-12

```
#include <stdio.h>
extern float da_pctg=50 ;
extern float net = 0.0 ;
void calculate(int pctg);
main()
{   int pay=5000 ;
    calculate(pay) ;
    printf("\nNet pay is %g",net) ;
}
void calculate(int pay)
{
    net = pay + (pay * da_pctg)/100.0 ;
}
```

RESULT

This program will display following result:

Net pay is 7500

ANALYSIS

Refer above mentioned program and note the following point.

1. Although net variable does not have extern keyword included its definition, but due to the fact that da_pctg and net have been declared before main function, they are taken as external variables.

2. The main function sends only, the value of pay to the calculate function.
3. Since da_petg is an external variable hence it remains accessible to all the function of the program. This is the reason, why the value of da_pctg becomes available in calculate function, without main function transferring it to the function.
4. The calculate function operates upon the received value and global variable da_pctg to calculate the total pay. This values gets stored in global variable net.

Since net is external variable hence its value becomes accessible in main function even if, calculate function doesn't return it to the main function.

Static Variables

Static variables are the variables, which remain local to the function. Their values cannot be accessed outside the function. They come into existence when function gets executed for the first time and remain into existence till the end of the program (note, not the function). They are declared as static by qualifying their definition by the keyword, static in the following format:

```
static data-type variable-name;
```

Following are few valid definition of static variables:

```
static int amt:
static float sum, total
static int col_total=0, row_total=0;
static char status='c';
```

Say a function, Increment-By-Ten has a static variable named total, which has been initialized to 100 (i.e. int total=100). Each time this function gets executed it increases the value of total by 10.

Say in due course of program, main() function calls Increment-By-Ten three times. First time when the function will get executed, value of total will not be lost, when the function ends. Second time when function gets executed value of total (i.e. 110) will get incremented by 10. Thus it will become 120. This value again will not be lost. Third time when the function executes, it will become 130.

To get more familiar with the usage of static variables, let's write few programs, for the given problems:

PROBLEM-13

Write a program, which accepts as many numbers as user wants and then sums them through a function.

PROGRAM-13

```
#include <stdio.h>
int addnum(int n) ;
main()
```

```
{
    int n, no, count, total=0 ;
    printf("\nHow many numbers are to be added ") ;
    scanf ("%i",&no) ;
    for (count = 1 ; count < no+1 ; ++count )
    {
        printf("\nGive number \n");
        scanf("%i",&n);
        printf("\nSum of Nos. is  %i",add_num(n));
    }
}
int add_num(int n)
{
    static int tot = 0 ;
    tot = tot + n ;
    return(tot) ;
}
```

ANALYSIS

To understand the dynamics of the program, go through the following points:

1. The main program accepts the numbers, while the summation is done in add_num function.
2. Since tot variable has been declared as static hence it doesn't die when the program control leaves the function each time. Rather its value is retained till the end of the program. Thus the cumulated value of the numbers, entered till now, gets displayed in each iteration of the loop. In the last iteration, total sum of the numbers, entered all together, gets displayed.
3. Had the variable tot not been declared static, it would have lost the previous sum and summation of the numbers would have had not been possible.

PROBLEM-14

Write a program to generate Fibonacci series. In Fibonacci series, each number remains equal to the sum of the previous two numbers. In general, any member of the series can be defined as Fi=Fi-1+Fi-2. Following is Fibonacci series:

1+1+2+3+5+8+13+------------+n

Let's write a program that asks the user, to give the number of terms in the series and then generates the series.

PROGRAM-14

```
#include <stdio.h>
long int fib (int n) ;
main()
{
    int n , i ;
    printf("\nHow many terms are required in the serise");
    scanf("%i",&n);
    for (i = 1 ; i < n+1 ; ++i)
    printf ("\ni = %i  f= %i ",i,fib(i));
}
long int fib(int n)
{   static int a = 1 , b= 1 ;
    int c ;
    c = (n < 3) ? 1 : (a+b) ;
    a = b ;
    b = c ;
    return (c);
}
```

Note that the variable a and b have been defined as static. Due to this they retain their values in each iteration. This value is used to calculate the next value of Fibonacci series in the next pass. If they are not declare as static they will always start with the value 1, when the program control comes to the functions and the series will never be generate.

RECURSION

In recursion, a function calls itself repeatedly until some specified condition is satisfied. This process is used for repetitive computation, in which action of current iteration is framed on the basis of the result of previous iteration. If recursion is to be used in a program, following two conditions must be fulfilled:

1. Problem must be written in recursive manner.
2. Problem must have a stopping condition.

In order to understand the concept let's write a program, which makes use of recursion.

PROBLEM-15

Let's write a program that accepts a number, say x in the main program and calculates the value of x^x in a recursive function. The resultant value should be printed in main function.

PROGRAM-15

```
#include <stdio.h>
int power(int x) ;
main()
{
    int no, rslt ;
    printf ("\nGive Number");
    scanf("%i",&no);
    printf("\nNo is %i",no) ;
    rslt = power(no);
    printf ("\n%i to the power of %i =  %i",no,no,rslt);
}
int power(int x)
{
    static int cnt=1 ;
    static int value=1 ;
    char junk ;
    if(cnt <= x)
    {
        value = value * x ;
        cnt=cnt+1 ;
        power(x);
    }
    else return(value);
}
```

ANALYSIS

To understand the dynamics of the program note the following points:

1. The function power is a recursive function. It keeps on calling itself till the time cnt<=x.
2. It multiplies its argument (x) x times so as to calculate the value of x^x .
3. The variable cnt is used for counting the number of times x has been multiplied by x, at a given point of time. Note that this has been made possible by declaring cnt variable as static. Its value increases by one, each time power(x) function executes.
4. The result of x * x is being stored in a variable named, value. Since it is a static variable hence its value doesn't get lost at the end of each iteration. Thus this value serves as base value for the next iteration.

5. When x has been multiplied by x, x times the value of x^x gets stored in value variable. The function returns this value to the main function through return statement, where it gets printed.

EXERCISES CHAPTER 13

Short Type Questions

A. Select most appropriate answers for the following questions:

1. How many functions can be there in a program?
   (a) At least one (b) As many as required
   (c) Practically there is no limit (d) All of the above
2. Which function does not require a calling function?
   (a) main (b) Function defined before main function
   (c) Function defined after main function (d) void function
3. Which of the following will not require a prototype function?
   (a) main (b) Function defined before main function
   (c) Function defined after main function (d) All the functions
4. Which of the following will not be terminated by a semicolon sign?
   (a) Function definition (b) Function calling statement
   (c) Function prototype (d) None of the above
5. Which type of variables will be accessible to all the functions of the program, provided they are suitably placed within the program?
   (a) Automatic (b) Static (c) External (d) Variables of main function.

B. Fill in the blanks.

6. A function prototype is always terminated by .... sign.
7. A function, which calls itself, is called .... function.
8. Using .... clause, at the time of declaring the variables, the variables can be declared as external variables.
9. Three types of storage classes can be declared in C program. They are ...., ... and ....
10. When a function is called, it is called by ....

C. State true or false.

11. All the functions, except main() function, do not execute on their own. They require a calling function.
12. Arguments of a called function are also called actual parameters.
13. For calling a function, actual arguments should either be equal to or more than the number of formal parameters.
14. The keyword extern is optional for declaring a variable as external variable. Actually the position of variable declaration, in the program, decides, whether a variable will be external or not.
15. Static variable remains alive till the end of the program.

D. Answer the following questions in short:

16. Is it necessary that each program should return a value to the calling function?
17. Can it so happen that some times a function returns an integer value and some times a float value, depending upon the situation?
18. In which situation, will you require a function prototype?
19. What will be the storage class of a variable, which comes into existence when function starts and dies when function ends?
20. Which keyword will be used to declare a variable as automatic variable?

Detailed Answer Type Questions

E. Answer the following questions in detail:

21. What is a function? State at least two advantages of using multiple functions in a program?
22. What is meant by passing arguments by value? Explain using a suitable example.
23. Write a program, which accepts temperature in centigrade in main function and converts it into Fahrenheit in another function. The converted values get printed in the main function.
24. Write a program, which accepts two numbers in main program and passes them to a function. The function calculates cube of both the numbers and their values get printed in main function.
25. Write a function, which accepts Roll number, Physics, Chemistry and Math marks in the main program.

    Another function, say result calculates the percentage. On the basis of percentage, it decides passing grade of the student. It returns grade to the main function, where it gets printed. Grade is decided as follows:

    (a) Grade F if percentage<50.

    (b) Grade B if percentage>=50 but less than 75.

    (c) Grade A if percentage>=75.

****

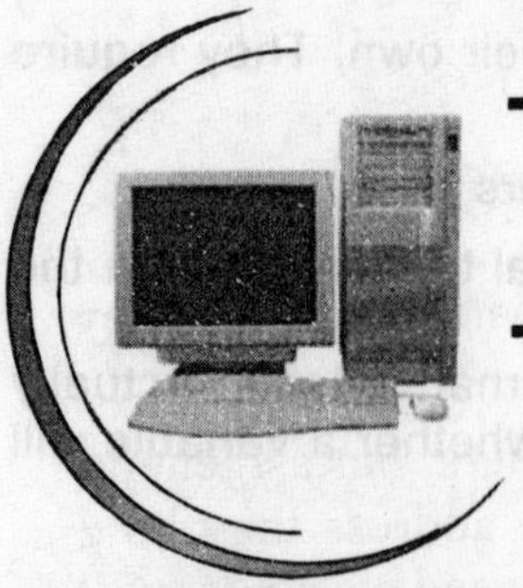

CHAPTER 14

Pointers

INTRODUCTION

Each variable that you define in your program is basically a memory location, which has a definite address. You can access this variable either by its name or by its address. For example, the variable speed, shown in figure 14.1, has the address AB7F. Thus this variable can either be accessed, using its name, speed or its address. AB7F.

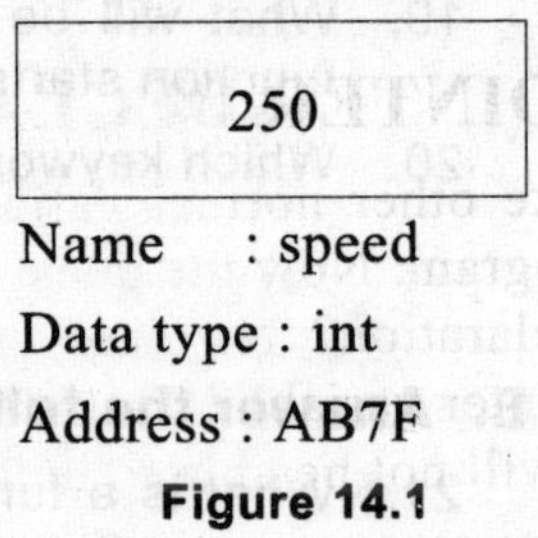

Figure 14.1

You are already familiar with the method of accessing the variables by their names (this is what we have been doing in last so many chapters). Now the question is, how do you access them through their addresses? Well, unlike other languages, C language provides few exclusive operators to operate upon addresses and complete address arithmetic. These operators and arithmetic is described in detail in this chapter.

WHAT IS POINTER

In general, pointer is something, which points to something specific. It could be teacher's finger pointing towards an equation written on the board or an arrow on the crossroads, showing the direction to be followed, for going to a locality. Now the question is, what a pointer is, in reference to C language? Well, pointer is a special variable, which holds the address of another variable. Thus if, somehow, you acquire the address contained in pointer, you can reach (access) the variable, whose address is stored in the pointer. The concept of pointer is illustrated in figure 14.2.

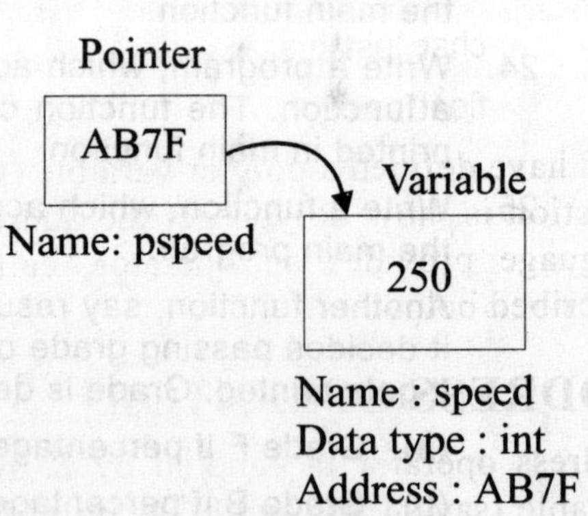

Figure 14.2

Refer this figure and note that pointer (pspeed) contain the address (AB7F) of some other variable (speed). Following this address, the variable (speed) can be accessed (i.e. its contents: 250).

POINTER IDENTIFICATION

Like normal variables, pointers are also identified by:

1. their names
2. their data type (which is always same as that of the variable, whose address they hold).

Although C language provides the liberty to assign any name to the pointers, but as general practice they are assigned the same name as that of the variable, whose address they hold (speed), with p prefixed to them (pspeed). For example, pointer to speed variable will generally be assigned the name, pspeed. This practice, at first glance, makes it clear that pspeed is a pointer and it points to the speed variable.

Data type of a pointer will always be same as that of the variable, to which it points. So, if the data type of speed variable is int then data type of pspeed will also be int. In other words you can say that a pointer of int data type will hold the address of int variable only. It cannot hold the address of the variables of other data types. Similarly the pointers of float or char data type will hold the addresses of float or char variables respectively.

POINTER DECLARATION

Like other normal variables, pointers should also be defined, before they are used in the program. Now the question is, how do you define pointers? Is "**int pspeed ;**" a valid pointer declaration? No here in this statement, simply prefixing p with speed doesn't make it pointer variable. This statement will simply define a normal int variable, with name pspeed. It will not be able to hold addresses in it.

To differentiate pointer with normal variables, they are prefixed with * sign. Thus general format for pointer declaration will be as follows:

```
        data-type *pointer-name;
e.g.    int *pspeed ;
        char *pstatus ;
        float*pamt ;
```

You have defined a pointer variable (pspeed) and are ready to hold a address into it. But the question is, how do you get the address of a variable (say speed) into it? Well, for that C language provides an operator, called Address operator. Details of this operator are described below.

ADDRESS OPERATOR

Address operator is denoted by & sign. It is a unary operator. It operates upon normal variable (say speed) and gives its address (say AB7F). Addresses thus obtained can always be stored in a pointer variable (which is exclusively meant for storing addresses). Usage of Addresses operator is illustrated below.

```
pointer variable=&variable-name ;
```

e.g. pspeed=&speed ;

Now if you display the value of pspeed, AB7F (i.e. address of variables speed, illustrated in figure 14.2) will get displayed.

You now, have the address of a variable stored in a pointer. Now the question is, if you have the address of a variable, how do you get the value stored in that variable? Well, in C language that is done through Indirection operator. Details of Indirection operator are given below.

INDIRECTION OPERATOR OR DE REFERENCING OPERATOR

Indirection operator is denoted by * sign. It is unary operator. It operates upon pointer (say pspeed) and gives the value (250) of the variable (speed), whose address is stored (speed) in pointer. The value thus obtained can always be stored in some other normal variable (say kmph, which is of int type). Usage of Indirection operator is illustrated below.

```
*pointer ;
normal-variable=*pointer ;
```

e.g. kmph=*pspeed;

Now if you display the value of kmph, 250(i.e. the value of speed variable) will get displayed.

PRINTING THE CONTENTS OF POINTER

You know that pointers contain addresses. Addresses are always expressed in Hexadecimal numbers. Hexadecimal numbers are printed through printf() function, using character x in format string. For example, to print the address stored in pspeed pointer, printf function can be used as follows:

```
printf("%x", pspeed) ;
```

Now you are familiar with the concept of pointers and the two operators (& and *), using which you operate upon pointers. So let's write few programs, which make use of pointers.

PROBLEM-1

Let's write a simple program, which illustrated the functioning of & and * operators.

PROGRAM-1

```
#include<stdio.h>
main()
{
    int speed=250 ;
    int *pspeed ;
    pspeed = &speed ;
    printf ("\nThe value of speed variable is %i",speed);
    printf ("\nThe address of speed variable is %x",pspeed) ;
    printf ("\nValue obtained through indirection operator%i",*pspeed) ;
}
```

RESULT

On execution, this program will generate following result:

The value of speed variable is 250

The address of speed variable is fc10 ***(Note: this value will change from time to time)***

Value obtained through indirection operator 250

Above illustrated result clearly shows:

1. **& operator gives the address of the variable, on which it operates.**
2. *** operator gives the value of the variable, whose pointer it operates upon.**

PROBLEM-2

Lets write a program to demonstrate that by interchanging the addresses contained within the two pointers, the values in variables do not get interchange.

PROGRAM-2

```
#include<stdio.h>
main()
{
    int data1=1000 ;
    int data2=2000;
    int *pdata1, *pdata2, *pdata3 ;
    pdata1 = &data1 ;
    pdata2 = &data2 ;
    printf ("\nValues before interchange operation") ;
    printf ("\nThe value of data1 variable is %i",data1) ;
    printf ("\nThe value of data2 variable is %i",data2) ;
    printf ("\nThe address of data1 variable is %x",pdata1) ;
    printf ("\nThe address of data2 variable is %x",pdata2) ;
    /* Interchange Pointer Values */
    pdata3= pdata1 ;
    pdata1 = pdata2 ;
    pdata2 = pdata3 ;
    printf ("\nValues after interchange operation") ;
    printf ("\nThe value of data1 variable is %i",data1) ;
    printf ("\nThe value of data2 variable is %i",data2) ;
    printf ("\nThe address of data1 variable is %x",pdata1) ;
    printf ("\nThe address of data2 variable is %x",pdata2) ;
}
```

RESULT

On execution, above mentioned program will generate following output:

Values before interchange operation

```
The value of data1 variable is 1000
The value of data2 variable is 2000
The address of data1 variable is fb6
The address of data2 variable is fb8
Values after interchange operation
The value of data1 variable is 1000
The value of data2 variable is 2000
The address of data1 variable fb8
The address of data2 variable is fb6
```

POINTER COMPARISON

You are now familiar with pointers and different types of operators related to them. You have also used pointers in different expressions and arithmetic operations. Now the question is, can we compare pointers? Yes, two pointers can be compared. Pointers can be used in conditional statements as usual variables. All the comparison operators can be used with pointers i.e. less than, greater than, equal to, etc.

For example, while writing a program for sorting an array, we can use two pointers and to test, which pointer is at higher address, we can compare them and take decision depending on the result.

To get familiar with the process of comparing the pointers, consider the two pointers to integer i.e. xp1 and yp2. We can compare *xp1 and *yp2 because *xp1 and *yp2 are simple values. They are the values that integer xp1, yp2 points to.

When we say *yptr1 > *yptr2, this is a comparison of simple two integer values. Whenever we are using the dereference pointer (pointers with *), all normal arithmetic and manipulation is valid. Whenever we are using pointers themselves, then certain type of operations are allowed and restrictions on other. Consider a sample program as follows:

PROBLEM-3

Let's write a program that accepts two numbers and compares them using pointer comparison method and prints larger number.

PROGRAM-3

```
#include <stdio.h>
#include <conio.h>
void main()
```

```
{
int x,y,*xptr1 , *yptr2 ;
printf(" Enter the value of x = ");
scanf("%d",&x);
printf("\n Enter the value of y = ");
scanf("%d",&y);
xptr1 = &x ;
yptr2 = &y ;
 if(*xptr1 > *yptr2)
{
 printf("\n x is greater then y ");
}
else
{
 printf("\n y is greater then x ");
}
getch();
}
```

POINTER CONVERSIONS

Pointer conversions are performed when pointers are used, including pointer assignment, initialization, and comparison.

Conversions that involve pointers must use an explicit type cast. The exceptions to this rule are the allowable assignment conversions for C pointers. In the following table, a const-qualified lvalue cannot be used as a left operand of the assignment.

Legal assignment conversions for C pointers

Left operand type	Permitted right operand types
Pointer to (object) T	• the constant 0 • A pointer to a type compatible with T • A pointer to void (void*)
Pointer to (function) F	• The constant 0 • Pointer to a function compatible with F

The referenced type of the left operand must have the same qualifiers as the right operand. An object pointer may be an incomplete type if the other pointer has type void*.

PASSING POINTERS TO FUNCTION (CALLING FUNCTION BY REFERENCE)

You are already familiar with the use of functions in the program and know that, when you call a function, the arguments are passed by value. That means actual arguments are copied to the formal arguments and the original copy of the value (i.e. actual arguments) remain intact. The changes done by the function, on formal arguments, in no way affect the original values. This is the reason that these changes/modifications remain local to the function.

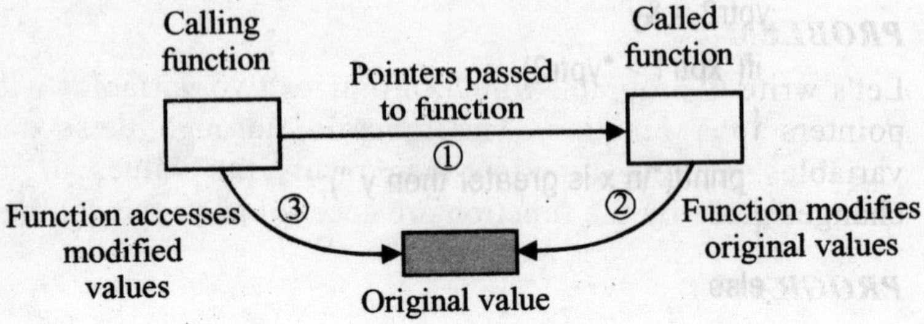

Figure 14.3

C language provides the facility to pass pointers as argument to the function. That means when you pass the pointers, addresses get passed to the function. Now the function operates upon the original values, through addresses, rather than on the copy. Since original values get changed hence when calling function access the values, it gets modified values. This method of passing the argument is called passing arguments by reference or calling function by reference. Concept is illustrated in figure 14.3.

In other words you can say that, when a function is called by reference, the modifications done by the function remain no more local to the function. They become accessible to the calling function also.

Now the question is, how do you define the function and write calling function and proto types? Well, their formats are given below.

Function Prototypes

```
        function data-type function-name(pointer -data-types pointers);
e.g.    void add-function(int*px1, int *px2);
```

Calling Statement

```
        function-name(pointers);
e.g.    add-function(&x1, &x2);
```

function definition

```
        function data-type function-name(pointer data types pointers);
        {
            statements
            return;
        }
```

```
e.g. void add-function(int &y1, &y2)
{
    Statements
    return
}
```

Now you are familiar with all the aspects of calling function by reference, so let's write few programs for the given problems:

PROBLEM-4

Let's write C program, which initializes two variables within the program and passes their pointers to a function. The function, through these pointers doubles the value of the variables. Calling function then prints the values of the variables, demonstrating that changes made by the function are accessible by the calling function.

PROGRAM-4

```
#include<stdio.h>
void double_value(int *p1, int *p2) ;
main()
{
    int val1=500 ;
    int val2=600 ;
    int *pval1, *pval2 ;
    pval1 = &val1 ;
    pval2 = &val2 ;
    double_value(pval1, pval2) ;
    printf ("\nThe value of val1 is now %i",val1 ) ;
    printf ("\nThe value of val2 is now %i",val2 ) ;
}
void double_value(int *p1, int *p2)
{
    *p1 = *p1 * 2 ;
    *p2 = *p2 * 2 ;
    return ;
}
```

RESULT

This program will generate following result:

```
The value of val1 is now 1000
The values of val2 is now 1200
```

Since values are being doubled in the function and are being printed in main program hence it is clear that modifications are globally accessable. Note that this could have never been possible if the values would have been passed, using call by value method.

PROBLEM-5

Say we have to write a program, which accepts a string (maximum 25 characters and no blanks in it) from the keyboard. It passes this string to a function, using pointers. Function counts number of voles in it. Calling function then prints the count of values.

PROGRAM-5

```
#include<stdio.h>
void count_vovles(char array[], int *num) ;
main()
{
    char strg1[25] ;
    int num=0 ;
    printf("\nType a string of less that 25 characters and press Enter\n");
    scanf("%s",strg1) ;
    count_vovles(strg1, &num) ;
    printf ("\nThe number of vovles are %i",num ) ;
}
void count_vovles(char array[], int *p2)
{
int cnt=0 ;
char x ;
while ( array[cnt] != '\0' )
    {
        x = toupper(array[cnt]) ;
        if (x=='A' || x=='E' || x=='I' || x=='O' || x=='U')
            *p2 = *p2 + 1;
            cnt++ ;
    }
        return ;
}
```

POINTERS AND ARRAYS

Pointers and arrays remain closely associated with each other. The name of the array works as pointer. It always points to the first element of the array. To understand the concept, consider the following array:

```
int mat[5]={700,500,900,400,300}
```

For this definition, **mat** will be a pointer pointing to the first element (i.e. pointing to 700).

Recall that the address of the first element of the array can also be expressed as &mat[0]. Thus you can say that &mat[0] and mat represent the same thing. thus if we wrint the value of *mat it will print 700, which is nothing but mat[0].

ACCESSING ELEMENTS OF ARRAY USING POINTERS

As, mentioned above, first element of the array can be accessed using the name of the array, as the name of the array points to the first element of the array. Now the question is, can other elements of the array be accessed using pointers? Yes the can be accessed easily. To access the elements of the array, we need to make use of pointer arithmetic. Pointer arithmetic is described below.

POINTER ARITHMETIC

Only two operations i.e. addition and subtraction are allowed to be performed on pointers. Following are the operators, using which these operations are performed.

1. Addition operator (+)
2. Increment operator (++)
3. Subtraction operator (-)
4. Decrement operator (--)

Pointer Addition

When addition operation is performed on a pointer, it points to the next variable in the sequence. To understand the concept, let's consider the following array:

```
int pay[10]={1000,7000,10000, 6000, 8000, 6500, 8300, 7600, 8200, 20000}
```

As you know, the array name, pay would point to the first element of the array. Now if you perform pointer addition operation on it. i.e. pay+1 or pay++, it will then point to the next element i.e. pay[1], which is 7000.

Similarly (pay+2) will point to the third element of the array i.e. pay[2], which is 10000.

Following this sequence, you can generalize the statement to conclude that pointer to the ith element can be written as (pay+(i+1).

Pointer Subtraction

When pointer subtraction is performed on a pointer, using - operator or -- operator, the pointer starts pointing towards previous elements. For example, if a pointer, say ptr is currently pointing to the fifth element of the array then (ptr-1) or ptr-- will make it point to the fourth element of the array.

Using Pointer Arithmetic

To understand the usage of pointer arithmetic, let's consider the following character array:

```
char ch[5]={'a', 'e', 'i', 'o', 'u'} ;
```

Following statements will hold good for the pointers of this array.

1. ch or &ch[0] will point to the first element of the array.
2. (ch+1) or &ch[1] will point to the second element of the array.
3. (ch+2) or &ch[2] will point to the third element of the array.
4. (ch+3) or &ch[3] will point to the fourth element of the array.
5. (ch+4) or &ch[4] will point to the fifth element of the array.

You know that Indirection operator(*) when operated upon pointer yields the value of the variable, to which the pointer points. So the following statements will hold good for the contents of the array:

1. *ch or ch[0] will provide value contained in the first element of the array.
2. *ch+1) or ch[1] will provide value contained in the second element of the array.
3. *(ch+2 or ch[2] will provide value contained in the third element of the array.
4. *(ch+3) or ch[3] will provide value contained in the fourth element of the array.
5. *(ch+4) or ch[4] will provide value contained in the fifth element of the array.

Now you are familiar with pointer arithmetic, so let's write program that demonstrates the validity of above written statements:

PROGRAM-6

```
#include<stdio.h>
main()
{
    char ch[5]={'a', 'e','i','o','u'};
    int j;
    printf("\nAddresses ") ;
    for(j=0; j<5; j++)
    {
        printf("\n&ch[%d]=%x",j,&ch[j]) ;
        printf("   (ch+%d)=%x", j,(ch+j)) ;
    }
```

```
        printf("\nValues ") ;
        for(j=0; j<5; j++)
        {
            printf("\nch[%d]=%c",j,ch[j]) ;
            printf("  *(ch+%d)=%c", j,*(ch+j)) ;
        }
}
```

RESULT

On execution, above mentioned program will produce following result:

```
Addresses
&ch[0] = fc0 (ch+0) = fc0
&ch[1] = fc1 (ch+1) = fc1
&ch[2] = fc2 (ch+2) = fc2
&ch[3] = fc3 (ch+3) = fc3
&ch[4] = fc4 (ch+4) = fc4
Values
ch[0] = a     *(ch+0) = a
ch[1] = e     *(ch+1) = e
ch[2] = i *(ch+2) = i
ch[3] = o     *(ch+3) = o
ch[4] = u     *(ch+4) = u
```

PROBLEM-7

Let's write a program, which accepts ages of 10 people and stores them in array. After that it checks all the value, if the age is less than 18 then it prints "Minor". On the other hand, if age is greater than 64, it print "Sinior Citizen". In rest of the cases it prints "Young". This program should make use of pointer arithmetic.

PROGRAM-7

```
#include<stdio.h>
main()
{
    int age[10] ;
    int i ;
```

```
        for (i=0 ; i<10 ; i++)
        {
                printf("\nGive age of person %d ",(i+1)) ;
                scanf ("%d", (age+i) ) ;
        }
        for(i=0 ; i<10 ; i++)
        {
                if (*(age+i) < 18)
                printf("\nAge %d is Minor " , (i+1) ) ;
                else if (*(age+i) > 64 )
                printf("\nAge %d is Senior Citizen " , (i+1) ) ;
                else
                printf("\nAge %d is Young " , (i+1) ) ;
        }
}
```

ANALYSIS

. To understand the usage of pointers in this program, observe the following points:

1. Generally to get the values read from the keyboard, in an array age[10], scanf statement is used within a for loop, in the following format:

   ```
   scanf("%d", &age[i])
   ```

Note that &age[i] is basically a pointer to the ith element. As per pointer arithmetic (age+1) is also a pointer to the ith element. So instead of above scanf statement, we have used the following statement:

```
scanf("%d", ( age+i));
```

2. Contents of array, age[10] elements can accessed in a for loop by referring the array elements through control variable, as follows:

   ```
   age[i]
   ```

Since in pointer arithmetic, age[i] can also be referred to as *(age+i) hence we have used this method for accessing the elements of the age array, throughout the second for loop.

POINTERS AND ONE DIMENSIONAL ARRAYS

You know that pointers and arrays are very closely associated with each other. Due to this close association, addresses of the elements can either be referred in normal way (such as & x[1], &x[2] etc.) or through pointers (such as (x+1), (x+2) etc.) Similarly the contents of the elements can either be referred in normal way (such as (x[1], x[2] etc.) or through pointers (such as *(x+1), *(x+2) etc.). Now the question is, can array be defined using pointers? For example, int x[10]; is a normal array declaration. Can this declaration be rewritten in some other way, which makes use of pointers (because array name acts as pointer pointing to the first element of the array)? Well, C language permits that. For example, if x[10] is an array of integers, it could be defined as follows:

1. int x[10] ; and /* Normal method */
2. int **x** ; also /* Using pointers */

Note that second method is a valid method of defining an array, which makes use of pointers. Also note that this methods does not talk anything about the number of elements present in the array, as int x[10] does (which states that there are 10 elements in the array). This is a fact that using second method, array x[20] or x[50] or x[100] will also be defined as int *x;. At first glance, this looks ambiguous. But truly speaking, it is not so. Because when you make such a statement, only 10 contiguous blocks of memory are reserved for the array. To create sufficient room for other elements, you need to include memory allocation statements within your program (before you operate upon memory elements).

This method of arranging memory at the time of execution of the program is called Dynamic Memory Allocation. It is done using malloc() function. This function remains available in "**stdlib.h**" library. Thus if you wish to make use of this function, you need to include a statement "#include <stdlib.h>" in the beginning of the program. Details of Dynaimc Memory allocation are given below.

DYNAMIC MEMORY ALLOCATION

Dynamic memory allocation is a process, which assigns required amount of memory for operations. This allocation is done, using malloc() function. The malloc() function is used in following manner:

```
int *x ;
    x=(int*) malloc (10* size of (int)) ;
```

This statement will reserve 10 contiguous blocks of memory. Each block of memory will be equivalent to the size of integer (the space that an integer variable occupies in memory. Note that it may vary from computer to computer but it is 2 bytes in most of the computers).

Here, in above statement, malloc() function will return a pointer to the block created by this statement. This pointer will initially point to the first element of the block. Note that this pointer has been assigned to the pointer variable x in the above statement. Thus (x+0) or x will point to the first element of the block. (x+1) will point to the second and (x+2) will point to the third element of the block. Similarly *x will refer to the first value, stored in this block, *(x+1) will refer to the second value and so on.

Note that sizeof() is a function, which returns the size of the mentioned date type, on present computer. Thus if an array of 20 float elements is to be created then malloc() function will have to be used as follows:

```
float *a
a=(float*) (20* sizeof(float));
```

Now you are familiar, with the method of declaring the single dimension arrays, using pointers and know that, for such an array, malloc() function is to be used, for creating enough space in the memory so as to store the array elements. Now let's write a program which makes use of this concept.

PROBLEM-8

Note that following piece of code will not work. It will give compilation error:

```
printf("\n How many elements are there in the array ? \n") ;
scanf("%i",&n) ;
int a[n] ;
```

Let's write a program to create an array in this way (it will be possible by declaring the array, using pointer and making use of malloc function), so as to accept as many integer numbers from the keyboard as user wishes and printing them in sorted descending order.

PROGRAM-8

```
#include <stdio.h>
#include <stdlib.h>
void reorder(int n,int *array) ;
main()
{
    int n , i , *mat ;
    printf("\n How many elements are there in the array ? \n") ;
    scanf("%i",&n) ;
    mat = (int * ) malloc(n * sizeof(int)) ;
    for (i = 0 ; i < n ; i++)
    {
        printf("\nGive Number %i ",(i+1)) ;
        scanf("%i",mat+i) ;
    }
    reorder(n,mat) ;
    for (i = 0 ; i < n ; i++)
    printf("%i ",*(mat+i)) ;
}
void reorder(int n, int *array)
{
    int i , j, temp ;
```

```
        for (j = 0 ; j < n-1 ; j++ )
        {
            for (i = 0 ; i < n-1 ; i++)
            {
                if ( *(array+(i+1)) >= *(array+i) )
                {
                    temp = *(array+i) ;
                    *(array+i) = *(array+(i+1)) ;
                    *(array+(i+1)) = temp ;
                }
            }
        }
        return ;
    }
```

ALLOCATING MULTIPLE BLOCKS OF MEMORY

You are now familiar with the functioning of **malloc** function and know that it allocates one block of memory randomly, for use, during the execution of the program. Now the question is, if large memory requirement is there then how to allocate multiple numbers of memory blocks? well, **calloc** function, in C language does this task. It is used in following format:

ptr = calloc(n, element-size) ;

This statement will allocate contiguous space of n number of memory blocks, each of the element-size bytes.

As a result of this statement, all bytes are initialized to zero and pointer to the first byte of allocated region is is returned.

If the mentioned memory space is not free in the main memory then a NULL pointer is returned.

Following statement shows the usage of calloc statement:

xptr1 = calloc(5, 250);

This statement will allocate 5 blocks of memory each of which is of the size 250 bytes.

RELEASING ALLOCATED MEMORY SPACE

All dynamically allocated memory blocks should be released, when their use is over and they are no more required.

When allocated memory blocks are released, memory space becomes free for further usage.

In C language, memory space is released using free function. It is used in following format:

free (pointer) ;

Here pointer is the same pointer to which the value was assigned at the time of allocating the memory block either through malloc or calloc function.

ALTERING THE SIZE OF ALLOCATED MEMORY

If during the execution of the program, it is realized that the allocated memory block is either small of large, its size can be altered using realloc function. The realloc function is used in the following format:

ptr = realloc(original-pointer, altered-size) ;

Here original-pointer is pointer, which was assigned the value at the time of executing malloc function. The altered-size is the size that is required now.

To understand the usage of realloc function assume that following statement was executed for creating dynamic memory block

xptr = malloc(100);

To alter this size to 500, following statement can be executed;

yptr=realloc(xptr,500);

Using, realloc function, newly allocated memory space can either be larger or smaller than original space.

If somehow, system is unable to allocate space in continuation to the previously created space, it creates entirely new space at other location and move the original data (if it is there) to newer location. Note that in this case the original memory addresses change.

If somehow the system is unable to reallocate new memory, it returns a NULL pointer. To understand the functioning of realloc function, let's write another program for the given problem.

PROBLEM-9

Let's write a program that dynamically allocates memory for accepting the elements of an integer array that is of the size that user wants.

This program first sorts the elements of the array in descending order and then prints them. Later it asks how many more elements have to be added to previously created array. It then reallocates dynamic memory space, accepts the elements from the user, reorders complete array and prints all its elements.

PROGRAM-9

```
#include <stdio.h>
#include <stdlib.h>
void reorder(int n,int *array) ;
```

```
main()
{
    int n ,m,o, i ,j, *mat ,*rmat ;
    clrscr();
    printf("\n How many elements are there in the array ? \n");
    scanf("%i",&n) ;
    mat = (int * ) malloc(n * sizeof(int)) ;
    for (i = 0 ; i < n ; i++)
    {
        printf("\nGive Number %i ",(i+1)) ;
        scanf("%i",mat+i) ;
    }
    reorder(n,mat) ;
    for (i = 0 ; i < n ; i++)
    printf("%i  ",*(mat+i)) ;

    printf("\n How many more elements are to be added in the array ? \n") ;
    scanf("%d",&m) ;
        o= m + n;
    rmat = (int *) realloc(mat, o * sizeof(int)) ;
        for (j = n ; j < o  ; j++)
    {
        printf("\nGive Number %d  ",j-(n-1)) ;
        scanf("%i",rmat+j) ;
    }
    reorder(o,rmat) ;
    for (j = 0 ; j < o ; j++)
    printf("%i  ",*(rmat+j)) ;
    free(rmat);
    getch();
}
void reorder(int n, int *array)
{
    int i , j, temp ;
    for (j = 0 ; j < n-1 ; j++ )
    {
```

```
            for (i = 0 ; i < n-1 ; i++)
            {
                if ( *(array+(i+1)) >= *(array+i) )
                {
                    temp = *(array+i) ;
                    *(array+i) = *(array+(i+1)) ;
                    *(array+(i+1)) = temp ;
                }
            }
        }
        return ;
    }
```

ARRAY OF POINTERS

In C language, we can have an array of pointers also. Following statement declares an array of 5 integer pointers:

int *mat[5];

This array is shown in figure 14.4

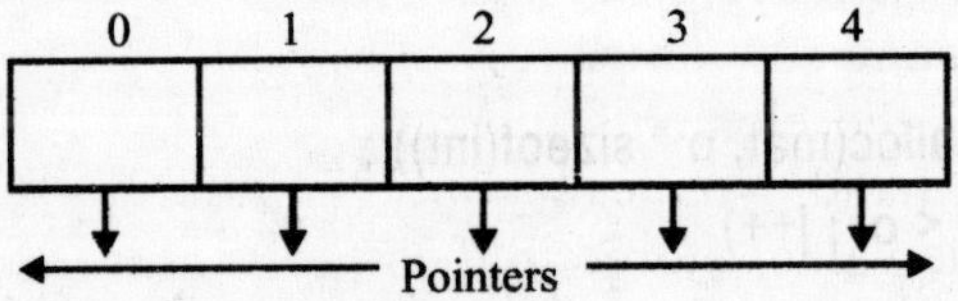

Figure 14.4

To understand the concept and usage of array of pointers, consider the following program:

PROGRAM-10

```
#include<stdio.h>
main()
{
    int *mat[5];
    int i ;
    int a=100,b=200,c=300,d=400,e=500;
    clrscr();
    mat[0]=&a;
    mat [1]=&b;
    mat [2]=&c;
```

```
        mat [3]=&d;
        mat [4]=&e;
        for(i=0;i<5;i++)
        printf("\n The Pointer mat[%d] points to the value %d\n",i,*mat[i]);
        printf("\n Base Address of array of pointer \"mat \" is %x\n", mat);
        for(i=0;i<5;i++)
        printf(" The Address contained in mat[%d] is %x  \n",i,mat[i]);
        getch();
}
```

POINTERS AND TWO DIMENSIONAL ARRAYS

You are already familiar with the concept of pointers and their relationship with one dimensional array. You know that the name of one dimensional array (say A) always points to the first element of the array. Applying pointer arithmetic i.e. adding 1 to it (i.e. A+1) yields the address of the second element of the array and so on.

Now the question is, can a relationship between pointers and two dimensional array be established? Well, the answer is yes. Since two dimensional array is a group of multiple single dimensional array hence pointer arithmetic can be devised to point to the second row, third row etc. of the two dimensional array and all the elements in them. Once you have correct pointers in hand, you can apply Indirection operator on them to get the values stored in them.

To understand the relationship between pointers and two dimensional arrays, consider the following definition of two dimensional array.

```
int p[3][4] ;
```

Using pointers, this definition can be rewritten as follows:

```
int (*p)[4] ;
```

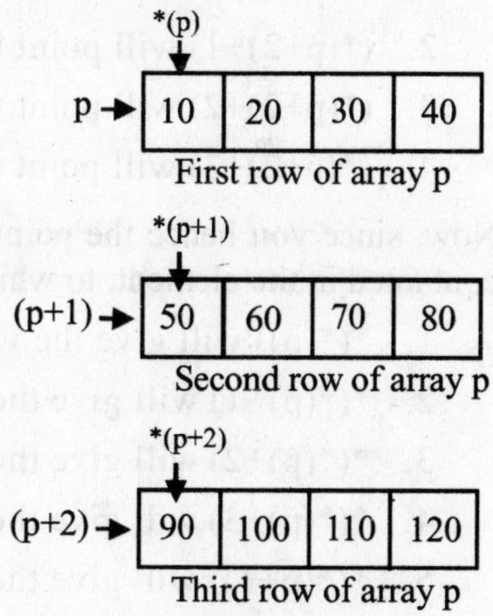

Figure 14.5

In this declaration, following things will hold good:

1. p will point to the first row of four elements.
2. (p+1) will point to the second row of four elements.
3. (p+2) will point to the third row of four elements.

Now the question is, what points to the elements of the rows? Well, to understand this, recall that p is a pointer to the first array. Thus *(p) will be an address. Add 0 to this and you get *(p)+0 i.e. *(p). This will give the address of the first element of the first row. Similarly if you add 1 to *(p) i.e. (*(p)+1) will give the address of the second element of the first row. Thus pointers to the elements of the first row can be obtained as follow.

1. (*(p)) points to be first element of the first row.
2. (*(p)+1) points to be second element of the first row.
3. (*(p)+2) points to be third element of the first row.
4. (*(p)+3) points to be fourth element of the first row.

Now for the elements of second row: The pointer (p+1) points to the second row of 4 elements. Thus *(p+1) will be an address. Using pointer arithmetic, add 1 to this i.e. (*(p+1)+1) will point to the second element of the first row. Thus pointers to the elements of second row can be obtained as follow:

1. (*(p+1)) will point to the first element of the second row.
2. (*(p+1)+1) will point to the second element of the second row.
3. (*(p+1)+2) will point to the third element of the second row.
4. (*(p+1)+3) will point to the forth element of the second row.

Similarly performing pointer arithmetic on (p+2) i.e. pointer to the third row, will yield the pointers to the elements of third row:

1. (*(p+2)) will point to the first element of the third row.
2. (*(p+2)+1) will point to the second element of the second row.
3. (*(p+2)+2) will point to the third element of the second row.
4. (*(p+2)+3) will point to the fourth element of the second row.

Now, since you hence the pointers, Indirection operator can be applied on them to get the value contained in the element, to which, they point to. This is illustrated and summarized below.

1. *(*(p)) will give the value contained in first element of the first row.
2. *(*(p)+1) will give the value contained in second element of the first row.
3. *(*(p)+2) will give the value contained in third element of the first row.
4. *(*(p)+3) will give the value contained in fourth element of the first row.
5. *(*(p+1)) will give the value contained in first element of the second row.
6. *(*(p+1)+1) will give the value contained in second element of the second row.
7. *(*(p+1)+2) will give the value contained in third element of the second row.
8. *(*(p+1)+3) will give the value contained in fourth element of the second row.
9. *(*(p+2)) will give the value contained in first element of the third row.
10. *(*(p+2)+1) will give the value contained in second element of third row.
11. *(*(p+2)+2) will give the value contained in third element of the third row.
12. *(*(p+2)+3) will give the value contained in fourth element of the third row

This pointer arithmetic has been applied in the following program. This program, declares an array of three row and four columns using pointer. The elements of this array are initialized using pointer first later their address and contents are printed, using pointers only.

PROGRAM-11

```
#include<stdio.h>
#include<stdlib.h>
#define row 3
#define col 4
main()
{
    int (*p)[4] ;
    int i,j ;
    int sum=10;
    p=(int*)malloc(row * col * sizeof(int));
    for (i=0;i<3;i++)
    for (j=0;j<4;j++)
    {
        *(*(p+i)+j)=sum ;
        sum = sum + 10 ;
    }
    for (i=0;i<3;i++)
    {
        printf("\n\n\nAddresses and the contents of the elements of row %d ",   i) ;
        for (j=0;j<4;j++)
        {
            printf("\nAddress of element %d is %x    ", j, (*(p+i)+j))  ;
            printf(" Value of the element %i is  %d",j, *(*(p+i)+j) );
        }
    }
}
```

To get more familar with the useage of pointer for accessing two dimensional arrays let's write few programs for the given problems:

PROBLEM-12

Let there be an array of 3 rows and 3 columns. Accept the values of its elements from the keyboard. Copy its rows into columns of another array (transpose) Print the new array. Make use of pointers for declaring the processing functions.

PROGRAM-12

```
#include<stdio.h>
main()
{
```

```
int (*mat1)[3] ;
int (*mat2)[3] ;
int i,j ;
int sum=10;
mat1=(int*)malloc(3*4*sizeof(int)) ;
for (i=0;i<3;i++)
{
    printf("\n Give values for row %d ",i) ;
    for (j=0;j<3;j++)
    {
        printf("\nGive value of element %d",j);
        scanf("%d",(*(mat1+i)+j)) ;
    }
}
for (i=0 ; i<3 ; i++)
for (j=0 ; j<3 ; j++)
*(*(mat2+j)+i)= *(*(mat1+i)+j) ;
for (i=0;i<3;i++)
{
    for (j=0;j<3;j++)
    {
        printf("%d  ",*(*(mat2+i)+j) );
    }
    printf("\n");
}
}
```

PROBLEM-13

Making use of pointer arithmetic, write a program to add the elements of two arrays (of [3][4] size) and print them.

PROGRAM-13

```
#include<stdio.h>
#include<stdlib.h>
#define row 3
#define col 4
main()
```

```
{
    int i, j ;
    int (*a)[col] ;
    int (*b)[col] ;
    int (*c)[col] ;
    a =(int*)malloc(row*col*sizeof(int));
    b =(int*)malloc(row*col*sizeof(int));
    c=(int*)malloc(row*col*sizeof(int));
    /* Taking elements of first array using pointers */
    for(i=0;i<row;i++)
    {
        printf("\nArray 1 : row %i element ",(i+1));
        for(j=0;j<col;j++)
        {
            printf("\nGive element %i ", (j+1));
            scanf("%i", (*(a+i)+j) );
        }
    }
    /* Taking elements of second array using pointers */
    for(i=0;i<row;i++)
    {
        printf("\nArray 2 : row %i element ",(i+1));
        for(j=0;j<col;j++)
        {
            printf("\nGive element %i ", (j+1));
            scanf("%i", (*(b+i)+j) );
        }
    }
    /* Summing up the two arrays and printing using pointers */
    for(i=0;i<row;i++)
    {
        for(j=0;j<col;j++)
        {
            *(*(c+i)+j)= *(*(b+i)+j) + *(*(a+i)+j);
```

```
            printf("%i   ", *(*(c+i)+j));
        }
        printf("\n");
    }
}
```

POINTER ARRAY

Recall that in the previous section we declared a two dimensional array as pointer to a group of one dimensional arrays. Using another method, the same two dimensional array can be defined as one dimensional array of pointers. Each element of this array would point to the beginning of separate one dimensional array (that put together would constitute two dimensional array). To understand the concept, refer figure 14.6.

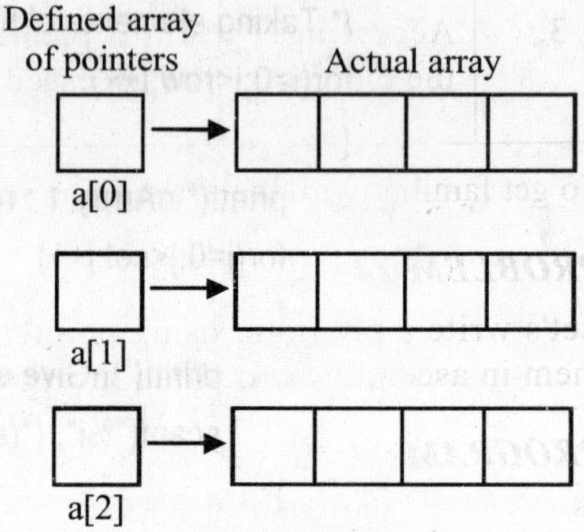

Figure 14.6

Say we wish to work with two dimensional array of 3 rows and 4 columns, as illustrated in figure, which is of int type. Then instead of defining the array as int a[3][4] or int (*a)[4], it can be defined as follows:

```
int *a[3];
```

The general format for defining an array of pointer is

```
data type * array-name[dimension] ;
```

Now, here in this definition, following points have to be noted:

1. In * array-name, *a is not written, within bracket, because if you do so, it will declare a pointer to a group of contiguous array blanks (refer previous sections).
2. Dimension of pointer array is one less than that, in which data is to be stored.
3. The first element of the pointer array will point to the beginning of the first row of two dimensional array. Second element will point to be beginning of second row and so on.
4. Since *a[3] is a pointer array hence a[0] will be the first pointer, pointing to the first row of two dimensional array. Similarly a[1] and a[2] will point to the beginning of second and third row.
5. Since you have the pointer (say a[1]), pointing to the beginning of row hence, adding a number (say2) to it will yield another pointer (i.e. (a[1]+2)), which will point to the corresponding element of that row (i.e. third element of second row).
6. As usual, using indirection operator (i.e.*) on any pointer (say (a[1]+2)) will refer to the contents of the element, to which it points to (i.e. third element of second row).
7. You can say that the elements of pointer array are pointers to pointers.

Now you are familiar with the two methods, which make use of pointers, for declaring the arrays, so a summary of their comparison is given in the following table:

Sr. No.	Subject	Pointer Variable Method	Pointer Array Method
1.	Declaration	data type (* pointer variable) [column value] e.g int(*x)[6]	Data type *Array[row value] e.g. *x[5]
2.	Mentioning rows/col	In declaration you mention the number of column in each row.	In declaration you mention the. number of rows in the array.
3.	Accessing the elements	Third element of the second will be accessed as *(*(x+1)+2).	Third element of the second row will get accessed as *(x[1]+2)

To get familiar with the usage of pointer arrays, let's write few programs, for the give problems.

PROBLEM-14

Let's write a program, using pointer array, which accepts 5 names from the keyboard, sorts them in ascending order and prints them.

PROGRAM-14

```
#include <stdio.h>
#include <stdlib.h>
#define size 5
void printarr ( char *x[ ]);
void sortarr ( char *x[ ]) ;
main()
{
    int i = 0 ;
    char *x[size]  ;
    printf("\n\n") ;
    for ( i =0 ; i < size ; i++)
    {
        x[i] = (char *) malloc (15 * sizeof(char)) ;
        printf("Give String %i " , i+1) ;
        scanf ("%s",x[i]) ;
    }
    printf("\n\n Unsorted Array is as follows ") ;
    printarr(x);
```

```
        printf("\n\n Sorted Array is as follows ") ;
        sortarr(x) ;
        printarr(x) ;
}
void printarr( char *x[ ])
{
        int i = 0 ;
        for ( i =0 ; i < size ; i++)
        {
                printf("\nString %i %s",i+1, x[i]) ;
        }
}
void sortarr( char *x[ ])
{
        int i , j ;
        char *temp ;
        for ( j = 0 ; j < size-1 ; j++)
        {
                for ( i = 0 ; i < size-1 ; i++)
                {
                        if ( strcmp( x[i+1],x[i]) < 0 )
                        {
                                temp = x[i+1];
                                x[i+1] = x[i] ;
                                x[i] = temp ;
                        }
                }
        }
        return ;
}
```

POINTERS TO FUNCTIONS

You know that arguments of a function (called formal arguments) receive values from the calling function (through actual arguments). These arguments could be of any data type like int, float, char, array, pointer etc. If any of the arguments is of pointer type then this pointer could point to any thing such as variable, array, function etc.

When a pointer to a function (let's call this function as

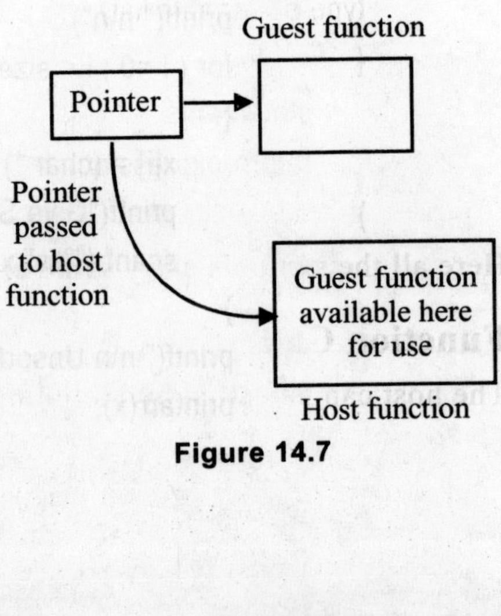

Figure 14.7

guest function) is passed to another function (let's call this function as host function) then the guest function becomes fully available in host function, as if it was a part of it. Concept of passing one function to another, using pointers is illustrated in figure 14.7.

The advantage of passing pointer to function, to another function is that using different pointers (say *p1 to x1 function *p2 to y2 function), different guest functions can be made available in host function to do multiple type of tasks.

Now the question is, how do you define, prototypes, formal arguments, actual arguments etc? Well, the general format for all these is given below.

Prototypes

General format for prototype host function is written as follows:

```
data-type-h Host-function-name (data type-g(*pointer)(data-type-a &variable-list), data-type-b &variable list) ;
```

Different symbols used in above format signify articles as mentioned below.

1. The host function will obviously return some value to the calling function. The data-type-h signifies the data type of that value, which host function returns.
2. Host function will obviously have some name, by which it will be identified throughout the program. Host-function-name is that name.
3. The data-type-g is the data type of that value which guest function returns.
4. Pointer is a pointer variable which points to guest function.
5. Guest function will obviously have an argument list, consisting of data-type and variables. They are being denoted through data-type-a & variable-list in the above format.
6. Apart from pointer to the guest function, host function may have other arguments also. Those arguments in terms of data type and variables are being denoted by data-type-b & variable list in the above mentioned format.

Function Definition

Function definition will be as follows:

```
data-type-h Host-function-name (data type-g(*pointer)(data-type-a&variable-list), data-type-b&variable list)
{
    statements
    return(expression);
}
```

Here all the symbols carry same meaning as mentioned in proto type section.

Function Call

The host can be called by including statement of the following type:

host-function-name(function name, data-type-b and variable list)

Here data-type-b and variable list have the same meaning, which was explained in prototype section.

To get familiar with the process of passing one function to another function, using pointers, let's write a program for the following problem:

PROBLEM-15

A construction company, develops blank land area, by doing land scaping, cement construction and wood work on it. The cost of development varies for circular areas and square plot areas.

Let's write a program to get type of area and length/radius from the keyboard and then depending upon the input calculates and prints the cost of construction.

PROGRAM STRATEGY

1. Shape of the plot main function.
2. We will have three functions i.e. circle- area, square-area and cost-construction.
3. As the names of the functions indicate, circle area will calculate circle area are return it to the calling program (an i++ value). Function square area will calculate square area and return it to the calling program (int value.

   Cost of construction will have provision for accepting length or radius and calculating and printing cost of landscaping, wood work and cement work. This function will return total cost of construction (a real value) to thje main function, where it will get printed.
4. The main function will call cost-construction function by passing pointer to either circle-area function or square- area function, depending upon the choice given by the user through keyboard.

PROGRAM-15

```
#include<stdio.h>
float circle_area(int r) ;
float square_area(int r) ;
float cost_construction( float (*ptr)(int r1), float r1, float r2, float r3);
main()
{
    int len ;
    float amt ;
    char shape ;
    printf("\nGive c for circular area and s for square") ;
    scanf("%c",&shape) ;
    if (shape=='c' || shape=='C')
        amt = cost_construction(circle_area, 10.00, 20.00, 30.00) ;
```

```
        else
        amt = cost_construction(square_area, 5.00,10.00,15.00) ;
        printf("\nTotal cost of construction = %f ",amt) ;
    }
    float cost_construction( float (*ptr)(int r1), float r1, float r2, float r3)
    {
        int len;
        float area, total, c1, c2, c3 ;
        printf("\Give radius or length of the plot ") ;
        scanf("%d",&len);
        area = (*ptr)(len) ;
        printf("\nTotal Area on which the construction is to be done %f",area);
        c1 = area * r1 ;
        c2 = area * r2 ;
        c3 = area * r3 ;
        printf ("\n Cost of Landscaping is %f", c1) ;
        printf ("\n Cost of Cement Consrruction is %f", c2) ;
        printf ("\n Cost of Woodwork is %f", c3) ;
        total = c1 + c2 + c3 ;
        return (total) ;
    }
    float circle_area (int r1)
    {
        int area ;
        area = (22 * r1 * r1 ) / 7 ;
        return (area) ;
    }
    float square_area (int r1)
    {
        float area ;
        area = (r1 * r1 ) ;
        return (area) ;
    }
```

EXERCISES CHAPTER 14

Short Type Questions

A. Select most appropriate answers for the following questions:

1. Which of the following is a pointer?
   (a) pa (b) &pa (c) *pa (d) int pa
2. If pa is a variable then which of the following will be an address?
   (a) pa (b) &pa (c) *pa (d) int pa
3. Which of the following will print the contents of a pointer variable, which has been declared as int *px?
   (a) printf("%i", px) (b) printf("%d", px) (c) printf("%x", px)
   (d) printf("%s", px)
4. If x[10] is an array of 10 integer elements then which of the following will point to the second element of the array?
   (a) x[2] (b) x[1] (c) (x+2) (d) (x+1)
5. If pa is a pointer then which of the following cannot be performed?
   (a) printing contents of pa (b) Accepting value of pa from keyboard
   (c) printing contents of the variable to which pa points to
   (d) Accepting contents of the variable to which pa points to

B. Fill in the blanks.

6. The statement .... will declare pi as pointer to character variable.
7. The statement .... will declare an array of 10 integer pointers.
8. The address of a variable v can be assigned to pointer pv by writing .... statement.
9. The operator .... is called Address operator.
10. If int *a[10] statement declares an array then .... will point to the third element.

C. State true or false.

11. A pointer declared as int *px can hold the addresses of integer variables only.
12. Pointers can be initialized in declaration statements.
13. The function malloc(), allocates memory space at run time.
14. If A[10]=700 then &(A+7) will also be 700.
15. The statement int *(a)[10] will declare a two dimensional array of 10 columns.

D. Answer the following questions in short:

16. If a=100 and pa=&a then what will be the value of *pa?

17. Which symbol is used for Indirection operator?
18. Are pointers passed by value to a function?
19. Which of the following two statements declare a two dimensional array as 4 contiguous blocks of memory locations: (a) int*x[10] (b) int (*x)[10]?
20. If x[10] is an array of integers then what x++ will signify?
21. What statement will you write to create an integer array of 5 rows and 3 columns, as contiguous blocks of memory locations, using pointer method?
22. An array has been declared as char (*x)[15]. What statement will you write for dynamic memory allocation, so as to accommodate 5 rows and 15 columns in it?
23. Two dimensional array has to be used in a program. If this array is to be declared, using array of pointers then what will be the dimension of pointer array?
24. An array has been declared as float *x ;. How will you refer the contents of its third element?
25. How will you define an array x[10][5] of integer elements, using pointers.

Detailed Answer Type Questions

E. Answer the following questions in details:

26. What is a pointer in reference to C language? How do you declare pointers? Explain using a suitable example.
27. Explain the role of Address and Indirection operators, using suitable examples.
28. Write a program to swap the values of two variables making use of pointers.
29. Explain the term "Calling function by reference "How it is done in C language"?
30. Differentiate between calling function by reference and calling function by value.
31. Write a program, which accepts principal amount, rate of interest and term of deposit in the main program. It passes these values to a function through pointers. Function operates upon these values to calculate total payable amount at the time of maturity. The amount gets displayed in main function.
32. Write a program that accepts names and age of 10 persons and prints the name of that person, who is youngest in age. Make use of pointer method to declare the array.
33. Write a program, which accepts sales figures of three organizations for the first three months of the year. The program should make use of pointer array method to define the array and should print the maximum cumulative sale (sum of three month's sale).
34. How do you pass one function to another function in C language? What are the advantages of this?
35. Write a program, which passes two functions f1 and f2 to another function f3. The function f1 calculates simple interest, f2 calculates compound interest. The function f3 calculates the difference between the two interest amounts for the same principal amount, year of deposit and same interest rate. All these values should be accepted through keyboard in main function.

****

CHAPTER 15

Structures and Unions

INTRODUCTION

You are already familiar with basic data types, such as int, float, double, char etc. available in C language. You also know that when multiple elements of same data type are logically grouped together then that group is called array. For example, int a[10] is a group of 10 elements. Each member in this group is of int data type. Now the question is, can multiple elements of different data types (say one integer element, two float elements and one character element) also be combined logically to form a group? Well, this is, what **structure** is all about.

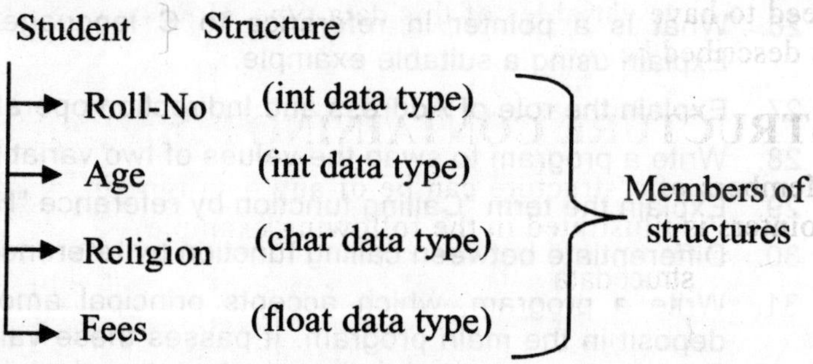

Figure 15.1

Structure is basically a logical group of multiple items of different data types such as int, float etc. Conceptual diagram of structure is illustrated in figure 15.1.

This figure illustrated a structure, named student. It comprises of four elements ie Roll-No, Age, Religion and Fees. Roll-No and Age are of int data type, while Religion and Fees are of char and float data types, respectively.

Individual elements that constitute the structure are called members. Thus structure illustrated in figure 15.1 comprises of four members.

DECLARING A STRUCTURE

All the structures that you use in the program need to be defined first. General format for defining the structure is given below.

```
struct structure-name
{   data-type-of-member-1  member-1-name ;
    data-type-of-member-2      member-2-name ;
```

```
        ........................................................................
        ........................................................................
        data-type-of-member-n      member-n-name ;
    };
```

Here "struct" is a keyword, which is to be written as such. The structure-name is the name that you wish to assign to the structure. The data-type and member name have obvious meaning. Thus structure, illustrated in figure 16.1 can be defined as follows:

```
struct student
{
    int roll_no ;
    int age ;
    char religion ;
    float fees ;
} ;
```

Note that when you define a structure, you basically define a derived data type. Now you need to have variables of this data type. How do you define variables of structure data type is described below.

STRUCTURE CONTAINING POINTERS

Members of a structure can be of any data type, including pointers. A structure containing pointers is illustrated in the following example:

```
struct data
{
    int  roll;
    char *name ;
    int  marks ;
};
```

STRUCTURE VARIABLES

After defining the structure, variables of this structure type can be defined in the following format:

```
storage class structure-name variable-name-1, variable-name-2........ variable-name-n ;
```

Here storage class can either be static, automatic or external. But it is optional. structure-name is name of that structure, which has already been defined and the following variables of that type are to be created. Variables-1 to variable-n are the variables, which are to be created.

For example, if three variables, say ram, shyam and geeta are to be created of student type then following statement will have to be included in the program:

```
struct student ram, shyam, geeta ;
```

An alternate method for defining the variables along with the definition of structure is also available in C language. This method is described below.

```
struct structure-name                    struct student
{                        e.g.            {
member definitions                       int roll-no ;
} variable-1 ..... variable-n;           int age ;
                                         char religion ;
                                         float fees ;
                                         } ram, shyam,geeta ;
```

STRUCTURE INITIALIZATION

Like variables of basic data types (int, float, char, etc.), variable of structure type can also be initialized at the time defined them. The general format for initializing the variables of structure type, at the time of their creation, is given below.

```
storage class struct structure-name variable={value-1, value-2... value-n};
```

In this format, value-1 is assigned to the first member, value-2 is assigned to the second member and so on. Following is a valid initialization statement:

```
struct student ram={110, 20, 'h', 375.50};
```

When this statement will get executed, structure member initialization for variable ram, will take place as follows:

1. roll_no=110
2. age=20
3. religion='h'
4. fees=37.5.50

Similarly another variable shyam can be initialized as follows:

```
struct student shyam={111, 21, 'c', 150.75};
```

ACCESSING STRUCTURE MEMBERS

Once the structure has been defined and variable have been created. Individual members for that variable can be accessed through Dot operator(.). Following is the general format for accessing any member of structure variable:

```
variable-name.member-name
e.g.    ram.roll_no              shyam.roll_no
        ram.age         or       shyam.age
```

```
ram.religion          shyam. religion
ram.fees              shyam.fees
```

You are now familiar with structures, their definition and methods of declaring variables of structure type. So let's write a simple program for the following problem:

PROBLEM-1

Write a program to define a structure named employee. The structure should have the following elements in it:

1. employee number (int type)
2. name (character array of 50 elements)
3. age (int type)
4. expression (int type)
5. salary (float type)

This program should create a variable alok of this data type accept members' values from keyboard and print them.

PROGRAM-1

```
#include <stdio.h>
struct employee {
        int empno ;
        char name[30] ;
        int age ;
        int experience ;
        float salary ;
        } alok ;
main()
{
printf("\n Give Employee Number " );
scanf ("%i",&alok.empno);
printf("Give Name" );
scanf (" %s",&alok.name);
printf("Give age " );
scanf ("%d", &alok.age);
printf("Give experience " );
scanf ("%i",&alok.experience);
printf("Give salary " );
```

```
scanf ("%f",&alok.salary);
printf("\nEmployee No %i ",alok.empno);
printf("\nName %s ",alok.name);
printf("\nAge %i ", alok.age);
printf("\nExperience %i ",alok.experience);
printf("\nSalary %g ",alok.salary);
}
```

STRUCTURE ASSIGNMENT

In C language, one structure variable can be assigned to another structure variable, which is of the same type. For example, if man1 and man2 are structure variables of employee type (structure mentioned in program 1) then following structure assignment statesmen can be written:

man2 = man1 ;

When this statement will get executed, values of all the members of boy1 will be assigned to the corresponding members of boy2 variable.

FINDING SIZE OF THE STRUCTURE

Each variable that you operate upon in your C program, occupies some space in memory. On most of the computers, integer occupies 2 bytes, character occupies 1 byte, float occupies 4 bytes and double occupies 8 bytes. Often this occupied space is called the size of the variable or length of the variable. Now the question is, what will be the size or length of a structure variable? Well, its size can be calculated by adding up the size of all its members. For example, any variable of employee type (mentioned in program 1), will be of following size:

size of empno member (2 bytes) + size of name member (30 bytes) + size of age member(2 bytes) + size of experience member (2 bytes) + size of salary member (4 bytes)

Thus the size of the variables, which are of employee type, will be 2 + 30 + 2 + 2 + 4 i.e. 40 bytes.

ARRAY OF STRUCTURES

To understand the requirement of array of structures, refer back to program-1. This program accepts data of one employee. Now the question is, what do we do, if the data of 50 employees has to be handled, within the program? Do we write 50 different variable names after alok? Well, that's not the way. To deal with 50 persons, an array of 50 elements, which are of this structure type, need to be defined. For example, below given statement creates an array of structure, which has 50 elements in it:

```
struct employee pepole[50];
```

Here 'people' is an array of 50 elements. Each element is a variable of employee (which is a structure) type.

ACCESSING MEMBERS OF STRUCTURE ARRAY

Once an array of structure has been defined, members can always be accessed in the following format:

array -name [index].member name

For example, following are few, valid member names of the array defined above:

people[0].employee_number

people[0].name

people[0].age

people[0].experience

people[0].salary

people[1].name

people[2].salary

people[49].experience etc.

Now you are familiar with array of structures, so let's apply this concept for handling multiple data items of structure data type in a program.

PROBLEM-2

Say account department has to keep track of savings done by 30 employees of the organization. For this it maintains following record of these employees.

1. employee_number
2. Name
3. Earnings
4. Expenditure

Let's write a program that accepts the data of all the employees and prints saving amount for them.

PROGRAM-2

```
#include <stdio.h>
void readdata(int i) ;
void calculate(int i) ;
struct employee {
        int empno ;
        char name[30] ;
        int earning ;
        int spend ;
        } emp[25] ;
```

```
main()
{
    int n ;
    printf("\nHow many employees are there ? " ) ;
    scanf ("%d",&n);
    readdata(n) ;
    calculate(n) ;
}
void readdata( int n)
{
    int i ;
    for (i = 0 ; i < n  ; i++)
    {
        printf("Give employee Number" );
        scanf ("%i",&emp[i].empno);
        printf("Give employee name " );
        scanf (" %[^\n]",emp[i].name);
        printf("Give earning amount " );
        scanf ("%i",&emp[i].earning);
        printf("Give Expenditure amount " );
        scanf ("%i",&emp[i].spend);
    }
    return ;
}
void calculate( int n)
{
    int i,diff;
    for (i = 0 ; i < n ; i++)
    {   diff = emp[i].earning - emp[i].spend ;
        printf("\nEmployee Number %i ",emp[i].empno);
        printf("\nName %s ",emp[i].name);
        printf("\nEarning %i ",emp[i].earning);
        printf("\nExpenditure %i ",emp[i].spend);
        printf("\nSaving %i ",diff);
    }
    return ;
}
```

STRUCTURE WITHIN STRUCTURE (NESTED STRUCTURE)

As mentioned earlier, members of any structure can be of any data type (i.e. int, float, char, array, pointer etc.). Since structure is also a derived type hence the question is, can a structure member be of structure data type? Well, the answer is yes. When a structure is placed within another structure, as its member item, the resultant structure is called nested structure.

To understand the concept of nested structures, consider two structures. Say first data structure named ddmmyy consists of three members i.e. day, month and year, which are of int data type. Such a structure can be defined as follows:

```
struct ddmmyy
{    int day ;
     int month ;
     int year ;
};
```

Say, second structure, named emp consists of four member i.e. emp_no, name, salary, date_of_joining, which are of int, character array of 50 elements, float and ddmmyy structure type. Such a structure can be defined as follows:

```
struct emp
{    int emp_no ;
     char name[50] ;
     float salary ;
     struct ddmmyy date_of_joining
};
```

It is quite obvious that a variable, named person1 of emp type can be defined as follows:

```
struct emp person1;
```

Accessing Members of Nested Structure

Members of nested data structures are accessed, using two dot operators. For example, member of emp structure defined above can be accessed as follows:

```
person1.emp_no
person1.name
person1.salary
person1.date_of_joining.day
person1.date_of_joining.month
person1.date_of_joining.year
```

Since you can now access the members of nested structures hence you can process them also. So let's write a program, for the following problem:

PROBLEM-3

Say ddmmyy and emp are two structures as mentioned above. Write a program that accepts data for 10 employees and prints the details of all those employees, who joined the organization after 10/10/2002.

PROGRAM-3

```
#include <stdio.h>
# define size 3
struct ddmmyy
{
    int day ;
    int month ;
    int year ;
} ;
struct emp {
   int emp_no ;
   char name[50] ;
   int salary ;
   struct ddmmyy doj ;
   } em[size] ;
main()
{
    int i ;
    for(i=0 ; i<size ; i++)
    {
        printf("\n Give Employee Number " );
        scanf ("%i",&em[i].emp_no);
        printf("Give Name" );
        scanf (" %s",&em[i].name);
        printf("Give salary" );
        scanf ("%i", &em[i].salary);
        printf("Give date of joining " );
        scanf ("%i",&em[i].doj.day);
        printf("Give month of joining " );
        scanf ("%i",&em[i].doj.month);
        printf("Give year of joining " );
        scanf ("%i",&em[i].doj.year);
    }
```

```
        for(i=0 ; i<size ; i++)
        {
            if (em[i].doj.year > 02)
                goto prt ;
                else  if (em[i].doj.year==2 && em[i].doj.month> 10)
                    goto prt ;
                    else if (em[i].doj.year==2 && em[i].doj.month==10 && em[i].doj.day> 10)
                    goto prt ;
                    else continue ;
            prt :
            printf("\nEmployee Number %i", em[i].emp_no);
            printf("\nName  %s ", em[i].name);
            printf("\nSalary %i", em[i].salary);
            printf("\nDate of joining %i",em[i].doj.day);
            printf("\nMonth of joining %i",em[i].doj.month);
            printf("\nYear of joining %i ", em[i].doj.year);
        }
    }
```

STRUCTURE CONTAINING POINTERS

Members of a structure can be of any data type, including pointers. A structure containing pointers is illustrated in the following example:

```
    struct data
    {
        int  roll;
        char *name ;
        int  marks ;
    };
```

POINTER TO STRUCTURE

You know that pointer is a variable, which points to another variable. The variable, to which it points to can be of any data type, i.e. int, float, char etc. You also know that structure is a derived data type. Now the question is, can a pointer point to a variable, which is of structure type? Well, the answer is yes. A pointer of structure type can always point to the variables, which are of structure type. The concept of pointer to structure is illustrated in figure 15.2.

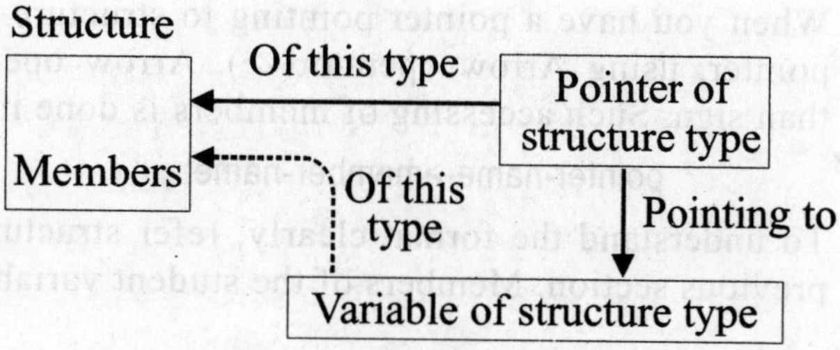

Figure 15.2

The concept illustrated in figure 16.2, when translated into C language, will result into following definitions and statements:

```
struct structure-name                /* Structure definition*/
{
    members
};
structure-name variable              /* To which pointer will point*/
structure-name *pointer-name /* pointer, which will hold the address of structure
variable*/
```

To understand the concept clearly, let's take an example.

```
struct data                                  struct data
{                                            {
    int roll_no;              or                 int roll_no;
    char name[50];                               char name[50];
    int marks;                                   int marks;
    int position;                                    int position;
};                                           } student ;
struct data student ;                        struct data *pstudent
struct * pstudent
```

ADDRESS OF THE FIRST ELEMENT

Address of the first element of structure type variable can be obtained using address operator. For above mentioned example, address of first element of student variable can be obtained as follows:

```
pstudent=&student;
```

ACCESSING MEMBERS THROUGH POINTERS

When you have a pointer pointing to structure variable, members can be accessed through pointer, using Arrow operator(->). Arrow operator consist of - sign followed by greater than sign. Such accessing of members is done in following format:

```
pointer-name->member-name;
```

To understand the format clearly, refer structure data and pointers pstudent, mentioned in previous section. Members of the student variable can be referred to as mentioned below.

Referring Using Pointer	**Normal referencing**
pstudent→ roll_no	student.roll_no
pstudent →name	student.name

pstudent ⟶ marks student.marks

pstudent ⟶ position student.position

Note that name is a character array of 50 elements. Now the question is, how do you access, individual elements (i.e. different characters of name) of the array? Well, that would be accessed as follows:

pstudent ⟶ name[0], pstudent ⟶ name [1], pstudent ⟶ name[2] etc.

Also note that these elements in normal referencing method will be referred to as follows:

student.name[0], pstudent.name [1], pstudent.name[2] etc.

Now you are familiar with pointer to structure, so let's write a program for the given problem.

PROBLEM-4

Say you have to accept roll number, name and marks of 50 students from the user and print all the details of the student, who secured highest marks.

PROGRAM-4

```
#include<stdio.h>
main()
{
    int i, count=0 ;
    int big=0 ;
    struct data
    {
        int roll_no ;
        char name[50] ;
        int marks ;
    };
    struct data student[5] ;
    struct data *pstudent[5] ;
    for (i=0 ; i<5 ; i++)
    {   pstudent[i]=&student[i] ;
        printf("\n Give Roll Number ") ;
        scanf("%d",&pstudent[i]->roll_no) ;
        printf("\n Give Name ") ;
        scanf("%s",pstudent[i]->name) ;
        printf("\n Give marks ") ;
        scanf("%d",&pstudent[i]->marks) ;
    }
```

```
        for (i=0; i<5 ; i++)
        {   if (pstudent[i]->marks > big)
            {   big=pstudent[i]->marks ;
                count = i ;
            }
        }
        printf("\nMerit Student") ;
        printf("\nRoll No %d ", pstudent[count]->roll_no) ;
        printf("\nName %s ", pstudent[count]->name) ;
        printf("\nMarks %d ", pstudent[count]->marks) ;
    }
```

STRUCTURES AND FUNCTIONS

You know that variables of any type can be passed to a function by the calling program. Now the question is, can individual structure elements or the complete structure be passed to a function? Well, the answer is yes, both the items (member and complete structure) can be passed to function. In turn if the need be, complete structure could also be returned by the function to the calling program.

Passing Structure Members to a Function

Truly speaking individual structure members are treated like normal variables. They can be very well passed to a function and a single value or no value could be returned via return statement. For doing this, actual arguments must include the names of structure members and formal arguments should match in number and data type. To understand the procedure, let's write a program for the following problem:

PROBLEM-5

Let's write a program that asks for the number of employees for whom the commission amount is to be calculated. Accordingly it takes employee number, name sale amount and percentage of commission applicable for him. It calculates and prints commission amount for the individuals and the net amount, which will have to be paid.

STRATEGY

To write the program for the above mentioned problem, we will follow the following strategy:

1. All the data items will be treated as members of a structure, named, record.
2. An array of structures with 100 elements will be created so as to make the program work for maximum 100 employees.
3. At the beginning of the program, we will ask for the number of employees, for whom the commission is to be calculated. Accordingly we will set for loops of the program.

4. We will have a function named readdata that will accept employee number, name, sale amount and percentage of commission. This function will be called as many times as there are employees, for whom the commission is to be calculated.
5. We will have another function named calculate, which will accept, sale amount and percentage of commission (which are basically members of structure) as argument. It will calculate the commission amount and return it back to the main program.
6. The main function will print the commission amount for the individuals and accumulate it also, so as to print the total commission to be paid at the end of the program.

PROGRAM-5

```
#include <stdio.h>
void readdata (int n) ;
float comm(int b, int d) ;
struct record
{  int  empno ;
     char name[30] ;
     int  sale ;
     int per  ;
}    emp[100] ;
main()
{
     int i, n ;
     float amt, total=0.0 ;
     printf("\n How many employees are there ? ") ;
     scanf("%i",&n) ;
     readdata(n) ;
     for (i=0 ; i< n ; i++)
     {
          amt = comm(emp[i].sale,emp[i].per) ;
          printf("\nCommission amount for %s is %f ", emp[i].name, amt);
          total = total + amt ;
     }
          printf("\nTotal comission to be given  = %f ",total);
}
void readdata( int n)
{
```

```
        int i ;
        for (i = 0 ; i < n  ; i++)
        {
            printf("Give empno" );
            scanf (" %[^\n]",emp[i].empno);
            printf("Give Name" );
            scanf (" %[^\n]",emp[i].name);
            printf("Give Sales amount " );
            scanf ("%i",&emp[i].sale);
            printf("Give percentage of commission" );
            scanf ("%i",&emp[i].per);
        }
        return ;
    }
    float comm(int b, int d)
    {   float amount ;
        amount  =  b * (d/100.00) ;
        return (amount) ;
    }
```

Passing Complete Structure to a Function

Like array, complete structure can also be passed to function. This is done with the help pointers. A pointer to the structure, when passed to a function passes the complete structure to the function. Note that passing pointer to the function results into passing arguments by reference (not by value).

Since passing of structure is done by reference hence function operates upon the original values and the modifications become visible is calling function.

It the need be, function can either return a single value to the calling program or pointer to the structure.

General format for passing complete structure to function is as follows:

Prototype

```
data-type function-name (structure-name *pointer-variable);
```

Calling Function

```
function-name (&structure-name)        /*Address of the structure gets passed
```

Function

data type function-name (struct structure-name *pointer-variable)

To be familiar with the process of passing complete structure to a function, let's write program for the given problem.

PROBLEM-6

Let's write a program, which accepts roll number, name and marks of the student from the user. If the marks are between 44 to 50 (both numbers excluded) it provides grace marks to make the marks 50. It also prints grace messages as follows:

1. "No grace marks required" if marks are more than 50.
2. "Grace marks given" if grace marks are awarded.
3. "Doesn't quality for grace marks", if marks are less than 45.

PROGRAM STRATEGY

We will follow following strategy for writing the program.

1. We will make use of a structure comprising of roll number, name, marks and grace marks.
2. Data will be accepted from the keyboard in main function.
3. The main function will pass the complete structure to other functions.
4. Other function will calculate the grace marks required to make the marks 50. It will return the grace marks to the main function.
5. Main function will print appropriate messages.

PROGRAM-6

```
#include<stdio.h>
struct record
{
    int roll ;
    int marks ;
    int gmarks ;
};
int gracem(struct record *point ) ;
main()
{
    struct record  student;
    struct record *pstudent ;
```

```
        int gm ;
        printf("\nGive Roll Number");
        scanf ("%d",&student.roll);
        printf("\nGive Marks");
        scanf ("%d",&student.marks);
        if(student.marks>44 && student.marks<50)
        {
            pstudent = &student ;
            gm = gracem(pstudent) ;
            printf("\nGrace marks given = %d",gm );
        }
        else if (student.marks >= 50)
            printf("\nNo grace marks required " );
            else
            printf("\nDoesn't qualify for grace marks " );
    }
    int gracem(struct record *pt)
    {   int gm=0 ;
        gm = 50 - pt->marks ;
        return (gm) ;
    }
```

Note that this program returns a single value. Now let's write a program in which the function modifies the structure value and doesn't return any value to the calling program. But the calling program, accesses the modified structures and makes use of modified values.

PROBLEM-7

Say account of 5 customers is to be maintained. Thus keeping record of their account number, name earnings, savings and tax.

If the balance i.e. (earning-saving)>5000 then tax @ 30% is paid.

PROGRAM STRATEGY

Main program accepts the input and passes pointer to the structure as argument to the function named, tax_calculation. This function calculates the tax value and updates the record. Main program accesses this value and prints it.

PROGRAM-7

```
#include<stdio.h>
struct record
{
    int accno;
    char name[20] ;
    int earning ;
    int saving;
    float tax ;
};
void tax_calculation(struct record *point ) ;
main()
{
    struct record  customer[5];
    struct record *pcustomer[5] ;
    int i ;
    int balance ;
    for(i=0 ; i<5 ; i++)
    {
        printf("\nGive Account Number");
        scanf ("%i",&customer[i].accno);
        printf("\nGive name");
        scanf ("%s",customer[i].name);
        printf("\nGive earning amount");
        scanf ("%d",&customer[i].earning);
        printf("\nGive saving amount");
        scanf ("%d",&customer[i].saving);
        balance = customer[i].earning - customer[i].saving;
        if(balance >  5000)
        {
            pcustomer[i] = &customer[i] ;
            tax_calculation(pcustomer[i]) ;
            printf("\nTax to be given is = %f", customer[i].tax);
        }
```

```
        else
        printf("\nNot a tax payee" );
    }
}
void tax_calculation(struct record *pt)
{
    float tax1=0.0 ;
    pt->tax = (pt->earning - pt->saving) * 30.00 / 100.00 ;
    printf("tax %f", tax1 );
    return ;
}
```

RETURNING STRUCTURES FROM FUNCTION

in C language functions can return complete structure to the calling function. In such cases function type is structure and return statement specifies the name of the structure being returned and its type matches with function type.

To get familiar with the process of returning structures to the functions, let's write a program for the following problem:

PROBLEM-8

Let's write a program that accepts two time values in hh, mm and ss format and adds them using time add function. This function returns added time in the form of complete structure.

PROGRAM-8

```
#include<stdio.h>
struct time
{
int hr;
int mt;
int sc;
};
struct time time_value[2], addedtime ;
main()
{
struct time timeadd (struct time t1, struct time t2) ; /* function Prototype */
int i ;
clrscr();
```

```
for (i=0 ; i<=1 ; i++)
{
printf("\n Give time components for time %d ", (i+1)) ;
printf("\n Give hours ") ;
scanf("%d",&time_value[i].hr) ;
printf("\n Give minutes ") ;
scanf("%d",&time_value[i].mt) ;
printf("\n Give seconds ") ;
scanf("%d",&time_value[i].sc) ;
}
addedtime = timeadd(time_value[0], time_value[1]) ;
printf("\n Added hour %d " , addedtime.hr) ;
printf("\n Added minute %d " , addedtime.mt) ;
printf("\n Added second %d " , addedtime.sc) ;
}
struct time timeadd (struct time t1, struct time t2)
{
int hour, minute, second , tot ;
struct time buffer ;
second = t1.sc  + t2.sc ;
tot = second / 60 ;
buffer.sc=second%60;
minute=t1.mt+t2.mt;
minute = minute + tot ;
hour = t1.hr + t2.hr ;
hour = hour + (minute/60) ;
buffer.hr = hour ;
buffer.mt=minute%60 ;
return (buffer) ;
}
```

SELF REFERENTIAL STRUCTURE

When an element of a structure is pointer that points to the structure itself then this structure is called Self Referential Structure.

Following is an example of self referential structure:

```
struct bnode
{
int info;
struct bnode *next;
};
```

Note that here we have a structure named bnode. It comprises of two elements. First element is info, which is of integer type. Other element is pointer named next, which is of pointer to structure named bnode.

To conceptualize a clear image of self referential structure, let's have three variables, named node1, node2 and node3 of bnode type. Creation of these three variables, in a program will be as follows:

```
bnode node1, node2, node3;
```

Conceptual diagram of these three variables is shown in figure 15.3.

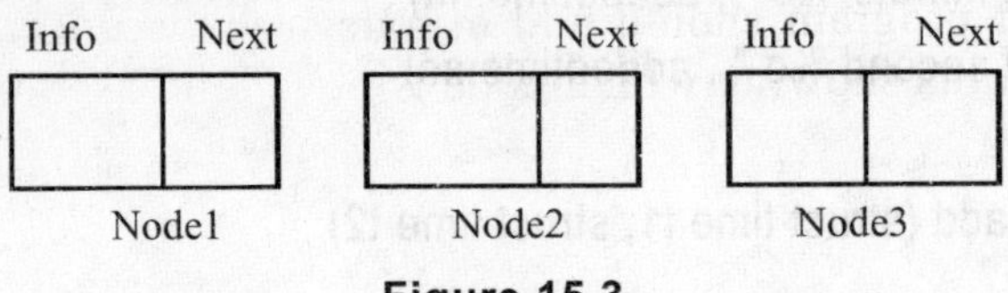

Figure 15.3

Say the contents of these nodes are as follows:

(i) Node1 has 100 stored in info and pointer next, points to node2.

(ii) Node2 has 200 stored in info and pointer next, points to node3.

(iii) Node3 has 300 stored in info and pointer next, points to node1.

Within the program data can be assigned as follows:

```
node1.info = 100 ;
node1.next=&node2;
node2.info = 200 ;
node2.next=&node3;
node3.info = 300 ;
node3.next=&node1;
```

All the three nodes now can be conceptualized as shown in figure 15.4.

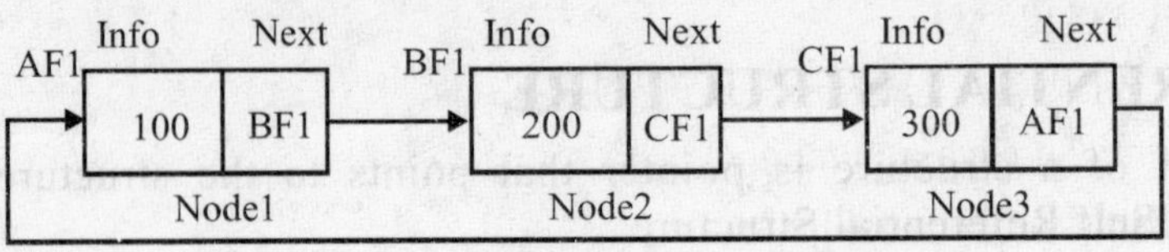

Figure 15.4

Above shown arrangement of nodes is basically a circular linked list, in which any node points to the next node in the sequence and the last node points to the first node to complete the circle.

Accessing members of the node

Now the question is how to access the members of the nodes? well, they can be accessed in any of the following ways:

```
node2.info     /* Accessing using node2 */
node1.next->info  /* Accessing using node1 */
```

To understand the usage of referential structures, let's write a program for following problem:

PROBLEM-9

Let's create a circular linked list of 5 elements and then display the contents of the list in normal way.

After displaying the list program should add a node in between two given positions and then again display the status showing which node is now pointing to which value.

PROGRAM-9

```
#include<stdio.h>
main()
{
    int i;
    int x,y;
    struct  bnode
    {
        int  info;
        struct bnode  *next;
    };
    struct bnode node[6] ;

    /* Creating a circular list of five elements*/
    printf("\n Create a Circular linked list of five elements ") ;
    for (i=0 ; i<5 ; i++)
    {
        printf("\n Give a number ") ;
        scanf("%d",&node[i].info) ;
        if(i==4)
```

```
            node[i].next=&node[0];
          else
            node[i].next=&node[i+1];
        }

        /* Displaying the list */
        for (i=0; i<5 ; i++)
        printf("\n Node values are %d", node[i].info) ;

        /* Inserting a new node */
        printf("\n Between which two nodes the new node is to be inserted ? ") ;
        scanf(" %d %d",&x,&y) ;
        printf("\n Give a number  to be stored in the new node") ;
        scanf("%d",&node[5].info) ;
        node[x-1].next=&node[5];
        node[5].next=&node[y-1];

        /*accessing list through array elements */
        printf("\n Accessing nodes in Normal way \n") ;
        for (i=0; i<6 ; i++)
        printf("\n Now node values are %d", node[i].info) ;

        /*Accessing List through pointers of the structure */
        printf("\n Accessing nodes through pointers " );
        for (i=0; i<6 ; i++)
        printf("\n Node%d points to  %d", (i+1), node[i].next->info) ;
    }
```

UNION

Union can be visualized as special type of structure, whose members share common memory space. Thus at any given point of time, only one member will remain present in the memory. So while working with them, you will have to keep track of the member, which is currently available in the memory. An attempt to access a member, which is not presently available in the memory, will produce absurd results. General format for defining the union is described below.

```
    union tunion-name {
    member1;
```

```
    member2;
    ------------
    ------------
    membern;
    };
```

Here "union" is the keyword, which is to be written as such, other items have the same meaning as the items of any structure. Following is a union definition:

```
union detail
{
    int size ;
    char color [10] ;
    float amount ;
};
```

Variables of union data type can be declared as follows:

```
storage-class union-name  variable-1, variable-2 -----, variable n ;
```

Here storage class is optional. The union is the keyword, which is to be written as such. The union-name is the name of that union, which has already been defined in the program and the following variables in the statement have be created, of this union type. Variable-1, variable-2 etc. are the names of variables, which have to be created of mentioned union type. For example, if shirt and trouser and the two variables, which have to be defined as detail (earlier defined as union) type then following statement will have to be written:

```
union detail
{
    int size;
    char color [10] ;
    float amount ;
} shirt, trouser ;
```

Individual members of any union can be accessed either through dot operator or arrow operator.

To get familiar with the concept of unions, their usage and behavior go through the following program. The program simply assigns the value to different members of the union and then accesses them. This program clearly illustrates that only one member of the union remains in memory at a time and other members stay out. It also illustrates that, if you try to access the value of those members, which are not currently present in memory, you get meaningless results.

PROGRAM-10

```
#include<stdio.h>
#include<stdlib.h>
union detail
{   int size ;
    int color[10] ;
    float amount ;
} ;
main()
{   union detail shirt ;
    /* Section -1 : Last accessed member in following section is amount
    so you will get the right value of amount. Other two valuse
    will be wrong, when displayed */
    shirt.size = 42 ;
    strcpy(shirt.color,"Blue") ;
    shirt.amount = 500.55 ;
    printf("\n\nShirt size is %d" , shirt.size) ;
    printf("\nShirt color is %s" , shirt.color) ;
    printf("\nShirt Amount is %f " , shirt.amount) ;
    /* Section -2 : Last accessed member in following section is color
    so you will get the right value of color. Other two valuse
    will be wrong, when displayed */
    shirt.size = 42 ;
    shirt.amount = 500.55 ;
    strcpy(shirt.color,"Blue") ;
    printf("\n\nShirt size is %d" , shirt.size) ;
    printf("\nShirt color is %s" , shirt.color) ;
    printf("\nShirt Amount is %f" , shirt.amount) ;
    /* Section -c : Last accessed member in following section is size
    so you will get the right value of size. Other two valuse
    will be wrong, when displayed */
    shirt.amount = 500.55 ;
    strcpy(shirt.color,"Blue") ;
    shirt.size = 42 ;
```

```
        printf("\n\nShirt size is %d" , shirt.size) ;
        printf("\nShirt color is %s" , shirt.color) ;
        printf("\nShirt Amount is %f" , shirt.amount) ;
    }
```

Result

When this program gets executed, it may display the following result:

```
Shirt size is 1800256
Shirt color is fF2
Shirt Amount is 500.55
Shirt size is 2771468
Shirt color is  Blue
Shirt Amount is 42368989.07234
Shirt size is 42
Shirt color is  fX4b
Shirt Amount is 42368080989.07234
```

Analysis

If you observe, above program and its result closely, you will analyze the following points:

1. Out of three given values, program displays only one correct value at a time. For example, in the first three lines of the result, only the amount value is correct. Rest of the values (i.e. size and color) are absurd.
2. You may note that the amount value is displayed correctly because the last member of the union that you accessed before displaying the result was amount.
3. When the last member accessed was color then correct color was displayed, other two values (i.e. size and amount) were absurd.
4. The same logic was true for size also.

From this observation we can conclude that member of the union, which you access last, its value remains in memory, rest of the values remain out.

Apart from the characteristic of union; that its members shares common memory space, rest of the things are similar to that of structure and it can be treated in the same manner. You can use union arrays, pointers to unions or pass a union to a function in the same way as you do for structures.

EXERCISES CHAPTER 15

Short Type Questions

A. Select most appropriate answers for the following questions:

1. Which type of items cannot be a member of a structure?
   (a) Array (b) Structure (c) Pointers (d) None of the above
2. Which keyword is used for defining a structure?
   (a) structure (b) STRUCTURE (c) STRUCT (d) None of above
3. Which operator is used for accessing the members of a structure?
   (a) Dot (b) Arrow (c) Both of the above (d) None of the above
4. You have structure-2 defined within structure-1. How many operators will be required to access the members of structure-1?
   (a) One (b) Two (c) Three (d) None of the above
5. You have structure x defined within y. How many arrow operators will you require to access the members of x?
   (a) One (b) Two (c) Three (d) None of the above

B. Fill in the blanks.

6. AB is a structure. A and B are its members. C is a variable of AB type. To refer B, you will have to write ....
7. A structure defined within an existing structure is called .... structure.
8. ABC is a structure. A pointer variable of this type can be declared by writing ....
9. When you pass a structure to a function, it is passed by ....
10. Unions are defined using .... keyword.

C. State true or false.

11. In structure, all the members should be of same data type.
12. Structure members can either be accessed using address operator or arrow operator.
13. While accessing members of a structure through pointers, you need to make use of arrow operator.
14. Structures are always passed to the function by value.
15. Members of union can be accessed using Dot operator.

D. Answer the following questions in short:

16. Is structure a derived data type?
17. If S1 is a structure then write a statement to create a variable v1 of this type.
18. In which situation, members of structure are accessed using arrow operator?
19. Write a statement to declare a variable var1, which is of structure st1 type and initialize its three members, m1, m2 and m3, which are of int, float and car type, with suitable values.
20. While printing the members of union, which member of union will get printed correctly, while others will not?

Detailed Answer Type Questions

E. Answer the following questions in details:

21. Define a structure S1, which has three members m1, m2 and m3 that are of int, float and double type. Create three variable v1, v2 and v3 of this type in the same statement.
22. Write a program to accept roll number, marks and name of 10 students.

    This program should calculate the grade for the students, using following rules:

    (i) Fail if marks<50.

    (ii) Good if marks>= 50 and <75.

    (iii) Excellent if marks>=75 <90.

    (iv) Outstanding if marks>=90.

    The program should make use of structure and grade should also be part of the structure.
23. Make few additions in above mentioned program, so that details of all those students get displayed, who have secured outstanding grade.
24. Differentiate between structure and union. Define a union, named "un" with three members a, b and c, which are of integer, float and char type respectively.
25. Write a program that has a structure named date, defined in it and another structure named, biodata. The biodata structure comprises of four members, i.e. employee number, name, date of joining and date of leaving (both dates defined as above mentioned date structure i.e. they are nested).
26. The program should accept data of 10 employees and calculate the total number of days for which the person served the organization.
27. Explain the concept of self referential structure, using a suitable example.
28. How will you identify self referential structure? Declare a self referential structure?
29. Write a program that passes pointer to the structure.
30. Write a program that returns a complete structure.

****

CHAPTER 16

Bitwise Operators

INTRODUCTION

As mentioned earlier, C language is a powerful and versatile language, it provides facilities for low-level programming and high-level programming too. These facilities are extended to the user through various operators, using which expressions are formed and manipulations are done.

Bitwise operators of C language are the operators, using which those types of operations are performed, which are generally, performed though low level languages. As the name indicates, using bitwise operators, bit of any number can be manipulated. For example, in C language, each integer is represented using 2 bytes i.e. 16 bits. Thus 12 will be represented as 0000 0000 0000 1100. In this combination of bits any bit can be manipulated to make it 1 or 0. Such types of requirements are very common while writing system pogroms for low-level activities. For bit manipulation C language provides following operators:

1. One's complements operator
2. Bitwise logical operators
3. Bitwise shift operators

Basic characteristic of these operators is that they operate only on integer operand. All above-mentioned types of operators are explained below.

Ones Complement Operator

One's complement of any binary number is achieved by replacing all its 0s by 1s and all 1s by 0s. For example 10110's one's complements will be 01001. Similarly ones complement of 110011 will be 001100.

In C language, tilde sign (i.e. ~) denotes bitwise complement operator. It is a unary operator. It operates upon an integer operand and gives its one's complement. Following example illustrates its usage.

```
 a = 1011  0001 1010 1100
~a =  0100 1110 0101 0011
```

Bitwise Logical Operators

C language provides following three logical bitwise operators:

1. Bitwise AND operator
2. Bitwise OR operator
3. Bitwise exclusive OR operator.

All the three operator require two integer type operands and they work on them bit by bit, starting from right most bits of the operands. Detailed functioning of these operators is explained below.

Bitwise And Operator

Bitwise AND operator is denoted by single ampersand sign i.e. & and is used in the following format:

```
operand-1 & operand-2
e.g.    a & b
```

It compares operand-1 with operand-2 bit by bit and gives 1 only at that position, where both the bits are 1. In all other cases it gives 0 . Its result are summarized in bitwise AND operator table. To understand its usage let's take and example. Say:

```
a = 1011 0001 1100 0101
b = 1011 1111 1011 1110
```

Then

```
a & b = 1011 0001 1000 0100
```

Bitwise AND operator Table

Operand–1	Operand-2	Operand –1 & Operand –2
0	0	0
0	1	0
1	0	0
1	1	1

Bitwise OR Operator

Bitwise OR operator is denoted by single pipe sign i.e. | and is used in the following format:

```
operand-1 | operand-2
e.g.    a | b
```

It compares operand-1 with operand-2 bit by bit and gives 0 only at that position, where both the bits are 0. In all other cases it gives 1. Its result are summarized in bitwise OR operator table. To understand its usage let's take and example. Say:

```
a = 1011 0001 1100 0101
b = 1011 1111 1011 1110
```

Then

```
a | b = 1011 1111 1111 1111
```

Bitwise OR operator Table

Operand–1	Operand-2	Operand –1 | Operand –2
0	0	0
0	1	1
1	0	1
1	1	1

Bitwise Exclusive OR Operator

Bitwise exclusive OR operator is denoted by ^ sign and is used in the following format:

operand-1 ^ operand-2

e.g. a ^ b

It compares operand-1 with operand-2 bit by bit and gives 1 only at that position, where one bit is 1 and other is 0. In all other cases it gives 0. Its result are summarized in bitwise exclusive OR operator table. To understand its usage let's take and example. Say:

a = 1011 0001 1100 0101

b = 1011 1111 1011 1110

Then

a ^ b = 0000 1110 0111 1011

Bitwise Exclusive OR operator Table

Operand–1	Operand-2	Operand –1 ^ Operand –2
0	0	0
0	1	1
1	0	1
1	1	0

Bitwise Shift Operator

Bitwise shift operator shifts the positions of bits in the given operand thus dropping out some bits either from right hand side or left hand side, depending upon the direction in which the shifting is done.

C language provides two types of shift operators i.e. left shift operator and right shift operator.

Left Shift operator

Left shift operator is denoted by << and is used in the following format:

operand << n

Hence operand is that integer number, in which bits have to shifted and n denoted number of positions that are to be shifted. For example, if n is 3 then bits will be shifted by 3 positions towards left. Thus 3 bits from left hand side will get dropped out and 3 positions on right hand side will get vacated and filled with 0s. To understand the usage of bitwise left shift operator. Consider the following example:

a = 1010 1100 1011 1001

a<< 2 = 1011 0010 1110 0100

NOTE :

10 ⟵ all other bits ⟶ 00

10 got dropped out; all other bits got shifted by 2 positions; 00 position got vacated and filled by 0s

Right Shift operator

Right shift operator is denoted by >> and is used in the following format:

operand >> n

Hence operand is that integer number, in which bits have to shifted and n denoted number of positions that are to be shifted. For example, if n is 2 then bits will be shifted by 2 positions towards left. Thus 2 bits from right hand side will get dropped out and 2 positions on left hand side will get vacated and filled with 0s. To understand the usage of bitwise right shift operator. Consider the following example:

a = 1010 1100 1011 1001

a>> 2 = 0010 1011 0010 1110

NOTE :

00	← all other bits →	10
position got vacated and filled by 0s	got shifted by 2 positions	got dropped out

Masking

Masking is basically a process, in which a given bit pattern is transformed into another bit pattern with the help of logical bitwise operator. The original bit pattern is one of the operands in this operation and other operand called masks is a carefully selected another bit pattern, which brings out the desired transformation. Operational aspect of masking is given below.

x = a & mask

or

y = a | mask

x = a & mask

a	=	0111 1010 0001 0101
Mask	=	0000 1111 0000 1111
x	=	0000 1010 0000 0101

x = a | mask

a	=	0111 1010 0001 0101
Mask	=	0000 1111 0000 1111
x	=	0111 1111 0001 1111

Masking is used for following purposes:

To copy a given portion of a bit pattern into a new variable while the remainder portion of the new number is:

(a) filled with 0s (using bitwise AND operator)

(b) Filled with 1s (using bitwise OR operator)

(c) Filled with inverted bits (using exclusive OR operator)

x = a & mask

a	=	1010 1100 1000 1100
Mask	=	1010 0000 0000 0000
b	=	1010 0000 0000 0000

x = a | mask

a	=	1010 1100 1000 1100
Mask	=	0000 1111 1111 1111
b	=	1010 1111 1111 1111

SPECIAL OPERATORS

C language provides few special operators called bitwise assignment operators. They are as follows:

&= ^= |= <<= >>=

These operators combine the preceding bitwise operations with ordinary assignments. Their usage is illustrated below:

	Expression	Equivalent
(i)	a & = 1010	a = a 1010
(ii)	a | = 1010	a = a | 1010
(iii)	a ^ = 1010	a = a ^ 1010
(iv)	a << = 3	a = a<< 3
(v)	a>> = 2	a = a>>2

To understand the functioning of bitwise operators, let's write a program for the following problem:

PROBLEM-1

Write a program that accepts two integer values from the user and performs following bitwise operations on them:

(i) Performs bitwise right shift operation of two places on first integer.

(ii) Performs bitwise left shift operation of one place on second integer.

(iii) Performs bitwise AND operation on first integer with another integer, 4.

(iv) Performs bitwise OR operation on first integer with second integer.

PROGRAM-1

```
#include<stdio.h>
main()
{
int i,j,k,m;
clrscr();
printf("Give first Integer value" );
scanf("%d",&i) ;
printf("Give second Integer value" );
scanf("%d",&j) ;
k = i>>2;
m = j<<1;
printf("\nValue  after performing bitwise shift operation  on i %d",k) ;
printf("\nValue after performing bitwise shift operation on j %d",m) ;
```

```
k = i & 4;
m = i | j;
printf("\nValue after performing bitwise AND operation on i with 4 %d",k) ;
printf("\nValue after performing bitwise OR  operation on i with j %d",m) ;
}
```

Sample Run Of The Program:

Give first Integer value **15**

Give second Integer value **17**

Value after performing bitwise shift operation on i **3**

Value after performing bitwise shift operation on j **34**

Value after performing bitwise AND operation on i with 4 **4**

Value after performing bitwise OR operation on i with j **31**

Result Confirmation

First Operation

(a) Integer 15 will be represented as 1111.

(b) Bitwise 2 right shift operations will take away 2 bits from right thus make it 11. Decimal equivalent of this number is 3.

Second Operation

(a) Integer 17 will be represented as 10001.

(b) Bitwise 1 left shift operation will add 0 at extreme right position thus make 100010. Decimal equivalent of this number is 34.

Third Operation

(a) Integer 15 will be represented as 1111.

(b) Integer 4 will be represented as 0100.

(c) Bitwise AND operation of these 2 numbers will yield 100. Decimal equivalent of this number is 4.

Fourth Operation

(a) Integer 15 will be represented as 01111.

(b) Integer 17 will be represented as 10001.

(c) Bitwise OR operation of these 2 numbers will yield 11111. Decimal equivalent of this number is 31.

Uses of Bitwise Operations

Occasionally, you may want to implement a large number of Boolean variables, without using a lot of space.

A 32-bit int can be used to stored 32 Boolean variables. Normally, the minimum size for one Boolean variable is one byte. All types in C must have sizes that are multiples of bytes. However, only one bit is necessary to represent a Boolean value.

You can also use bits to represent elements of a (small) set. If a bit is 1, then element i is in the set, otherwise it's not.

You can use bitwise AND to implement set intersection, bitwise OR to implement set union.

Facts About Bitwise Operators

Consider the expression x + y. Do either x or y get modified? The answer is no.

Most built-in binary operators do not modify the values of the arguments. This applies to logical operators too. They don't modify their arguments.

There are operators that do assignment such as +=, -=, *=, and so on. They apply to logical operators too. For example, |=, &=, ^=. Nearly all binary operators have a version with = after it.

EXERCISES **CHAPTER 16**

Short Type Questions

A. Select most appropriate answers for the following questions:

1. Which of the following operators are exclusively used in low level programming?
   (a) Arithmetic (b) Bitwise
   (c) Logical (d) Sting
2. Which of the following operator will perform bitwise right shift operation?
   (a) > (b) < (c) >> (d) <<
3. Which of the following operator is used for bitwise AND operation?
   (a) & (b) && (c) | (d) ||
4. Which of the following operator is used for bitwise OR operation?
   (a) & (b) && (c) | (d) ||
5. Which of the following operation will give 1 when 0 and 1 bit are operated together?
   (a) AND (b) OR (c) Shift (d) Mask

B. Fill in the blanks.

6. Bitwise .... operation will give 1 when both the bits are 1.
7. When bitwise AND operation will be performed on two integers 11110 and 100, it will result into ....
8. When bitwise OR operation will be performed on two integers 110101 and 111, it will result into ....
9. When 3 left shift bitwise operations will be performed on 1000111 it will result into....................................
10. When 2 right shift bitwise operations will be performed on 10001, it will result into....................................

C. State true or false.

11. >> is a valid bitwise shift operator.
12. ^ is valid bitwise operator.
13. Masking is a valid bitwise operation in C language
14. 1100 & 1100 will give 1100.
15. 1111>>4 will give 0000.

D. Answer the following questions in short:

16. Which bitwise operator gives 1 when both the bits are 1 and in any other condition gives 0?
17. Which bitwise operator gives 0 when both the bits are 0 and in any other condition gives 1?
18. Which bitwise operator gives 0 when both the bits are either 0 or 1 and in any other condition gives 1?
19. %% is left shift operator.

Detailed Answer Type Questions

E. Answer the following questions in detail:

20. What is the use of bitwise operators in C language?
21. Explain the functioning of bitwise AND operator? Which symbol is used to denote it in C language?
22. Explain the functioning of bitwise OR operator? Which symbol is used to denote it in C language?
23. Explain the functioning of bitwise Exclusive OR operator? Which symbol is used to denote it in C language?
24. Explain the functioning of bitwise left shift operator? Which symbol is used to denote it in C language?

25. Explain the functioning of bitwise right shift operator? Which symbol is used to denote it in C language?
26. What is bitwise masking operation? Explain using a suitable example.
27. Write a program in C Language, which takes an integer and performs Exclusive bitwise OR operation on it with another integer 123.
28. Write a program in C Language, which demonstrate the functioning of bitwise AND and OR operations.
29. Write a program in C language that takes an integer from the user and displays number of 1s, present in its binary equivalent number.
30. Write a program that accepts an integer from the user and asks how many left or right bitwise shift operations are to be carried out on the number. After carrying out the operation it displays the result.

****

CHAPTER 17

File Processing Techniques

INTRODUCTION

Up till now we had been dealing with the programs, which held the input-data temporarily. As soon as the program came to end, the data got lost. For example, if you enter student's roll number, name and marks, using scanf statement, the data will remain available till the time program is running. As soon as the program will end, these values will not be available. While writing programs for real life situations, you will often come across situations, when you will have to hold the data permanently. For holding the data permanently, you have to read the data from the keyboard (as we used to do), write it in a file and later, whenever required, read the data from file. C language supports different types of file handling operations for using files. Their details are described in this chapter.

TYPE OF FILES

C supports three different types of data files, using which you can hold the data permanently on media and make use of it as and when required. These files are:

1. Text files
2. Variable Record length files.
3. Constant record length files

Text Files

Text files are also called stream oriented data files. In these files the data is written as stream of characters and it is read as stream of characters. A typical Text file many look like as follows:

> Bell Infotech System is a software development organization. It has high turnover with high growth rate. It is committed to deliver quality products and promote software culture in India and abroad.

Figure 17.1

Recall the nature of the files that you create through text editors and note that the text file mentioned above is just equivalent to any text editor file.

REMARK

1. Since text files are ASCII files hence you can view them on your computer screen.
2. You can create a text file through your system text editor and read them through a C program also.

   or

   You can create a text file through a C program and read it through your system text editor.

PERFORMING FILE OPERATIONS

Be it any type of file, read and write operations have to be performed in the sequence mentioned below:

Writing in a File	Reading the File
(a) Establishing a Buffer area	(a) Establish a buffer Area
(b) Open the file	(b) Open the file
(c) Write the data into file	(c) Read the file
(d) Close the file	(d) Close the file.

Establishing a Buffer Area

While working with files in C language, you have to establish a Buffer area first. Buffer area is a memory area, where the information is temporary held then it is transferred to/from file. General format for establishing a buffer area is as follows:

```
FILE *pointer-variable;
```

Here FILE (all upper case letters) is a special structure type that establishes the buffer area and the pointer-variable is the name of pointer variable that points to the beginning of the buffer area. Note that the structure type, FILE is already defined in stdio.h file. This pointer is often referred to as stream pointer or simple stream.

Opening a Data File

After defining the buffer area, you have to open the data file, so that read/write operations could be performed. The library function fopen opens the file. General format for fopen function is as follows:

```
pointer-variable=fopen(file-name,mode);
```

Here pointer-variable is the name of pointer variable that was defined at the time of establishing the buffer area. fopen is the name of the function, which is to be written as such and file-name is the name of the file that you want to open. Mode is a string, which indicates the mode, in which the file is to be opened. It can be opened in any one of the following modes:

Mode	Meaning
"r"	Opens the file for read operations only.
"r+"	Opens an existing file for both reading and writing.
"w"	Opens the file for writing only. If the mentioned file already exists then it will destroy that file and create a fresh file for writing.
"w+"	Opens the file for both reading and writing. If the mentioned file already exists then it will destroy that file and create a fresh file for writing.
"a"	Opens the file for appending. If the file with mentioned file name does not exist then a fresh file will be created.
"a+"	Opens the file for reading and appending. If the file with mentioned file name does not exist then it creates a fresh file for operations.

NOTE

1. fopen function returns a pointer to the beginning of the buffer area associated with the file. A Null value is returned, if somehow the file could not be opened.
2. After opening the file, it is identified with pointer variable rather than by its name. In the subsequent file operations, such as writing the file, reading the file or closing the file, we mention the corresponding pointer variable name, instead of the file name.

Examples

1. If you wish to open a file named bell.dat, in read mode only then you will have to include the following lines in the program, before you perform any file operation:

```
FILE *Pt1;
Pt=fopen("bell.dat", "r");
```

2. Following statements will open the file in write mode:

```
FILE *PT2 ;
Pt2= fopen("marks.dat","w");
```

3. If an already existing file named, student.dat has to be opened in append mode then following statements could be used for opening the file:

```
FILE * PT3;
Pt3= fopen ("student.dat", "a");
```

Closing the Files

After performing all the operations on files, all the opened files should be closed. Although, when the program ends, C closes all the opened files itself. But on the other hand, if you do not close the file then you may run the risk of loosing the data. So it is a good programming practice to close all the opened files before you end the program. General format for closing the file is as follows:

```
fclose (pointer-variable);
```

Here pointer-variable is that variable name, which was mentioned at the time of opening the file. For example, if you wish to close all the three files mentioned above then you will can include the following statements in the program:

```
fclose (pt1) ;  /* close bell.dat file*/
fclose (pt3) ;  /* close student.dat file*/
```

Writing in a Text File

C provides, putc function, using which you can write a single character in the file. General format for putc function is as follows:

```
putc (character, pointer-variable);
```

Here character is a character or character variable whose value is to be written in the file. The pointer-variable is that pointer variable, which refers to the file, in which the value is to be written. For example, if you wish to write "B" in marks.dat file (mentioned above) then you can use putc function as follows:

```
putc ("B", pt2);
```

READING THE TEXT FILE

C provides getc function for reading a character from the text file. General format for getc function is as follows:

```
getc (pointer-variable) ;
```

Here pointer-variable refers to that file, from which you wish to read the character. For example, if you wish to read a single character form bell.dat file (mentioned above) then you can include the following statements in the program:

```
Char x;
----------------
----------------
x=getc (pt1);
```

Note that in this example getc function reads a character from the file and assigns it to character variable x.

Now you are familiar with the characteristics of text files and the functions, using which you can operate upon them. So let's write few programs to perform different types of functions.

PROGRAM-1

Let's write a program, which accepts stream of characters from keyboard and stores them in test.dat file. The program continues to accept the input, till you press Tab and Enter keys.

```
#include <stdio.h>
main()
{
    char c ;
    FILE *point ;
    point = fopen("test.dat" , "w") ;
    printf("\nEnter text & to stop press Tab & Enter keys\n");
do
  { c = getchar() ;
    putc(c,point) ;
  }
while (c != '\t') ;
fclose(point) ;
}
```

Sample Execution of the Program

When you execute the program, the program will display the following message

```
Enter text & to stop press Tab & Enter keys
```

After this you can enter the following text:

```
Bell is a renowned software organization.
It is committed to deliver quality produces.
Its website can be visited at bispl.com.
<Tab> <Enter>
```

REMARK

1. You can view the contents of this file in Notepad program.
2. Note that the program will put a tab (\t) character in the last line, which in this case will mark the end of the file.
3. If you run this program again then the file will be recreated. These lines will get lost and whatever you enter now, will get stored in the file. You may note that this happens because of "w" mode (in open statement), which opens the file, but if the file already exists, then it destroys it and creates a new file with same name.

PROGRAM-2

Now let's write a program that reads the file created above and displays the contents on the screen. The program should also have the provision to display the total number of characters in the file (including blanks)

```
#include <stdio.h>
main()
{
    int i = 0 ;
    FILE *point ;
    char c ;
    point = fopen("test.dat","r");
do
  {  i++ ;
    c = getc(point) ;
    putchar(c) ;
  }
while ( c != '\t') ;
fclose(point) ;
printf ("\nTotal No. of characters in the file are = %i " , i);
}
```

Sample Execution of the Program

When you execute above mentioned program, it will open the text.dat file for reading and display the following result (if you have entered the data mentioned above)

```
Bell is a renowned software organization.
It is committed to deliver quality produces.
Its website can be visited at bispl.com.
Total No of characters in the file are 142
```

NOTE

1. **Refer above mentioned output and note the following points:**
   - **Program counts \n (which is not visible but present at the end of each line) as one character.**
   - **Program also counts \t character, (which is also invisible), which marks the end of file, as one character.**

PROGRAM-3

Say we have to write a program that appends the text to the already existing file, text.dat For such requirements, you can write the following program:

```
#include <stdio.h> ;
main() {
    FILE *point ;
    char c ;
    point  = fopen("test.dat" , "a") ;
    printf("\nNow Enter New lines\n ");
do
  {
    c =getchar() ;
    putc(c,point) ;
  }
while (c!='\t') ;
fclose(point) ;
}
```

Sample Run of the Program

When you execute the above mentioned program then it will display the following message and wait for an input.

```
Now Enter New lines
```

Say we enter the following lines:

```
Bell is high growth rate organization.
Bell is company of high tech professionals.
Tab <Enter>
```

An Interesting Result

If you view the file in Notepad then following lines will get displayed:

```
Bell is a renowned software organization.
It is committed to deliver quality produces.
Its website can be visited at bispl.com.
Bell is high growth rate organization.
Bell is company of high tech professionals.
```

On the other hand if you execute program-2 to view the appended file, it will show you the old contents only, giving you an impression that in spite of running the program-3, no lines have been added in the test.dat file.

Reason

This happens because this file has two tabs in it. The first one is at the beginning of fourth line and the other one is in the sixth line (invisible). Recall that program-2 has been designed to read the file till it encounters a tab character in the file. So as soon as it finds the first tab character (i.e. fourth line) it comes to halt. In spite of, more lines present in the file, you cannot display all the lines, using program-2. For that you have to write a program with different logic.

END OF FILE FUNCTION

Above mentioned results clearly indicate that finding the end of file through characters may lead to problems so there is a need for a function, which when executed, should be able to trace the end of file. For such requirements, C provides a function called feof. Its general format is as follows:

```
        feof (pointer-variable);
e.g.    fefo (pointer 1);
```

Note that this function returns a value 0 (zero i.e. false) if it is not the end of file. It returns a non zero value (true), if the end of file has been reached.

Now you are familiar with functioning of feof function, so we will make use of it in writing a program, which displays the contents of an already existing file and then asks for more input to append it at the end of file.

PROGRAM-4

```
#include <stdio.h> ;
main()
{
FILE *point ;
char c ;
point  = fopen("test.dat" , "a+") ;
printf ("\nContents that already exist in the File are as follows : \n");
do
  {
     c = getc(point) ;
     putchar(c) ;
  }
while ( feof(point) == 0 ) ;
```

```
printf("\nNow Enter New line\n ");
do
{
    c =getchar() ;
    putc(c,point) ;
}
while (c!='\t') ;
fclose(point) ;
}
```

Sample Execution of the Program

When you execute this program, it will open the file, test.dat in "a+" mode i.e. for read and append. After opening the file it will display all the lines, as follows:

```
Bell is a renowned software organization.
It is committed to deliver quality produces.
Its website can be visited at bispl.com.
Bell is high growth rate organization.
Bell is company of high tech professionals.
Now enter new lines.
After this you can enter the following text:
This program is working fine.
It displays complete file and asks for input.
Tab <Enter>
```

If you execute the program again then above added lines will also get displayed and the process will repeat.

READING AND WRITING FILES USING GETW AND PUTW FUNCTIONS

The **getw** and **putw** are exclusively integer oriented functions. Using putw function an integer value is written the file while getw reads an iteger from a file.

The putw function is used in the following format:

putw(integer,fp) ;

Here integer is the integer value that is to be written in the file. fp is the pointer to the data file, which has been opened for writing.

The getw function is used in the following format:

variable = getw(fp) ;

Here variable is an integer variable that will hold the integer value that will be read from the file. fp is the pointer to the data file, which has been opened for reading..

To understand the usage of putw function let's write a program for the following problem:

PROGRAM-5

Say we have to write a program that accepts, roll number, age and marks of the student from the keyboard and writes in a data file.

This program should works in a loop so that user can enter as many records as he wants.

```
#include <stdio.h>
#include <stdlib.h>
main ()
{
    int roll, age, marks;
    int q = 1
    FILE *f1 ;
    f1=fopen("details.dat","w") ;
    while (q!=0)
    {
        printf("\nGive roll number of the student ");
        scandf("%d"&roll);
        putw(roll,f1) ;
        printf("\nGive age of the student ");
        scandf("%d"&age);
        putw(age,f1) ;
        printf("\nGive marks of the student ");
        scandf("%d"&marks);
        putw(marks,f1) ;
        printf("\nGive 1 to continue and 0 to stop ");
        scandf("%d"&roll);
    }
    fclose (f1);
}
```

To understand the usage of getw function let's write a program for the following problem:

PROGRAM-6

Say we have to write a program that reads the file created in the last program and prints the roll number, age and marks of all the students.

```
#include <stdio.h>
#include <stdlib.h>
main ()
{
int roll, age, marks;
int  number ;
FILE *f1 ;
f1=fopen("details.dat","r") ;
while ( (roll=getw(f1))  !=EOF)
{
    printf("\nRoll number of the student is %d ", roll);
    age=getw(f1);
    printf("\nAge of the student is %d ", age);
    marks=getw(f1);
    printf("\nMarks  of the student are %d ", marks);
}
fclose (f1);
}
```

VARIABLE RECORD LENGTH FILES

Unlike text files, which contain only characters, variable record length files contain numbers, characters and strings also. For example, you may wish to store following data in the data file so that the total salary of the employee could be calculated:

Name	Basic Pay	DA	House Rent
Manoj Kumar Gupta	5000	3000.50	600
Ajay	7000	5500.70	800
Rita Das	4000	5500.00	500

It is quite obvious that if you store above mentioned data in text file, you will not be able to treat Basic Pay, DA, House rent etc. as numeric fields and will not be able to perform calculations on them. For such type of requirements C language provides variable length files.

In such type of files, individual field is written as an individual data item and thus an ASCII file gets generated. To get an idea of its shape, consider above mentioned data. If you store the data in variable length file then the file will get arranged as follows:

Manoj Kumar Gupta

5000

3000.50

600

Ajay

700

5500.700

800

Rita Das

4000

5500.00

500

Characteristics of Variable Record Length Files

1. Since each data item is written in a separate line hence each data item is terminated by new line character. You may note that we will make use of this feature while writing the data in variable length files.
2. A typical characteristic of this file is that the data items, within the individual field can be of different length. For example, consider the names, Manoj Kumar Gupta (17 characters), Ajay (4 characters), Ritu Das (8 characters), all have different lengths.
3. While writing the record in the file, you have to individually write the field. For example, if you have to write the record of Rita Das in the file, you will have to write four different fields i.e. Name, Basic Pay , DA and House Rent.
4. If you wish to read the record from the file then you will have to read the fields individually, in the same sequence, in which they were written. For example, to read the record of Rita Das, you will have to read four fields in the same sequence i.e. Name, Basic Pay, DA and House Rent.
5. Since these files are ASCII files hence they can be very well displayed on the screen, using Notepad program.

Writing in Variable Length Files

For writing data into variable Record length files, C language provides fprintf function. General format of fprintf function is same as that of printf function, except an additional information of file pointer, which refers to the file, in which the data is to be written. So the general format of fprintf function is as follows:

```
fprintf (file-pointer, "format", variable)
```

For example, for writing the basic pay (basic_salary) in the file (pointer as pt1), you will have to write the following statement:

```
fprintf (pt1,"% i\n", basic_salary);
```

Note that the format, used in fprintf function is same as that in printf function. It has been terminated by new line character i.e. \n so that one data item is written in one line.

Reading Variable Length File

For reading the data from variable record length file, C language provides fscanf function. General format of fscanf function is same as that of scanf function, except that it also contains, file pointer, which refers to the file, from which the data is to be read. So the general format of fscanf function is as follows:

```
fscanf (file-pointer, "format", variable);
```

For example, for reading the basic_salary from the file (pointer pt1), you will have to write the following statement:

```
fscanf (pt1, "%i", & basic_salary);
```

REMARK

1. File open and file close statements for variable length files work in the same way as they do for text files.
2. feof function, which checks the end of the file can also be used for variable length files.

Now you are familiar with basic characteristics of variable record length files and different types of functions, which are generally used to operate upon them. So now, let's make use of those functions to create variable record length file, write data into it and then write another program to read the data from the file.

PROGRAM-7

Let's write a program, which accepts, Name, Basic Pay, DA and House Rent for different persons from the keyboard and writes it in the file. After writing one set of data, it asks the user if he wishes to continue. If he opts to continue, program accepts data for other person, else it closes the file and stops.

```
#include <stdio.h>
main()
{
 FILE *pt1 ;
 char name[30] ;
 int basic, hrent, n = 0 ;
 float da ;
 int q = 1 ;
 pt1 = fopen("pay.dat", "w") ;
 while ( q != 0 )
```

```
    {
        printf("\nGive Name" ) ;
        scanf(" %[^\n]",name);
        printf("\nGive Basic Pay") ;
        scanf("%i",&basic);
        printf("\nGive Da") ;
        scanf ("%f",&da) ;
        printf("\nGive House Rent") ;
        scanf("%i",&hrent) ;
        /* Writing Data in the File */
        fprintf(pt1 , "%s\n",name) ;
        fprintf(pt1 , "%i\n",basic) ;
        fprintf(pt1 , "%f\n",da) ;
        fprintf(pt1 , "%i\n",hrent) ;
        printf("\nRecord Written %i",++n) ;
        printf("\nGive 0 to STOP any other No. to Continue " ) ;
        scanf("%i",&q) ;
    }
    close(pt1) ;
}
```

This program, when executed, will create a fresh file, named pay.dat and keep on accepting the records of different employees (i.e. Name, Basic Pay, DA and House Rent) till the time you enter 0 against the following prompt:

Give 0 to STOP, any other No. to continue

REMARK

1. **If you wish you can view this file using Notepad program.**

PROGRAM-8

Now let's write a program to read all the records from the data file, created by above.

```
#include <stdio.h>
main()
{
    FILE *pt1 ;
    char name[30] ;
    int basic, hrent ;
    float da ;
```

```
    pt1 = fopen("pay.dat", "r") ;
    while ( feof(pt1) == 0 )
    {
        fscanf(pt1 , "%s",name ) ;
        if (feof(pt1) != 0 )
            break ;
        fscanf(pt1 , "%i",&basic) ;
        fscanf(pt1 , "%f",&da) ;
        fscanf(pt1 ,"%i",&hrent) ;
        printf("\nName is %s ",name);
        printf("\nBasic Pay is %i",basic);
        printf("\nDa is %f",da) ;
        printf("\nHouse Rent is %i",hrent) ;
    }
    close(pt1) ;
}
```

FIXED RECORD LENGTH FILES

In fixed record length files, the data is stored as blocks of fixed number of bytes. For example, if name occupies 30 bytes, Basic occupies 2 bytes, DA occupies 4 bytes and house rent occupies 2 bytes (i.e. total = 38 bytes) then all the records will occupy 38 bytes, irrespective of the length of name and figures.

A fixed record length file may have following shape:

1st Record	2nd Record	3rd Record	--------------	n[th] Record

CHARACTERISTICS OF FIXED RECORD LENGTH FILES

1. These files are not ASCII files so you cannot view their contents, using any text editor like Notepad program. Their contents can only be viewed with the help of corresponding program.
2. For performing read write operation, you have to read or write the entire record, instead of reading or writing the individual fields.
3. Fixed record length is generally defined with the help of structures, so structures play an important role in reading and writing operations of fixed record length files.

Writing in Fixed Record Length Files

For writing a record in fixed record length file, C provides fwrite function. Its general format is given below.

```
fwrite (& customer, size of (record), 1 ftp1);
```

Here customer is the structure variable, "size of (record)" signifies the record length, 1 signifies that you wish to write one record at a time and ftp1 is the pointer, which is associated, with the file, in which you want to write the records.

Reading the Record Form Fixed Record Length Files

For reading a record from fixed record length file, C provides fread function. Its general format is given below.

```
fread (&student, size of (record), 1 ftp1)
```

All the arguments mentioned here have same meaning as that mentioned in fwrite function.

Now you are familiar with the characteristics of fixed record length files and the functions, using which you can perform different types of operations on them. So let's write programs that write data in them and read data from them.

PROGRAM-9

Say we want to store, following details of all the students of the class, in a fixed record length file:

Roll Number	(Integer i.e. 2 bytes)
Name	(Character 30 bytes)
Marks	(Integer i.e. 2 bytes)

```
#include <stdio.h>
struct record
{
    int roll ;
    char name[30] ;
    int marks ;
} student ;
main()
{
    int flag = 1 ;
    FILE *pt1 ;
    pt1 = fopen("marks.dat","w") ;
    while (flag==1) {
    printf ("\nGive Roll Number of the student or 0 to stop");
    scanf("%i",&student.roll) ;
    if (student.roll == 0 )
        break ;
```

```
        printf("\nGive Name of the student");
        scanf(" %[^\n]",student.name);
        printf("\nGive Marks");
        scanf("%i",&student.marks);
        fwrite(&student,sizeof(student),1,pt1) ;
    }
    fclose(pt1) ;
    printf("\nEND OF THE PROGRAM " );
    }
```

This program will keep on accepting input from the user and writing the records in the file, till the user enters roll number as 0 (zero). You may note that here single fwrite statement, writes all the three fields in the file. For writing three fields you do not have to make use of three statements, as you have to do in variable record length files. You may also note that this is possible because, you are writing the complete record not the individual fields.

PROGRAM-10

Now let's write a program that reads the data file created above.

```
    #include <stdio.h>
    #include <string.h>
    struct record
    {
        int roll ;
        char name[30] ;
        int marks ;
    }   student ;
    main()
    {
        FILE *pt1 ;
        pt1 = fopen("marks.dat","r");
        while (feof(pt1) == 0 )
        {
            fread(&student,sizeof(student),1,pt1) ;
            if (feof(pt1) != 0 )
                break ;
            printf ("\nRoll Number of the student is %i",student.roll) ;
            printf("\nName of the student is %s", student.name);
```

```
        printf("\nMarks are %i",student.marks);
    }
    fclose(pt1) ;
    printf("\nEND OF THE PROGRAM " );
}
```

READING AND WRITING FILES RANDOM LY

All the time up till now we had been performing sequential read and write operations in the file. That means we created the file, wrote first record into it then second record then third and so on. At last, we closed the file and terminated the program.

Similarly while performing the read operation, we read the first record first, then second record and then the third one and the process continued till the time end of file condition was encountered.

But there are times when records have to be written or read from the file in random fashion. For example, first write the second record and then the first and then the third one. Similarly while reading the file no sequential pattern may be followed. Records may be read in any desired order, irrespective of the sequence, in which they were written.

When no certain sequence is followed while reading or writing in the file, file is said to be accessed randomly.

Now the question is how do we read or write in the file randomly? Well, C language provides few functions, using which data files can be accessed randomly. These functions are described below.

fseek Function

The fseek function sets the location of record pointer to the desired location in the file. It is used in the following format:

fseek (file_pointer, offset, location);

Here file_pointer is the pointer to the file (already opened), in which random read or write operations have to be performed.

Offset is the position, at which the record pointer is to be placed so that read or write operations will be performed at this position. For example if the offset value is set to 10 then the next read or write operation will be performed from 10th location of the file. Note that first position in the file is 0.

Location can acquire any of the following values:

- 0: Indicates that offset value is to be taken from the beginning of the file.
- 1: Indicates that offset vale is to be taken from the current location of the record pointer.
- 2: Indicates that offset value is to be taken from the end of the file.

When the file is opened the record pointer is automatically placed at the beginning of the file i.e. at 0th location.

After this, record pointer can be moved to any desired location of the file, using fseek function.

To understand the functioning of fseek function, few fseek statements and their effects are summarized in the following table:

Statement	Effect
fseek (fp1,0,0)	Takes record pointer to the beginning of the file.
fseek (fp1,24,0)	Takes record pointer to the 24th position from the beginning of the file.
fseek (fp1,12,1)	Takes record pointer to the 12th location from the current record pointer's position. For, example, if currently the record pointer is placed at 24th position from the beginning of the file, this command will place it at 36 position from the beginning.
fseek (fp1,-12,1)	Takes record pointer back by 12 positions from the current record pointer's position. For example, if record pointer is currently at 36th position then this command will place it at 24th position.
fseek (fp1,-12,2)	Takes record pointer back by 12 positions from the end of file position.

ftell function

The ftell function returns current position of the record pointer. For example, if currently record pointer is placed at 50th position, ftell function will return 50. It is used in the following format:

```
ftell (fp);
```

Here fp is the pointer to the file (already opened), whose record pointer's position is to be known.

rewind function

The rewind function resets record pointer's position back to the beginning of the file. It is used in the following format:

```
rewind(fp1);
```

Here fp is the pointer to the file (already opened), whose record pointer is to be taken back to the beginning of the file.

Random Writing Logic

1. Open the file.
2. Get the data.
3. Decide the location, at which the record is to be written.
4. Place the record pointer to the decided location, using fseek function.
5. Write the record.
6. If required, perform step 2 to step 5 in a loop.
7. Close the file after exiting the loop.

To understand the process of writing randomly in file, let's write a program for the folloing problem:

PROGRAM-11

Write a program to store roll number (2 bytes), name (30 bytes) and marks (2 bytes) of the students randomly in the data file. Roll number of the students are such that they are indicative of the location, where the record will be written in the file.
For example, record bearing roll number 5 will be fifth record of the file. Similarly roll number 3 record will be third record in the file and so on.

```
#include <stdio.h>
struct record
{
    int roll ;
    char name[30] ;
    int marks ;
}   student ;
main()
{
    int flag =  1 ;
    int pos ;
    FILE *pt1 ;
    clrscr();
    pt1 = fopen("marks.dat","w") ;
    while (flag==1) {
    printf ("\nGive Roll Number of the student or 0 to stop");
    scanf("%i",&student.roll) ;
    if (student.roll == 0 )
      break ;
```

```
            printf("\nGive Name of the student");
            scanf(" %[^\n]",student.name);
            printf("\nGive Marks");
            scanf("%i",&student.marks);
             pos = (student.roll - 1) * sizeof(student) ;
            fseek(pt1,pos,0);
            fwrite(&student,sizeof(student),1,pt1) ;
        }
        fclose(pt1) ;
        printf("\nEND OF THE PROGRAM " );
        }
```

Logic For Random Reading

1. Open the file for reading.
2. Decide which record is to be read.
3. Calculate the offset position.
4. Place the record pointer to the offset position (calculated in last step).
5. Read the record.
6. If required, set a loop to read other records of the file.
7. Close the file after exiting the loop.

To understand the process of reading the file randomly, let's write a program for the following problem:

PROGRAM-12

Let's write a program to randomly read the file created in the last program. The program should accept the roll number of the student from the keyboard, fetch the corresponding record from the file and display other the details of the student.

Program should work in a loop so as to display records as many number of times as user wants.

```
#include <stdio.h>
#include <string.h>
struct record
{
   int roll ;
   char name[30];
   int marks ;
} student ;
main()
```

```
{
int q = 1 ;
int rollin;
long pos ;
FILE *pt1 ;
clrscr();
pt1 = fopen("marks.dat","r") ;
while (q==1)
    {
        printf("Please Enter the Roll no = ");
        scanf("%d",&rollin);
        pos = (rollin - 1) * 34 ;
        fseek(pt1,pos,0);
        fread(&student,sizeof(student),1,pt1) ;
        printf ("\nRoll Number of the student is %i",student.roll) ;
        printf("\nName of the student is %s", student.name);
        printf("\nMarks are %i",student.marks);
        printf("\nGive 1 to continue or 0 to stop :");
        scanf("%d",&q);
    }
getch();
fclose(pt1) ;
}
```

MULTIPLE FILE OPERATIONS

While dealing with real life situations, you will often come across situations, in which you will have to read the data from one file and write in another file. In such type of situations, you can open multiple files, in the same way as you open single file and then operate upon them. Following program reads the transaction file and writes the details in master file.

PROGRAM-13

Say variable record length file, named trans.dat has already been created and contains following data in it:

(a) Employee Number

(b) Employee's name

(c) Basic Salary

(d) DA

(e) House Rent

(f) Conveyance Allowance

(g) Cpf

(h) Tax

Program has to read the data from this file and write the data into another fixed length file, named mast.dat, which has following record structure:

(a) Employee number

(b) Employee name

(c) Total earnings

(d) Total deductions

(e) Net salary

Here total earnings are calculated as follows:

Basic Salary + Da + House Rent + Conveyance Allowance

Total deductions are calculated as follows:

(Cpf +Tax)

and net salary is (Total Earning – Total Deductions)

Program for these specifications is written below.

```
#include <stdio.h>
struct rec1
{    int empno ;
     char name[30] ;
     int basic ;
     float da ;
     int hrent ;
     int conv ;
     float cpf ;
     float tax ;
}    trans ;
struct  rec2
{    int empno ;
     char name[30] ;
     float earn;
     float ded;
     float net ;
```

```
}    mast ;
struct rec1 rtrans( struct rec1 trans) ;
void wmast (struct rec2 mast) ;
FILE *pt1 ;
FILE *pt2 ;
int flag = 0 ;
main()
{    pt1 = fopen("trans.dat", "r" ) ;
     pt2 = fopen("mast.dat", "w") ;
     while ( flag == 0 )
     {    trans = rtrans (trans) ;
          if (flag == 1)
               break ;
          mast.empno = trans.empno ;
          strcpy(mast.name,trans.namer) ;
          mast.earn = (trans.basic + trans.da + trans.hrent + trans.conv) ;
          mast.ded  = (trans.cpf + trans.tax ) ;
          mast.net = ( mast.earn - mast.ded ) ;
          wmast (mast) ;
     }
     fclose(pt1) ;
     fclose(pt2) ;
}
struct rec1 rtrans( struct rec1 trans)
{    fscanf (pt1, "%i",&trans.empno) ;
     if (feof(pt1) !=0 )
     {    flag = 1 ;
          return ( trans ) ;
     }
     fscanf (pt1, "%s", trans.name) ;
     fscanf(pt1 , "%i",&trans.basic) ;
     fscanf (pt1, "%f",&trans.da) ;
     fscanf (pt1, "%i",&trans.hrent) ;
     fscanf (pt1, "%i",&trans.conv ) ;
     fscanf (pt1, "%f",&trans.cpf) ;
     fscanf (pt1, "%f",&trans.tax) ;
```

```
        return(trans) ;
}
void wmast (struct rec2 mast)
{       static no = 0 ;
        fwrite (&mast, sizeof(mast) , 1 , pt2 ) ;
        printf("\nRecord written = %i ", ++no ) ;
        return ;
}
```

PROGRAM-14

Following is the program using which you can view the contents of "mast.dat" file.

```
#include <stdio.h>
struct  rec1
{       int empno ;
        char name[30] ;
        float earn;
        float ded;
        float net ;
} mast ;
main()
{       FILE *pt1 ;
        pt1 = fopen("mast.dat", "r") ;
        while ( feof(pt1) == 0 )
        {       fread (&mast, sizeof(mast) , 1 , pt1 ) ;
                if (feof(pt1) !=0 )
                        break ;
                printf("\nEmpno is %i ",mast.empno) ;
                printf("\nName is %s ",mast.name) ;
                printf("\nEarnings are %f ",mast.earn) ;
                printf("\nDeductions are %f ",mast.ded) ;
                printf("\nNet Salary is %f ",mast.net) ;
        }
        fclose(pt1) ;
}
```

EXERCISES CHAPTER 17

Very Short Answer Type Questions

A. Select the most appropriate choice for the following questions:

1. Which of the following activity will be performed first while operating upon a file?
   (a) Opening a file (b) Establishing a buffer
   (c) Closing the file (d) Writing in a file.
2. Which of the following activity will be performed last while operating upon a file?
   (a) Opening a file (b) Establishing a buffer
   (c) Closing the file (d) Reading the file.
3. Which of the following activity has to be done as many number of times as record is read form the file?
   (a) Establishing a buffer (b) Opening a file
   (c) Checking EOF (d) Closing the file.
4. Which of the following clause in used for opening a file?
   (a) Fopen (b) Fileo
   (c) File open (d) Open file.
5. In which of the following modes, will you open a file for adding the records at the end of the file?
   (a) rt (b) wt
   (c) atn (d) att.
6. Which of the following can be used to write a character in binary file?
   (a) putchar (b) putc
   (c) putcf (d) write
7. Which of the following will be used for checking the end of the file?
   (a) feof (b) eof
   (c) end (d) fileend.
8. When feof function will be used?
   (a) While reading form file (b) while writing in file
   (c) While reading form keyboard. (d) Both (a) and(c).
9. Which of the following can be used for writing data in variable length files?
   (a) printf (b) frtintf
   (c) writefile (d) printfile
10. Which of the following can be used for reading data from variable length file?
    (a) scanf (b) fscanf (c) gescan (d) filescan.

B. Fill in the Blanks:

11. ....function can be used to write record in fixed length file.
12. .... function can be used for reading records from fixed length file.
13. To perform read operation on a file, you should open it in .... mode.
14. .... command should be written to open file x.dat in writing mode.
15. Function ....is used to place the record pointer to the desired location of the data file.
16. .... function is used for checking the end of file.
17. .... Clause is used for closing the file.

C. State, True or False:

18. It is mandatory to open a file before you write in it.
19. End of file is to be checked each time you write a record into it.
20. ftell is a function that tells if a file is open or not.
21. rewind is function that puts the record pointer to the end of the file.
22. You can place the record pointer to 100th position from the end of the file, using fseek function.
23. All the files should be closed before the end of the program.
24. It is mandatory to close all the opened files.

Short Answer Type Questions

D. Answer the Following Questions in Short:

25. Which character terminates each field of variable record length file?
26. In which type of files it is possible to access the records randomly?
27. Write a command for establishing a buffer for opening a file.
28. Write a command for opening x.dat file in append mode.
29. Differentiate between w and w++ mode of file operations.
30. What is the use of r+ mode?
31. What will the following commands do?

    FILE = *PT1

    Pt1 =fopen("JAM.DAT", "a+");
32. What will following command do?

    putc("Z"; pt2)
33. What will the following command do?

    getc(pointx)
34. With which type of file fscanf()command is related to?

Long Answer Type Questions

E. Answer the Following Questions in Detail:

35. What all types of files are supported in C?
36. What are ASCII files (or variable length files) and what is their importance?
37. How are variable length file created? Write a program to create a variable length file containing names of all those students, who study in a class.
38. What are text files? How are they different from variable length files?
39. Describe the role of fseek, ftell and rewind functions.
40. Give examples of opening variable length file and writing data in it.
41. State different modes, in which a file could be opened.
42. Write a program that counts the number of characters up to the first $ in input stream.
43. Write a program that reads a text file and creates another file that is identical except that every sequence of consecutive blank spaces is replaced by a question mark.
44. Write a program to append text in an already existing text file.
45. Write a program to open variable length file and write the information (Salesman code and Sales done by him) in it.
46. Write a program to create a fixed record length file, which, comprises of salary and bonus fields. The program should have provision for writing the records randomly.
47. Write a program to read the file, created in previous example.
48. Write a program to create a fixed record length file, with following information stored in it:
    (a) Train number.
    (b) Train name.
    (c) Arrival Time (hr-mnt-sec)
    (d) Departure Time (hr-mnt-sec)
49. Write a program to read the above mentioned file, to calculate and display the stay time of the given train number (user enters it from the keyboard).

****

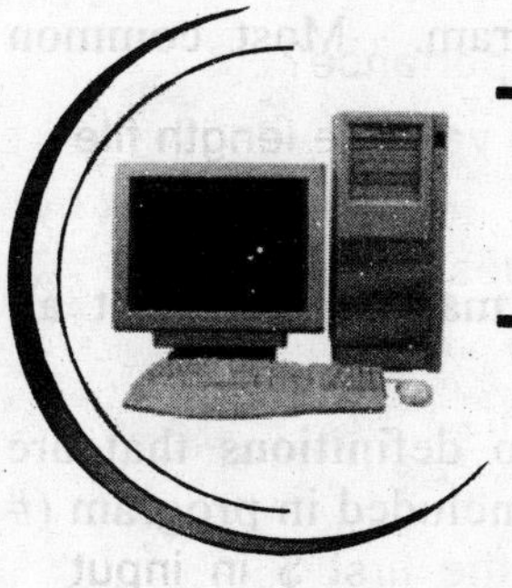

CHAPTER 18

The Standard C Preprocessor

INTRODUCTION

C compiler is basically a combination of two functional programs: the Preprocessor and Translator. The preprocessor, often referred to as *cpp* reads the source code and prepares it for the translator. For translating the code, it scans for special instructions, known as preprocessor commands or preprocessor directives. Preprocessor commands tell the preprocessor to look for special code libraries, make substitution in the code and prepare it for translation into machine language. Preprocessor is also called macro processor because it also allows you to define *macros*, which are brief abbreviations for longer constructs. The output of preprocessor is called translation unit.

Translation unit serves as input for translator. Translator does the actual translation of source code into machine language and writes it into a file called object module. Object module is thus a program in machine language. Concept of preprocessor and translator is illustrated in the figure 18.1.

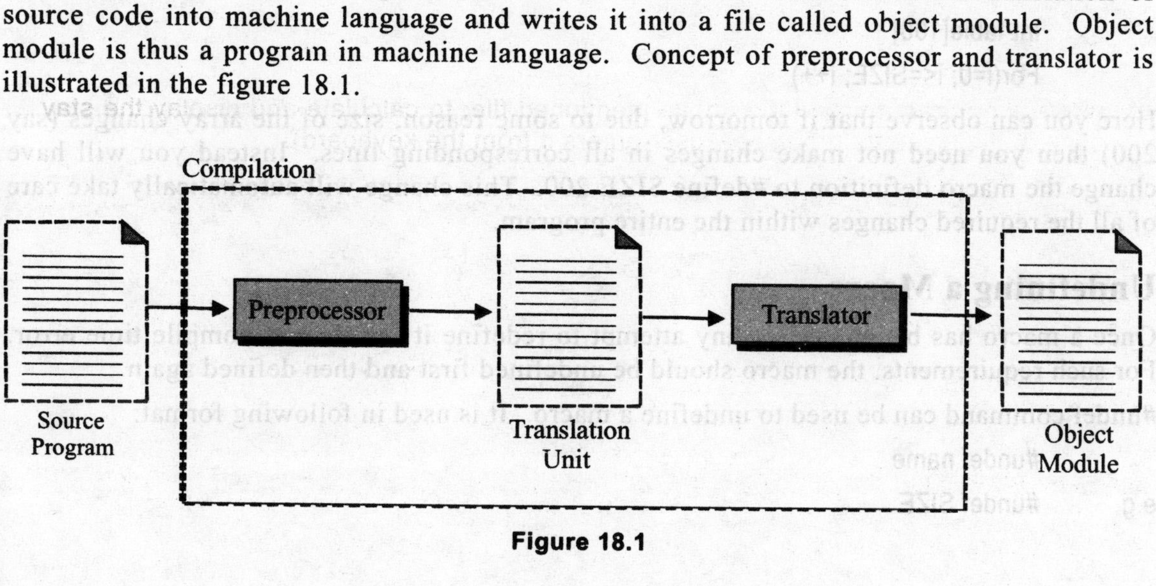

Figure 18.1

PREPROCESSOR DIRECTIVES

Preprocessor directives are included at the beginning of the program. All preprocessor directives start with # sign. For example, #include<stdio.h> is a preprocessor directive and it tells the compiler to include standard I/O library in the program. Most common preprocessor directives are described below.

#include Direcive

You are already familiar with #include directive and have been making use of it all throughout the book, in the format #include<file name>.

A very good usage of this directive can be that all useful macro definitions that are frequently required can be put into a file (say def.h) and that file be included in program (# include<def.h>).

#define Direcive

To define a preprocessor macro, you can use #define command. Using this command, a sequence of taken is assigned a name. The name is called a macro name and the token is referred to as macro body. A macro definition is defined in the following format:

```
#define name body
#define SIZE 100
```

When the preprocessor encounters this directive, it replaces the name by the body. For example, if you have defined SIZE as 100 then within the program you can use following type of statements:

```
int table [SIZE];
for(i=0; i<=SIZE; i++)
```

These statements will, in fact, be treated as follows:

```
int table[100]
For(i=0; i<=SIZE; i++)
```

Here you can observe that if tomorrow, due to some reason, size of the array changes (say 200) then you need not make changes in all corresponding lines. Instead you will have change the macro definition to #define SIZE 200. This change will automatically take care of all the required changes within the entire program.

Undefining a Macro

Once a macro has been defined, any attempt to redefine it results into compile time error. For such requirements, the macro should be undefined first and then defined again.

#undef command can be used to undefine a macro. It is used in following format:

```
        #undef name
e.g.    #undef SIZE
```

Few Important Issues

Following are two important issues related to macro. They need to be kept in mind while making use of them else they may result into error:

1. Macros must be written in a single line. If the macro is too long to fit in a single line, you must use continuation sign. For C macros, backslash(\) immediately followed by new line serves as continuation sign. Remember, if any white space is left between backslash and new line then backslash in not treated as continuation character, rather it is treated as part of macro body. Following example demonstrates the use of continuation character:

```
#define PRT\
printf("This is the end of the file")
```

2. A special care need to be taken while defining the body, because when a macro call is made the entire body is substituted at the called place. For example, following definition will give an error, when macro is called:

```
# define SIZE=100
```

When you use following statements, within the program:

```
int array[SIZE];
```

it be treated as follows:

```
int array[=100];
```

which is grammatically incorrect.

MACROS TO SIMULATE FUNCTIONS WITHOUT ARGUMENTS

When we simulate a function with a macro, the macro definition replaces the function definition. The macro name serves as the header and the macro body serves as function body. The name of the macro is used to replace function call. To get familiar with this consider following program and the function:

```
void disp();
#include <stdio.h>
main ()
{int a=100, b=200, c=300 ;
a=a+b+c;
printf("%i\n",a);
disp();
}
void disp()
{ printf("Job Done"); }
```

Using macro the function can be simulated in the program as follows:

```
#include <stdio.h>
#define DISP \
printf("\Job Done \n")
main ()
{
    int a=100, b=200, c=300 ;
    a=a+b+c;
    printf("%i\n",a);
    DISP;
}
```

Note that here you do not have to declare function, function header and the return statements. It makes the task quite simple.

MACROS TO SIMULATE FUNCTION WITH ARGUMENTS

Macro definitions can also be used to simulate functions with arguments. How it is done, is illustrated in the following example:

```
#include <stdio.h>
#define MIN(x,y) ((x)<(y) ? (x) : (y))
main ()
{
    int a=0, b=200, c=300 ;
    a=MIN(b,c);
    printf("%i\n",a);
}
```

In such cases the replacement is done in two steps as explained below.

STEP 1

```
main ()
{
    int a=0, b=200, c=300 ;
    a=  ((x)<(y) ? (x) : (y)) ;
    printf("%i\n",a);
}
```

STEP 2

```
main ()
{
     int a=0, b=200, c=300 ;
     a= ((b)<(c) ? (b) : (c)) ;
     printf("%i\n",a);
}
```

Following are the points to be noted, in the relation to macros for function with arguments:

1. **To include parameters in macro the opening parenthesis must be placed immediately at the end of the macro name. There should be no white space between them. It you place white spaces between them you will get an error. Following example will result into error.**

   ```
   #define PRD  (x,y) (x)*(y)
   ```

2. **It is highly recommended that the formal parameters within the body of macro must be written within parenthesis. If you don't do so, you may often not get correct result. To understand the point, consider the following wrong definition, which in no way seems to be wrong.**

   ```
   # define PRD(a,b) a*b
   ```

Now if the program passes two arguments (x+1) and (y+2) then the expression will be executed as x+1*y+2. If the values of x and y were 5 and 10 respectively then it will be evaluated as: 5+1*10+2 i.e. 62 instead of 120, which is incorrect.

PREDEFINED MACROS

C language provides many predefined macros. Few commonly used predefined macros are listed in the following table along with the example of their usage:

Command	Meaning	Example
DATE	Provides a sting constant in the form "Mm Dd Yyyy" containing the date of translation.	printf("line %d\n",_DATE_);
FILE	Provides a string constant containing the name of the source file.	printf("file %d\n",_FILE_);
LINE	Provides an integer constant containing the current statement number in the source file.	printf("date %d\n",_LINE_);
TIME	Provides a string constant in the form "Hh:Mm:Ss" containing the time of the translation.	printf("time %d\n", TIME_);

CONDITIONAL COMPILATION

C preprocessor provides the facility of conditional compilation. Conditional compilation allows you to control the compilation process by including #if command in the program. Syntax of #if command is as fallow:

Format-1	Format-2
#if expression	#if expression
code to be included, if	code to be included
expression is true.	#endif
#else	
code to be included, if	
expression is false.	
#endif.	

RULES

1. If given expression is found true, commands in if branch get executed.
2. If given expression is found false, commands, in else branch get executed.
3. If the need be, any of the two sections can be blank i.e. they may not contain any command.
4. Expression should not be include within parenthesis, as is done in case of if else statements of C language.
5. Code in if or else branch cannot be compound statement. The commands #else and #endif serve as delimiters.

To get familiar with conditional compilations, let's take an example.

Say you wish to test your program under 2 conditions, named Local and Abroad. While testing under local conditions, you wish to include local.h file in your program and if you are testing for abroad conditions, you may wish to include abroad.h file. For this, you can include conditional compilation directive at the beginning of the program, as shown below:

```
#if condition=local
    # include<local.h>
#else
    # include<abroad.h>
#endif
```

Multi-Way Command

You know that #if command evaluates single condition and depending upon the result either if branch command is executed or else branch command is executed.

But there could be times, when more than one conditions have to be evaluated and depending on the result, one command is to be executed. To implement such type of situations, C provides #elif command. This command works in conjunction with #if….#else command. It enables you to check another condition if the condition associated with nearest #if command fails. Its usage is shown below.

```
#define CODE0 0
#define CODE1 1
#define CODE2 0
---------------
---------------
---------------
#if (CODE0)
    # include<code0.h>
#elif (CODE1)
    # include<code1.h>
else
#include<code2.h>
#endif.
```

COMMAND LINE ARGUMENTS

All the programs that we have dealt so far directly get executed, without taking values from the command line. But main is a function and as a function, it can have parameters. Now the question is, who supplies values to the main function, which supplies values to all other functions? Well, these values are passed through command line and the values are called command line arguments.

Command line arguments are the parameters to main program. They are supplied at the time of execution of the program, along with the name of the program at the command line. For example, the main program may print the month name at the beginning of the program. Instead of hard coding the month name in the program, it can be given as command line argument to make the program more flexible.

Defining Command-Line Arguments

To define command line arguments, you have to define the main function with two arguments. First argument as integer and other argument as array of pointers to char (strings) to point to the values that user will supply at the time of executing the program. The number of elements in the array is stored in the first arguments and pointer to the user values are stored in array. The main function for such requirement could be written as follows:

```
main(int argc, char *argv[] )
    {
        ---
        ---
    }
```

Note that any name can be chosen for the arguments but traditionally they are called argc (argument count) and argv (argument vector) and used by majority of programmers.

Usage of command line arguments is illustrated in the following program:

```
#include <stdio.h>
#include <stdlib.h>
#include <string.h>
main (int argc, char *argv[])
{
int i ;
printf("\nNo. Of Arguments %i", argc);
printf(" \nFile Name %s",argv[0]);
for (i=1 ; i<argc ; i++)
printf("\nNext argument is %s",argv[i]);
}
```

If you compile above mentioned program and make an executable file of it with the name, showarg then it will have to be executed as mentioned below:

```
showavg <list of arguments>
e.g. showarg India 1947 2009
```

With these command line arguments, the output of the program will be as follow:

```
File name showarg
Next arguments is India
Next argument is 1947
Next argument is 2009
```

EXERCISES **CHAPTER 18**

Short Type Questions

A. Select most appropriate answer for following questions:

1. At which stage C preprocessor works?
   (a) Before translation (b) Before linking
   (c) Before execution (d) Before debugging.
2. What name is given to the output of preprocessor?
   (a) Translation unit (b) Executable module
   (c) Object module (d) Source program.
3. Which of the following serves as input for C preprocessor?
   (a) Translation unit (b) Executable module (c) Object module (d) Source program.
4. C compiler comprises of how many parts?
   (a) 1 (b) 2 (c) 3 (d) 4
5. Which of the following directive will be used to attach a library file in your program?
   (a) #include (b) #exclude (c) #define (d) #if
6. Using which directive a macro can be undefined?
   (a) #Udefine (b) #Undefine (c) #include (d) #cancle
7. Which of the following preprocessor directive becomes quite effective while using arrays in the program?
   (a) #include (b) #DEFINE (c) #if (d) #ARRAY

B. Fill in the blanks:

8. C .... and .... put together form C compiler.
9. The program that gets generated after compilation is generally referred to as........
10. .... directive can be used for assigning a name to a number ....
11. .... and .... are two predefined macros of C preprocessor.
12. For conditional compilation .... can be used.
13. To more use of command line argument .... parameters should be used in main()function.
14. main(int a, char * x[]) will get values of its parameters form ....
15. For multi way conditional compilation. .... , ...and......directives have to be used.

C. State, true or false for following statements:

16. C preprocessor translates high level language.
17. C preprocessor works as macro.

18. A C program can be compiled conditionally using preprocessor commands.
19. Functions without parameters can be simulated using preprocessor directives.
20. Functions with parameters can be simulated using preprocessor directives.
21. Values of predefined macros can be printed using printf statements in C program.
22. #DEFINE is a predefined macro.
23. To more use of command line arguments, main function should be written with arguments.
24. While making use of command line arguments the first argument in main should be an integer.
25. While making use of command line arguments the second argument in makes should be array of integer pointers.

D. Answer the following questions in short:

26. Which preprocessor directive will you use for including a header file in your program?
27. Write general syntax for using # include directive in your program.
28. Write two directives used for conditional compilation.
29. Write a command for printing the value of predefined macro___DATE___in your C program.
30. What is the use of __LINE___prefefined macro?

Detailed Answer Type Questions

E. Answer the following questions in detail:

31. What do you understand by C preprocessor? Why it is used?
32. Explain the term, source program, Translation Unit and Object Module, in relation to C preprocessor.
33. What is the use of # define directive and how it is related to the use of array and for loops in the program? Explain using a suitable example.
34. What do you understand by conditional compilation? How it is performed in C program? Explain using required directives.
35. Give an example, simulation of function without arguments in a C program, using preprocessor directives.
36. Give an example of simulation of function with arguments in a C program, using suitable preprocessor directives.
37. What do you understand by command line arguments? How do you handle them, using preprocessor directives in your program?
38. What is the use of #undefined directive. In which circumstances will you require it and why?
39. Write a short note on C preprocessor.
40. Explain the use of # if, #else, #endif and #elseif.

****

Computer Fundamentals And Programming In C Lab (CM-107)

Practical Assignments

1.0 WINDOWS

Assignment 1.1: Start Windows Operating System.

Assignment Activities: Perform following activities to complete the assignment:

1. Carryout all the steps described for booting the system, on page 71 in chapter 4 and get Windows Desktop appear on your monitor screen.
2. Move few icons on the desktop by dragging them to some other place.
3. Rearrange the icons, using following steps:
   - Right click the mouse on some blank portion of the desktop. When you do so, a shortcut menu will appear on the screen.
   - Select "Arrange Icon By" option from this menu. When you do so, another popup menu will appear on the screen.
   - Select "Name" option from that menu.
   - This procedure will rearrange the icons on desktop.

ASSIGNMENT 1.2 : Start a program, using the All Programs option of the Start menu.

Assignment Activities: Invoke Disk Cleanup program to complete the assignment. Perform following steps to invoke it:

1. Click the mouse on "Start" button, present on desktop. When do so, Start menu will appear on monitor screen.
2. First select "All Programs" option from this menu and then "Accessories", then "System Tools" and then "Disk Cleanup" option from the submenus that appear one after the other.

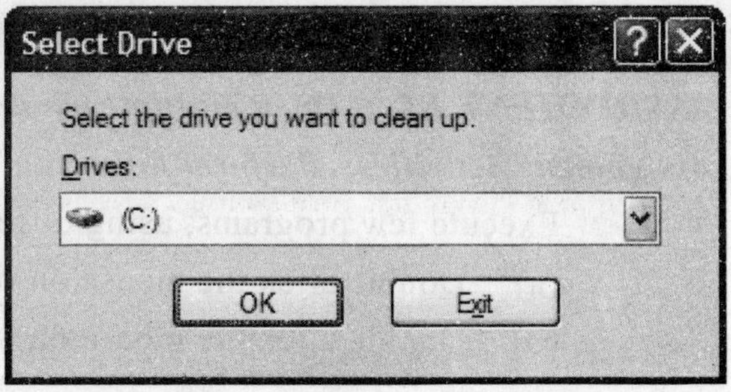

Figure F-1

3. When you do so, a dialog box as illustrated in figure F-1, will appear on the screen.
4. Now select the drive that is to be cleaned.
5. At last, click the mouse on "OK" button.

When you do so, all unnecessary files will get deleted from the disk and disk performance will be better.

ASSIGNMENT 1.3 & 1.4 : Minimize, Maximize, Close Resize a window.

Assignment Activities: Perform following steps to complete this assignment:

1. Double click the mouse on any program icon (say, My Computer icon), present on desktop. When do so, a program window will appear on monitor screen.
2. Drag the window by its title bar to move the window.
3. Drag the left border line of the window, towards right, to decrease the width of the window.
4. Drag the right border line of the window, towards right, to increase the width of the window.
5. Drag the right border line of the window, towards left, to decrease the width of the window.
6. Drag the top border line of the window, down, to decrease the height of the window
7. Drag the bottom border line of the window down, to increase the height of the window.
8. To change the height and width of the window, in proportion, drag it by corner.
9. Click the mouse on Maximize button to maximize the window. When you do so, Maximize button will change to Restore button.
10. Click the mouse on Restore button to restore the maximized window.
11. Click the mouse on Minimize button to minimize the window.
12. Right click the mouse on window button, present in program manager area. When you do so, a menu will pop up on the screen. Select Restore option from this menu. This process will restore the minimized window.
13. Click the mouse on Close button to close the window.

ASSIGNMENT 1.5 : Open multiple windows and switch between windows.

Assignment Activities: Perform following operations to complete this assignment.

1. Execute few programs, using different methods:
   (a) Double click the mouse on time that gets displayed in system tray.
   (b) Double click the mouse on "My Computer" icon present on desktop.

(c) First click the mouse on "Start" button and then select any option from Start menu.

(d) Click the mouse on any icon present in Quick Launch toolbar.

Each step mentioned above will invoke a program. All the programs thus invoked will be in running state. This clearly demonstrates multitasking feature of Windows.

Now right click the mouse at some blank space in Task Manager. When you do so, a shortcut menu will appear on the screen. Select "Tile Windows Horizontally" option from this menu. This process will arrange all the windows neatly on desktop.

2 Now switchover from one program to another by either clicking the mouse on title bar of the window or by clicking the mouse on the corresponding button in Task Manager area.

ASSIGNMENT 1.6 & 1.9 : Locate a file, using Search option of Start menu.

Assignment Activities: Perform following operations to complete this assignment.

1. Search procedure is given on page 85 of chapter 4. Follow that procedure and find the location of following files and folders on the disk.

   calc.exe, mspaint.exe, notepad. exe, winword.exe, iexplore.exe

ASSIGNMENT 1.7 : Operate the Calculator in Accessories..

Assignment Activities: Perform following operations to complete this assignment:

1. Invoke "Calculator" program by first clicking the mouse on "Start" button and them selecting "All Program/Accessories/Calculator" options from the menus that appear one after the other.

   When you do so, calculator, as shown in figure F-2 will appear on monitor screen.

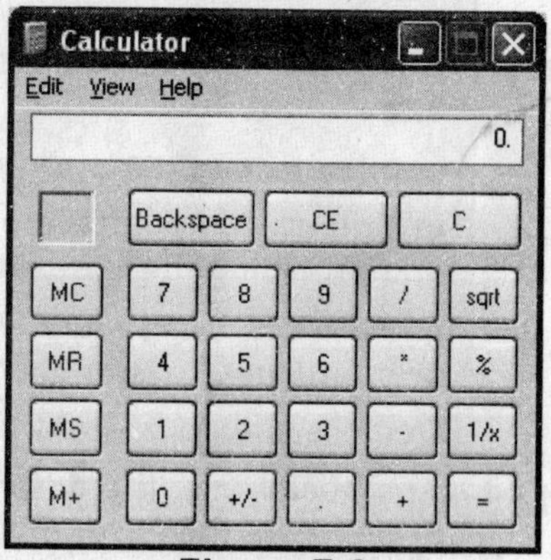

Figure F-2

2. Switchover to Scientific and Standard mode by selecting corresponding options from calculator's View submenu.
3. Enter a number either by pressing number keys of the keyboard or by clicking the mouse on calculator's number buttons.

   Click the mouse on + sign and enter another number.

   Now click the mouse on = sign to display the sum of two numbers.
4. Do other types of calculations also.
5. Operate upon binary numbers and do binary calculations in scientific calculator.

ASSIGNMENT 1.8 (a) : Working With Notepad Program.

Assignment Activities: Perform following operations to complete this assignment:

1. Invoke "Notepad" program by first clicking the mouse on "Start" button and them selecting "All Program/Accessories/Notepad" options from the menus that appear one after the other.

   When you do so, Notepad window, as shown in figure F-3 will appear on monitor screen.

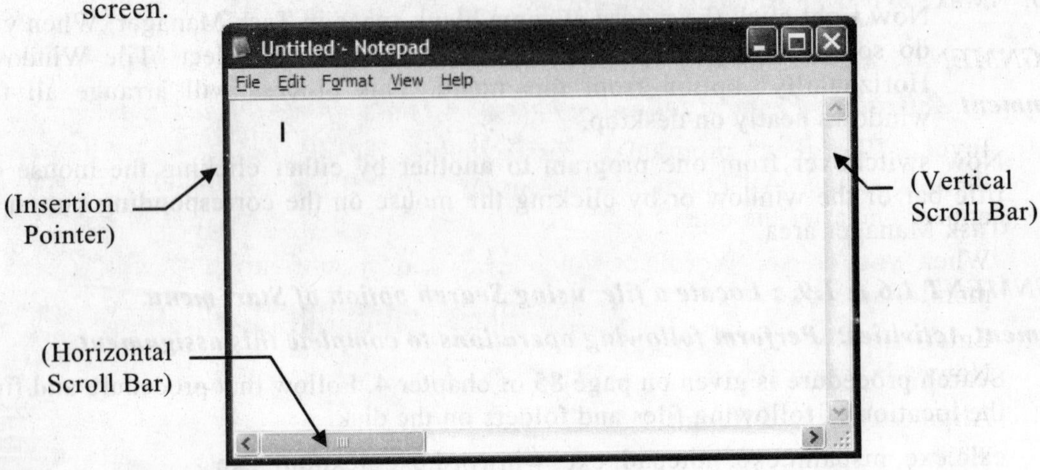

Figure F-3

2. Enter following text in Notepad window:

> Computer is electronic equipment. It is mainly used for automating manual tasks.
>
> In offices computers are used for preparing letters, documents and reports.
>
> In hotels, computers are used for advance booking of rooms, preparing bills and providing other services.
>
> In railways computers are used for rail reservation, printing of tickets and preparation of reservation charts.
>
> Doctors use computers for diagnosing the illness and treatment of deceases.
>
> Architects use them for map designing and city planning. In meteorology department they are used for weather forecasting.

3. Select some portion of the text by dragging the mouse over it.
4. Cancel the selection by clicking the mouse on unselected portion of the text.
5. Copy some portion of the text by using "Copy" and "Paste" options of Edit submenu.

6. Move some portion of the text by using "Cut" and "Paste" options of Edit submenu.
7. Cancel the effect of last operation by selecting "Undo" option from Edit submenu.
8. Make use of "Replace" option present in Edit submenu for finding a given word and replacing it with another word.
9 Save the text in a file.
10. Make exit from Notepad program.

ASSIGNMENT 1.8 (b) : Working With WordPad Program.

Assignment Activities: Perform following operations to complete this assignment:

1. Invoke "WordPad" program by first clicking the mouse on "Start" button and them selecting "All Program/Accessories/WordPad" options from the menus that appear one after the other.

   When you do so, WordPad window, as shown in figure F-4 will appear on monitor screen.
2. Enter the text, given in Notepad section above.
3. Align text in different ways.
4. Change the font size of first two lines of the text.
5. Change the font type for the last two lines of the text.
6. Save the text in a file and exit from the WordPad program.

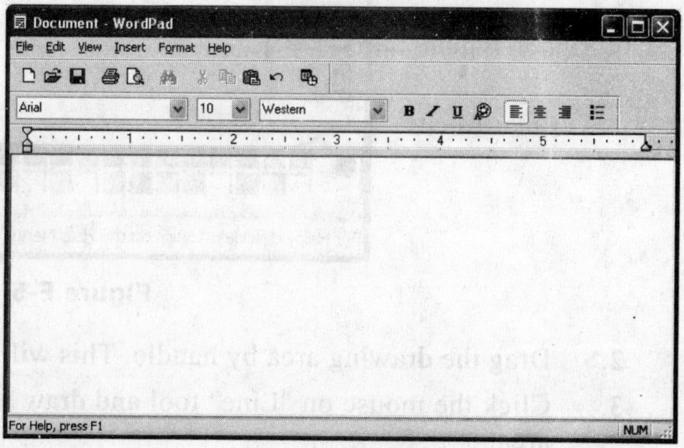

Figure F-4

7. Reopen the saved file and try other options of WordPad program.

ASSIGNMENT 1.8 (c) : Working With Paint Program.

Assignment Activities: Perform following operations to complete this assignment:

1. Invoke Paint Program by first clicking the mouse on "Start" button and them selecting "All Program/Accessories/Paint" options from the menus that appear one after the other.

   When you do so, Paint windows, as shown in figure F-5 will appear on monitor screen.

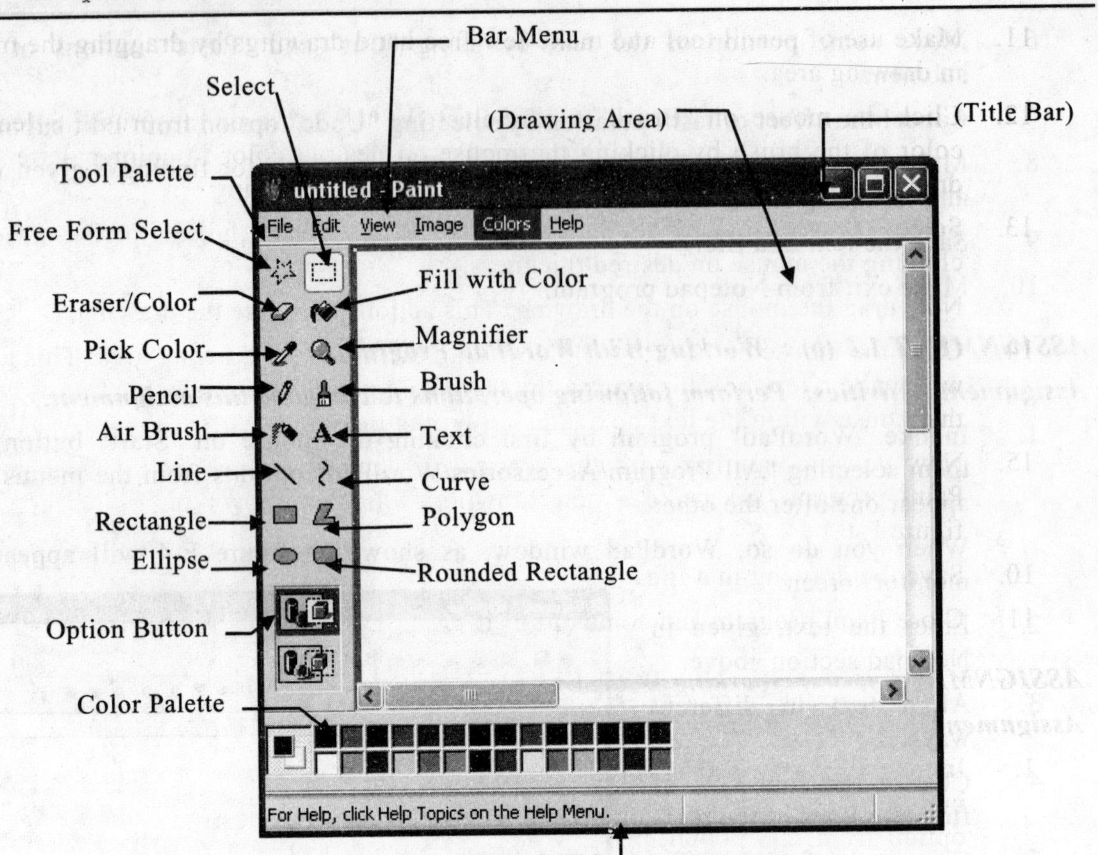

Figure F-5

2. Drag the drawing area by handle. This will change the size of drawing area.
3. Click the mouse on "Line" tool and draw a line by dragging the mouse in drawing area.
4. Draw another line of different thickness and color by selecting desired options.
5. Draw straight line. For this, press Shift key while dragging the mouse.
6. Draw an ellipse, by selecting "Ellipse" tool from tool box and dragging the mouse in drawing area.
7. Draw a circle by selecting "Ellipse" tool from toolbox and dragging the mouse in the drawing area, with shift key pressed.
8. Now first click the mouse on "Fill with color" button tool and then on green color swatch of color palette. At last, click the mouse within the circle that you had made in the last step. Circle will get filled with green color.
9. Perform similar steps to draw shapes like rectangle, polygon etc.
10. Click the mouse on "Curve" tool and drag the mouse in spiral path. This action will make a spiral.

11. Make use of pencil tool and make few free hand drawings by dragging the mouse in drawing area.
12. Click the mouse on "Brush" tool. Select the thickness of the brush. Select the color of the brush by clicking the mouse on desired color in color palette. Now drag the mouse in drawing area and make free hand drawing.
13. Select "Eraser" tool by clicking the mouse on it. Select the size of the eraser by clicking the mouse on desired thickness.

    Now drag the mouse on the drawing. This action will erase the drawing.
14 Click the mouse on "Text" tool. Now drag the mouse in drawing area. This action will make a text box for writing the text. To type the text, click the mouse within the text box and start typing the text.
15. Now you are familiar with the process of drawing shapes in Paint program. So make a new drawing, which is shown in figure F-6.

Figure F-6

10. Save the drawing in a file.
11. Close Paint program and come out of it.

ASSIGNMENT 1.10 : Working With Windows Explorer Program.

Assignment Activities: Perform following operations to complete this assignment:

1. Invoke Windows Explorer program by first right clicking the mouse on "Start" button. When you do so, a popup menu will get displayed. Select "Explorer" option from this popup menu. When you do so, Windows Explorer window, as shown in figure F-7 will appear on monitor screen.

Delete Button

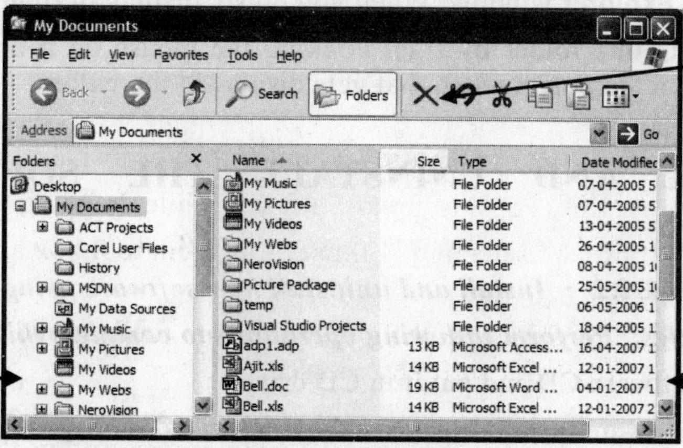

Left Pane

Right Pane

Figure windows-7

2. Click the mouse on any folder in left pane of the window. Contents present within the folder will get displayed in the right pane.
3. Click the mouse on "Desktop" icon, present in left pane of the window.

4. Perform following steps to make a new folder on desktop:
   (i) Right click the mouse on some blank space in right pane of the windows. When you do so, a popup menu will get displayed.
   (ii) First Select "New" option from this popup menu and then "Folder" option from the menu, which appears thereafter. This will create a new folder with the name "New Folder"
   (iii) Now type any desired name. Say you type "test". By doing so, a new folder with name, test will get created on desktop.
5. Drag a file icon and drop it on test folder icon. When you do so, file will move to test folder.
6. Undo the effect of Move operation by selection "Undo" option from "Edit" submenu.
7. Press Control key and repeat step (5). This process will copy the file in test folder
8. Copy few more files into folder, using above mentioned procedure.
9. To go into test folder, double click the mouse on its icon. When you do so, all the files present in it will get displayed in right pane.
10. To delete a file, right click the mouse on any icon. When you do so, a popup menu will appear on the screen. Select "Delete" option from this menu.
11. To rename any file, right click the mouse on its icon. When you do so, a popup menu will appear on the screen. Select "Rename" option from this menu and type the new name of the file.
12. To come out of test folder, click the mouse on "UP" button present in toolbar of Windows Explorer window. When you do so, display in right pane will change.
13. Now delete this folder by right clicking the mouse on it and selecting "Delete" option from the popup menu that gets displayed thereafter.

2.0 INSTALL AND UNINSTALL THE SOFTWARE AND HARDWARE

ASSIGNMENT 2.1 & 2.2 : Install and uninstall new software using control panel

Assignment Activities: Perform following operations to complete this assignment:

1. Get the software CD and put it in CD drive.
2. Follow software installation procedure described on page 90 of chapter 4
3. After installation, invoke the software to ensure that it is working properly.
4. Now uninstall the software.

ASSIGNMENT 2.3 & 2.4 : Install and uninstall new hardware using control panel

Assignment Activities: Perform following operations to complete this assignment:

1. Get the new hardware and connect it to the computer at proper place.
2. Follow installation procedure described on page 90 of chapter 4
3. After installation, work with hardware to ensure that it is working properly.
4. Now uninstall the hardware.

ASSIGNMENT 2.5 : Install a modem using control panel.

Assignment Activities: Perform following operations to complete this assignment:

1. Get the new modem and connect it to the compute using proper cable.
2. Connect the Internet line to the appropriate port of the modem.
3. Follow installation procedure described on page 94 of chapter 4
4. After installation, invoke Internet Explorer to check that Internet is accessible and the modem has been installed properly.

ASSIGNMENT 2.6 : Install a printer using control panel.

Assignment Activities: Perform following operations to complete this assignment:

1. Get a new printer and connect it to the compute, using proper cable.
2. Switch the computer on.
3. Follow installation procedure described on page 92 of chapter 4
4. After installation, print few pages on the printer to insure that it has been installed properly.

3.0 USAGE OF SYSTEM TOOLS

ASSIGNMENT 3.1 : Find out drive space.

Assignment Activities: Perform following operations to complete this assignment:

1. Carry out all the activities given on page 96 of chapter 4 to find the available space on C: disk drive.

ASSIGNMENT 3.2 : Carryout disk defragmentation

Assignment Activities: Perform following operations to complete this assignment:

1. Carry out all the activities given on page 97 of chapter 4 to defragment any disk drive present on the system.

ASSIGNMENT 3.3 (a) : Change resolution, color and appearance

Assignment Activities: Perform following operations to complete this assignment:

1. Carry out all the activities given on page 98,99 of chapter 4 to change the resolution, color and appearance.

ASSIGNMENT 3.3 (b) : Set screensaver for the system.

Assignment Activities: Perform following operations to complete this assignment:

1. Carry out all the activities given on page 97 of chapter 4 to set the screensaver for the system.

ASSIGNMENT 3.4 : Change system date and time

Assignment Activities: Perform following operations to complete this assignment:

2. Carry out all the activities given on page 99 of chapter 4 to change the system date and time.

4.0 DOS

ASSIGNMENT 4.1, 4.2 & 4.3 : Practice Internal and external commands. Create and use batch file. Know use of Edit editor.

Assignment Activities: Perform following operations to complete this assignment:

1. Switch on the computer and boot it with MS-DOS operating system.
2. Make a directory with the name TEST.
3. Go into TEST directory.
4. Make a file, INDIA.TXT using Edit editor and enter following text into it:

> India is the world's largest, oldest, continuous civilization.
>
> India never invaded any country in her last 10000 years of history.
>
> India is the world's largest democracy.
>
> Varanasi, also known as Benares, was called "the ancient city" when Lord Buddha visited it in 500 B.C.E, and is the oldest, continuously inhabited city in the world today.
>
> India invented the Number System. Zero was invented by Aryabhatta.
>
> The World's first university was established in Takshashila in 700BC. More than 10,500 students from all over the world studied more than 60 subjects. The University of Nalanda built in the 4th century BC was one of the greatest achievements of ancient India in the field of education.
>
> Sanskrit is the mother of all the European languages. Sanskrit is the most suitable language for computer software - a report in Forbes magazine, July 1987.
>
> Ayurveda is the earliest school of medicine known to humans. Charaka, the father of medicine consolidated Ayurveda 2500 years ago. Today Ayurveda is fast regaining its rightful place in our civilization.

5. Perform following operations on this file.
   (a) Add few lines at top, bottom and in middle.
   (b) Delete few lines from the text.
   (c) Copy some portion of the text to some other part.
   (d) Move some portion of the text to other location.
   (e) Save the text in the file and exit.
6. Execute DIR command and observe the output.
7. Make a duplicate copy of INDIA.TXT file with another name, INDIA1.TXT.
8. Display the contents of INDIA.TXT file on VDU.
9. Rename the file INDIA.TXT to BHARAT.TXT.
10. Make another directory with the name JUNK.
11. Copy BHARAT.TXT file into JUNK directory with same name.
12. Copy BHARAT.TXT file into JUNK directory with another name, BHATRAT.BAK.
13. MOVE to JUNK directory.
14. Execute DIR commands to see how many files are there.
15. Now execute CD .. command first and then print the current directory name so as to know the effect of CD .. command.
16. Remove the file BHARAT.BAK.
17. Try to remove JUNK directory, you will get an error.
18. Perform all necessary steps and remove JUNK directory.
19. Take a floppy and format it.
20. Make the floppy bootable.
21. Copy few files from TEST directory to floppy.
22. Move one file from hard disk to floppy.
23. Remove the file that you had copied on floppy.
24. Display the names of the files present on floppy.
25. Delete all the files from floppy.
26. Reboot the system from floppy.
27. Give C: command to make hard disk as default disk.
28. Print the name of working directory.
29. Go to root directory.
30. Go to TEST directory.
31. Take another floppy that has few files in it. Using DISKCOPY command, copy all the contents of previous floppy to this floppy.

32. Move around the system. Go to other drives.
33. Perform DEL A:*.* command for floppy and note the message that appears against this command.
34. Execute TREE command and view the complete directory structure.
35. View the Label of floppy.
36. Change the label of the floppy.
37. Clear the contents present on VDU screen, using CLS command.
38. Change the system prompt, using PROMPT command.
39. Confirm the presence of COMMAND.COM, IO.SYS and MSDOS.SYS files on bootable floppy.
40. Make an exit from the system and switch it off.
41. Edit AUTOEXEC.BAT file. Put some commands into it and execute it.

5.0 C PROGRAMMING

ASSIGNMENT 5.1 : Acquaintance with editing, compiling and executing programs.

Assignment Activities: Perform following operations to complete this assignment:

1. Invoke C environment on your computer. Procedure is given on page 163
2. Enter program given on page 161 into the system. Procedure for entering the program is given on page 163.
3. Compile the program. Procedure for compiling the program is given on page 164.
4. Execute the program. Procedure for executing the program is given on page 165.

ASSIGNMENT 5.2 : Exercises on printf and scanf functions.

Assignment Activities: Perform following operations to complete this assignment:

1. To get familiar with putchar function, enter, compile and execute Program-2 given on page 181 and ensure the correctness of the output.
2. To get familiar with getchar function, enter, compile and execute Program-3 given on page 182 and ensure the correctness of the output.
3. To get familiar with printf and scanf functions, enter, compile and execute Program-4 given on page 184 and ensure the correctness of the output.
4. Enter, compile and execute Program-5 given on page 186 and ensure the correctness of the output.

ASSIGNMENT 5.3 : Exercises on selective structures.

Assignment Activities: Perform following operations to complete this assignment:

1. To get familiar with the usage of if then else statement, enter, compile and execute Program-2 given on page 191 and ensure the correctness of the output.

2. To get familiar with nested if statements, enter, compile and execute Program-3 given on page 195 and ensure the correctness of the output.
3. To get familiar with the usage of Switch statement, enter, compile and execute Program-7 given on page 200 and ensure the correctness of the output.
4. To get familiar with the usage of goto statement, enter, compile and execute Program-9 given on page 203 and ensure the correctness of the output.

ASSIGNMENT 5.4 : Exercise on repetitive structures

Assignment Activities: Perform following operations to complete this assignment:

1. To get familiar with while loop functioning, enter, compile and execute Program-1 given on page 208 and ensure the correctness of the output.
2. To get familiar with do while loop functioning, enter, compile and execute Program-2 given on page 209 and ensure the correctness of the output.
3. To get familiar with for loop functioning, enter, compile and execute Program-4 given on page 212 and ensure the correctness of the output.
4. To get familiar with nested for loops, enter, compile and execute Program-8 given on page 214 and ensure the correctness of the output.
5. To get familiar with breaking of loops, enter, compile and execute Program-9 given on page 216 and ensure the correctness of the output.
6. To get familiar with the functioning of continue statement, enter, compile and execute Program-10 given on page216 and ensure the correctness of the output.

ASSIGNMENT 5.5 : Exercise on arrays and strings.

Assignment Activities: Perform following operations to complete this assignment:

1. To get familiar with the declaration of one dimensional array and the process of accessing its elements, enter, compile and execute Program-3 given on page 224 and ensure the correctness of the output.
2. To get familiar with the process of one dimensional array initialization, enter, compile and execute Program-4 given on page 225 and ensure the correctness of the output.
3. To get familiar with the declaration of two dimensional array and the process of accessing its elements, enter, compile and execute Program-8 given on page 236 and ensure the correctness of the output.
4. To get familiar with the process of two dimensional array initialization, enter, compile and execute Program-9 given on page 237 and ensure the correctness of the output.

5. To get familiar with the process of sorting an array, enter, compile and execute Program-5 given on page 227 and ensure the correctness of the output.
6. To get familiar with the process of accepting strings within the program, enter, compile and execute Program-2 given on page 250 and ensure the correctness of the output.
7. To get familiar with the process of handling multiple strings within the program, enter, compile and execute Program-4 given on page 252 and ensure the correctness of the output.
8. To get familiar with various string related functions, enter, compile and execute Program-5 given on page 254 and ensure the correctness of the output.

ASSIGNMENT 5.6 : Exercise on functions.

Assignment Activities: Perform following operations to complete this assignment:

1. To get familiar with the process of using functions within the program, enter, compile and execute Program-1 given on page 268 and ensure the correctness of the output.
2. To get familiar with the function prototypes, enter, compile and execute Program-2 given on page 270 and ensure the correctness of the output.
3. To get familiar with the process of calling the function by value, enter, compile and execute Program-3 given on page 270 and ensure the correctness of the output.
4. To get familiar with the functions that return multiple values, enter, compile and execute Program-8 given on page 278 and ensure the correctness of the output.

ASSIGNMENT 5.7 : Exercises on recursion.

Assignment Activities: Perform following operations to complete this assignment:

1. To get familiar with the recursive functions, enter, compile and execute Program-15 given on page 289 and ensure the correctness of the output.

ASSIGNMENT 5.8 : Exercises on global variables.

Assignment Activities: Perform following operations to complete this assignment:

1. To get familiar with the usage of global variables, in C programs, enter, compile and execute Program-12 given on page 285 and ensure the correctness of the output.

ASSIGNMENT 5.9 : Exercises on C preprocessor directives.

Assignment Activities: Perform following operations to complete this assignment:

1. Make use of macros, as explained on page 391.
2. Write macro to simulate function with arguments, as explained on page 392.

3. Make use of command line arguments as explained on page 396.

ASSIGNMENT 510 : Exercise pointers.

Assignment Activities: Perform following operations to complete this assignment:

1. To get familiar with the process of declaring pointers and accessing values through them, enter, compile and execute Program-1 given on page 294 and ensure the correctness of the output.
2. To get familiar with the process of passing pointers to the functions (i.e. calling the function by reference) enter, compile and execute Program-3 given on page 296 and ensure the correctness of the output.
3. To get familiar with pointer arithmetic, enter, compile and execute Program-5 given on page 300 and ensure the correctness of the output.
4. To get familiar with the process of dynamic memory allocation, enter, compile and execute Program-7 given on page 303 and ensure the correctness of the output.
5. To get familiar with the relationship of pointers and two dimensional arrays, enter, compile and execute Program-9 given on page 308 and ensure the correctness of the output.
6. To get familiar with pointers to functions, enter, compile and execute Program-12 given on page 313 and ensure the correctness of the output.

ASSIGNMENT 5.11 (a) : Exercise on Structures and unions.

Assignment Activities: Perform following operations to complete this assignment:

1. To get familiar with the process of declaring structures and accessing its members, enter, compile and execute Program-1 given on page 327 and ensure the correctness of the output.
2. To deal with array structures, enter, compile and execute Program-2 given on page 329 and ensure the correctness of the output.
3. To deal with nested structures, enter, compile and execute Program-3 given on page 332 and ensure the correctness of the output.
4. To get familiar with the process of accessing structure members through pointers, enter, compile and execute Program-4 given on page 335 and ensure the correctness of the output.
5. To get familiar with the process of passing complete structure to the function, enter, compile and execute Program-6 given on page 339 and ensure the correctness of the output.
6. To get familiar with the process of returning a structure from the function, enter, compile and execute Program-8 given on page 342 and ensure the correctness of the output.

7. To get familiar with self referential structure, enter, compile and execute Program-9 given on page 345 and ensure the correctness of the output.
8. To get familiar with the process of declaring unions and accessing its members, enter, compile and execute Program-10 given on page 348 and ensure the correctness of the output.

ASSIGNMENT 5.11 (b) : Exercise on files.

Assignment Activities: Perform following operations to complete this assignment:

1. To get familiar with the process of creating a binary file, enter, compile and execute Program-1 given on page 365.
2. To get familiar with the process of reading a binary file, enter, compile and execute Program-2 given on page 366.
3. To create a data file that exclusively holds integer values in it, enter, compile and execute Program-5 given on page 370.
4. To read the data from a file that exclusively holds integer values in it, enter, compile and execute Program-6 given on page 371.
5. To create variable record length data file, enter, compile and execute Program-7 given on page 373.
6. To read variable record length data file, enter, compile and execute Program-8 given on page 374.
7. To create fixed record length data file, enter, compile and execute Program-9 given on page 376.
8. To read fixed record length data file, enter, compile and execute Program-10 given on page 377.
9. To get familiar with the process of writing records randomly in fixed record length file, enter, compile and execute Program-11 given on page 380.
10. To get familiar with the process of reading records randomly from fixed record length file, enter, compile and execute Program-12 given on page 381.

ASSIGNMENT Extra : Exercise on Bitwise Operators

Assignment Activities: Perform following operations to complete this assignment:

1. To get familiar with bitwise operations, enter, compile and execute Program-1 given on page 356.

****

Information Technology Lab (CM-110)

(Self Study Material and Practical Assignments)

Information Technology Lab (CM-110)

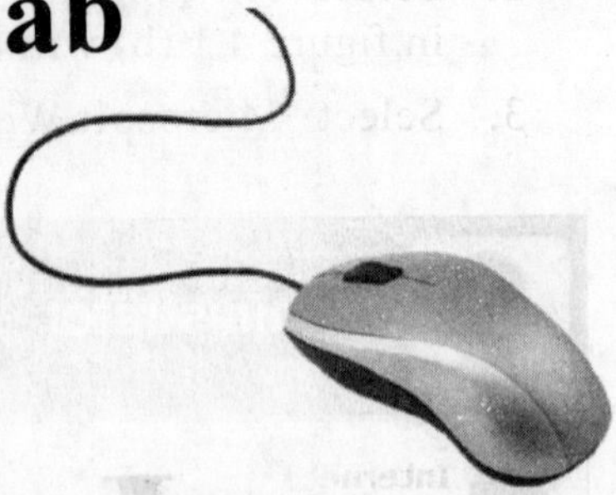

MS-Word

(Self Study Material and Practical Assignments)

INTRODUCTION

Quite some time back, typewrites were very popular in offices, organizations and factories. They were used for preparing documents like letters, reports, memos etc. But ever since computers became popular, they replaced typewriters. Today the situation is that majority of organizations are using computers for their typing work. Advantages of using computers are many. Many typing related activities, which can be performed through computers, cannot be performed through typewriter. For example, including pictures with the text, checking spelling mistakes, reformatting the document after typing it etc. are few activities that cannot be performed in typewriters but can be very easily performed in computers. Use of computers for typing related activities is explained in this chapter.

INTRODUCTION TO WORD PROCESSING

In computer terminology, all typing related activities, such as setting the margins, typing the document, formatting the text, including different types of objects such as pictures, tables, charts etc. in the document, are called word processing. The software, using which such types of activities are performed on computer is called word processor.

INTRODUCTION TO MS-WORD

MS-Word is word processing software. It is mainly used for entering text into computer and formatting it in the form of letters, notes, memos or reports. MS-Word has been designed and developed by Microsoft Corporation of USA. It is GUI based, easy-to-use interactive software, which takes care of most of the typing related requirements. It provides numerous facilities to make the text entry easy and document attractive. Its operational details are described below.

GETTING STARTED WITH MS-WORD

For getting started with MS-Word, perform following steps after making sure that computer is booted with Windows operating system:

1. Click the mouse on "Start" button. When you do so, Start menu, as shown in figure 4.1 (a) will appear on the screen.
2. Select "All Program" option from this menu. When you do so, a submenu as shown in figure 4.1 (b) will appear on the screen.
3. Select "Microsoft Word" option from this submenu.

(a) (b)

Figure Word-1

When you do so, a window, as illustrated in figure Word-2, will get displayed on the screen. This window is called Word Window.

INTRODUCTION TO WORD WINDOW

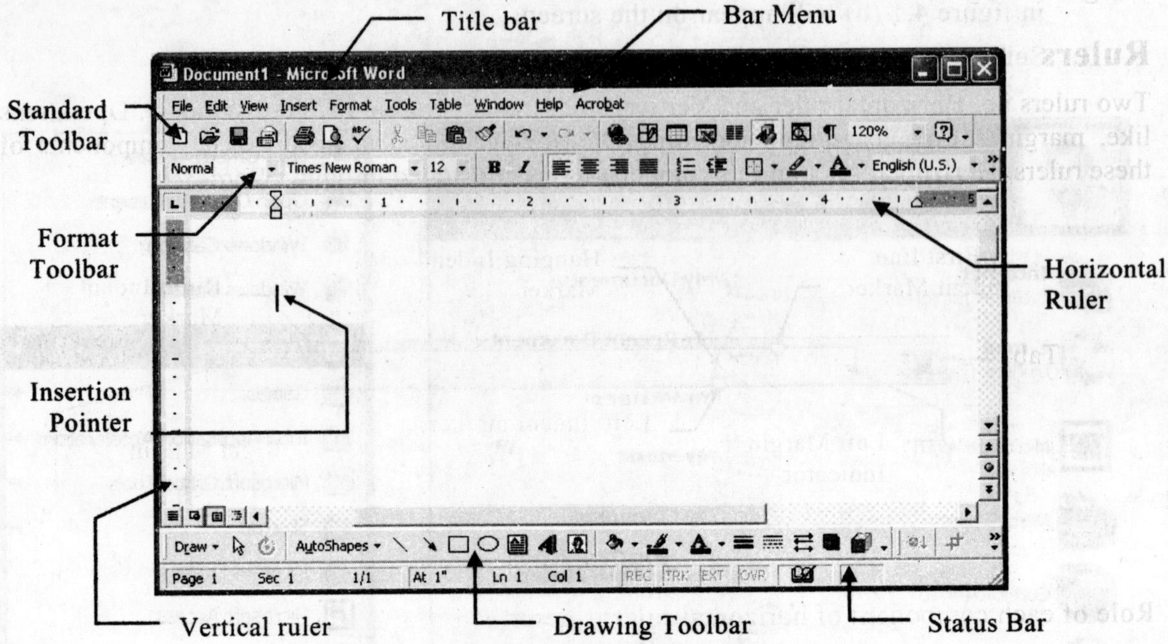

Figure Word-2

Refer figure Word-2 and note that Word window comprises of many objects. Some of the objects like Title bar, Minimize button, Maximize button, System menu button, Bar menu etc. are common objects that remain present in each windows. These objects require no further explanation. But some of the objects are local to Word window. A brief introduction of such objects is given below.

Standard Toolbar

Standard toolbar comprises of many buttons. These buttons relate to frequently performed activities, which are performed while typing the text. To know, which button performs which activity, rest the mouse pointer on the button for a while. When you do so, a message, called tool tip will get displayed. Tool tip generally gives an indication of the activity that would get performed by the button. To perform any activity through a button, you need to click the mouse on that button. For example, when you click the mouse on "Save" button, typed text gets saved in a file.

Format Toolbar

Buttons for text formatting functions remain present in Format toolbar. For example, font, font size, font style etc. for the text can be set, using Format toolbar buttons.

Drawing Toolbar

Different types of shapes, such as square, rectangle circle, ellipse, stars etc. can be drawn using Drawing toolbar buttons.

Rulers

Two rulers i.e. Horizontal ruler and Vertical ruler remain present in Word Window. Operations like, margin setting, paragraph indenting etc. are performed using different components of these rulers. Horizontal ruler and its components are illustrated in figure Word-3.

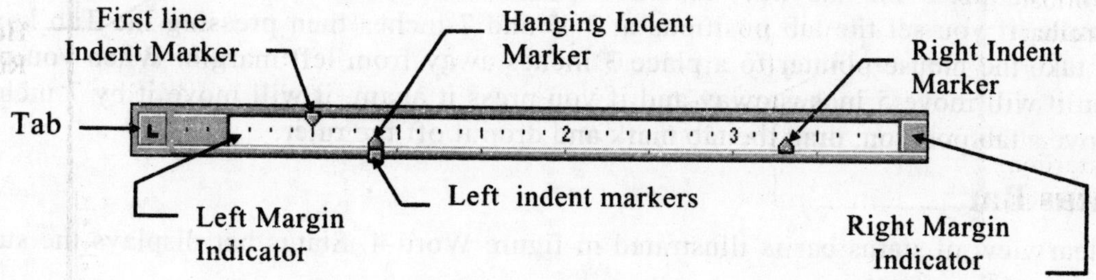

Figure Word-3

Role of each component of horizontal ruler is described below.

Left And Right Margin Indicators

These indicators are used for setting the respective margins of the document. For example, if Right Margin Indicator's position is set to one inch then the width of the left margin, for the whole document will be one inch. To change the width of the margin, you can drag the respective indicator to the desired place.

Hanging Indent Marker

Usually all the paragraphs of the document start from left margin but Hanging Indent Marker provides the facility to start the current paragraph from a different position. It could be dragged to a new position to define the starting place for the current paragraph. For example, if the right margin has been set to 1 inch and Hanging Indent Marker has been positioned at 1.5 inch then all the paragraphs other than the current paragraph will start from 1 inch but the current paragraph will start from 1.5 inch.

First Line Indent Marker

First line Indent Marker provides the facility to start the first line of the paragraph from a place other than that from where rest of the lines of the paragraph start. For example, all the lines of the paragraph may start from the left margin (say 1 inch) but first line for the paragraph may start from 1.5 inch from the left margin. To set the position of the first line of the paragraph, First Line Indent Marker can be dragged to the desired position.

Left Indent Marker

Left Indent Marker facilitates simultaneous movement of First line Indent Marker and Hanging Indent Marker. When you drag it, both the markers move together in the same direction and by the same distance.

Tab

Tab button, present in horizontal ruler, facilitates setting of tab positions for the Tab key of the keyboard. To set the tab positions, first click the mouse on Tab button and then click it at the desired position in the ruler. This will put a mark in the ruler and set the tab position. When you press the tab key, insertion pointer will jump to the set tab position. For example, if you set the tab positions at 3, 5 and 7 inches then pressing the Tab key once will take the mouse pointer to a place 3 inches away from left margin. When you press it again it will move 5 inches away and if you press it again, it will move it by 7 inches. To remove a tab position, drag the tab mark and drop it off the ruler.

Status Bar

A clear view of status bar is illustrated in figure Word-4. Status bar displays the status of the current document.

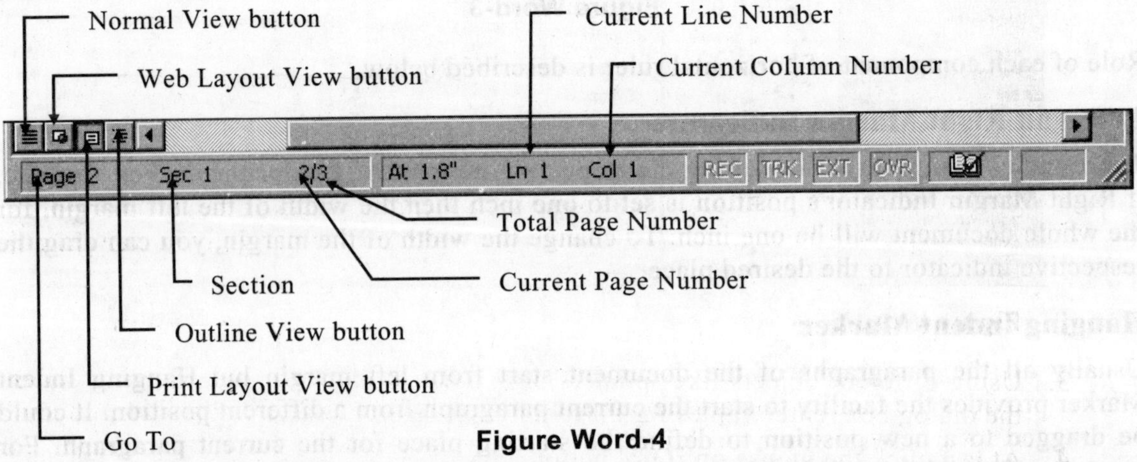

Figure Word-4

Refer figure Word-4 and note that there are four view mode buttons in Status bar. These buttons are used for switching over from one mode of display to another. To switch over to desired mode, click the mouse on corresponding button.

Information like, total number of pages in the document, current page number, current line number, current character position etc. also get displayed in the status bar.

Type Area

The blank white space, present in the Word window is called Type Area. Whatever you type gets typed in this area.

Insertion Pointer

A small blinking vertical line initially appears at the beginning of the type area. It is called Insertion Pointer. It basically indicates current position in the document. Whatever you type from the keyboard, gets entered at current insertion pointer position.

PAGE SETUP

Before typing the text, page specifications like, page size, width of the margins, header footer distance etc. need to be decided, so that typed text gets accommodated accordingly. Perform following steps to decide the page specifications:

1. Select "File" option from the bar menu. When you do so, File submenu, as shown in figure Word-5 will appear on the screen.
2. Select "Page Setup..." option from File submenu. On selecting this option, a dialog box, as shown in figure Word-6, will appear on the screen.

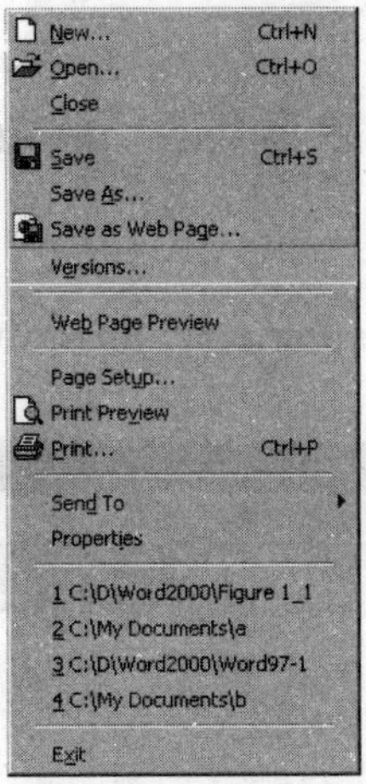

Figure Word-5

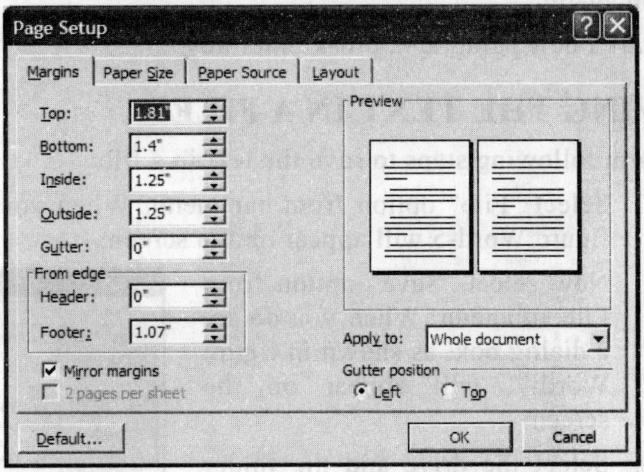

Figure Word-6

3. Using different objects like spinners, text boxes, radio buttons, tabs etc. present in the dialog box, enter values for all required settings.
4. At last click the mouse on "OK" button.

When you do so, page setup will change as per values entered above and whatever you type from the keyboard will get arranged on the page, accordingly.

ENTERING THE TEXT

When you press any key of the keyboard, character gets typed at current cursor position. Thus by pressing different keys of the keyboard, you can type the complete letter, document, or report.

While entering the text, when insertion pointer reaches the right margin, it automatically gets placed in first column of the next line. When current VDU screen becomes full of text, document automatically shifts upwards (this process is called scrolling) and blank line appears at the bottom of the screen, where you can further enter the text.

When current page becomes full, insertion pointer gets automatically placed at the beginning of the next page. Thus, continuing in this way, you can enter the text, page after page.

While entering the text, you can always make use of Del and Backspace keys to erase characters, words or sentences.

To insert the text in between two characters, words, sentences or paragraphs, click the mouse at the place where the text is to be inserted. When you do so, insertion pointer will get placed there. Now whatever you type will get typed in between and the text on the right hand side will automatically shift.

To overwrite on already entered text, first double click the mouse on OVR button of status bar and then type the text. To come out of Insert mode, double click the mouse on the same button again.

To start a new paragraph, press Enter key.

SAVING THE TEXT IN A FILE

Perform following steps to save the text in a file:

1. Select "File" option from bar menu. When you do so, File submenu, as shown in figure Word-5 will appear on the screen.
2. Now select "Save" option from File submenu. When you do so, a dialog box, as shown in figure Word-7, will appear on the screen.
3. Select the drive and the folder in which the file is to be saved.
4. Enter the name of the file in "File Name" text box.
5. Click the mouse on "Save" button.

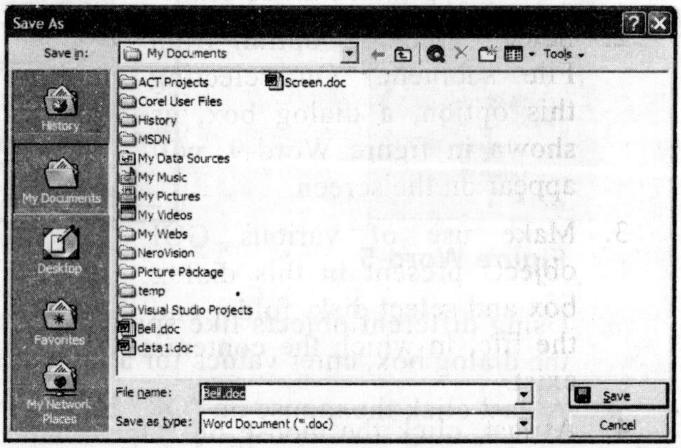

Figure Word-7

When you do so, current text will get saved on the selected disk, in specified folder and file.

CLOSING THE FILE

Perform following steps to close currently opened file:

1. Select "File" option from the bar menu. When you do so, File submenu, as shown in figure Word-5 will appear on the screen.

2. Select "Close" option from File submenu.

If no additions or modifications have been made in the document, ever since it was last saved, file will get closed. On the other hand, if they were made, an Alert box, as shown in figure Word-8, will appear on the screen.

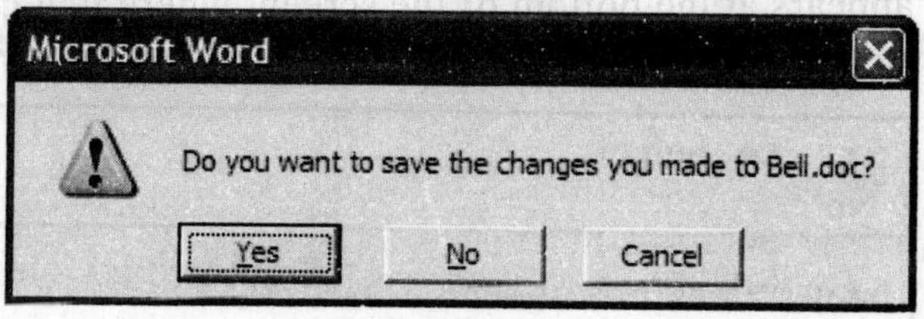

Figure Word-8

3. Click the mouse on "Yes" button if you wish to save the additions and modification on the disk. Select "No" button for not saving them. If you wish to cancel the idea of closing the file, click the mouse on "Cancel" button.

You are now familiar with the method of defining the page layout, entering the text and saving it in a file. Whatever text you save in the file, remains permanently available for use.

OPENING AN EXISTING DOCUMENT

Following are the steps for opening an existing file:

1. Select "File" option from the Bar menu. When you do so, File submenu, as shown in figure Word-5 appears on the screen.
2. Select "Open...." option from File submenu. On selecting this option, a dialog box, as shown in figure Word-9, will appear on the screen.
3. Make use of various GUI objects present in this dialog box and select disk, folder and the file, in which the contents exist.

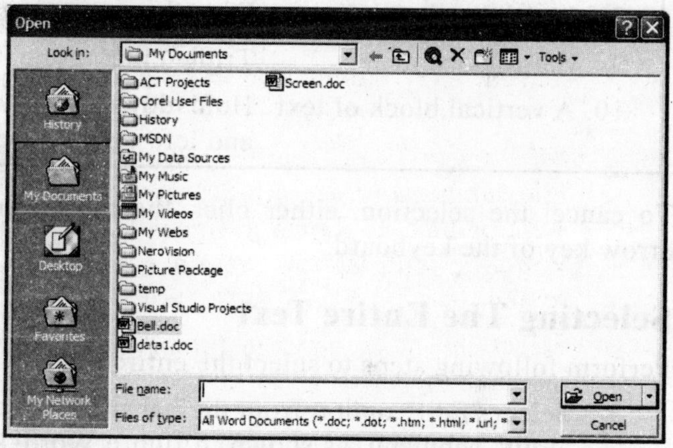

Figure Word-9

4. At last, click the mouse on "Open" button. On doing so, contents of selected file will get displayed in Word window.

EDITING OPERATIONS

After opening the file you may wish to make few modifications in it. For example, you may wish to delete few lines or you may wish to copy a part of the text from one place to another or you may wish to move few lines of paragraphs from here to there. For performing all such types of editing operations, you will have to first select the text on which you wish to perform the operation. MS-Word provides different mechanisms for selecting different portions of the text. They are explained below.

Selecting The Text

For selecting different parts of the document, perform actions, as mentioned below.

Sr. No	To Select	Action
1.	A word	Double click on the word.
2.	A portion of the text	Drag the mouse over the text that is to be selected.
3.	A graphic picture	Click the mouse on the picture.
4.	A line	Click the mouse on the left hand side of that line.
5.	Multiple lines	Drag the mouse vertically in the left margin, starting from the first line to the last line of the selection.
6.	A sentence	Hold down the CTRL key and click the mouse anywhere in between the sentence that is to be selected.
7.	A paragraph	Triple click anywhere in-between the paragraph.
8.	Multiple paragraphs	Drag the mouse pointer in the left margin.
9.	Entire document	Triple click in the left margin.
10.	A vertical block of text	Hold down ALT key and drag the mouse Up/Down and left/ right, covering the vertical block.

To cancel the selection, either click the mouse anywhere in the document or press any arrow key of the keyboard.

Selecting The Entire Text

Perform following steps to select the entire text:

1. Select "Edit" option from the bar menu. When you do so, "Edit" submenu, as shown in figure Word-10, will appear on the screen.
2. Select "Select All" option from Edit submenu.

When you do so, complete text will get selected.

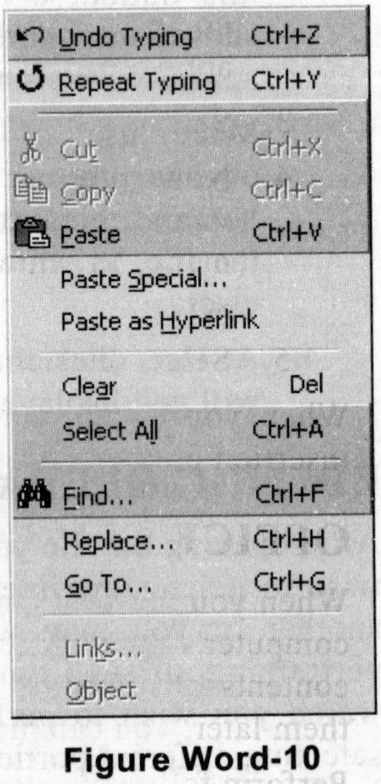

Figure Word-10

Deleting Text

Different parts of the text can be deleted differently. Various deletion operations are explained below.

1. To delete a word after the insertion pointer, press CTRL and DEL keys together.
2. To delete a word before the insertion pointer, press CTRL and Backspace keys together.

3. To delete a desired portion of text (either text or graphics), select it, using any of the methods mentioned above and then press DEL key.

Copying The Text

Perform following steps to copy a portion of text to some other place in the document:

1. Select the text you wish to copy.
2. Select "Edit" option from the bar menu. On doing so, "Edit" submenu, as illustrated in figure Word-10, will appear on the screen.
3. Select "Copy" option from this submenu.
4. Now take the insertion pointer to the place, where you wish to copy the selected text.
5. Select "Edit" option again from the bar menu and get Edit submenu, as illustrated in figure Word-10, on the screen.
6. Now select "Paste" option from this submenu.

When you do so, selected text will get copied at current insertion pointer's position.

Moving The Text

Perform following steps to move a portion of text from it's original place to some other place in the document:

1. Select the text that you wish to move to other location of the document.
2. Now right click the mouse on selected portion. When you do so, a popup menu, as shown in figure Word-11 will appear on the screen.
3. Select "Cut" option from this menu.
4. Now right click the mouse at that place of the document, where the text is to be moved. When you do so, popup menu, as shown in figure Word-11, will reappear on the screen.
5. Select "Paste" option from this menu.

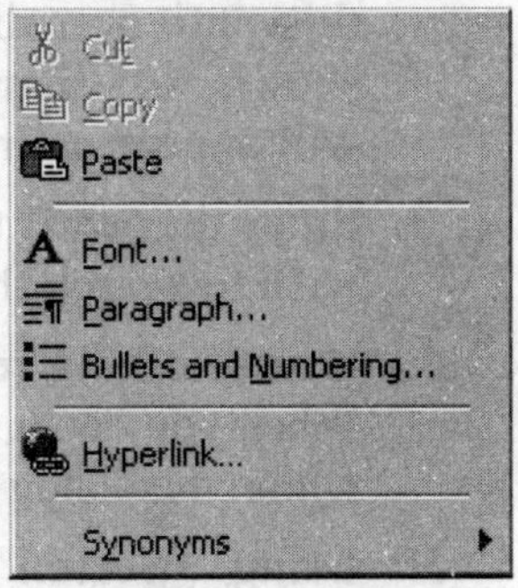

Figure Word-11

When you do so, selected text will shift its place from its original position to current insertion pointer's position.

OFFICE CLIPBOARD

When you perform cut or copy option, the selected text gets copied into specific portion of computer's memory, called Clipboard. When you perform these operations again, previous contents of clipboard get lost. If you wish to retain these contents so that you could use them later, you can make use of Office Clipboard feature of MS-Word.

Perform following steps to make Office Clipboard feature on:

1. Select "View" option from the bar menu. When you do so, View submenu, as shown in figure Word-16, will appear on the screen.
2. Select "Toolbar" option from View submenu. When you do so, another submenu will appear on the screen.
3. Select "Clipboard" option from this submenu. When you do so, a clipboard panel will get displayed. For each Cut/Copy operation that you perform, an icon for it will get made in it.
3. To paste any clipboard content at current insertion pointer's position, click the mouse on its icon, present in clipboard panel.

FINDING THE GIVEN WORD IN THE TEXT

Perform following steps to search the presence of a given word:

1. Select "Edit" option from the bar menu. When you do so, Edit submenu, as shown in figure Word-10, will appear on the screen.
2. Select "Find..." option from this submenu. On selecting this option, a dialog box, as shown in figure Word-12, will appear on monitor screen.

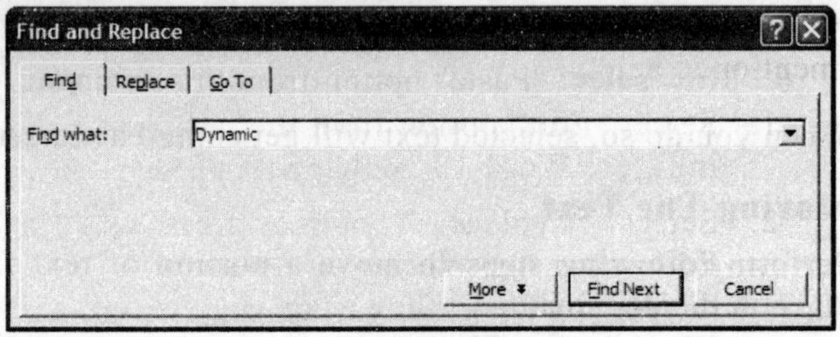

Figure Word -12

3. Enter the word that you wish to find in "Find what" text box. For example, if you wish to search the word "Dynamic", enter "Dynamic" in "Find what" text box.
4. If more details, related to search need to be specified, click the mouse on, "More" button. When you do so, more options related to search, as shown in figure Word-13 will appear within the dialog box.
5. Using "Search" drop down list, specify the direction of search as All, Down or Up.
6. If you wish that MS-Word should differentiate between upper case letters and lower case letters, check "Match Case" check box. For example, when you check this check box, MS-Word will treat Dynamic, DYNAMIC and dynamic as 3 different words.

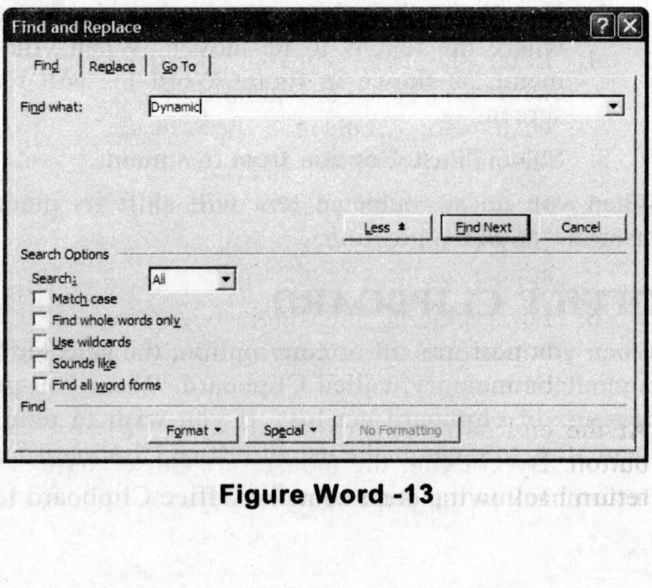

Figure Word -13

7. If complete word match is to be found, check "Find Whole Word Only" check box. In such cases partial matches will not be reported as found. For example, say you are searching the word "garden" then it will not be reported found, when MS-Word comes across, the word "gardener".
8. To perform the search according to the parameters defined above, click the mouse on "Find Next" button.

When you do so, MS-Word will search the first occurrence of the specified word and temporarily halt the search there and highlight the word in the text. Clicking the mouse on "Find Next" button again will search the next occurrence. Following this procedure, search can be continued for finding other occurrences of the same word.

REPLACING THE WORD WITH ANOTHER WORD

For finding the occurrence of a word and replacing it with another word, MS-Word provides replace facility. Replacement of a word using this facility can be done as mentioned below:

1. Select "Edit" option from the bar menu. When you do so, Edit submenu, as shown in figure Word-10, will appear on the screen.
2. Select "Replace..." option from Edit submenu. When you do so, a dialog box, as shown in figure Word-14, will appear on the screen.
3. Enter the word that is to be replaced, in "Find What" text box. For example, if the word "Dynamic" is to be replaced with other word, enter "Dynamic" in the text box.
4. Enter the new word in "Replace with" text box. For example, if you wish to replace the word "Dynamic" with the word "Energetic", enter "Energetic" in "Replace with" text box.

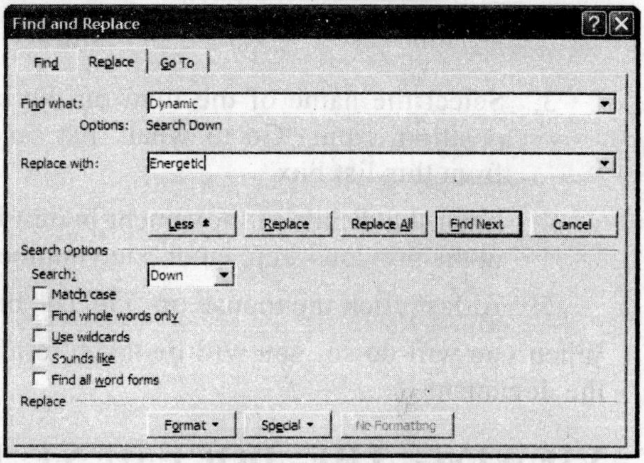

Figure Word -14

5. If you wish to specify more details related to replacement, click the mouse on "More" button. When you do so, other options, as shown in figure Word-14, will appear on the screen.
6. For replacing the single occurrence of the word, click the mouse on "Replace" button and for changing all the occurrences in one-go, click it on "Replace All" button.

At the end of replacement operation, "Cancel" button automatically changes to "Close" button. By clicking the mouse on "Close" button, you can close the search operation and return back to the document.

GOING TO A SPECIFIC LOCATION

Perform following steps to go to a specific location of the document. This location could either be a given page number, line or table etc.

1. Select "Edit" option from the bar menu. When you do so, Edit submenu, as shown in figure Word-10, will appear on the screen.
2. Select "Go To..." option from this submenu. On selecting this option, a dialog box, as shown in figure Word-15, will appear on monitor screen.

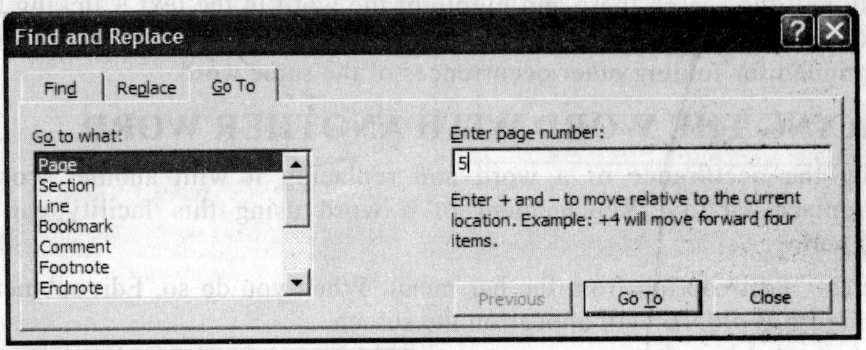

Figure Word-15

3. Select the name of the item on the basis of which you would like to change your position, from "Go to what" list box. For example, say you select "Page" option from this list box.
4. Enter the details of movement in edit box. For example, if you selected "Page" option in the previous step, enter page number, to which you wish to go, in the text box.
5. At last click the mouse on "Go To" button.

When you will do so, you will be taken to aforementioned place of the document.

VIEWING THE DOCUMENT IN DIFFERENT WAYS

The document that you have typed in MS-Word can be viewed in different ways. Perform following steps to display it in some other fashion:

1. Select "View" option from the bar menu. When you do so, View submenu, as shown in figure Word-16 will appear on monitor screen.
2. Select either "Web Layout" or "Print Layout" or "Outline" or "Full Screen" option from view submenu.

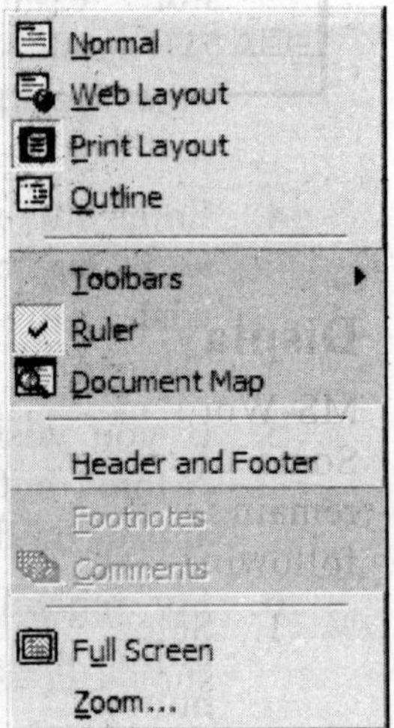

Figure Word -16

When you do so, current document will get displayed accordingly. Which option will display the document in which fashion, is shown in figure Word-17

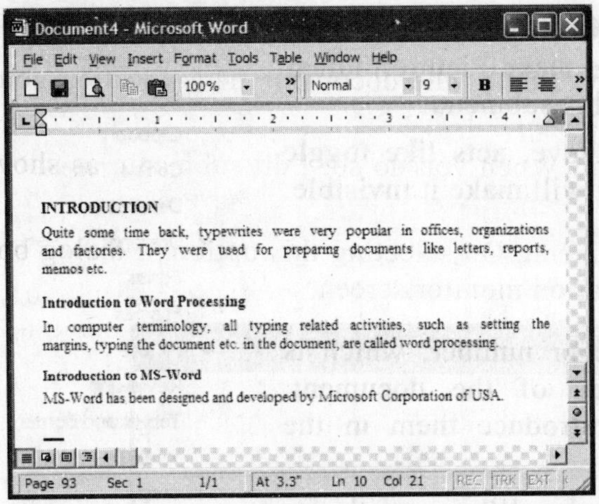

Normal View

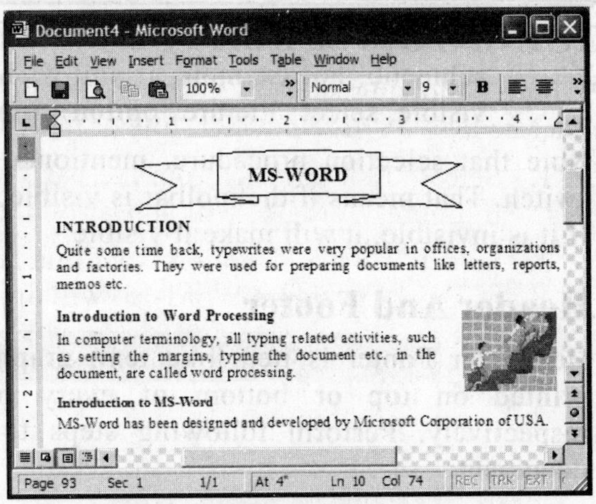

Web Layout View

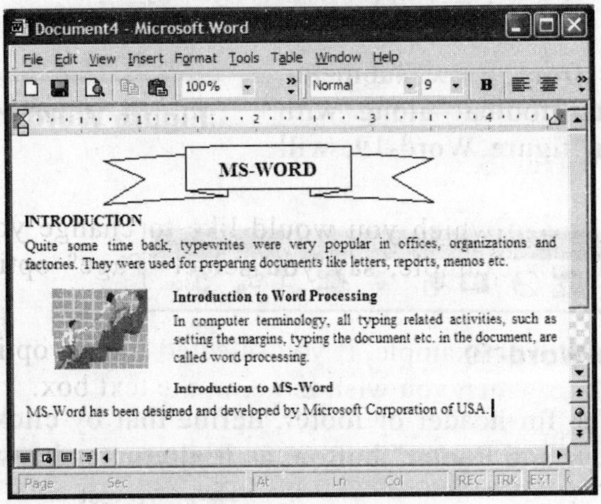

Print Layout View

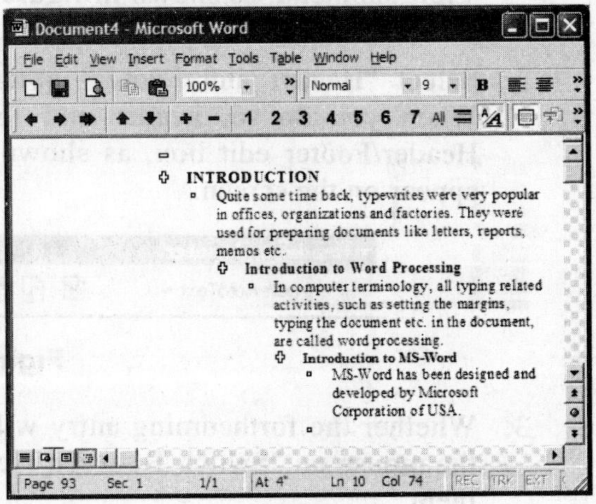

Outline View

Figure Word-17

Displaying Toolbars

MS-Word offers many classified toolbars for performing different class of operations. Some of the toolbars, by default, remain visible within MS-Word window, while others remain invisible. Any toolbar can be made visible or invisible on the screen by performing following steps:

1. Select "View" option from the bar menu. When you do so, View submenu, as shown in figure Word-16 will appear on the screen.

2. Select "Toolbars" option from View submenu. When you do so, another submenu, as shown in figure Word-18 will appear on monitor screen.

3. To make a toolbar visible, select its name from this submenu. For example, if you wish to make Picture toolbar visible, select "Picture" option from this submenu.

Note that selection procedure, mentioned above, acts like toggle switch. That means if the toolbar is visible, it will make it invisible. If it is invisible, it will make it visible.

Header And Footer

Header or Footer is item like text, graphic or number, which is printed on top or bottom of every page of the document, respectively. Perform following steps to introduce them in the document:

1. Select "View" option from the Bar menu. When you do so, View submenu, as shown in figure Word-16, will appear on the screen.
2. Select "Header and Footer" option from View submenu. When you do so, header and footer toolbar along with Header/Footer edit box, as shown in figure Word-19, will appear on the screen.

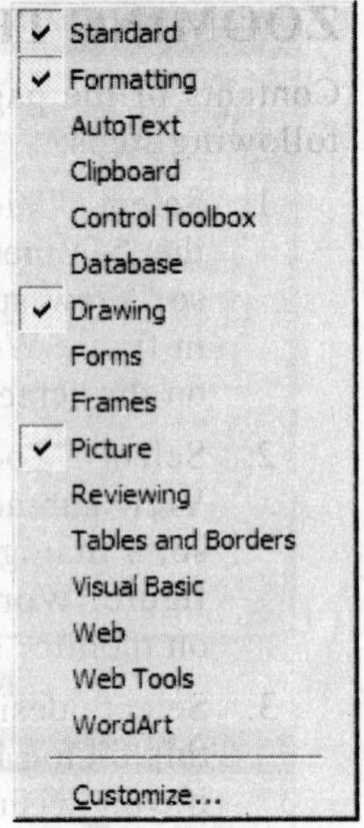

Figure Word -18

Figure Word-19

3. Whether the forthcoming entry will be for header or footer, define that by clicking the mouse on "Switch Between Header and Footer" button, as it alternates between them.
4. Enter header/footer text in the respective area.
5. If you wish to include current date or time as header or footer, click the mouse on respective buttons present in "Header and Footer" toolbar.
6. To include the page number, take the insertion pointer to that place, where you wish the page numbers to appear and then click the mouse on "Page Number" button, present in "Header and Footer" toolbar.
7. Generally the page numbers start from 1 and are numbered as 1, 2, 3 etc. In case you want them to start from some other number or want them to appear in different format, such as (a, b, c etc.), click the mouse on "Format Page Number" button. When you do so, another dialog box will appear on the screen. Define all the options of your choice through that dialog box.
8. At last click the mouse on "Close" button.

When you do so, defined header, footer page numbers etc. will be visible in the pages.

ZOOMING THE DOCUMENT

Contents of the page can be magnified or squeezed as per requirement by performing the following steps:

1. Select "View" option from the bar menu. When you do so, View submenu, as shown in figure Word-16 will appear on the screen.
2. Select "Zoom" option from View submenu. When you do so, a dialog box, as shown in figure Word-20 will appear on monitor screen.
3. Select desired option from this dialog box. For example, if you wish to 2 times zoom the document, select "200%" option. If you wish to display multiple pages in the same space, select "Many pages" option.

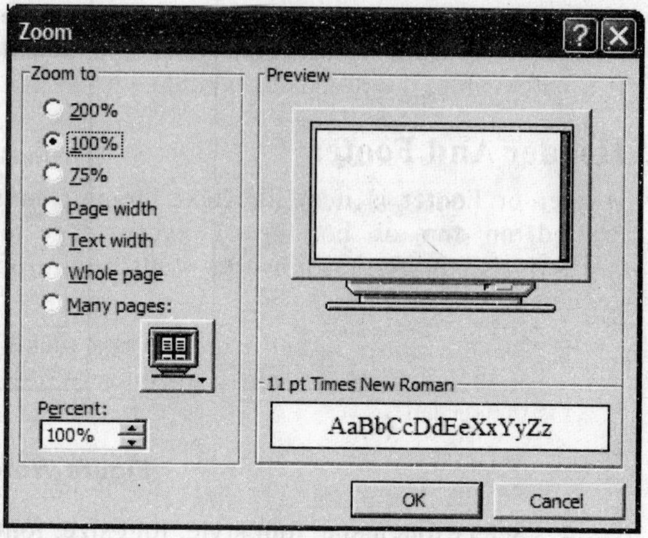

Figure Word -20

When you do so, display will change accordingly.

FORMATTING THE DOCUMENT

Formatting the document means arranging the contents of the document (such as text, graphics etc.), in such a way that the document looks attractive. For example, changing the font, font size, line spacing, paragraph spacing etc. are the activities, which fall into the category of formatting. How formatting operations are done in MS-Word, is explained below.

Changing The Font, Font Style, Font Size Etc.

Perform following steps to change font, font style, font size etc. either for the whole document or selected part of the text:

1. Select the text, for which font related changes are to be done.
2. Select "Format" option from the Bar menu. When you do so, "Format" submenu, as shown in figure Word-21(a) will appears on the screen.
3. Select "Font" option from Format submenu. When you do so, a dialog box, as shown in figure Word-21 (b) will appear on the screen.

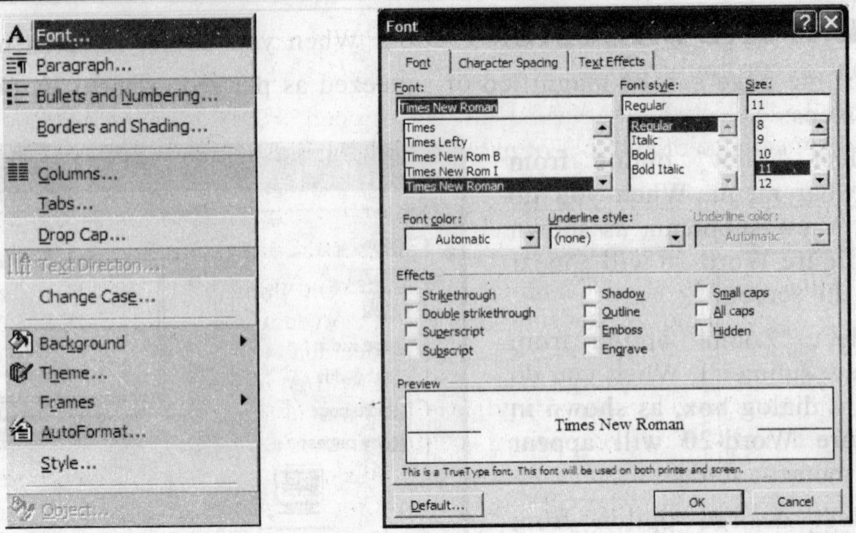

(a) (b)

Figure Word-21

4. Select font name, font style, font size, font color etc. from the respective list boxes.
5. If the selected text is to be made bold, italic, underlined etc. select respective options.
6. At last, click the mouse on "Ok" button.

When you do so, font related changes will get done in selected text.

Aligning The Paragraph

Perform following steps to align a paragraph:

1. Select the paragraph, which is to be aligned.
2. Select "Format" option from the bar menu. When you do so, "Format" submenu, as shown in figure Word-21(a) will appear on the screen.
3. Select "Paragraph" option from Format submenu. When you do so, a dialog box, as shown in figure Word-22, will appear on the screen.
4. Using "Alignment" drop down list, of this dialog box, select the type of alignment that you wish to apply to the paragraph. For example, if you wish to right aligned the paragraph, select "Right" option from Alignment drop down list.

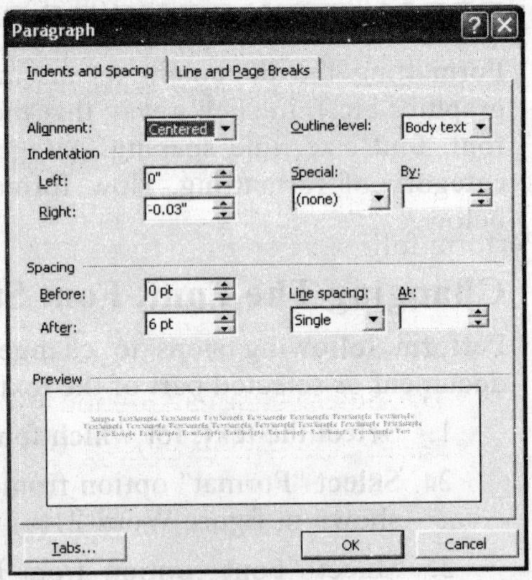

Figure Word -22

5. At last click the mouse on "OK" button. When you do so, selected text will get aligned accordingly.

When you do so, selected paragraph will get aligned as per options chosen, during the process. Visual appearance of all types of paragraph alignments is shown in figure Word-23.

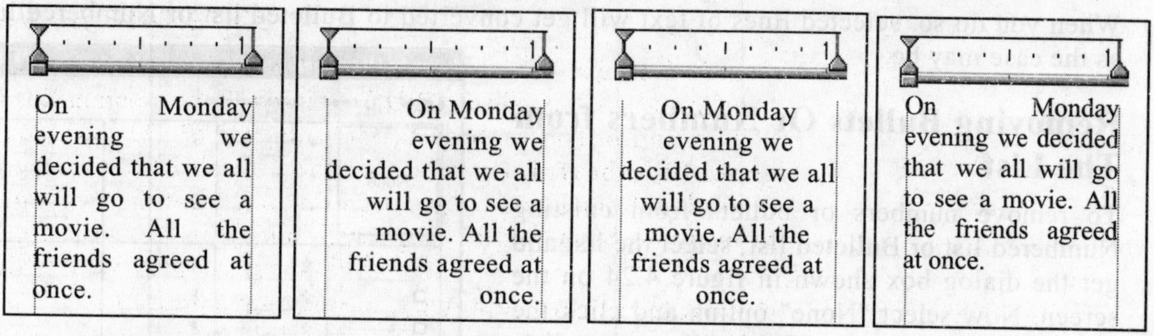

Left Aligned (a) | Right Aligned (b) | Center Aligned (c) | Justified (d)

Figure Word-23

Bullets And Numbering

In MS-Word, text can also be formatted in the form of lists. Number list and Bulleted lists, shown below are examples of such lists:

- Hardware
- Software
- Firmware
- Users

Bulleted List

1. Hardware
2. Software
3. Firmware
4. Users

Numbered List

Perform following steps to format the text in the form of list:

1. Enter each item of the list in separate line.
2. Select all the items, by dragging the mouse over them.
3. Select "Format" option from the bar menu. When you do so, Format submenu, as shown in figure Word-21(a), will appear on the screen.
4. Select "Bullets and Numbering" option from this submenu. When you do so, a dialog box, as shown in figure Word-24 will appear on the screen.
5. If you wish to format the text as Bulleted list, click the mouse on "Bulleted" tab. If you wish to format it as "Numbered" list, click the mouse "Numbered" tab. When you do so, various options for specifying other details of the list will appear within the dialog box. Select the desired option.

6. If you wish to put graphic bullets in the list, click the mouse on "Picture" button. When you do so, many graphic bullets will appear in the dialog box. Select the desired bullet and click the mouse on "OK" button.
7. At last, click the mouse on "OK" button.

When you do so, selected lines of text will get converted to Bulleted list or Numbered list, as the case may be.

Removing Bullets Or Numbers from The List

To remove numbers or bullets from existing Numbered list or Bulleted list, select the list and get the dialog box shown in figure 4.24 on the screen. Now select "None" option and click the mouse on "OK" button. This will convert lists into plain text.

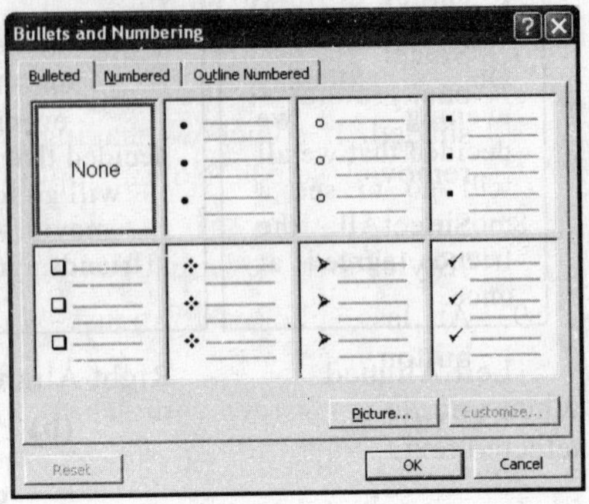

Figure Word - 24

Introducing Borders And Shading

Perform following steps to introduce borders around the selected text and shading in it:

1. Select the text, around which the border is to be introduced.
2. Select "Format" option from the bar menu. When you do so, Format submenu, as shown in figure Word-21(a), will appear on the screen.
3. Select "Borders and Shading..." option from Format submenu. When you do so, a dialog box as shown in figure Word-25, will appear on the screen. Somehow, if the options being displayed within the dialog box are different, click the mouse on "Borders" tab.
4. Select the border type, mentioned under "Setting" section of this dialog box. Somehow, if the border is to be removed, select "None" option.

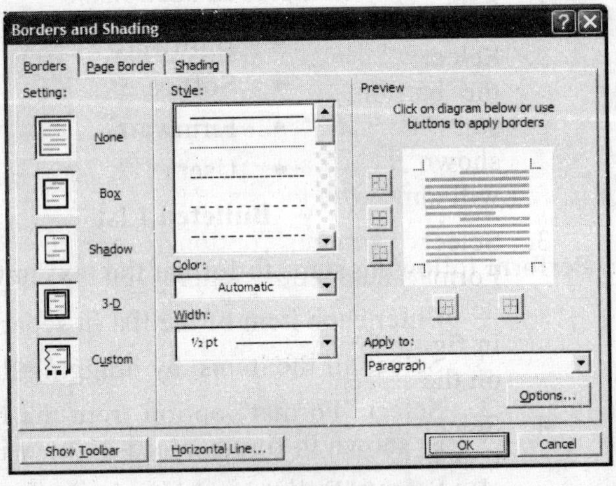

Figure Word - 25

5. Select the style, color and width or the line, using which the border is to be made, through "Style", "Color" and "Width" drop down list boxes respectively.

Introducing Shading

6. Click the mouse on "Shading" tab. When you do so, options shown within the dialog box will change as shown in figure Word-26.
7. Select the color, using which the background of the border is to be shaded. If somehow shading is to be removed, select "No Fill" option.
8. Select pattern of the color, using "Style" drop down list box.
9. At last, click the mouse on "Ok" button.

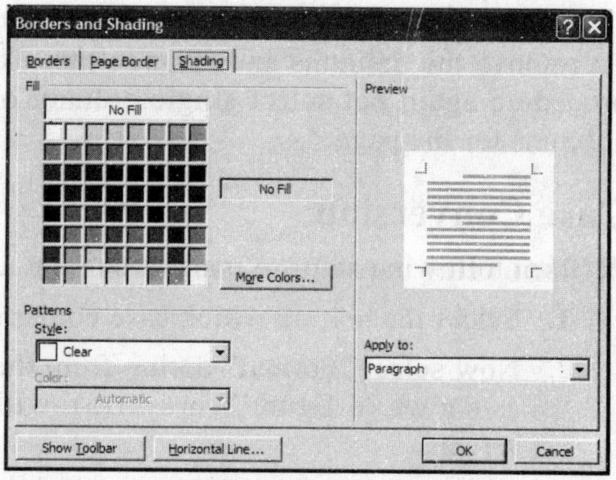

Figure Word - 26

When you do so, border with selected colored background, will get introduced around the selected text.

Columns

Instead of text running in straight lines from left margin to right margin, it can be arranged in columns, as is done in newspapers and magazines. Perform following steps to arrange the text in multiple columns:

1. Select the text that is to be arranged in columns.
2. Select "Format" option from the bar menu. When you do so, "Format" submenu, as shown in figure Word-21(a) will appear on the screen.
3. Select "Columns" option from Format submenu. When you do so, a dialog box, as shown in figure Word-27, will appear on the screen.
4. Select the number of columns that have to appear across the width of the page by clicking the mouse on desired option present in "Preset" section of this dialog box.

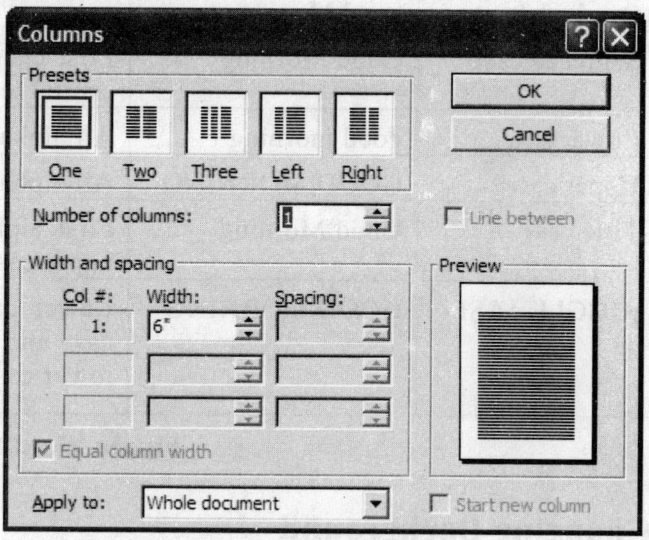

Figure Word - 27

5. Select the width of the column and spacing between the columns, using respective spinners present in this dialog box.

6. At last, click the mouse "Ok" button. When you do so, text will get arranged in columns.

To remove the columns and arrange the text in normal fashion, perform above mentioned procedure again but select single column option this time, while selecting the number of columns for the page.

Case Conversion

Perform following steps to make case related conversions in the typed text:

1. Select the text, in which case conversion is to be done.
2. Now select "Format" option from the Bar menu. When you do so, Format submenu, as shown in figure Word-21(a), will appear on the screen.
3. Select " Change Case..." option from Format submenu. When you do so, a dialog box, as shown in figure Word-28 will appear on the screen.
4. Select the desired option from this dialog box and click the mouse on "OK" button.

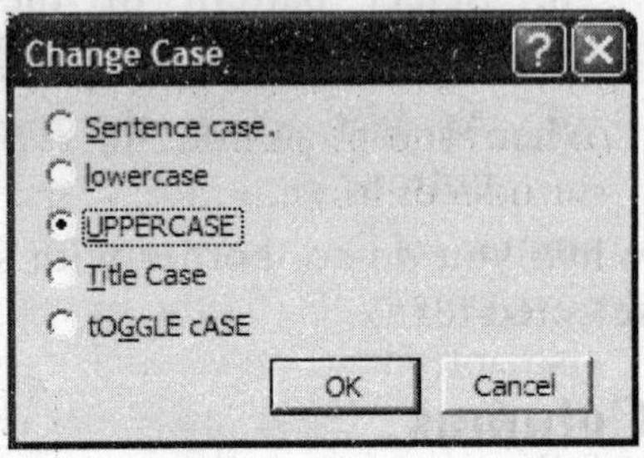

Figure Word - 28

When you do so, case of the selected text will change accordingly. The effect of each type of case conversion is shown in figure Word-29.

Option	Example	Remark
Original Text	good Morning	
Sentence case	Good Morning	First character of sentence gets converted into capital letter.
Lower case	good morning	All alphabets get converted to lower case.
Upper case	GOOD MORNING	All alphabets get converted to upper case.
Title case	Good Morning	First alphabet of each word gets converted to upper case.
tOGGLE cASE	GOOD mORNING	Lower case alphabets get converted to upper case and upper case alphabets get converted to lower case

Figure Word-29

Changing Background

The text that you type is generally written on white background. If you wish, you can change the white background to colored background, by performing following steps:

1. Select "Format" option from the bar menu. When you do so, "Format" submenu, as shown in figure Word-21(a) will appear on the screen.
2. Select "Background" option from Format submenu. When you do so, a color swatch, as shown in figure Word-30, will appear on the screen.
3. Select the color from this swatch by clicking the mouse on desired color.

When you do so, the background for the whole document will change.

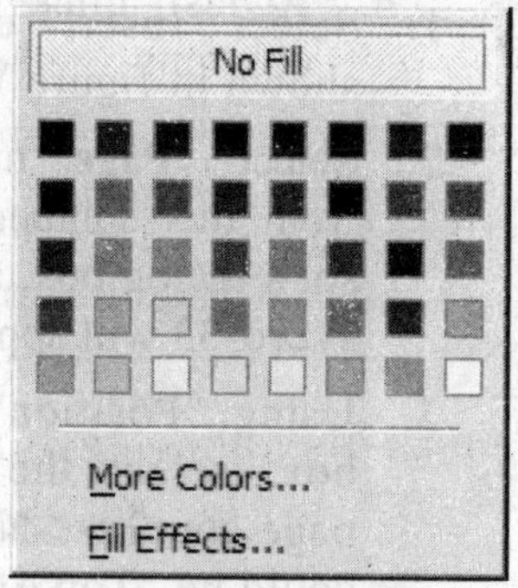

Figure Word -30

Page Breaks

When you enter the text in MS-Word and the current page becomes full, it automatically introduces a page break, called soft page break. It takes the mouse pointer to the beginning of the next page, so that whatever you type now, gets typed on the next page. Apart from soft page breaks, you can also introduce additional page breaks, at any desired location of the document. These page breaks are called hard page breaks. Perform following steps to introduce a hard page break, at desired location:

1. Position the insertion pointer, at the place, where you wish to introduce the page break.
2. Select "Insert" option from the Bar menu. When you do so, Insert submenu, as illustrated in figure Word-31, will appear on the screen.
3. Select "Break..." option from Insert submenu. On selecting this option, a dialog box, as shown in figure Word-32, will appear on monitor screen.
4. Select "Page Break" option from this dialog box.
5. At last, click the mouse on "OK" button.

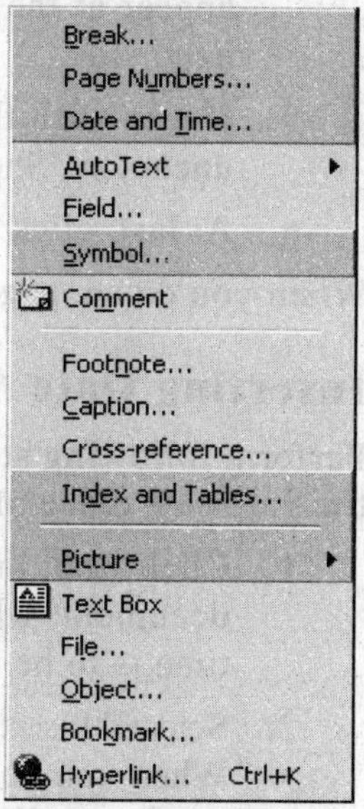

Figure Word -31

When you do so, this Page break will appear like dotted line, in the Normal view mode.

All types of page breaks appear as thick line in Print Layout View mode.

To remove hard page break, select the page break in Normal view mode by clicking the mouse on it and then press Backspace or Del key.

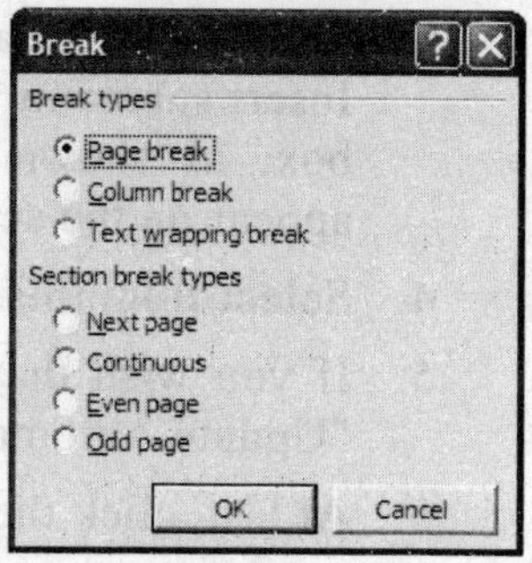

Figure Word -32

Inserting Page Numbers

Each page of the document can bear a unique number. Perform following steps to introduce page numbers in the document:

1. Select "Insert" option from the Bar menu. When you do so, Insert submenu, as shown in figure Word-31, will appear on the screen.
2. Select "Page numbers..." option from this submenu. When you do so, a dialog box, as shown in figure Word-33 will appear on the screen.

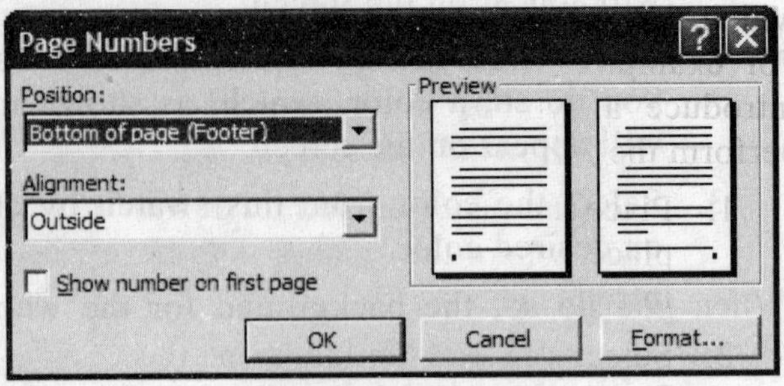

Figure Word -33

3. Using "Position" drop down list box, select the position of the page number. Note that either it could be "Top of page" or it could be "Bottom of Page".
4. Using "Alignment" drop down list, select the alignment of the page number. Note that page number could either appear at the center of the page or on the left hand side of the page or on the right hand side.
5. If you wish that page number should not appear on the first page of the document, uncheck "Show number on first page" check box.
6. At last, click the mouse on "OK" button.

When you do so, page numbers will appear accordingly, in the document.

Inserting Date And Time

Perform following steps to insert system date and time at some place of the document:

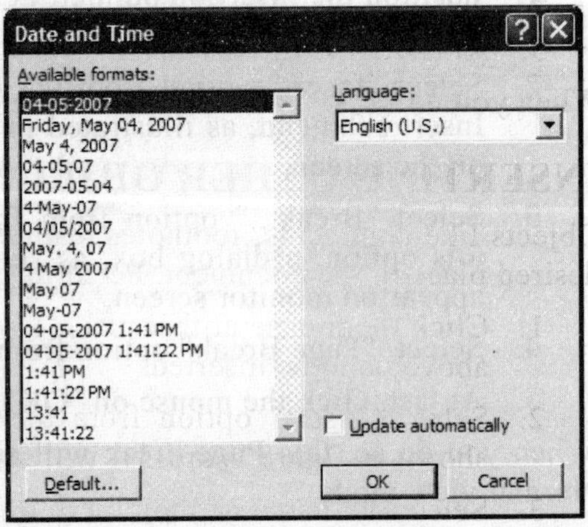

Figure Word -34

1. Click the mouse at that place of the document, where current system date and time is to be inserted.
2. Select "Insert" option from the Bar menu. When you do so, Insert submenu, as shown in figure Word-31, will appear on the screen.
3. Select "Date and Time" option from Insert submenu. When you do so, a dialog box, as shown in figure Word-34 will appear on the screen.
4. Select from this dialog box, the format, in which date and time are to be inserted.
5. If you wish that current date and time should keep on changing with time, check "Update Automatically" check box.
6. At last, click the mouse on "Ok" button.

When you do so, current system date and time will get inserted at current cursor position.

INSERTING SYMBOLS IN THE TEXT

MS-Word provides the facility to introduce even those characters in the document for which there is no corresponding key on the keyboard. Such characters are called symbols. For example, Trade Mark (™), Copyright (©) mark etc. are examples of symbols. To introduce a symbol in the document, perform the following steps:

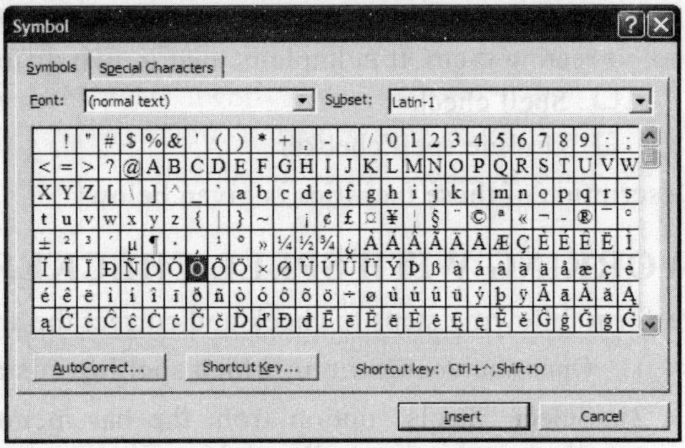

Figure Word -35

1. Place the insertion pointer at the place, where the symbol is to be introduced.
2. Select "Insert" option from the Bar menu. When you do so, Insert submenu, as shown in figure Word-31 will appear on the screen.
3. Select "Symbol..." option from Insert submenu. When you do so, a dialog box, as shown in figure Word-35, will appear on the screen
4. Select the symbol of your choice by clicking the mouse on the symbol.
5. At last, click the mouse on "Insert" button.

When you do so, symbol will get introduced at current insertion pointer position.

INSERTING OTHER OBJECTS IN THE DOCUMENT

Objects like comments, footnotes, captions, pictures, text boxes etc. can be inserted at any desired place in the document. Perform following steps to introduce them:

1. Click the mouse at that place of the document, where any of the objects, mentioned above, is to be inserted.
2. Select "Insert" option from the bar menu. When you do so, Insert submenu, as shown in figure Word-31, will appear on the screen.
3. Select the name of the object from Insert submenu. When you do so, a dialog box, for getting other details of the object from you, will appear on the screen.
4. Provide those details.
5. At last, click the mouse on "Ok" button.

When you do so, the object will get inserted at current cursor position.

SPELLING AND GRAMMAR CORRECTION

It is likely that while typing the document, few spelling or grammar mistakes may go unnoticed into the document. It is always desirable to correct all the mistakes before the document is finalized. One method of finding the spelling and grammar mistakes is the manual method, in which the whole document is read again. Obviously this method doesn't guarantee 100% correctness. It is possible that the person reading the document may overlook some of the mistakes or he himself many not know the correct spelling. Thus mistakes may still persist in the document. To overcome this problem and ensure 100% correctness, MS-Word has automated the process of finding spelling and grammar mistakes and correcting them. It is implemented in two different forms:

- ❑ Spell checker
- ❑ On-line spell checker

Description of these facilities is given below:

WORKING WITH SPELL CHECKER

Perform following steps to check and correct the spelling mistakes in the document:

1. Open the document, in which spelling mistakes have to be found and corrected.
2. Select "Tools" option from the bar menu. When you do so, Tools submenu, as illustrated in figure Word-36, will appear on the screen.
3. Select "Spelling and Grammar" option from Tool submenu. On selecting this option, a dialog box, as shown in figure Word-37, will appear on the screen.

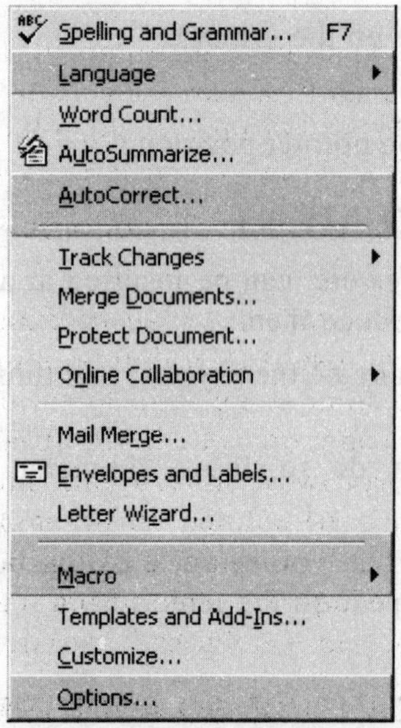

Figure Word-36

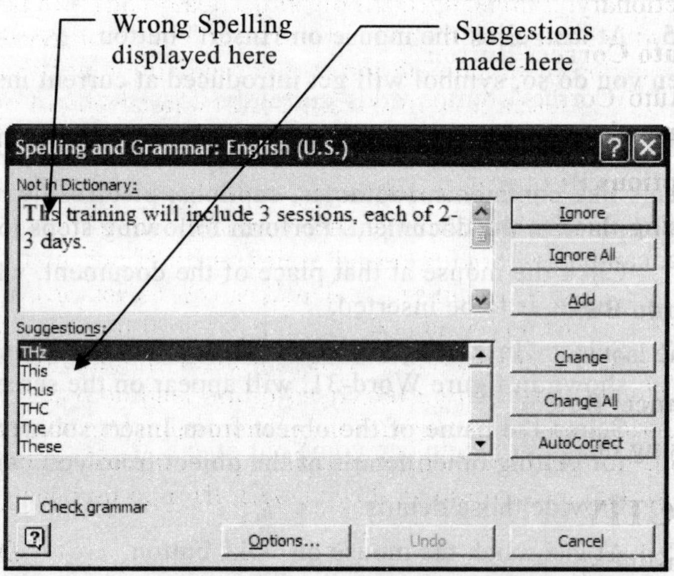

Figure Word-37

Note that there are many buttons in this dialog box. Explanation of these buttons is given below.

Ignore & Ignore All Buttons

While performing spelling check, few words like colour, Rakesh, centre etc. may be reported as spelling mistakes. To retain such type of errors, you need to make use of "Ignore" button.

Ignore button ignores current word only. If the same spelling appears again, it is again reported as error. But instead of making use of "Ignore" button, if you select "Ignore All" button, all the reappearances will be automatically ignored.

Change And Change All Buttons

A list of correct spellings, for currently misspelled word gets displayed in "Suggestions" list box. If you wish, you can either choose a suggestion from that list or you can reenter the word. Be it any case, to incorporate the change, you need to click the mouse on "Change" button. Note that this replacement occurs only for currently misspelled word. If same spelling mistake appears again, above mentioned procedure has to be repeated. On the other hand, if same replacement is to be done throughout the document, you need to make use of "Change All" button.

Add Button

Any word, which is correct and (and is being reported as spelling mistake) is not present in the dictionary, can be added to the dictionary by selecting "Add" button. The word can either be added to the main dictionary, named, CUSTOM.DIC or any other personal dictionary.

Auto Correct Button

"Auto Correct" button adds currently done correction in "Auto Correct" list so that next time when you enter the wrong spelling, it gets automatically corrected.

Options Button

Using this button, various parameters like the choice of dictionary, capitalization of words etc. can be set for checking the spellings.

Undo Button

The last spelling correction made, can be undone by selecting "Undo" button.

Cancel Button

Using this button, you can come out of spell checker.

ACTIVATING ON-LINE SPELL CHECKER

On-line spell checker is a facility, using which the spelling of a word is checked as soon as it is typed. If the spelling is found incorrect the word is underlined with red zigzag line. If you wish, it could also suggest correct spellings for this word. Note that On-line spell checker marks incorrect spellings, only when it is made on. To switch it on, follow the following steps:

1. Select "Tools" option from the Bar menu. When you do so, Tools submenu gets displayed on the screen.
2. Select "Options" option from this submenu. When you do so, a dialog box, as illustrated in figure Word-38, will appears on the screen.
3. Check "Check Spellings as you type" check box.
4. Now select "OK" button.

When you do so, On-line spell checker gets activated. Now, whenever you type a misspelled word, red colored zigzag line automatically underlines it.

To correct the spelling, right click the mouse on wrong spelling. When you do so, a popup menu containing the list of suggestions, appears on the screen. Correct spelling can be chosen from this list by clicking the mouse on appropriate suggestion.

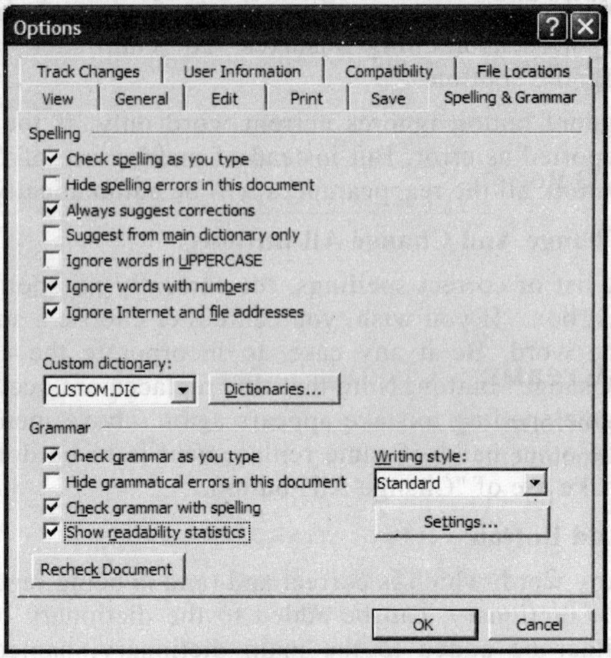

Figure Word -38

WORD COUNT

Word Count is a facility of MS-Word, which displays count statistics of the document. Perform following steps to know, how many pages, lines, paragraphs, characters etc. are there in the document:

1. Select "Tools" option from the bar menu. When you do so, Tools submenu, as shown in figure Word-36, will appear on the screen.
2. Select "Word Count" option from Tools submenu. When you do so, a dialog box, as shown in figure Word-39, will appear on monitor screen. This dialog box will have all necessary count statistics in it.
3. After viewing the statistics, click the mouse on "Close" button.

When you do so, dialog box will get closed.

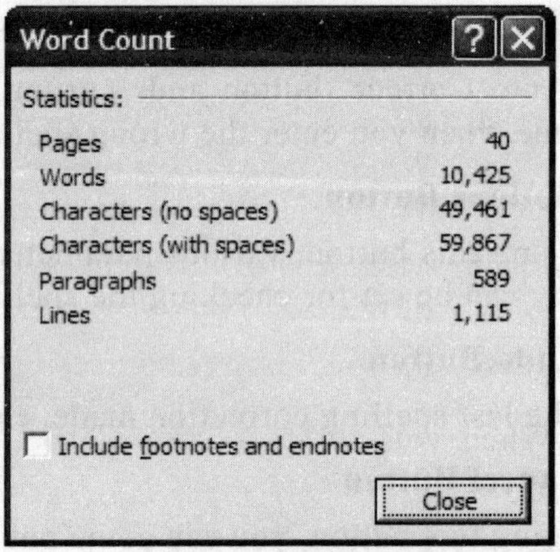

Figure Word -39

INTRODUCTION TO TABLE

Tables are the best means for illustrating classified data. They consist of rows and columns.

A blank table is shown in figure Word-40. The unit space formed by the intersection of rows and column is called cell. Thus a table consisting of 3 rows and 4 columns will have 12 cells in it. MS-Word provides facility for creating tables and entering data in them. The method of creating the table and entering data is given below:

4 columns

3 Rows

Figure Word-40

Creating A Blank Table

Perform following steps to create a blank table in the document:

1. Place the insertion pointer at the place, where the table is to be created.
2. Select "Table" option from the bar menu. When you do so, "Table" submenu, as shown in figure Word-41(a), will appear on the screen.
3. Select "Insert" option from Table submenu. On selecting this option, another submenu, as shown in figure Word-41(b), will appear on the screen.
4. Now select "Table" option from this submenu. When you do so, a dialog box, as shown in figure Word-42, will appear on the screen.
5. Make use of different spinners present in the dialog box and specify the dimension of the table. Say you specify 4 column and 3 rows.
6. At last, click the mouse on "OK" button.

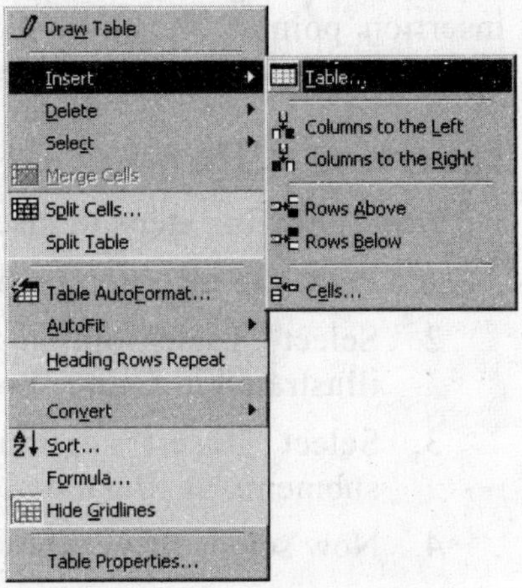

(a) (b)

Figure Word -41

When you do so, a blank table structure, as shown in figure Word-40, will get created.

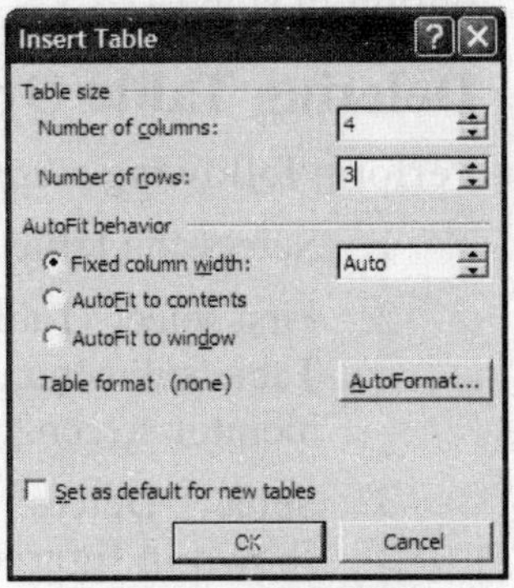

Figure Word -42

Drawing The Table

Instead of making a table by adopting the procedure mentioned above, you can directly draw a table using "Draw Table" option of Table submenu. Perform following steps to draw a table of your choice:

1. Select "Table" option from the bar menu. When you do so, "Table" submenu, as shown in figure Word-41(a), will appear on the screen.

2. Select "Draw Table" option from Table submenu. On selecting this option, Table and Border toolbar, as shown in figure Word-43 will appear on the screen.
3. Make use of different tools of this toolbar and draw the table of your choice.

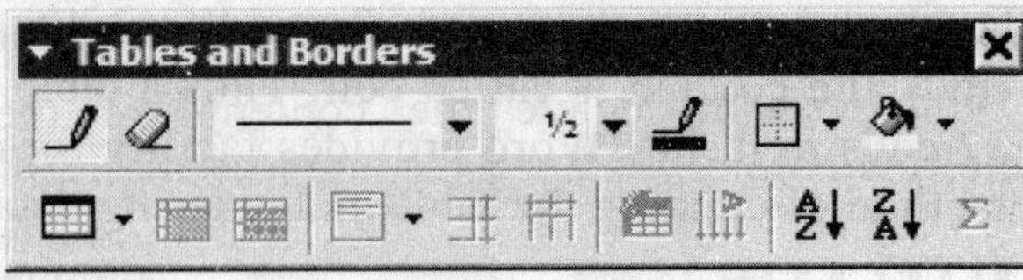

Figure Word -43

Entering Data In Table

To type the data in the table, click the mouse in desired cell and start typing the data from keyboard. Using arrow keys, you can move within the cell. Pressing Tab key moves insertion pointer ahead by 1 cell, while Shift and Tab keys pressed together take the insertion pointer back by one cell.

Inserting A Row

Perform following steps to insert a row in an already existing table:

1. Place the insertion pointer in the row, above which you wish to insert a new row.
2. Select "Table" option from the Bar menu. When you do so, a Table submenu, as illustrated in figure Word-41(a), will appear on the screen.
3. Select "Insert" option from this submenu. On selecting this option, another submenu, as illustrated in figure Word-41(b), will appear on the screen.
4. Now select "Row Above" option from this submenu.

When you do so, a blank row, above the insertion pointer, will get created in the table.

Inserting A Column

To insert a column in an already existing table, place the insertion pointer in the column, left to which, a new column is to be inserted. After this, perform all the steps mentioned in "Inserting a row" section but select "Column to the Left" option instead of "Row above" option in step (4).

Deleting Table Or Row Or Column

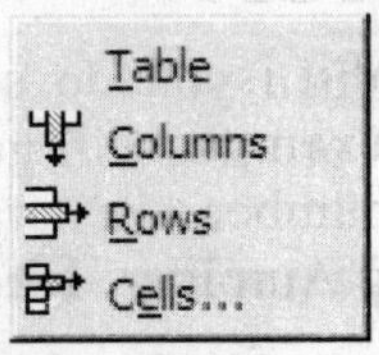

Figure Word - 44

Perform following steps to delete the table, row(s) /column(s):

1. Select the table or row or column that is to be deleted.
2. First select "Table" option from the bar menu. When you do so, Table submenu, as shown in figure Word-41(a) will appear on monitor screen.
3. Select "Delete" option from Table submenu. When you do so, another submenu, as shown in figure, 4.44, will appear on monitor screen.
4. Select "Table", "Rows" or "Columns" option from this submenu.

When you do so, the selected table, row or column will get deleted.

If you wish to delete the contents of the table/rows/columns and not the entire table/row/column, select the contents and press Del key.

AUTO FORMAT

Auto Format is a facility of MS-Word that provides many predefined table formats. Each table format suggests a different style and color scheme for the table. This style can be applied to any existing table. Perform following steps to make use of this facility:

1. Create a table, using above mentioned procedure and select it.
2. Select "Table" option from the bar menu. When you do so, Table submenu, as shown in figure Word-41(a) will appear on monitor screen.
3. Select "Table AutoFormat" option from Table submenu. When you do so, a dialog box, as shown in figure Word-45 will appear on the screen.
4. Select the desired style from "Table Style" list box. The style that you select will get displayed in Preview list box.
5. Select other desired options from this list box.
6. At last click the mouse on "Ok" button.

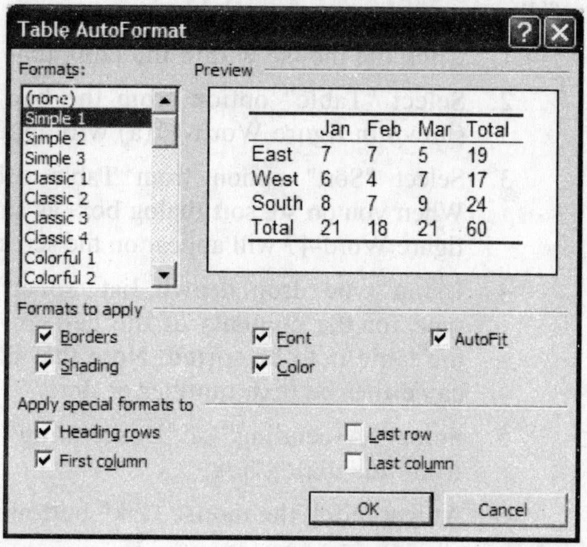

Figure Word - 45

When you do so, selected style will get applied to the table.

AUTOFIT

AutoFit is a facility of MS-Word that fits the text within the cell as per your requirement. For example, if you wish that the width of the cell should be flexible and it should vary as per number of characters entered in the cell, you can do that, using AutoFit facility.

Perform following steps to make use of this facility:

1. Click the mouse on any cell of the table, on which you wish to apply AutoFit facility.
2. Select "Table" option from the bar menu. When you do so, Table submenu, as shown in figure Word - 41(a) will appear on monitor screen.

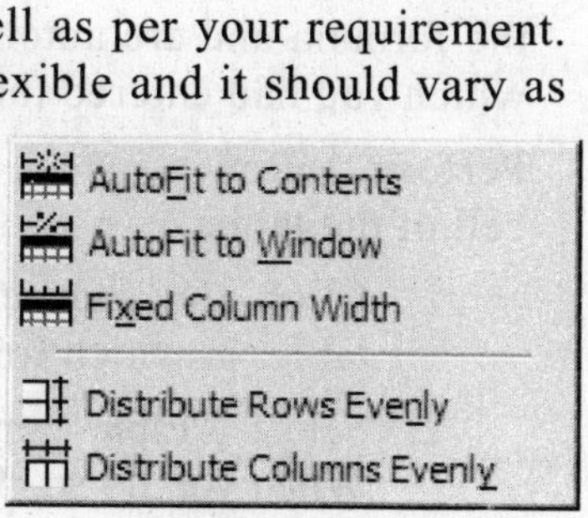

Figure Word - 46

3. Select "AutoFit" option from Table submenu. When you do so, another submenu, as shown in figure Word - 46 will appear on the screen.
4. Select desired auto fit option from this submenu.

When you do so, selected AutoFit option will get applied to the table and its effect will become visible when you enter text in the table.

SORTING THE TABLE

Table can be sorted in ascending or descending order on first column of the table. Perform following steps to sort the table:

1. Click the mouse within the table that is to be sorted.
2. Select "Table" option from the bar menu. When you do so, Table submenu, as shown in figure Word-41(a) will appear on monitor screen.
3. Select "Sort" option from Table submenu. When you do so, sort dialog box, as shown in figure Word-47 will appear on the screen.
4. Using type drop drown list, specify data type for the contents of the cell, on which the table is to be sorted. Note that contents can either be text, number or date.
5. Select "Ascending" or "Descending" option from this dialog box.
6. At last, click the mouse "Ok" button.

When you do so, table rows will get rearranged and presented in sorted order.

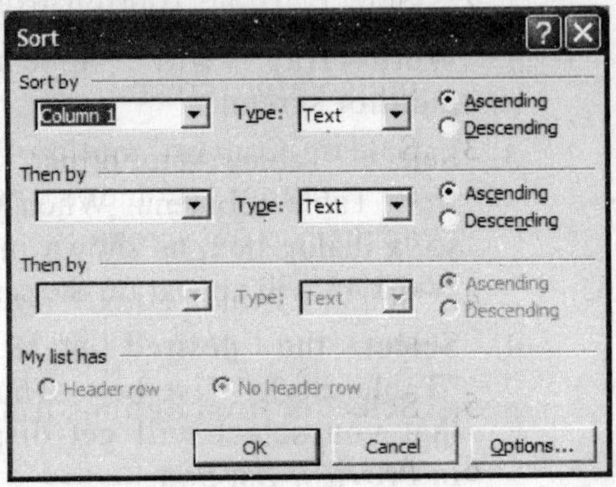

Figure Word - 47

Formula

If the need be a formula can be defined for a cell of the table. This formula can be based on the contents of other cells of the table. When you do so, values are automatically calculated based on the formula and are automatically put in the cell in which you had entered the formula.

Perform following steps to define a formula in a cell of the table:

1. Click the mouse within that cell of the table, in which formula is to be defined.
2. Select "Table" option from the bar menu. When you do so, Table submenu, as shown in figure Word-41(a) will appear on monitor screen.

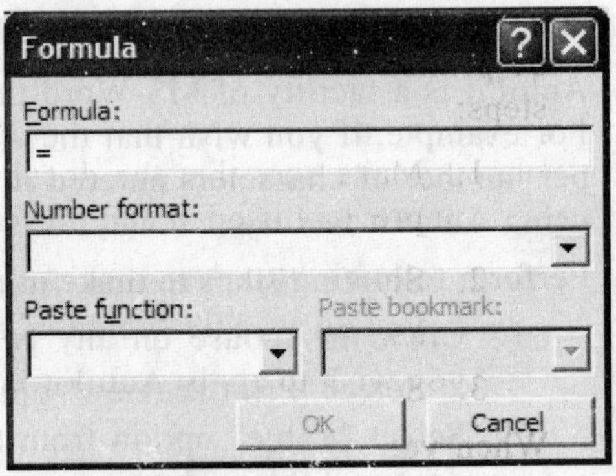

Figure Word - 48

3. Select "Formula" option from Table submenu. When you do so, Formula dialog box, as shown in figure Word-48 will appear on the screen.
4. Write the formula in Formula edit box.
5. At last, click the mouse "Ok" button.

When you do so, value will be automatically calculated and put in the cell.

CONVERTING TABLE INTO SIMPLE TEXT

Text that has been typed in the cells of the table can be converted to simple text by performing following steps:

1. Click the mouse within the table.
2. Select "Table" option from the bar menu. When you do so, Table submenu, as shown in figure Word-41(a) will appear on monitor screen.
3. Select "Convert" option from Table submenu. When you do so, another submenu, as shown in figure Word-49 will appear on the screen.

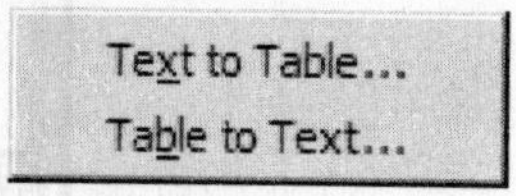

Figure Word -49

4. Select "Table to text" option from this submenu. When you do so, a dialog box, as shown in figure, Word-50 will appear on the screen.
5. Select desired options from this dialog box.
6. At last, click the mouse "Ok" button.

When you do so, text within the table cells will get converted to simple text, as per choices made during conversion.

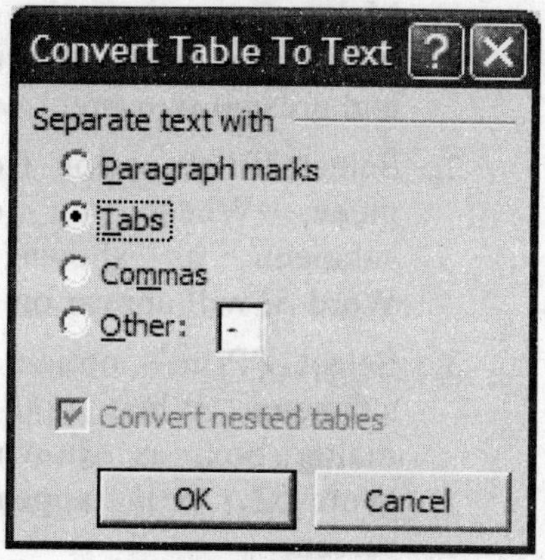

Figure Word -50

PRINT PREVIEW

You may wish to view the document, in the form it will be printed on the printer. To do this, perform following steps:

1. Make sure that the document, which you wish to preview is open and present in current window.
2. Select "File" option from the bar menu. When you do so, File submenu, as shown in figure Word-5, will appear on the screen.
3. Select "Print Preview" option from File submenu.

When you do so, current page of the document, as it will get printed on the printer will appear on the screen. Sample of such a page is shown in figure Word-51.

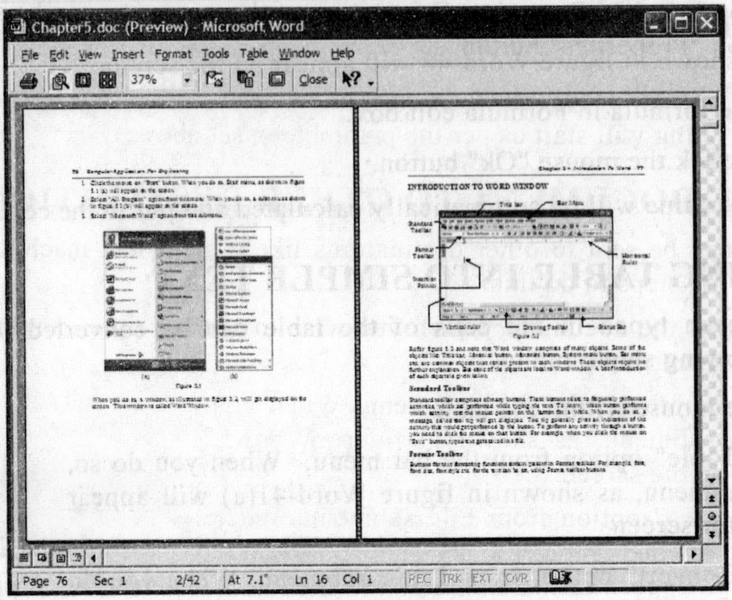

Figure Word-51

PRINTING THE DOCUMENT

Perform following steps to print the document on printer:

1. Make sure that the document, which you wish to print is open and present in current window.
2. Select "File" option from the bar menu. When you do so, a submenu, as shown in figure Word-5, will appear on the screen.
3. Select "Print" option from File submenu. When you do so, a dialog box, as shown in figure Word-52, will appear on the screen.

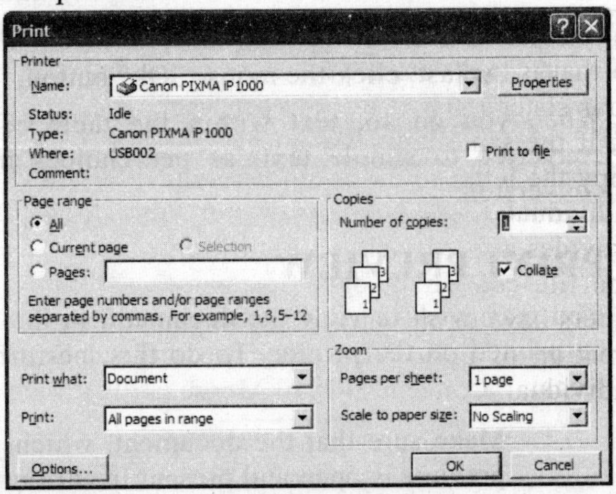

Figure Word -52

4. Click the mouse on "Name" drop down list and select the name of the printer, on which the document is to be printed.
5. If all the pages of the document are to be printed, select "All" option present in "Page range" section of the dialog box else specify the page range as **s-e**. Here s denotes the starting page number and e denote the last page number that is to be printed.
6. Specify number of copies that need to be pointed, using "Number of Copies" spinner.

7. Advanced options like Page size, Orientation of the paper etc. can be set by clicking the mouse on "Properties" button.
8. After defining all the options, as per requirement, click the mouse on "OK" button.

When you do so, printing will start as per the parameters, set above.

SENDING THE DOCUMENT TO OTHER DESTINATIONS

Current document can be sent to other destinations like e-mail, Fax machine, PowerPoint etc. Perform following steps to do this:

1. Make sure that the document, which you wish to send to other destinations is open and present in current window.
2. Select "File" option from the bar menu. When you do so, File submenu, as shown in figure Word-5, will appear on the screen.
3. Select "Send To" option from File submenu. When you do so, another submenu, as shown in figure Word-53, will appear on the screen.
4. Select the desired destination from this submenu.

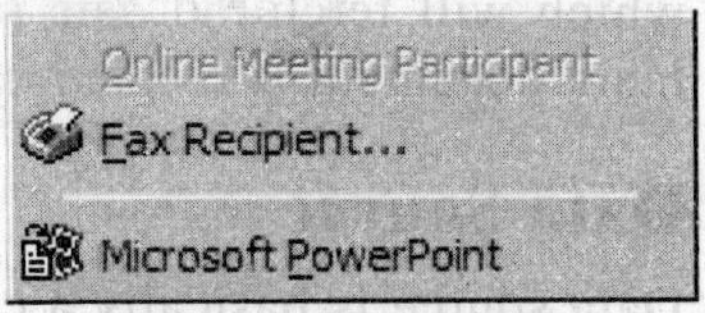

Figure Word -53

When you do so, current document will be forwarded to the selected destination.

INTRODUCTION TO MAIL MERGE

In the last chapter you learned the method of typing a letter in MS-Word and formatting it so that it looks attractive. Now if you have to write a letter to your friend, inviting him to your sister's marriage, you can very well prepare the letter in MS-Word. But the question is, if the same letter has to be sent to say 25 or 30 friends then what do you do? Do you copy the letter to 25 or 30 different files and change the names and addresses of friends in individual files? No, this is not the right solution. If you are working in MS-Word, it provides a facility called Mail Merge. Using this facility you can create two different files, one file containing data (i.e. names and addresses of all the friends to whom invitation letters have to be sent) and other containing letter (with name and address left blank). After creation of these files, they are merged together, so that one letter is created for each individual. Concept of Mail Merge is illustrated in Word-54.

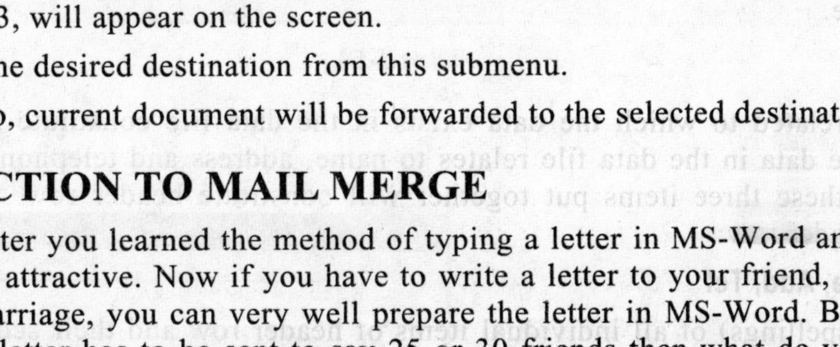

Figure Word- 54

TERMS AND TERMINOLOGY OF MAIL MERGE

Before we describe operational details of Mail Merge, it is necessary to get familiar with few important terms and their meanings.

Main Document

Format of the letter, which is to be sent to each individual, is called main document. Refer figure Word-1 and note that invitation letter format is nothing but main document.

Main document basically consists of two items; one is the text that will appear in the letter (such as "You are cordially invited to my sister's marriage ....) and other are the variables, which will fetch the data (such as name, address etc. of friends) from the data file. How main document is created, is explained later in this chapter.

Data Source

Data source is basically a combination of two items i.e. Header row and Data. Refer figure Word-1 and note that combination of item like name, address etc. and the data is nothing but data source.

Header Row

Those items, related to which the data exists in the data file constitute header row. For example, if the data in the data file relates to name, address and telephone number of the persons then these three items put together will constitute header row. Following is an example of header row:

Name, Add, Tel

Here names (spellings) of all individual items of header row and their sequence in header row are important, wherever they will be referred, they will be referred by same name and the data in the data file will have to be put in the same sequence.

Data

Data consists of those values, which are to be included in the letters. For example, if the letters are to be sent to 4 persons then there will be 4 rows of data. Each row will contain values for each individual item of the header row. Table shown here clearly illustrates header row and data.

Header Row →	**Name**	**Add**	**Tel**
Data →	Rakesh	1 Park street Lko.	2787531
	Rani	23 Dover Lane Delhi	2608529
	Rupa	43 Mall Avenu Allahabad	23405091
	Soni	69 Kanpur Road Lko	26589063

For generating letters through Mail Merge facility of MS-Word, you need to create main document, data source and data, first. After this, data is merged with the main document and letters are printed. Operational details for creating these items are given below.

CREATING THE MAIN DOCUMENT

Perform following steps create the main document:

1. Select "Tools" option from the bar menu. When you do so, Tools submenu, will appear on the screen.
2. Select "Mail Merge..." option from Tools submenu. On selecting this option, Mail Merge Helper screen, as shown in figure Word-55, will appear on the screen.
3. Click the mouse on "Create" button. When you do so, a drop down list, as shown in figure Word-56 will appear on the screen.
4. Select "Form Letters" option from this list. When you do so, a dialog box as shown in figure Word-57, will appear on the screen.

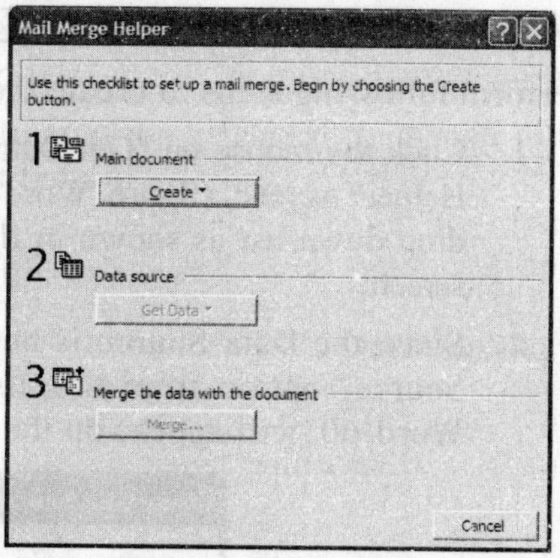

Figure Word - 55

5. If you wish to create the document in current window, click the mouse on "Active Window" button else click it on "New Main Document" button. In both the cases, Mail Merge Helper screen, as shown in figure Word-57,will appear on the screen.

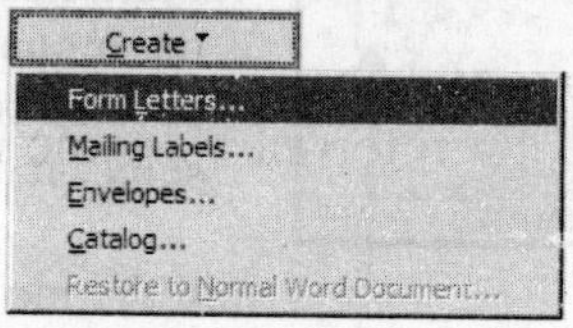

Figure Word-56

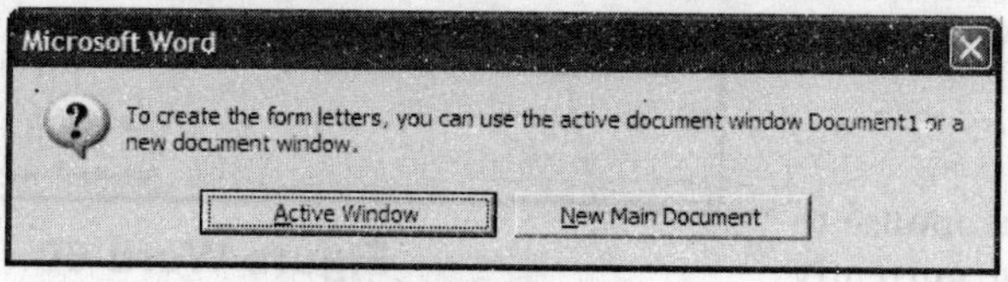

Figure Word-57

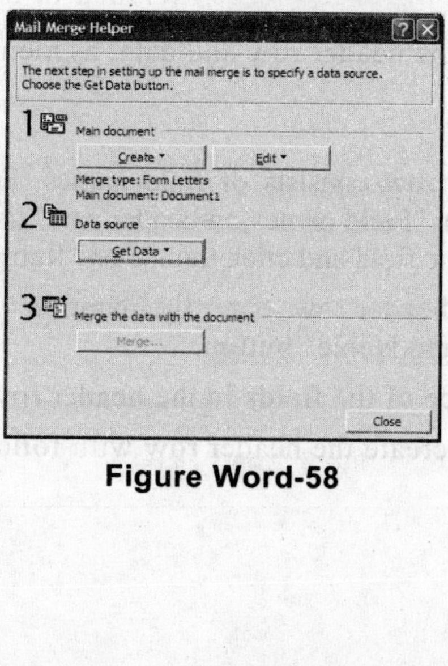

Figure Word-58

Note that main document consists of text and the field names (header row constituent). So in order to create the main document, you will have to write the text and the field names also. But the field names have not yet been created. So let's first create the data source and then create the main document.

CREATING THE DATA SOURCE

Figure Word -59

Perform following steps to create the data source:

1. Click the mouse on "Get Data" button, present in "Mail Merge Helper" screen (figure Word-58). On selecting this option, a drop down list as shown in figure Word-59 will appear on the screen.
2. Since the Data Source is being created for the first time hence select "Create Data Source" option from this list. When you do so, a dialog box, as shown in figure Word-60, will appear on the screen.

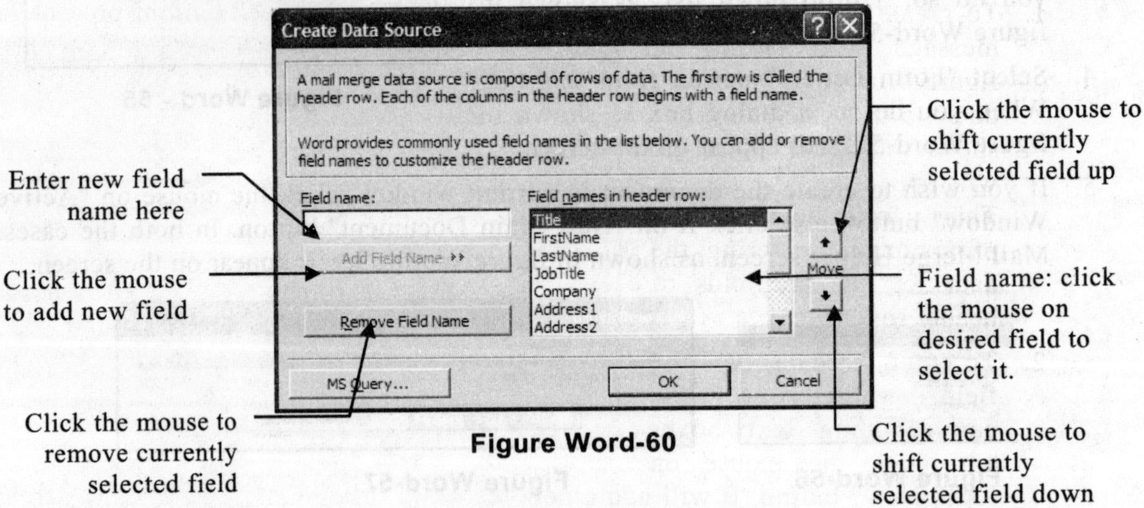

Figure Word-60

Using this dialog box, create the header row and data, as mentioned below.

Creating Header Row

1. You know that header row consists of field names. Field names currently present in header row are shown in "Field names, in header row" list box. To remove any field from the header row, select the field and click mouse on "Remove field Name" button.
2. To add a new field in header row, enter the name in "Field name" text box and click the mouse on "Add Field Name" button.
3. To change the sequence of the fields in the header row, make use of arrow buttons.

   For example, say you create the header row with following field names:

   Name, Add, Tel

4. Click the mouse on "OK" button. When you do so, usual "File Save" dialog box appears on the screen. Mention drive, folder and file name for saving the header row. Say for example, you specify the file name as "DataRow". To end the saving process, click the mouse on "Save" button. When you do so, a message box, as shown in figure Word-61, will appear on the screen.

Figure Word-61

Creating The Data

1. To create the data, click the mouse on "Edit Data Source" button, present in the message box, shown in figure Word-61. When you do so, a data entry form, as shown in figure Word-62, will appear on the screen. This form will have provision for entering the data for all the fields of header row.

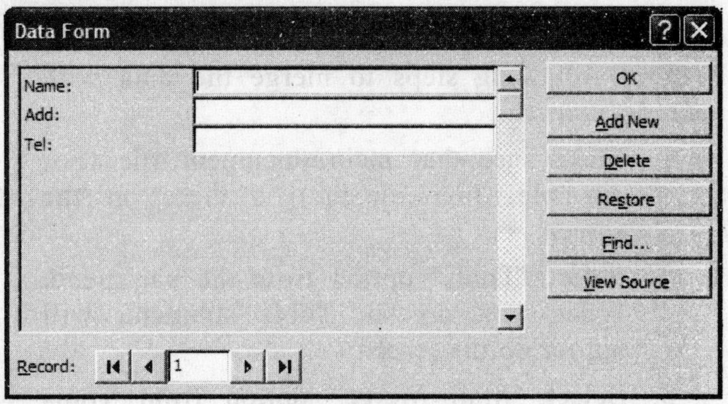

Figure Word -62

2. To enter the data, type the field values in the corresponding text boxes and click the mouse on "Add New" button. It will add a new record to the file and create blank screen for entering the next record.

After entering the complete data, click the mouse on "OK" button. When you do so, Mail Merge tool bar, as shown in figure Word-10 will appear on the screen and you will be taken back to the main, blank document, which, you had created at the beginning. Now you need to enter the text and header row field names in the document so that letters for all individuals could be generated.

Figure msword-63

EDITING THE MAIN DOCUMENT

Perform following steps to edit the main document:

1. Type the text of the letter, in normal way, as you type the contents of other documents
2. To add the header field name in the text, take the mouse pointer at the place, where the field is to be added and click the mouse on "Insert Merge Field" button, present in Mail Merge toolbar (Figure Word-63). When you do so, header row field name will get displayed, as shown in figure Word-64.
3. Select the field by clicking the mouse on it. When you select the field, MS-Word will put the field name at the current insertion pointer's position as, <<Name>>. Remember that these signs are not less than or greater than signs, they cannot be entered through keyboard. They can only be included through Mail Merge toolbar.

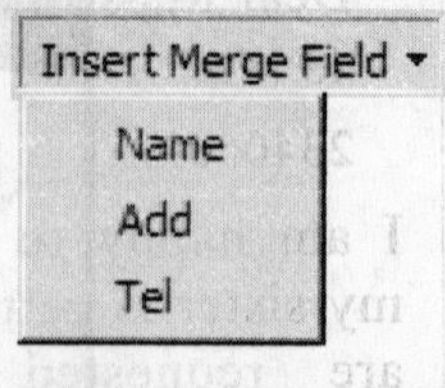

Figure Word -64

Say, for example, you prepare the main document, as shown in figure Word-65.

To

Dear <<Name>>

<<Add>>

<<Tel>>

I am happy to inform you that my sister is getting married. You are requested to grace the occasion by your presence.

Vimal Singh

Figure Word -65

MERGE DATA SOURCE WITH MAIN DOCUMENT

Perform following steps to merge the data with main document:

1. Make sure that main document file (For example, Invitaton.doc) is there on the screen.
2. Select "Tools" option from the bar menu. When you do so, Tools submenu will appear on the screen.
3. Select "Mail Merge" option from Tools submenu. When you do so, "Mail Merge Helper" screen, as shown in figure Word-65, will appear on the screen.
4. Click the mouse on "Merge" button present in that screen. When you do so, a dialog box, as shown in figure Word-66, will appear on the screen.
5. Using different objects of this dialog box specify printing related details.
6. At last, click the mouse on "Merge" button present in the dialog box.

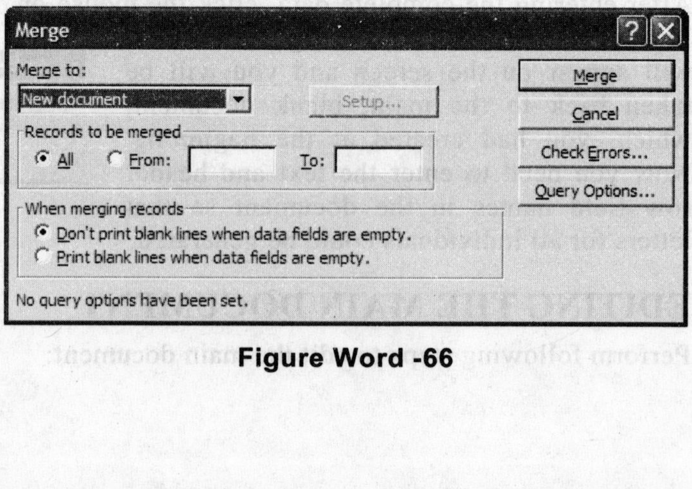

Figure Word -66

When you do so, letters for all the persons, will get generated on the screen. If you wish, you can print them on printer in the same way as other document. Sample letters for the example, taken in this chapter are illustrated below.

To

Dear Rupa

43 Mall Avenu Allahabad

23405091

I am happy to inform you that my sister is getting married. You are requested to grace the occasion by your presence.

Vimal Singh

To

Dear Rupa

43 Mall Avenu Allahabad

23405091

I am happy to inform you that my sister is getting married. You are requested to grace the occasion by your presence.

Vimal Singh

To

Dear Rupa

43 Mall Avenu Allahabad

23405091

I am happy to inform you that my sister is getting married. You are requested to grace the occasion by your presence.

Vimal Singh

To

Dear Rupa

43 Mall Avenu Allahabad

23405091

I am happy to inform you that my sister is getting married. You are requested to grace the occasion by your presence.

Vimal Singh

Figure Word-67

PRACTICAL ASSIGNMENTS

Assignment -1: Entering, Formatting And Printing The Document

Perform, following activities in lab sessions:

1. Set left and right margins for the entire document.
2. Type the following piece of text in 11 points, Times New Roman font, without caring about its formatting:

> The Crossover
>
> A new business opportunity is coming up at the junction of hardware and software embedded technology
>
> An Indian boy selling newspapers at Stockholm railway station was unusual enough for Sunil to investigate. The boy turned out to be a student at the Royal Institute of Technology, Sweden. He talked excitedly about an idea for a pace marker that lasted much longer than the ones available in the market. "Why don't you come and develop this product in my laboratory?" asked Sunil.
>
> The lab is a center of excellence for embedded systems at Tata Consultancy services (TCS) in Bangalore. Sunil had set it up only a year ago, after quitting Sasken Communication Systems. "I had approached TCS with this idea of an embedded systems lab and TCS had agreed," say Sunil. Despite being the largest software services company in India, TCS had not worked on embedded system other than in telecommunications. It was slow off the blocks, but the company was trying to make up for lost time.
>
> Sunil's lab's mandate was not to provide services. It would to research, develop technologies, and build product; not just software but complete devices. Whenever a product came out, it would be sold under the TCS brand name. The first device could be patient health monitoring system. The next one could be a box that would increase spectrum utilisation in CDMA (code division multiple access) networks. The third device could be the boy's pacemaker.
>
> The embedded system lab is also building competencies in three areas: wireless LAN (local area network), multimedia and medical electronics. TCS is about to take over a wireless LAN firm in Demark. This firm has a key technology that will strengthen the TCS portfolio.

3. Now perform following steps to edit and format the text:
   (i) Find the word utilisation in the document and replace it with utilization.
   (ii) Put the heading, "The Crossover" in 24 points bold, Arial Black.
   (iii) Make the text, starting with the words "**A new business opportunity......**" till "**embedded technology**" as subheading. Put it in 14 points bold, italic and underlined.

(iv) Find the first appearance of the word "Sunil" and change its color to red and make it italic bold.

(v) Import the clip art from clip art gallery.

(vi) Align the paragraphs.

Format the document as shown below.

Print the document on printer.

Save the document in a file.

The Crossover

A new business opportunity is coming up at the junction of hardware and software embedded technology

An Indian boy selling newspapers at Stockholm railway station was unusual enough for Sunil to investigate. The boy turned out to be a student at the Royal Institute of Technology, Sweden. He talked excitedly about an idea for a pace marker that lasted much longer than the ones available in the market. "Why don't you come and develop this product in my laboratory?" asked Sunil.

The lab is a center of excellence for embedded systems at Tata Consultancy services (TCS) in Bangalore. ***Sunil*** had set it up only a year ago, after quitting Sasken Communication Systems. "I had approached TCS with this idea of an embedded systems lab and TCS had agreed," say Sunil. Despite being the largest software services company in India, TCS had not worked on embedded system other than in telecommunications. It was slow off the blocks, but the company was trying to make up for lost time.

Sunil's lab's mandate was not to provide services. It would to research, develop technologies, and build product; not just software but complete devices. Whenever a product came out, it would be sold under the TCS brand name. The first device could be patient health monitoring system. The next one could be a box that would increase spectrum utilization in CDMA (code division multiple access) networks. The third device could be the boy's pacemaker.

The embedded system lab is also building competencies in three areas: wireless LAN (local area network), multimedia and medical electronics. TCS is about to take over a wireless LAN firm in Demark. This firm has a key technology that will strengthen the TCS portfolio.

Assignment–2 : Creating Tables In The Document.

4. Prepare following letter in MS-Word:

To Date: 12/9/06

Mr. A. K. Tandon
Bharat Book Depot
77 Mal Avenue
Lucknow

Subject: Supply of Computer Books.

Dear Sir,

This has reference to the specimen of books, submitted by you for our approval. We are pleased to place order for following books.

Sr. No.	Title of the Book	Details of the Book			No. of Copies
		Author	Edition	Publisher	
1.	Fundamentals	Anurag	1st	BPB	4
2.	Windows	Rahul	2nd	New Age Publication	2
3.	Word	Sanjeev	1st	New Age Publication	6
4.	Excel	Ajit	2nd	MBD	5
5.	PowerPoint	Manav	1st	BPB	10

We agree to 35% discount that you have offered under your terms and conditions. These books may please be delivered, latest by 1-10-2006 in our library.

Kindly submit the bill in duplicate along with the books, so that the payment could be made at the earliest.

Thanking you

Sincerely yours

R.K. Pandey
(Librarian)

5. Print the letter on printer.

Assignment 3 : Generating Letters Using Mail Merge.

1. Invoke MS-Word on your computer.
2. Make use of Mail Merge facility.
3. Create following data source:

Name	Add	Tel
Rakesh	1 Park street Lko.	2787531
Rani	23 Dover Lane Delhi.	2608529
Rupa	43 Mall Avenue Allahabad.	23405091
Soni	69 Kanpur Road Lko.	26589063

4. Create main document, as mentioned below.

To
Dear <<Name>>
<<Add>>
<<Tel>>

I am happy to inform you that my sister is getting married. You are requested to grace the occasion by your presence.

Vimal Singh

5. Merge data source with main document and generate letters.
6. Print the letters on printer.
7. Save the letters in a file.
8. Generate letters for only Rupa and Soni.

****

Information Technology Lab

(CM-110)

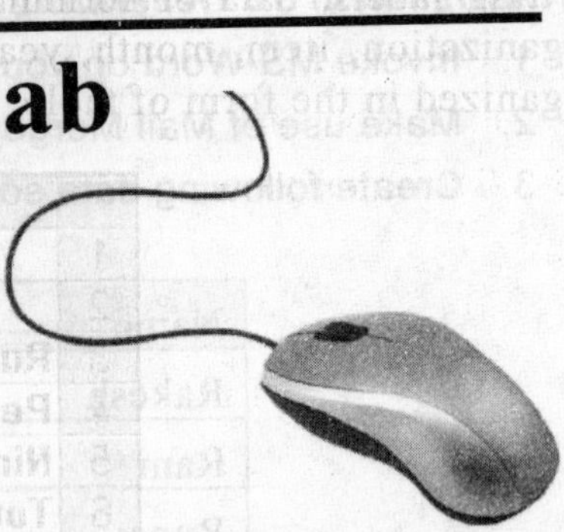

MS-Excel

(Self Study Material and Practical Assignments)

INTRODUCTION

Data collection, its organization and presentation in easy-to understand forms like tables, graphs, charts etc. for the purpose of analysis are day-to-day activities of any working setup. For example, a sales organization, at the end of financial year, may collect sales figures from all its regional offices for analyzing company's sales performance and deciding the targets for the next year. Similarly a manufacturing organization may collect all input costs involved in manufacturing an item to estimate fund requirements and to calculate the profitability.

When data volumes are small, such activities are either performed manually or using equipments like calculator etc. But when data volume becomes large and presentation requirements are complex, these tools become limitation. Other sophisticated tools are required to handle such situations. MS-Excel is one such software-tool, which facilitates maintaining large data volumes on computer, organizing them in the form of tables, charts, reports etc. and performing "What if" analysis. Working details of MS-Excel are described in this chapter.

MS-EXCEL - A WORK BOOK

MS-Excel is workbook software, which has been designed and developed by Microsoft Corporation of USA.

Workbook software comprises of multiple worksheets with data editing facilities and inbuilt calculation abilities. Data editing facilities of workbook ensure proper organization of data and calculation abilities facilitate its automatic updation.

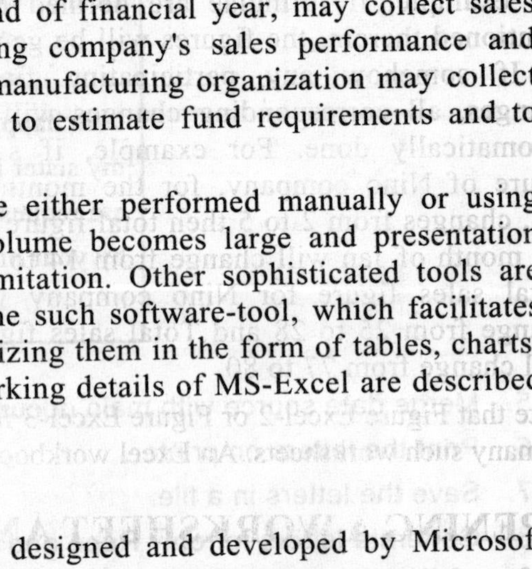

Figure Excel-1

A simple worksheet is illustrated in Figure Excel-1. It looks like a page of child's mathematics copy that has squares drawn in it. Squares are used for writing labels, data or formulae in them. When data pertaining to similar entities like organization, item, month, year etc. is put in same column or row, it automatically gets organized in the form of table. Such a table is illustrated in Figure Excel -2.

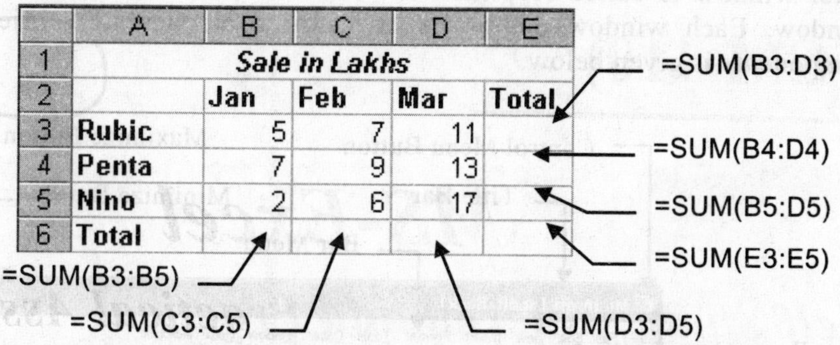

Figure Excel-2

When formulae are defined in worksheet, automatic calculations are done and results are generated.

For example, if formulae are defined in the worksheet, shown in Figure Excel-2, as mentioned therein, the figures will be generated automatically, as shown in Figure Excel - 3. If somehow any participating figure changes, all corresponding changes will be automatically done. For example, if sales figure of Nino company, for the month of Jan, changes from 2 to 5 then total figure for the month of Jan will change from 14 to 17. Total sales figure for Nino company will change from 25 to 28 and Total sales figure will change from 77 to 80.

	A	B	C	D	E
1			*Sale in Lakhs*		
2		Jan	Feb	Mar	Total
3	Rubic	5	7	11	**23**
4	Penta	7	9	13	**29**
5	Nino	2	6	17	**25**
6	Total	**14**	**22**	**41**	**77**

Figure Excel-3

Note that Figure Excel-2 or Figure Excel-3 illustrates a single worksheet. A workbook comprises of many such worksheets. An Excel workbook comprises of 255 such worksheets.

OPENING A WORKSHEET AND ENTERING DATA

Perform following steps to invoke MS-Excel on your computer:

1. Click the mouse on "Start" button. When you do so, Start menu, as shown in figure 4.2 will appear on the screen.
2. Select "All Programs" option from this menu. When you do so, a submenu, as shown in figure 4.3 will appear on the screen.
3. Select "Microsoft Excel" option from this submenu.

When you do so, MS-Excel window, as shown in Figure Excel--4, will appear on the screen.

INTRODUCTION TO MS-EXCEL WINDOW

Refer Figure Excel-4 and note that Excel window comprises of two nested windows. The outer window is called Application window and the inner windows is called Document window. Each window comprises of many components. A brief introduction of their components is given below.

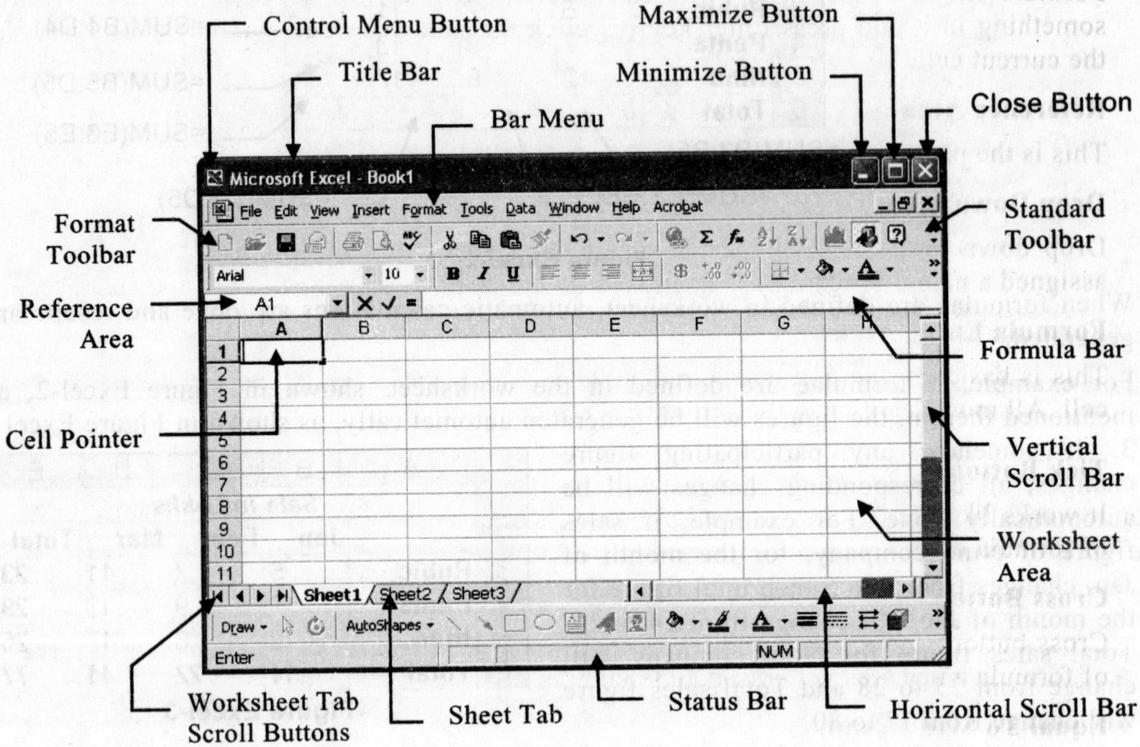

Figure Excel-4

Application Windows

Components of MS-Excel Application window are as follows:

Title Bar

Title bar comprises of usual components like system menu button, name of the current document, minimize, maximize and close button.

Status Bar

Status bar at the bottom of MS-Excel window comprises of message area and few buttons. Message area generally displays status of current activities. Buttons display the status of various action keys of the keyboard. For example, Num Lock is on or off, Caps Lock key is active or not etc. are few situations that are indicated by these buttons.

Document Window

Document window comprises of few common components like bar menu, toolbars, scroll bar etc. and few special components, which are local to Excel window. You are already familiar with the role and functioning of all the common components. Role and functioning of all special components of MS-Excel window are explained below.

Formula Bar

Formula bar is a place where you can enter the contents of the cell. Whenever you type something in it and press Enter key (or click the mouse on tick symbol) it gets written in the current cell.

Reference Area

This is the place where the address of current cell gets displayed.

Drop Down List

Drop down list is basically a list of all those items of the worksheet, which have been assigned a name. When mouse is clicked on the arrow button, names get displayed.

Formula Entry Area

This is basically the text entry area. Whatever you type here is later transferred to current cell. All modifications in the cell entries are done in this area.

Tick Button

It works like "Enter" key of the keyboard. When mouse is clicked on this button, contents of formula entry area get transferred to the current cell.

Cross Button

Cross button works like "Cancel" button. When mouse is clicked on this button, contents of formula entry area get erased and that area becomes blank.

Equal To Sign Button

When mouse is clicked on this button, function wizard appears on the screen and starts functioning.

Worksheet Area

Worksheet area comprises of rows and columns. Partial area of the worksheet remains visible on the screen. Other portion of it can be brought on the screen by scrolling the worksheet, using vertical and horizontal scroll bars.

All together there are 65536 rows and 256 columns in a worksheet. Refer Figure Excel--4 and note that rows are labeled as 1,2,3,4,5 etc. and columns are labeled as A, B, C, D, E etc. Thus the last row will be labeled as 65536 and the last column will be labeled as IV

Intersection of a row and column forms a rectangular space, called Cell. Each cell is identified by its address and the address of the cell is defined as column number and the name of the row that form the cell. For example, the cell formed by fifth column (i.e. E)

and third row (i.e. 3) will be defined as E3. Similarly the cell formed by fourth column (i.e. D) and second row (i.e.2) will be defined as D2.

Worksheet area is used for data entry. As per standard rules of MS-Excel, contents of a cell are considered as single data item. In other words you can say that a cell of the worksheet can hold single data item only.

Worksheet Tab

As mentioned earlier, a workbook comprises of 256 worksheets. Each worksheet has a corresponding tab in MS-Excel window. Refer Figure Excel-4 and notc that these tabs are placed just below the worksheet area. These tabs are named as Sheet1, Sheet2, Sheet3 ... etc.

When you invoke MS-Excel, first worksheet appears in the window and Sheet1 tab remains highlighted.

Worksheet Tab Scroll Buttons

Refer Figure Excel-4 and note that not all 255 worksheet tabs (as there are 256 worksheets in a workbook) remain visible on the screen. Due to space limitation, only few of them appear on the screen. To scroll the list of these tabs, worksheet tab scroll buttons remain present in the window.

Figure Excel-5 clearly shows that there are four worksheet tab scroll buttons. Sequential scroll buttons scroll the tabs forward and backward one by one. For example, if currently Sheet3 is visible on screen and you click the mouse on "Sequential scroll forward" button, sheet4 tab will become visible. Similarly "Sequential scroll backward" button will move the tabs in backward direction.

Step scroll buttons, scroll the tabs in steps. For example, if tabs for sheet1, sheet2, sheet3 etc. are visible on the screen and you click the mouse on " Steps forward scroll" button, set of tab buttons i.e. Sheet4, sheet5, sheet6 etc. will be visible on the screen. Similarly "Step backward scroll" button will scroll the worksheet tabs in other direction.

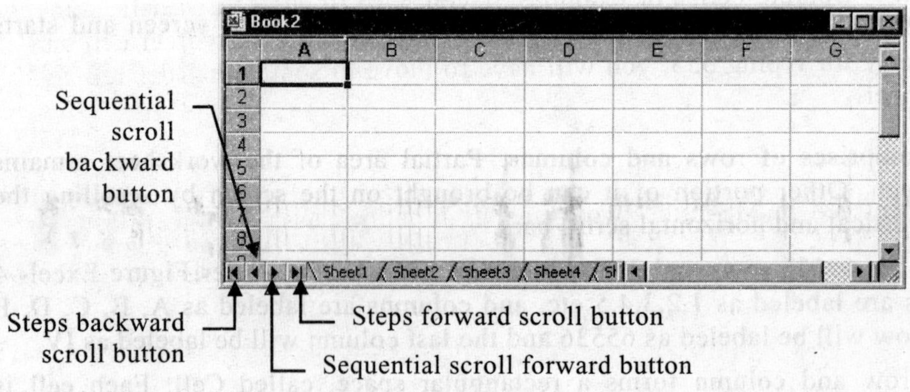

Figure Excel-5

Cell Pointer

Refer Figure Excel--4 and note that the thick border around the cell (A1) is cell pointer. Cell pointer can be moved anywhere in the worksheet with the help of arrow keys of the keyboard. The cell, on which cell pointer resides, is referred to as current cell. When you enter the data, it gets entered in the current cell.

Now you are familiar with MS-Excel window, its components, worksheet and the workbook. Now the question is how do you move around in the worksheet or workbook? Well, the procedure for these activities is explained below.

MOVING AROUND IN A WORKBOOK

You can move around in the workbook in any one of the following ways:

1. Make use of the arrow keys to move the cell pointer to the desired location. The position of cell pointer will be your current position in the worksheet.
2. Click the mouse on the cell, to which you wish to move. When you do so, cell pointer will get immediately placed there and the clicked cell will become current cell.
3. Click the mouse in Reference area of formula bar and type the address of the desired cell. After this, when you will press Enter key, cell pointer will move to the cell whose address you had typed in the reference area.
4. To move to any other worksheet, click the mouse of its sheet tab. For example, if you wish to move to the third worksheet, click the mouse on "Sheet3" tab, located just below the worksheet area. If the desired worksheet tab is not visible on the screen, make use of "Worksheet tab scroll" buttons, to make it appear there.

ENTERING DATA IN WORKSHEET

Data entry in worksheet is quite different from the text entry that is done in MS-Word. In MS-word, you continuously keep on typing the text but in MS-Excel worksheet you need to type each data item in a separate cell. For example, if you wish to enter three data items, say Ravi, 200, 555 then you will have to type Ravi in one cell then move to other cell and type 200 there. Similarly for typing 555, you will have to move to some other desired cell and then type the number.

DATA TYPES

The data that can be entered in MS-Excel worksheet is broadly classified into following two categories:

1. Constants
2. Formula

Constants

The values, which do not change on their own are called constants, For example, if you enter "Ravi" in cell A1, it will not change unless you deliberately modify it (to say,

Ravina). Similarly other values like 200, 255 etc. will also be treated as constants because they will not change automatically.

Type Of Constants

Constants can further be classified into following categories:

1. Numbers
2. Text
3. Date
4. Time

Numbers

Any combination formed by ten digits i.e. 0 to 9 is treated as number or numeric constant. For example, 200 is a number. Similarly 555 is another number or another numeric constant. Use of following special characters is allowed in the formation of numbers:

+ - ( ) / * $ %

While making use of these special characters in the numbers, following rules apply:

1. MS-Excel ignores + sign in all the numbers that are preceded by it. For example, it will treat +176 as 176. Similarly +975 will be treated as 975.
2. Any number preceded by a hyphen (-) is treated as negative number. For example, -753 is a negative number.
3. $ sign can precede the number. For example, $200, $735 etc. are valid numbers or valid numeric constants.
4. To increase the readability of the numbers, MS-Excel allows the use of comma in between the digits of the numbers. For example, 10,357, 1,567 etc. are valid numbers.
5. MS-Excel also accepts numbers in scientific notation. For example $10e^6$, $10e^3$ etc. are valid numbers in scientific notation.
7. Use of parenthesis is also allowed in forming the numbers. For example, (7), (200+700), (300-55) etc. are valid numbers.

Text

Any data that is neither number nor date nor time, is treated as text in MS-Excel. For example, Ravi, Ravina, January, Month etc. are all examples of text. Note that a cell can hold at most 255 character long text. Blank is also treated as single character text.

Date

MS-Excel allows date entries in the cells of the worksheet. It treats them as separate identities. Thus date mathematics becomes possible in MS-Excel. In date data, day, month and year values are either separated by hyphen (-) or slash (/). Following are few valid dates:

22/06/1975, 16/MAY/1975, 10-3-1988 etc.

Time

Time is a valid data type in MS-Excel. For entering time values in MS-Excel worksheet, following rules apply:

1. Time values can either be as per 12 hours clock or 24 hours clock.
2. If time values are as per 12 hours clock, they should be followed by AM or PM. For example, 7 AM, 8 PM etc. are valid time values.
3. Instead of AM, PM, A and P can also be used respectively. For example, 7A, 8P are also valid time values.
4. If time value includes hours, minutes and seconds then colon (:) should be used as separator between them. For example, 10:45 AM, 1:10:05 PM etc. are valid time values.
5. Excel automatically displays time in 24 hours clock. For example, if you enter 2 PM, it will automatically convert it to 14:00.
6. Date and time values can be entered together in a cell by including a blank in between them. For example, 10/5/2006 11:55, 3/5/1957 10:20 PM etc. are few valid date and time entries.

Formula

Formula is basically a user defined function, which can be formed as per our own requirements by making use of constants, mathematical operators, standard MS-Excel functions (there are numerous standard, predefined functions available in MS-Excel, for use), and cell addresses. For example, (A1*C1)+200 is a valid formula. Similarly SUM(A1:A10) is another valid formula.

To differentiate formulae with text, all formulae should start with = sign in MS-Excel. For example, above mentioned formulae should be entered as =(A1*C1)+200, =SUM(A1:A10) respectively.

Type Of Formulae

MS-Excel formulae can be broadly classified into following categories:

1. Numeric Formulae
2. Logical Formulae
3. Text Formulae

A brief introduction of all these types of formulae is given below.

Numeric Formulae

Formulae that make use of arithmetic operators are called Numeric Formulae. For example, =(A+B)-C1 is a numeric formula because it makes use of arithmetic operator + and -. Following is the list of arithmetic operators that are allowed in MS-Excel.

Sign	Operations Performed
+	Addition
-	Subtraction (or negation when placed before a value, say - 149)
/	Division
*	Multiplication
%	Percentage (Placed after a value e.g. 25%)
^	Exponentiation (e.g. 20^2)

Following are few valid numeric formulae:

=(A1+B1+C1+D1), =(B10-C10), =(A1*B1)/C1, =(C1+C5)*25%, (5^3)+B1

Logical Formulae

Formulae that make use of logical operators are called Logical Formulae. They are basically used for making logical comparison. The result of comparison is either TRUE or FALSE. They produce no other result. For example, =(A1>B1) is a logical formula because it makes use of logical operator >.

Following is the list of logical operators that are available in MS-Excel:

Sign	Meaning	Sign	Meaning
=	Equal to	>=	Greater than or equal to
>	Greater than	<=	Less than or equal to
<	Less than	<>	Not equal to

To get familiar with the use of logical operators and the result produced by logical formulae, assume that cell A1 contains 1000 and cell B1 contains 500. Formulae entered in different cells of the worksheet will generate result as summarized in the following table:

Cell	Formula	Result
C1	=(A1=B1)	FALSE
C2	=(A1>B1)	TRUE
C3	=(A1<>B1)	TRUE
C4	=(A1>=B1)	TRUE
C5	=(A1<B1)	FALSE
C6	=(A1<=B1)	FALSE

Text Formulae

Those formulae, which make use of text operators, are called Text Formulae.

Only one text operator, called concatenation operator, is available in MS-Excel. It is denoted by & sign and it operates upon two text items to join them together. For example, if cell A1 contains "Andhra" and B1 contains "Pradesh" then =(A1&B1) will produce AndhraPradesh.

ORDER OF EVALUATION

As per standard rules, evaluation of operators starts from right and gradually proceeds towards left. For example, formula =300-5+50*3 will generate 445.

Making use of parenthesis can always change the order of evaluation. For example, formula=(300-5+50)*3 will generate 1035.

Within the parenthesis, evaluation proceeds from right to left.

In case of nested brackets, innermost bracket is resolved first. After this, next outer bracket is resolved and evaluation proceeds in the same way. While evaluating an expression, operators are evaluated in following sequence:

Sr. No.	Operator	Description
1.	-	Negation (-25)
2.	%	Percent
3.	^	Exponentiation
4.	* and /	Multiplication and Division
5.	+ and -	Addition and Subtraction
6.	&	Text joining
7.	=, <, >, <>	Comparison operators

DEFAULT FORMATTING

While entering the data in worksheet, it gets automatically formatted. The rules for default formatting are as follows:

1. Numeric values get right aligned.
2. Text values get left aligned.
3. Date and time values get right aligned.
4. Formulae get left aligned.

	A	B	C	D
1	125.6	Ajit	03/05/1976	9:45:17
2				

Figure Excel-6

Default alignments of all these data items is shown in Figure Excel-6

ENTERING AND EDITING FORMULA

You are now familiar with MS-Excel worksheet and the types of data that can be entered in it. To get familiar with the process of preparing a worksheet, let's take a simple example. Say, we have to prepare a worksheet, in which rate and quantity are entered manually and the amount is calculated automatically, using the formula (rate * quantity).

Perform following steps for preparing this worksheet.

1. Type "Rate" in cell A1. The word, Rate is a text constant and will be treated as label or heading. Its purpose is to communicate that the value written below is rate.
2. Type the word "Quantity" in cell B1. This label will also serve the purpose of heading.
3. Type the word "Amount" in cell C1. This text will also serve the purpose of heading.
4. Since quantity and rate values have to be entered in cell A2, B2 respectively and the amount is to be calculated by multiplying values in these cells and the result is to be displayed (automatically) in cell C2 hence enter the formula, =(A2*B2) in cell C2.
5. Now, when you enter the values in cell A2 and B2, result will get automatically displayed in cell C2. For example, if you enter 50 in cell A2 and 3 in cell B2 then the result, 150 (i.e. 50*30) will automatically appear in cell C2.

Now, if you change the values either in A2 or B2 or in both the cell, value in cell C2 will automatically update itself, according to the formula. For example, if you change the value in cell B2, from 3 to 5, the value in cell C2 will change from 150 to 250. This worksheet is illustrated in figure Excel-7.

	A	B	C
1	Rate	Quantity	Amount
2	50	3	150
3			

Figure Excel - 7

The formula that you enter in a cell can either be edited in cell, by double clicking the mouse in the cell and changing the contents there or by placing the cell pointer on the cell and editing the contents in the Formula Bar.

REFERENCING A GROUP OF CELLS

Refer above mentioned example and recall that in cell C1, we made use of the formula, =(A2*B2), Note that this formula makes use of the cell addresses, which refer single cell. For example, A2 refers a single cell. Similarly B2 refers other cell. But there would be times when group of cells will participate in the formula. For example, column A may contain 12 different sales values i.e. A1 may contain sales value for the month of Jan, A2 may contain sales value for the month of Feb and so on. Thus to add all the 12 values, you will have to write a formula =(A1+A2+A3 -----+A12). This is lengthy and uncomfortable way. To make the task simple, MS-Excel provides many reference operators. Using these operators, you can refer group of cells (more then one cell) and make the formula short. An explanation of these operators is given below.

Range Operator

As the name indicates, Range operator, refers a group of cells, which fall within the given cell addresses.

Range operator is denoted by colon sign (:). It requires two operands and is used as Op1:Op2. Here Op1 is the first operand, which refers the address of the cell from where the range starts. Similarly Opt2 is the second operand, which refers the address of the cell, where the range ends. For example, (A1:A12) will signify all the cells starting from cell A1 to cell A12 (i.e.12 cells). Similarly (A5:G5) will signify all the cell from A5 to cell G5 (i.e. 7 cells).

Union Operator

As the name indicates, Union operator refers to all those cells, which are referred in the expression.

Union operator is denoted by a comma (,). It requires two operands and is used as op1, op2. Here op1 refers a cell address and op2 refers to another cell address. Thus (A7, B10) will refer two cells i.e. A7 and B10. Similarly (A7, A9, A11) will refer three cells A7, A9 and A11. In the same way (A5:A10), (B15:B20) will refer 12 cells i.e. all the cells starting from A5 to A10 (6 cells) and the cells starting from B15 to B20 (another 6 cells).

Intersection Operator

Intersection operator refers to all those cells, which are common between the two given ranges.

Intersection operator is denoted by a blank space. It requires two ranges as operands and is used as (R1 R2). Here R1 and R2 are two ranges. For example, (A1:A10 A7:A15) will result into 4 cells i.e. A7, A8, A9 and A10.

CELL REFERENCING

Consider the use of cell addresses in a formula. For example, in the worksheet shown in Figure Excel-7, the formula = (A2*B2) was written. Here by writing A2 or B2, You are referring to the values present in these cells. When you refer the contents of the cell, it is called cell referencing. Note that just writing the cell addresses and referring their values is not the only way of cell referencing. MS-Excel provides following three methods of cell referencing:

1. Relative referencing
2. Absolute referencing
3. Mixed referencing

Relative Referencing

As the name indicates, in relative referencing, cells are referred in relation to the current cell position. To understand the concept of relative referencing, consider the worksheet shown in Figure Excel-8. If you put the formula =(B2+C2+D2) in G2, it will show 1000 in G2. But it would, in the background, convey following aspects related to the current cell position (i.e. G2):

1. Take the value of the cell, which is 5 cells away towards left, from current cell.
2. Take the value of the cell, which is 4 cells away towards left, from the current cell.
3. Take the value of the cell, which is 3 cells away towards left, from the current cell.
4. Add all the three values and put the result in the current cell.

	A	B	C	D	E	F	G	H
1	Name	Jan	Feb	Mar			Total	Tax
2	LG	200	300	500				
3	BP	300	700	200				
4	RK	400	300	100				
5								
6	Tax Rate	0.1						

Figure Excel-8

In MS-Excel, whenever cell addresses are written in normal way (i.e. A1, C2, D7 etc.), relative referencing automatically takes place.

Note

Since in relative referencing all cell positions are referred in relation to current cell position, hence the same formula, when copied into another cell, (which would then be the current cell) will refer other cells and produce different result.

Absolute Referencing

As the name indicates, in Absolute Referencing the position of the cell or cells being referred does not depend upon the current cell position. Such type of referencing is done by prefixing $ sign with row and column names in a cell address.

For example, $B$2, $C$3, $D$4 etc. are examples of relative referencing. Note that B6 is an example of relative referencing, while $B$6 is an example of absolute referencing.

To understand the concept of relative referencing, consider the worksheet shown in Figure 6.8 and assume that values in G2, G3 and G4 are to be multiplied by fixed value of tax rate, present in cell B6. For this, formulae as mentioned in the table will have to be entered in the cells, mentioned therein.

Cell	Formula
H2	=G2*$B$6
H3	=G3*$B$6
H4	=G4*$B$6

Note

Since in absolute referencing, the position of the cell being referred does not depend upon the current cell position hence when a formula containing absolute referencing (only) is copied to other cell, it produces same result.

Mixed Referencing

As the name indicates, in Mixed Referencing, the cell addresses are partly relative and partly absolute. This is done by either prefixing a $ sign with row name or column name. For example, $B4, B$4 both are examples of mixed referencing (but with a difference). In $B4, column reference is absolute but row reference is relative, while in B$4, it is just opposite i.e. column reference is relative and row reference is absolute.

Note

Since in mixed referencing, the position of cell being referred, partially depends upon the position of the current cell and partially doesn't depend upon it hence a formula, which contains mixed references, when copied to other cell may or may not produce the same result, depending upon where the formula is copied.

PREPARING A WORKSHEET

To get familiar with different types of referencing methods, let's prepare a worksheet, which is illustrated in Figure Excel-8. Say we have to enter labels and data, as shown therein.

Assume that row totals have to be calculated and put in corresponding cells of column G. Tax values have to be calculated by multiplying total by tax rate (present in B6). For this, perform following steps:

1. Enter all the labels, as illustrated in Figure Excel-8.
2. Enter all the data items, as illustrated in Figure Excel-8.
3. Enter formula, =(B2+C2+D2) in G2
4. Enter formula, =(B3+C3+D3) in G3
5. Enter formula, =(B4+C4+D4) in G4
6. Enter formula, =(G2*$B$6) in H2
7. Enter formula, =(G3*$B$6) in H3
8. Enter formula, =(G4*$B46) in H4

	A	B	C	D	E	F	G	H
1	Name	Jan	Feb	Mar			Total	Tax
2	LG	200	300	500			1000	100
3	BP	300	700	200			1200	120
4	RK	400	300	100			800	80
5								
6	Tax Rate	0.1						

Figure Excel-9

After entering these formulae, the worksheet will show the values, as illustrated in Figure Excel-9.

SAVING THE WORKBOOK

Perform following steps to save the workbook on the disk:

1. Click the mouse on "File" option, present in the bar menu. When you do so, File submenu, as shown in Figure Excel-10, will appear on the screen.
2. Select "Save As" option from the File submenu. When you do so, a dialog box, as shown in figure 4.7 will appear on the screen.
3. Now select drive and the folder, in which you wish to save the worksheet.
4. Enter the name of the file, in which you wish to save the workbook in "File Name" text box.

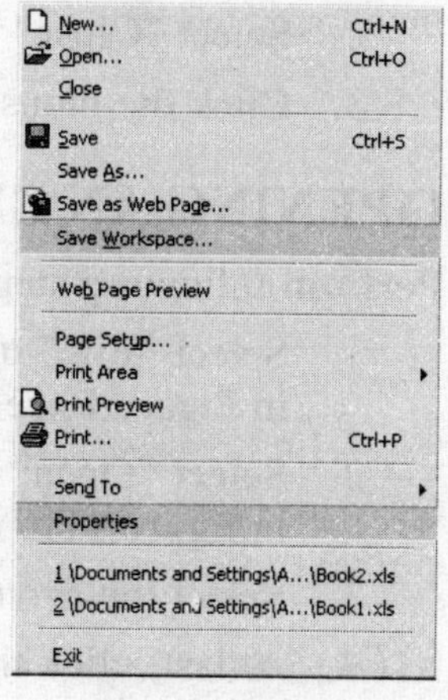

Figure Excel-10

5. At last, click the mouse on "Save" button, present in the dialog box.

When you do so, file will get saved on the disk.

Note

When you save a workbook, it is saved in a file that has the name, assigned by you. But MS-Excel assigns .XLS extension to it. For example, if you save the workbook in a file named, mywork, it will be saved in a file mywork.xls.

CLOSING THE WORKBOOK

Perform following steps to close the workbook:

1. Click the mouse on "File" option, present in the Bar menu. When you do so, File submenu, as shown in Figure Excel-10 will appear on the screen.
2. Select "Close" option from File submenu. If current modifications have not yet been saved on the disk, an alert box, as shown in Figure Excel-11, will appear on the screen.

   On the other hand, if current modifications have been saved on the disk, the workbook will get closed.

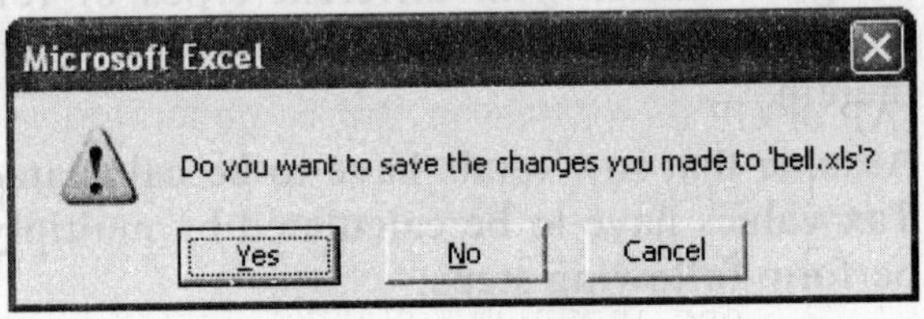

Figure Excel-11

3. If you wish to save the current editing session on the disk, click the mouse on "Yes" button else click it on "No" button. If somehow you wish to abort the closing process, click the mouse on "Cancel" button.

EXITING FROM EXCEL

Exit from Excel can be made in any one of the following ways:

1. Select "Exit" option from the File submenu.
2. Select "Close" option from the System menu.
3. Click the mouse on "Close" button, present in title bar.

OPENING AN EXISTING WORKBOOK

Perform following steps to open an existing workbook:

1. Select "File" option from the Bar menu. When you do so, File submenu, as shown in Figure Excel-10, will appear on the screen.
2. Select "Open" option from File submenu. When you do so, a dialog box, as shown in figure 4119 will appear on the screen.
3. Select the drive, folder and the file, in which the workbook exists.
4. At last, click the mouse on "Open" button.

PREPARING WORKSHEET WITH SERIES

MS-Excel provides various mechanisms for generating following types of series:

1. Arithmetic Progression series (1, 2, 3, 4 , 4, 5 .... etc.)
2. Geometric Progressing series (3, 9, 24, 81 ...... etc.)
3. Full month name series (January, February, March .... etc.)
4. Short month name series (Jan, Feb, Mar ..... etc.)
5. Full day name series (Sunday, Monday ...... etc.)
6. Short day name series (Sun, Mon, Tue ..... etc.)
7. Date series (1/1/2006, 1/2/2006 ...... etc.)

Methods of generating, such types of series are explained below:

Generating AP Or GP Series

AP or GP type of series can be generated as follows:

1. Enter starting values in the cell and press Enter key.
2. Now select all those cells, which have to be filled with the series (including the one, in which you have entered the value), by dragging the mouse over them.
3. Now click the mouse on "Edit" option, present in bar menu. When you do so, Edit submenu, as shown in Figure Excel-12(a) will appear on the screen.
4. Select "Fill" option from this submenu. When you do so, another submenu, as shown in Figure Excel-12(b), will appear on the screen.

Now select "Series" option from this submenu. When you do so, a dialog box, as shown in figure, Eexcel-12(c) will appear on the screen.

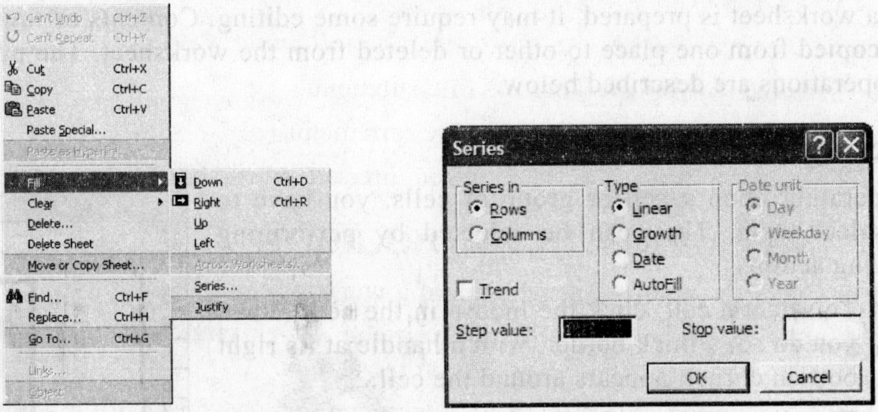

(a) (b) (c)

Figure Excel-12

6. If you wish to generate AP series, select "linear" option and for generating GP series, select "Growth" option.

7. Enter suitable value for increment, in "Step value" edit box.
8. At last, click the mouse on "OK" button.

When you do so, series will get generated.

Generating Day or Date Series

Perform following steps to generate the series of day name, month name etc.:

1. Enter the first term of the series in a cell and press Enter key. Say you enter Sun in cell D4.
2. Now click the mouse in the cell, in which you had entered the value. Thus you will have to click the mouse in D4 cell.
3. Now drag the mouse by handle, in any desired direction, (i.e. right, left, up, or down) over as many cells as there have to be terms in the series. Say you drag the mouse over 4 cells.

	A	B	C	D	E	F	G	H
1				Thu				
2				Fri				
3				Sat				
4	Thu	Fri	Sat	Sun	Mon	Tue	Wed	
5				Mon				
6				Tue				
7				Wed				
8								

Figure Excel-13

When you do so, a series of short day names will get generated, as shown in Figure Excel-13.

NOTE

Similarly, by entering January, Sunday etc. as first term of the series, you can generate month full-name, day full-name series etc.

EDITING CELLS

Once a worksheet is prepared, it may require some editing. Contents of few cells may have to be copied from one place to other or deleted from the worksheet. The procedures for all such operations are described below.

Selecting The Cells

For operating upon a cell or group of cells, you have to first select them. They can be selected by performing following actions:

1. To select a cell, click the mouse in the cell. When you do so, a thick border, with a handle at its right bottom corner, appears around the cell.
2. To select a range of cells, drag the mouse over the range. A selected cell range is shown in Figure Excel-14.

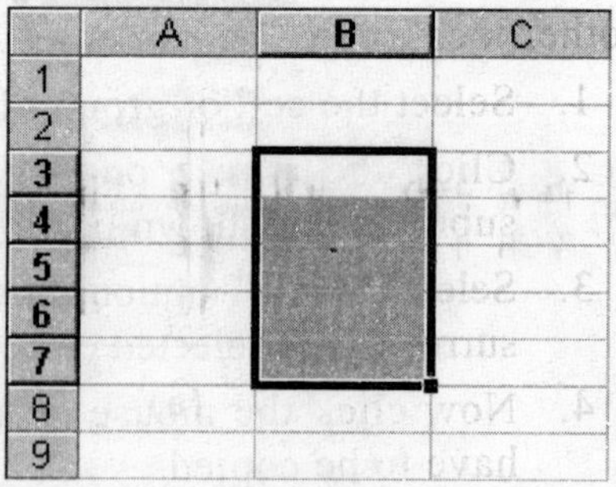

Figure Excel-14

3. To select the entire column, click the mouse on column name. For example, clicking the mouse on A will select the entire, first column.

4. To select a group of contagious columns (say E, F, G and H) drag the mouse on their column names.
5. Another method of selecting contagious group of columns (say E, F, G and H) is to press shift key of the keyboard, click the mouse on first column of the group (i.e. E in this case) and then click it on last column of the group (i.e. H in this case, with shift key pressed).
6. To select a non contagious group of columns (say A, C, D and I), keep CTRL key of the keyboard, pressed and click the mouse on name of each column, which is to be selected (i.e. A, C, D and I in this case.)
7. To select the entire row (say fifth row), click the mouse on row name (5 in this case)
8. To select the contagious or non-contagious group of rows, perform all the steps, mentioned above but instead of clicking the mouse on column names, click the mouse on row names.
9. To select the complete worksheet click the mouse on blank cell, which remains present towards left of column label A and just above row label 1.

Changing The Contents Of Cell

Contents of a cell can either be edited in Formula Bar or within the cell itself. Both the procedures are given below:

1. To modify the contents in Formula Bar, click the mouse in the cell, whose contents have to be modified. When you do so, cell contents will appear in the Formula Bar. Now using DEL or Backspace keys etc. you can modify the contents. At last, press Enter key.
2. To modify the contents, within the cell, double click the mouse in that cell, whose contents have to be modified. When you do so, insertion pointer will appear in cell. Now using different keys of the keyboard, modify the contents, within the cell. At last press Enter key.

Copying The Contents Of The Cell

Contents of a cell or group of cells can always be copied from their original place to another location of the worksheet. For this, perform following steps:

1. Select the cell or group of cells, which is to be copied.
2. Click the mouse on "Edit" option, present in bar menu. When you do so, Edit submenu, as shown in Figure Excel-12(a) will appear on the screen.
3. Select "Copy" option from Edit submenu. When you do so, a moving frame will surround the selected cells, indicating that this portion of the worksheet will get copied.
4. Now click the mouse on the cell (or the first cell of the range), where the contents have to be copied.
5. Click the mouse on "Edit" option of the bar menu again and get Edit submenu on the screen.

6. Select "Paste" option from Edit submenu.

When you do so, contents of selected range will get copied at current location. Note that if you are copying labels or data from one place to another, they will get copied as such, without any modifications done (internally). But if you copy the formula or formulae, they may get copied with some modifications or without modifications, depending upon the types of cell references (relative, absolute or mixed) used in the formulae. To understand the concept, let's consider following three cases of copying the formula:

Copying Formula, Containing Relative References

To understand the concept of relative referencing more clearly and observing its changing behavior in the event of copying the formula, perform following steps:

1. Enter three different values in cell A1, B1 and C1. Say you enter 100, 200 and 300 respectively in them.
2. Now enter the formula =(A1+B1+C1) in cell D1. When you do so, the value 600 will get displayed in the cell D1
3. Now copy this formula, in cell D1, to another cell, say E1. When you do so, to your surprise, the result will not be 600 (as the same formula produce 600 in D1). It will be 1100.

   Take a look in the Formula Bar and you will find that the formula (=A1+B1+C1) has been copied as =B1+C1+D1 (which will correctly produce 1100). The reason for this change is explained below.

Note that A1, B1 and C1 are relative references. The formula = A1+B1+C1 in cell D1 indicates that values in the third left cell second left and first left cell have to be added together and the sum has to be put in the current cell. Now if this formula is copied in cell E1, then it would mean the same thing. Thus for this cell the participating cells will be B1 (third left cell that has 200 in it), C1 (second left cell, which has 300 in it) and D1(first left cell, which has 600 in it). Thus the sum of these three cells will result into 1100.

Copying Formula Containing Absolute References

To understand the concept of absolute referencing more clearly and observing its behavior in the event of copying the formula, perform following steps:

1. Enter three different values in three different cells. Say you enter 100, 200 and 300 in cells A1, B1 and C1 respectively.
2. Now enter the formula =($A$1, $B$1, $C$1) in cell D1. When you do so, the value 600 will get displayed in it.
3. Now copy this formula, in cell D1, into another cell E1. When you do so, the same value, 600 will get displayed in cell E1.

Take a look in the Formula Bar and you will notice that formula has been copied as =$A$1+$B$1+$C$1. This time there is no change in the formula. This is because all these references (like $A$1, $B$1 etc.) are absolute references. They do not depend upon the current location. They directly point to cell, in question.

Copying Formula Containing Mixed References

To understand the concept of Mixed References, more clearly and observing its behavior, while copying the formula from one cell to another, perform following steps:

1. Enter three different values in three different cells. Say you enter 100, 200 and 300 in cells A1, B1 and C1 respectively.
2. Now enter the formula = A$1+$B1+C$1 in cell D1. When you do so, the value 600 will get displayed in it.
3. Now copy the formula in cell D1, into cell E1. When you do so, the value 1000 will get displayed in it.

   Take a look in the Formula Bar and you will notice that the formula has been copied as B$1+$B1+D$1. This is because in cell reference A$1, column is relative reference and row is fixed reference. Due to this when you copy the formula, relative part (i.e. column) changes but row part remains same. Thus A$1 gets copied as B$1. Same thing happens while copying C$1. Thus it gets copied as D$1.

On the other hand something different happens when $B1 gets copied. Note that in this cell reference, row reference is absolute (it will not change and column reference is relative). Since the cell reference is being copied in same row hence the row reference doesn't change (in this case). Thus $B1 gets copied as $B1.

The complete formula gets copied as =B$1+$B1+D$1. Note that here cell B1, containing 200 is participating twice and cell D1 contains 600. Thus the formula produces 1000.

Now let's consider another case, say formula in D1 is now copied to cell D2. In this case the formula will get copied as =A$1+$B2+c$1. Since A1 contains 100, B2 contains 0 and C1 contains 300. Hence value 400 will get displayed in D2.

Moving The Contents Of A Cell

To move the contents using Bar menu, follow all the steps that have been described for copying but choose "Cut" option instead of "Copy" option.

Deleting The Contents Of The Cell

Perform following steps to delete the contents present in the cell:

1. Select the cell or range of the cells, from which the contents have to be removed.
2. Select "Edit" option from bar menu. When you do so, Edit submenu, as shown in Figure Excel-12(a) will appear on the screen.
3. Now select "Clear" option from this submenu. When you do so, another submenu will appear on the screen.
4. Select "Contents" option from this submenu.

When you do so, the contents of the selected cell or cells will get erased.

Undo The Changes

Perform following steps to cancel the effect of previous command:

1. Click the mouse on "Edit" option present in bar menu. When you do so, Edit submenu, as shown in Figure Excel-12(a) will appear on the screen.
2. Select "Undo" option from Edit submenu.

When you do so, the effect of previous command will get cancelled and the worksheet will retain the status, as it had before executing the previous command.

Note

Previous command can be repeated, either by selecting "Redo" option from the Edit submenu or by clicking the mouse on "Redo" button present in Standard toolbar.

Finding And Replacing The Contents In The Worksheet

Given content can be searched in the worksheet for its presence and if the need be, it could also be replaced by other content. For example, the presence of the word, **Bonus** can be searched in the worksheet and if required, it could be replaced by other word, say, **Incentive.**

Find and Replace are two different facilities of MS-Excel, available in Edit submenu. Replace facility is extension of Find facility and is executed in the same way as Find facility is done. The procedure for finding the given contents and replacing it by other contents is given below.

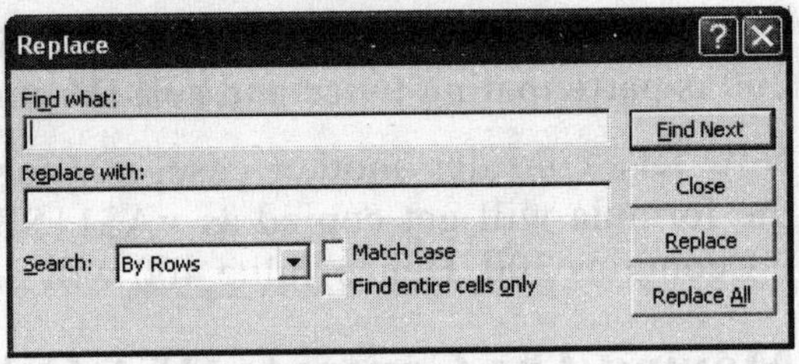

Figure Excel-15

1. Select "Edit" option from the bar menu. When you do so, Edit submenu, as shown in Figure Excel-12(a) will appear on the screen.
2. Select "Replace" option from Edit submenu. When you do so, a dialog box, as shown in Figure Excel-15 will appear on the screen.
3. Enter the contents to be searched, in "Find what" text box. For example, if you wish to search the word, Bonus in the worksheet, type this word in "Find what" text box.
4. Type the word, with which the word being searched is to be replaced, in "Replace with" text box. For example, if the word Bonus is to be replaced with Incentive, type Incentive in "Replace with" text box.
5. Specify the direction of search by selecting either "By Rows" option or "By columns" option from "Search" dropdown list.
6. To make the search, case sensitive, check "Match case" check box.
7. To start the process, click the mouse on "Find Next" button. When you do so, MS-Excel will search the given contents (Bonus in above mentioned example) and halt the search temporarily, if it finds a match.

8. To replace the searched occurrence, with the given word, click the mouse on "Replace" button.
9. If you wish to replace all the occurrences of the given word with another word, in one shot, click the mouse on "Replace All" button.
10. At last, click the mouse on "Close" button.

MANIPULATING THE WORKSHEET

Operations like changing the height and width of rows and columns, inserting new rows and columns etc. are the operation, which are frequently required, while preparing a worksheet. Operational details of these activities are given below.

Changing Height Of The Row

Perform following steps to alter the height of the row, so that bigger font characters could be accommodated in it:

1. Select the row or group of rows, for which the height has to be changed.
2. Select "Format" option from the bar menu. When you do so, Format submenu, as shown in Figure Excel-16(a), will appear on the screen.

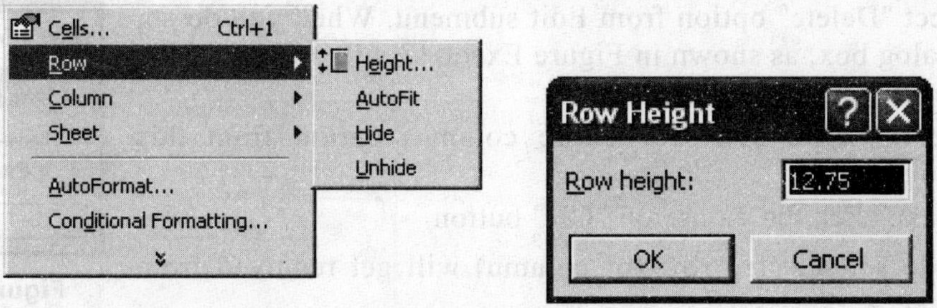

(a) (b) (c)

Figure Excel-16

3. Select "Row" option from Format submenu. When you do so, another submenu, as shown in Figure Excel-16(b), will appear on the screen.
4. Select "Height" option from this submenu. When you do so, a dialog box, as shown in Figure Excel-16(c) will appear on the screen.
5. Now enter the desired height in "Row height" text box, of this dialog box.
6. At last, click the mouse on "OK" button.

When you do so, the height of selected rows will change.

Changing The Width Of The Column

The procedure for changing the width of the column is same as that of changing the height of the row (mentioned above), except that you need to select "Column" option from the Format submenu (Figure Excel-16(a)) and "width" option from the submenu that appears thereafter.

Inserting Blank Row Or Column

Perform following steps to insert blank row or column in the worksheet:

1. Place the cell pointer on the row (or column), above (or left) which the blank row (or column) is to be inserted.
2. Click the mouse on "Insert" option present in the bar menu. When you do so, a submenu, as shown in Figure Excel-17, will appear on the screen.
3. Select "Rows (or columns)" option from Insert submenu.

When you do so, a new blank row (or column) will get inserted just above (or towards left of) the current row (column).

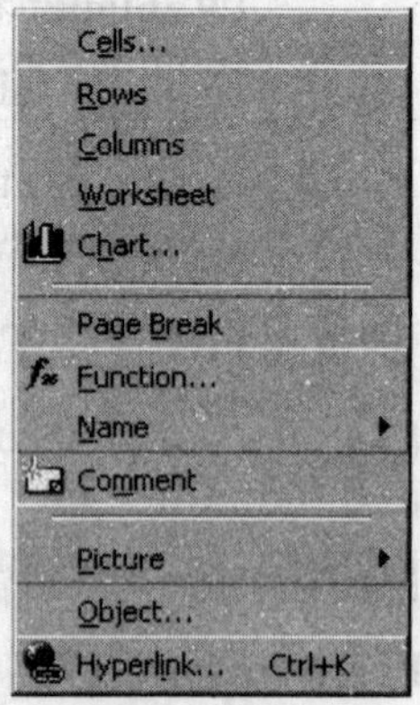

Figure Excel-17

Deleting Row Or Column

Perform following steps to delete unwanted row(s) or column(s) in the worksheet:

1. Select the row(s) or column(s) that need to be deleted.
2. Click the mouse on "Edit" option of the bar menu. When you do so, Edit submenu, as shown in Figure Excel-12(a) will appear on the screen.
3. Select "Delete" option from Edit submenu. When you do so, a dialog box, as shown in Figure Excel-18 will appear on the screen.
4. Select "Entire row" (or entire column) option from this dialog box.
5. At last, click the mouse on "OK" button.

When you do so, selected row (or column) will get removed from the worksheet.

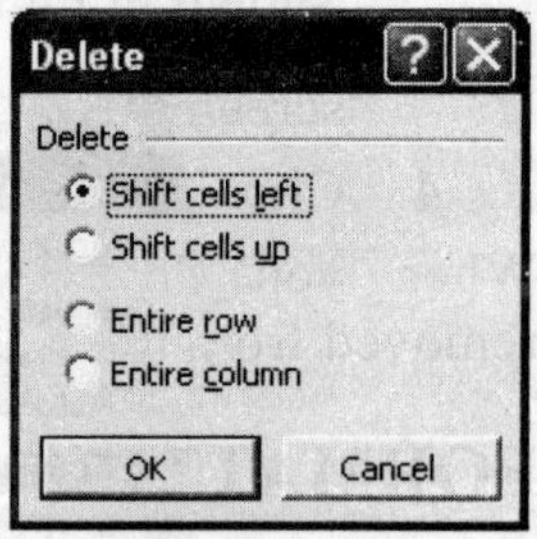

Figure Excel-18

Inserting A New Blank Worksheet

Perform following steps to insert a new blank worksheet in the workbook:

1. Click the mouse on that tab of the worksheet, left to which a new blank worksheet is to be inserted. For example, if a new worksheet is to be inserted in between Sheet4 and Sheet5, click the mouse on Sheet5 tab.
2. Select "Insert" option from the Bar menu. When you do so, Insert submenu, as shown in Figure Excel-17 will appear on the screen.
3. Select "Worksheet" option from Insert submenu.

When you do so, a blank worksheet will get inserted in the workbook.

Renaming The Worksheet

Recall that the worksheets of the workbook are named as Sheet1, Sheet2, Sheet3 etc. Perform following steps to rename any worksheet:

1. Right click the mouse on that name (sheet tab), which is to be changed. For example, if fifth worksheet is to be renamed, click the mouse on the tab named Sheet5. When you do so, a popup menu, as shown in Figure Excel-19 will appear on the screen.
2. Select "Rename" option from this submenu. When you do so, the sheet name will get highlighted.
3. Type the new name and press Enter key.

When you do so, the name of the worksheet will change.

Figure Excel-19

Deleting A Worksheet

Perform following steps to remove any worksheet from the workbook:

1. Select the worksheet, which is to be deleted by clicking the mouse on its sheet tab. For example, if fifth worksheet is to be deleted, click the mouse on Sheet5 tab.
2. Click the mouse on "Edit" option of the bar menu. When you do so, Edit submenu, as shown in Figure Excel-12(a) will appear on the screen.
3. Select "Delete Sheet" option from Edit submenu. When you do so, an alert box, as shown in Figure Excel-20 will appear on the screen.
4. Click the mouse on "OK" button.

When you do so, current worksheet will get removed from the workbook.

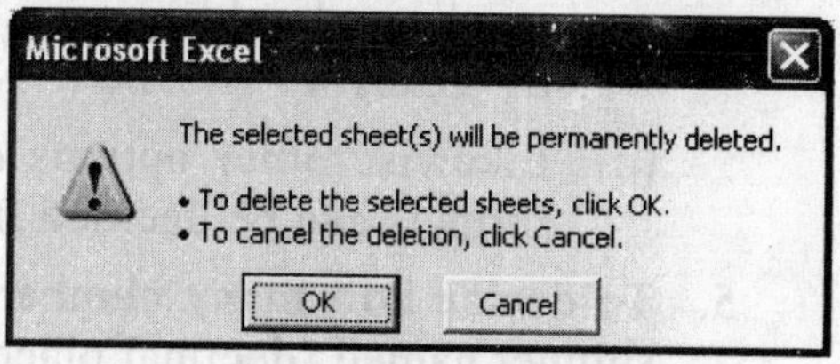

Figure Excel-20

FORMATTING CELLS

You are already familiar with the default formatting that automatically takes place, when you enter text, numbers, formulae etc. in the cells (already explained earlier). If the need be the default format for the selected range or the entire worksheet can be changed. In addition to this, many other things like adding comma or $ sign in numbers, changing alignment of text in cells, applying borders around selected cells etc. can also be done through formatting facility available in MS-Excel. Different types of formatting operations are described below.

Applying Number Format

Perform following steps to specify the format for the numerical values that would be entered in the cell or range of cells:

1. Select the cell or range of cells, on which you wish to apply the Number format.
2. Select "Format" option from the Bar menu. When you do so, Format submenu, will appear on the screen.
3. Select "Cells" option from Format submenu. When you do so, a dialog box, as shown in Figure Excel-21 will appear on the screen. If somehow different options appear in the dialog box, click the mouse on "Number" tab.

4. To apply the Number format, select the desired option from "Category" list box. For example:

   (a) To decide the way, numbers will appear in the cells, click the mouse on "Custom" option, present in "Category" list box. When you do so, a list of formats will appear within the dialog box. Select the desired format.

   (b) To decide the Date or Time formats, click the mouse on "Date" or "Time" option (respectively), present in category list box. When you do so, many date and time formats will appear, within the dialog box. Select the desired format.

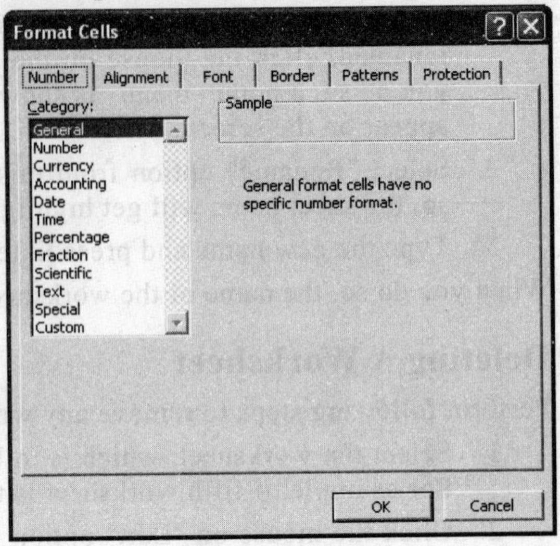

Figure Excel-21

   (c) Where and at what place the comma should be used in numbers and in what color or format the negative numbers should appear, can be decided by selecting "Number" option present in "Category" list box.

   (d) Likewise other options can be selected from "Category" list box and related formats can be decided from the options that appear thereafter.

5. To decide how many numbers will appear after the decimal point, make use of the spinner named "decimal places".
6. Click the mouse on "OK" button.

When you do so, all chosen formats will get applied to the selected cells. If the data already exists in the cells, it will get automatically formatted else when the data will be entered in these cells, the format will get applied on them.

Applying Alignment

Recall that the contents entered in the cell are either left aligned or right aligned. But if the need be, they can be top or bottom aligned or oriented at certain angle, as shown in Figure Excel-22(a). Note that applying Alignment format to the desired cells does this. Perform following steps for applying this format:

1. Select the cell or range of cells, on which you wish to apply the Alignment format.
2. Select "Format" option from the bar menu. When you do so, Format submenu will appear on the screen.
3. Select "Cells" option from Format submenu. When you do so, a dialog box, as shown in Figure Excel-21 will appear on the screen.
4. Click the mouse on "Alignment" tab. When you do so, the dialog box options will change, as shown in Figure Excel-22(b).

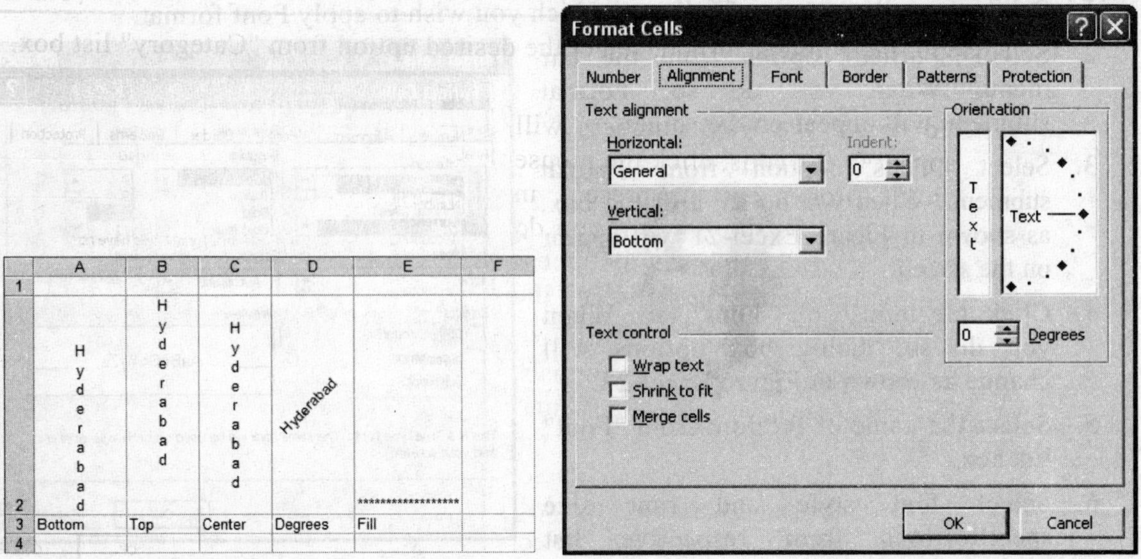

(a) **(b)**

Figure Excel-22

5. If the contents of the cell are to be aligned horizontally, select the desired alignment (such as, left, right center etc.), using "Horizontal" drop down list, present in the dialog box. If you wish to fill the whole cell with repeated occurrence of a character, select "Fill" option from this drop down list.
6. If the cell contents are to be vertically aligned, select the desired option, (such as, Top, Bottom, Justify etc.) from "Vertical" drop down list.
7. If the contents of the cell are to be placed diagonally, set the angle of inclination through "Degree" spinner, present in orientation section of the dialog box.
8. If the length of the text is larger than the width of the cell and you wish to wrap the text so that it is accommodated in multiple lines, within the cell, check the "Wrap text" check box.
9. If you wish to shrink the longer text so that it fits within the width of the cell, check, "Shrink to fit" check box.
10. To merge, adjacent cells, so that longer text is accommodated properly, check "merge" cells check box.
11. At last, click the mouse on "OK" button.

When you do so, chosen alignment option will get applied to the selected cells.

Applying Font Formats

The data that you enter in worksheet is always entered in preset font, font style and font type. These specifications can always be changed either for selected cells or entire worksheet. Perform following steps to apply font format:

1. Select the cell or range of cells, on which you wish to apply Font format.
2. Select "Format" option from the bar menu. When you do so, Format submenu will appear on the screen.
3. Select "Cells" option from Format submenu. When you do so, a dialog box, as shown in Figure Excel-21 will appear on the screen.
4. Click the mouse on "Font" tab. When you do so, dialog box options will change as shown in Figure Excel-23.
5. Select the name of the font from "Font" list box.
6. Select font style and font size specifications from respective list boxes.

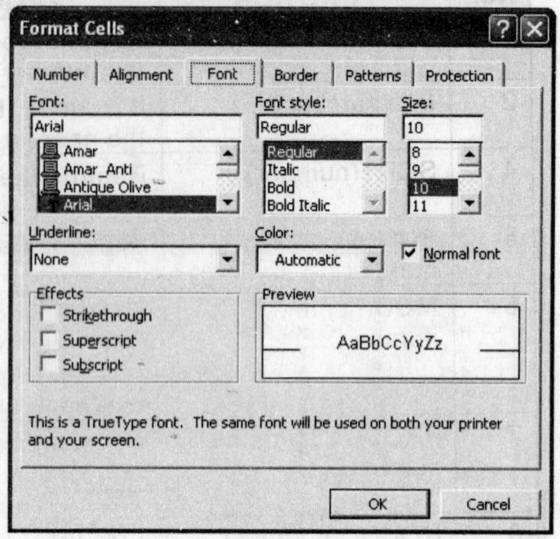

Figure Excel-23

7. If the characters have to be underlined, select a suitable line type from "Underline" drop down list box.
8. If the text has to be striked out, check "strikethrough" check box, present in effects section of this dialog box.
9. At last, click the mouse on "OK" button.

When you do so, chosen font specifications will get applied to the selected cell.

FUNCTIONS

MS-EXCEL has numerous inbuilt formulae in it. The formulae are called functions or Excel functions. Each formula operates upon the given value (either taken from cell or written directly in the function itself) and produces specific result. These functions can either be written directly in the cell or can be included in the formula that you define. Functions are written in following format:

Function-name (arguments)

Here function-name is the name of the function and arguments are the list of values, separated by comma, on which the function has to operate.

For example, SUM is a valid MS-Excel function. It takes cell addresses or constant numeric values as arguments and returns total. For example, SUM (10, 20, 30) will return 60. Similarly, it can be used as SUM(A1+B1+C1) here A1, B1 and C1 are the cell addresses. If they contain 100, 150 and 200 respectively then this function will return 450.

As mentioned above, you can also use functions in your own formulae. For example, =1000-SUM (A1+B1+C1) is a valid formula. Few commonly used MS-Excel functions are described in the following table:

No.	FUNCTION	PROCEDURE	EXAMPLE	RESULT
1	ABS(number)	Returns absolute value of the number.	=ABS(-200)	200
2	INT(number)	It rounds the number to the nearest integer.	=INT(200.37)	200
4	SQRT(number)	Returns the square root of the number.	=SQRT(64)	8
5	SUM(number1, number2....)	Adds all the number	=SUM(140,30)	170
6	MOD(number1, number2...)	This function divides the first number with the second number and returns the remainder.	=MOD(127,5)	2
7	PRODUCT(number1, number2...)	It multiples all the numbers given and returns the product	=PRODUCT(5,6)	30
8	ROUND(number1, number2...)	It rounds the number to the specified number of digit.	=ROUND(122.66,1) =ROUND(122.6679, 2)	122.7 122.66
9	AVERAGE(number1, number2...)	It returns the average (arithmetic mean) of its arguments.	=AVERAGE(15,17)	16
10	COUNT(value1, value2)	It counts the numbers, which are provided to it as arguments.	=COUNT(1,8,4,9,1)	5
11	MAX(number1, number2)	It returns the largest value in given set of values	=MAX(100,135)	135
12	MIN(number1, number2)	It returns the smallest value in given set of values.	=MIN(100,135)	100
13	LEN(text)	Returns the number of characters in a text string	=LEN("INDIA")	5
14	LEFT(text, value)	This function returns as many leftmost characters of the given text string as specified by value.	=LEFT("INDIA",2)	IN
15	RIGHT(text, value)	This function returns as many rightmost character of the given text string as specified by value.	=RIGHT("INDIA",2)	IA
16	LOWER(text)	Converts all the uppercase letters in the lowercase	=LOWER("INDIA")	india
17	UPPER(text)	Converts a text string to uppercase	=UPPER("India")	INDIA

No.	FUNCTION	PROCEDURE	EXAMPLE	RESULT
18	TRIM(text)	It removes all the spaces from the text string, except for single space between the words.	=TRIM("Hi Dear")	Hi Dear
19	REPT(text, number of times)	It repeats the text, given number of times	=REPT("S",5)	SSSSS

PRINTING THE WORKSHEET

Perform following steps for printing the worksheet:

1. Select "File" option from the bar menu. When you do so, File submenu, as shown in Figure Excel-10 will appear on the screen.
2. Select "Print" option from this submenu. When you do so, a dialog box, as shown in Figure Excel-24, will appear on the screen.
3. Make use of "Name" drop down list box and specify the name of the printer, on which the worksheet is to be printed.
4. Make use of "From" and "To" spinners to specify the pages of the worksheet that are to be printed.
5. Make use of "Number of copies" spinner and specify the number of copies that are to be printed.
6. If the printing is to be done in a file, check "Print to File" check box.
7. After selecting all the required options, click the mouse on "OK" button.

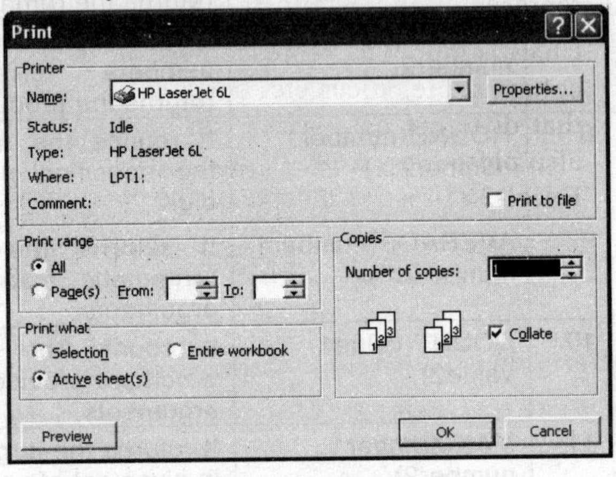

Figure Excel-24

When you do so, printing will start and the worksheet will get printed.

INTRODUCTION TO CHARTS

Representing data in the form of chart is one of the most popular methods, which is used, for the purpose of data analysis. Excel provides many tools and facilities, using which you can transform the data into charts. In this chapter we will mainly deal with charting capabilities of MS-Excel. Let's take the example of following data and analyze it. The data pertains to sales and expenditure figures of three companies viz. TEK, SUN and NET.

	A	B	C	D	E
1	Sales and Expenditure Figure				
2					
3			TEK	SUN	NET
4	SALES		1,000	15,000	20,000
5	EXPND		4,000	8,000	7,000
6	TAX		2,000	4,000	1,000

Figure Excel- 25

When you go through the data carefully you may find the following facts from the data:

1. Maximum sale has been made by the company NET, which paid the lowest tax.
2. Highest expenditure has been made by the company SUN, which has paid the highest tax.
3. The company TEK has made a loss, while the other two companies have incurred a profit.

From the above analysis, it is quite clear that data table is an effective medium for data analysis. But you have to do lot of calculations to bring out the hidden facts. On the other hand, if you transform the same data into a chart, no calculations have to be done. Hidden facts get revealed themselves. So you can say that chart is more effective medium of data representation. Details of MS-Excel charts are described below.

Chart is graphical representation of data. Data values are represented in terms of bars, lines, columns, pie, slices etc. Different bars, columns, lines etc. are colored in different colors so that different data series can be distinguished from one another. Standard data values are also plotted horizontally and vertically so as to get the exact idea of their magnitude. Figure Excel-26 illustrates some of the charts that have been plotted in MS-Excel.

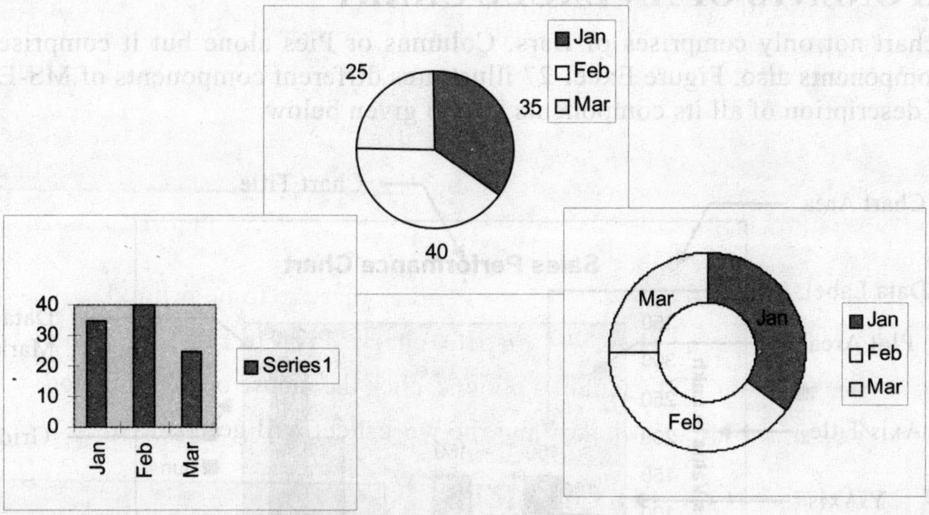

Figure Excel-26

INTRODUCTION TO MS-EXCEL CHARTS

Excel supports 18 different types of charts to represent the data in different forms. Different parts of the chart can also be labeled. Which type of chart will suit best, for the given data will depend upon what the data pertains to and what type of analysis is to be done.

Before we go into the operational aspects of drawing the chart, let's first, get introduced to different types of charts that can be generated in MS-Excel.

TYPES OF CHARTS

1. Area Chart and 3-D - Area chart.
2. Bar Chart and 3-D - Bar chart.
3. Column Chart and 3-D - Column chart.
4. Line Chart and 3-D - Line chart.
5. Pie Chart and 3-D - Pie Chart.
6. Doughnut Chart and
7. XY Scatter Chart.

Apart from above mention charts, MS-Excel provide following 3-D Charts:

8. 3-D Cylinder Chart.
9. 3-D Cone Chart.
10. 3-D Pyramid Chart.
11. 3-D Surface Chart.

COMPONENTS OF AN EXCEL CHART

Excel chart not only comprises of Bars, Columns or Pies alone but it comprises of many other components also. Figure Excel-27 illustrates different components of MS-Excel chart. A brief description of all its components is also given below.

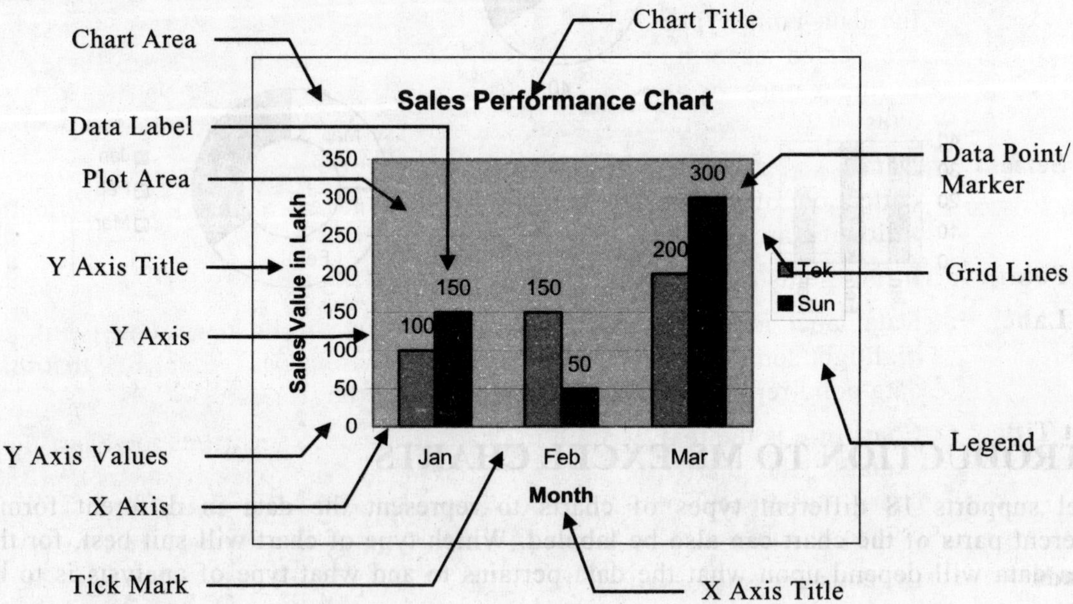

Figure Excel- 27

Chart Area : Chart Area is the entire area that is reserved for accommodating the chart and other components such as legends, titles etc.

Plot Area : Plot area is part of chart area, which contains the chart.

Y Axis : It is the vertical line whose length and segments represent different values, which you will be making use of, to show the variation of different identities (such as sales, expenditure, profit figures etc.) when you plot the chart.

X Axis : A horizontal line, which meets Y axis at right angle, on which you show the variation of another component (such as time, month, year etc.) of the chart. Its length and segments represent different intervals of values.

Y Axis Title : Y axis title identifies the values, which have been illustrated on Y axis. For example, simply writing 10, 50, 100, 150 etc. on Y axis doesn't convey the full details of the values. But a Y axis title 'Sales value in Lakh clearly illustrates that the figures written on Y axis represent Sales figures and that too in Lakh.

X Axis Title : Similar to Y axis title, X axis conveys details of the X axis values.

Tick marks : They are the small lines, used to divide both the axes into small segments, in order to form a scale.

Grid Lines : Grid lines are the lines that can be thought of as an extension of tick marks. They help in reading the values of the data points. They are scaled according to the values of the axes.

	A	B	C	D	E
1		Jan	Feb	Mar	
2	Sales	100	50	150	
3	Expenditure	150	100	200	
4					

Figure Excel-28

Data Series : Data series is a collection of related values that are plotted on a chart. For example, following are two data series:

Data Point : It represents one value of the data series.

Data Label : Data label is some piece of text, which is written near data point, to highlight some aspect of it. For example, writing 'Max' identifies that this data point represents the maximum value of the series.

Chart Title : Chart title is the text, written in chart area, which identifies the chart. For example, the chart title, 'Sales Performance Chart' clearly states that the chart has been plotted to represent sales performance of the company/companies, graphically.

Legends : Legends are some sort of labels that identify different series that have been plotted in the chart. Generally these labels are attached to a symbol or color or pattern that is associated with the series of the chart. It is used to distinguish one data series from another.

MAKING A CHART USING CHART BAR

In order to make a chart, using chart bar, firstly you have to display the chart bar on the screen and then perform the required steps. The procedure to display the chart bar is explained below:

Displaying The Chart Bar

Perform following steps to display the Chart Bar on the screens, if it is not there:

1. Select "View" option from the bar menu. When you do so, View submenu, as shown in figure Excel-29(a), will appear on the screen.
2. Select "Toolbar" option from View submenu. When you do so, another submenu, as shown in figure Excel-29(b), will appear on the screen.
3. Select "Chart" option from this submenu. On doing so, a chart bar, as shown in figure Excel-30, will appear on the screen:

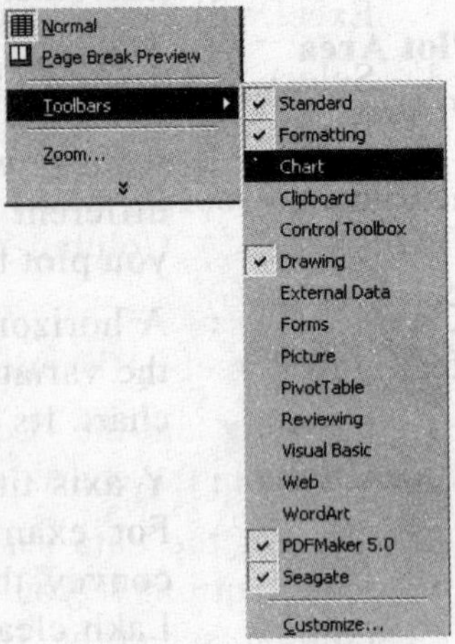

(a) (b)

Figure Excel-29

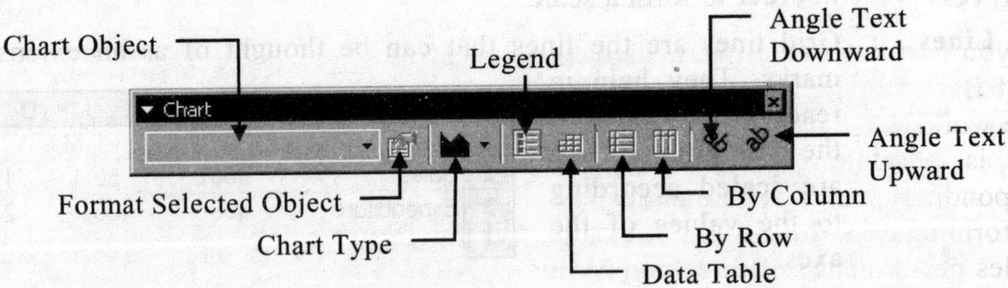

Figure Excel-30

Making A Chart

Perform following steps to prepare the desired chart:

1. Select that portion of the data that has to be transformed into chart. Let's take the example of the data pertaining to three companies viz. Tek, Sun & Net that is shown in figure Excel-31(a). Select the range A2:D6.

	A	B	C	D
1	Profit & Losss Copmparision Sheet			
2		Tek	Sun	Net
3	Sales	5000	12000	25000
4	Spend	4000	5000	7000
5	Tax	2000	3000	4000
6	Profit	-1000	4000	14000

(a)

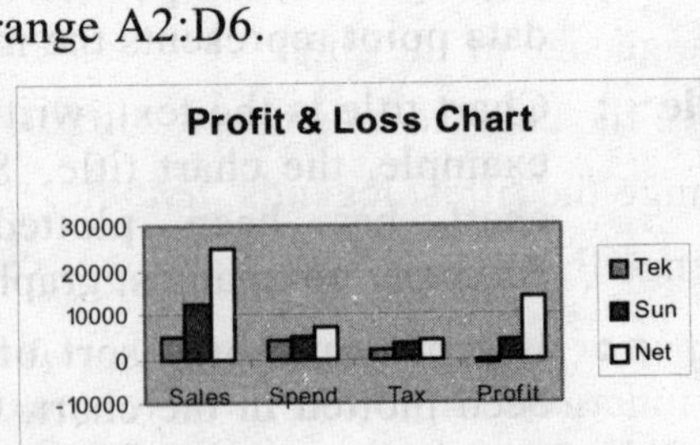

(b)

Figure Excel-31

2. Now select "Chart Type" button from the chart bar. On selecting this button, MS-Excel will display a chart list as shown in figure Excel-32.
3. Select the desired chart type from this list. Say you select Column Chart option from this list.

When you do so, MS-Excel will automatically plot the chart and include it as an object in the worksheet. A Column chart made for the options chosen above is shown in figure Excel-31(b).

Refer figure Excel-31(b) and note the following points:

1. Clicking on the 'Legend' button will display or hide the legend in the chart.
2. To plot the data series according to the row, click on 'By Row' button. If you want to plot the series according to the column, select the 'By Column' named button.
3. To display the chart text diagonally, select 'Angle text' button.

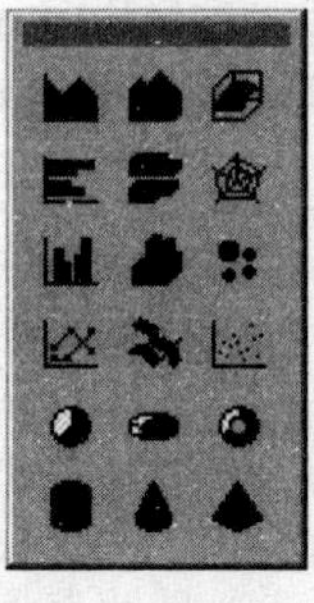

Figure Excel- 32

CHANGING CHART VALUES

Once you have created a chart, its data points (columns in case of Column charts, bars in case of Bar charts, slices in case of Pie charts etc.) get automatically linked to the values (of the worksheet), based on which they were created. Due to this link, on-line updating of charts is possible. In On-line updating, if you change the values in worksheet, corresponding change is automatically reflected in the chart, without giving any command or performing extra function. For example, if you have plotted a column chart for depicting the sales performance of three companies viz. Tek, Sun and Net, in which Tek's sales was Rs. 5000. Now if you change the value from 5000 to 10000 then immediately the height of Tek's column (representing sales figure) will increase.

INTRODUCTION TO FORMATTING OPERATIONS

While working with MS-Excel charts, you may be required to perform following types of functions:

1. Change size of the chart.
2. Move the chart to a different suitable location.
3. Change the titles, legends, text etc.
4. Change the font, font size and style etc. of the text.

All such types of operations are called formatting functions. Remember that for most of the formatting functions, first you have to select the chart and then that particular component of the chart that has to be modified and then perform formatting operation on it. The procedure for selecting the chart and its components is described below.

Selecting The Chart

Chart can be selected by clicking the mouse on it. When you select the chart, handles appear around the chart, as shown in figure Figure Excel-33

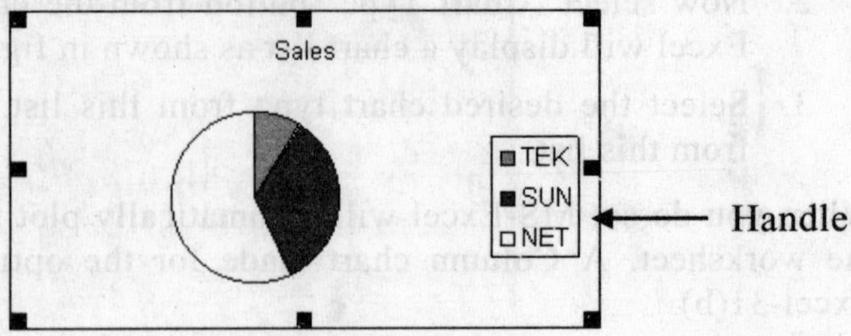

Figure Excel- 33

Selecting Items In A Chart

Perform following steps to select an item of the chart:

1. Select the chart by clicking the mouse on the chart.
2. Now click the mouse on the item that you want to select.

For example, if you wish to select the legend of the chart, first select the chart by clicking the mouse on it and then click it on the legend. When you click the mouse on the item, it gets surrounded with a border with handles, which indicates that this component of the chart has been selected for modification.

Canceling The Selection

To cancel the selection press Esc (escape) key or click the mouse on any blank space of the worksheet.

Deleting A Chart

To delete a chart, first select the chart and then press "Del" key of the keyboard.

Moving The Chart

To move the chart from one location to another, simply select the chart and drag the mouse to the new location. As you drag the mouse, chart will also move along with the mouse pointer. When you release the mouse button the chart will get located at new location.

Sizing The Chart

To change the size of the chart (increase/decrease), first select the chart and then place the mouse pointer at any handle. The mouse pointer will change to a double-headed arrow pointer. Now drag the mouse. Dragging the mouse will change the size of the chart.

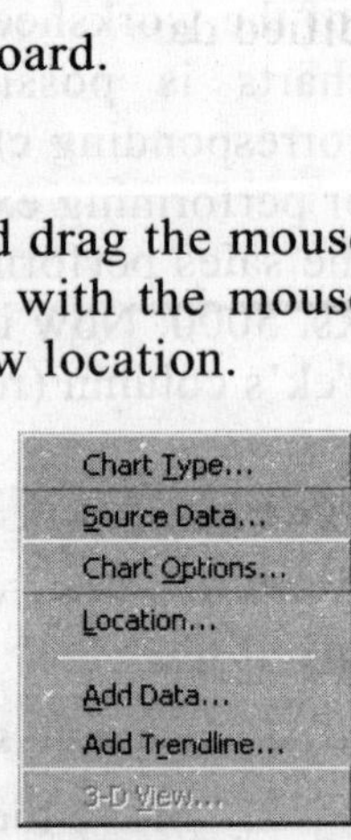

Figure Excel-34

Changing The Title In The Chart

Perform following steps to make changes in the title:

1. First select the title that needs to be altered.
2. Now select "Chart" option from the bar menu. When you do so, a submenu, as shown in Figure Excel-34, will appear on the screen.
3. Now select "Chart Options" option from this submenu. When you do so, a dialog box, as shown in Figure Excel-35, will appear on screen.

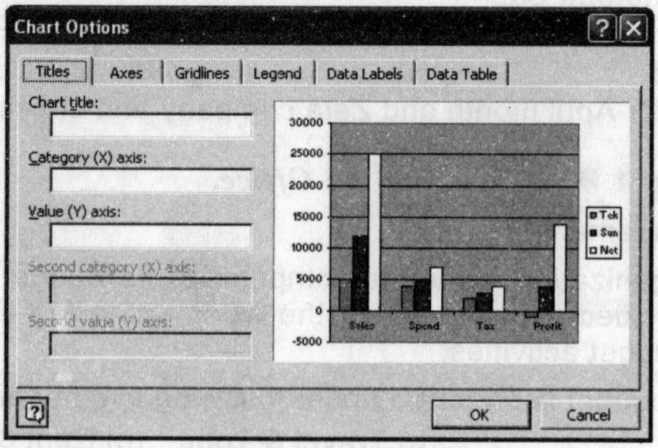

Figure Excel-35

4. Click the mouse in 'Chart Title' text box and enter the title. If you wish to change the title of the chart. If you wish to make changes in X axis title or Y axis title, select corresponding text boxes and enter new titles in the desired text box.
5. At last, click the mouse on "OK" button.

When you do so, selected chart will get updated automatically.

Making Other Modifications In The Chart

Other modifications can be made in the chart by clicking the mouse on other tabs like "Axes", "Gridlines", "Legends", "Data Labels" etc. present in the dialog box and entering modified data in corresponding text boxes that appear within the dialog box.

PRACTICAL ASSIGNMENTS

Assignment 1: Creating a Simple Worksheet.

1. Perform following operations to get familiar with the process of creating worksheet:
   (i) Invoke MS-Excel on your computer.
   (i) Enter all the labels, formulae and data that are shown in Figure 6.2 and create a simple worksheet.
   (iii) Modify sales figures and observe its effect on total.
   (iv) Save the worksheet on disk.
   (v) Open the worksheet and perform following operations:
      (a) Add a new column after Mar to accommodate April figures.
      (b) Add a new row above Total row to accommodate a new company, named Zeta.

(c) Modify all formulae accordingly to get the sum of all the four months and four companies.

(d) Add data for April month and Zeta company and check your results.

Assignment 2: Creating A Worksheet For An Office.

2. Read following requirement first:

   Assume that an organization wishes to computerize its Budget Preparation & Analysis activities. It has decided to computerize the work, using MS-Excel. Say following are the details of the budget activities:

   (i) Organization's budget is prepared under following five heads:

   (a) Salary (b) Travel & Tour (c) Rent & Maintenance

   (d) Electricity & Telephone (e) Miscellaneous

   (ii) Following figures are clearly shown in the budget:

   (a) Amount under each head is classified into two categories i.e. Officers and Staff. Totals of these amounts are also shown in the budget.

   (b) Previous year figures are also included in same format in the report (as that of current year, mentioned in previous point).

   (iii) Apart from above mentioned figures, following analysis is also included in budget:

   (a) The difference between current year figures and last year figures, for each head.

   (b) Percentage increase/decrease for each head.

   To perform this activity, using Excel, make a worksheet as shown below.

Budget For The Year 2006-2007										
(Figure In Lakhs)										
Head	**Last Year**			**Current Year**			**Difference**			**Total % Diff.**
	Officers	**Staff**	**Total**	***Officers***	**Staff**	**Total**	**Officers**	**Staff**	**Total**	
Salary										
Travel & Tour										
Rent & Maintenance										
Electricity & Telephone										
Miscellaneous										
Total										

3. Perform following activities, for preparing the worksheet.

(i) Wherever Totals are there, use formula for them.

(ii) Make use of formula to calculate differences.

(iii) Make use of formula to calculate all the percentages.

(iv) Enter relevant data in the worksheet and test the validity of formulae used and worksheet.

4. Save the worksheet in a file.
5. Print the worksheet on printer.
6. Exit from MS-Excel

Assignment 3 : Plotting Chart For Given Data.

1. Assume that five students of a collage scored marks in their final examination, as mentioned below.

Student Name	Subject		
	Physics	Chemistry	Maths
Rahul	88	90	98
Soni	80	82	86
Ranjna	90	69	96
Atul	70	75	85
Vipul	75	76	77

2. Enter this data in Excel worksheet to present it in the form of a table.
3. Enter formula in the worksheet to calculate total marks for Rahul.
4. Copy above mentioned formula for other students.
5. Plot a Pie chart for Rahul to show subject wise contribution.
6. Plot a Bar chart to show subject wise comparison of marks for Atul and Vipul.
7. Plot a Doughnut chart to show subject wise comparison of marks for Rahul and Soni.

Assignment 4 : Plotting Another Chart For Given Data.

8. Assume that target and achievement figure of three companies are as follows:

Company	Budget	Achievement
JET	500	498
SPARK	800	980
FUSION	300	600

9. Enter above mentioned data in MS-Excel worksheet.

10. Enter a formula in suitable cell to calculate the difference between target and achievement.
11. Copy this formula for other two companies.
12. Plot a column chart to show budget and achievement figures of all the three companies.
13. Modify the chart and:
    (i) Include "Performance Chart For 2007" as chart title in the chart.
    (ii) Include "Company" as X axis title in the chart.
    (iii) Include "Value in Lakh" as Y axis title in the chart.
14. Change achievement figure of FUSION Company from 60 to 1000 and observe the change in the chart.
15. Select achievement column of SPARK Company and drag it downwards and observe its effect on corresponding data in worksheet.
16. Move the chart to some other location.
17. Change the size of the chart.
18. Convert column chart into bar chart.
19. Copy the chart in some other worksheet.
20. Delete the charts.

****

Information Technology Lab
(CM-110)

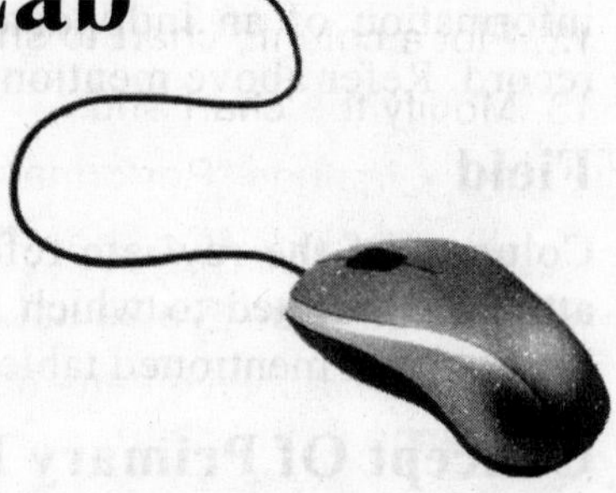

MS-Access

(Self Study Material and Practical Assignments)

INTRODUCTION

MS-Access is database management system. It has been designed and developed by Microsoft Corporation of USA for performing data storage and retrieval type of activities on computer. It stores data in the form of tables and provides means for defining the selection criterion for retrieving the data and presenting it in the form of report. What are tables, how they are defined and how data is entered and retrieved from them are the topics, which are described in this chapter.

INTRODUCTION TO TABLE

Table is basically collection of rows, divided into one or more columns. Each row consists of complete information of a single identity (such as individual, object, place etc.) and each column of the row represents an attribute, related to which the information is maintained within the table.

For example, a table containing data of ten meritorious students, who secured first ten positions in the examination, is illustrated below:

Roll No.	Name	Sex	City	Age	Marks
101	Ravi	M	Delhi	17	855
170	Jyoti	M	Hyderabad	18	846
210	Rahul	M	Mumbai	19	835
525	Seema	F	Mumbai	17	795
750	Jyoti	F	Lucknow	20	780
810	Suman	F	Hyderabad	18	780
825	Alok	M	Chennai	19	775
888	Saket	M	Hyderabad	18	760
860	Sachin	M	Mumbai	21	747
920	Tarun	M	Delhi	19	735

Record

Each row of the table is referred to as record. In other words, you can say that complete information of an individual identity that is being maintained within the table, is called record. Refer above mentioned table and note that it contains 10 records.

Field

Columns of the row are referred to as fields. In other words, you can say that all those attributes, related to which information is being maintained in the rows are called fields. Refer above mentioned table and note that each record consists of 6 fields.

Concept Of Primary Key

The field that uniquely identifies the record is called Primary Key. Refer above illustrated data. It consists of 10 records and 6 fields. In this data, Roll Number field uniquely identifies the record. For example, when you say, get me the record of roll number 170 then there is no confusion. In response, record of Jyoti, male student is given to you. On the other hand, if you ask for record of Jyoti, confusion prevails. It is not sure, whether record of roll number 170 is to be fetched or record of roll number 750 is to be fetched because both of them have the same name. Similarly neither sex field nor city nor age nor marks field can uniquely define the record. In other words, it can be said that value of Primary Key doesn't get repeated in the table.

DATA TYPES

Refer previously illustrated table and note that Roll Number is a field, which consists of numbers. Similarly Name field consists of alphabets. Now the question is what all types of data can be accommodated in MS-Access fields? Well, an introduction of the data types, supported in MS-Access is given below.

Text

Text data consist of alphabets, numbers, special characters etc. For example, India, 77 Park Avenue, Hyderabad-08 etc. are examples of Text data.

Fields that hold text data are called Text fields. In MS-Access, text fields can hold maximum up to 255 characters. Default length of text field is 50 characters.

Memo

Like text data, memo data also consists of alphabets, numbers, special characters etc. But they can consist of more than 255 characters. Those fields, which hold Memo data, are called Memo fields. In MS-Access, practically there is no limit to the length of Memo fields. They are generally utilized for storing long history or remarks associated with the record.

Number

Number data consists of numerical figures. For example, 175, 266.87, 23.4298 etc. are examples of Number data.

Fields that hold numbers are referred to as, Number fields. Number fields can either hold integer numbers or real numbers (number with decimal point).

Date/Time

Date and Time data consists of valid date and time values respectively. In date, day, month, year values are separated by forward slash. For example, 05/03/2006, 10/12/2004 etc. are valid date values. Similarly 10:15:05AM, 10:25:30PM etc. are valid time values.

Currency

Currency data consist of financial figures. For example, 100.25, 77.75 etc. are financial figures. Those fields, which hold financial figures, are called Currency fields. In MS-Access these fields are accurate up to 15 digits on left of the decimal point and 4 digits on the right of decimal point. While doing calculations, rounding off is prevented in this type of field.

Auto Number

These fields are basically, serial number fields, in which serial number is automatically entered (by MS-Access).

Yes/No

Those fields, which hold logical data, are called Yes/No fields. Valid logical values that can be held in them are T and F. If you enter Yes in this field, T gets stored in the table. On the other hand, if you enter No, F gets stored.

OLE

Objects like, MS-Excel Worksheet, graphical pictures, sound clips, video clips etc. are example of OLE data. Those fields that hold OLE data are called OLE fields. In MS-Access these fields basically hold the links to OLE objects, which have been created by other softwares.

Hyperlink

Hyperlink is basically a link to other object. When you click the mouse on hyperlink, linked object is accessed. Those fields, which contain hyperlinks, are called Hyperlink fields.

Lookup Wizard

It is a special type of field, which when defined, allows you to select the values, which have already been entered. For example, if the examination of the students is to be held only in Hyderabad, Bangalore and Chennai then these three cities can be entered in a table and examination center choice of the student, in some other table, can be defined as lookup wizard field, so that while entering student's data, no other city than these three cities is entered.

TABLE STRUCTURE

Now you are familiar with characteristics of MS-Access tables and the field types that are allowed in MS-Access. Now the question is, what is "table structure"? Table structure is the format of the record, which clearly defines the names of the fields, type of data that they will hold, length and format of the data that will be contained in them.

For performing data storage and retrieved activities in MS-Access, you need to first decide the table structure. To get familiar with this process, let's define the table structure for the data, which is illustrated in the last table:

Name of the field	Field Type	Width of the field	Number of places after decimal
Roll	Number		0
Name	Text	30	
Sex	Text	1	
City	Text	15	
Age	Number		0
Marks	Number		0

Once table structure is finalized, tables can be created, data can be entered and retrieved as per requirements.

CREATING TABLE

MS-Access provides many ways of creating a table structure. Some of them are as follows:

1. In Datasheet view
2. Using Table wizard
3. Using Design view

Most versatile method is, "Using Design View" method. Perform following steps to create a table in Design view:

1. Click the mouse on "Start" button, present on desktop. When you do so, Start menu, as shown in figure 4.1(a), will appear on the screen.
2. Select "All Programs" option from Start submenu. When you do so, another submenu, as shown in figure 4.1(b), will appear on the screen.

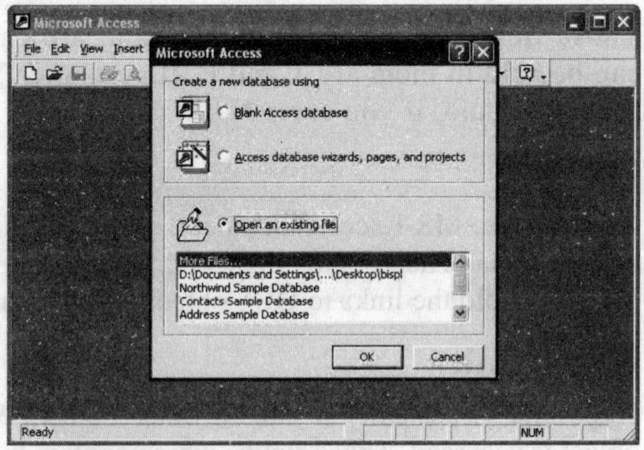

Figure Access-1

3. Select "Microsoft Access" option from this submenu. When you do so, a window with a dialog box, as shown in figure Access-1, will appear on the screen.
4. Create a blank database, by selecting "Blank Access database" option and clicking the mouse on "OK" button.

   When you do so, a dialog box, as shown in figure ms-access-2, will appear on the screen.
5. First select the drive and the folder, in which you wish to create the database and then enter the name that you wish to assign to this blank database (being created) in "File name" text box.

6. At last, click the mouse on "Create" button. Say, you create a blank database with the name "MYDB".

When you do so, a dialog box, as shown in figure ms-access-3, will appear on the screen. If somehow the options within the dialog box are different, click the mouse on "Table" option.

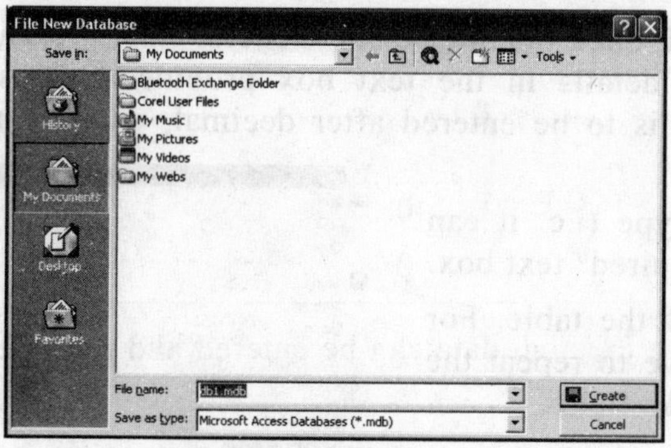

Figure Access- 2

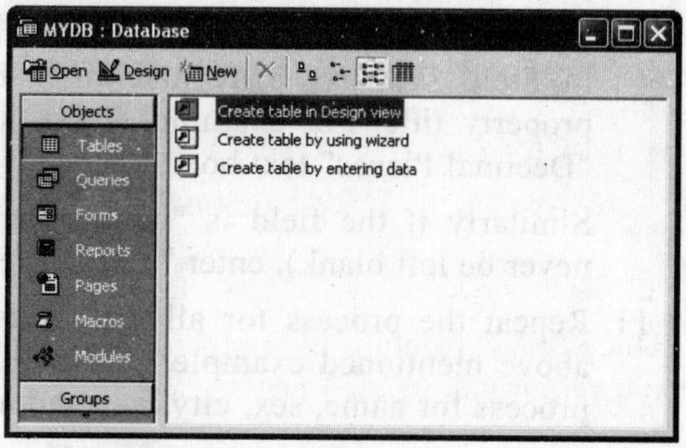

Figure Access- 3

7. Select "Create table in Design view" option and click the mouse on "Open" option, present in database design toolbar.
   When you do so, Data Design window, as shown in figure Access-4, for entering the table structure, will appear on the screen.

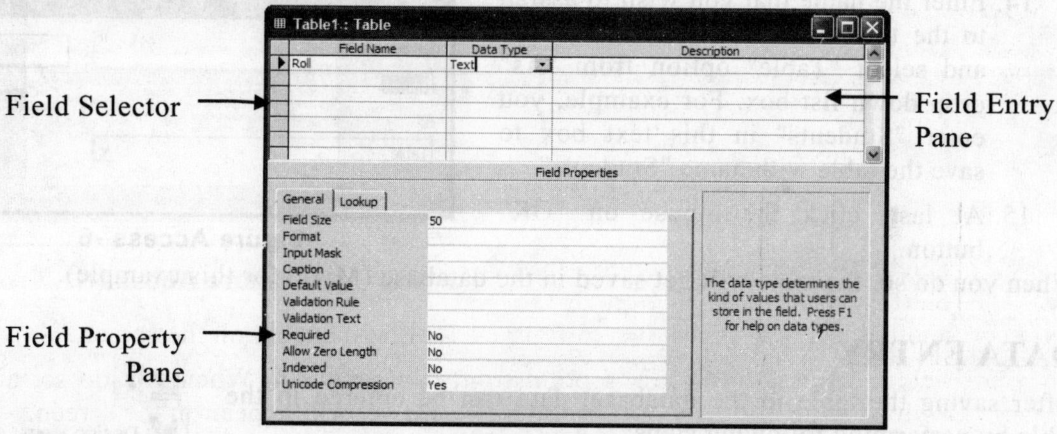

Figure Access-4

Refer Data Design View window and note that it consists of following three panes:

(a) Field Entry pane (for entering field details)

(b) Field Property pane (for entering field property details)

(c) Help pane (for displaying help messages related to current entry)

8. Enter the field name in "Field Name" column. Say you enter roll (for the example taken above) in this column. When you do so, a drop down list will automatically appear in "Data Type" column.
9. Now select the field type from the drop down list, present in "Data Type" column. Say you select Number for the example mentioned above.
10. To set the properties for the current field, click the mouse on "General" tab, present in Field Property pane and enter the details in the text box provided against property title. For example, if no digit is to be entered after decimal, enter 0 in "Decimal Places" text box.

    Similarly if the field is "must enter" type (i.e. it can never be left blank), enter "Yes" in "Required" text box.
11. Repeat the process for all the fields of the table. For above mentioned example, you will have to repeat the process for name, sex, city, age and marks fields.
12. To save the table structure in a file, click the mouse on "File" option present in bar menu. When you do so, File submenu, as shown in figure Access-5 will appear on the screen.

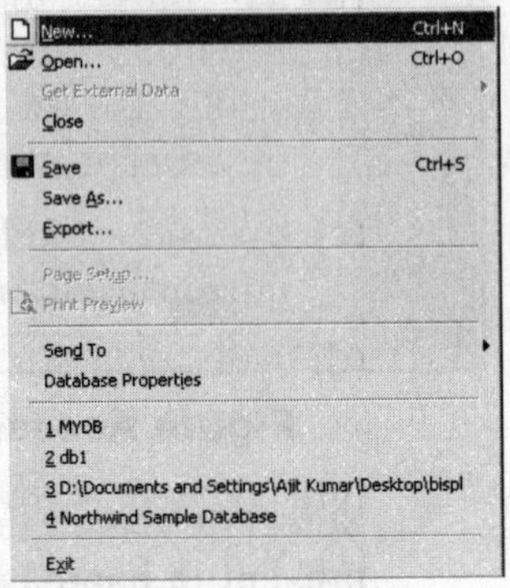

Figure Access -5

13. Select "Save As" option from File submenu. When you do so, a dialog box, as shown in figure Access-6, will appear on the screen.
14. Enter the name that you wish to assign to the table in "Save Table" text box and select "Table" option from "As" drop down list box. For example, you enter "Students" in this text box to save the table with name "Students".
15. At last, click the mouse on "OK" button.

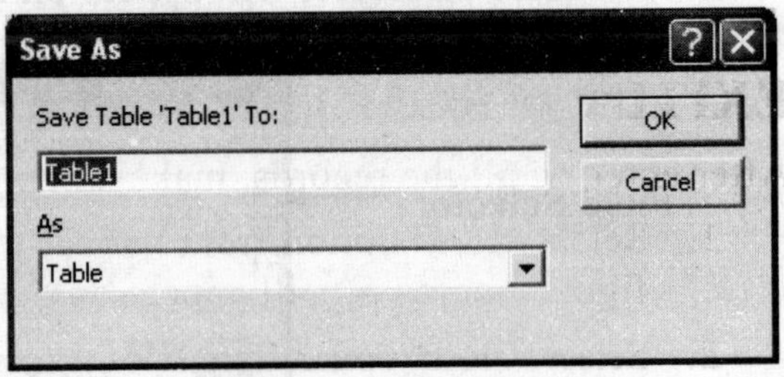

Figure Access -6

When you do so, the table will get saved in the database (Mydb for this example).

DATA ENTRY

After saving the table in the database, data can be entered in the table by performing following steps:

1. Click the mouse on "View" button, present in Data Design View window. When you do so, a list of options, as shown in figure Access-7, will appear on the screen.

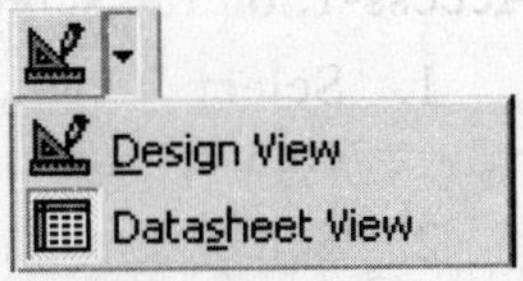

Figure Access -7

2. Select "Datasheet View" option from this list. When you do so, Datasheet view window, as shown in figure Access-8, will appear on the screen.

3. To enter the data in the table, using Datasheet view window, make use of following procedures:

   (a) To enter the data in any field, click the mouse in the corresponding blank space (cell) and type the data. When the field becomes full, no more characters will be accommodated in the field.

   (b) To move to the next field or previous field of the same record, make use of right and left arrow keys respectively.

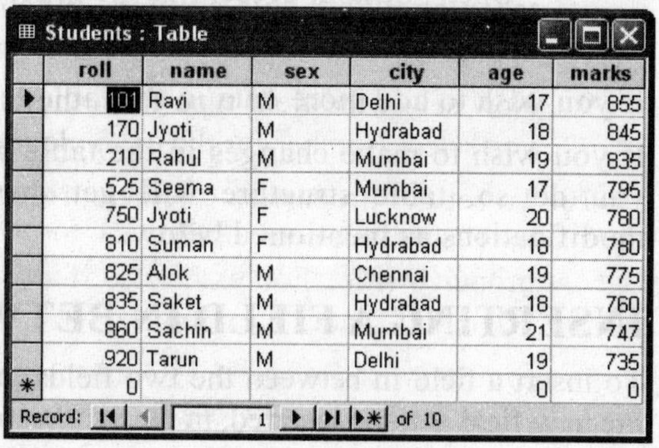

Students : Table

roll	name	sex	city	age	marks
101	Ravi	M	Delhi	17	855
170	Jyoti	M	Hydrabad	18	845
210	Rahul	M	Mumbai	19	835
525	Seema	F	Mumbai	17	795
750	Jyoti	F	Lucknow	20	780
810	Suman	F	Hydrabad	18	780
825	Alok	M	Chennai	19	775
835	Saket	M	Hydrabad	18	760
860	Sachin	M	Mumbai	21	747
920	Tarun	M	Delhi	19	735
0				0	0

Record: 1 of 10

Figure Access-8

   (c) To make modifications within the current field, make use of DEL and Backspace keys.

   (d) After entering the data in the last field of the current record, press Enter key. When you do so, a blank place is created ahead to enter the next record.

   (e) To move to the next or previous record, make use of Down and Up arrow keys.

   (f) While entering the data in any field, if data mismatch occurs, MS-Access gives an error message and the data entry stops. In such a situation, either correct the mistake and enter the correct data or click the mouse on View button, select Data Design View and correct the field specifications.

EXITING FROM THE TABLE

After entering all the records, make an exit from the table by performing following steps:

1. Select "File" option from the bar menu. When you do so, File submenu, as shown in figure Access-5, will appear on the screen.
2. Select "Close" option from File submenu. When you do so, MS-Access will close the table.

OPENING AN EXISTING TABLE

To open an existing table, first invoke MS-Access and get the dialog box, shown in figure Access-1, on the screen. After this, perform following steps:

1. Select "Open an existing file" option. When you do so, names of all the databases created, up till now, will appear in the dialog box.
2. Select the name of the database that you wish to open. Say, you open "mydb" database, which was created in the example mentioned above.
3. Click the mouse on "OK" button. When you do so, a dialog box, as shown in figure Access-3, will appear on the screen. If somehow, the options shown, within the dialog box are different, click the mouse on "Table" option. When you do so, the names of all the tables, created within, current database (mydb in this example) will get listed, within the dialog box.

4. Select the name of the table, which you wish to open and click the mouse on "Open" button, present in the toolbar of the dialog box.

When you do so, selected table, will get displayed in Datasheet view mode.

If you wish to add more data in the table, enter the data in Datasheet view.

If you wish to make changes in the table structure, click the mouse on View button. When you do so, table structure will get displayed in Data Design View. Now make the modifications as mentioned below.

INSERTING A FIELD IN BETWEEN TWO FIELDS

To insert a field in between the two fields, place the insertion pointer on the field, above which the new field is to be inserted, in Design View. After this perform any one of the following step:

1. Open that table which is to be modified in design view mode.
2. Now click the mouse on that field above which the new field is to be inserted.
3. Either click the mouse on "Insert Rows" button present in "Table Design" toolbar, or select "Rows" option from Insert submenu.

When you do so, a blank field will get created. Now type the details in the same way as you had typed at the time of creating the existing fields.

DELETING A FIELD FROM TABLE

To delete a field from the table, place the insertion pointer on the field, which is to be deleted and perform any one of the following steps:

1. Select "Delete" option from Edit submenu.

   or

2. Click the mouse on "Delete Rows" button, present in "Table Design" toolbar.

When you do so, a confirmation box, for the confirmation of deletion of the field appears on the screen. To delete the field, click the mouse on "Yes" button else click it on "No" button.

CHANGING THE SEQUENCE OF THE FIELD

To change the current place of a field, drag the field and drop it at the new location.

Note that after changing the sequence of the field in the table, the data in the data table also changes its sequence.

RENAMING THE FIELD

To rename any field, simply edit its name and then save the table.

EDITING THE RECORDS

Note that above mentioned procedures were for editing the table. Now the question is how do you edit data? Well, for this, open the database and the table, related to which the data is to be edited and then click the mouse on "View" button present in the toolbar. When you do so, data in the table, as shown in figure Access-8, will appear on the screen, in Datasheet view.

To perform different types of operations perform procedures mentioned below.

ACCESSING THE DESIRED RECORD

Refer figure Access-9 and note that for navigating the records, a navigation toolbar remains present at the bottom of Datasheet view window.

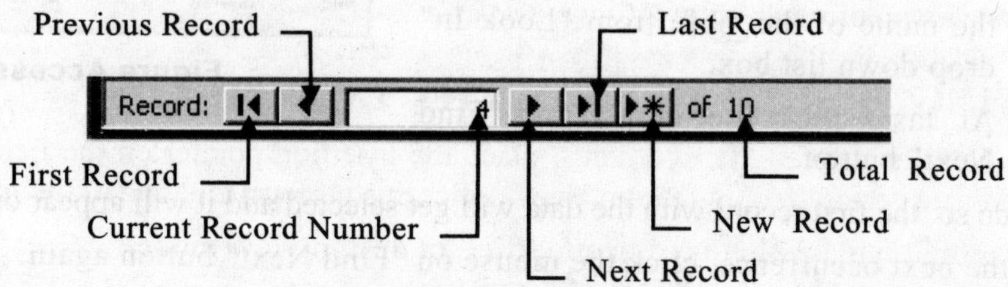

Figure Access-9

Using this toolbar, any record of the database can be accessed and made current.

To access any record of the table, enter the record number in the edit box and press Enter key. For example, if you wish to access, 50th record, enter 50 in the edit box and press Enter key. When you do so, 50th record will appear in Datasheet view within the window.

Refer figure Access-9. Role and function of other components (buttons) of record navigation toolbar are illustrated and labeled there. Click the mouse on these buttons and access other records of the table.

Alternate Methods Of Accessing Records

MS-Access offers many ways of accessing the record. One way of accessing was described above. Other methods are described below.

Figure Access- 10

1. Click the mouse on "Edit" option, present in bar menu. When you do so, Edit submenu will appear on the screen. Select "Go To" option from Edit submenu. When you do so, a submenu, as shown in figure Access-10 will appear on the screen.
2. Perform following steps to find a record, with the given field value:

   (a) Select the column (field name), on the basis of which, the record is to be accessed. For this, click the mouse on field name. For example, if you wish to find the first occurrence of the record containing Mumbai in city field, click the mouse on "City" field.

   (b) Now either select "Find" option from Edit submenu or press CTRL and F keys together.

   When you do so, a dialog box, as shown in figure Access-11 will appear on the screen.

(c) Enter the data on the basis of which the record is to be accessed, in "Find What" text box. For example, for finding the first record with city Mumbai, enter "Mumbai" in this text box.

(d) If you wish to search the occurrence of the given data, throughout the table (not only in the selected field), select the name of the table from "Look In" drop down list box.

(e) At last, click the mouse on "Find Next" button.

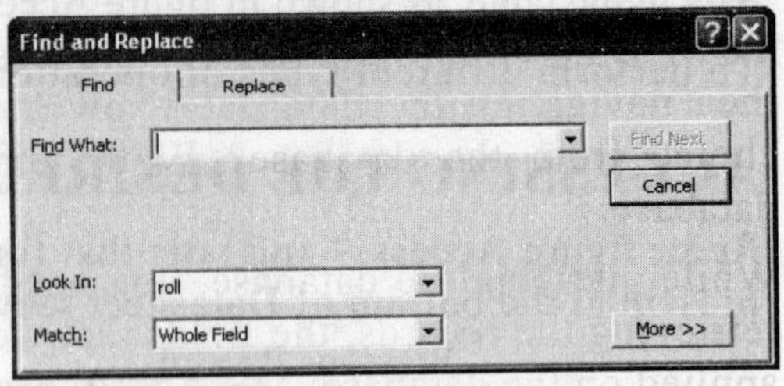

Figure Access- 11

When you do so, the first record with the data will get selected and it will appear on the screen.

To search the next occurrence, click the mouse on "Find Next" button again.

You can continue clicking on "Find Next" button till the time all the records get selected one by one.

MODIFYING THE DATA

Perform following steps to modify the data:

1. Access the record, in which contents have to be modified, using navigation toolbar.
2. Using arrow keys, access that field, in which modifications are to be done.
3. Using Del and Backspace keys modify the data.

DELETING A RECORD

To delete a record, from the table, select the record, which is to be deleted and then perform any one of the following actions:

1. Select "Delete" option from Edit submenu.

   or

2. Click the mouse on "Delete Record" button, present in "Table Datasheet" toolbar.

When you do so, a confirmation dialog box for the confirmation of deletion of the records, will appear on the screen. If you wish to delete the record, click the mouse on "Yes" button else click it on "No" button.

APPENDING RECORDS

To add more records at the end of the table, click the mouse on "New Record" button, present in "Table Datasheet" toolbar. When you do so, Insertion pointer gets placed at the end of the table (in first field of the blank record). Now enter the data.

QUERYING THE DATABASE

You are now familiar with the process of creating the database, entering data into it and then navigating the database. Now the question is how do you retrieve records of your choice from the database? Well, this is done through a process, called querying the database.

While querying the database, you need to specify your choices like, selection criterion for retrieving the records, the fields that would appear in the output etc. Once these choices are applied on the database, MS-Access provides the required output.

The process of querying the database is explained below.

CREATING QUERIES

Perform following steps to create a query in Design view:

1. Open the database, which contains the table, from which the records are to be retrieved. For example, if you wish to retrieve the records from "students" table open "mydb" database. When you do so, MS-Access window with a dialog box, as shown in figure Access-3, will appear on the screen.

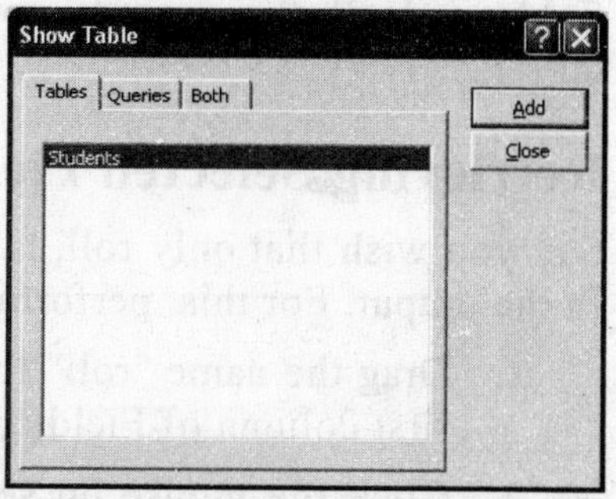

Figure msaccess-12

2. Now click the mouse on "Query" option, present in this dialog box. When you do so, following two options, will appear, within the dialog box:
   - ❑ Create Query in Design View
   - ❑ Create Query by using Wizard
3. Select "Create Query in Design View" option, and click the mouse on "Open" button, present in dialog box toolbar. When you do so, a dialog box, as shown in figure Access-12, will appear on the screen.
4. Select the name of the table from which the data is to be retrieved. First click the mouse on "Add" button and then on "Close" button present in "Show Table" dialog box. When you do so, a query window, as shown in figure Access-13, will appear on the screen.

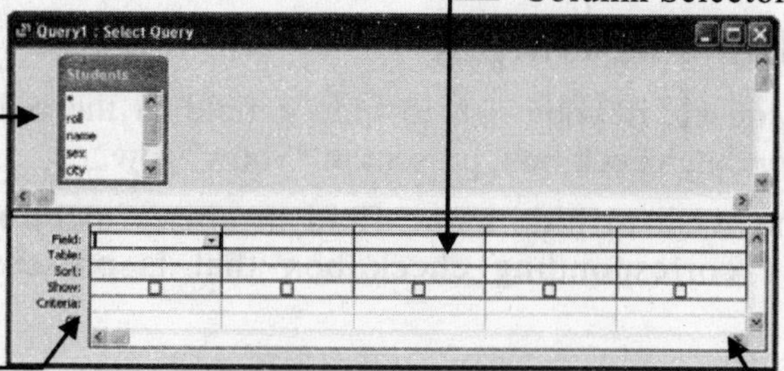

Figure Access-13

Using this query window, you can design queries, execute them and retrieve the data, as per your requirement.

Few examples of this are given below.

Retrieving All The Records And All The Fields From Database

To retrieve all the records and all the fields of the database, drag the character, "*" from field list and drop it in the first column of field row. Note that here * carries special meaning and refers to all the fields of the table.

To run this query, click the mouse on "Run" button, present in "Query Design" toolbar. When you do so, it will generate the output, as shown in figure Access-14. Refer this output and note that all the fields and all the records appear in the output.

Query1 : Select Query

roll	name	sex	city	age	marks
101	Ravi	M	Delhi	17	855
170	Jyoti	M	Hydrabad	18	845
210	Rahul	M	Mumbai	19	835
525	Seema	F	Mumbai	17	795
750	Jyoti	F	Lucknow	20	780
810	Suman	F	Hydrabad	18	780
825	Alok	M	Chennai	19	775
835	Saket	M	Hydrabad	18	760
860	Sachin	M	Mumbai	21	747
920	Tarun	M	Delhi	19	735
0				0	0

Record: 1 of 10

Figure Access- 14

Retrieving Selected Fields Of All The Records

Say you wish that only roll, name and marks field should appear in the output. For this, perform following steps:

1. Drag the name "roll" from field list box and drop it in the first column of Field row.
2. Click the mouse on second column of Field row. When you do so, a drop down list will appear in that column. Select the name "name" from that list.
3. Drag the name "marks" from field list box and drop it in third column of Field row.

To run this query, click the mouse on "Run" button present in "Query Design" toolbar. When you do so, it will generate the output, as shown in figure Access-15.

Query1 : Select Query

roll	name	marks
101	Ravi	855
170	Jyoti	845
210	Rahul	835
525	Seema	795
750	Jyoti	780
810	Suman	780
825	Alok	775
835	Saket	760
860	Sachin	747
920	Tarun	735
0		0

Record: 1

Figure Access-15

Hiding A Field In The Output

After designing the query, if you wish to hide a field in the output, uncheck the corresponding check box, present in "Show" row.

For example, if you wish to hide name field in above mentioned query, uncheck the corresponding check box that is present in "Show" row.

When you run this query, output, as shown in figure Access-16 will appear on the screen.

Query...

roll	marks
101	855
170	845
210	835
525	795
750	780
810	780
825	775
835	760
860	747
920	735
0	0

Record:

Figure Access-16

Obtaining Sorted Output From The Query

Say you wish that roll, name and age fields should appear in the output and the output should be sorted in descending order of age field. For this, perform following steps:

1. Include the three fields, roll, name and age in the output by either dragging them from field list and dropping them in three consecutive columns of Field row or by clicking the mouse one by one in first three columns of field row and selecting the names of the fields from the drop down lists that appear thereafter.
2. To sort the output on age fields, click the mouse in corresponding column of sort row. When you do so, a drop down list will appear in that column.
3. Select "Descending" option from that list.

To run the query, click the mouse on "Run" button present in "Query Design" toolbar. When you do so, output, as shown in figure Access-17, will appear on the screen.

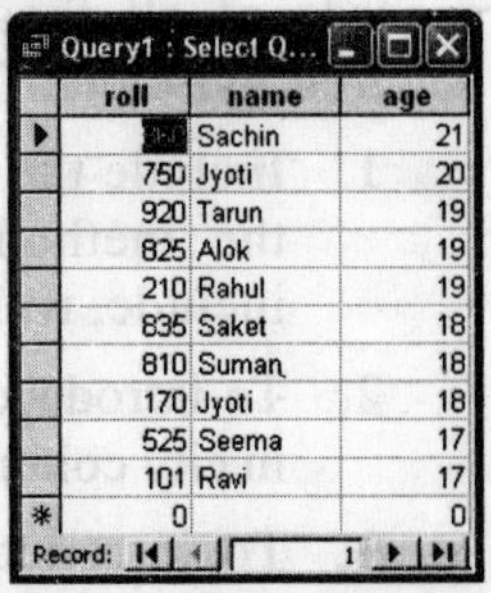
Query1 : Select Q...

	roll	name	age
▶	[illegible]	Sachin	21
	750	Jyoti	20
	920	Tarun	19
	825	Alok	19
	210	Rahul	19
	835	Saket	18
	810	Suman	18
	170	Jyoti	18
	525	Seema	17
	101	Ravi	17
*	0		0

Record: 1

Figure Access-17

Applying A Selection Criteria In Query

If the need be, selection criteria could be introduced in the query so that not all the records of the database appear in the output but only those records are retrieved, which satisfy the selection criteria.

For example, say you wish to retrieve only those records in which marks >795. Perform following steps for this:

1. Include all the fields of the table in the output by dragging them from field list and dropping them in consecutive columns of Field row.
2. Enter >795 in marks column of criteria row.

To run the query, click the mouse on "Run" button, present in "Query Design" toolbar. When you do so, output, as shown in figure Access-18, will appear on the screen.

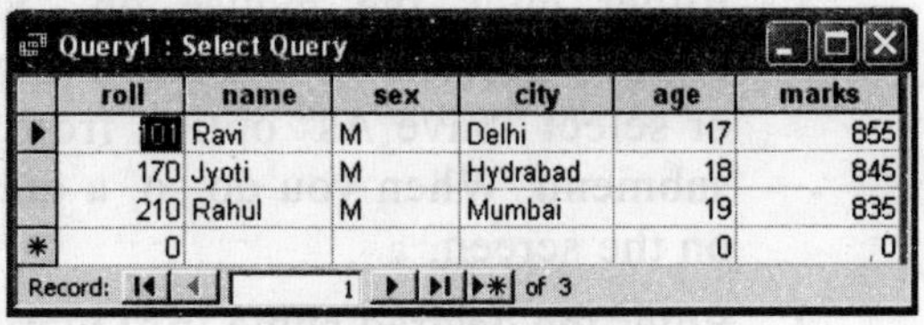
Query1 : Select Query

	roll	name	sex	city	age	marks
▶	101	Ravi	M	Delhi	17	855
	170	Jyoti	M	Hydrabad	18	845
	210	Rahul	M	Mumbai	19	835
*	0				0	0

Record: 1 of 3

Figure Access-18

Applying Multiple Selection Criteria Using OR Operator

Two or more conditions can also be introduced within the query to define the selection criteria precisely. For example, if you wish to select the records of those students who are either female or have secured more than 835 marks, perform following steps:

1. Include the names of all those fields, which are required in the output, using any of the methods, described earlier. Say you include roll number, name, sex and marks fields.
2. To introduce female condition enter ="F" in sex column of criteria row.
3. To introduce marks condition, enter >835 in marks column of OR row.

To run the query, click the mouse on "Run" button present in "Query Design" toolbar. When you do so, output, as shown in figure Access-19, will appear on the screen.

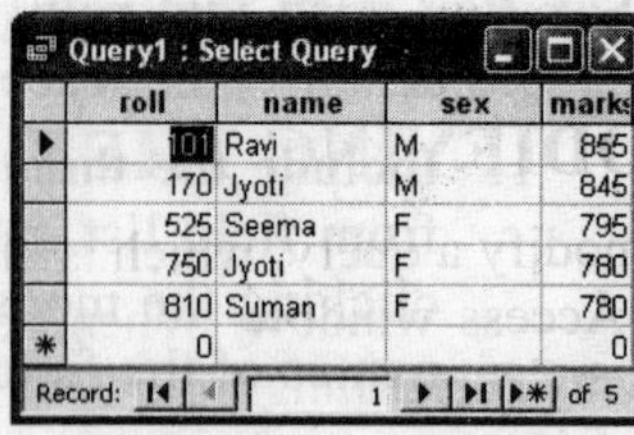

Figure Access-19

Applying Multiple Selection Criterion

More than one condition can be applied to retrieve the records from the table. For example, you may wish to retrieve the records of all those students who live in Mumbai and have secured more than 750 marks, perform following steps:

1. Include the names of all those fields, which are required in the output, using any of the methods, mentioned above. Say you include, roll, name, city and marks fields.
2. To introduce, city condition, enter="Mumbai" in city column of criteria row.
3. To introduce marks condition, enter >750 in marks column of criteria row.

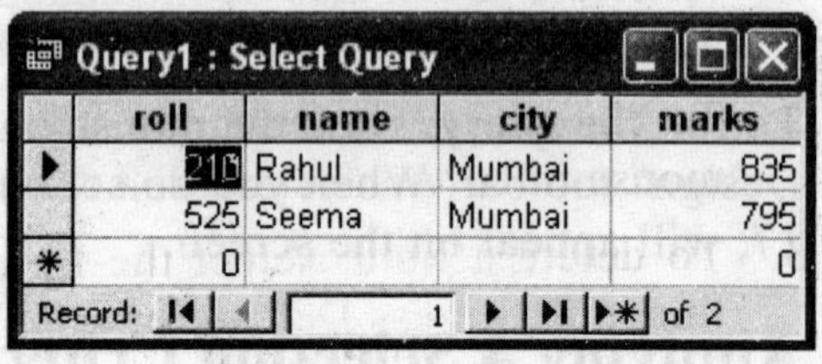

Figure Access-20

To run the query, click the mouse on "Run" button, present in "Query Design" toolbar. When you do so, output, as shown in figure 9.20, will appear on the screen.

SAVING THE QUERY

Perform following steps to save the query in the database:

Figure Access-21

1. Either click the mouse on "Save" button, present in Standard toolbar or select "Save As" option from File submenu. When you do so, a dialog box, as shown in figure Access-21, will appear on the screen.
2. Enter the desired name in "Query Name" text box, present in this dialog box.
3. Click the mouse on "OK" button. For example, say you save the last query with the name myq.

When you do so, the query will get saved in the database for further use.

OPENING AN EXISTING QUERY

To open the query, open the database, in which the query exists (if not yet opened) and get the dialog box, shown in figure Access-3 on the screen. Click the mouse on "Query" button. When you do so, the names of all the queries, present within the opened database will get listed in that dialog box.

Select the name of the query, which you wish to open and click the mouse on "Open" button, present in the toolbar. When you do so, the selected query will get opened and executed to show the result. For example, if you open the myq query, which was saved in the last section, it will display the results, as shown if figure Access-20.

MODIFYING THE QUERY

To modify a query, which is already opened, simply click the mouse on "View" button, present in MS-Access window. When you do so, the query, will get displayed in Query Design window. Now by performing following activities, query can be modified as per requirement:

1. To add a new field, in the query, drag the new name from field list and drop it in the blank column of Field row. If the need be, visibility factor, sort order, selection criteria etc. can also be introduced in the query by following the methods, described above.
2. To change the current place of a field in the query, select the field by clicking the mouse in column selector. After this, drag the field and drop it at desired location.
3. To delete a field, select the field by clicking the mouse in column selector. After this, either press Del key or select "Delete" option from Edit submenu.
4. Note that in the result obtained from the query (query executed), field names appear as headings, at the top of each column. For example, if you have designed query to extract roll, name and marks data from the table then "roll" "name" and "marks" will appear as headings of the three columns in the output. If you wish to change these headings, you can do so by prefixing the field names by new headings and a colon sign (:). For example, if you wish that "Roll Number" should appear as heading, instead of roll then you should write "Roll Number:roll" in the query column of Field row. Similarly if you wish that instead of name, Student Name should appear as heading, in the output, you should write "Student Name: name" in the query.

FORM

Form is a utility, using which you design screens for data entry and data retrieval. Forms consist of fields, field headings and GUI objects like graphics, radio buttons, check boxes, list boxes etc. If the need be, you can also include generated fields (which are calculated on the basis of the data entered in previous fields) in the form. How do you create these forms, how do you utilize them for data entry and data retrieval operations, is explained below.

CREATING A FORM USING FORM DESIGN VIEW WINDOW

Creating forms in Design View is the best method for creating forms because it gives you full control over the appearance of the form. Perform following steps to create the form in design view:

1. Open that database, which contains the table, for which, you wish to create the form. Say you open "Mydb" database, which was created earlier. When you do so, MS-Access will display database view window as shown in figure Access-3.
2. Select "Form" tab from that window and click the mouse on "New" icon present in

the toolbar. When you do so, a dialog box, as shown in figure Access-22 will appear on the screen.

3. First select "Design View" option present this dialog box and then select the name of the table or query for which you wish to design the form, from the combo box present in this dialog box. After this, click the mouse on "OK" button. For example, say you select "Student" table and click the mouse on "OK" button. When you do so, MS-Access will display Form Design View window, as shown in figure Access-23.

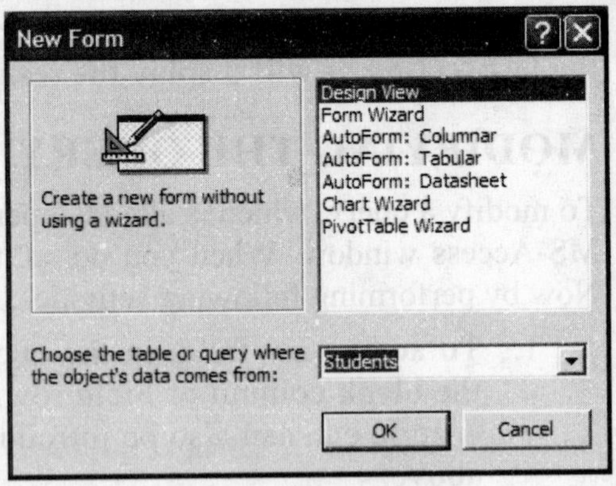

Figure Access-22

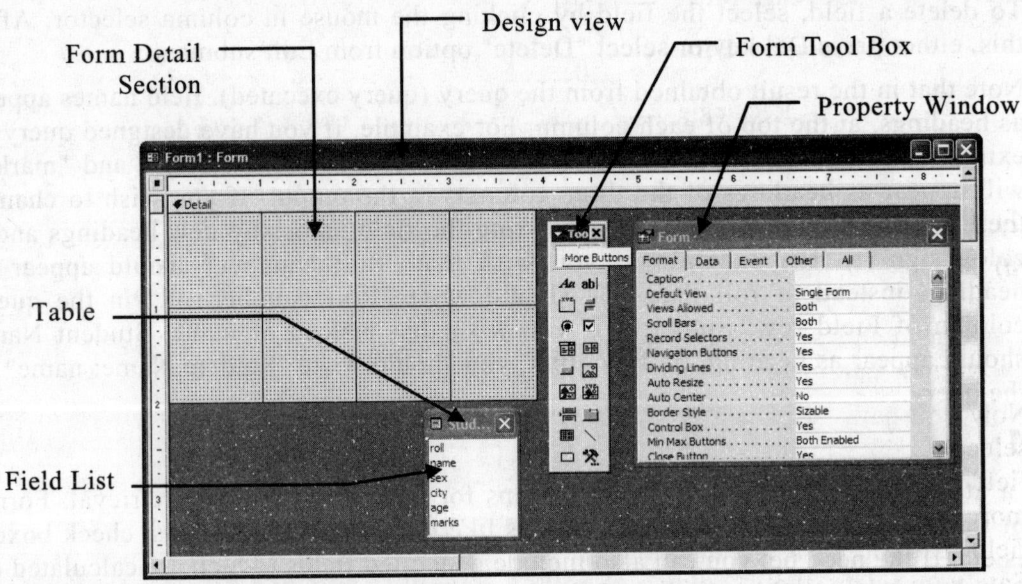

Figure Access-23

Refer Form Design View window, shown in figure Access-23 and notice that this window contains many elements for designing the form. An introduction to these elements is given below.

(a) Form Detail Section- Form Detail Section, is the base of the form, on which all the fields, controls etc. are placed.

(b) Form Toolbox- Form toolbox consists of various controls. To design the form, you have to select the controls from here and then drag and drop them in Form Detail Section. An elaborated view of form toolbox is shown in figure Access-24.

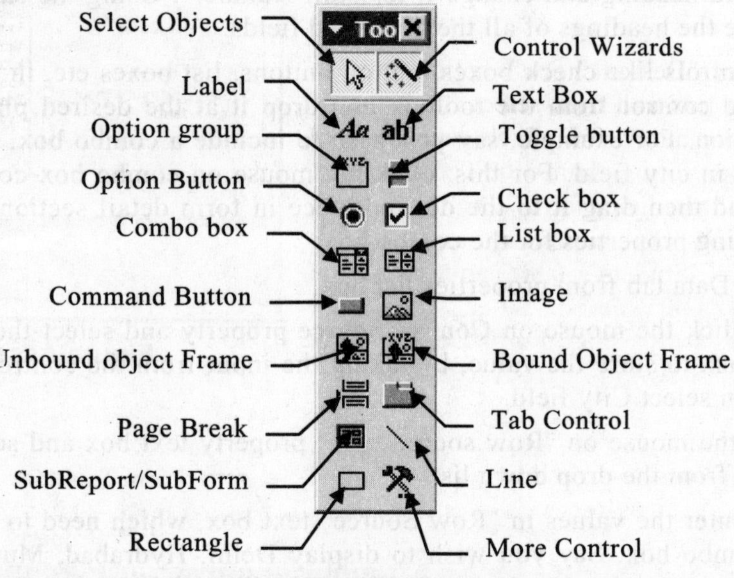

Figure Access-24

(c) ***Field List***: Field list consists of field names that can be included in the form.

(d) ***Property list box***- Property list box is the list box, which displays the properties and the current values for the controls, which you have currently selected in form detail section. By changing the value of any property, you can change various parameters associated with the control.

4. Now you have to place the fields in form detail section. To add the fields of the selected table, in form detail section, drag the name of the desired field from the field list box and drop it at the desired place in form detail section. Note that if more fields are to be added in the form then this process has to be repeated for each field that you wish to add in the form. Say you select three fields i.e. roll, name and marks. When you do so, form detail section will look like as shown in figure Access-25.

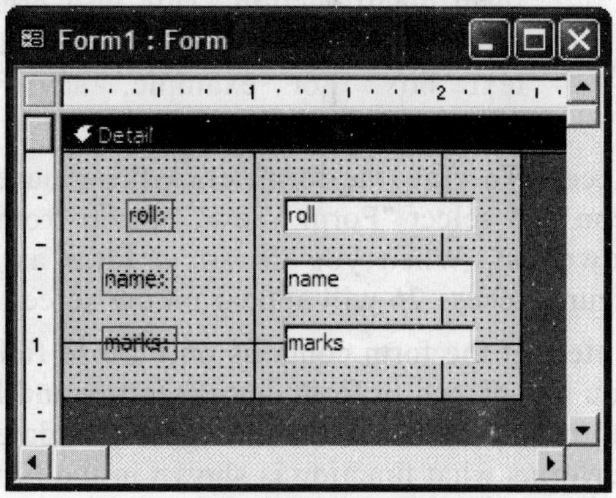

Figure Access-25

5. Refer detail section and note that the field headings are same as the names of the fields, which were assigned to them, while creating the table. If you wish to change the field headings, either click the mouse on field heading and enter the new heading or change the Caption property value to new

heading that you wish to assign to the field. For example, say you click the mouse on roll field heading and change it to "Roll Number". Using the same process you can change the headings of all the described fields.

6. To add controls like check boxes, option buttons, list boxes etc. in the form, select the desired control from the toolbox and drop it at the desired place in the form detail section. For example, say you wish to include a combo box, on the form for data entry in city field. For this, click the mouse on combo box control present in toolbox and then drag it to the desired place in form detail section. After this, set the following properties for the combo box:

   (a) Select Data tab from properties list box.

   (b) Now click the mouse on Control Source property and select the field in which you wish to store the value, by taking the input from the control. For example, say you select City field.

   (c) Click the mouse on "Row source type" property text box and select Value List option from the drop down list.

   (d) Now enter the values in "Row Source" text box, which need to be displayed in the combo box. Say you wish to display Delhi, Hydrabad, Mumbai, Lucknow and Chennai values in the combo box. For this, click the mouse on Row Source text box and enter **"Delhi"; "Hydrabad"; "Mumbai"; "Lucknow"; "Chennai"** into it.

   (e) If you wish you can set default value for the combo box. To enter the default value, click the mouse on Default Value text box and enter the value in it. For example, say you enter the value "Delhi" in Default Value text box.

7. If you wish, you can also add heading in the form. To do so, click the mouse on Label control present in the form toolbox. This will change the mouse pointer to cross hair band cursor. Now drag the mouse in the form detail section. This will create a text box. After this, type the desired text in this text box. For example, say you type "Student Data Entry Form".

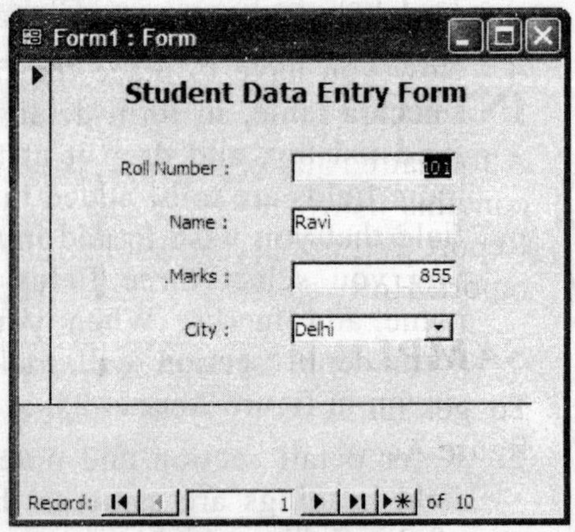

Figure Access-26

Access-To view the form, click the mouse on View icon and select "Form View" option from the drop down list. When you do so, a form as shown in figure Access-26 will appear on the screen.

Note that the form contains only those fields, which you had placed in form detail section and has a series of buttons at the bottom. Using these buttons, you can either navigate the database or enter new records in it. Which button performs what function is shown in the figure Access-27.

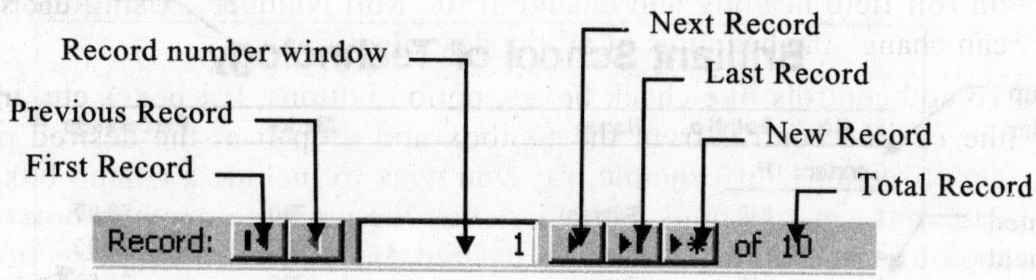

Figure Access-27

Moving Between Records In Form View

As mentioned above, form buttons can be used to move around in the database. Refer figure Access-27 and note that Navigation buttons are the six controls, which are used for moving between the records. Two leftmost buttons helps you to move to the first and previous records respectively. The three rightmost buttons help you to move to the next record, to the last record or add a new record in the table. The "Record Number" text box displays, which records is the current record.

EXITING FROM MS-ACCESS

To exit from MS-Access, follow any one of the following methods:

1. Select "Exit" option from File submenu.

or

2. Click the mouse on "Close" button, present in MS-Access windows title bar.

INTRODUCTION TO REPORTS

A formatted and organized presentation of data is called report. Apart from data, report also contains many headings that make the report more meaningful. MS-Access has an inbuilt Report Writer that takes the data from the table or query and presents it in the form of report. How reports are generated in MS-Access is described in this chapter.

SAMPLE REPORT

To get familiar with MS-Access report and its components, consider a report shown in figure Access-28. This report is created in MS-Access.

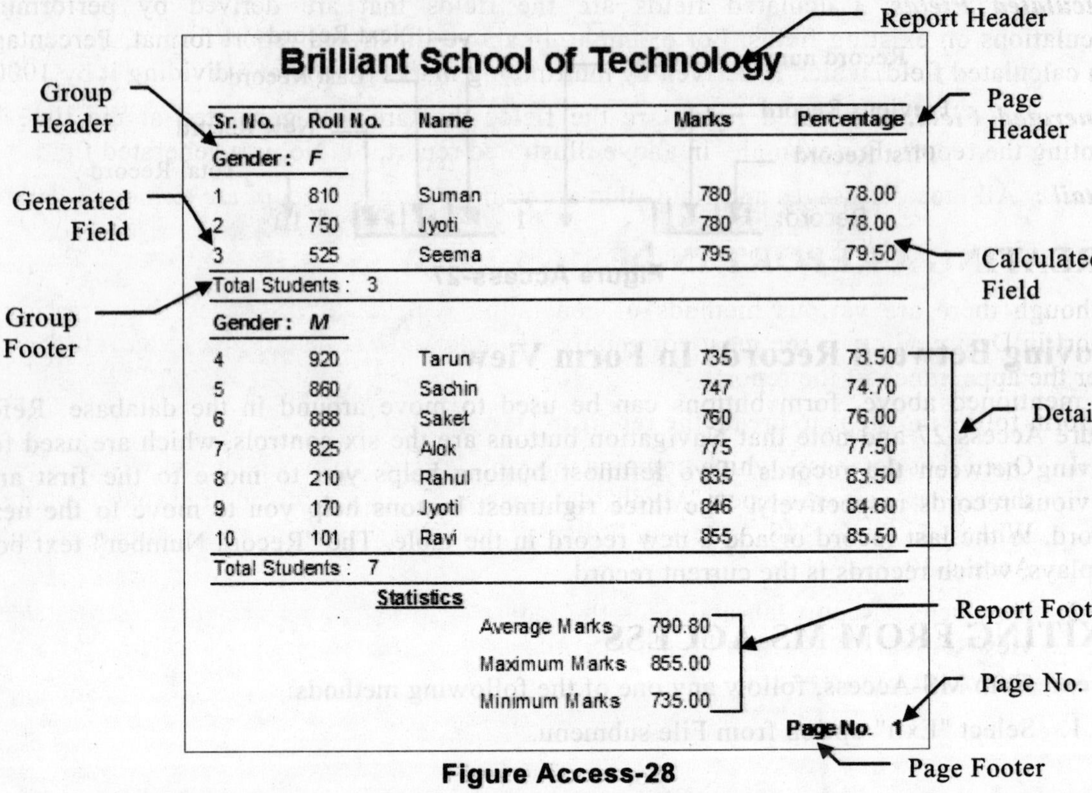

Figure Access-28

Refer report format shown in figure Access-1 and note that the report consists of various components. Details of these components are as follows:

Report Header: Report heading is printed only once, at the top of the first page of the report. Generally the title of the report is printed as report header.

Report Footer: Report Footer is printed only once, at the bottom of the last page of the report. Report summary or end message etc. are generally printed as report footer.

Page Header: Page header is that message, which is printed at the beginning of each page. If it is the first page then it is printed, below the report heading.

Group Header: Group is basically a cluster of records, which are clubbed together on the basis of some common field. For example, in above illustrated report, the records are clubbed together on the basis of sex field. Thus the records of the same sex appear together in the report and the report is said to be grouped on sex field. Group header is basically a title or remark, which is printed at the beginning of each group. Refer above illustrated figure and note that " Gender: <sex >" is the group header in the report.

Group Footer: Group footer generally comprises of few titles, remarks, totals, statistics etc., which are printed at the end of each group.

Calculated Fields: Calculated fields are the fields that are derived by performing calculations on existing fields. For example, in above illustrated report format, Percentage is a calculated field, which is derived by multiplying marks by 100 and dividing it by 1000.

Generated Field: Generated fields are the fields that are self generated at the time of printing the report. For example, in above illustrated report, Sr. No. is a generated field.

Detail : All those messages and fields that are printed for each record are termed as detail.

CREATING A REPORT IN DESIGN VIEW

Although there are various methods of generating reports in MS-Access but creating a report in Design View is the most commonly used method because it gives you full control over the appearance of the report.

Perform following steps to create the report in Design View:

1. Open that database, which contains the table or query, for which you wish to create the report. Say, you open "Mydb" database, which was created in previous chapter. When you do so, MS-Access will display database view window as shown in figure Access-30.
2. Now select Report tab and click the mouse on "New" icon present in the database view toolbar. When you do so, MS-Access will display New Report dialog box, as shown in figure Access-29.

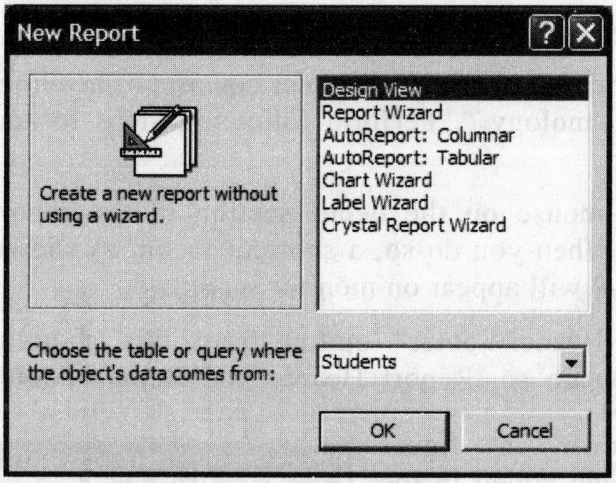

Figure Access-29

3. Select "Design View" option from this dialog box. After this, select the name of the table or query, for which you wish to design the report, from the combo box present in the dialog box. For example, say you select "Student" table. After this, click the mouse on "OK" button. When you do so, MS-Access will display Report Design View window as shown in figure Access-30.

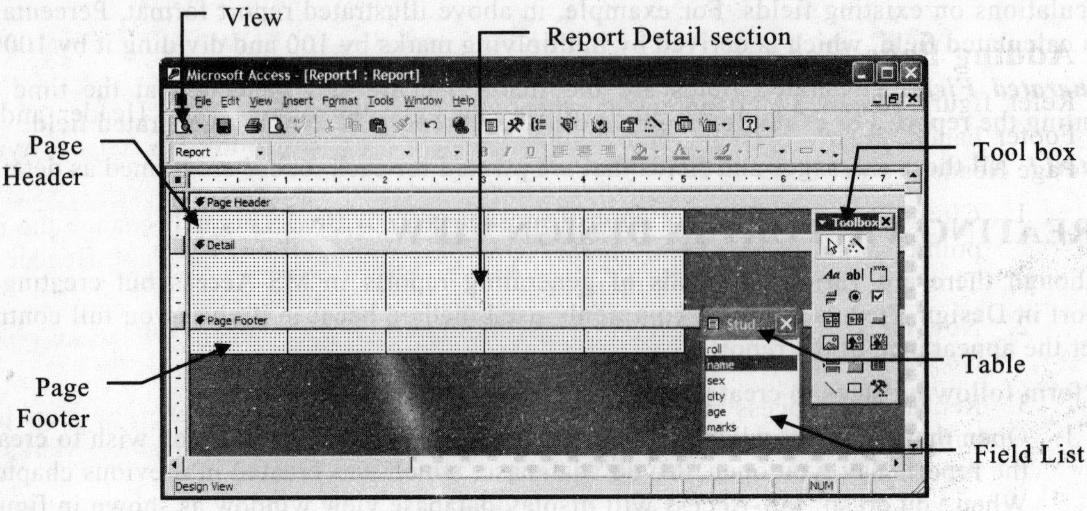

Figure Access-30

Now the report layout can be designed, using this window. The procedure for adding required components in the report layout, is given below.

Adding Report Header

Refer figure Access-1 and note that report header consists of heading, "Brilliant School of Technology ". Perform following steps to add this header in the report:

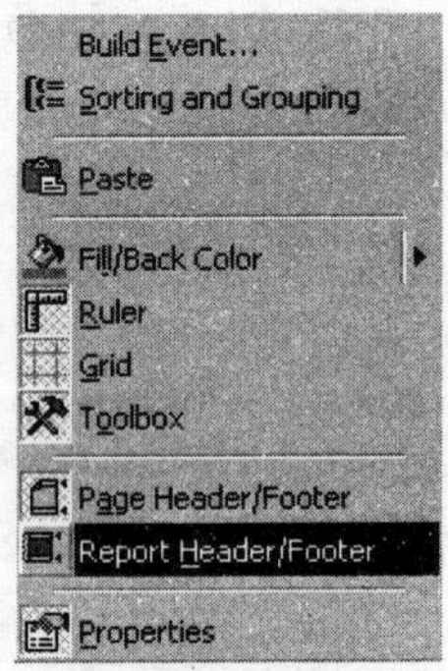

Figure Access-31

1. Right click the mouse on the detail section of the report layout window. When you do so, a shortcut menu, as shown in figure Access-4 will appear on monitor screen.

2. Select "Report Header/Footer" option from this shortcut menu. When you do so, Report Header and Report Footer bands, as shown in figure Access-32, will get added in the report layout.

3. To type the report heading in Report Header band, click the mouse on Label control, present in Tool Box. This will change the mouse pointer to cross hair band cursor. Now drag the mouse in the report header band. When you do so, a text box will get

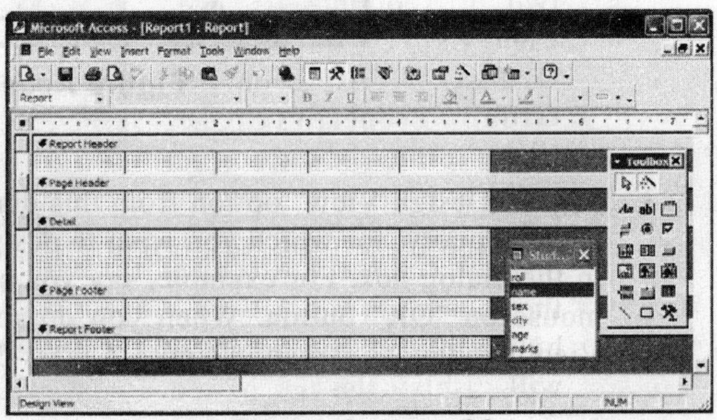

Figure Access-32

created. Click the mouse in text box and type the heading. Say you type "Brilliant School Of Technology".

Adding Page Header

Refer figure Access-3 and note that when you open the report, Page Header and Page Footer bands already exist in report layout format. Perform following steps to type the Page Header/Footer text:

1. Click the mouse on label control present in Tool Box. This will change the mouse pointer to cross hair band cursor. Now drag the mouse in the Page Header band. This will create a text box there.
2. Now click the mouse in the text box and type the Page heading. Say you type "Sr. No." as first label.
3. Repeat this process for every heading that you wish to include in the page header band. Say you add following more headings: Roll No., Name, Marks, and Percentage in the page header band.

Adding Group Header/Footer

Refer figure Access-1 and note that the report has to be grouped on sex. Perform following steps to add group header and group footer in the report:

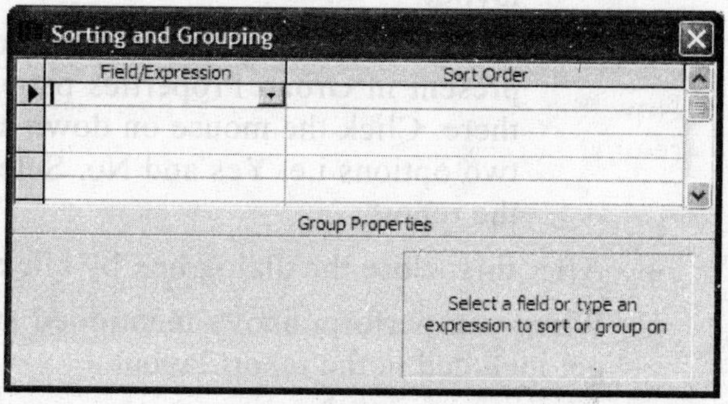

Figure Access-33

1. Right click the mouse on the detail section of the report. When you do so, a shortcut menu, as shown in the figure Access-4, will appear on monitor screen.
2. Select "Sorting and Grouping" option from this shortcut menu. When you do so, a dialog box, as shown in the figureAccess-6 will appear on the screen.
3. The dialog box, shown in figureAccess-6 contains two columns i.e. **Field/Expression** and **Sort Order.** It also contains **Group Properties** pane. Click the mouse on Field/Expression column. When you do so, it will display a combo box. Click the mouse on down arrow button. When you do so, it will display the list of the

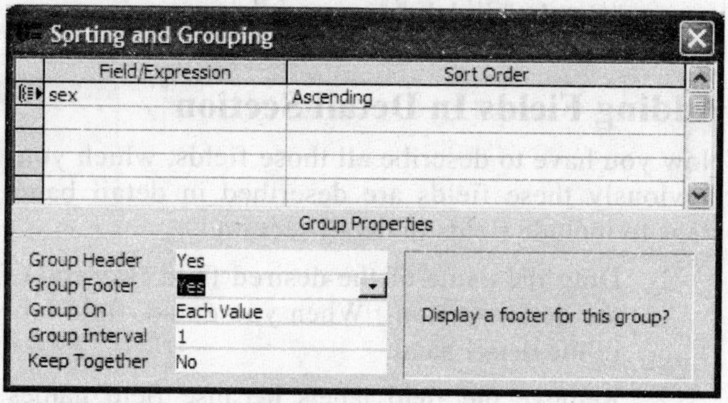

Figure Access-34

field names. Select the field, on which you wish to group the report. Say you select sex field. When you do so, above illustrated dialog box will take the shape as shown in figure Access-34.

Refer dialog box, shown in figure Access-34 and note that when you select the name of the field, Ascending automatically appear in the Sort Order column and various properties appear in the Group Properties pane of the dialog box.

- If you wish to change the sort order, click the mouse on Sort Order column. When you do so, it will display a combo box. Click the mouse on down arrow button. When you so, it will display two options i.e. Ascending and Descending. Select any one of the two options. Say you select "Descending" option.
- After this, click the mouse on Group Header text box present in Group Properties pane. When you do so, a combo box will appear there. Click the mouse on down arrow button. When you do so, it will display two options i.e. Yes and No. Select "Yes" option to add Group Header band in the report layout.
- To include Group footer band click the mouse on Group Footer text box present in Group Properties pane. When you do so, a combo box will appear there. Click the mouse on down arrow button. When you do so, it will display two options i.e. Yes and No. Select "Yes" option to add Group Footer band in the report.

4. After this, close the dialog box by clicking the mouse on "Close" button.

   When you perform above-mentioned steps, Group Header and Group Footer bands get included in the report layout.

5. Now you need to describe the text and the field names, which will appear as Group Header. Refer figure Access-1 and note that " <sex> " is the group header that has to be included in the report. To include it as group header, select the name of the field, drag it and drop it in the Group Header band. Note that when you drop the name of the field, a label for that field also appears along with the field name. Type "Gender" in label box.

Adding Fields In Detail Section

Now you have to describe all those fields, which you would like to print for all the records. Obviously these fields are described in detail band of report layout. Perform following steps to include fields in detail section:

1. Drag the name of the desired field (say roll) from the Table window and drop it in the detail section. When you do so, field labels along with fields will get included in the detail band.
2. Remove the field labels because field names have already been included in page heading. To delete the field label from detail section, select the label and press Del key.

3. Repeat this process for all other fields that have to be included in the detail band. For our report, we will have to repeat above mentioned steps for name and marks fields.

Adding Generated Field In Detail Section

Refer report shown in figure Access-1 and note that before every record, serial number is also printed. Since serial number is not a field of the table hence a special provision will have to be made in the layout. Perform following steps to make provision for serial number in the report:

1. Click the mouse on Text box control present in the toolbox of the report and make a text box by dragging the mouse at appropriate place. This will create a text box.
2. Now right click the mouse on it. When you do so, a shortcut menu, as shown in figure Access-34, will appear on the screen.
3. Select "Properties" option from that menu. When you do so, Property dialog box, as shown in figure Access-35 will appear on monitor screen.
4. Click the mouse on "Data" tab and enter **=1** in "Control source" combo box.
5. Now click the mouse on "Running Sum" text box. When you do so, it will display a down arrow button. Click the mouse on that button. This will display a list of options. Select "Over All" option from that list.
6. After setting the properties, select the text label and press Del key. This will remove undesired label.

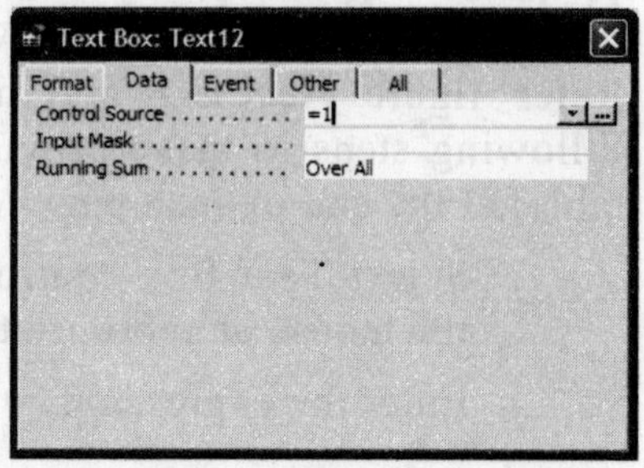

Figure Access-35

This process will add a running serial number field in the detail section.

Adding Calculated Fields In Detail Section

Refer figure Access-1 and note that in the detail section, last field in the report is Percentage field. This is a calculated field and is generated by multiplying marks by 100 and dividing by 1000. Perform following steps to make provision for this field in the report:

1. Click the mouse on Text Box control, present in the tool box. This will change the mouse pointer to cross hair band cursor. Now drag the mouse in detail section. This will create a text box. Now type the expression **=[marks]* 100 / 1000** in this text box.
2. Place the text box at appropriate place in the detail section by dragging it to the desired place. Say you place the text box below the Percentage label, present in page header band.

Defining Group Footer Contents

Refer figure Access-1 and note that group footer consists of the title, "Total Students" and the count of the students. Perform following steps to include these items in group footer:

1. Select Label control from the toolbox. When you do so, this will change the mouse pointer to cross hair band cursor. Now drag the mouse in Group Footer band. This will create a text box. Now type the heading "Total Students" in this text box.
2. Click the mouse on Text Box control present in the toolbox. This will change the mouse pointer to cross hair band cursor. Now drag the mouse in the group footer band. This will create a text box in group footer band. Now type the expression **=Count(*)** in this text box, to count total number of students in this group.
3. Delete all undesired labels if there are any.

Defining Page Footer

Refer figure Access-1 and note that page footer consists of page number. Perform following steps to make provision for printing page numbers (which is not a field of the table) at the end of each page:

1. Select Text Box control from the report toolbox and make a text box by dragging the mouse at appropriate place in the page footer.
2. Enter the expression = **[Page]** in the text box.

Defining Report Footer Contents

Refer figure Access-1 and note that report footer consists of two types of objects i.e. Text ("Statistics", "Average Marks", "Maximum Marks", "Minimum Marks") and calculation on marks field (i.e. average marks, maximum marks, minimum marks)

To include text ("Statistics", "Average Marks", "Maximum Marks", "Minimum Marks") in report footer make labels in report footer band and type the desired text. This will make provision for all the labels. To make provision for including corresponding values, perform following steps:

1. Select Text box control present in toolbox. Now drag the mouse at the location, where you want to place the average marks and make text box. Delete unwanted label also.
2. Now click the mouse in the text box and enter **=Avg([marks])** in the text box.
3. To include maximum and minimum marks, perform same steps which are mentioned above and enter **=Max([marks])** to calculate maximum marks and **=Min([marks])** to calculate minimum marks.

After performing all the steps mentioned above, your report format will get ready. Now you need to run the report and view the output.

Viewing The Report

Perform following steps to view the report:

1. Click the mouse on "View" icon present in Design View toolbar. When you do so, a list of option will appear on the screen.

2. Select "Layout Preview" option from the list.

When you do so, report, as shown in figure Access-1 will appear on the screen.

SAVING THE REPORT

To save the report layout on the disk, perform all those steps, which you had performed for saving other objects. Note that the process of saving other objects like table, query etc. has already been explained before.

PRINTING THE REPORT

After defining the report layout and saving it, you can print the report on printer. Perform following steps to print the report:

1. Click the mouse on "File" option present in bar menu. When you do so, File submenu will appear on the screen.
2. Select "Print" option from File submenu. When you do so, a dialog box, as shown in figure Access-Access-
3. Set the properties as per your requirements and click the mouse on "Ok" button.

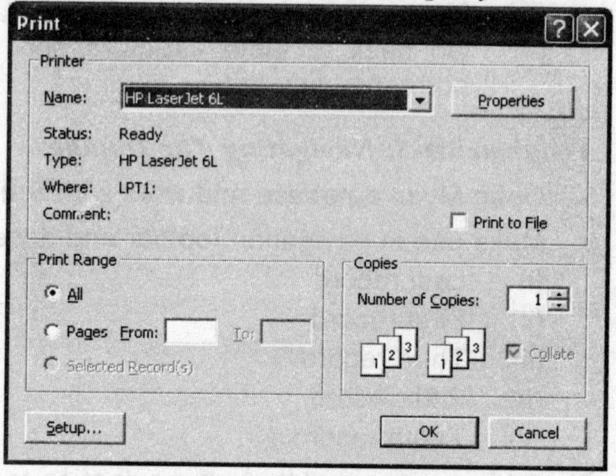

Figure Access-36

When you do so, currently opened report will get printed on the printer.

PRACTICAL ASSIGNMENTS

Assignments-1 : Creating A Database

1. Invoke MS-ACCESS and create a blank database with name Mydb.

Assignments-2 : Creating A Table

2. Create a table, with name Student. Its structure is described on page 184 of this book.

Assignments-3 : Entering Data In Table

3. To get familiar with data entry process, perform following operations:
   (i) Refer data, which is given on page 181 of this book.
   (ii) Enter first five records in Student table.
   (iii) Close the database.
   (iv) Exit from MS-Access.
   (v) Reload MS-Access.
   (vi) Open Mydb database again and make use of Student table.
   (vii) Enter remaining records of the given data.

Assignments-4 : Modifying The Database

4. To get familiar with database modification process, perform following steps:
   (i) Open Mydb database and work with Student table.
   (ii) Add a new field Fname at the end of the structure. Fname field should be character field of 50 characters.
   (iii) Move Fname field next to Name field.
   (iv) Now enter data in Fname field.
   (v) Go back to table structure and delete Fname field and observe its effect on corresponding data.

Assignments-5: Navigating The Database

5. Open Mydb database and work with Student table.
6. Make use of navigation toolbar and access following records:
   (i) Last record
   (ii) First record
   (iii) Third record
   (iv) Fifth record
   (v) Tenth record
7. Add a new record through navigation toolbar.
8. View first record and then newly created record.
9. Delete newly created record.

Assignments-6: Querying The Database

10. To get familiar with the process of retrieving the record of our choice, perform following operations:
    (i) Open Mydb database and work with Student table.
    (ii) Select all the records of all the students.
    (iii) Select all the records of male students.
    (iv) Select all the record of female students.
    (v) Select roll number and name of those students who are more than 18 years old.
    (vi) Select roll number, name and marks of all those female students who secured more than 750 marks.
    (vii) Select roll number and name of those students who are either male or less than 20 years in age.
    (viii) Select names of all those students who are from Delhi.
    (ix) Select records of all those students who belong to Lucknow and their name is Jyoti.
    (x) Select the record of that student who secured highest marks.

Assignments-7: Designing A Form

11. To get familiar with form designing process, perform following operations:
    (i) Open Mydb database and select Student table.
    (ii) Design a form, as shown in figure Access-26.

(iii) Display the form in Form View mode.
(iv) Access records through this form.
(v) Add few more records in the database through this form.
(vi) Delete all those records that you added in this session.

Assignment-8 Generating A Report:

1. To get familiar with MS-Access report printing procedure, perform following operations:
   (i) Open the mydb database, which was created in previous lab sessions?
   (ii) Make use of student table.
   (iii) Generate a report, which is shown at the beginning of this chapter.
   (iv) View the report in print preview mode.
   (v) Print the report on printer.

Assignment-9 Generating A Report For The Output Of A Query.

2. Perform following operations to generate another report:
   (i) Open mydb database, which was created in previous lab sessions.
   (ii) Make use of student table.
   (iii) Generate a report for all those students only who secured more than 790 marks. At the end of the report, a summary should also be printed as shown below:

Merit Report				
Sr. No	**Roll Number**	**Name**	**Age**	**Marks**
1				
2				
3				
4				
5				

Summary

Maximum Marks ####

Minimum Marks ####

****

Information Technology Lab

(CM-110)

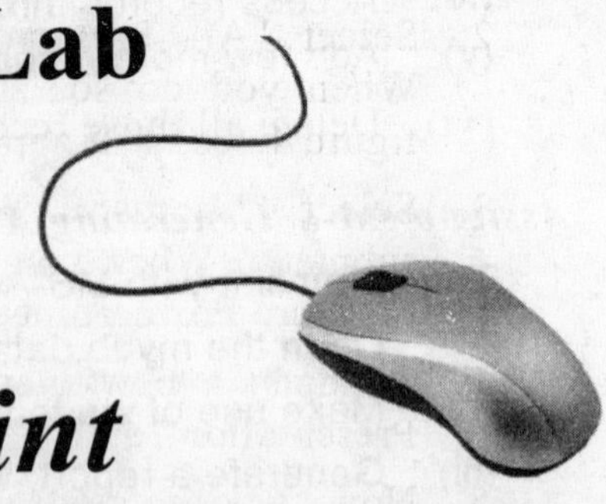

MS-PowerPoint

(Self Study Material and Practical Assignments)

INTRODUCTION

Be it internal activities of any office or external affairs of an organization, effective communication plays a major role in their success. In order to make the communication effective, innovation and creativity both have to be built into the presentation. Unless the presentation is interesting, audience will not pay attention to the speaker.

Computer is a modern tool, which helps in building impressive presentations and presenting a subject before the audience in interesting way. PowerPoint is one of the most popular software, which is used for making computer-based presentations.

MANUAL PRESENTATION

When a speaker talks on a subject, before the audience it is said that he is making a presentation. For example, when Managing Director of an organization addresses Sales Mangers to tell them sales plan of the next year, it is said that he is making a presentation. Similarly in an exhibition, exhibiter makes a presentation of his product before the crowd. All these are of manual presentations.

POWERPOINT PRESENTATION

PowerPoint presentation is basically a series of slides, containing information of the subject, which is to be put before the audience. They appear on computer screen, one after the other, either automatically or on a click of mouse.

ELEMENTS OF POWERPOINT PRESENTATION

In order to make the presentation impressive, PowerPoint presentation slides may contain multimedia elements like text, graphics, audio, animation, video etc. in them. These elements put together open multi channels of communication and make the presentation more convincing.

GETTING STARTED WITH POWERPOINT

Perform following steps to start work in PowerPoint:

1. Click the mouse on "Start" button, present on desktop. When you do so, Start menu, as shown in figure 4.1(a), will appear on the screen.
2. Select "All Programs" option from Start menu. When you do so, another submenu, as shown in figure 4.1(b) will appear on the screen.
3. Select "Microsoft PowerPoint" option from this submenu. When you do so, a dialog box, as shown in figure Powerpoint-1, will appear on the screen.
4. To open a new blank presentation, select "Blank Presentation" option from this dialog box.
5. Now click the mouse on "OK" button. When you do so, a dialog box for selecting the slide layout, as shown in figure Powerpoint-2, will appear on the screen.
6. Select the desired layout from this dialog box. Say you select "Text & ClipArt" layout.
7. Now click the mouse on "OK" button. When you do so, selected layout, within the PowerPoint window, as shown in figure Powerpoint-3, will appear on the screen.

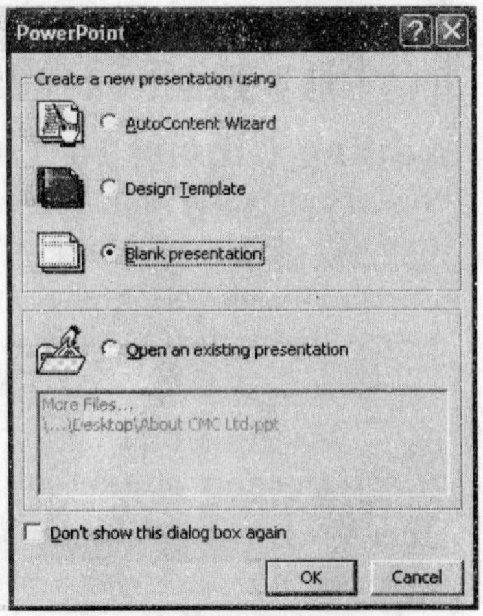

Figure Powerpoint - 1

Now you can add desired contents in the slides. The procedure for including different items in the slide is explained below.

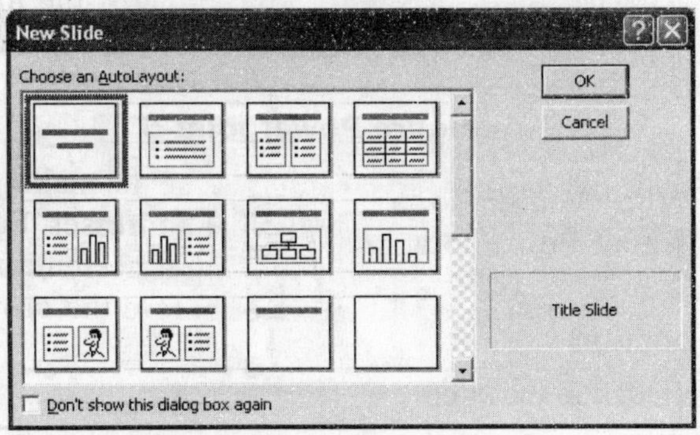

Figure Powerpoint-2

Figure Powerpoint-3

Adding Title In The Slide

To add title in the slide, click the mouse in Title placeholder and Type the title. To change the font, font size and font style drag the mouse on text and select desired specifications, using respective objects (like drop down lists, buttons etc.), present in Format toolbar.

Adding Text In The Slide

Click the mouse within Text placeholder and type the text. To change the font specifications, follow the method mentioned above.

Adding Clipart In The Slides

PowerPoint has an inbuilt graphics library of its own. Perform following steps to include pictures from that library, into the slide:

1. Double click the mouse within ClipArt placeholder. When you do so, ClipArt dialog box, as shown in figure Powerpoint-4, will appear on the screen.
2. Select a category of the clipart from this dialog box, by double clicking the mouse on desired category icon. When you do so, all the clip arts available in the selected category appear on the screen, as shown in figure Powerpoint-5.

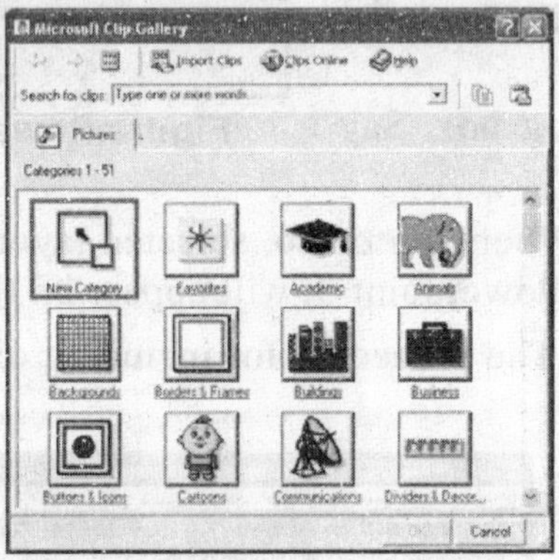

Figure Powerpoint-4

Figure Powerpoint-5

3. Click the mouse on desired clipart. When you do so, a graphical popup menu, as shown in figure Powerpoint-6, will appear on the screen.
4. Now click the mouse on "Insert Clip" option.

When you do so, the selected clip art will get included in the slide.

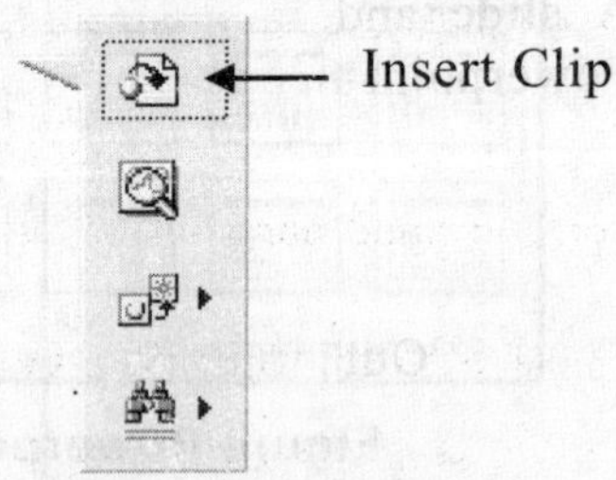

Figure Powerpoint -6

Including Notes

To include a brief description or remarks about the slide, so as to make the slide more informative, click the mouse in "Click to add notes" placeholder and type the contents.

Note that these contents (notes) are for documentation purpose only. They do not get displays when the slide show goes on.

ADDING NEXT SLIDE TO THE PRESENTATION

After completion of the first slide, next slide can be added to the presentation by performing following steps:

1. Select "Insert" option from the bar menu. When you do so, Insert submenu, as shown in figure Powerpoint-7(a) will appear on the screen.
2. Select "New Slide" option from Insert submenu. When you do so, a dialog box, as shown in figure Powerpoint-2 for selecting the slide layout, will appear on the screen.
3. Select the desired layout from this dialog box and click the mouse on "OK" button. When you do so, placeholders as shown in figure Powerpoint-3, will appear within PowerPoint window.
4. Now add the desired contents, like text, graphics, notes etc. to the slide, following the methods, mentioned above.

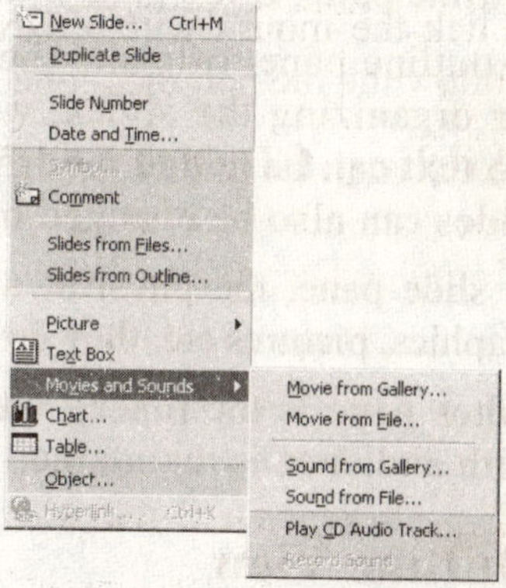

(a) (b)

Figure Powerpoint -7

Following above mentioned method, you can add as many slides to the presentation as you want.

DIFFERENT SLIDE VIEWS

Once the slides of the presentation are made, they can be viewed in different modes. PowerPoint offers following modes for viewing the slides:

1. Normal View
2. Outline View
3. Slide View
4. Slide Sorter View
5. Slide Show View

Each mode serves a different purpose and offers ease of operations, while performing specific type of task. A brief introduction of each mode is given below.

Normal View

A slide and its contents, as they would appear in Normal View are shown in figure Powerpoint-8.

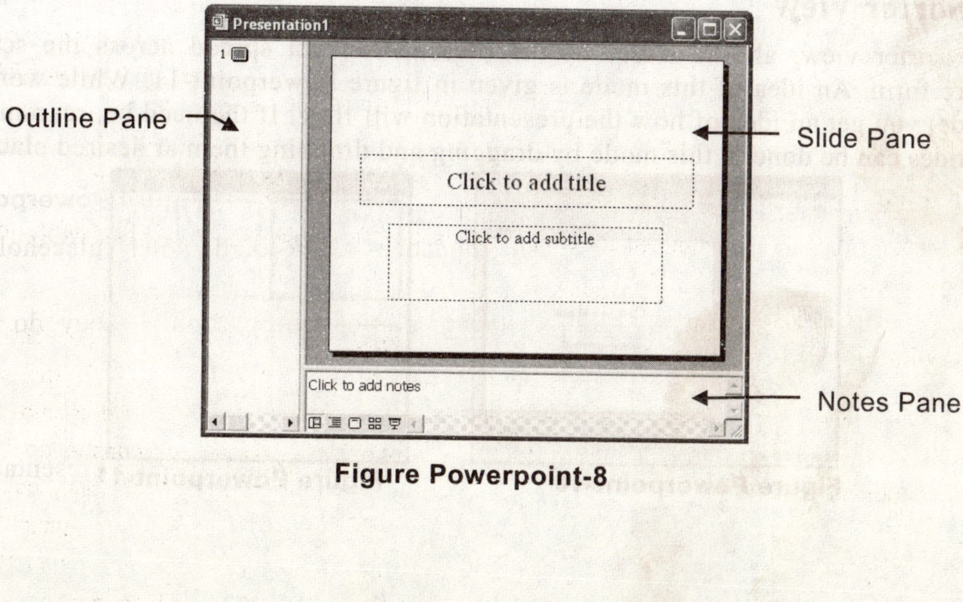

Figure Powerpoint-8

Refer this figure and note that Normal View comprises of three panes. These panes are Outline pane, Slide pane and Notes pane.

In outline pane, title and the text get displayed in hierarchical order. It is generally utilized for organizing the slides, within the presentation and text within the slides. For example, the text can be added modified, shifted or deleted in outline pane. Similarly position of the slides can also be changed by dragging and dropping them at desired place.

In slide pane, the physical appearance of the slide gets displayed. Note that if slide includes graphics, pictures etc. they do not get displayed in outline pane. They are visible in slide pane.

Notes pane is the place, where speaker notes or important information that is to be shared with audience is maintained.

Outline View

A slide and its contents, as they will appear in Outline View, are shown in figure Powerpoint-9.

Refer this figure and note that it is basically a rearrangement of Normal View. In this view, outline pane occupies larger space and Slide Pane becomes smaller.

For rearranging the contents and the slides, outline view comes handier than Normal View.

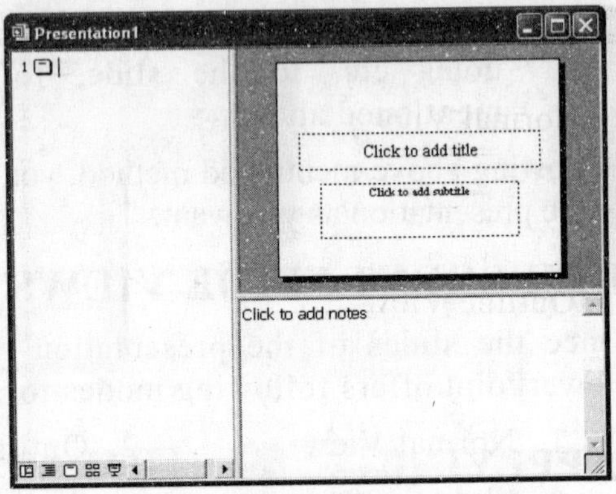

Figure Powerpoint -9

Slide View

As the name indicates, in Slide View, single slide gets displayed at a time. Physical appearance of the slide gets displayed in a larger area. To modify the contents, slide can be displayed in Slide View mode and then changes can be made. An idea of Slide View mode is given in figure Powerpoint-10.

Slide Sorter View

In slide sorter view, all the slides of the presentation get spread across the screen in miniature form. An idea of this mode is given in figure Powerpoint-11. While working in this mode, you get an idea of how the presentation will flow. If the need be, rearrangement of the slides can be done in this mode by dragging and dropping them at desired place.

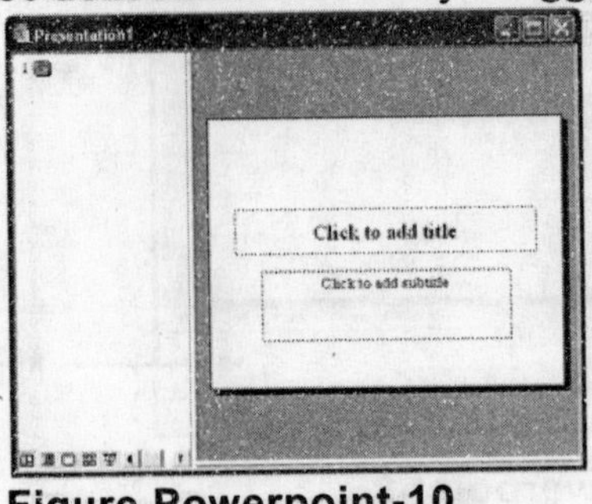

Figure Powerpoint-10

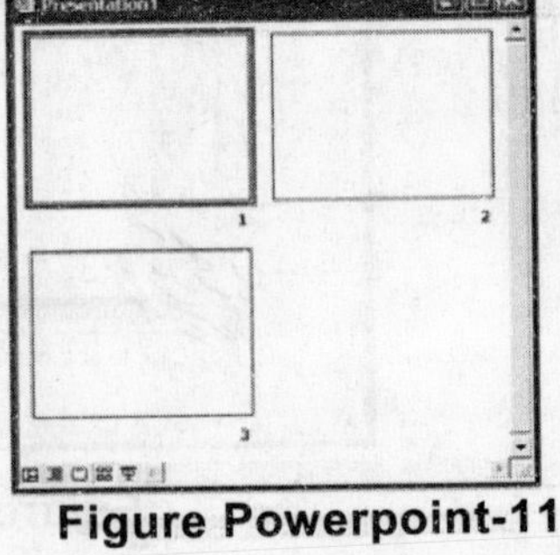

Figure Powerpoint-11

Slide Show View

In this mode, all the slides of the presentation appear one after the other on the screen either automatically or on a click of mouse. More details of this mode are given later in this chapter.

Switching From One View Mode To Other

Refer figure Powerpoint-12 and note that at the bottom left corner of PowerPoint window there are five view buttons. Each button corresponds to a view mode. To switchover to a view mode, you need to click the mouse on corresponding button. For example, if you are it Normal View mode and wish to switchover to Slide Sorter view mode, you will have to click the mouse on Slide Sorted view button.

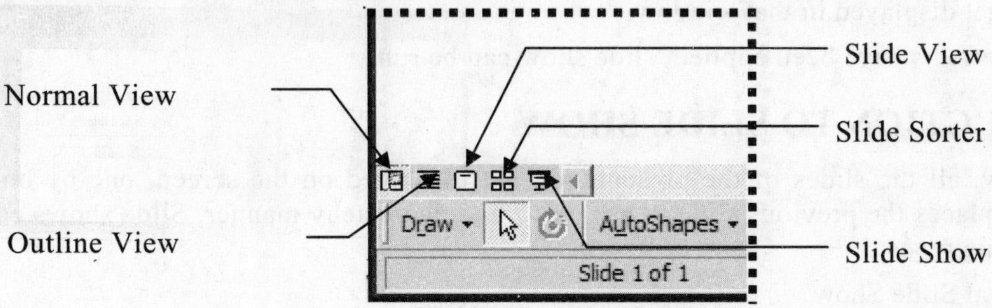

Figure Powerpoint-12

APPLYING ANIMATION

To make the presentation interesting, objects of the slides can be animated. In PowerPoint, animation is applied through "Animation Effects" toolbar. Usually it doesn't remain present on the screen but it can be made to appear by right clicking the mouse on any toolbar and then selecting "Animation Effects" option from the popup menu that appears thereafter. Animation Effects toolbar is illustrated in figure Powerpoint-13.

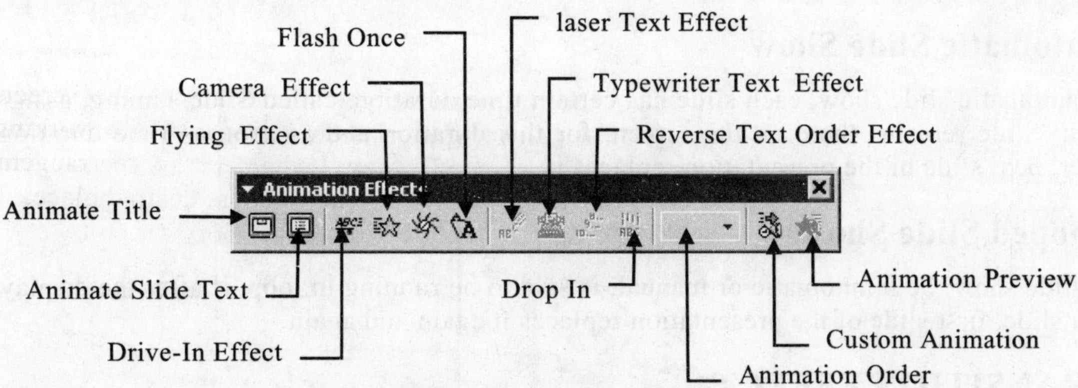

Figure Powerpoint-13

Perform following steps to apply animation in any slide:

1. Make the slide appear in Normal view mode.

2. To animate the title of the slide, click the mouse on "Animate Title" button, present in Animation Effects toolbar. On the other hand, if you wish to animate the text of the slide, select "animate Slide Text" button.
3. Select the desired animation effect by clicking the mouse on corresponding button (such as Drive-In effect, Flying effect etc.) present in Animation Effects toolbar.
4. If more than one objects are to be animated on the slide, their animation order can be selected through "Animation Order" drop down list, present in the toolbar.
5. To preview the effect of selected animation, click the mouse on "Animation Preview" button, present in the toolbar.
6. When you do so, a small window will appear on the screen and animation effects will get displayed in that window.

Once all the effects have been applied, slide show can be run.

INTRODUCTION TO SLIDE SHOW

In slide show, all the slides of the presentation get displayed on the screen, one by one. Next slide replaces the previous slide in attractive and eye-catchy manner. Slide shows can be of following types:

1. Manual Slide Show
2. Automatic Slide Show

Basic characteristics of both types of slide shows are described below.

Manual Slide Show

In manual slide show, one slide replaces the other slide only when space bar is pressed or mouse is clicked. Till the time any of these two events don't take place, slide remains visible on the screen.

Automatic Slide Show

In automatic slide show, each slide has certain time duration, called Slide Timing, assigned to it. Slide remains there on the screen, for this duration and as soon as time duration is over, next slide of the presentation replaces it.

Looped Slide Shows

A slide show, be it automatic or manual, is said to be running in loop, if after the display of last slide, first slide of the presentation replaces it again and again.

TRANSITION EFFECT

The way one slide replaces the other slide, during the slide show is called Transition Effect. For example, the next slide may take entry on the screen from left hand side and gradually replace the previous slide. Similarly, in other transition effect the first slide may tear apart from the middle, as if stage curtains are sliding left and right and the next slide is slowly becoming visible in back.

PowerPoint offers many transition effects, which can be selected and applied to one, many or all slides of the presentation.

Applying Transition Effect And Slide Timings

Perform following steps to apply slide timings and transition effect to the slides of the presentation:

1. Open the presentation and display the slide, in which the transition effect or slide timing is to be applied, in Normal View mode.
2. Select "Slide Show" option from the bar menu. When you do so, Slide Show submenu, as shown in figure Powerpoint-14(a) will appear on the screen.

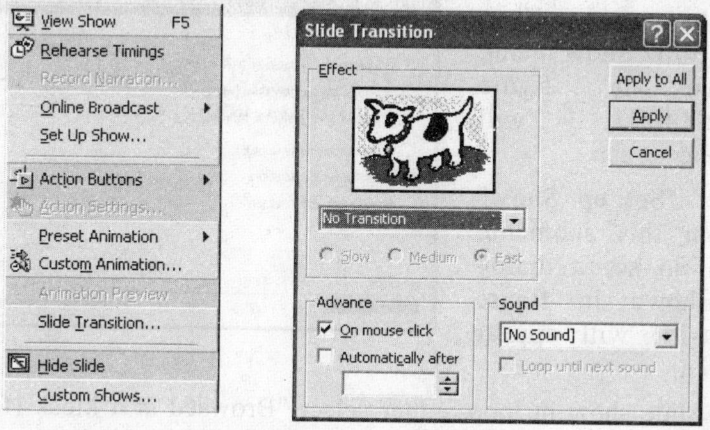

(a) (b)

Figure Powerpoint-14

3. Select "Slide Transition" option from this submenu. When you do so, a dialog box, as shown in figure Powerpoint-14(b) will appear on the screen.
4. Select the desired transition effect from "Effect" dropdown list.
5. Select the speed of the transition (i.e. how fast the replacement of one slide by the other has to be done) by clicking the mouse on Slow, Medium or Fast radio button.
6. If the slide show has to advance on the click of the mouse, check "On mouse click" check box.
7. If slide timing is to be assigned to the slide, check "Automatically after" check box and specify the time duration (for which the slide has to stay on the screen), using corresponding spinner.
8. If sound is to be produced on its appearance on screen, select a sound clip from "Sound" drop down list.

9. If the sound clip is to be played till the time other sound is invoked, check "Loop until next sound" check box.
10. If these settings are to be applied to the current slide only, click the mouse on "Apply" button. On the other hand, if the settings are to be applied to all the slides of the presentation, click it on "Apply to All" button.

When you do so, selected transition effect and chosen slide timing will get applied to the slides.

SETTING UP THE SLIDE SHOW

After making the slides and applying transition effects, certain parameters related to slide show need to be set. Perform following steps to set those parameters:

1. Open the presentation, for which the parameters need to be set.
2. Select "Slide Show" option from the bar menu. When you do so, Slide Show menu, as shown in figure Powerpoint-14(a), will appear on the screen.
3. Now select "Set up Show" option from this submenu. When you do so, a dialog box, as shown in figure Powerpoint-15, will appear on the screen.

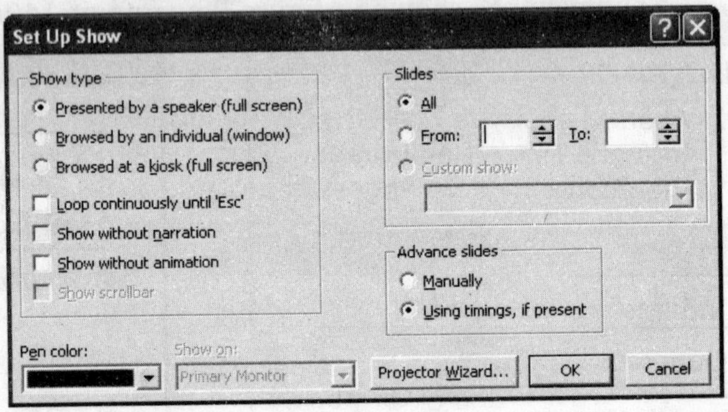

4. To run the slide show in loop, either select "Browsed at a kiosk (full screen)" radio button or check "Loop Continuously until Esc" check box.
5. If narration and animation, present in the presentation are to be displayed, check the corresponding check boxes.
6. If all the slides of the presentation have to participate in the slide show, select "All" radio button else select "From", button and specify the slide numbers that have to appear in the slide show. For this, make use of the "From" and "To" spinners, present in the dialog box.
7. If the slide show has to run in manual mode (slides advance on the click of mouse or on pressing space bar), select "Manually" radio button. For automatic slide show, select "Using timings, if present" radio button.
8. At last, click the mouse on "OK" button.

When you do so, slide show will get ready to run as per the specifications set by you.

RUNNING THE SLIDE SHOW

To run the slide show, follow any one of the methods described below:

1. Select " Slide Show" option from " View" submenu.

or

2. Select "View Show" option from "Slide Show" submenu.

or

3. Click the mouse on "Slide Show" button, present at the left bottom part of PowerPoint window.

PRACTICAL ASSIGNMENTS

Assignment 1 : Preparing A Presentation.

1. Assume that you have to talk about India in an international seminar. For this, you have to make PowerPoint presentation comprising of many slides. Titles of these slides and their contents are suggested below:

Title	Contents
India is a great country	Few sentences in appreciation of India.
Geographical facts	Few facts like Himalayas in north, Indian ocean in south, area, population etc.
Unity in diversity	Different states and their cultures. Feeling of unity that prevails.
Highlights	Important aspects of India and its strong points.
Famous tourist spots	Names and highlights of famous tourist spots of India. For example, Taj Mahal, sea beaches of Goa, Palaces of Jaipur etc.
Famous temples	Locations of famous temples and stories associated with them.
Events	Few famous events like independence day, festivals like Diwali, Holi etc.
Personalities	World renowned personalities and their contributions.
Indian culture	Greatness of Indian culture and its difference from other cultures.
East or west India is best	All those aspects, which make India better than other countries.
Developments of India	Progress that India has made in last decade.
My dream India	What India should be after 10 years.

2. Collect above mentioned details and write them on paper.

3. Create all slides mentioned above.
4. Now run the slide show and test the presentation.
5. Add clip arts in few slides.
6. Run the slide show again.
7. Apply transition effect on the slides.
8. Run the slide show again.
9. Make animation toolbar on and apply animation in first slide.
10. Run the slide show again.
11. Apply slide timings to the slides and run the presentation in automatic mode.
12. Run the slide show in loop.

****

Information Technology Lab (CM-110)

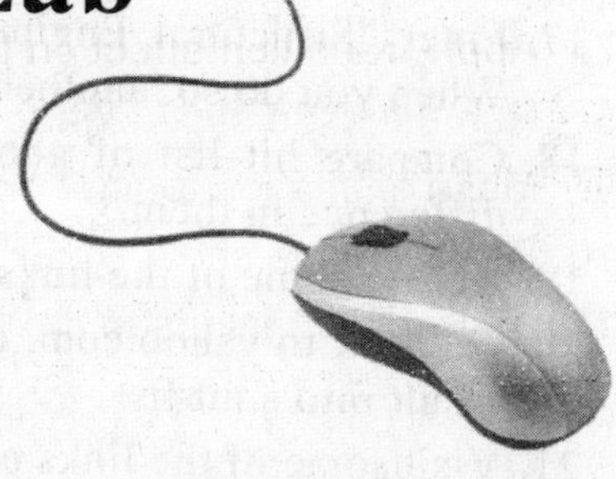

Internet

(Self Study Material and Practical Assignments)

INTERNET STUDY MATERIAL REFERENCE

Detailed description of Internet and related topic is given in chapter 5. Please study that chapter and solve the exercisers given at the end of the chapter before attempting following assignments.

PRACTICAL ASSIGNMENTS

Assignment-1: Web Surfing

1. Get connected to Internet
2. Invoke web browser.
3. Access yahoo.com web site.
4. Click the mouse on any link present in the web page.
5. Click the mouse on "Back" button present in browser window. This button will take you back to yahoo.com web site.
6. Now click the mouse on another link, present in the page.
7. Now enter excite.com in address bar and press Enter Key. This process will take you to another web site.
8. Now right click the mouse on any link. When you do so, popup menu will appear on the screen.
9. Select "Open in New Window" option. This will display web page in new window.
10. Repeat above mentioned procedure for few other links present on excite.com web site.

Assignment-2: Web Searching

11. Get connected to Internet if you are not connected to it.
12. Invoke you web browser.
13. Go to google.com web site. It provides very popular search engine.

14. Enter "Structural Engineering" in edit box and click the mouse on "Google Search" button.
15. Access at least three links of hit list and compare the contents.
16. Go to excite.com web site.
17. Enter "Structural Engineering" in edit box and click the mouse on "Search" button. When you do so, another hit list will get displayed.
18. Compare hit list of google.com with the hit list of excite.com. You will find some difference in them.
19. Access some of the links present in hit list.
20. Go back to yahoo.com, enter "How computer works" in search edit box and search will result into a hit list.
21. Visit some of the links of this hit list.

Assignment-3: Creating An E-Mail Account.

22. Get connected to Internet.
23. Invoke the web browser.
24. Go to yahoo.com web site.
25. Click the mouse on mail link.
26. Create a new e-mail account for yourself.
27. Recall that procedure for opening an e-mail account is given in this chapter.

Assignment-4: Reading e-mail

28. Get connected to Internet.
29. Invoke the web browser.
30. Go to yahoo.com web site.
31. Click the mouse on mail link.
32. This will take you to login web page.
33. Enter your login name and password.
34. Read the test mail received into your account.

Assignment-5: Sending e-mail.

35. Get connected to Internet.
36. Invoke the web browser.
37. Go to yahoo.com web site.
38. Click the mouse on mail link.
39. Enter your login name and password.
40. Opt for "Compose" option.
41. Write a letter to your friend, saying that you are master of Internet now.
42. Attach a picture with this letter and send the letter to your friend.

****

APPENDIX-1

EBCDIC Code Table

Dec	Hex	Code	Dec	Hex	Code	Dec	Hex	Code	Dec	Hex	Code
0	00	NUL	32	20		64	40	space	96	60	-
1	01	SOH	33	21		65	41		97	61	/
2	02	STX	34	22		66	42		98	62	
3	03	ETX	35	23		67	43		99	63	
4	04		36	24		68	44		100	64	
5	05	HT	37	25	LF	69	45		101	65	
6	06		38	26	ETB	70	46		102	66	
7	07	DEL	39	27	ESC	71	47		103	67	
8	08		40	28		72	48		104	68	
9	09		41	29		73	49		105	69	
10	0A		42	2A		74	4A	[	106	6A	|
11	0B	VT	43	2B		75	4B	.	107	6B	,
12	0C	FF	44	2C		76	4C	<	108	6C	%
13	0D	CR	45	2D	ENQ	77	4D	(	109	6D	_
14	0E	SO	46	2E	ACK	78	4E	+	110	6E	>
15	0F	SI	47	2F	BEL	79	4F	| !	111	6F	?
16	10	DLE	48	30		80	50	&	112	70	
17	11		49	31		81	51		113	71	
18	12		50	32	SYN	82	52		114	72	
19	13		51	33		83	53		115	73	

Dec	Hex	Code	Dec	Hex	Code	Dec	Hex	Code	Dec	Hex	Code
20	14		52	34		84	54		116	74	
21	15		53	35		85	55		117	75	
22	16	BS	54	36		86	56		118	76	
23	17		55	37	EOT	87	57		119	77	
24	18	CAN	56	38		88	58		120	78	
25	19	EM	57	39		89	59		121	79	‘
26	1A		58	3A		90	5A	!]	122	7A	:
27	1B		59	3B		91	5B	$	123	7B	#
28	1C	IFS	60	3C		92	5C	*	124	7C	@
29	1D	IGS	61	3D	NAK	93	5D	)	125	7D	‘
30	1E	IRS	62	3E		94	5E	;	126	7E	=
31	1F	IUS	63	3F	SUB	95	5F	^	127	7F	"
128	80		160	A0		192	C0	{	224	E0	\
129	81	a	161	A1	~	193	C1	A	225	E1	
130	82	b	162	A2	s	194	C2	B	226	E2	S
131	83	c	163	A3	t	195	C3	C	227	E3	T
132	84	d	164	A4	u	196	C4	D	228	E4	U
133	85	e	165	A5	v	197	C5	E	229	E5	V
134	86	f	166	A6	w	198	C6	F	230	E6	W
135	87	g	167	A7	x	199	C7	G	231	E7	X
136	88	h	168	A8	y	200	C8	H	232	E8	Y
137	89	i	169	A9	z	201	C9	I	233	E9	Z
138	8A		170	AA		202	CA		234	EA	
139	8B		171	AB		203	CB		235	EB	
140	8C		172	AC		204	CC		236	EC	
141	8D		173	AD		205	CD		237	ED	
142	8E		174	AE		206	CE		238	EE	

Dec	Hex	Code	Dec	Hex	Code	Dec	Hex	Code	Dec	Hex	Code
143	8F		175	AF		207	CF		239	EF	
144	90		176	B0		208	D0	}	240	F0	0
145	91	j	177	B1		209	D1	J	241	F1	1
146	92	k	178	B2		210	D2	K	242	F2	2
147	93	l	179	B3		211	D3	L	243	F3	3
148	94	m	180	B4		212	D4	M	244	F4	4
149	95	n	181	B5		213	D5	N	245	F5	5
150	96	o	182	B6		214	D6	O	246	F6	6
151	97	p	183	B7		215	D7	P	247	F7	7
152	98	q	184	B8		216	D8	Q	248	F8	8
153	99	r	185	B9		217	D9	R	249	F9	9
154	9A		186	BA		218	DA		250	FA	
155	9B		187	BB		219	DB		251	FB	
156	9C		188	BC		220	DC		252	FC	
157	9D		189	BD		221	DD		253	FD	
158	9E		190	BE		222	DE		254	FE	
159	9F		191	BF		223	DF		255	FF	

APPENDIX-2

ASCII Code Table

Character	Binary	Decimal	Character	Binary	Decimal
NUL	00000000	00	SO	00001110	14
SOH	00000001	01	SI	00001111	15
STX	00000010	02	DLE	00010000	16
ETX	00000011	03	DC1	00010001	17
EOT	00000100	04	DC2	00010010	18
ENQ	00000101	05	DC3	00010011	19
ACK	00000110	06	DC4	00010100	20
BEL	00000111	07	NAK	00010101	21
BS	00001000	08	SYN	00010110	22
HT	00001001	09	ETB	00010111	23
LF	00001010	10	CAN	00011000	24
VT	00001011	11	EM	00011001	25
FF	00001100	12	SUB	00011010	26
CR	00001101	13	ESC	00011011	27
FS	00011100	28	6	00110110	54
GS	00011101	29	7	00110111	55
RS	00011110	30	8	00111000	56
US	00011111	31	9	00111001	57
SP	00100000	32	:	00111010	58
!	00100001	33	;	00111011	59

Character	Binary	Decimal	Character	Binary	Decimal
"	00100010	34	<	00111100	60
#	00100011	35	=	00111101	61
$	00100100	36	>	00111110	62
%	00100101	37	?	00111111	63
&	00100110	38	@	01000000	64
'	00100111	39	A	01000001	65
(	00101000	40	B	01000010	66
)	00101001	41	C	01000011	67
*	00101010	42	D	01000100	68
+	00101011	43	E	01000101	69
,	00101100	44	F	01000110	70
-	00101101	45	G	01000111	71
.	00101110	46	H	01001000	72
/	00101111	47	I	01001001	73
0	00110000	48	J	01001010	74
1	00110001	49	K	01001011	75
2	00110010	50	L	01001100	76
3	00110011	51	M	01001101	77
4	00110100	52	N	01001110	78
5	00110101	53	O	01001111	79
P	01010000	80	h	01101000	104
Q	01010001	81	i	01101001	105
R	01010010	82	j	01101010	106
S	01010011	83	k	01101011	107
T	01010100	84	l	01101100	108
U	01010101	85	m	01101101	109

Character	Binary	Decimal	Character	Binary	Decimal
V	01010110	86	n	01101110	110
W	01010111	87	o	01101111	111
X	01011000	88	p	01110000	112
Y	01011001	89	q	01110001	113
Z	01011010	90	r	01110010	114
[	01011011	91	s	01110011	115
\	01011100	92	t	01110100	116
]	01011101	93	u	01110101	117
^	01011110	94	v	01110110	118
_	01011111	95	w	01110111	119
`	01100000	96	x	01111000	120
a	01100001	97	y	01111001	121
b	01100010	98	z	01111010	122
c	01100011	99	{	01111011	123
d	01100100	100	|	01111100	124
e	01100101	101	}	01111101	125
f	01100110	102	~	01111110	126
g	01100111	103	DEL	01111111	127

APPENDIX-3

Programs

Problem 1

Write a program to print the sum of two integer numbers that are entered through keyboard.

Program 1

```
#include <stdio.h>
main()
{
    int num1, num2, tot = 0;
    printf ("\nGive First Integer Number ");
    scanf ("%i" , &num1) ;
    printf("\nGive Second Integer Number ") ;
    scanf("%i", &num2) ;
    tot= num1 + num2 ;
    printf ("\nSum = %i ", tot) ;
}
```

Problem 2

Write a program to subtract two floating numbers that are entered through keyboard.

Program 2

```
#include <stdio.h>
main()
{
    float num1, num2, rslt = 0.0;
    printf ("\nGive First Flaot Number ");
    scanf ("%f" , &num1) ;
    printf("\nGive Second  Float Number ") ;
    scanf("%f", &num2) ;
```

```
        rslt= num1 - num2 ;
        printf ("\nResult = %f ", tot) ;
    }
```

Problem 3

Write a program to calculate m to the power n , where the values of m and n are taken from the keyboard.

Program 3

```
    /* This program calculate m to the power n */
    #include<stdio.h>
    main()
    {
        int m, n, count, rslt=1 ;
        printf("\nEnter the value of m & n");
        scanf("%i %i", &m,&n);
        count=1;
        while(count<=n)
        {
            rslt=rslt*m;
            count++;
        }
        printf("\nThe answer is %i ",rslt);
    }
```

Problem 4

Write a program that accepts radius of the circle from the keyboard and prints area and circumference of the circle.

Program 4

```
    void main()
    {
        int r;
        float area, cir;
        printf("\nEnter radius of the circle : ");
        scanf("%d",&r);
        area=3.14*r*r;
```

```
cir = 2 * 3.14 * r ;
printf("Radius = %d and area=%f", r, area);
printf("\Circumference =  %f ", cir);
}
```

Problem 5

Write a program to read a number from the keyboard and print, if it is a positive number or negative number.

Program 5

```
/*Program to check if the given number is positive or negative */
#include<stdio.h>
main()
{
    int x;
    printf("\nEnter the number :");
    scanf("%d",&x);
    if(x>0)
    printf("\nNuber is Positive);
    else
    printf("\nNumber is Negative");
}
```

Problem 6

Write a program to print the sum of all the numbers till a given number.

Program 6

```
/*Program to print the sum of all the numbers up to a given number*/
#include<stdio.h>
main()
{
    int target, tot=0, i ;
    printf("\nEnter the target number :");
    scanf("%d",&target );
    for (i=1 ; i <= target ; i++)
    tot = tot + i ;
```

```
        printf("\ntoatal %i ", tot );
    }
```

Problem 7

Write a program to print the average of all the numbers up to a given number.

Program 7

```
/*Program to print the average of all the numbers up to a given number*/
#include<stdio.h>
main()
{
    int target, i, num ;
    float tot = 0.0,  avrg = 0.0 ;
    printf("\nEnter the target number :");
    scanf("%d",&target );
    for (i=1 ; i <= target ; i++) .
    {
        printf("\nGive No %i ", i  );
        scanf ("%i", &num );
        tot = tot + num ;
    }
    avrg = tot / target ;
    printf("\nAverage =  %f ", avrg );
}
```

Problem 8

Write function to compute the GCD of two numbers.

Program 8

```
/* Use of a function that computes the GCD of two numbers*/
#include<stdio.h>
#include<conio.h>
#include<process.h>
int a,b;
void main()
{
```

```
    printf("\n Enter the two numbers of which gcd is to be calculated\n");
    scanf("%d\n %d",&a,&b);
    gcd();
}
void gcd()
{
    if(a==b)
    {
        printf("\ngcd of the two no. is %d",a);
        getch();
        exit(0);
    }
    else if(a<b)
    {
        b=b-a;
        gcd();
    }
    else
    {
        a=a-b;
        gcd();
    }
}
```

Problem 9

Write a program to convert Centigrade temperature in Fahrenheit.

Program 9

```
#include <stdio.h.>
main()
{
    float farenheit;    /* the temperature in Farenheit degrees  */
    flaot centigrade;   /* the temperature in Centigrade degrees */
    printf("Centigrade to Farenheit Conversion\n\n");
    printf("\nGive  temprature in Centigrade  ")
```

```
        scanf("%f", &centigrade) ;
        farenheit = 32 + (centigrade * 9)/5;
        printf(" C =%4d   F =%4d  ",centigrade,farenheit);
    }
    #include <stdio.h>
```

Problem 10

Write a program to convert Fahrenheit temperature in Centigrade.

Program 10

```
    main()
    {
        float  farenheit;    /* the temperature in Farenheit degrees  */
        float  centigrade;   /* the temperature in centigrade degrees */
        printf(" Farenheit  To Centigrade Conversion\n\n");
        printf("\nGive  temprature in Farenheit  ");
        scanf("%f", &farenheit) ;
        centigrade  =( farenheit -32 ) * 5.0 / 9.0 ;
        printf("  F =%f  C =%f     ",farenheit, centigrade) ;
    }
```

Problem 11

Write a program to convert given millimetres to meters and centimetres.

Program 11

```
    /* Program to Convert millimetres to meters, & centimetres*/
    #include<conio.h>
    #include<stdio.h>
    #include<string.h>
    void main()
    {
        float mm, cm, mtr ;
        clrscr();
        printf("\n Enter a Quantity in Millimeters");
        scanf("%f",&mm);
        cm = mm /10.00 ;
```

```
mtr=mm/1000.00;
printf("\nMillimeter= %f Centimeter %f Meters = %f ", mm, cm, mtr );
getch();
}
```

Problem 12

Write a program to calculate Cosine values for angle 0 to 180.

Program 12

```
/* Program to calculate Cosine values for angle 0 to 180*/
#include<conio.h>
#include<stdio.h>
#include<math.h>
#define PI 3.1416
void main()
{
    int i;
    float angle;
    clrscr();
    printf("\n The cosine of different angle");
    printf("\n\n angle \t COS (angle)\n\n");
    for(i=0;i<=180;i=i+10)
    {
        angle=(PI/180)*i;
        printf("\n %3d\t %7.5f",i, cos(angle));
    }
    getch();
}
```

roblem 13

/rite a program to print the largest number among given three numbers.

'rogram 13

```
#include<stdio.h>
void main()
{
```

```
        int A, B, C;
        printf("\nEnter First  number :");
        scanf("%d",&A);
        printf("\nEnter Second  number :");
        scanf("%d",&B);

        printf("\nEnter Third  number :");
        scanf("%d",&C);

        if(A>B)
            if(A>C)
                printf("\n %d is largest number ",A);
            else
                printf("\n %d is largest number ",C);
            else
                if(B>C)
                    printf("\n %d is largest number ",B);
                else
                    printf("\n %d is largest number ",C);
}
```

Problem 14

Write a program to convert a given binary number to equivalent decimal number.

Program 14

```
/*THIS PROGRAM CONVERTS A BINARY NUMBER TO DECIMAL*/
#include<conio.h>
#include<stdio.h>
#include<math.h>
#define m 15
main()
{
    int n,a[m],count=0,p,i,sum=0,temp;
    clrscr();
    printf("\n GIVE THE NUMBER IN THE BINARY FORM (only 1 & 0 are allowed) ");
```

```
scanf("%d",&n);
p=n;
do
{
    a[count]=n%10;
    count++;
    n=n/10;
}
while(n>0);
for(i=0;i<count;i++)
{
    temp=a[i]*pow(2,i);
    sum=sum+temp;
}
printf("\n\n THE DECIMAL EQUIVELENT OF %d IS : %d",p,sum);
getch();
}
```

Problem 15

Write a program c to compute and print partial sum of harmonic series

1 + 1/2 + 1/3 + ... +1/N

The value of N is entered through keyboard.

Program 15

```
#include <stdio.h>
main()
{   int i, target ;
    float sum = 0;
    printf("\nGive target number ");
        scanf("%i",&target) ;
        for (i=1; i <= target; i++)
        {               sum += 1.0/i;
            printf("%d:  %4.6f\n", i, sum);
        }
}
```

Problem 16

Write a program to evaluate equation $V=P(1+r)^n$ for various combination of P, r and n P=1000,2000,....

Program 16

```
/* Program to evaluate equation V=P(1+r)ⁿ for various combination of */
/* P, r and n P=1000,2000,.... */
/* 10000; r=.10,.11,.12.......20; n=1,2,3, 10; */
#include<conio.h>
#include<stdio.h>
#include<math.h>
void main()
{
    int i,j,k, count=0;
    float v[30] ,p,r,n;
    clrscr();
    printf("\n");
    for(i=1;i<=3;i++)
    {   p=1000*i;
        for(j=1;j<=3;j++)
        {
            r=0.10+i*0.01;
            for(k=1; k<=3;k++)
            {
                n=k;
                v[count]=p*pow((1+r),n);
                count++;
            }
        }
    }
    for(i=0;i<count;i++)
    printf("\n %f", v[i]);
    getch();
}
```

Problem 17

Write a program that accepts a number from the keyboard and checks if it is a prime number or not.

Program 17

```
/* Program to check if a given number is a prime number nor not */
#include <stdio.h>
main()
{
    int n ;
    printf("Enter a number: ");
    scanf("%d", &n);
    if(n == 2)
    printf("%d is prime", n);
    else if(n % 2 == 0 || n < 2)
    printf("%d is not prime", n);
    else
    {
        int x;
        for(x = 0; x < (int)sqrt((double)n); x++)
        if(n % x == 0)
        {
            printf("%d is not prime", n);
            return;
        }
        printf("%d is prime", n);
    }
}
```

Problem 18

Write a program to find the sum of odd and even numbers starting from 1 to 100.

Program 18

```
/* Program to find the sum of odd and even numbers starting from 1 to 100*/
#include<conio.h>
#include<stdio.h>
```

```
void main()
{   int num,i,j;
    int evensum=0,sumodd=0;
    clrscr();
    printf("\n The sum of odd numbers is\n");
    printf("0");
    for(i=1;i<99;i=i+2)
    {
        sumodd=sumodd+i;
        printf("+ %d",i);
    }
    printf("= %d\n\n\n",sumodd);
    printf("The sum of even number\n\n");
    printf("0");
    for(i=2;i<=100;i=i+2)
    {
        evensum=evensum+i;
        printf("+ %d",i);
    }
    printf("= %d", evensum);
    getch();
}
```

Problem 19

Write a program to print 'a'...'z' and digit'0'...'9' and their ASCII integer value in Decimal.

Program 19

```
/* Program to print 'a'...'z' and digit'0'...'9' and their ASCII integer value in Decimal*/
#include<conio.h>
#include<stdio.h>
void main()
{
    char ch='a';
    int i;
    clrscr();
```

```
        printf("\n The ASCII value of \n");
        for(i=0;i<26;i++)
        {
            printf("\n n%c=%d",ch,ch);
            ch=ch+1;
        }
        ch='0';
        printf("\n");
        for(i=0;i<=9;i++)
        {
            printf("\n%c=%d",ch,ch);
            ch=ch+1;
        }
        getch();
    }
```

Problem 20

Write a program to generate all the prime numbers up till a given number.

Program 20

```
    #include <stdio.h>
    main()
    {
        int n,i=1,j,c;
        printf("\nEUpto which number prime numbers have to be generated");
        scanf("%d",&n);
        printf("\nFollwing  are the prime numbers: \n");
        while(i<=n)
        {
            c=0;
            for(j=1;j<=i;j++)
            {
                if(i%j==0)
                c++;
            }
```

```
            if(c==2)
            printf("%d       ",i) ;
            i++;
        }
        getch();
}
```

Problem 21

Write a program for reversing the digits of a given number.

Program 21

```
/*Program for reversing the digits of a given number.*/
#include<stdio.h>
void main()
{
    int no1, no2;
    printf("\nEnter a number :");
    scanf("%d",&no1);
    no2=0;
    while(no1!=0)
    {
        no2=no2*10+no1%10;
        no1=no1/10;
    }
    printf("\n%d",no2);
}
```

Problem 22

Write a C program to find and output all the roots of a given quadratic equation for non-zero coefficients.

Program 22

```
#include<conio.h>
#include<stdio.h>
#include<math.h>
void main()
```

```
{
    float a,b,c;
    float temp,root1,root2;
    printf("Enter non zero Coefficient for equation aX^2+bX+c=0");
    scanf("%f%f%f",&a,&b,&c); /*scaning values for coefficients*/
    if(a!=0 && b!=0 && c!=0) /*condition for checking non zero coefficients */
    {
        temp=(b*b)-(4*a*c);
        if(temp<0)
        {
            printf("The equation has indeterminant roots");
        }
        else
        {
            root1=((-b)-sqrt(temp))/(2*a); /*calculates first root */
            root2=((-b)+sqrt(temp))/(2*a); /*calculate second root */
            printf("\n First root=%f",root1);
            printf("\n Second root=%f",root2);
        }
    }
    else
    {
        printf("Enter non zero coefficients");
    }
    getch();
}
```

Problem 23

Write a C program to simulate a simple calculator that performs arithmetic operations like additions, subtraction, multiplication, and division only on integers. Error message should be reported, if any attempt is made to divide by zero.

Program 23

```
#include<conio.h>
#include<stdio.h>
```

```
void main()
{
    int a,b,ch=0, result;
    printf("Enter two nos. for operation=");
    scanf("%d%d",&a,&b);/*scaning values of two numbers */
    printf("\nEnter Choice of Operation");
    printf ("\n1.Addition\n2.Subtraction\n3.Multiplication\n4.Division\nChoice=");
    scanf("%d",&ch);
    switch(ch)  /*switches value of ch */
    {
        case 1:  /*For addition*/
            result=a+b;
            printf("\nResult=%d",result);
            break;
        case 2:  /*For subtraction*/
            result=a-b;
            printf("\nResult=%d",result);
            break;
        case 3:  /*For Multiplication*/
            result=a*b;
            printf("\nResult=%d",result);
            break;
        case 4:  /*For Division */
            if (b==0)
        {
            printf("Error as B can not be Zero");  /*Shows error if bis Zero*/
        }
        else
        result=a/b;
        printf("\nResult=%d",result);
        break;
        default:
        printf("\nWrong Choice");
```

```
    }
    getch();
}
```

Problem 24

Write a C program to generate and print first 'N' Fibonacci numbers.

Program 24

```
#include<conio.h>
#include<stdio.h>
void main()
{   int i,n,a=1,b=1,c=0;
    printf("\nEnter limit for fibbonaci series=");
    scanf("%d",&n);
    printf("\nFibbonaci Series=");
    printf("%d,%d",a,b);
    for (i=0;i<n-2;i++)/*calculate fibbonaci series*/
    {   c=a+b;/*adds previous two nos.*/
        a=b;
        b=c;
        printf(",%d",c);
    }
    getch();
}
```

Problem 25

Write a C program to find the GCD and LCM of two integers and output the results along with the given integers. Use Euclid's algorithm.

Program 25

```
#include<conio.h>
#include<stdio.h>
int gcd(int a,int b)   /*function to find gcd of any no.*/
{
    int t;
    while(b!=0)
```

```
        {
            t=b;
            b=a%b;
            a=t;
        }
        return a;
    }
    void main()
    {   int a,b,lcm,gcd1;
        clrscr();
        printf("Enter any two to find LCM and GCD ");
        scanf("%d%d",&a,&b);
        gcd1=gcd(a,b);
        lcm=a*b/gcd1; /*calculates LCM*/
        printf("The LCM=%d\nThe GCD =%d",lcm,gcd1);
        getch();
    }
```

Problem 26

Write a C program to evaluate the given polynomial $f(x)=a_4x^4+a_3x^3+a_2x^2+a_1x^3+a_0$ for given value of x and the coefficients using Horner's method. (Using single dimension arrays to store coefficients)

Program 26

```
    #include<conio.h>
    #include<stdio.h>
    void main()
    {
        int a[50],x,n,i=0,result;
        clrscr();
        printf("\nEnter maximum power of n=") ;
        scanf("%d",&n);
        printf("\nEnter cofficients of the polynomial");
        for(i=0;i<=n;i++)
        {
```

```
        printf("\nEnter cofficient of X^%d=",i);
        scanf("%d",&a[i]);
    }
    printf("\nEnter value of X=");
    scanf("%d",&x);
    result=a[n];
    for(i=n-1;i>=0;i--)
    result=result*x+a[i];  /*calculating polynomial using horner method*/
    printf("\nThe value of the polynomial=%d",result);
    getch();
}
```

Problem 27

Write a program to print transpose of a square matrix.

Program 27

```
#include<stdio.h>
#include<conio.h>
void main()
{
    int a[10][10],m,i,j,temp;
    /* actual size of matrix is m*n
    i,j  - for scanning of array
    temp - for interchanging of a[i][j] and a[j][i] */
    printf("\n How many rows are  there in your square matrics :");
    scanf("%d",&m);
    /* Reading elements of matrix */
    printf("\n\nEnter the values :\n\n");
    for(i=0;i<m;i++)
    {
        printf("\nGive row  %i elements seprated by blank ", (i+1));
        for(j=0;j<m;j++)
        scanf("%d",&a[i][j]);
    }
    printf("\nOriginal square matrix is \n\n ");
```

```
for(i=0;i<m;i++)
{
    printf("\n");
    for(j=0;j<m;j++)
    printf("%d\t",a[i][j]);
}
/* Finding transpose */
for(i=1;i<m;i++)
    for(j=0;j<i;j++)
    {
        temp=a[i][j];
        a[i][j]=a[j][i];
        a[j][i]=temp;
    }
/* printing of all elements of final matrix */
printf("\n\nTranspose matrix is : \n\n");
for(i=0;i<m;i++)
{
    printf("\n");
    for(j=0;j<m;j++)
    printf("%d\t",a[i][j]);
}
getch();
}
```

Problem 28

Write a program to find if the given array is symmetric array or not. Note that a symmetric array is an array that equals to its transpose.

Program 28

```
#include<stdio.h>
#include<conio.h>
int symmetry(int a[][10],int m);
void main()
{
```

```
    int a[10][10],m,i,j,result;
    printf("\n Enter the size of matrix :");
    scanf("%d",&m);
    /* Reading matrix elements */
    printf("\n Enter the values :");
    for(i=0;i<m;i++)
        {
            printf("\nEnter elements of row %i separated by blank ",(i+1));
            for(j=0;j<m;j++)
            scanf("%d",&a[i][j]);
        }
        result=symmetry(a,m);
        if(result==0)
            printf("\n Not symmetrical");
        else
            printf("\n Symmetrical");
        getch();
}
int symmetry(int a[][10],int m)
{
    int i,j;
    for(i=1;i<m;i++)
        for(j=0;j<i;j++)
            if(a[i][j]!=a[j][i])
            return(0);
    return(1);
}
```

Problem 29

Write a program to find the position of a substring into the main string.

Program 29

```
#include<stdio.h>
#include<string.h>
int search(char[],char[]);
```

```
void main()
{
      char a[100],b[40];
      int loc;
      printf("\n Enter the main string :");
      gets(a);
      printf("\n Enter the search string :");
      gets(b);
      loc = search(a,b);
      if(loc==-1)
            printf("\nnot found");
      else
      printf("\nfound at location %d",loc+1);
      getch();
}
int search(char a[],char b[])
{
      int i,j,k;
      i=0,j=0;
      while(a[i]!='\0')
      {
            while(a[i]!=b[0] && a[i]!='\0')
                  i++;
            if(a[i]=='\0')
                  return(-1);
                  k=i;
            while(a[i]==b[j] && a[i]!='\0' && b[j]!='\0')
            {
                  i++;
                  j++;
            }
            if(b[j]=='\0')
                  return(k);
```

```
            if(a[i]=='\0')
                return(-1);
            i=k+1;
            j=0;
        }
    }
```

Problem 30

Write a program to concatenate two given strings.

Program 30

```
#include<stdio.h>
#include<string.h>
void concatenate(char[],char[]);
void main()
{
    char s1[50],s2[30];
    printf("\n Enter First strings :");
    gets(s1);
    printf("\n Enter Second strings :");
    gets(s2);
    concatenate(s1,s2);
    printf("\nConcatnated string is :%s",s1);
    getch();
}
void concatenate(char s1[],char s2[])
{
    int i,j;
    i=strlen(s1);
    for(j=0;s2[j]!='\0';i++,j++)
        s1[i]=s2[j];
    s1[i]='\0';
}
```

Problem 31

Write a program to enter a text line from the keyboard and print total number of characters (including blanks), words and special characters in the text line.

Program 31

```
#include<stdio.h>
#include<ctype.h>
void main()
{
    char a[80];
    int words,special,characters,i;
    words=special=characters=0;
    printf("\n Enter text here : ");
    gets(a);
    for(i=0;a[i]!='\0';i++)
    {
        characters++;
        if(isalnum(a[i]) && (i==0 || ! isalnum(a[i-1])))
            words++;
        if(!isspace(a[i]) && !isalnum(a[i]))
            special++;
    }
    printf("\n No of characters in the text (including blanks)  = %d",characters);
    printf("\n No of words in the text = %d",words);
    printf("\n No of special characters in the text = %d", special);
}
```

Problem 32

Write a program for displaying the moves that would be made in solving Tower of Hanoi puzzle.

Program 32

```
#include<stdio.h>
#include<conio.h>
void tower(int n,char x,char y,char z);
void main()
```

```
{
    int n;
    printf("\n Enter number of plates:");
    scanf("%d",&n);
    tower(n-1,'1','2','3');
    getch();
}
void tower(int n,char x,char y,char z)
{
    if(n>0)
    {
        tower(n-1,x,z,y);
        printf("\n%c -> %c",x,y);
        tower(n-1,z,y,x);
    }
}
```

Problem 33

Write user defined functions in C language to:

(a) Input N real numbers into a single dimension array.

(b) Compute their mean.

(c) Compute their variance.

(d) Compute their standard variation.

Using these functions, write a C program to input N real numbers into a single dimension array and compute their mean, variance & standard deviation. Output the computed results with suitable headings.

Program 33

```
#include<stdio.h>
#include<conio.h>
#include<math.h>
void read(float a[20],int n)
{
    int i;
    printf("\nEnter %d numbers=",n);
```

```
        for (i=0;i<n;i++)
        scanf("%f",&a[i]);
}
//---------------------------------
float mean(float a[20],int n)
{
        float sum=0, mean1=0;
        int i;
        for(i=0;i<n;i++)
        sum=sum+a[i];
        mean1=sum/n;
        return mean1;
}
//---------------------------------
float varience(float a[20],int n)
{
        int i;
        float mean1,var,sum=0;
        mean1=mean(a,n);
        for (i=0;i<n;i++)
        {
                sum=sum+ pow((a[i]-mean1),2);
        }
        var=sum/n;
        return var;
}
//---------------------------------
float standard(float a[20],int n)
{
        float stvar=0;
        stvar=sqrt(varience(a,n));
        return stvar;
}
```

```
//---------------------------------
void main()
{   float a[20],mean1,var,stvar;
    int n,i,j;
    clrscr();
    printf("Enter total no in array=");
    scanf("%d",&n);
    read (a,n);//takes input
    mean1=mean(a,n);//calculates mean
    printf("\nMean of %d numbers=%f\n",n,mean1);
    var=varience(a,n);//calculates varience
    printf("\nVarience of %d numbers=%f\n",n,var);
    stvar=standard(a,n);//calculates standard varience
    printf("\nStandard Varienceof %d numbers =%f\n",n,stvar);
    getch();
}
```

Problem 34

Write C program to read a matrix A(MxN) and to calculate the following:

(a) Sum of the elements of the specified row.

(b) Sum of the elements of the specified column.

(c) Sum of all the elements of the matrix.

Output the computed results with suitable headings.

Program 34

```
#include<stdio.h>
#define maxrow 10
#define maxcol 10
void rowtot(int row, int col, int mat[maxrow][maxcol]);
void coltot(int row, int col, int mat[maxrow][maxcol]);
void arrtot(int row, int col, int mat[maxrow][maxcol]);
main()
{
    int mat[maxrow][maxcol] ;
    int row,col;
```

```
    int ch ;
    int i,j;
    printf("\nHow many rows ") ;
    scanf("%i",&row) ;
    printf("\nHow many columns ") ;
    scanf("%i",&col) ;
    for(i=0;i<row;i++)
    for(j=0;j<col;j++)
    {
        printf("\nGive Element of %i row and %i column",(i+1),(j+1)) ;
        scanf("%i",&mat[i][j]) ;
    }
    rowtot(row, col, mat) ;
    coltot(row, col, mat) ;
    arrtot(row, col, mat) ;
}

void rowtot(int row, int col, int mat[maxrow][maxcol])
{
    int i, j, ch, tot =0 ;
    printf("\nGive the row to be totalled " );
    scanf("%i",&ch);
    for(j=0 ; j<col ; j++)
    tot = tot + mat[ch][j] ;
    printf("\nSum of row %i = %i ",ch ,tot) ;
}

void coltot(int row, int col, int mat[maxrow][maxcol])
{
    int i, j, ch, tot =0 ;
    printf("\nGive the column to be totalled ");
    scanf("%i",&ch);
    for(j=0 ; j<col ; j++)
```

```
        tot = tot + mat[j][ch] ;
        printf("\nSum of column %i = %i ",ch, tot) ;
    }
    void arrtot(int row, int col, int mat[maxrow][maxcol])
    {
        int i, j, ch, tot =0 ;
        for(i=0 ; i<row ; i++)
        {
            for(j=0 ; j<col ; j++)
            tot = tot + mat[i][j] ;
        }
        printf("\nSum of the array elements = %i ",tot) ;
    }
```

Problem 35

Write C user defined functions:

(a) To read the elements of a given matrix of size MxN.

(b) To print the elements of a given matrix of size MxN.

(c) To compute the product of two matrices.

Using these functions, write a C program to read two matrices A(M x N) and B(PxQ) and compute the product of A and B after checking compatibility for multiplication. Output the input matrices and the resultant matrix with suitable heading headings and format.

(Using two dimension arrays where array size M, N, P, Q $\leq$3)

Program 35

```
    #include<conio.h>
    #include<stdio.h>
    void read(int a[20][20],int m,int n)
    {
        int i,j;
        for(i=0;i<m;i++)
        {
            for(j=0;j<n;j++)
            scanf("%d",&a[i][j]);
        }
```

```
}
void product(int a[20][20],int b[20][20],int c[20][20],int m,int q,int n)
{
    int i,j,k;
    for (i=0;i<m;i++)
    {
        for(j=0;j<q;j++)
        {
            c[i][j]=0;
            for(k=0;k<n;k++)
            c[i][j]=c[i][j]+a[i][k]*b[k][j]; //performing multiplication
        }
    }
}

void display(int a[20][20],int m,int n)
{
    int i,j;
    for(i=0;i<m;i++)
    {
        for(j=0;j<n;j++)
        printf("%d ",a[i][j]);
        printf("\n");
    }
}

void main()
{
    int j,k,a[20][20],b[20][20],c[20][20],m,n,p,q;
    clrscr();
    printf("Enter rows and colums in A matrix A(M X N)=");
    scanf("%d%d",&m,&n);
    printf("Enter rows and colums in B matrix B(P X Q)=");
```

```
scanf("%d%d",&p,&q);
if (n==p && p<=3 && m<=3) //checking condition for multiplication
{
    printf("\nEnter numbers in  matrix A");
    read(a,m,n);//reading value of matrix A
    printf("\nEnter numbers in  matrix B");
    read(b,p,q);//reading value of matrix B
    product(a,b,c,m,q,n);//calculates product
    printf("\nMatrix A=\n");
    display (a,m,n);
    printf("\nMatrix B=\n");
    display (b,p,q);
    printf("\nMatrix AXB=\n");
    display (c,m,q);
}
    else
{
    printf("\nMatrix Can not be multiplied");
}
getch();
}
```

Problem 36

Write a number guessing program. This program should generate a random number and should give chance to the user to guess it in a continuous loop. If the number given by the use is higher then it should display Too High. If the number given is lower, then it should display Too Low. It the number given matches the number then it should display Good Job Done and it should also display the total number of chances taken to guess the number.

Program 36

```
#include <stdlib.h>
#include <string.h>
#include <stdio.h>
#include <time.h>
#define NO  (100)
```

```
void ParseCmdLine(int argc, char *argv[], int *max);
int main(int argc, char *argv[])
{
   int guess, target, goes = 0, max = 100;
   char buffer[NO];

   ParseCmdLine(argc, argv, &max);

   srand( (unsigned) time(NULL) );
   do {
     printf("The number is between 1 and %d.\n", max);
     printf("Guess The Number?\n\n");

     target = rand() % max + 1;
     do {
     printf("\nEnter the number you think : ");
        fgets(buffer, NO - 1, stdin);
        while ( !sscanf(buffer, "%d", &guess) ) {
          printf("Enter a number! ");
          fgets(buffer, NO - 1, stdin);
     }

        if ( guess < target )
          printf("Too Low! ");
        else if ( guess > target )
          printf("Too High! ");
        ++goes;
     } while ( guess != target );
     printf("Good Job Done, it was %d!\n", target);
     printf("You took %d chances.\n\n", goes);
     printf("Do You wish to play more? (y/n) ");
     fgets(buffer, NO - 1, stdin);
   } while ( buffer[0] == 'y' || buffer[0] == 'Y' );
```

```
    printf("Thanks!\n");
    return EXIT_SUCCESS;
}
void ParseCmdLine(int argc, char *argv[], int *max) {
    char *endptr = NULL;
    if ( argc == 2 ) {
      *max = strtol(argv[1], &endptr, 0);
      if ( *endptr ) {
          printf("You did not enter a valid maximum number.\n");
          exit(EXIT_FAILURE);
      }
      else if ( *max < 2 ) {
      printf("Maximum number must be at least two!\n");
          exit(EXIT_FAILURE);
      }
    }
}
```

Problem 37

Write a program that finds the largest number in the array, using pointer.

Program 37

```
/* This program finds largest number in the array using pointer*/
#include<stdio.h>
#define TOT 5
main()
{
    int *ptr,max,n;
    int marks[TOT];
    max=0;
    ptr=marks;
    for(n=0;n<TOT;n++)
    {
        printf("Enter the numbers\n");
        scanf("%d", &marks[n]);
```

```
        }
        n=0;
        while(n<TOT)
        {
            if (max < *ptr)
            max=*ptr;
            n++;
            ptr++ ;
        }
        printf("\nLargest number=%d\n",max);
    }
```

Program 38

Write a program in C using structures which maintains the records of students (roll_no, name, hostel_no, physics marks, chemistry marks, math marks).Write functions which perform following tasks:

1. Find the student who scored the maximum marks(Topper)

2. Finds average marks in Physics.

3. Finds average marks in Chemistry.

4. Finds average Marks in Mathematics.

5. Finds students, who live in a particular Hostel.

6. Adds 10% bonus marks to al the students in individual subject.

Problem 38

```
    #include<stdio.h>
    #include<conio.h>
    #include<alloc.h>
    #include<process.h>
    #include<string.h>
    #define NULL1 0
    struct student
    {
        int roll_number;
        char name[30];
        int hostel_no;
```

```
        float physics;
        float chemistry;
        float maths;
        struct student *next;
    };
    void get_data(struct student **);
    void maximum(struct student **);
    void average(struct student **,char*);
    void hostel(struct student **);
    void bonus(struct student **);

    void main()
    {
    struct student *p=NULL1;
    int choice;
    while(1)
    {
        clrscr();
        printf("\n\t1. ENTER RECORD OF STUDENT");
        printf("\n\t2. MAX MARKS OF TOPPER");
        printf("\n\t3. AV_MARKS_PHYSICS");
        printf("\n\t4. AV_MARKS_MATSH");
        printf("\n\t5. AV_MARKS_CHEMISTRY");
        printf("\n\t6. DISPLAY RECORD OF STUDENT ACCORDING TO HOSTEL NO.");
        printf("\n\t7. ADD BONUS MARKS");
        printf("\n\t8. EXIT");
        printf("\n\tENTER YOUR CHOICE(1,2,3,4,5,6,7,8):");
        scanf("%d",&choice);
        switch(choice)
        {
            case 1:get_data(&p);
                break;
            case 2:maximum(&p);
```

```
            break;
        case 3:average(&p,"PHYSICS");
            break;
        case 4:average(&p,"MATHS");
            break;
        case 5:average(&p,"CHEMISTRY");
            break;
        case 6:hostel(&p);
            break;
        case 7:bonus(&p);
            break;
        case 8:exit(1);
            break;
        default:printf("\n\tError!!!!!");
            printf("\n\tWRONG CHOICE ENTERED....");
            getch();
            break;
        }
    }
}

void get_data(struct student **p)
{
    struct student *q=*p;
    struct student *r,*s;
    char choice;
    int roll_number;
    char name[30];
    int hostel_no;
    float physics;
    float chemistry;
    float maths;
    do
```

```
{
    q=*p;
    r=(struct student *)malloc(sizeof(struct student));
    printf("\n\t*****STUDENT RECORD*****");
    printf("\n\tNAME:");
    fflush(stdin);
    gets(name);
    strcpy(r->name,name);
    printf("\n\tROLL NUMBER :");
    scanf("%d",&roll_number);
    r->roll_number=roll_number;
    printf("\n\tHOSTEL NO.:");
    scanf("%d",&hostel_no);
    r->hostel_no=hostel_no;
    printf("\n\tPHYSICS MARKS:");
    scanf("%f",&physics);
    r->physics=physics;
    printf("\n\tCHEMISTRY MARKS:");
    scanf("%f",&chemistry);
    r->chemistry=chemistry;
    printf("\n\tMATHS MARKS:");
    scanf("%f", &maths);
    r->maths=maths;
    r->next=NULL1;
    if(*p==NULL1)
    *p=r;
    else
    {
while(((r->physics+  r->maths+  r->chemistry)  <=(q->physics  +  q->maths  +  q-
>chemistry)) && q!=NULL1)
    {
        s=q;
        q=q->next;
    }
```

```
        if(q==*p)
        {
            r->next=q;
            *p=r;
        }
        else
        {
            r->next=q;
            s->next=r;
        }
    }
    printf("\n\tDO YOU WANT TO ADD MORE RECORDS(Y/N):");
    fflush(stdin);
    scanf("%c", &choice);
    }
    while(choice=='y'|| choice=='Y');
}
void maximum(struct student **p)
{
struct student *q=*p;
if(q==NULL1)
printf("\n\tNO RECORDS CURRENTLY STORED");
else
    {
    printf("\n\t******MAXIMUM MARKS OF TOPPER******");
    printf("\n\tPHYSICS: %f",   q->physics) ;
    printf("\n\tCHEMISTRY: %f", q->chemistry);
    printf("\n\tMATHS: %f",     q->maths);
    printf("\n\tTOTAL: %f",     (q->physics+q->chemistry  + q->maths));
    }
    getch();
}
void average(struct student **p,char *c)
```

```
{
    struct student *q=*p;
    int i=0;
    float total=0;
    if(q==NULL1)
    printf("\n\tNO RECORDS CURRENTLY STORED");
    if ((strcmpi("PHYSICS",c))==0)
    {
        total=0 ;
        while(q!=NULL1)
        {
            total=total+q->physics;
            i++;
            q=q->next;
        }
    }

    else
    {
        if((strcmpi("CHEMISTRY",c))==0)
         {
                total=0 ;
            while(q!=NULL1)
            {
                total=total + q->chemistry;
                i++;
                q=q->next;
            }
         }
        else
        {

            total=0 ;
```

```
                while(q!=NULL1)
                {
                        total=total+ q->maths;
                        i++;
                        q=q->next;
                            }
            }
        }

printf("\nAVERAGE MARKS IN %s : %f",c, (total/i));
    getch();
}

void hostel (struct student **p)
{
    struct student *r=*p;
    int n;
    if(r==NULL1)
    printf("\n\tNO RECORDS CURRENTLY STORED");
    else
    {
    printf("\n\tENTER THE HOSTEL NO.:");
    scanf("%d", &n);
    printf("\n\t******STUDENT RECORD******");
    while(r!=NULL1)
    {
    if(r->hostel_no==n)
    {
    printf("\n\tNAME : % s", r->name);
    printf("\n\tROLL NUMBER : %d", r->roll_number);
    printf("\n\tPHYSICS MARKS : %f", r->physics);
    printf("\n\tCHEMISTRY MARKS : %f", r->chemistry);
    printf("\n\tMATHS MARKS : %f\n", r->maths);
```

```
}
r=r->next;
}
}
getch();
}

void bonus(struct student **p)
{
struct student *q=*p;
int n;
if(q==NULL1)
printf("\n\tNO RECORDS CURRENTLY STORED") ;
else
{
printf("\n\tENTER THE STUDENT ROLL NUMBER:");
scanf("%d", &n);
while(q!=NULL1 && q->roll_number!=n)
q=q->next;
if(q->roll_number==n)
{
q->physics=q->physics+(0.10 * q->physics);
q->chemistry=q->chemistry+(0.10 *q->chemistry);
q->maths=q->maths+(0.10 * q->maths);
}
else
{
printf("\n\tNO RECORD CORESPONDING TO THIS ROLL NUMBER EXISTS");
getch();
}
}
}
```

****